The Deadly Ethnic Riot

The Deadly
Ethnic Riot

Donald L. Horowitz

UNIVERSITY OF CALIFORNIA PRESS
Berkeley . Los Angeles . London

University of California Press
Berkeley and Los Angeles, California

University of California Press, Ltd.
London, England

© 2001 by
The Regents of the University of California

Portions of Chapter 2 were originally published in
a somewhat different form in the *Annual World
Bank Conference on Development Economics*,
1998 (© 1999 The World Bank). Portions of
Chapter 4 were originally published in a slightly
different form in *Comparative Politics 6* (October
1973) (© 1973 The City University of New York).
Both are reprinted with permission.

Library of Congress Cataloging-in-Publication Data

Horowitz, Donald L.
    The deadly ethnic riot / Donald L. Horowitz.
        p.   cm.
    Includes bibliographical references and index.
        ISBN 0-520-22447-7 (cloth : alk. paper)
        1. Riots.   2. Violence.   3. Ethnic Relations.
    4. Ethnicity.   5. Culture conflict.   6. Social
    conflict.   I. Title.

HV6474.H67 2001
303.6'23 — dc21   99-086512

Manufactured in the United States of America

09   08   07   06   05   04   03   02   01   00

10   9   8   7   6   5   4   3   2   1

The paper used in this publication meets the minimum requirements of ANSI/NISO Z39.48-1992
(R 1997) *(Permanence of Paper).* ♾

For Hannah and Alexis

Peace becomes mankind; fury is for beasts.
Ovid

Contents

Preface

"On the analyst's couch, a neurosis," declares Freud; "in real life, swinish behavior." This book is an attempt to bring the detachment of the analyst, although not of the psychoanalyst, to one of the most swinish forms of human behavior: the murder of strangers by crowds. It is simultaneously a book about violence and a book about ethnicity.

Anyone who studies severely divided societies at close range will probably encounter the deadly ethnic riot sooner or later. Deadly riots are not ubiquitous, merely episodic, but when these attacks occur a good many people lose their lives in the most brutal sort of killing, typically accompanied by mutilation, and many more become refugees. The deadly ethnic riot has an element of fury that signals widespread hostility and portends worse. This form of violence produces memories that linger, coloring group relations long afterward. The possibility of ethnic violence lurks in the consciousness of people who, to outward appearances, go about their business in the market or the office in complete tranquility.

This is a study of the who, when, where, how, what, and why of ethnic riot behavior: of the participants and organization, targets, timing and precipitants, supporting conditions, locations, methods, and effects of violent episodes. The goal is to explain the major elements in ethnic riot behavior. Since there are usually many possible target groups, why do some ethnic groups rather than others get attacked? In recurrent sequences of riots, are target choices consistent? How do the killers conquer their fear before violence begins? What events tend to precede and precipitate such violence? What conditions in a society are especially conducive to violent attacks? Does one type of precipitating event rather than another alter the identity of the ethnic groups chosen as targets? What determines the scale and spread of violence? Why are atrocities prevalent? What conditions govern whether the riot will be followed by other forms of violence, and by which groups? What conditions facilitate riots as opposed to, say, acts of terrorism? What are the consequences of the riot for ethnic-group relations, public policy, and change in the political system? This is, in short, a study of the morphology of the ethnic riot.

It is also a study of riot dynamics. Every aspect of the riot is related to every other aspect. The nature of a precipitating event may dictate the rapidity with which violence occurs. This, in turn, may govern where it occurs, and where it occurs may determine, within limits, the identity of the targets. Where the precipitant occurs may also have an impact on the precipitant-threshold required to ignite violence, if some localities happen to be more hospitable to violence than others are. Likewise, the aims and identity of riot leadership may be reflected in the character of the precipitants as well as in the choice of target groups. What arouses some categories of participant does not necessarily arouse others. Conceivably, what the precipitant lacks in intensity may be made up by the conflict-laden structure of group relations — and perhaps vice versa if the precipitating events are unusually powerful. There is a considerable degree of circularity in the riot process. What observers separate out for analysis the participants regularly put together for action. Organizing the study around the structure of violent episodes facilitates the pursuit of questions of this kind.

No inquiry into riots should fail to account for their absence. The study of violence proceeds most fruitfully when it asks those deceptively simple questions that illuminate the violent episode: Why here and not there? Why now and not then? Why these methods of killing and not others? Why these targets and not others? After the fact of violence, its destructive fury makes its course appear to have been foreordained. All the more reason to take nothing as given and to proceed on the basis of such naive questions.

Since the riot involves passion and calculation, the sources of explanation reside in realms appropriate sometimes to psychological and sometimes to strategic behavior. Violence has so many wellsprings of action that the varied repertoire of the fox, rather than the single-mindedness of the hedgehog, is more appropriate to the explanatory task.[1] Any theory will need to draw its sustenance from the diverse disciplines that speak to the phenomenon. That does not mean that we shall fail to reach ultimate questions about the scale and explosiveness of the deadly ethnic riot, its

1. See Isaiah Berlin, *The Hedgehog and the Fox*, rev. ed. (London: Weidenfeld & Nicolson, 1978). Cf. Albert O. Hirschman, "The Search for Paradigms as a Hindrance to Understanding," *World Politics* 22, no. 3 (April 1970): 329–43.

sheer brutality, its ability to attract participants, its selectivity between groups and its indiscriminateness within groups, or its mix of impulsive and instrumental elements, for assuredly we shall reach them. But we shall tiptoe up to these questions, first building up a picture of the indispensable elements and strongly facilitative conditions of the riot and then testing these findings against a control group of quiescent cases. This will be an aggressive encounter with the facts.

In unraveling this phenomenon, I have had a great deal of support: material, intellectual, and moral. Fellowships from the John Simon Guggenheim Foundation and the National Humanities Center helped get the project off the ground. Further support was provided by grants from the United States Institute of Peace, the Carnegie Corporation, the Duke University Research Program in Comparative Studies, and the Charles A. Cannon Charitable Trust, which funds the Bost Research Professorship at Duke Law School. The project benefited from documentary research conducted at the Rhodes House Library, Oxford, assisted by a grant from the American Philosophical Society, and from periods devoted to writing when I was a visiting fellow at Wolfson College, Cambridge, and at the University of Canterbury Law School in New Zealand, as well as when I was a resident at the Rockefeller Foundation's Villa Serbelloni in Bellagio, Italy. Finishing touches were applied while I was a visitor at the University of Hong Kong Law Faculty and a Suntory and Toyota Center (STICERD) Distinguished Visitor at the London School of Economics. I am indebted to all of these institutions.

I have also had the inestimable benefit of Joan Ashley's ability to produce a seamless manuscript out of frayed drafts; of superb research assistance from Susan Redick Gruber, Layna Mosley, Zephyr Rain Teachout, and Claire Kramer; and of the resourcefulness of librarians at Duke University, particularly Michael Minor, Avinash Maheshwary, Janeen Denson, Melanie Dunshee, Katherine Topulous, and Janet Sinder. Various chapters were presented at seminars at the UCLA Center for Social Theory and Comparative History, the Harvard University Center for International Affairs, the Harvard Center on South Asian Studies, the Harvard Seminar on Nationalism, the Yale University Comparative Politics Seminar, the Princeton University Comparative Politics Seminar, the Duke University Seminar on Nationalism, the Midwest Consortium on International Security Studies, the Albert Einstein Institution, the University of Washington Seminar on Riots and Pogroms, the Hoover Institution, and the International Seminar on Violence in Punjab, sponsored by the Institute for Development and Communication, Chandigarh.

I am grateful to my hosts on those occasions and to those who provided especially useful comments on those presentations or on chapters they were kind enough to read. Most notable among these are Samuel P. Huntington, Ashutosh Varshney, Marilynn Brewer, Ian Shapiro, Nancy Bermeo, Peter Klopfer, and John Staddon. Along the way, an array of people has made inestimable contributions to the research by helping, knowingly or unknowingly, to obtain or interpret some crucial pieces of data or to facilitate the writing. Among those in whose debt I find myself in this respect are Pamela B. Gann, Steven I. Wilkinson, Christopher McCrudden, Sir David Williams, Shruti Kapil, Pramod Kumar, R. William Liddle, Lee Poh Ping, Monnie Lee, Brendan O'Leary, Nicole Boyce, Gordon R. Walker, Anwar Fazal, and Michael J. Lacey. With all this help, the deficiencies of this book can hardly be attributed to a scarcity of opportunity.

In the production process, the University of California Press made everything easier. I am especially appreciative of the high professionalism and cool efficiency of both Kay Scheuer, who edited the manuscript, and David Peattie of BookMatters, who managed the project.

Finally, I express my habitual but unflagging gratitude to my wife, Judy, whose aversion to violence and to ethnocentrism failed to diminish her indispensable encouragement.

Donald L. Horowitz

A Note on Place Names

Many territories in which riots have occurred have undergone name changes. Most such changes were introduced at independence or after a new regime took power. To avoid confusion, I have resisted the temptation to use multiple names for the same territory. In general, I use the later name (for example, Sri Lanka rather than Ceylon, Malaysia rather than Malaya), even in referring to riots preceding the change of name. I use Zaire, rather than the Congo, however, to avoid confusing the Congo whose capital is Kinshasa with the Congo whose capital is Brazzaville. I also continue to refer to Burma, rather than to Myanmar, and to Bombay, rather than to Mumbai, because the latter names remain relatively unfamiliar. The choices I have made are intended to emphasize recognizability and consistency over time, so multiple riots in the same place will not appear to have occurred in several places.

CHAPTER I

Say It with Murder

A DEADLY ETHNIC RIOT is an intense, sudden, though not necessarily wholly unplanned, lethal attack by civilian members of one ethnic group on civilian members of another ethnic group, the victims chosen because of their group membership. So conceived, ethnic riots are synonymous with what are variously called "communal," "racial," "religious," "linguistic," or "tribal" disturbances.[1] Examples are the anti-Ibo riots in Nigeria in 1966, the anti-Chinese riots in Malaysia in 1969, the anti-Bengali riots in Assam and Tripura, India, in 1980, the anti-Uzbek riots in Kyrghyzstan in 1990, and the anti-Madurese riots in West Kalimantan, Indonesia, in 1997 and 1999. The list can easily be extended, for ethnic riots are probably the most common form of collective violence,[2] by some estimates the form that took more lives than any other in the twentieth century.[3]

The deadly ethnic riot is a passionate but highly patterned event. In the first instance, such an episode has at least an immediate cause. It is triggered by events — precipitants — that are regarded as sufficient to warrant violence. The ethnic riot is not a random phenomenon.

Once the riot begins, it takes an interpersonal and brutal form.

1. For present purposes, the term *ethnic group* includes groups based on all such indicia of ascriptive differences. The rationale for this inclusive usage is discussed in Donald L. Horowitz, *Ethnic Groups in Conflict* (Berkeley and Los Angeles: University of California Press, 1985), pp. 41–54. For a comparable definition of a religious riot, see Natalie Zemon Davis, *Society and Culture in Early Modern France* (Stanford: Stanford University Press, 1975), p. 153.

2. See R. P. Richardson, "An Analysis of Recent Conflicts" (mimeo., Arlington, Va., 1970), pp. 43–44.

3. See Harold Isaacs, "Power and Identity: Tribalism in World Politics," *Headline Series* of the Foreign Policy Association, no. 246 (October 1979): 11–12. Some commentators have noted that peace is more common than violence, even in divided societies, an observation unquestionably true but, for reasons explained later in this chapter, less significant than it may seem.

Members of one ethnic group search out members of another. The search is conducted with considerable care, for this is violence directed against an identifiable target group. When found, members of the target group are murdered and usually tortured or mutilated as well. Despite an atmosphere of sadistic gaiety that frequently surrounds the killings, this is no lighthearted or ritualized test of strength — it is deadly serious.

Such an episode has its own temporal and spatial rhythms, of accelerating and declining activity, of localized or radiating destruction. Depending on a number of variables, including the effectiveness of law enforcement agencies, an ethnic riot may be as brief as a day or two or as long as several weeks; it may be confined to one place, or it may set a whole state aflame. Once controlled, it may stay controlled, or it may smolder on, only to resume at another opportunity.

The ethnic riot has a structure and a natural history. In fact, violent events in general are structured by implicit rules governing provocation, initiation, choice of targets, intensity of violence, and termination.[4] As a patterned event, the ethnic riot has meaning. Like the willingness to die for a cause, the willingness to kill for a cause constitutes a kind of statement about the cause, the killer, the victim, and the act of killing. Ethnic violence is revealing of the ethnic conflict from which it springs and of the nature and consequences of collective violence. "Rumania says it with murder," writes Countess Waldeck of the anti-Jewish violence in Bucharest in 1941.[5] But what, exactly, does it say — or, rather, what do the killers say? The task is to decode the message.

THE MORPHOLOGY AND DYNAMICS OF VIOLENCE

Until fairly recently, questions about the precipitants, targets, supporting conditions, organization, participants, locations, and effects of ethnic riots have not been asked systematically. Behavior that breaches norms depends on "processes that seem at once too familiar and too opaque to be readily discernible."[6] Since it departs from normative expectations, riot behavior is in that sense mystifying; since it nonetheless happens frequently, commonsense notions develop about it. And so

4. Peter Marsh, Elisabeth Rosser, and Rom Harré, *The Rules of Disorder* (London: Routledge & Kegan Paul, 1978), pp. 109–10.

5. R. G. Waldeck, *Athene Palace* (New York: Robert M. McBride, 1942), p. 343.

6. Anne Campbell, "The Streets and Violence," in Anne Campbell and John J. Gibbs, eds., *Violent Transactions: The Limits of Personality* (Oxford: Basil Blackwell, 1986), p. 115.

it produces a paradox: violence is either beyond explanation or not in need of explanation.

The gap is filled in by some hoary myths and assumptions, difficult to dislodge even in serious treatments of ethnic violence. For each such notion, invoked when violence strikes, there is usually an equal and opposite notion, in some cases more than one.

Consider the timing of riots. In a severely divided society, it is said, an ethnic riot can happen at any time. On the other hand, it is asserted with equal conviction that ethnic riots happen only in economically stressful times. Implicit in the latter view are some possible causes of violence.[7]

Or take the question of the events that precipitate riots. For some, any small spark will suffice to set off a spontaneous riot in a severely divided society: "long antagonisms express themselves in trifles."[8] The precipitant, on this view, has no independent importance; it is just a signal. Neither is any special importance attributed to the precipitant by those who assert that riots are organized by powerful people in order to gain advantage or deflect hostility away from themselves.[9] The precipitant, in that case, is just a convenient excuse. But there is another view, according to which the precipitating agent and the underlying reason for the riot have a large area of overlap, perhaps even identity. If, for example, police action precipitates violence, it is highly probable, on this view, that underlying the violence are grievances against the police.[10] So the precipitant actually evokes the violence and therefore may have great significance for understanding the riot.

The same range of views is discernible regarding the ethnic identity of the targets and the reasons particular groups are victimized. The victims of ethnic violence are often characterized as helpless scapegoats: any convenient minority will do. On the other hand, since people attack those who are threateningly different or those who are materially more suc-

---

7. For the view, on the other hand again, that riots are the product of uneven economic modernization, see Asghar Ali Engineer, *Communalism and Communal Violence in India: An Analytical Approach to Hindu-Muslim Conflict* (Delhi: Ajanta, 1989), pp. 4–46.

8. Winston S. Churchill, *The World Crisis, 1911–1914* (New York: Scribner, 1923), Vol. 1, p. 52. For an example, see Margaret J. Wyszomirski, "Communal Violence: The Armenians and the Copts as Case Studies," *World Politics* 27, no. 3 (April 1975): 430–55, at p. 443.

9. See Paul R. Brass, *Theft of an Idol: Text and Context in the Representation of Collective Violence* (Princeton: Princeton University Press, 1997), p. 9.

10. Robert M. Fogelson, *Violence as Protest* (Garden City, N.Y.: Anchor Books, 1971). For a critique of such views, see Donald L. Horowitz, "Racial Violence in the United States," in Nathan Glazer and Ken Young, eds., *Ethnic Pluralism and Public Policy: Achieving Equality in the United States and Britain* (London: Heinemann, 1983), p. 194.

cessful, cultural distance or economic power is said to attract violence. All of these conceptions are frequently encountered.

Chance or determinism; spontaneity or a hidden hand; weakness or strength: these opposite poles define the state of the implicit, common-sense theory of ethnic violence. Needless to say, these conflicting theories cannot all be correct. More than that, some versions are invalid on their face. If a riot can happen at any time, or at any time there is the least spark, ethnic violence would be very much more common than it already is. The argument that makes violence a happenstance event is an argument that proves too much.

On a few issues, there is at least informed speculation. Students of violence agree, for example, that its various forms are convertible from one to another under certain conditions.[11] Hence what begins as a localized outbreak can prove to be an enormously significant event for a society. But no one has specified the conditions that turn an ethnic riot into protracted civil war or terrorism. The difficulty of identifying the conditions conducive to a change from one form of ethnic violence to another is compounded by the fact that either the initiators or the victims of the violence may respond to its occurrence by turning to other forms of violence. Ibo were victims who turned to a strategy of armed secession; Sri Lankan Tamils were victims who turned to terrorism and separatist warfare.

From the standpoint of riot prevention, the timing of violence is an important issue. It is an issue with two components. Riots are preceded by precipitating events. At the same time, certain features of the social and political environment may facilitate rioting without being proximate causes of the riot. Generally, they do this by removing restraints on the expression of violence. Although it may sometimes seem that there is no particular rhyme or reason for the outbreak of violence in a conflict-prone society, that any incident can provoke bloodshed, in fact, precipitants and supporting conditions fall into determinate classes, identification of which will aid in the understanding of ethnic violence and in the capacity to predict it.

Selective targeting appears to be practically universal in ethnic riots. In every case, there is more than one potential target group, but in virtually every violent episode one ethnic group is targeted and others are bypassed. Ibo but not Yoruba were victimized on four successive occa-

---

11. Ted Robert Gurr, *Why Men Rebel* (Princeton: Princeton University Press, 1970), pp. 4–5, and studies cited therein.

sions in northern Nigeria. Bengalis but generally not Marwaris were recurrently attacked in Assam, Tamils but not Muslims in Sri Lanka, Chinese but not Indians in Malaysia. There are some exceptions and qualifications, to be sure, but what stands out are the ubiquity of selective targeting and the consistency of targets over time.

Given selective targeting, the theory of target choice becomes a central element in the study of ethnic violence. The various notions mentioned above, which have been advanced to explain target choices, cannot be confirmed. Take the assertion that unusually prosperous or advantaged ethnic groups, such as trading minorities, tend to be targeted. In comparative perspective, this is only a minor factor in target selection, operative under certain, specific conditions of riot leadership. Quite often, prosperous minorities are not targeted even during the most brutal riots. The scapegoat hypothesis, emphasizing the weakness and vulnerability of targets of violence, is equally impossible to substantiate on a comparative basis. Groups targeted in riots are generally far from weak. The nature and location of the riot precipitants may affect target choice, but these are probably not decisive in most cases. Indeed, to constitute a precipitant, an event must implicate a group already regarded as a significant potential recipient of violence, so that in a sense the identification of targets precedes the occurrence of the precipitant. Targeting, in short, is an issue on which there is much conventional wisdom, most of it inaccurate.[12]

While the participants take selective targeting to be natural — since they do not consider alternative target groups to be worthy of a violent response — we may consider the grounds of target selection to be problematic and in need of careful explanation. The systematic elaboration of a theory of target selection promises to make a significant contribution to the understanding of violence and of the underlying sentiments that form the basis of ethnic conflict.[13]

The study of target choice also promises to aid in the resolution of an issue that has long troubled social psychologists. Hostility that might produce violence is more often generated by potential victims who are strong and powerful; but, because they are strong and powerful, they

12. For a first cut at some psychological issues associated with problems of selective targeting, see Donald L. Horowitz, "Direct, Displaced, and Cumulative Ethnic Aggression," *Comparative Politics* 6, no. 1 (October 1973): 1–16. See also the comments on it in Michael Billig, *Social Psychology and Intergroup Relations* (New York: Academic Press, 1976), pp. 175–76.

13. This elaboration is the subject of Chapters 4, 5, and 6.

usually can inhibit violent action against them. On the other hand, potential victims who are weak and vulnerable are obviously easier targets, but there may be insufficient hostility against those who are most accessible to violence.[14] This dilemma of target choice is greatly illuminated by the comparative analysis of riot episodes.

The location of ethnic riots within a country is equally problematic. There is a time and a space dimension to the location problem. The same locations experience violence, usually between the same groups, more than once over the years, while other locations, in which the same groups reside, are left out. At any given moment of violence, however, riots may be localized. Malaysia, for example, experienced rioting in Penang but not in Kuala Lumpur in 1967 and rioting in Kuala Lumpur but not in Penang a year and a half later. The ethnic antagonists were the same in the two cases, and the overall structure of ethnic relations was fairly uniform in the two cities. Why was the rioting confined in each case to one city and not the other? The same question may be asked of Hindu-Muslim riots in India, which have occurred in many cities, often on a repeat basis, but have not always spread contemporaneously from one city to another. Theories of contagion, widely advanced to explain the spread of black protest violence from one American city to another in the 1960s, until hundreds of cities had had riots, may be less pertinent to the deadly ethnic riot.[15] Why are there not even more ethnic riots and riot locales than there already are?

The prevalence of atrocities also requires explanation. Various forms of ethnic violence differ on two dimensions of deadliness: scale and brutality. In some types of violence, as I shall soon point out, few people are killed; in others, many are. In some types of ethnic violence, regardless of the magnitude of casualties, the killing is notably brutal. For example, lynching in the United States south, although usually involving single vic-

14. For some perspectives on this issue, see Richard H. Walters, "Implications of Laboratory Studies of Aggression for the Control and Regulation of Violence," *The Annals* 364 (March 1966): 60–72, at pp. 69–70; Ralph Epstein, "Aggression toward Outgroups as a Function of Authoritarianism and Imitation of Aggressive Models," *Journal of Personality and Social Psychology* 3, no. 5 (May 1966): 574–79, at p. 577. Cf. Leonard Berkowitz, *Aggression: A Social-Psychological Analysis* (New York: McGraw-Hill, 1962), pp. 139–40.

15. See, e.g., Manus I. Midlarsky, "Analyzing Diffusion and Contagion Effects: The Urban Disorders of the 1960s," *American Political Science Review* 72, no. 3 (September 1978): 996–1008. Cf. Ladd Wheeler and Anthony R. Caggiula, "The Contagion of Aggression," *Journal of Experimental Social Psychology* 2, no. 1 (January 1966): 1–10.

tims, was commonly characterized by mutilations. Although the scale and brutality of killing vary independently from one type of ethnic violence to another, ethnic riots are extreme on both counts. Many people are killed, and atrocities are committed in the course of the killing. There have been many theories of aggression and violence, but few, if any, that undertake to account for the particular cruelty of the atrocity-killing that is an integral part of the ethnic riot.

An inquiry into such questions is theoretically important and practically useful. Despite the sporadic social science preoccupation with the nature of violence, ethnic riots have not usually been separated out for analysis. In the past, bodies of literature in several disciplines tended to subsume the ethnic riot in broader categories: "turmoil" — meaning unorganized mass violence — in political science, "aggression" in social psychology, and "hostile outbursts" or crowd behavior in the sociology of collective behavior.[16] Yet there is good reason to believe that collective violence or even rioting is not all of a piece, that there are patterns of timing, targeting, and location that are specific to ethnic riots, and that much is to be gained by giving separate treatment to this type of violence. If those patterns are to be understood, the questions asked and the categories used must be less general than those asked and used in aggregate data studies of violence.

Consider an example. There has been a tendency, particularly in the literature on turmoil, to merge antigovernment and intergroup violence,

16. Gurr defines turmoil as "relatively spontaneous, unorganized political violence with substantial popular participation, including violent political strikes, riots, political clashes, and localized rebellions." *Why Men Rebel*, p. 11. Compare Gurr's earlier definition, which listed "ethnic clashes," used the word "strife" for "political violence," and included "political demonstrations and strikes," implying that "turmoil" need not be violent. "A Comparative Study of Civil Strife," in Hugh Davis Graham and Ted Robert Gurr, eds., *Violence in America: Historical and Comparative Perspectives* (Washington, D.C.: Government Printing Office, 1969), Vol. 2, p. 444. For related political science perspectives, see Douglas Hibbs, *Mass Political Violence: A Cross-National Causal Analysis* (New York: John Wiley, 1973), p. 8; Ivo K. Feierabend and Rosalind L. Feierabend, "Aggressive Behaviors within Polities, 1948–1962: A Cross-National Study," *Journal of Conflict Resolution* 10, no. 3 (September 1966): 249–71; Ivo K. Feierabend and Betty Nesvold, with Rosalind L. Feierabend, "Political Coerciveness and Turmoil," *Law and Society Review* 5, no. 1 (August 1970): 93–118. For a summary of social psychology literature, see Berkowitz, *Aggression: A Social-Psychological Analysis*. For the sociological literature on collective behavior, see Neil J. Smelser, *Theory of Collective Behavior* (New York: Free Press, 1962), pp. 222–69; Kurt Lang and Gladys Engel Lang, *Collective Dynamics* (New York: Thomas Y. Crowell, 1961); Ralph H. Turner and Lewis M. Killian, eds., *Collective Behavior* (Englewood Cliffs, N.J.: Prentice Hall, 1957), pp. 83–161.

sorting participants into "dissidents" on one side and "regime" on the other.[17] Much political violence in the contemporary world is, of course, dissident violence, directed against a regime, but not all is. In point of fact, most ethnic violence is not directed against a regime but against members of other groups. More than that, I shall show later that official *support* for violence is actually a common facilitator of ethnic riots. On this question, therefore, submergence of ethnic riots in the larger category of turmoil misleads by 180 degrees.[18] There is, then, analytical utility in separating out violence directed against other groups.

As the most extreme and passionate manifestation of ethnic conflict, the ethnic riot also lifts the curtain on group sentiment. The violence permits a glimpse, under intense light, at points of friction in intergroup contact, at ethnic aspirations and apprehensions, and at some previously only implicit group conceptions of the right ordering of an ethnically heterogeneous polity. The ethnic riot thus provides clues, not only to the character of violence, but to the substance of group relations. Ethnic violence can help clarify something of which social scientists speak only on rare occasions and in circumlocutions: the nature of antipathy.

There are excellent practical reasons, too, for focusing on the ethnic riot. These reasons derive from the widespread, destructive character of ethnic riots and their propensity to develop into more serious and destabilizing forms of violent activity. Ethnic riots are particularly deadly. Unlike assassinations, the riot does not aim at single victims. Unlike most episodes of terror, it is not limited to times, places, and targets pinpointed in advance. Although ethnic riots are not always quite as spontaneous as they may appear, the mass hostility they reflect imparts to them a consid-

17. See Gurr, *Why Men Rebel*, passim. See also the following definition of turmoil: ". . . serious, widespread disturbance, anomie, popular mass participation, *and government retaliation*." Feierabend and Feierabend, "Aggressive Behaviors within Polities," p. 256 (emphasis supplied). Hibbs, *Mass Political Violence*, pp. 7–8, includes riots in a study of events which have "an anti-system character." Cf. Donald G. Morrison and Hugh Michael Stevenson, "Political Instability in Independent Black Africa: More Dimensions of Conflict Behavior within Nations," *Journal of Conflict Resolution* 15, no. 3 (September 1971): 347–68. The merger of varying forms of collective violence is very common. See, e.g., John Ladd, "The Idea of Collective Violence," in James B. Brady and Newton Garver, eds., *Justice, Law and Violence* (Philadelphia: Temple University Press, 1991), pp. 19–47.

18. See the trenchant remarks of James DeNardo, *Power in Numbers: The Political Strategy of Protest Rebellion* (Princeton: Princeton University Press, 1985), p. 5, and of Mark R. Beissinger, "Nationalist Violence in the Former Soviet Union, 1987–1992: An Event Analysis" (paper presented at the annual meeting of the American Association for the Advancement of Slavic Studies, October 29, 1995), p. 7.

erable potential for destruction of life and property. Since the ethnic riot is a cataclysmic, discontinuous event, it is also, not surprisingly, a harbinger of other forms of violence, and it can serve as a source of dramatic political change. The riot thus not only signals dislocations in the polity but often provides the conditions for further disruption and change.

THE RIOT AS CAUSE, EFFECT, AND PROCESS

The deadly ethnic riot is, then, a pivotal event. It is both cause and effect, and it can also be viewed as a process that, in some respects, has its own dynamics. It is worthwhile taking a closer look at these three sides of the riot: causal, consequential, and processual.

THE RIOT AS CAUSE

The riot has at first palpable physical effects. Riots exact their toll in casualties. Sometimes, as in the southern Philippines (1971–72), Chad (1979), Tripura (1980), or Ghana (1994), the deaths number in the thousands; sometimes, as in Burundi (1972), in the tens of thousands; and sometimes, as in India-Pakistan (1947), in the hundreds of thousands.[19] More often a few dozen or a few hundred people are killed. By world standards, an ethnic riot in which 100 people are killed is a very serious disorder.[20] Unless modern weapons have been used — and they rarely are — such a riot probably lasted several days and nights, perhaps a week

19. For deaths in the southern Philippines, see *Washington Post*, June 30, 1972, p. A30; for Chad, see Isaacs, "Power and Identity," p. 12. For Tripura, see *Far Eastern Economic Review*, July 4, 1980, p. 23. For Burundi, see Victor D. DuBois, "To Die in Burundi, Part I: The Eruption of Intertribal Strife: Spring 1972," *American Universities Field Staff Reports*, Central and Southern Africa Series 16, no. 3 (September 1972): 1–15; "Letter from Burundi," *Swiss Review of World Affairs*, July 1972, p. 67. The Indo-Pakistan partition riots have yielded various estimates. Penderel Moon, *Divide and Quit* (Berkeley and Los Angeles: University of California Press, 1962), p. 293, puts the "casualty" (death?) figure for east and west Punjab at a number approaching, but below, 200,000.

20. Lewis F. Richardson, *Statistics of Deadly Quarrels* (Pittsburgh: Boxwood Press, 1960), ch. 2, has shown that, in terms of death toll, wars tend to be at one end of a continuum, riots at the other. Of course, this assumes that they are both, in some sense, single events. In a study of 330 violent conflicts for which fatality estimates were available, R. P. Richardson has concluded that the lowest fatality levels occurred in coups d'état (often no fatalities at all); civil disorders (riots), military revolts, insurrections, and border conflicts occupied a middle ground, averaging slightly more than ten fatalities; while guerrilla wars, civil wars, and limited international wars involved major fatality levels. Richardson, "An Analysis of Recent Conflicts," p. 133.

or more, spreading over at least one major town or rural area, inflicting total casualties many times the death figure, bringing all public and private business to a halt in the affected area and in a surrounding area as well, producing a stream of refugees (some of whom will never return to their homes), likely requiring curfews, and generating all manner of inconvenience, indignity, and outrage.

In gauging the magnitude of an episode of ethnic rioting, then, the cold body count is likely to mislead. In any event, all such casualty figures are estimates, notoriously inaccurate ones at that. Even granted the best of intentions, with which few governments can be credited after the fact of civil disorder, the problem of accounting for the missing, the burned-to-death, the secretly buried, and the unceremoniously drowned is insuperable. At the same time, the incentives to rewrite the performance of the security forces in more effective terms are temptingly great. Official figures of deaths tend to be at the low end of the scale.

Somewhat more reliable are figures on refugees. These provide a more revealing picture of the impact of a disorder. The Sri Lankan riot of 1977 took about 100 lives in the course of a fortnight, but it displaced well over 50,000 people from the Sinhalese south.[21] The 1983 riot in Sri Lanka resulted in at least 471 deaths and created 100,000 refugees.[22] An anti-Indian riot in Durban, South Africa (1949), in which roughly 200 people were killed, lasted the better part of a week, injured more than 1,000, rendered more than 20,000 homeless, involved the burning or looting of whole blocks of Indian shops and homes, and created a variety of dislocations, including absenteeism from industry that continued long after the violence was over.[23] A week of rioting in 1959 in Luluabourg, Zaire, left fewer than 100 dead but triggered a massive exodus from the area, numbering 50,000 in the first two months but ultimately closer to one million.[24] It took the Lebanese civil war 12 years to displace that many people. The northern Nigerian riots of 1966 had produced well over a million displaced persons by the following year.[25] The India-

21. *Far Eastern Economic Review*, February 10, 1978, p. 28; September 9, 1977, p. 32.

22. Ibid., August 18, 1983, p. 17; T. D. S. A. Dissanayake, *The Agony of Sri Lanka* (Colombo: Swastika Press, 1983), p. 93.

23. Union of South Africa, *Report of the Commission of Enquiry into Riots in Durban* (Cape Town: Government Printer, 1949), pp. 4–5.

24. Thomas Turner, "Congo-Kinshasa," in Victor A. Olorunsola, ed., *The Politics of Cultural Sub-Nationalism in Africa* (Garden City, N.Y.: Anchor Books, 1972), p. 223.

25. S. Aluko, "Displaced Nigerians," part II, *West Africa*, April 15, 1967, pp. 495–98, at p. 495.

Pakistan partition riots, with a death toll between 100,000 and 200,000, produced an estimated 10 million refugees.[26] The 1980 violence in Tripura involved the killing of perhaps 1,000 people in a week's time, but it created some 200,000 refugees.[27] Between 258 and 500 people were killed in less than a week in Bombay-Bhiwandi (1984) — about the same death toll as inflicted in several years of Basque terrorism in Spain — but at least 50,000 were left homeless.[28] On the basis of these and similar figures, it is a reasonable conjecture that the ratio of refugees to officially reported deaths in ethnic violence averages at least 100 to one.

As these consequences might suggest, the riot reverberates throughout the political system long after the debris has cleared. The violent outburst may change the course of the system altogether or simply accelerate earlier trends. There are times when violence leads to public introspection, to a determination to see what went wrong and to set it right. The outbreak of violence may inhibit the management of conflict in some cases, facilitate it in others. One thing it will not do is to leave the conflict where it was. After the killing, it is no longer possible to bury the ethnic problem by denying its existence. The riot constitutes a statement of group intentions by conduct — even the conduct of a relative few — and it exposes the malevolence of those intentions, belying the former tranquility inferred from the routine interethnic contact of the marketplace or the government office.[29] One way to measure the importance of group violence is to assess the lingering bitterness and suspicion and aloofness, the residue of distrust and the lust for revenge, that riots introduce or accentuate in ethnic relations.

As I intimated earlier, states experiencing extensive riots are also likely to experience other kinds of political violence.[30] It is easy to see why this is so. Ethnic violence can serve as the proving ground of extremist organizations, which sometimes provide its leadership. The riot may test their

26. Richardson, *Statistics of Deadly Quarrels*, p. 43. This number may be low.

27. *Far Eastern Economic Review*, June 20, 1980, p. 34.

28. Asghar Ali Engineer, *Bhiwandi-Bombay Riots: Analysis and Documentation* (Bombay: Institute of Islamic Studies, 1984), pp. 163, 166.

29. Another effect of violence may be to render the groups in conflict more homogeneous internally than they had previously been. Intraethnic social divisions, based on class, caste, region, or dialect, may seem less important after the killing than they did before. Cf. Lewis A. Coser, *The Functions of Social Conflict* (Glencoe, Ill.: Free Press, 1956), pp. 87–95.

30. Michael C. Hudson, "Conditions of Political Violence and Instability: A Preliminary Test of Three Hypotheses," *Sage Professional Papers in Comparative Politics* 1, no. 5 (1970): 243–94, at p. 264.

mettle, cement their esprit de corps, and aid their recruitment efforts. In India, the Rashtriya Swayamsevak Sangh, a Hindu paramilitary organization, was born out of Hindu-Muslim violence and contributed a considerable share to later violent episodes. Likewise, in the 1960s, as conflict grew between indigenes and migrants in many Indian cities, a spate of *senas* (private armies) was formed, each representing a single ethnic group. In Bombay, one of these, the Shiv Sena, has been active in several violent episodes, including the very destructive anti-Muslim riots of the 1980s and 1990s. In Northern Ireland and the Philippines, ethnic violence that was at first relatively spontaneous grew more and more calculated as the organizations developed, made international contacts, obtained better arms and explosives, and articulated more far-reaching political claims. Violence may thus give enduring organizational expression to the polarization of sentiment.

Not surprisingly, therefore, ethnic riots are a frequent forerunner of secessionist warfare, of terrorism, and of several major forms of political change, including coups, martial law, and suspension of democratic liberties. Civil and secessionist wars in Nigeria, Bangladesh, Chad, Burma, Iraq, the Sudan, martial law in the Philippines, restrictions on democracy in Malaysia, expulsion of the ethnic opposition from the Sri Lankan parliament, and the transition to one-party rule in a veritable array of states were all proximately related to ethnic violence. The question is not whether ephemeral episodes of ethnic rioting can have long-term effects, but what determines which effects they will have.

THE RIOT AS EFFECT

A recurring crossnational feature of ethnic riots is their bizarre fusion of coherence and frenzy. That fusion helps to explain the ethnic conflict out of which violence arises.

The riot is not an unstructured mêlée, in which it is impossible to disentangle attackers from their victims. Rather, the ethnic riot consists of a series of discernible actions, identifiable initiators and targets, attacks and (rarely) counterattacks. Riots spring from highly patterned occurrences and conditions, and they reflect clear-cut structures of ethnic-group relations. Communities do not generally slip gradually or imperceptibly — or randomly — into ethnic violence. Moreover, after the event, participants typically exhibit an utter lack of remorse for their conduct. The Ibo "had it coming to them," it was said after the killings of 1966; the anti-Muslim riot in Ahmedabad, India, in 1969 "was very necessary," said a Hindu mill owner afterward.[31] These are quite characteristic postmortem evaluations. The riot is more like purposive, concerted activity than it is like sleepwalking.

Yet it is concerted activity of a certain furious sort. Virtually everywhere, as I have indicated, atrocities are committed. Victims are often slashed to death or burned alive. When Sikhs attacked Muslims in the Punjab (1947), the "penises of their Muslim male victims were hacked off and stuffed into their mouths or into the mouths of murdered Muslim women."[32] This behavior fits well within the normal range for such events. The more general fury is captured by a description of the Durban riots that reads like many other such descriptions. Mobs of Africans formed *impis*, traditional fighting bands, "chanting the Zulu warcry . . . ." Indian houses were set afire, their inhabitants burned to death inside or clubbed to death outside. The aim was "to destroy the Indian and all that belonged to him."[33] Such activities proceed at a high pitch of manic enthusiasm.

An amalgam of apparently rational-purposive behavior and irrational-brutal behavior forms the leitmotiv of the ethnic riot and distinguishes it from some other forms of ethnic violence, such as the Nazi extermination of Jews, which generally proceed in a coolly calculative spirit.[34] The amalgam of purpose and brutality reflects the spontaneous quality of riot behavior, which proceeds not in response to government orders but in response to the heat of the moment and the feelings of the participants. And that is precisely why violence of this kind is a consistently more reliable guide to intergroup relations than ethnic violence that is more carefully planned and executed, as terrorism is, for example. The very spontaneity of the riot also liberates it from the institutional constraints that shackle the full expression of ethnic sentiment in the conduct of govern-

31. The quotations are drawn from K. Whiteman, "Enugu: The Psychology of Secession, 20 July 1966 to 30 May 1967," in S. K. Panter-Brick, ed., *Nigerian Politics and Military Rule: Prelude to the Civil War* (London: Athlone Press, 1970), p. 116; and Ratna Naidu, *The Communal Edge to Plural Societies* (Delhi: Vikas, 1980), p. 103. For similar sentiments, see Elliott M. Rudwick, *Race Riot at East St. Louis, July 2, 1917* (Carbondale: Southern Illinois University Press, 1964), pp. 51–52; Michael Feldberg, *The Philadelphia Riots of 1844: A Study of Ethnic Conflict* (Westport, Conn.: Greenwood Press, 1975), pp. 133–36.

32. Leo Kuper, *Genocide: Its Political Use in the Twentieth Century* (New Haven: Yale University Press, 1981), p. 66, quoting Larry Collins and Dominique LaPierre, *Freedom at Midnight* (New York: Simon & Schuster, 1975), p. 251.

33. Union of South Africa, *Report of the Commission of Enquiry into Riots in Durban*, pp. 4, 5.

34. See Daniel Jonah Goldhagen, *Hitler's Willing Executioners: Ordinary Germans and the Holocaust* (New York: Alfred A. Knopf, 1996).

ment, or the armed forces, or even ethnically based political parties. The riot produces a more faithful, albeit extreme, reflection of group sentiment than does behavior in an institutional setting. Inferences can be drawn from the identity of the targets and the occasions and locations of the violence. The fusion of coherence and frenzy mirrors, too, the dual character of the underlying ethnic conflict, a conflict motivated simultaneously by collective self-interest and collective passion.[35]

Insofar as the riot constitutes the acting out of ethnic-group sentiment, it is a useful vehicle for understanding the nature of ethnic antipathy. Everywhere, no doubt, the actual killing is the work of a relatively small fraction of people, numbering in the hundreds or thousands. But a great many group members who would shrink from killing are nonetheless willing to condone the violence and provide a sympathetic explanation of it, because it is an extreme manifestation of their own feelings. Without such support, as I shall show, deadly ethnic riots would be very much less frequent than they are, and inferences drawn from them might be much less reliable.

The riot is not merely patterned internally, but is also patterned cross-nationally. There are regularities across riot episodes. These strikingly similar patterns permit a significant measure of generalization about ethnic conflict, not for particular societies alone, but as a general phenomenon.

THE RIOT AS PROCESS

Riots are thus reflections of ethnic conflict by violent means, on the whole fairly faithful reflections. But the infliction of violence is also a process with a logic of its own. The incidence and magnitude of ethnic violence are governed, in part, by the sheer structure of opportunities for violence (such as the availability of targets), by logistics, by the organization of participants and the nature of leadership, by police behavior, by the respect commanded by authority and how it is employed, by tactical imperatives common to all fighting, and by the presence of criminals eager to take advantage of a violent situation. Some such conditions may bear only a tenuous relationship to ethnic conflict.[36]

---

35. For details, see Horowitz, *Ethnic Groups in Conflict*, pt. II.

36. This point of view has been stated most articulately by Richard D. Lambert: "The precise relationship between communal violence and communal tension is . . . difficult to define. Between them is a process of social mechanics which transforms tension into violence. It is not always possible to take the areas or social groups most frequently involved

There are, then, dangers of both overinference and underinference in interpreting the significance of riot behavior for ethnic relations in general. Violence is neither a perfectly crisp dramatization of antecedent conflict nor a wholly autonomous process that bears no relationship to enduring sources of tension.

On the one hand, some of the environmental conditions that foster violence may also be concomitants of ethnic conflict. The belief that the police are partial, the presence of ethnic organizations willing to lend a hand to killing, and previous experience of violence may form part of the underlying conflict, just as they may simultaneously make new violence more likely. Moreover, variable intensities of interethnic hostility tend to produce variations in the intensity of the resulting violence. It is no accident, for example, that anti-Bengali riots in Assam (1979–83) were as widespread and destructive as they were, for they reflected powerful levels of intergroup hostility.

On the other hand, the dynamics of violence as a process can subtly shape and skew antecedent patterns of conflict. The city or town in which a riot begins typically is indicative of the patterning of conflict. But whether that riot then spreads to other cities or towns may depend at least as much on the vicissitudes of communication, the balance of force, and the casualty count at the first location as it does on ethnic conflict in the other areas. Some features of riot behavior — particularly, timing, targeting, and location — reflect antecedent ethnic conflict more faithfully than others, but it is still necessary to be alert to the distortions introduced by the very exigencies of violence.

The dialectic between conflict in general and violence in particular is

---

in violence and infer that these are the areas or social groups experiencing the greatest social tensions. The situation is analogous to an earthquake where the rifts in the surface represent the violence, and the pressures far below the earth the tensions. The location of the rifts depends upon weak points throughout the sub-strata and at the surface. The points of greatest stress may be far below and far removed. So it is in the case of tensions and violence. There are weak points in the society where violence may appear, originating from many different pressures. The points of weakness in social organization where violence may break out depend upon such factors as past traditions of violence, decay in respect for authority, disbelief in the efficiency or impartiality of the police, elements of the population with little to lose and much to gain in the immediate rewards of looting, the presence of transient groups marked as strangers, degree of organization toward violence, and the presence of catalytic groups with or without organization. Many of these factors are not necessarily concomitants of basic tensions either in terms of geographic location or in terms of the groups within the society most directly affected. The origins and nature of tensions must be studied in greater depth and on a different level . . . ." "Hindu-Muslim Riots" (Ph.D. diss., University of Pennsylvania, 1951), pp. 17–18.

nicely illustrated by a question explored in greater depth further on: why some groups are victimized time and again in riots, while others, despite what may appear to be enmity between them and the attackers, are not harmed. In the northern Nigerian riots of 1945, 1953, and 1966, the Ibo received the brunt of the rage of the Hausa attackers, while the Yoruba for the most part escaped it. This is true notwithstanding the many facts that arguably point to frictions between Yoruba and Hausa similar to those between Ibo and Hausa: the presence of relatively well-placed Yoruba as well as Ibo strangers in northern Nigeria; conduct by both groups that could have been interpreted as political provocations to the Hausa; an alliance of Ibo and Yoruba parties before independence that could easily have been regarded as antinorthern; then a coalition at the outset of independence between Hausa and Ibo parties that left the Yoruba party in opposition; and so on. The Ibo may have been disliked more than the Yoruba, but even this does not tell us why the Yoruba received so little aggression when so much was being dished out. The selection of the Ibo as recipients of this enormous violence can be explained. Chapter 5 attempts to do so. Nevertheless, the explanation for so gross a disparity between Ibo and Yoruba victims is not readily apparent in the earlier relations between these groups and the Hausa.

This disparity may be a distortion introduced by the exigencies of violence. But, conceivably, it is not. Perhaps the putative indicators of conflict between Hausa and Yoruba, convincing to outsiders when enumerated, are not causal conditions that actually motivate participants in conflict behavior, or perhaps some such indicators are causally more important than others. If so, our initial assessment of the strength of the underlying conflict between Hausa and Yoruba may have been exaggerated. Violence may still distort conflict relations, emphasizing some, suppressing others, but perhaps the distortions are not as substantial as anticipated.

Like riot causes and effects, riot processes are patterned.[37] Riots are, for example, commonly preceded by a period which I shall call the *lull*, a time of apprehensive quiet during which rumors and warnings may circulate and potential victims may take steps to provide for the safety of their persons and property, while preparations for the attack go forward in inconspicuous ways. Despite the occurrence of such transition periods, an ethnic riot usually has an identifiable precipitating event or events, a

---

37. See Richard D. Lambert, "Ethnic/Racial Relations in the United States in Comparative Perspective," *The Annals* 454 (March 1981): 189–205, at p. 205.

clear beginning, discernible groups of people who initiate the violence and others who receive it. This may be reflected in the sequence of casualties brought to hospitals and morgues, the first set of victims belonging predominantly to one group and subsequent victims to the other. Sometimes, too, a great riot is preceded by a smaller, anticipatory riot, in which attackers test the determination of the forces of law and order as a prelude to the far bigger assault some days or weeks later. Often a great riot is followed by a second round, weeks later, in which rioters attempt a repetition of sorts. Marked similarities in riot process on dimensions such as these are identifiable across time and space; they are as visible in nineteenth- as in twentieth-century riots and in Asian, African, and North American riots.[38] Violence creates the appearance of confusion, but within the confusion there is structure.

A riot on a significant scale has a complex pattern. For the most part, this seems to be a function of divergent motives among a growing number of participants. Arson and looting, for example, may not occur at the same time or place; some participants may be more interested in destruction, others in theft.[39] Despite variations of this kind, it is possible to construct a coherent picture of the elements of riot behavior as a joint function of violence as a process and as a reflection of ethnic-group conflict.

THE FORMS OF ASCRIPTIVE VIOLENCE

The ethnic riot, as I have defined it, entails a substantial measure of relatively spontaneous physical assault by members of one group on members of another. Although elements of organization may be present, for the participants there appears to be a strongly affective aspect. High levels of anger are displayed and atrocities are typically committed in the course of the riot. The main targets are people and the property that is associated with them, rather than institutions. This has the effect of excluding from the definition violence directed primarily at impersonal targets, such as government buildings,[40] although in practice these two varieties of violence may shade off into each other. The choice of targets

38. For nineteenth- and twentieth-century American evidence, see Feldberg, *The Philadelphia Riots of 1844*, pp. 99–161; Rudwick, *Race Riot at East St. Louis*, p. 27.

39. Margaret J. Abudin Stark et al., "Some Empirical Patterns in a Riot Process," *American Sociological Review* 39, no. 6 (December 1974): 865–76.

40. Compare the broader definitions of Hudson, "Conditions of Political Violence and Instability"; Gary T. Marx, "Issueless Riots," *The Annals* 391 (December 1970): 21–33, at p. 24.

by group membership also excludes violence in which victims, including ethnically differentiated victims, are chosen by reference to their individual identification or prior personal conduct.

This conception of ethnic riots — for which I shall also use *ethnic violence* as a synonym — is generally narrower than the common conception, but in one respect it is broader. Common understanding of the riot tends to view it as an entirely spontaneous, uncontrolled, emotion-laden event. This is one side of the phenomenon. But it is important not to be too precise in limiting ethnic riots to wholly unorganized, non-goal-oriented behavior, lest we exclude a significant class of cases in which organization plays a stronger role. In some of the literature on political violence, riots have generally been thought to exclude organized violence,[41] but few riots occur with no organization whatever, and some are rather well organized. The degree to which ethnic violence is organized and the identity of the organizers may well be linked to variations in target selection, timing, and other aspects of riot behavior. For that reason, lack of organization is not one of the definitional properties of this class of cases. On the other hand, ethnic violence, as the term is used here, does not refer to highly organized long-term hostilities designed to effect secession or revolution, although it may be the prelude to that form of violence. Compared to internal war, then, ethnic riots are more concentrated in time and space, more episodic (albeit sometimes recurrent), and apparently less instrumental and calculative.

Similarly, the definition includes nothing about goals. The definition emphasizes the event rather than any objectives toward which violent means might be directed. The immediate aims of this violence are to inflict physical injury and death and sometimes to seize, damage, or destroy property owned by or associated with members of the target group.[42] Even variations on these limited objectives are possible, however. In certain cases, alternatives to physical harm have been offered to victims. The broader goals of violence that is laden with passion are, however, by no means obvious enough to compel incorporation in a definition. They need to be inferred from behavior during violent episodes.

The ethnic riot is a close cousin of several other events involving ethnic actors using violence: violent protest demonstrations, pogroms,

41. Gurr, *Why Men Rebel,* p. 11; Ted Robert Gurr, "Psychological Factors in Civil Violence," *World Politics* 20, no. 2 (January 1968): 245–78, at pp. 275–76.

42. For the pervasiveness of the purpose to injure or hurt in both calculative and impulsive aggression, see Leonard Berkowitz, "Some Varieties of Human Aggression," in Campbell and Gibbs, eds., *Violent Transactions,* pp. 87–89, 101.

feuds, lynchings, genocides, terrorist attacks, gang assaults, ethnic fights, and ethnic warfare. Some episodes may fit one or more of these categories and yet also shade over into ethnic rioting. There is sometimes a practical difficulty of deciding how to characterize a given event. Despite areas of overlap, ethnic riots, as I use the term, are not synonymous with these events.

VIOLENT PROTESTS

The violent protest is usually easy to distinguish from the ethnic riot, but not always. When Gurkha militants bombed police posts and set fire to government buildings in 1987, as part of their campaign for a state separate from West Bengal, or when Muslims in the Malaysian state of Sabah burned shops and cars and attacked police in 1986, in order to destabilize a government representing Christian Kadazans, these events were both ethnic and violent, but they were not the sort of interpersonal civilian assaults characterized here as riots. In south India, in 1965, there were marches against the declared intention of the central government to make Hindi the official language. Effigies and Hindi books were burned; Hindi signs in railway stations were defaced.[43] This was an archetypical violent protest demonstration. So, too, was an episode of violence in Namibia, where, in 1973, Ovambo burned down a municipal building to protest the establishment of an advisory council by the South African government.[44] A year earlier, in the midst of a strike, some 60 Ovambo attacked a police patrol and burned down cattle corrals.[45] There were deaths on both sides, but this I would also classify as a violent protest demonstration. The targets of the violence were not civilians, and they obviously were not chosen merely because of their group membership.

To obtain a more direct sense of the analytical and practical difference between these two forms, it is instructive to contrast the antiblack violence that occurred periodically in the United States from 1900 to 1920, and sporadically afterward, with the African-American violence of the 1960s.[46] The targets of the earlier violence were persons, chosen by their ethnic membership. There were significant casualties. For example, in

43. See Robert L. Hardgrave, Jr., "The Riots in Tamilnad: Problems and Prospects of India's Language Crisis," *Asian Survey* 5, no. 8 (August 1965): 399–407.

44. *Washington Post*, March 8, 1973, p. C5.

45. Ibid., January 31, 1972, p. A5.

46. See Horowitz, "Racial Violence in the United States," in Glazer and Young, eds., *Ethnic Pluralism and Public Policy*, pp. 187–211.

East St. Louis, in July 1919, there were at least 39 blacks killed in just a couple of days of violence.[47] The violence of the 1960s took a completely different course. For the most part, this was not interpersonal violence, though occasionally a white who found himself in the riot area was attacked. Property damage was in the hundreds of millions of dollars, but the death toll was relatively low, and most of those who died were shot by the police or National Guard: 21 of 23 deaths in Newark, for example. The anti-Chinese riots in Kuala Lumpur in 1969 probably involved about the same number of deaths as did all the ghetto disorders of the 1960s taken together, and the 1966 anti-Ibo riots in northern Nigeria took perhaps ten times that number of lives. I note this contrast not to suggest that the test of a riot is the number of casualties, but rather to indicate that, in riots that aim at interpersonal targets, many more deaths are likely than are likely in violent activity that aims only at property destruction and defiance of authority. The ghetto violence of the 1960s was in the latter category.

Despite the connections between the two types, there is much to be gained by distinguishing them. To separate out interpersonal ethnic violence obviously allows us to ask questions about why people kill others and whom they choose to kill, questions it makes no sense to ask of the protest category.

POGROMS

The pogrom is not so much a complementary species of interethnic violence as it is a subcategory of the ethnic riot. If *pogrom* is taken to mean a massacre of helpless people, then it obviously connotes something about the situation of the targets and the outcome of the violence. Since my definition of ethnic riot does not turn on the outcome or retaliatory capacity of the target group, what others may call a pogrom I shall call a riot if the other definitional properties are present.[48]

47. Rudwick, *Race Riot at East St. Louis*, p. 50.

48. Some episodes labeled pogroms, however, entail the active participation of state officials, in which case they may shade over into genocide, a category explicated below. See Leonidas E. Hill, "The Pogrom of November 9–10, 1938 in Germany," in Paul R. Brass, ed., *Riots and Pogroms* (New York: New York University Press, 1996), pp. 89–113; Robert Melson, "A Theoretical Inquiry into the Armenian Massacres of 1894–1896," *Comparative Studies in Society and History* 24, no. 3 (July 1982): 481–509. For another view of riots and pogroms, see Paul R. Brass, "Introduction: Discourses of Ethnicity, Communalism, and Violence," in Brass, ed., *Riots and Pogroms*, pp. 1–55, at pp. 32–34. Much harder to classify is the planned ethnic massacre carried out by professional killers. See, e.g., M. J. Akbar, *Riot after Riot* (New Delhi: Penguin, 1988), pp. 45–60.

FEUDS

A feud is different again. The literature on feuding is in a somewhat confused state. There is no agreement on whether the term *feud* is properly confined only to intraethnic violence.[49] If the term is extended to interethnic violence, the feud is still not synonymous with the ethnic riot, however. A feud is usually conceived as entailing repeated acts of revenge. It is characterized by reciprocal, measured, generally proportional violence,[50] even if it sometimes entails doing a bit more to an opponent than was done by an opponent on the previous occasion.[51] No such norms confine the riot, which is a form of unrestrained violence. Whereas the hostilities that comprise the feud are prolonged and intermittent, a single episode suffices for a riot. Whereas aggressors and victims change roles during a feud — that is the meaning of reciprocal revenge — such a role reversal is unnecessary and unusual for riot behavior. The infliction of riot violence is usually quite one-sided, and revenge is rarely taken by targets of a riot episode. Moreover, the targets need not be related closely to those individuals viewed as provoking the violence, as they tend to be in a feud. Whereas the violence of a feud is confined to a circumscribed category of opponents,[52] riot violence is inflicted indiscriminately on members of a larger target group. Neither the exchange of violence, nor the norm of proportionality, nor individually discriminate targeting is a necessary feature of an ethnic riot.[53]

LYNCHINGS

An ethnic riot, as presently defined, also differs from a lynching, as that term is generally understood. Lynchings had their origin in a crude form

49. See Jacob Black-Michaud, *Feuding Societies* (Oxford: Basil Blackwell, 1975); see also E. L. Peter, Foreword to ibid.

50. Leopold Posposil, "Feud," in David Sills, ed., *International Encyclopedia of the Social Sciences* 5 (New York: Free Press, 1968), pp. 389–93; Black-Michaud, *Feuding Societies*, pp. 27–28; Keith M. Brown, *Bloodfeud in Scotland, 1573–1625* (Edinburgh: John Donald, 1986), pp. 28–29; C. R. Hallpike, *Bloodshed and Vengeance in the Papuan Mountains* (Oxford: Clarendon Press, 1977), p. 211. For a different view of the feud, see Thomas M. Kiefer, *The Tausug: Violence and Law in a Philippine Modern Society* (New York: Holt, Rinehart, & Winston, 1972), pp. 68, 81–82, 105; Christopher Boehm, *Blood Revenge: The Anthropology of Feuding in Montenegro and Other Tribal Societies* (Lawrence: University Press of Kansas, 1984), pp. 110, 216–19.

51. Boehm, *Blood Revenge*, pp. 57, 113.

52. Ibid., p. 172.

53. Nevertheless, the line between feud and riot is not always easy to discern. See *Far Eastern Economic Review*, March 4, 1974, p. 28, reporting interclan violence in Papua–New Guinea.

of punishment for alleged crimes. Although lynching came to be a form of ethnic violence, it was not that originally, and for quite some time not all lynching victims in the United States south were ethnic strangers; some were white.[54] Where the victim of a lynching was black, he (on rare occasions, she) was typically chosen because of his ethnic group membership *plus* some alleged individual crime or breach of the mores of ethnic relations. In one reported case, for instance, a black leader who happened to walk past the scene of a lynching immediately after it was over was actually received with some courtesy by mob members.[55] Presumably, the killers were eager to make the point that the alleged violation of mores was indispensable to lynching and that nonviolators were exempt from that form of violence. Sometimes, however, kinsmen of the accused were lynched when the violator himself could not be located.[56]

By contrast, a riot victim is a member of an ethnic group, chosen randomly because of group membership. To put the point another way, in a lynching there is identity between putative precipitating agent and target that typically does not prevail in a riot. There are exceptions. Lynch mobs have been known to attack members of the target group other than the alleged violators.[57] By the same token, rioters have been known occasionally to focus special attention, nonrandomly, on particularly disliked members of the target group, often settling old scores in the process.[58] Still, these are cases at the margins. The cores of the two phenomena are different.

GENOCIDES

If genocide is taken to mean an attempt to kill an entire people "by direct extermination and other means, including deliberately creating condi-

---

54. Horowitz, "Racial Violence in the United States," pp. 188–90.

55. See Arthur F. Raper, *The Tragedy of Lynching* (Chapel Hill: University of North Carolina Press, 1933), pp. 289–90.

56. Orlando Patterson, "The Feast of Blood: Race, Religion and Human Sacrifice in the Post-Bellum South" (unpublished paper, Department of Sociology, Harvard University, 1997), p. 5.

57. See Hadley Cantril, *The Psychology of Social Movements* (New York: John Wiley & Sons, 1941), p. 94.

58. See Aswini K. Ray and Subhash Chakravarti, *Meerut Riots: A Case Study* (New Delhi: Sampradayikta Virodhi Committee, 1968?), p. 2; Government of Burma, *Final Report of the Riot Inquiry Committee* (Rangoon: Superintendent of Government Printing, 1939), pp. 95, 102; Ghanshyam Shah, "Communal Riots in Gujarat," *Economic and Political Weekly*, Annual Number, January 1970, p. 193.

tions increasing mortality and diminishing birth rates,"[59] then the ethnic riot differs in a number of respects. The random identity of the victims within the targeted ethnic category is the same, but there is no necessary intention in ethnic riot behavior to kill a whole people. In addition, the riot does not embrace the more indirect means that are contemplated by this definition of genocide. Physical assault is the method of the riot. And the participation of state authorities in genocide is not necessary to the ethnic riot. A riot can, however, form an episode in a larger genocidal campaign, and there are here, as elsewhere, ambiguities of classification, exacerbated by definitions that conflate the two phenomena.[60] Some or all of the large-scale killing of Hutu in Burundi (1972 and 1988), like the killing of Armenians in Turkey (1894–96, 1915), has been regarded as both riot behavior and genocide.[61]

TERRORIST ATTACKS

Ethnically motivated terrorist attacks differ from riots in their much greater organization and planning and their generally (but not uniformly) more scrupulous choice of targets. The terrorist kills as a matter of policy. He or she may or may not be imbued with passion. The terrorist kills exactly when and where he chooses to kill; and, if he chooses assassination as his vehicle, he knows the personal identity of his victim. The terrorist bomb is another matter, but even it may be placed so as to discriminate, in some measure, among various targets. However, the ethnic terrorist who plants a bomb is typically willing to take the risk of killing some members of his own group, in the interest of the larger strategic

59. Helen Fein, "A Formula for Genocide: Comparison of the Turkish Genocide (1915) and the German Holocaust (1939–1945)," in Richard F. Tomasson, ed., *Comparative Studies in Sociology*, Vol. 1 (Greenwich, Conn.: JAI Press, 1978), pp. 271–94, at p. 271.

60. Including that of the United Nations Genocide Convention. See Helen Fein, "Accounting for Genocide after 1945: Theories and Some Findings," *International Journal on Group Rights* 1, no. 2 (January 1993): 79–106, at pp. 80–81. See generally Kuper, *Genocide: Its Political Use in the Twentieth Century*; Frank Chalk and Kurt Jonassohn, *The History and Sociology of Genocide* (New Haven: Yale University Press, 1990); Ervin Staub, *The Roots of Evil: The Origins of Genocide and Other Group Violence* (Cambridge: Cambridge University Press, 1989); Robert F. Melson, *Revolution and Genocide: On the Origins of the Armenian Genocide and the Holocaust* (Chicago: University of Chicago Press, 1992).

61. In addition to the works cited in note 60, see René Lemarchand, *Burundi: Ethnocide as Discourse and Practice* (Cambridge: Cambridge University Press, 1994), pp. 127–28; Fein, "A Formula for Genocide"; Wyszomirski, "Communal Violence: The Armenians and the Copts as Case Studies."

objective. The ethnic rioter, on the other hand, takes pains, as we shall see, to kill only members of the target group. The violence of the terrorist is more precise in some ways; that of the rioter is more precise in others.

Terrorism comes in many guises,[62] and sometimes the pattern of a terrorist attack can resemble the ethnic riot. In 1979, for example, more than 1,000 Nagas crossed the state border between Nagaland and Assam, set fire to 260 homesteads in five villages, and killed about 50 Nepalese settlers and indigenous Bodo plains tribals of Assam.[63] The violence took place in an area claimed by Nagaland and was aimed at discouraging residents of Assam from cultivating the land. The mobilization of more than 1,000 Naga warriors and the likely connivance of the Nagaland government in organizing the attack suggest that this was no spontaneous riot, but rather state-sponsored terrorism.[64]

Some of the most important and enduring terrorist movements have been ethnically based. Among the most prominent of these are segments of the Irish Republican Army, operating in Northern Ireland, and the Basque Euskadi Ta Askatasuna, operating in Spain. There has been Corsican terrorism, Sri Lankan Tamil terrorism, and Sikh terrorism. Ethnic conflict often gives rise to terrorist activity. Similarly, terrorist organizations may be formed, or their membership augmented, in the aftermath of ethnic rioting. And terrorist attacks or assassinations may precipitate ethnic rioting, as they certainly did in Sri Lanka (1983) and in Delhi (1984). Yet, entangled as these two forms sometimes are, they are hardly the same thing.

One of the consequences of the deliberation and pinpointing of targets that characterize terrorist activity is the relatively lower death toll from terrorist attacks than from ethnic riots. As I have indicated, this is not intrinsic to terrorist violence, but it is typical of established movements. In Spain, the death toll over many years was measured at fewer than 400, about the same number of deaths suffered by Bengalis in Tripura on a single day: June 8, 1980.[65] In Northern Ireland, from 1969 to 1981, there were 2,161 deaths in 1,715 separate fatal incidents, a ratio of 1.2

62. For the diversity of the phenomenon, see Martha Crenshaw, "The Causes of Terrorism," *Comparative Politics* 13, no. 4 (July 1981): 379–400.

63. *Far Eastern Economic Review*, January 29, 1979, p. 27.

64. International law conceptions of terrorism stress its antistate character. See John Dugard, "International Terrorism: Problems of Definition," *International Affairs* 50, no. 1 (January 1974): 67–81. There is, however, a strong case for recognizing the phenomenon of state-sponsored or state-condoned terrorism. See H. Jon Rosenbaum and Peter C. Sederberg, eds., *Vigilante Politics* (Philadelphia: University of Pennsylvania Press, 1976).

65. *Far Eastern Economic Review*, June 20, 1980, p. 34. The official death toll was 378; the unofficial toll numbered much higher.

deaths to the incident.[66] This clear indication of individual selectivity is a clue that differentiates the terrorist attack from the ethnic riot.

GANG ASSAULTS

It is not difficult to distinguish between ethnic terrorism and attacks on ethnic strangers by gangs whose membership is ethnically based. Terrorists typically adhere to a political ideology, are better trained, possess more sophisticated weapons, usually have a strategic rationale for their attack, and execute it with greater tactical skill. Gang attacks differ on these dimensions, but they are not themselves a homogeneous category. One subspecies involves the ethnically differentiated youth gang that attacks ethnic strangers with an arbitrariness in its choice of victims that resembles the ethnic riot.[67] Such a gang attack is generally not a response to precipitating events. Another subspecies involves the ethnically differentiated criminal gang that makes extortionate demands on ethnic strangers, demands enforced by violence. Recurrent activity by such gangs may lead to episodes of ethnic rioting, as it did in the southern Philippines (1970–72),[68] but the gang attack has different aims. Gangs also have a strong element of organization extending far beyond any given episode of violence.

ETHNIC FIGHTS

There are other events even harder to classify, because they resemble ethnic riots and yet lack the depth of feeling necessary for killing or, alternatively, are subject to restraints that inhibit killing. Such events tend to occur in highly structured environments, such as mining camps or plantations with ethnically segmented, sometimes seasonal, often overwhelmingly male, work forces.[69] The settings in which they occur suggest that, despite their ethnic character, they may have dynamics different

66. Michael Poole, "The Demography of Violence," in John Darby, ed., *Northern Ireland: The Background to the Conflict* (Belfast: Appletoe Press, 1983), p. 169. By 1988, more than 2,600 had been killed. *Irish Times*, August 6, 1988, p. 2.

67. For an example, see Dennis Wederell, "Letter from Auckland," *Far Eastern Economic Review*, January 19, 1979, p. 94.

68. See Peter G. Gowing, "Muslim Filipinos between Integration and Secession" (paper presented at the annual meeting of the Association of Asian Studies, Chicago, March 30–April 1, 1973).

69. Robert Gordon, "The Celebration of Ethnicity: A 'Tribal Fight' in a Namibian Mine Compound," in Brian M. du Toit, ed., *Ethnicity in Modern Africa* (Boulder, Colo.: Westview, 1978), pp. 213–31.

from those of an ethnic riot. In spite of (or because of) the proximity of
the participants to each other, these attacks involve few serious casualties. In their sudden, rather spontaneous, interpersonal character, and
their choice of targets by ethnic membership, such events would qualify
as ethnic riots. What they lack is the intensity required for killing and
atrocity.

THE BALANCE AMONG FORMS

To say, as I have, that the various forms of interethnic violence differ on
several dimensions — nature of targets, severity and number of casualties,
centrality of revenge, randomness or selectivity of individual victims, and
degree of planning — is not to suggest that the forms are structurally
unrelated to each other. On the contrary, there may be some common
underlying causes. Furthermore, the existence of one form of violence
may be a function of the absence of another. In the West, ethnic violence
does not take the form of warfare or of ethnic riots, as defined here,
although ethnic riots are by no means historically absent. Outside the
West, both warfare and riots are more common than ethnic terrorism.
This would seem to suggest some element of functional substitutability of
one form for another, where the requisite conditions for the latter do not
exist. That is to say, there is reason to suppose that the West has ethnic
terrorism because it lacks the conditions for the other forms of ethnic
violence or that the non-West has ethnic warfare and riots because it
lacks the conditions for ethnic terrorism.

What these conditions are, and why they are present in one world
region but not in another, are important research questions. This is an
example of how focused attention on one form of violence can contribute to an overall understanding of violence, and I shall return to the
conditions underlying the worldwide regional distribution of ethnic riots
in the last two chapters.

HYBRID FORMS

It is worth emphasizing the occasional existence of hybrid forms of violence, even while keeping an eye on one form. In highly organized ethnic
warfare, as in Liberia, Georgia, and Bosnia in the 1990s, or in Eritrea in
the 1970s and '80s, there is considerable opportunity for the pursuit of
genocide, riot, violent protest, terrorism, and feud. The line between
warfare and riot is often elusive, and riots occur within warfare or alter-

nate with it, as in the Congo Republic (1993–94), or the southern Philippines (1971 and 1974).[70] Anti-Armenian riots in Dushanbe, Tajikistan (1990), began as antiviolent government protests,[71] whereas anti-Chinese violence in Jakarta (May 1998) turned to more general looting and burning.[72] A series of violent episodes in Papua–New Guinea (1989) straddled the line between feud and riot. Riots gave way to genocide in Burundi (1988).[73] In the United States, Miami (1980) and Los Angeles (1992) were mainly violent protests, but they had some Cuban and Korean victims, respectively. Riots do not always occur in a pure, natural state, uncontaminated by other forms.

A hybrid form was the violence in Zahedan, Iran (1979), and in the Sind, Pakistan (1972).[74] Following the overthrow of the shah, the Khomeini regime appointed a Persian governor for the Zahedan region. Baluch, who are Sunni, complained that the regime and the governor favored their neighbors, the Sistani, who, like the Persians, are Shiites. When Revolutionary Guards began to disarm Baluch, Baluch attacked. Their targets were Sistani *and* Revolutionary Guards. The violence partook of both ethnic riot and antiregime protest. In the Sind, violence was triggered by passage of a bill making Sindhi the sole official language of the province. Urdu-speakers protested, at first attacking police but later attacking Sindhis as well.

The point of dealing with the bounded phenomenon, in spite of hybridity and alternation in some cases, is to avoid the mistaken causality that can occur when one sets out to understand the large, blended phenomena that Giovanni Sartori calls cat-dogs.[75] In the end, riots almost surely share some causal elements with other forms of ethnic violence, but it will not be possible to know which conditions are common and which are distinctive if we begin with a dependent variable based on

70. Kajsa Ekholm Friedman and Anne Sundberg, "Ethnic War and Ethnic Cleansing in Brazzaville" (unpublished paper, Department of Social Anthropology, University of Lund, 1994); Peter G. Gowing, *Muslim Filipinos — Heritage and Horizon* (Quezon City: New Day, 1979), pp. 193–95.

71. BBC Summary of World Broadcasts, February 14, 1990, SU/0688/B/1.

72. I am drawing here on my interviews in Jakarta, August 9–14, 1998, and on inferences from I. Sandyawan Sumardi, "The Early Documentation No. 1: Pattern of Riots in Jakarta and Surrounding Areas," Report of the Volunteer Team for Humanity, mimeo., June 9, 1998.

73. Lemarchand, *Burundi: Ethnocide as Discourse and Practice*, pp. 118–27.

74. Radio Tehran, December 19–23, 1979, in FBIS-MEA-79–246, December 20, 24, 1979, pp. 13, 14, 20–22, 35–39; *Statesman* (Calcutta), July 11, 1972, p. 1.

75. Giovanni Sartori, "Comparing and Miscomparing," *Journal of Theoretical Politics* 3, no. 3 (July 1991): 243–57, at pp. 247–49.

merged phenomena. The category of undifferentiated ethnic violence, to which most studies refer, is far too capacious to permit systematic comparison without the risk of vague findings such as those attributing all such disorders to "strain" resulting from "change."[76] Disaggregation of violent phenomena is required.

DEPLOYING THE DATA

Reports of ethnic riots are abundant, because ethnic riots are frequent. Many countries of Asia and Africa have experienced serious episodes of ethnic rioting. Especially since 1989, they have been joined by countries in the former Soviet Union and Eastern Europe. According to figures compiled by Ted Robert Gurr, as early as 1961–65 perhaps one-fourth of all "turmoil" was initiated by ethnic groups in Africa (where the figure was 32 percent) and Asia (19 percent).[77] More recent data show a slightly higher incidence of ethnically identified events as a fraction of "direct action" conflict events, peaceful and violent.[78] For 1984–95, the sub-Saharan African figure was 38 percent, and the Asian figure was 23 percent. There are good reasons to believe that these percentages, even though merely suggestive, understate the incidence of ethnic rioting. Governments everywhere are embarrassed by the image of a crumbling nationhood evoked by ethnic violence. A great many act on their embarrassment and suppress news of its outbreak. Some violent events are not reported at all in the standard sources used in aggregate data studies, because they occur in what the international news media regard as backwaters.[79] Nevertheless, when disorder surfaces, it generates interest in

76. See Charles Tilly, *Big Structures, Large Processes, Huge Comparisons* (New York: Russell Sage Foundation, 1984), pp. 53–54.

77. Gurr, "A Comparative Study of Civil Strife," p. 454. I discuss Gurr's concept of "turmoil" as embracing spontaneous, unorganized violence in the next section.

78. The data are drawn from Reuters and coded by the KEDS/PANDA system in use at the Project on Non-Violent Sanctions at the Harvard Center for International Affairs. "Direct action" is similar to Gurr's "turmoil," in that it includes various forms of "indeterminate action," such as strikes, protests, and violent encounters. Many thousands of events were coded worldwide for the project. I am indebted to Doug Bond for making these data available.

79. A favorite such source is the *New York Times*. But the *New York Times Index* contains no entry whatever for Guinea (even under "French West Africa") in January 1956— or any other month in that year—or for Assam (even under "India") in January 1968, although both experienced ethnic disorders in those months. This is not necessarily an adverse reflection on the *Times*—only on those who think they can utilize it as a source that provides comprehensive or representative coverage. Gurr has made a conscious attempt at inclusiveness, but others have been less alert to this problem. Note the systematic

uncovering causes and patterns of action. Violent episodes have therefore produced a large but still incomplete body of documentary material that lends itself to comparative analysis.

The field is fertile but untilled. The accumulated body of data ranges from local newspaper accounts and the more detailed narratives of regional or specialist periodicals, to reports of official commissions of inquiry or of unofficial organizations that have conducted their own investigations, and to books, memoirs, partisan tracts, and parliamentary debates. This corpus of detailed, descriptive material, which sometimes includes eyewitness interviews gathered by investigatory bodies, constitutes a surprisingly copious and largely untapped resource for comparative analysis. There have been studies of violent episodes in a single country and perceptive attempts to compare an outbreak at one time and place with an outbreak at another.[80] At the other end of the continuum, there have been several very ambitious undertakings in the formulation of general theories of collective violence. These macropolitical studies, relying heavily on international newspaper reportage, have tended to ask large questions about violence in general. Between the case study and the aggregate-data study, a few subjects, notably genocide, have been treated extensively. But there has been no previous multicountry study of the ethnic riot, certainly none relying on data adequate for multiple observations on most of the significant issues.

Adequate reports exist for approximately 150 riots in 50 countries. All but a few of these episodes took place in the post–World War II period, and the majority are from the period from 1965 to 2000. There is, of course, some unevenness of detail in the data sources. For many incidents, there are complete accounts covering all the questions to be pursued, in multiple sources that lend themselves to factual cross-checking; for others, there is useful material on only some of the issues. The immediate precipitants of riots, for example, are almost universally described at some length, whereas the planning of violence, where planning is present,

---

bias likely to be introduced into studies of, for example, modernization and the incidence of communal violence when those studies are based on aggregate data culled from the news media. Since less modernized areas are also less fully reported, the results of the research are, in more ways than one, predictable.

80. See, e.g., Stanley J. Tambiah, *Leveling Crowds: Ethnonationalist Conflicts and Collective Violence in South Asia* (Berkeley and Los Angeles: University of California Press, 1996); Steven Ian Wilkinson, "The Electoral Incentives for Ethnic Violence: Hindu-Muslim Riots in India" (Ph.D. diss., M.I.T., 1998); Naidu, *The Communal Edge to Plural Societies*, pp. 91–123; Rudwick, *Race Riot at East St. Louis*; H. Otto Dahlke, "Race and Minority Riots," *Social Forces* 30, no. 4 (May 1952): 419–25.

tends to be clandestine and thus less frequently reported in detail. In virtually every case, there is more than one source, and in all there is some good assurance of reliability. The data on each episode are far more extensive and much higher in quality than the usual events-data sources, which tend to rely on the international press and events-data banks.

To say that riot narratives are abundant is not to imply that the distribution of reports is evenly spread across countries. Some countries report their ethnic violence with more frequency, in greater depth, and in more varied sources than others do. In some small measure, differential reporting may be associated with skewed patterns of riot behavior. Consider the case of India, which, officially and unofficially, provides frequent, detailed narratives of ethnic riots. Many Indian riots are therefore included in the data set, more, in fact, than those of any other country. Riots in India, especially Hindu-Muslim riots, have often been precipitated by events occurring during public processions. Riots elsewhere are also precipitated by processions, but the overall frequency of the procession precipitant, as a fraction of all riot precipitants, may be somewhat lower elsewhere than in India. This would introduce a serious bias into findings about the frequency distribution of various precipitants. But it is no limitation whatever on classification. Although I make statements of the "more common, less common" or "most common, least common" variety, knowledge of the potential for skewing in the data leads me to do so judiciously.[81] For the most part, I am concerned to provide answers to questions of *what*, rather than *how much*.[82] The narrative accounts provide a good deal of confidence for this sort of statement.[83]

81. As pointed out in note 79, above, a comparable problem is present in studies that draw conclusions from events-data banks derived from standard newspaper sources. The fact that the data set is ready-made, rather than constructed by the investigator, provides no ground for confidence about the absence of skewing sufficient to justify the validity of quantitative statements. Cf. Alexander L. George, "Case Studies and Theory Development: The Method of Structured Focused Comparison," in Paul Gordon Lauren, ed., *Diplomacy: New Approaches in History, Theory, and Policy* (New York: Free Press, 1979), p. 60, on "conditional generalizations rather than frequency distributions."

82. The case for such questions is cogently presented, for comparative politics generally, by Giovanni Sartori, "Concept Misformation in Comparative Politics," *American Political Science Review* 64, no. 4 (December 1970): 1033–53. See also Arend Lijphart, "Comparative Politics and the Comparative Method," *American Political Science Review* 65, no. 3 (September 1971): 682–93, at p. 683.

83. Abundant though the materials are, they obviously suffer from the usual sources of distortion: deficiencies of observation and articulation, selective perception, observer bias, loss of information during interpretation, and so on. The problems of verification are as serious with riots as with other social phenomena, but they are not more serious, and the heterogeneity of sources ought to mitigate these problems. Certainly, there is no case for abandoning the quest for a scholarly account altogether. But see Brass, *Theft of an Idol*, p. 5.

In addition to exploiting the narrative accounts, I have conducted interviews with participants, organizers, victims, observers, and suppressors of violent episodes in six countries: one episode in Guyana, two in Malaysia, two in Sri Lanka, one in Singapore, one in Indonesia, and a series in Romania. Although these interviews are not the main data source, they provide direct support for inferences that could otherwise be drawn only from behavior in the large, and sometimes they open windows on mechanisms that underlie the violence but that might be missed in the narrative accounts. A few examples illustrate what I mean.

Quite by accident, I was able on one occasion to interview a lucky survivor of a Sri Lankan riot, a Tamil who had understandably contrived to be misidentified as a Sinhalese. He provided a report of his rather lengthy encounter with those who contemplated killing him (and who nearly did so). His account illuminates the great care taken by rioters to be accurate in their identifications, even, as in this case, at the expense of losing a chance to kill someone the crowd thought probably should be killed. I theorize about this behavior of rioters and its significance in Chapter 4.

On another occasion, in Malaysia, I conducted interviews with participants in a riot soon after it occurred. They provided data on their own rapid mobilization for a violent response to a sudden precipitant. One might have inferred the existence of the most skeletal, ephemeral organization (bordering on none) from reports of the quick sequence of events, but the interviews make this explicit, and they clarify the relation of antecedent social organization to rapid mobilization. These issues are discussed in Chapter 7.

Soon after this violence, further anti-Chinese violence was averted in a neighboring Malaysian state, when police arrested leaders of a rural organization called Tentera Sabilullah or Holy War Army. When I interviewed close observers, including some likely members of this organization, what emerged, among other things, were the close connections between supernatural beliefs and the conquest of fear by prospective participants in deadly violence. These connections are explored in Chapter 3.

Years later, I spent several days with participants, police, and victims of anti-Roma (Gypsy) violence in a large swath of rural Romania. Some of the victims were spending a cold, wet winter living in holes in the ground. A close look at the sites of the violence shows the anti-Roma episodes to be more like lynchings than riots, serving to sharpen up the distinction (and its occasional blurring) discussed in this chapter. In Chapter 12, using the Romanian materials, I examine the emergence of violent alternatives to riots.

These illustrations suggest that it is no disadvantage that the written and oral sources are not coterminous. As plentiful, rich, and representative of the range of riot behavior as the narrative accounts may be, resort to interviews slices into the phenomenon at a usefully different level of analysis.[84]

To study violence implies the need to study quiescence. Some have gone further and asserted that, since peace is more prevalent than violence, it is more important to focus on peace than on violence.[85] This carries things too far. Like violence, quiescence needs study, although not more study than violence. Because of the difficulty of proving negatives, however, quiescence is hard to study apart from violence. I have tried to develop a strategy for explaining why phenomena do not happen and have applied it in Chapter 12 to a control group of 50 additional negative cases. These are cases in which riots do not occur when they might be expected, or, having occurred, fail to recur, or give way to alternative forms of violence, or occur only in very mild degrees. The strategy is to focus on what might be called near misses.

The whole inquiry unfolds issue by issue, culminating in a bigger picture of the riot as an amalgam of passion and calculation in the final chapter.[86] Decades ago, William H. Riker suggested that examinations of large phenomena occurring over long time periods and involving indefinite numbers of actors are more likely to produce inconclusive results than are close studies of small phenomena of brief duration that can be "precisely bounded . . . ."[87] Bounding the ethnic riot is a bit more difficult than might be imagined, as we shall soon see; and I make no claim for the superiority of Riker's strategy in all cases. However, where there are abundant data at the level of the episode, there is much to be gained by exploiting them in this way.

There is always a question of how rare or well done to serve up those data. On most issues, I permit the data to do much of the talking and to

84. On the benefits of data at different levels, see Gary King, Robert O. Keohane, and Sidney Verba, *Designing Social Inquiry* (Princeton: Princeton University Press, 1994), pp. 30–31, 48.

85. James D. Fearon and David D. Laitin, "Explaining Interethnic Cooperation," *American Political Science Review* 90, no. 4 (December 1996): 715–35.

86. For the utility of the disaggregative strategy, see King, Keohane, and Verba, *Designing Social Inquiry*, p. 218.

87. William H. Riker, "Events and Situations," *Journal of Philosophy* 54, no. 3 (January 31, 1957): 57–70, at p. 69. For similar views, see Valery A. Tishkov, *Ethnicity, Nationalism and Conflict in and after the Soviet Union: The Mind Aflame* (London: Sage, 1997), p. 153; Charles W. Anderson, "Comparative Policy Analysis: The Design of Measures," *Comparative Politics* 4, no. 1 (October 1971): 117–31, at pp. 120–21.

some extent "delay the reduction of detail to abstract categories," making "that reduction part of the analysis itself . . . ."[88] I am especially circumspect about reducing the detail on precipitating events in Chapter 8, for these are the events that show exactly how riots develop. If, in all this, we are able to observe what rioters do and to listen carefully to what they say about their enterprise, we shall be struck by recurrent similarities and, ironically enough, be in a better position to produce a theoretical account, one that does not coincide with the lay understanding, whether of rioters or others.

One of the most damning reproaches that can be made against a discipline with theoretical pretensions is that its categories of explanation are those of the laity,[89] that it cedes its own sense of importance to the flow of events. Appropriately, most disciplines reward those who display originality by reordering reality. As I show in the next section, the study of violence has been characterized by considerable reactivity to the occurrence of violent events of various classes. Theory has twisted and turned in response to events and the changing identity of the protagonists. This does not make for good theory, but neither does the opposite temptation: an excessively spare and speculative a priorism. "To set forth symmetrical crystals of significance, purified of the material complexity in which they were located, and then attribute their existence to autogenous principles of order, universal properties of the human mind, or vast a priori *Weltanschauungen*, is to pretend a science that does not exist and imagine a reality that cannot be found."[90] There is no escape, Clifford Geertz trenchantly observes, from "inspecting events," and "it is not in our interest to bleach human behavior of the very properties that interest us before we begin to examine it . . . ."[91]

We shall inspect first, infer second, and bleach not at all. The result is a considerable immersion in the gore of the violent episode. Underpinning this venture is a conviction of the need to be faithful to the evidence *and* to reshape it, on the premise that it is better to prove that an argument is sound than to sound as if an argument is proved.

88. Tilly, *Big Structures, Large Processes, Huge Comparisons*, p. 119.

89. I agree with Russell Hardin, *One for All: The Logic of Group Conflict* (Princeton: Princeton University Press, 1995), pp. 9–14, who characterizes theory as transcending the commonsense understanding of the actors whose actions it interprets. But this injunction does not explain how such transcendence is to be achieved.

90. Clifford Geertz, *The Interpretation of Cultures* (New York: Basic Books, 1973), p. 20.

91. Ibid., p. 17.

THE STATE OF VIOLENCE THEORY

If we ask why ethnic riots occur, or why they occur when or where they occur, or why particular groups of people initiate them and others are victimized in them, or any of the other questions that need to be asked about such events, the answer from theories of violence developed during and after the 1960s will be at once too broad and too narrow. Too broad, because the theories are explicitly designed to explain, in the first instance, all collective violence and, in the second instance, all "turmoil" or some such equivalent. Rarely do they descend to treat riots separately. Too narrow, because, despite their ambitions to be comprehensive, the theories emphasize, in their explanatory schema, a rather limited conception of grievance or an equally limited conception of instrumental political rationality among those who organize and participate in violence. Both in their scope and in the substance of their explanations, the prevailing theories have a particularly poor fit with the phenomenon of ethnic riots. To appreciate why such theories offer so little to anyone seeking to understand ethnic riots, it is necessary to examine briefly the origins and outlines of the major perspectives that emerged in the decades after World War II. We shall have a chance to assess some newly emerging approaches — not yet full-blown theories — against the comparative evidence in Chapter 13.

Several bodies of theory were potentially available to help explain political violence. Freudian theory had dealt with the issue of aggression and had applied the psychoanalytic model to crowd behavior, but it had relatively little to say about nonregressive political violence per se.[92] The collective behavior approach, principally the work of sociologists, was more directly pertinent to political violence.[93] Collective behaviorists had studied episodes of violence. They called attention to the formation of what appeared to be common purposes in crowds, to the dynamics of interactions within crowds, and to such politically relevant matters as mass organization and precipitating events. Nevertheless, neither psychoanalytic theory nor collective behavior theory proved particularly influential with most students of political violence after about the mid-1960s.

Psychoanalytic theory was not readily amenable to empirical testing,

92. Sigmund Freud, *Group Psychology and the Analysis of the Ego*, trans. and ed. James Strachey (New York: Norton, 1961).

93. See the works on collective behavior cited in note 16, above.

and it is not surprising that it should be neglected in political violence studies, with the notable exception of studies of the personality of individual terrorists.[94] Collective behavior, however, is another matter.

The study of crowds has been characterized by false starts, going back to Durkheim's conception of "collective effervescence," a state of "psychic exultation" that exists in crowds acting at moments of social discontinuity.[95] Durkheim understood that crowd members are capable of conduct of which they are incapable individually, that emotions echo in crowds, and that the passions that seize crowds can produce action either heroic or barbaric. Durkheim's heirs were the collective behaviorists. There is much to criticize in the collective behavior literature, which had subsumed most mass violence under the rubric of "hostile outbursts": the occasional implication of incoherent action, the frequent emphasis on rather rigid stages that must be traversed by crowds in a specified order, and the suggestion that crowds are inevitably acting in contradiction to values accepted in the wider society.[96] Rioting crowds, we shall see, are aroused but not incoherent, they can move into action quickly, and they draw support from social approval.

Nevertheless, collective behaviorists were focused on aspects of the riot that unfortunately got lost as their work was eclipsed by a new wave of theory. In their absence, the understanding of crowds has gone by default.[97] The term *hostile outburst* is an important clue to the relative

94. See, e.g., Gustave Morf, *Terror in Quebec: Case Studies of the FLQ* (Toronto: Clare, Irwin, 1970); Jerrold M. Post, "Hostilité, Conformité, Fraternité: The Group Dynamics of Terrorist Behavior," *International Journal of Group Psychotherapy* 36, no. 2 (April 1986): 211–24.

95. Emile Durkheim, *The Elementary Forms of Religious Life*, trans. Karen E. Fields (New York: Free Press, 1995), p. 228. See Edward A. Tiryakian, "Collective Effervescence, Social Change, and Charisma: Durkheim, Weber and 1989," *International Sociology* 10, no. 3 (September 1995): 269–81, at p. 273. I am grateful to Edward A. Tiryakian for steering me back to Durkheim.

96. See, e.g., Smelser, *Theory of Collective Behavior*, pp. 13–18, 101–12, 248–53; Turner and Killian, *Collective Behavior*, p. 58; and the critique of S. D. Reicher, "The St. Paul's Riot: An Explanation of the Limits of Crowd Action in Terms of a Social Identity Model," *European Journal of Social Psychology* 14, no. 1 (January–March 1984): 1–21, at pp. 17–19. Much early work in collective behavior would not survive an encounter with research that has been done since, as is recognized by one of the leading collective behaviorists of the 1950s and '60s. See Ralph H. Turner, "Race Riots, Past and Present: A Cultural-Collective Behavior Approach," *Symbolic Interaction* 17, no. 3 (1994): 309–24.

97. There is a small revival of interest in the crowd. It is evident, for example, in Turner's emphasis on the nullification of customary meanings that makes extraordinary action possible. See "Race Riots, Past and Present," p. 318. It is also manifest in Tambiah's and Reicher's concern with the crowd's interpretation of its environment. See Tambiah, *Leveling Crowds*; Reicher, "The St. Paul's Riot."

insignificance of the collective behavior school in the later development of theories of political violence. Hostile outbursts and the dynamics of crowd behavior — including the prominent role of rumor, often false rumor, in propelling mass action — imply a substantial degree of irrationality among participants in violent acts. The study of crowds, especially in the version associated with Gustave Le Bon,[98] was heavily imbued with explanation based on misperception, closed channels of communication, and the so-called group mind. It was based, in other words, on irrational behavior.

The theories that emerged in the 1960s and 1970s, on the other hand, proceeded from an assumption of collective rationality inimical to the adoption of concepts developed by the collective behaviorists.[99] The origins of the theories seem to reside in the particular violence to be explained in the 1960s. It was one thing to attribute irrationality to sailors attacking Mexican Americans in California or to white mobs attacking blacks in Chicago or East St. Louis decades earlier.[100] It was quite another to impute the same irrationality to African Americans struggling against urban ghetto conditions or to guerrillas struggling in behalf of peasants against Latin American oligarchies.[101] The two predominant explanations emerging in the 1960s and 1970s are those frequently described as the relative deprivation and resource mobilization approaches. These two differ dramatically on many dimensions, but they share a common assumption of the basic collective rationality of the participants in violence.

Grievance models of political violence generally utilize the concept of relative deprivation, defined in terms of a perceived disparity between expectation and gratification. There are many variations around this theme. Certainly, the literature does not embody a single view of relative deprivation. But the various formulations share an underlying assumption that people behave violently because they feel aggrieved. In Gurr's

98. Gustave Le Bon, *The Crowd: A Study of the Popular Mind* (London: Ernest Benn, 1896).

99. No effort was made, however, to differentiate individual motives for participating from collective interests in the violence. Compare Mancur Olson, *The Logic of Collective Action* (Cambridge: Harvard University Press, 1965).

100. Ralph H. Turner and Samuel J. Surace, "Zoot-Suiters and Mexicans: Symbols in Crowd Behavior," *American Journal of Sociology* 62 (1956): 14–24.

101. "Sharing [a] liberal perspective, social scientists of diverse theoretical persuasions often restricted their analyses of 1960s and 1970s movements to an exposition of grievances." Ralph H. Turner, "Collective Behavior and Resource Mobilization as Approaches to Social Movements," in Louis Kriesberg, ed., *Research in Social Movements, Conflicts and Change: A Research Annual*, Vol. 4 (Greenwich, Conn.: JAI Press, 1981), p. 7.

concise formulation, "Discontent arising from the perception of relative deprivation is the basic, instigating condition for participants in collective violence."[102]

The intellectual origins of the relative deprivation literature lie heavily in the psychological conceptualization of individual aggression as the product of anger induced by frustration, where frustration results from impediments placed in the path of goal-directed behavior.[103] Frustration-aggression theory is, in turn, an outgrowth of stimulus-response psychology.[104] On this view, violence does not stem from impulses generated by participation in a crowd — still less could it derive from some primal instinct or unresolved problems in childhood — but rather is always "instigated" by an external "thwarting agent." The expression of an emotion, anger, is not, then, irrationally produced. Rather, violence is, in this paradigm, a response to grievance.[105]

This view of the matter takes some issues off the table. Most obviously, if violence is a response to interference with the attainment of goals, a key emotion — let us call it antipathy — is removed as a causal factor in violent behavior. Although intergroup violence is embraced as a subtype of political violence to be explained, and social psychology is prominent in the relative deprivation strand of violence theory, the theory does not link up with the social psychology of prejudice. The careful documentation of violent episodes in some collective violence studies also neglects the atrocities, tortures, and mutilations that characterize so much of mass violent behavior, and it pays no attention to the specification of target groups.

Frustration-aggression theory may be said to share the same general orientation, but hardly to the same extent. Frustration-aggression theory finds numerous ways of taking account of both antipathy and impulsive behavior. It smuggles antipathy back into theoretical constructs by means of variables such as "prior dislike" of a target of aggression.[106] Prior dislike is part of a systematic concern with the characteristics of potential targets and the mechanisms by which they evoke aggressive responses. Frustration-aggression theorists also place considerable emphasis on the

102. Gurr, *Why Men Rebel*, p. 13.

103. For a very useful summary, see Berkowitz, *Aggression: A Social-Psychological Analysis*.

104. John Dollard et al., *Frustration and Aggression* (New Haven: Yale University Press, 1939).

105. See, e.g., Gurr's "strategy for incumbents," which involves, above all, redressing grievances. *Why Men Rebel*, pp. 352–53.

106. For example, Berkowitz, *Aggression: A Social-Psychological Analysis*, pp. 152–60.

variable ability of potential aggressors to inhibit their aggression, and they often argue that much violence is inflicted by people who lack sufficient self-control to inhibit the expression of aggressive responses.[107] In frustration-aggression theory, there is room for individual variation in aggressiveness and certainly no notion that aggression results from responses to objective conditions per se. Although relative deprivation theories were cast in terms of subjective expectations, they in fact had neither the means nor the inclination to take an array of subjective states into account. Deprivation studies tended to infer subjective discontent from "measures of objective welfare . . . ."[108]

In the resource mobilization literature, violence is also considered to be instrumental to a goal, however vaguely formulated the goal may be.[109] Violence may be a strategy employed to extract benefits from those who control resources,[110] a way of securing influence in the political process for groups without routinized access, a mode of "aggressive political participation."[111] In this formulation, violence is not — or at least not only — a response to deprivation, and resource mobilization theories pay more attention to how violence is organized and why individuals participate. There is an assumption that violence *is* organized, perhaps even centrally directed, and it has been remarked critically that such a perspective is more useful in explaining planned activity like strikes and protest demonstrations than more spontaneous activity like riots.[112]

---

107. Berkowitz, "Some Varieties of Human Aggression."

108. David Snyder, "Collective Violence: A Research Agenda and Some Strategic Considerations," *Journal of Conflict Resolution* 23, no. 3 (September 1978): 499–534, at p. 510.

109. See, e.g., William A. Gamson, *The Strategy of Social Protest* (Homewood, Ill.: Dorsey Press, 1975); Anthony Oberschall, *Social Conflict and Social Movements* (Englewood Cliffs, N.J.: Prentice-Hall, 1973); Anthony Oberschall, "Group Violence: Some Hypotheses and Empirical Uniformities," *Law and Society Review* 5, no. 1 (August 1970): 61–92.

110. E. Marx, *The Social Context of Violent Behavior: A Social Anthropological Study in an Israeli Immigrant Town* (London: Routledge & Kegan Paul, 1976).

111. Edward N. Muller, *Aggressive Political Participation* (Princeton: Princeton University Press, 1979).

112. Turner, "Collective Behavior and Resource Mobilization as Approaches to Social Movements," pp. 11–12; Snyder, "Collective Violence," pp. 506–07, 527; Herbert Kitschelt, "Resource Mobilization Theory: A Critique," in Dieter Rucht, ed., *Research on Social Movements* (Boulder, Colo.: Westview Press, 1991), pp. 323–47, at pp. 333, 335. For a good example of planned protest, see Owen M. Lynch, "Rioting as Rational Action: An Interpretation of the April 1978 Riots in Agra," *Economic and Political Weekly*, November 28, 1991, pp. 1951–56.

Disappointingly little has come of the prodigious literature on violence. No theory is clearly supported by empirical evidence. Few if any specific findings can be said to be firmly established. Relative deprivation theories, repeatedly tested against data from the urban violence of the 1960s and early 1970s in the United States, have fared poorly. Indicators of black disadvantage do not predict the location or the severity of the violence. Cities that experienced disorder are difficult to distinguish from those that did not. And if linear relationships are absent, so, too, are the curvilinear relationships postulated by theories that predict violence when a period of progress in meeting expectations is followed by a sharp period of decline. The data on black economic progress do not fit the theories. The ratio of nonwhite to white median income increased steadily during the riot years; other measures of nonwhite economic welfare were also on the increase; and the indicators turned down (especially for the black poor) in the 1970s, after the riots gave way to quiescence.[113] The same was true for the British violence of the early 1980s, which coincided with improvement in the conditions of minorities in income, housing, and employment, and trends toward convergence between the minority position and that of the general population.[114] The American and British data suggest a considerable disjunction between objective conditions and the occurrence of violence, which can scarcely support any version of relative deprivation theory, certainly not any that bases subjective expectations on objective indicators.

There are several instructive reasons for this shortfall of results. Some of the most important derive from the very same forces that propelled the proliferation of violence studies in the first instance.

First and foremost was the ambition of many of the projects, which were aimed at explaining violence in general or something close to it. Whereas the natural sciences have tended to disaggregate animal aggression by context and objective (such as predation or defense of territory), the social sciences have often seen human aggression as a unitary phenomenon. The 1960s were certainly a violent decade, and in some sense, no doubt, that violence — or, more properly, those types and episodes of violence — *were* interlinked. But it was surely a non sequitur to conclude from the probability of *some* linkage that all collective violence (or any-

113. The evidence is reviewed in Horowitz, "Racial Violence in the United States," pp. 192–98, 201–02. Hibbs, *Mass Political Violence*, pp. 48, 52, also finds relative deprivation theory insupportable in crossnational perspective.

114. See Horowitz, "Racial Violence in the United States," p. 206, for citations to British data.

thing approaching it) could be captured by a single theory.[115] The concatenation of violent events that stimulated attempts to explain them
thus also stimulated the creation of a theory that was altogether too
grand to do what it aimed to do.

Second, having framed the subject matter broadly, the theorists, it
might be thought, needed immediately to sort the phenomenon of violence into types. Not all did sense the need to do this,[116] and those who
made crude first cuts at categorization of violent events generally put
together some kinds of violence that would better have been kept separate. One typology distinguishes broadly between confrontations that
pit "protesters" against "authorities" and those that oppose "two hostile
population groups, such as employers and employees or whites and
blacks . . . ."[117] Labor violence and ethnic violence are thus grouped
together, a strange merger. Another set of categories is based primarily on
the structure of violence (organized or spontaneous) and secondarily, for
organized violence, on participation (limited or widespread).[118] This
yields, parsimoniously, three categories of violent phenomena: turmoil
(strikes, riots, political clashes), conspiracy (terrorism, coups, assassinations), and internal war (guerrilla war, civil war, revolution). The apparent objectives of the violence are, then, immaterial to the categories. As
revolution, intended to seize power in the state, is merged with separatist
warfare, designed to secede from the state, so the carefully planned military coup is bracketed with the sometimes planned, sometimes anomic,
political murder, and crowd violence against the state is placed under the
same rubric as crowd violence against members of other groups. If
apparently disparate types of violence such as these are to be explained
together, it is obvious that the explanations adduced will be at a high
level of generality; and indeed they are. This is theoretical parsimony at a
price in precision. The crudeness of the categories reinforces the difficulties created by attempting to explain all of collective violence in the first
instance.

115. Compare Oberschall, "Group Violence," p. 62: ". . . a satisfactory theory of
group violence ought to have some general applicability," transcending any typology of violence.

116. For example, Feierabend, Nesvold, and Feierabend, "Political Coerciveness and
Turmoil," p. 106, group under the umbrella of "political aggression" and "political instability" such events as "civil war, riots, mass executions, and guerrilla warfare," plus "general strikes, attempted assassinations, and demonstrations."

117. Oberschall, "Group Violence," p. 85. See also Oberschall, *Social Conflict and
Social Movements*.

118. Gurr, *Why Men Rebel*, pp. 10–11.

Third, the theorizing was done top down. Not only were the theories grand, in the sense of comprehensive, but they were constructed on a thin base of lower-level theorizing. For example, there were several competing theories of the coup d'état, none of them particularly ascendant, certainly none confirmed.[119] There were, likewise, very few theories of terrorism that had gained a measure of acceptance.[120] Fragments of riot theories were floating around in assorted corners of the social sciences, generally proceeding along lines that did not intersect. One of the virtues of the 1960s–'70s violence literature is that it uncovered and brought into contact for the first time some of these separate theoretical strands, but the strands were still too fragmentary, too undeveloped, too unconfirmed, or too implausible to support a theory of violence at a higher level. Given the inadequate state of the subfields, top down was not a good strategy.

Fourth, the prevalent explanatory models were indifferent to large areas of the landscape they sought to map. I have already noted that the resource mobilization approach, with its emphasis on the organization of discontent, left little scope for relatively spontaneous violence. Relative deprivation theory, on the other hand, had no difficulty embracing unorganized violence, but had great difficulty accounting for the violence of those who are generally not deprived relative to other groups, such as Basques, Sikhs, or members of upper castes who engage in violence against ex-untouchables in various Indian states. Relative deprivation theory and resource mobilization theory also assume that violence is generally directed against authority, against power holders. The ethnic riot, against other groups, is not necessarily, not even predominantly, directed against power holders. Neither was lynching in the United States or genocide in Nazi Germany or Ottoman Turkey. Relative deprivation theory was subject to underdog bias. And none of the major theoretical statements was designed to develop a theory of the targets of violence or to separate the *where* from the *when* of violence, which tended to be linked in an undifferentiated conception of the causes or correlates of violence.

If there is ever to be a single, coherent theory of collective violence, it will be created after there are a substantial body of theory and some reliable findings about the specific varieties of collective violence: about rev-

119. The main theories are canvassed in Donald L. Horowitz, *Coup Theories and Officers' Motives: Sri Lanka in Comparative Perspective* (Princeton: Princeton University Press, 1980).

120. See Crenshaw, "The Causes of Terrorism," pp. 379–80.

olutions, about terrorism, about coups, about riots.[121] That day has still not arrived, and the fact that it has not arrived argues for a strategy of proceeding from the bottom up, rather than the top down. It also counsels leaving open some issues prematurely assumed away by macrolevel theorists of violence. In particular, I leave open at the outset the extent to which violence is organized and, if so, for what purpose; the possibility that the infliction of harm is an end, not necessarily a means to some other end; and the related possibility that the violence is generated by antipathy and that the cruelty so prominently displayed in the violence results from that antipathy, or from poorly controlled impulses, or from both.

121. For concurrence and a fine summary of the literature, see Rogers Brubaker and David D. Laitin, "Ethnic and Nationalist Violence," *Annual Review of Sociology* 24 (1998): 423–52.

CHAPTER 2

Ethnic Boundaries, Riot Boundaries

A STUDY OF ETHNIC RIOTS requires conceptual clarity about ethnicity and about riots. By conceptual clarity, I mean something beyond mere definitions of terms — a starting sense of what the two phenomena are and where they begin and end. It is altogether too easy to take both as perfectly bounded, reified entities, hard substances, as it were, that can be diced and sliced without spilling out their contents. In the case of the two phenomena, this is far from true, and it is best to understand their fluidity, internal and external, before dissection begins.

The issues of ethnic boundaries and riot boundaries are important for understanding violence. On both issues, the views of rioters diverge markedly from the views of those who study them. Rioters take group boundaries and characteristics to be deeply embedded. Their conceptions are very much at odds with those of many theorists, for whom group boundaries are problematic, fluid, mutable, even manipulable. On the other hand, rioters act on conceptions of violent events that see them as much less well bounded than most outside observers do. I shall show in later chapters that an elastic conception of where the event begins and ends forms a deep underpinning of the violence. Whether they are acting on the basis of firm target-group boundaries or rendering event boundaries indistinct, rioters proceed according to their own theory.

COGNITIVE AND STRATEGIC BASES OF ETHNICITY

Several schools of thought advance conflicting theories of ethnic conflict, but in various permutations and combinations.[1] The issues on which

---

1. This section is a revised and expanded version of parts of an essay written under the auspices of the World Bank: "Structure and Strategy in Ethnic Conflict: A Few Steps toward Synthesis," in Boris Plescovic and Joseph E. Stiglitz, eds., *Annual World Bank Conference on Development Economics, 1998* (Washington, D.C.: The World Bank, 1999), pp. 345–70.

they differ are several, but the differences can be reduced to hard views of ethnic conflict versus soft views, where *hard* and *soft* refer to the nature of group affiliations and the ends of conflict behavior. For a hypothetical theorist who adheres to all the hard positions (no one does), ethnic groups are ascriptive, firmly bounded entities, based on a strong sense of commonality, producing considerable loyalty, persisting over time, providing large affective rewards to group members, inclined to ethnocentrism and to hostility to and a desire to dominate outsiders, liable to conflict behavior based on passion (even to the exclusion of calculation), and engendering a great willingness on the part of group members to sacrifice for collective welfare. For an equally hypothetical theorist who adheres to all the soft positions (again, no one does), ethnic groups are entities whose boundaries are problematic and malleable, whose solidarity is based on material rewards they provide for their members rather than on diffuse affection, whose behavior, based on the interests of their members, is vulnerable to strategic manipulation, whose apparent affect can often be reduced to calculation, and whose severe conflicts with others often result less from irreconcilable objectives than from strategic dilemmas. These are hard and soft positions in the sense that the first sees ethnic affiliations as made of stone, while the second sees them as made of putty.

The range of issues on which disagreement is possible on these continua is very great. At least three issue-clusters can be distinguished.

One has to do with the very concept of an ethnic group and the features it may or may not share with other affiliations. Is an ethnic group inevitably a given, or is it merely a vehicle created, say, for the extraction of resources from an environment? Where do ethnic groups come from, anyway? Once we discover that group boundaries change, that some ethnic groups die while others are born, what is left of the idea that groups are merely given? On the other hand, once we discover that ethnic affiliations seem to possess competitive advantages over other forms of affiliation in attracting the loyalty of their members, can they simply be regarded as receptacles of social purposes more or less fungible with other affiliations? What is at stake, in short, is the very idea of ethnicity as a distinctive affiliation.

A second cluster relates to the opposition of passion and interest as wellsprings of human behavior. Here sides have been chosen in debate, and they are powerfully antagonistic. Where some analysts see love and hatred, others see straightforward calculation. Where some see expressiveness, others see instrumental action. Where some see perceptual distortion driven by affect, others see appropriate response resulting from the situation. Each side tries to reduce one to the other.

A third cluster concerns the extent to which the collectivity should be considered the central actor, the unit of analysis. A deeply embedded groupness, characterized by diffuse sentiments, altruism, and the willingness of individuals to make sacrifices, is characteristic of the hard position. In contrast is the soft view that ethnic groups can be decomposed into the motives of their members, that they are instruments for the pursuit of those motives, and that their actions need to be explained in terms of individual calculations of utility in specific contexts rather than some transcendent collective purpose. On the whole, the importance accorded leaders is greater among adherents of the soft persuasion; the role of mass sentiments and behavior is greater among hards. To the antinomies that make progress in this field difficult is thus added the methodological issue of the proper locus of investigation, macrosocietal or microstrategic.

Riot behavior can and will shed light on some of these issues, but it is not necessary to wait until the findings are in to develop a sense of the formation and content of ethnic affiliations. The foundations of ethnic loyalty reside in the need of individuals to belong to groups. Individuals require the cooperation that groups provide. They possess a deep sociality.

That sociality, however, is not maximally inclusive. Whenever groups form, their members sense the existence of boundaries that divide them from other groups. Both the impulse to form groups and the impulse to differentiate them from others are so strong that they are easily activated. No sense of birth connection, no sense of common history, no sense of prior intracategory similarity is necessary at the outset. In a laboratory setting, random assignment to categories will activate a sense of groupness.[2] Once categories develop, cleavages follow. The tendency to cleavage is so well established as to be undeniable. Groups use their perceptual apparatus to categorize people into classes and to exaggerate the similarities among themselves and their differences from others, a phenomenon well known in social-judgment theory as assimilation and contrast effects.

This phenomenon involves a cognitive simplification of values arrayed along a continuum. Subjects simplify the array by compressing small differences to a point approaching their mean value (this is called assimilation effects) and by exaggerating larger differences to make them greater

2. Henri Tajfel, *Human Groups and Social Categories* (Cambridge: Cambridge University Press, 1981).

than they are (contrast effects).[3] Another way to put this is to say that, in a series, differences among items judged to belong to the same general class (for example, heavy in weight) are perceptually reduced, while those judged to belong to a different class from the first (for example, light in weight) are judged to be more different from the first class and more similar to each other than they actually are. These cognitive propensities constitute intraclass assimilation and interclass accentuation or contrast.[4] The same propensities apply to judgments of neighboring groups. The presence of multiple outgroups leads the subject group to sort them into those judged similar to and different from itself, compressing differences between itself and those groups seen to be somewhat different but still relatively close to itself, and exaggerating differences between itself and those groups seen to be different and close to an extremely different group in the same environment.[5] There are ineluctable perceptual processes involved in establishing group boundaries, and there are many examples of groups that are amalgams of somewhat different subgroups that merged in the presence of outsiders seen to be still more different.

With cleavage comes comparison. Ingroups are said to have certain qualities; outgroups, others. Generally, insiders evaluate their own collective qualities and cultural products more highly than those of outsiders,[6] and they apportion rewards so as to favor themselves and to disfavor outsiders, even when it costs them some portion of the reward to create the intergroup difference in apportionment.[7] They behave this way even in the absence of any hint by experimenters of intergroup competition and even in the face of the possibility of positive-sum outcomes if they wish to choose them. Groups are given to ingroup bias, and they appear to be motivated by a desire for favorable collective evaluation. Although some theories suggest that groups derive value from their ability to satisfy the goals of individuals within them, the opposite appears to

3. J. Richard Eiser, *Social Judgment* (Pacific Grove, Calif.: Brooks/Cole, 1990).

4. Leslie A. Zebrowitz, *Social Perception* (Pacific Grove, Calif.: Brooks/Cole, 1990), p. 53.

5. David A. Wilder and John E. Thompson, "Assimilation and Contrast Effects in the Judgments of Groups," *Journal of Personality and Social Psychology* 54, no. 1 (January 1988): 62–73.

6. See, e.g., Melville Leonard Edelstein, *What Do Young Africans Think?* (Johannesburg: South African Institute of Race Relations, 1972); A. A. Dubb, "The Impact of the City," in W. D. Hammond-Tooke, ed., *The Bantu-Speaking Peoples of South Africa* (London: Routledge & Kegan Paul, 1974); Charles K. Ferguson and Harold H. Kelley, "Significant Factors in Overevaluation of Own Group's Product," *Journal of Abnormal and Social Psychology* 69, no. 2 (August 1964): 223–28.

7. Henri Tajfel, "Intergroup Behavior, Social Comparison and Social Change" (Katz-Newcomb Lectures, University of Michigan, Ann Arbor; mimeo., 1974).

be the case: individuals derive value from the groups to which they belong.[8] They derive satisfaction from the success of the group, even when their own individual contribution to that success is palpably absent.[9] By the same token, the willingness of individuals to sacrifice for group interests and participate in collective action is predicted more by a sense of collective deprivation than it is by individual deprivation.[10] The improvement of the group's condition, in other words, may be a more powerful motivation for participation in collective effort than is improvement of the participating individual's condition. This finding casts doubt on the aptness of methodological individualism as a starting assumption — or at least the sole starting assumption — in understanding group dynamics.

Given the compelling power of group affiliations, it is not surprising that individuals should find them useful vehicles for the pursuit of their own interests as well. It would be surprising if they did not. It is not possible, however, to reduce groups to their fulfillment of individual goals or to reduce affect to instrumental behavior. Both are present.

So far, all of this pertains to groups but not specifically to ethnic groups. Members of ethnic groups partake of all of these tendencies to cleave, to compare, to specify inventories of putative collective qualities, to seek a favorable evaluation, to manifest ingroup bias, to exaggerate contrasts with outgroups, and to sacrifice for collective interests. Ethnic groups also seem to carry matters further. They appear frequently to engender more loyalty from their members than competing group-types do and to engage in severe conflict with other ethnic groups.

To appreciate the special power of ethnic loyalty, one must see ethnic groups as groups like all others but also as groups possessing qualities that not all other groups possess in the same measure. The most important of these qualities is a strong sense of similarity, with roots in perceived genetic affinity, or early socialization, or both. Belonging to a group implies thinking of oneself as possessing characteristics that are somehow representative of the social category the group embraces.[11] This feature, it can be hypothesized, is what leads individuals to sub-·

8. Marilynn B. Brewer, "The Social Psychology of Intergroup Relations: Can Research Inform Practice?" *Journal of Social Issues* 53, no. 1 (Spring 1997): 205; Marilynn B. Brewer, "The Social Self: On Being the Same and Different at the Same Time," *Personality and Social Psychology Bulletin* 17, no. 5 (October 1991): 476.

9. Marilynn B. Brewer, "In-Group Bias in the Minimal Intergroup Situation: A Cognitive-Motivational Analysis," *Psychological Bulletin* 86, no. 2 (March 1979): 322.

10. Brewer, "The Social Self," pp. 478–79.

11. Marilynn B. Brewer and Norman Miller, *Intergroup Relations* (Buckingham, England: Open University Press, 1996), p. 22.

merge their own identities in the collective identity, to favor ingroup members and make sacrifices for them. One sees oneself, so to speak, in other group members. Similarity engenders empathy and in extreme cases even obliterates the boundary between one individual group member and another. There is ample evidence that people have affection for others whom they believe to be similar to themselves in tastes, attitudes, and values.[12] They are also attracted to those they believe are attracted to them in turn, but this seems to be because "interpersonal attraction is a very sound basis for assuming commonality; it results in exaggerated perceptions of similarity."[13] People assume ingroup members are similar to each other — that, after all, is the result of assimilation effects — and that assumption strengthens their attraction to them, even when they have no actual knowledge of their qualities.[14] The irony here is that egocentrism leads people to favor those seen to be like themselves, and this leads beyond egocentrism to ethnocentrism and sacrifice — in other words, to a broader concept of self and self-interest.

Ethnicity is a powerful affiliation, both because similarity is valued and because genetic (or putatively genetic) origins and early socialization are potent sources of similarity or, in any case, of cues that signal similarity: appearance, customs, gestures, language, clothing, tastes, and habits. The assumption of similarity follows quickly once groups are formed, even in laboratories, and reinforces group identity. How much more powerful is the assumption of similarity when it derives from birth or common experiences of childhood. The hallmark of the ethnic group, even if relatively recently established, is its intergenerational character. Despite the variable porosity of group boundaries, most people are born into the group in which they will die.

Underlying genetic similarity and early socialization is, of course, the family. The family is the unit that provides constant replenishment of ethnic-group members. It is the first group to which individuals belong,

12. Donn Byrne, T. L. Clore, and G. Smeaton, "The Attraction Hypothesis: Do Similar Attitudes Affect Anything?" *Journal of Personality and Social Psychology* 51, no. 6 (December 1986): 1167–70; Cookie Stephan, "Attribution of Intention and Perception of Attitudes as a Function of Liking and Similarity," *Sociometry* 36, no. 4 (December 1973): 463–75; Donn Byrne, "A Theory of Attraction: A Reinforcement Model," in Leonard Berkowitz, ed., *Advances in Experimental Social Psychology*, Vol. 4 (New York: Academic Press, 1969), pp. 67–89.

13. Michael A. Hogg and John C. Turner, "Interpersonal Attraction, Social Identification and Psychological Group Function," *European Journal of Social Psychology* 15, no. 1 (January–March 1985): 61.

14. Brewer and Miller, *Intergroup Relations*, pp. 29–31.

and, because of the long period of human maturation, its influence is extraordinarily durable. At an early age, children express fear toward strangers, and they learn the difference between family members and others. There is little doubt that they internalize the significance of the birth principle in cooperative organization and the significance of distinctions based on birth. In most conditions, they certainly appreciate that, however attenuated, genetic connections are a surer source of similarity than any others are. Ethnic groups, whatever their actual composition, purport to be founded on descent, and they, too, offer a greater sense of similarity than do groups founded on other premises. Given the general preference for people with similar attributes, this fact alone accounts for ethnic affinity. Experimental studies show that the greater the felt similarity within a group, the greater the degree of ingroup bias.[15] Within ethnic groups, felt similarity is likely to be great, and that should lead to expectations that ingroup bias and differentiation from outgroups will also be great. The ascriptive character of ethnic affiliations accounts for their potency.

Among family choices bearing on ethnicity, marriage is perhaps the most important. Endogamy gives concreteness to conceptions of ethnic affinity. If two subgroups that previously did not practice intermarriage begin to do so, the reason is that they are beginning to see the line between them as insignificant, in contrast to the line between them and others. Although marriage patterns can and do change, there are spiral effects that flow from them. Groups in accelerating conflict tend to practice less exogamy. This leads to less porous boundaries between them, and the resulting attenuation in ties facilitates (or is at least no barrier to) further conflict. Severely conflicted groups rarely have significant rates of marriage between them. Groups with low levels of conflict (such as many in Latin America) have porous boundaries, both created by and facilitating exogamy, thus bolstering ties that can be a barrier to conflict.

In addition to being the fount of descent affiliations, the family is the source of behavioral lessons likely to be transferred to ethnic relations. Diffuse, unflinching mutual support and affection are the widespread model for family relations (however discrepant reality may be). It is likely that this model is invoked for ethnic affiliations that are grounded in the same birth principle and that grow out of family affiliations.

The extent of actual similarities of traits within ethnic groups and actual differences between them is undoubtedly highly variable. They

15. Brewer, "In-Group Bias in the Minimal Intergroup Situation," p. 318.

need not be substantial. There may be fairly similar inventories of actual cultural attributes across group lines. Nevertheless, it is common for a few traits that mark one group off from another to be built on and exaggerated as interaction proceeds.[16] Once minimal attraction has done its work, intergroup similarity will not impede intergroup rivalry.[17] Cleavage drives culture, more than culture drives cleavage.

Notice that this account, although referable to birth, gives ample play to the social construction of ethnicity. Just as intergroup boundaries are constructed in the laboratory, so are they constructed in social life. The scope of group boundaries is not foreordained, and boundary change is common.[18] In the process of boundary enlargement or contraction, cultural and political elites play their part, just as social constructivists claim, emphasizing those features in the situation of their audience, including those affinities and disparities that conduce to one or another definition of the group and its boundaries.[19] Those with interests seek to harness passions.

Some social constructivists, however, go further, claiming that elites do not merely steer the process in the light of existing ethnic juxtapositions, but that they more or less shape them, that the determination is made in the material interest of elites, and that they also have wide latitude to foment conflict and violence. These broader claims are highly contestable.[20] The constraints of the field in which group interactions occur limit what elites can do and what interests they can pursue. The strong cognitive basis of ethnic affinities and disparities is underappreciated by many constructivists. By the same token, the freedom of elites to foment conflict and violence is limited by their followers' definition of the situation and by what they would be willing to fight over. Hindu nationalists

---

16. See, e.g., Myron Weiner, *Sons of the Soil: Migration and Ethnic Conflict in India* (Princeton: Princeton University Press, 1978), pp. 240–41.

17. Rupert J. Brown, "The Role of Similarity in Intergroup Relations," in Henri Tajfel, ed., *The Social Dimension: European Developments in Social Psychology* (Cambridge: Cambridge University Press, 1984), pp. 603–23.

18. See May Edel, "African Tribalism: Some Reflections on Uganda," *Political Science Quarterly* 80, no. 3 (September 1965): 857–72; Crawford Young, *Politics in the Congo* (Princeton: Princeton University Press, 1965); Edward M. Bruner, "The Expression of Ethnicity in Indonesia," in Abner Cohen, ed., *Urban Ethnicity* (London: Tavistock, 1974), pp. 251–80; Leroy Vail, ed., *The Creation of Tribalism in Southern Africa* (Berkeley and Los Angeles: University of California Press, 1989).

19. Donald L. Horowitz, "Cultural Movements and Ethnic Change," *The Annals* 433 (September 1977): 6–18.

20. See Nelson Kasfir, "Explaining Ethnic Political Participation," *World Politics* 31, no. 3 (April 1979): 365–88, at pp. 375–76.

in India often attempt to incite attacks on Muslims, but they rarely succeed in the southern states of Kerala and Tamil Nadu, where caste affiliations have more resonance than does the Hindu-Muslim polarity.[21] Constructivism can survive without seeing ethnicity as an altogether opportunistic and infinitely malleable affiliation.

The account I have given also takes seriously the claims of primordialists that ethnicity is a thick, *Gemeinschaft* affiliation, without acceding to the extreme claims of some primordialists about its mysterious, ineffable, invariably conflict-producing quality. Primordialists argue that ethnicity is connected to the things without which people cannot live, among them traditionality, the persistence of the past into the present, and a sense of collective self-consciousness.[22] A sense of community of this sort necessarily generates awareness of other communities and spills over, they aver, into conflict and violence. The contribution of primordialists is to emphasize the emotive power of ethnic affiliations. A good explanation of ethnic phenomena needs to come to terms with the thick, compelling character of group membership, but it also needs to explain the sensitivity of ethnic boundaries and ethnic conflict to changing contexts, which primordialists have usually neglected.

A hard emphasis on the responsiveness of ethnic groups to the deep needs of group members is not at odds with a keen sense of the variability of ethnic phenomena.[23] It follows that group members may entertain sentiments so intense that observers identify them as primordial, even though group identities are socially constructed, recently constructed, founded on relatively little in the way of palpable differences, and mutable as environmental conditions change. Intergroup sentiments can and

---

21. Steven Ian Wilkinson, "The Electoral Incentives for Ethnic Violence: Hindu-Muslim Riots in India" (Ph.D. diss., M.I.T., 1998).

22. Edward Shils, "Primordial, Personal, Sacred and Civil Ties," *British Journal of Sociology* 8, no. 1 (March 1957): 130–45; Edward Shils, "Nation, Nationality, Nationalism and Civil Society," *Nations and Nationalism* 1, no. 1 (1995): 93–118; Clifford Geertz, "The Integrative Revolution: Primordial Sentiments and Civil Politics in the New States," in Clifford Geertz, ed., *Old Societies and New States* (New York: Free Press, 1963); Walker Connor, "Beyond Reason: The Nature of the Ethnonational Bond," *Ethnic and Racial Studies* 16, no. 3 (July 1993): 373–89; Walker Connor, *Ethnonationalism: The Quest for Understanding* (Princeton: Princeton University Press, 1994); Harold R. Isaacs, *Idols of the Tribe* (New York: Harper & Row, 1975). In placing all these writers together and labeling them *primordialist* (a label to which not all would subscribe), I am aware of the danger of creating an "imagined community" of primordialists.

23. Cf. Jack David Eller and Reed M. Coughlin, "The Poverty of Primordialism: The Demystification of Ethnic Attachments," *Ethnic and Racial Studies* 16, no. 2 (April 1993): 183–202.

do change. Whereas Georgians formerly had a high opinion of Abkhaz as people with a rich traditional culture, these stereotypes have given way to a view of Abkhaz as wild and uncivilized.[24] Some antipathies and some affinities are durable, and some are not. The determinants of such variations remain open to explanation.

Ethnicity has given rise to widely divergent interpretations — that it is primordial, or, on the other hand, that it is conjured and wholly instrumental, or, on the other hand again, that it emerges from evolutionary hard wiring[25] — because it seems so powerfully important to people and so powerfully conflict producing and at the same time so flimsy, insubstantial, and changeable. Ethnicity is inspissate: it is a thickened version of a substance, the origins of which are invariably much thinner, a substance that a profound change of context may thin out yet again.

Stereotypes of group characteristics, aptitudes, and disabilities amplify whatever intergroup differences have been identified. Many of the traits imputed to outgroup members are threatening. The putative differences that accompany intergroup differentiation also provide reason for group mobilization. The favorable outcomes that ethnic groups seek in competition are endangered by the presence of traits, such as diligence, clannishness, intractability, or intelligence, that they sense in their adversaries, even as they prefer their own mix of attributes. Where stereotypes are invidious, which is to say threatening to positive group evaluation, conflict is likely to be severe.

If we return to the emergence of cleavage and ask why the tendency is so persistent, we might speculate that differentiation results from a decline in the benefits of cooperation as group size increases. But another explanation can be inferred from the behavior that immediately accompanies cleavage: ingroup bias that seeks favorable evaluation through discriminatory action. Perhaps this behavior simply manifests a desire to reap a disproportionate share of rewards in a given environment. Such a desire would not be at odds with the quest for a favorable evaluation, since the relative superiority of evaluation would provide a justification for unequal distribution. The desire for disproportionate reward would also comport with observed political behavior in ethnically divided

---

24. Yurii Anchabadze, "Georgia-Abkhazia: The Hard Road to Agreement" (paper presented at the conference "Georgians and Abkhazians: The Search for Agreement and the Role of the International Community," Brussels, Belgium, June 12–14, 1997), p. 6.

25. Paul C. Stern, "Why Do People Sacrifice for Their Nations?" in John L. Comaroff and Paul C. Stern, eds., *Perspectives on Nationalism and War* (Amsterdam: Gordon & Breach, 1997).

societies, in which a part of the society claims to be the whole, to place the status of ethnic strangers at sufferance, to demand a variety of privileges, to dominate the environment, and, if possible, to establish a status hierarchy.

A clear implication of the view of ethnic identity as deriving from human needs for cooperation, affiliation, and reward is that ascriptive groups and group relations are universal. They antedate globalization, the modern state, the industrial revolution, even the printing press. No doubt, all of these developments can make group relations better or worse, not least by altering the contexts in which they take place, but group formation and what follows from it do not depend on them.

Nothing I have said here, it should be emphasized, obviates the possibility that individuals may sense more affinity with groups other than the ethnic group into which they were born. Some people may find that, for them, occupational cleavages displace ethnic cleavages. On the similarity principle, professors may prefer the company of professors, physicians of physicians, to the company of members of their own ethnic group or family. Some individuals may find that they have more than one strong birth affiliation. A Belgian may be born Flemish and Catholic, as opposed to other Belgians who are born Walloon and Catholic or born Flemish and secularist in the Freemason tradition that, passed down from generation to generation, produces a birthlike affiliation in Belgium. Likewise, beneath these overarching levels of affiliation, there are likely to be subethnic ties as well. A Fleming from the southeast of Flanders may also see himself or herself as a Limburger and may view Antwerpers as possessing a certain unwonted arrogance. Affiliations may be multiple at the same level, or they may be tiered.

These variations depend on particular social developments. In the first case, the growth of a complex set of educational structures — and a society that takes those structures very seriously — may strongly differentiate academics and doctors from other occupational groups. In the second case, a history of religious warfare and then Enlightenment ideas produced *familles spirituelles* based on religious orientation, which were overlaid on, but did not correspond to, those based on language. In the third case, since many ethnic groups are amalgams (that is, are built from the ground up), the residue of sentiment attaching to the earlier, lower-level materials may be more or less salient, depending in large measure on how significant overarching conflicts are.

In many countries, the first and second variations — occupational identities (or class identities) and crosscutting but still birth-based identities — are not strongly present. The first is a function of an industrial or postindustrial, highly complex division of labor. The second is a function of specific histories. Sweeping continental religious and ideological movements of the sort that, because of their inconclusive results, produced multiple affiliations in Belgium are not universal, and so neither are their comparable contemporary deposits. Still, such movements are present where, for example, Islam and Christianity or Islam and Hinduism cross-cut ethnic affiliations, as the former do for the Yoruba in Nigeria and the latter do for many groups in India. But in many countries where such developments did not break ethnic lines, ethnicity, while it always encounters competing affiliations, does not encounter affiliations quite so powerful in their pull. In such cases, a single ethnic cleavage can rend a polity. Usually, however, especially after relatively recent amalgamation, subethnic affiliations are available for invocation when the context shifts to a lower level. This fact provides a policy handle for the mitigation of ethnic conflict, for subethnic affiliations can be utilized to dilute the overwhelming saliency of ethnic affiliations.

A view of ethnicity as a strong affiliation is not incompatible with variation in the boundaries of groups and in their political saliency. Constructed identities and visceral antipathies can coexist. The deadly ethnic riot shows ethnicity in its hardened state, but it is a state that flows directly out of the dependence of ethnic alignments on context. One recurrent feature of riot behavior is the strong tendency to bipolarity before the riot. One group narrows the focus of its enmity and targets another, rather than multiple other groups. To some considerable degree, this phenomenon may be attributable to the emergence of bipolar patterns of political competition, competition between a political majority and minority, each constituted along ethnic lines. In many societies, this competition takes the form of aggregating groups and subgroups felt to have the requisite affinities to form a majority vis-à-vis other aggregates, with contrasting attributes, that attempt to form a majority of their own. This development is recognizable as an ascriptive variant of the effort to produce a minimum winning coalition, one in which a bit more than half the state can claim much more than half of the rewards that political victory provides.[26] But even where electoral politics does not prevail, if ethnicity is salient, there is a struggle to produce aggregates of sufficient strength to take control of the state by nonelectoral means.

26. William R. Riker, *The Theory of Political Coalitions* (New Haven: Yale University Press, 1962), pp. 32–101.

In Asia, Africa, Eastern Europe, and the former Soviet Union, there are many states that are characterized by a predominant ethnic cleavage. That many of these have two or three large ethnic agglomerations confronting each other is due to a combination of social perception and strategic imperatives in a bounded environment.

The importance of social perception is suggested by the fact that, despite a tendency to expand group identity to a level of up to half the population of a state,[27] many smaller groups survive although they do not approach the 50 percent mark, and in some cases subgroups actually split off from larger groups of which they formerly were a part. Not all boundary change is upward.

Still, there is no denying the utility of the larger affiliations or the general trend toward them. Much intergroup differentiation takes place in anticipation of competition within the political system of the state.[28] That strategy, as well as social perception, is involved is indicated not merely by the trend toward larger groups. There is also a trend toward bifurcation of polities and a frequent proclivity (albeit far from ineluctable) for tripolar conflicts to become bipolar, as third groups, those that are smallest or most divided internally, are pressured to align with one of the other two groups. Ethnic interactions occur in bounded environments; they are heavily conditioned, as Rogers Brubaker says, "by the properties of political fields . . . ."[29] If this were all there was to it, if groups were organized only for politics in institutional settings, the isomorphism of the two processes would be illusory, for the two would amount to the same thing. Both might be reducible to the minimum winning coalition theorem. But what is striking is that intergroup differentiation has the same characteristics even in noninstitutional settings, including experimental settings. This might lead, upon further exploration, to a conclusion that the minimum winning coalition theorem is actually an instance of the more general human tendency to cleave, compare, and apportion rewards in a biased fashion. In institutional and in laboratory settings, maximal inclusiveness is a disfavored outcome.

The tendency to bifurcation is particularly dangerous in ethnic politics, since it is conducive to zero-sum outcomes that greater fluidity of

27. See Sun-Ki Chai, "A Theory of Ethnic Group Boundaries," *Nations and Nationalism* 2, no. 2 (1996): 281–307.

28. Ibid.

29. Rogers Brubaker, *Nationalism Reframed: Nationhood and the National Question in the New Europe* (Cambridge: Cambridge University Press, 1996), p. 17.

alignments makes less probable. Tripolar conflicts become much more dangerous when the third party is induced to align with one of the other two contestants. Interestingly, experimental research, too, has begun to suggest that significant differences in conflict behavior can be detected in two-way as against three-way relationships. In an important study, random division of subjects into two groups produced the expected competitive orientation and strong manifestation of ingroup bias, but division into three groups did not produce ingroup bias in the majority of subjects.[30] Bipolar interactions seem to elicit much stronger competitive cues and discriminatory impulses than a more complex set of alignments does. This propensity offers a significant opening for the amelioration of conflict by preventing bifurcation.

Of course, we already know that the combination of a defined political field and the perceptual tendency to simplify the number of groups in the environment through assimilation and contrast effects can easily produce polarities. We shall witness many examples of violence that proceeded from growing bipolarity and a focus of antipathy by one group on another. A growing sense of opposition between two groups is the necessary, but not sufficient, condition for ethnic violence.

THE ONTOLOGY OF THE RIOT

In spite of our ability to conceptualize the riot as a single event, its boundaries are never as clear as the conception of a unit of action or a distinct incident would suggest. There are spatial and temporal connections to yet other incidents that quickly undermine the notion that each incident is separate. Similarly, within the single event lie subevents that are themselves candidates for separate status. The violence is said to begin and end, to have external boundaries, and to be singular, that is, to have no internal boundaries. But, of course, both propositions are problematical: the external differentiation and the internal coherence of the riot event are open to question. Riot boundaries are, if anything, more amorphous than group boundaries.

Some riots may merge into others, and some episodes of killing may not be coherent enough to be called a single riot. If, on February 1, members of group A kill three members of group B and then, on February 15

---

30. Margaret Hartstone and Martha Augoustinos, "The Minimal Group Paradigm: Categorization into Two versus Three Groups," *European Journal of Social Psychology* 25, no. 2 (March–April 1995): 179–93.

to 18, kill 30 members of group B, is this one riot or two?[31] Were the killings of February 1 a warmup, a precondition, or an integral part of the events of two weeks later? Or reverse the sequence. If a few people are killed two weeks or two months after many people have been killed, what is the relationship of the two sets of killings? Are they really one riot? Farther afield, what are the connections among riots occurring years apart, with participants drawn from the same opposing groups of initiators and victims?

These are variants of two common patterns. The first I shall call *two-wave* riots, events of the same general character, with accelerating or decelerating magnitudes, separated by a few weeks or months. The second I shall refer to as *recurrent riots*, usually separated by years, sometimes by many years, and, because of that separation, generally thought to be independent events, subject to different causes. Earlier riots are no doubt connected in various ways to those that occur years later. The memory of the earlier violence may shape the disposition to engage in violence again, may affect the conception of an appropriate occasion for violence, may even create a desire to finish the job. For all that, however, it is difficult to see how riots years apart can be regarded as the same event without losing the concept of an event altogether. Two-wave riots, on the other hand, certainly do challenge the everyday, certain sense of firmly bounded, discrete events.

Perhaps more often than not, two-wave riots consist of a first outbreak of violence that is milder than the second.[32] Many Hindu-Muslim riots in India have two such rounds. The two Bombay-Bhiwandi riots (1984) were separated by about five weeks.[33] The two Meerut riots (1987) were separated by a month. In the second round, the precipitants were so powerful that police auxiliaries joined crowds of Hindus in killing about 400 Muslims.[34] In 1982, Meerut had had a riot in three

---

31. For an example of what might have been one riot or two in an even more restricted time frame, see E. G. Ghurye, *Social Tensions in India* (Bombay: Popular Prakashan, 1968), p. 309.

32. One unusual African riot, between Konkomba and Nanumba in the north of Ghana (1981), came in three waves. In the first wave, in mid-April, fewer than ten people were killed. In early May, some 600 were killed. In June, perhaps 500–800 were killed. The violence produced at least 30,000 refugees. Colin Legum, ed., *Africa Contemporary Record, 1981–82* (New York: Africana, 1982), p. B421; *Africa Diary,* September 10–16, 1981, p. 10657; *West Africa,* April 28, 1981, p. 1001; July 20, 1981, pp. 1629–31.

33. *Indian Express* (New Delhi), June 26, 1984, p. 6.

34. Asghar Ali Engineer, "Meerut: The Nation's Shame," *Economic and Political Weekly,* June 20, 1987, pp. 969–71; *Far Eastern Economic Review,* June 11, 1987, p. 52.

parts, all within less than two months. That riot showed strong signs of organization, and it required 4,000 paramilitary police to put it down. Mild violence in Karachi in October and November of 1986 preceded much more severe violence in December of that year.[35] The anti-Muslim riot in southern Chad in 1979 began with the killing of 20 Muslims in late February. It was followed by the killings of hundreds or thousands a week later.[36] Two mild rounds preceded a more deadly one in Uzbekistan (1989) by a matter of weeks. A mild round preceded serious violence in Luluabourg, Zaire (1959), by two months.[37] The anti-Alevi violence in Turkey in December 1978 followed less serious attacks in the preceding months.[38] In Singapore, there were skirmishes, with a few casualties, in June 1964. These constituted a practice session for the more deadly riot of September of that year.[39] In 1977 and again in 1983, in Sri Lanka, small riots, with a few killed, were followed weeks later by large riots, with many killed, after new precipitating events.[40] Often the first such riot looks in retrospect like an intimation of what is to come, a prelude, a warning to the prudent.

What differentiates the two outbreaks is some combination of greater ability or willingness of the forces of order to control one episode than to control the other, greater opportunity for the rioters to organize one or the other, and/or the occurrence of some significant precipitant of new violence after the first wave is concluded. After an episode of violence, the atmosphere is likely to be quite propitious for another episode. The first riot is anticipatory, a tryout that, if successful, makes massive violence feasible.

Another variant is typified by the Malaysian violence of 1969. In May, hundreds of Chinese were killed. At the end of June, a much smaller

---

35. Farida Shaheed, "The Pathan-Muhajir Conflicts, 1985–6: A National Perspective," in Veena Das, ed., *Mirrors of Violence: Communities, Riots and Survivors in South Asia* (Delhi: Oxford University Press, 1990), pp. 200, 207.

36. *Africa News*, March 16, 1979, p. 2; Virginia Thompson and Richard Adloff, *Conflict in Chad* (Berkeley: University of California Institute of International Studies, 1981), pp. 84–89.

37. Henri Nicolai, "Conflits entre groupes africains et décolonisation au Kasai," *Revue de l'Université de Bruxelles*, XIIe Année (1960): 140–41.

38. Feroz Ahmad, *The Making of Modern Turkey* (London: Routledge, 1993), p. 172.

39. Michael Leifer, "Communal Violence in Singapore," *Asian Survey* 40, no. 10 (October 1964): 1115–21.

40. Tamil Refugees Rehabilitation Organization, *Communal Disturbances in Sri Lanka: Sansoni Commission, Written Submissions* (mimeo., March 28, 1980), pp. 137–40; T. D. S. A. Dissanayaka, *The Agony of Sri Lanka: An In-Depth Account of the Racial Riots of 1983* (Colombo: Swastika Press, 1983), pp. 56–57.

number of Indians, earlier viewed as siding with the Chinese, were killed in what amounted to a postscript to the earlier violence.[41] Similar simmering violence, with fewer casualties in the later stages, occurred in Burma (1938), Cairo (1981), Mauritius (1968), Jamshedpur, India (1979), Moradabad, India (1980), Aligarh, India (1978–79), and Tripura, India (1980).[42] Mauritius and Aligarh actually had several small aftershocks. In Sri Lanka (1983) and in West Kalimantan (1997), there were mild outbreaks in the weeks before *and* the weeks after the massive killings. If the later round is milder, the atmosphere may still be conducive to violence, but now the instrumentalities of force have the advantage, and major new precipitating events have not occurred.

Whether these sequences constitute one or two or three riots is difficult to decide. Differences of time always challenge conceptions of singularity.[43] As I shall suggest in a moment, a closer look within each violent encounter could even produce a finding that the circumstances of each individual killing were different. Different locations can also yield the conclusion that there are different riots in progress simultaneously. It is not uncommon for violence to occur first in Town X and the next day in Town Y, three or four miles away. Here, too, the boundary of the event is in doubt and, in some sense, rightly so; for it is certainly plausible to speculate that the riot in Town Y, while inspired by the previous day's events or facilitated by the concentration of the police at Town X, may derive from different local sources of hostility, involve different sets of organizers and participants, and target different categories of victim. Space, like time, raises the external boundary question.

Within what seems to be a single episode, there may be stages, shifts in

41. John Slimming, *Malaysia: Death of a Democracy* (London: John Murray, 1969), p. 64.

42. Government of Burma, *Final Report of the Riot Inquiry Committee* (Rangoon: Superintendent, Government Printing and Stationery, 1939), ch. 10; *African Recorder*, October 8–21, 1981, pp. 5746–47; *Africa Report* 13, no. 4 (April 1968): 23; ibid., 13, no. 5 (May 1968): 27; S. K. Ghosh, *Communal Riots in India* (New Delhi: Ashish, 1987), p. 222; *Keesing's Contemporary Archives*, December 7, 1979, p. 29969; *Far Eastern Economic Review*, July 4, 1980, p. 11.

43. The violence may develop over such a long period, and so intermittently, as it did in Tuva (1990), that it may be difficult to locate the riot altogether. At first, in Tuva, there were fights and kidnappings around May. In the succeeding months, there were apartment blocks and cars burned, rocks thrown, people beaten, and then, in August, some combustible fluids aimed at Russian houses. By then, some 88 people had been killed in an accumulation of small incidents that continued right through November. Could it be said that the riot lasted for half a year? Perhaps there was no single riot but a great many small riots. Or perhaps the requisite intensity of violence for even one riot was never quite achieved, at least according to the definition advanced in Chapter 1.

crowd action, stops and starts that render problematic the determination that there is a single episode. Examine closely one of the simplest (and mildest) of deadly riots for which good data are available, the Singapore riot of 1950.[44] The first incidents were discernible in the early afternoon. They involved property damage, mainly to automobiles, and some theft. Slowly, personal assaults increased, and the first deaths were inflicted between six and seven in the evening. This is a common progression, from less to more serious violence. The pattern is consistent with the reduction of inhibitions on violence if the first events proceed with impunity.

The first targets were Europeans and Eurasians, but some others were also assaulted. By late afternoon, several different crowds of 200 or more were looking for rather differently defined sets of targets. This is by no means the usual pattern, particularly in events that proceed simultaneously.[45] Some rioters sought to attack Europeans in general. Other attackers were focused on Dutch victims only, conspicuously excluding British victims. Still others continued to cast their nets more widely, for Europeans and Eurasians. In general, targeting became more precise as time went on. There was a respite for about four hours before dawn of the second day, at which point violence resumed. Slowly, the police and army began to regain control. By 10 P.M., the violence stopped, only to begin again at 8 A.M. the next day. On the third day, there were fewer incidents, and by 3 P.M. the violence was over.

It is legitimate to ask how many riots these were. If rioters, having made a decision to stop for the night, make another decision to begin in the morning, are each day's events properly considered part of a larger event? Riots may be divisible into daily cycles of activity, rather than constituting a continuously developing single episode. Combine these cycles with changes in targeting over time and space. Rioters at Time One

44. "Statement of Andrew Howat Frew, ASP, to the Riot Inquiry Commission," Singapore, February 27, 1951 (mimeo.), copy in the Rhodes House Library, Oxford.

45. For consistency in targeting, see Chapter 4, below. At slightly different times and locations, variations, though rare, are possible. In Sri Lanka (1958), the attacks on Sri Lankan Tamils in many locations were preceded by an attack on Indian Tamils at Welimada and followed some weeks later by a Tamil-Muslim clash at Akkaraipattu. Government of Ceylon, *Administration Report of the Inspector-General of Police for 1958*, part III (Colombo: Government Press, 1960), pp. A154–A156. In Dushanbe, Tajikistan (1990), the targets of some rioters were Armenians; of others, Russians or all Slavs; and, of yet others, all non-Tajiks. *Moscow Trud*, February 15, 1990, in FBIS-SOV-90–033, February 16, 1990, p. 56.

would have killed a person, a Briton, for example, whom rioters at Time Two would have let pass unharmed. Even concurrently, rioters in one place were interested in killing all Europeans, rioters in another place in killing only Dutch, and rioters in a third place in killing not just Dutch or Europeans but Eurasians as well. This, as I say, is unusual, because generally target choices are precise and consistent. In this case, perhaps each group of rioters was conducting a separate riot.[46]

A not dissimilar process has been documented for the rhythms of the Watts violence in Los Angeles (1965).[47] This was not a riot that aimed to kill ethnic antagonists. Burning and looting were the main activities, but areas experiencing one did not necessarily experience the other. After the first day, the violence did not spread to contiguous areas, and newly affected areas went through cycles of variable intensity and duration, mainly at night. Differentiated patterns over time and space suggest different motivations among categories of participant, sufficiently to raise the possibility that within the larger events "several smaller, simultaneously mini-riots may be occurring . . . ."[48]

Every event can thus be decomposed into other events. Although riot data are rarely adequate to allow sophisticated disaggregation of this kind, multiple crowds are not uncommon.[49] Similarly, every event can be linked with another into a larger event. There is no iron law determining eventness. This conundrum causes problems for riot study, for unit

46. It is interesting to speculate on the sources of differential target choice. The precipitating events could reasonably have been identified with the Dutch, the British, or the Eurasians, or all three, which may have produced the confusion. The occasion was a custody proceeding, in which the Dutch consulate was active, the Dutch mother was actually a Eurasian, and the court awarding custody to her was British. But some attackers had clearly been inspired by Indonesian leaders in Singapore, and many Indonesians were later arrested for participating. "Statement of Andrew Howat Frew," p. 30. Perhaps it was they, who, for reasons related to Indonesia, specially sought out the Dutch. In 1946, however, there had been a small riot in Singapore between Malays and local Indonesians, on one side, and Dutch and Menado sailors, on the other, over advances the latter made to Malay women. Malayan Security Service, *Political Intelligence Journal*, serial 6 of 1946, July 15, 1946, p. 2, copy in the Rhodes House Library, Oxford, MSS Ind. Ocn. s. 251. Perhaps, then, the 1950 violence was connected to the 1946 violence, bringing us back to the uncertain external boundaries of a riot, even as we raise the possibility of internal boundaries.

47. Margaret J. Abudu Stark et al., "Some Empirical Patterns in a Riot Process," *American Sociological Review* 39, no. 6 (December 1974): 865–76.

48. Ibid., p. 874.

49. See, e.g., Government of Burma, *Final Report of the Riot Inquiry Committee*, pp. 33–41; Karl von Vorys, *Democracy without Consensus: Communalism and Political Stability in Malaysia* (Princeton: Princeton University Press, 1975), pp. 332–33.

homogeneity is required in the dependent variable.[50] It is particularly problematic to perform correlations based on events data, for the mode of counting occurrences as one or several events can easily bias the conclusions. If, for example, the proposition is advanced that casualties are greater in riots with multiple precipitants, skepticism is warranted, for riots with multiple precipitants may be multiple riots; and, all else equal, several riots will produce more casualties than one will.

Difficulty in locating the boundary of an event does not, of course, preclude all conclusions based on what goes on inside whatever boundary is located or is chosen arbitrarily. For some purposes — but not for all purposes — it will not matter whether one, two, or three riots have occurred. If it always mattered, it would be impossible to analyze events like the partition violence in India-Pakistan (1946–47) or the northern Nigerian violence of 1966. These violent episodes were so massive and overlapping that most divisions into discrete events would seem fictitious.

There is a further problem that derives from alternative histories of the event. Does a conception of the event properly include the action which precipitated it? If so, how is that action to be identified? This is a crucial matter for the participants, because if the precipitating action is itself brutally violent, it can operate both to cause and to justify the violence that then results. Were the 1983 anti-Tamil riots in Sri Lanka produced by — and even part and parcel of — the Tamil guerrilla attack on the armed forces that preceded the riots, in which Sinhalese did the attacking? Or was the guerrilla attack in turn a reaction to the earlier torture of Tamil youths by Sri Lankan security forces? Alternative interpretations of where one event stops and another begins "constitute the meaning of the violence for people located in different social positions."[51] Time consists of antecedent and subsequent, but time by itself does not demarcate temporal boundaries.

How, then, is this task to be accomplished? There are essentially three approaches to the problem of demarcating events, each with characteristic difficulties.

The first is to solve the problem by definitional fiat. The very unusual

50. Gary King, Robert O. Keohane, and Sidney Verba, *Designing Social Inquiry: Scientific Inference in Qualitative Research* (Princeton: Princeton University Press, 1994), pp. 91–94. For very general cautions about units of analysis, see Robert K. Yin, *Applications of Case Study Research* (London: Sage, 1993), p. 10; Royce Singleton, Jr., et al., *Approaches to Social Research* (New York: Oxford University Press, 1988), pp. 69–72.

51. Veena Das, "Communities, Riots, Survivors: The South Asian Experience" (Punitham Tiruchelvam Memorial Lecture, Sri Lanka Tamil Women's Union, Colombo, September 5, 1988; mimeo.), p. 9.

study of violence that attends to this problem, if only in passing, solves it by deciding arbitrarily that, for example, "reports of multiple disturbances in a city which are separated by less than five days [are] recorded as a single event."[52] Such arbitrary demarcations open the possibility of recording as one what, for some purposes, ought to be counted as several. Sometimes the definition of a term can properly be arbitrary. But to demarcate arbitrarily a phenomenon that is chosen for investigation because its coherence suggests its individuation — or its appropriateness as a dependent variable — can skew the findings.

The second solution is that of more self-conscious events-data researchers, most often in international relations, although occasionally in studies of violence. They tend to define events in terms of transitive action. In a typical formulation, an event is "an activity which an actor undertakes at a specific time and which is generally directed towards another actor for the purposes of conveying intent or interest (even noninterest) in some issue."[53] True enough, perhaps, but not responsive to the problem of whether to aggregate or disaggregate candidates for event status. Since an event is said to be "an activity," this defines one unknown in terms of another.

The third approach is to be found in lively debates about the individuation of events in ontological theory. Although some philosophers are "multipliers," whose conceptions proliferate the number of events,

52. Seymour Spilerman, "The Causes of Racial Disturbances: Tests of an Explanation," *American Sociological Review* 36, no. 3 (June 1971): 427–42, at p. 430 n. 5. Many other efforts at definition touch the problem of individuation obliquely, if at all. See, e.g., Seymour Spilerman, "The Causes of Racial Disturbances: A Comparison of Alternative Explanations," *American Sociological Review* 35, no. 4 (August 1970): 627–49, at p. 630; William R. Morgan and Terry Nichols Clark, "The Causes of Racial Disorders: A Grievance-Level Explanation," *American Sociological Review* 38, no. 5 (October 1973): 611–24, at pp. 612–13; Robert M. Fogelson, "Violence and Grievances: Reflections on the 1960s Riots," *Journal of Social Issues* 26, no. 1 (Winter 1970): 141–64, at pp. 144–47; Stanley Lieberson and Arnold R. Silverman, "The Precipitants and Underlying Conditions of Race Riots," *American Sociological Review* 30, no. 6 (December 1965): 887–98, at p. 887.

53. Edward E. Azar, "Ten Issues in Events Research," in Edward E. Azar and Joseph D. Ben-Dak, eds., *Theory and Practice of Events Research* (New York: Gordon & Breach, 1975), pp. 1–18, at pp. 2–3. To the same effect, see Edward E. Azar et al., "Making and Measuring the International Event as a Unit of Analysis," in Edward E. Azar, Richard A. Brody, and Charles A. McClelland, *International Events Interaction Analysis: Some Research Considerations* (Beverly Hills, Calif.: Sage Professional Papers in International Studies, 1972), pp. 59–77, at p. 61; C. F. Hermann, "What Is a Foreign Policy Event?" in Wolfram F. Hanrieder, ed., *Comparative Foreign Policy: Theoretical Essays* (New York: David McKay, 1991), pp. 295–321, at p. 310.

whereas others are "unifiers," whose views compress potential events,[54] there are many more than two positions on these questions.

An event can be regarded as a change in the condition of an object or objects.[55] One possibility, then, is to focus on the source of the change and to individuate an action or event if it has a single cause.[56] Another is to conclude that two candidates for event status are identical if and only if they occupy the same space and time.[57] Both of these views present major problems for deciding whether to discriminate between possible riot events or to denominate them a single event.

The single-cause view raises the question of what caused what. It is often equally plausible to say that each subevent causes another subevent, which causes yet another. The hope that the boundaries of a riot could be defined by identifying its (single) cause can be defeated by decomposing one cause into many. This is a game easy to play with riot data and often played by political actors seeking to control the interpretation of the violence afterward. More fundamentally, one of the major things we seek to learn about events is what causes them. This view requires us to answer that question in advance.

The identity-of-space-and-time view is predicated on the similarity of events to objects, which are defined by the space-time matrix. That is, an object is unitary if and only if it exists in the same time and space. If an event truly is a change in an object, then the same time-space criterion of individuation should apply. Two events would be identical if they occurred in the same time and space. W. V. Quine, who argues for this position, concedes that the boundaries of an event may well be vague, but so are the boundaries of objects. It is not easy to say where a mountain begins and ends, but a mountain does at least have a summit, where its individuating center is located.[58] Unfortunately, the problem of individuating riots relates mainly to their boundaries, although not only to their boundaries. If the identity of time and space forms the criterion,

54. Irving Thalberg, "Singling Out Actions, Their Properties and Components," *Journal of Philosophy* 68, no. 21 (November 4, 1971): 781–87.

55. Monroe C. Beardsley, "Actions and Events: The Problem of Individuation," *American Philosophical Quarterly* 12, no. 4 (October 1975): 263–76; Donald Davidson, "Reply to Quine on Events," in Ernest LePore and Brian P. McLaughlin, eds., *Actions and Events* (Oxford: Basil Blackwell, 1985), pp. 172–76, at p. 176.

56. A view advanced and now abandoned by Donald Davidson. See Davidson, "Reply to Quine on Events," p. 175.

57. W. V. Quine, "Events and Reification," in LePore and McLaughlin, eds., *Actions and Events*, pp. 162–71.

58. Ibid.

even this is uncertain for riots. In the 1950 riot(s) in Singapore, is the single location Singapore as a whole, or one neighborhood, or one street? One is nearly tempted to say that the answer depends on whether the various streets and neighborhoods were equally affected by the violence — which would be to define the space by the riot rather than the other way around.

It may be that riots are complexes or congeries of events of uncertain number. This would bother most ontologists, but it should not necessarily disturb us, provided we are able to individuate the complex or congeries reliably. The study of ontology has been fixed on some rather simple events. A riot is a more complex phenomenon than those that ontologists usually consider as candidates for separate-event status. If it is true that a riot is a concatenation of events, it might well be categorized as a "temporally discontinuous"[59] and also, for that matter, a spatially discontinuous event. The components may be events, and so may the whole. But how does one know?

Surely it matters why the prospect of decomposing one event into more than one seems plausible initially. In the Singapore case, where the ethnic identity of the targets varied somewhat from time to time and place to place, something turns on how we account for those variations. If, on the one hand, differing groups of participants acted variously at varying times and places because of varying motives, perhaps there was more than one riot. If, on the other hand, the complexity of the events precipitating the riots gave rise to a variety of plausible target choices, which perpetrators of violence could opt for as they saw fit, then perhaps it was still a single riot. There is some truth, as we shall see, in both of these hypothesized explanations for what happened in Singapore: some classes of participant seem deliberately to have taken greater aim at the narrower category of Dutch targets; and, apart from this, the events producing the violent response also gave the rioters a choice, depending on whether they attributed responsibility to the British, the Dutch, all Europeans, or Europeans and Eurasians. To be required to know all of this in advance, however, is to be required to know too much, merely to put a boundary around the riot, for this is not likely to be known until after the riot is studied.

It is, then, very easy to reason into circles on these matters. Small wonder that the arbitrary definition has considerable appeal. As William

---

59. Judith Jarvis Thomson, *Acts and Other Events* (Ithaca: Cornell University Press, 1977), p. 53.

Riker suggests,[60] events consist of a continuous stream of actions and motions, which are then structured into units categorized as events.

Yet it takes little probing to discern some criteria for categorizing and individuating units. Judith Jarvis Thomson uses the example of cleaning a house,[61] an activity that can stop and start, that has multiple components and phases, but that can nonetheless be bounded with some degree of certainty. The deadly ethnic riot resembles the housecleaning in its purposiveness, its temporal and spatial fitfulness, its open-textured choice of methods and objects of action, and its complexity of constituent acts. If several people undertake the same housecleaning, they may emphasize different methods, focus on different objects, and even hinder each other in the process, just as several crowds may perform as variously as the Singapore crowds did. As violence may start up again before too long, the house may be cleaned again before too long; and the two cleanings may even run into each other, without quite undoing the idea of separate cleaning episodes. In each case, the action as a whole has a certain coherence, because of its common general purposes, its characteristic, if slightly variable, methods, and the ability to declare it done, although subject to recurrence. If the violent purpose and methods subsist, the riot persists. And it persists until the forces of order have regained the kind of control that makes members of the target group feel more or less secure on the streets, even if that security is later interrupted again.

This implies a proper reluctance to proliferate (that is, count multiply) riots in instances like Singapore (1950), although we might later conclude that several streams of activity were occurring within such an event. Boundary problems remain, especially when a riot spreads quickly to another city. But this is preferable to the proliferation of riot units within what are plausibly single episodes, merely on the basis of what we know about them at an early point in the inquiry; for what we know then may well be completely fortuitous.

Riker suggests the utility of the concept of *a situation*, defined as "motion and action imagined to a standstill,"[62] with, in other words, time factored out. He sees events as bounded by initial and terminal situations, provided that all the actors in the initial situation are included in or accounted for in the terminal situation. Building on this notion, Riker

60. William Riker, "Events and Situations," *Journal of Philosophy* 54, no. 1 (January 1957): 57–70.
61. Thomson, *Acts and Other Events*, pp. 50–57.
62. Riker, "Events and Situations," p. 60.

lays down canons for reducing the ambiguity of events.[63] None of these, it is fair to say, provides any certain means to ascertain the boundaries of events, for alternative conceptions of the initial and terminal situation can always be advanced. Yet, following the notion of the riot as a congeries of events, loosely bounded at the beginning by characteristic phases of transition from nonviolence to violence and at the end by the restoration of order by force of arms, we can still view the Singapore violence of 1950 as a single *episode*, even if we take liberties by describing it as a single event.

Conceiving of the riot as something akin to a housecleaning — and there is bitter irony in that term — implies that it has characteristic rhythms, which is indeed what I shall argue. Typically included are some precipitating events. The absence of separate precipitating events should generally lead us to conclude that succeeding violence is attached to antecedent violence and so also argues for viewing Singapore (1950) as a single riot. The presence of fresh precipitants should also lead us to individuate episodes of violence, as in the two waves of riots in Sri Lanka (1977 and 1983). To acknowledge riot sequences and use them in individuation is not to impute causation but rather to concede that, in some way that requires examination, rioters act on the antecedent events, obviously finding them significant.

The boundaries of a phenomenon may also be fixed by the disadvantages of alternative boundary delimitations for explanatory purposes. In the case of riots, the approach of the multipliers and the approach of the unifiers both create major problems.

Consider first the prospect of compressing several possible riots and treating them as a single riot. The case for doing this is well made by those who know how important, below the surface of events, are the parts played by historical recollection, tradition, and culturally embedded motifs. In the anti-Muslim riot in east Delhi, India (1990), for example, there was at work a clear recollection of the 1947 partition riots, which apparently affected the behavior of some participants.[64] Causally important as such memories may be, it would be thoroughly self-defeating to utilize the external connections of one candidate for event status to another such candidate so as to suppress their individuation. No doubt it is all too easy to neglect such connections, which are frequently hid-

63. Ibid., pp. 65–69.

64. Shalini D'Souza and Arundhuti Roy Choudhury, "The Riots and the Perception of the People: Notes from the Field," *Social Action* 44, no. 1 (January 1994): 114–25, at p. 117.

den — and in the next chapter I shall stress some such connections relating to the phenomenon of *amok* — but the very ubiquity of connections means that their presence should not defeat the individuation of an event, lest there be, in the end, no separate events.

An excess of connectedness, too little individuation, destroys the concept of an event and shifts attention from immediate causes to remote causes. To link one candidate riot-event to another requires linkage to connective tissue, at least some of which will be nonviolent. If violence is the category, if the study is of riots and not of general social conditions, then discrete units have to be found.[65] Failure to individuate riots adequately also deemphasizes agency, for the less sharply discriminated the event is, the less well it will be accounted for in terms of who did what to whom. Keeping the focus of our inquiry requires that we avoid excessive sophistication in linking, at the threshold, potential exemplars of the phenomenon to other exemplars or other phenomena, no matter how sophisticated this linkage may become once we are embarked on the task of explanation.

The opposite course, proliferating the number of riots by promiscuous individuation, also has something to commend it. By multiplying riots, it is possible to increase the number of observations. Even if the units are not wholly independent of each other, as in the case of riots, there is often some information to be added by providing separate treatment.[66] The decomposition of the Singapore (1950) riot, performed above and extended later, suggests the utility of such an approach.

Nevertheless, promiscuous individuation has major problems attached to it. The first consists of the paucity of appropriate microlevel data. Singapore (1950) is not unique in its detailed documentation, but it is unusual. It is much more difficult to measure and maintain consistency with respect to smaller units than it is with respect to larger.[67] Furthermore, individuation on a liberal basis risks closing off some very important variations by definition. One of the sources of neighborhood variation in riot patterns in Singapore (1950) was heterogeneity of leadership and participation: those leaders and rioters of Indonesian background

65. Cf. Gyanendra Pandey, "In Defence of the Fragment: Writing about Hindu-Muslim Riots in India Today," *Representations*, no. 37 (Winter 1992): 27–55.

66. A strategy recommended by many authors, including King, Keohane, and Verba, *Designing Social Inquiry*, p. 222. How to sort out the effects of mutual dependence of the units on the data obtained is a tricky question, however.

67. Steven Ian Wilkinson, "What Large Datasets Can Tell Us about the General Explanations for Communal Riots" (paper presented at the annual meeting of the Association for Asian Studies, March 31, 1995), pp. 10–11.

were more interested in targeting the Dutch. If we were to decide that variable targeting was an indication of a separate riot, we might also be deciding, *sub silentio*, that riot leaders and participants — the cause of that variation — tended strongly to be homogeneous. On the other hand, treating homogeneity as a variable would lead to the next questions: When are leadership and participation homogeneous, and when are they heterogeneous? When are targets homogeneous and when are they heterogeneous?

The more there is a tendency to individuate each group of killings or even each killing, the closer such a strategy approaches a reductio ad absurdum, because the subject is, after all, *collective* violence. As we shall see, collective violence differs from individual violence on a number of dimensions, such as the frequency of atrocities, and these differences should not be obscured.

Both too little individuation and too much remove questions from the table. Too little individuation, which unifies any events that are connected, ties events together, so as to preempt the inquiry into proximate causes. Too much individuation suppresses variation. The truisms that everything is related to everything else and that every incident is unique are just that: truisms.

COMPOSING THE DECOMPOSABLE

It is just as easy to cast doubt on the very existence of the two elements that make up the ethnic riot as it is to accept them uncritically. The riot as an event can easily be decomposed into more than one, or two riots can plausibly be reduced to one. Equally, what looks like a single ethnic group can be divided into subgroups that until recently saw themselves as separate groups, or two antagonistic groups can be reduced historically to one. As the riot episode consists of an array of actions and events suspended in a molecular relation to each other, the group is a configuration produced by shifting combinations of collective perceptions of affinities and disparities and of attempts to secure strategic advantage in a bounded environment.

It is scarcely surprising that what looks thick should turn out so recently to have been thin and that what looks well bounded should turn out to be disorderly and rough-edged. For a variety of reasons — ameliorative efforts, for example — it is important to keep in mind the uncertain configurations of phenomena that appear fully fashioned. Yet it is not likely that what can be decomposed by analysts will be decomposed in the same way by participants. In mass activity, historical inaccuracy is the rule.

The fragility of group boundaries will not be acknowledged in the violence, occurring, as it does, at a moment of maximal emotional attachment to the group. Rioters reify group boundaries and attribute characteristics to whole groups, even to groups relatively recently formed, such as Mohajirs, an amalgam of migrants from India to Pakistan at the time of partition. Corporate identities and reputations can be established quickly, and, once they are established, collective repertoires are attributed to relatively new groups in the same way as they are attributed to old groups. For rioters, unlike theorists, plasticity is not destiny.

By the same token, to show that an episode can be bounded in a certain way after the fact does not mean that the participants will be equally inclined to individuation. Rioters have their own conception of the violent event. Their ontology is very different from that of analysts. I shall show later that rioters connect to the violence events that precede it, viewing them as one transaction in which pre-riot events justify their violent behavior. In the section on rumors in Chapter 3, we shall get our first glimpse of such mechanisms at work, and I shall argue in Chapter 13 that this tendency to merge what we might think of as separate events is indeed crucial to the killing.

The Riot Episode

THE DEADLY ETHNIC RIOT is an event with a structure, a process, and a character. It has overall rhythms. The riot is preceded by certain typical events that facilitate the transition to violence. Progressing from the rumors and plans that mark the slide into violence, the rioters soon arrive at the time for mass killing. Within these outlines there are phases, times in which characteristic rumors give rise to characteristic interpretations, followed by times in which certain preparations are made; and then there is the violence itself, with its characteristic intensity and sadism. In apparently disparate circumstances, these phases of the episode and the action that goes on within them recur.

THE RHYTHM OF THE RIOT

There is no single course taken by every riot as it develops, but there is a rough sequence in many riots that characterizes the transition from peace to mass violence and back. The riot is preceded by a chain of identifiable precipitants, events that persuade people that violence is necessary and appropriate. The various classes of precipitant require separate discussion, for they help in classifying the occasions for violence. There is, however, one precipitating event that usually comes last in the chain and transcends the particular occasion. That event is the dissemination of rumors. As we shall see, the rumors are highly patterned, and they move people to violence by acting on individual cognition and motivation as well as on group dynamics.

Viewed at close range, the rhythm of the riot is decidedly uneven. After the precipitants, there may be an unsettling event, perhaps a scuffle or a fight, conceivably a bit of burning. Quite possibly, no one will be killed on this first day of disturbance unless there has been a significant and intense buildup to the violence. Then, the violence may be interrupted for a period, which I call *the lull.* The first acts of violence that follow the lull are typically somewhat more deliberate than those that preceded it. They may or may not be lethal, but they are likely to be sporadic and isolated. If they are uncontrolled, however, they soon develop into a massive deadly attack. A common pattern is the progression from attacks on property, usually including burning of homes or shops, to vicious attacks on people, perhaps beginning with a bystander or passerby of the target group. Eventually, the violence is controlled by forces of order or by the fatigue or satisfaction of the rioters, but it is more likely to end gradually, with a diminishing number of stray attacks, than it is to end all at once.[1]

Overall, the riot thus follows something resembling a bell-shaped curve of growing and then receding intensity over time.[2] In some cases, intense violence comes sooner than in others, particularly if large numbers of people have already assembled for some purpose and the violence grows out of their assembly.[3] Once the riot becomes intense, any disposition the targets may have felt to resist and counterattack will almost certainly disappear. In the relatively few cases of significant early resistance, there are reports of victims who then became "pathetically passive and allowed themselves to be slaughtered like sheep."[4] The ethnic riot is one-

1. In constructing this sequence, I have relied, in addition to published sources, on interviews in Penang and in Colombo and on reports on the Penang riot of 1967 prepared by field liaison officers of the Malaysian Chinese Association and later made available to me by the MCA. For examples of such sequences, see "Statement of Andrew Howat Frew, ASP, to the Riot Inquiry Commission," Singapore, February 27, 1951 (mimeo.), copy in the Rhodes House Library, Oxford, pp. 1–30; S.K. Ghosh, *Communal Riots in India* (New Delhi: Ashish, 1987), pp. 126–30, 151–60; *Report of the Presidential Commission of Inquiry into the Incidents Which Took Place between 13th August and 15th September 1977,* Sessional Paper No. VII, July 1980 (Colombo: Government Publications Bureau, 1980), pp. 89–255; T.D.S.A. Dissanayaka, *The Agony of Sri Lanka: An In-Depth Account of the Racial Riots of 1983* (Colombo: Swastika Press, 1983), pp. 70–93; Asghar Ali Engineer, "Meerut: The Nation's Shame," *Economic and Political Weekly,* June 20, 1987, pp. 969–71.

2. To take just one example, the Sri Lanka riot of 1977 developed in Trincomalee with small disturbances on August 17, followed by a day of quiet on August 18 and six days of intense violence, reaching its peak on August 22 and trailing off through August 24. *Report of the Presidential Commission of Inquiry into the Incidents Which Took Place between 13th August and 15th September 1977,* pp. 254–55.

3. As in Malaysia (1969). See John Slimming, *Malaysia: Death of a Democracy* (London: John Murray, 1969), pp. 16–28.

4. Union of South Africa, *Report of the Commission of Enquiry into Riots in Durban* (Cape Town: Government Printer, 1949), p. 4. To the same effect, see Elliott M. Rudwick, *Race Riot at East St. Louis, July 2, 1917* (Carbondale: Southern Illinois University Press, 1964), pp. 38, 53. But see Paul R. Brass, *Theft of an Idol: Text and Context in the*

sided, because it is brought on by events believed to warrant violence by one side against another and because that side strikes when it has a clear advantage.

While the violence proceeds, there is a strong, although not exclusive, concentration on male victims of a particular ethnic identity.[5] The elderly are often left aside, and sometimes, though less frequently, so are children. Rapes certainly occur in ethnic riots, sometimes a great many rapes,[6] but the killing and mutilation of men is much more common than is the murder or rape of women. Women are sometimes pushed aside or forced to watch the torture and death of their husbands and brothers.[7]

As the riot proceeds, core participants are joined by others interested in attacking hapless victims. There is a tendency toward broadened participation once it seems safe to participate.[8] If the riot lasts several days, there is a likelihood of turnover in the crowd, as some participants tire and withdraw and their places are taken by others.[9]

This is a general, if sketchy, outline of the riot process, some pieces of which will receive more elaborate dissection than others. Fused in the violence are an underlying sense of justification, illustrated by the one-sidedness of the killing and by the content of rumors preceding it, and a sense of impunity, an ability to conduct the killing free of retribution. The

---

Representation of Collective Violence (Princeton: Princeton University Press, 1997), pp. 214–21, describing confrontations between Hindu and Muslim crowds in Kanpur (1992) before the one-sided phase of Hindu killing of Muslims.

5. See, e.g., Haja Maideen, *The Nadra Tragedy: The Maria Hertogh Controversy* (Petaling Jaya, Malaysia: Pelanduk, 1989), p. 262; Amrita Basu, "When Local Riots Are Not Merely Local: Bringing the State Back In, Bijnor, 1988–92," *Economic and Political Weekly*, October 1, 1994, pp. 2605–21, at pp. 2611, 2613. In Kishinev (1903), 38 of the 49 Jews killed were men and boys. Edward H. Judge, *Easter in Kishinev: Anatomy of a Pogrom* (New York: New York University Press, 1992), p. 72. This is within the normal range for such an episode.

6. See, e.g., Basu, "When Local Riots Are Not Merely Local," pp. 2611–12; Union of South Africa, *Report of the Commission of Enquiry into Riots in Durban*, p. 4; *Report of the Presidential Commission of Inquiry into the Incidents Which Took Place between 13th August and 15th September 1977*, pp. 126, 135, 137, 215, 222, 234, 235.

7. For the full range of treatment of women and children, see Uma Chakravarti and Nandita Haksar, *The Delhi Riots: Three Days in the Life of a Nation* (New Delhi: Lancer International, 1987), pp. 33, 545, 583–90.

8. Richard Lambert, "Hindu-Muslim Riots" (Ph.D. diss., University of Pennsylvania, 1951), pp. 58, 97, 223.

9. A process well documented by Christopher Hibbert, *King Mob: The Story of Lord George Gordon and the Riots of 1780* (New York: Dorset Press, 1989), pp. 36–39, 44, 48, 61, 81–82.

ability to engage in violence is tested in the first, relatively mild incidents — just as anticipatory riots test the possibilities for more serious violence — and confirmed by growing violence and broader participation.

BEFORE THE RIOT: THE CRITICAL ROLE OF RUMOR

A rumor is a short-lived, unverified report, usually anonymous in its origin.[10] No rumor that is disseminated widely enough to help precipitate collective violence can be understood as merely a chance falsehood or, as is commonly thought, a bit of misinformation that gains currency because official news channels have been remiss in putting out the truth. Concealed threats and outrages committed in secret figure prominently in pre-riot rumors. Since verification of such acts is difficult, they form the perfect content for such rumors, but difficulty of verification is not the only way in which they facilitate violence. Rumors are structurally embedded in the riot situation, because they are satisfying and useful to rioters and their leaders, and so efforts to counter rumors may be misdirected. Rumor is likely to prevail over accurate information.[11] The direct and authoritative contradiction of a false rumor that large numbers of Armenians had been resettled in scarce housing was of no interest to the Tajik crowd that set upon Armenians in Dushanbe (1990).[12] Rumor prevails because it orders and organizes action-in-process.

THE NATURE AND FUNCTION OF RIOT RUMORS

Rumors form an essential part of the riot process. They justify the violence that is about to occur. Their severity is often an indicator of the

10. See Jan Harold Brunvand, *The Vanishing Hitchhiker: American Urban Legends and Their Meanings* (New York: W.W. Norton, 1981), pp. 12, 20, 194.

11. See Kajsa Ekholm Friedman and Anne Sundberg, "Ethnic War and Ethnic Cleansing in Brazzaville" (unpublished paper, Department of Social Anthropology, University of Lund, 1994), p. 7.

12. BBC Summary of World Broadcasts, February 14, 1990, SU/0688/B/1. The rumor was that 2,500 to 5,000 Armenians had been resettled in new housing in Dushanbe after anti-Armenian riots in Azerbaijan. In fact, only 39 Armenians had been resettled temporarily, with their own relatives rather than in new housing, and these had in any case already left for Armenia. For another failure of government efforts to counter rumors, see V.V. Singh, *Communal Violence* (Jaipur: Rawat, 1993), p. 118. For an unusual case in which rumors of the destruction of a temple were effectively countered by evidence that it still stood, see M.J. Akbar, *Riot after Riot* (Harmondsworth: Penguin, 1988), pp. 124–25. This, however, was a rumor pertaining to Hindu-Sikh conflict in Punjab, which has taken violent forms other than riot.

severity of the impending violence. Rumors narrow the options that seem available to those who join crowds and commit them to a line of action. They mobilize ordinary people to do what they would not ordinarily do. They shift the balance in a crowd toward those proposing the most extreme action. They project onto the future victims of violence the very impulses entertained by those who will victimize them. They confirm the strength and danger presented by the target group, thus facilitating violence born of fear. Rumors, then, are not stray tales. They perform functions for the group and for individuals in it.[13]

Since rumors facilitate ethnic violence in so many ways, it has been argued that rumors are disseminated deliberately by those who foment violence and that rumors remain in a more or less pristine form.[14] No doubt some instigators of violence use rumor, but a rumor will not take hold unless there is a market for it, a need in an emerging situation; and rumors change in the telling, becoming sharper in their factual assertions and more meaningful to recipients.[15] A story that a black man had shot a white in East St. Louis in 1917 "was embellished as it passed among the crowd; within minutes people asserted that the shooting was intentional and the victim had died."[16] What is remarkable is not that an interested agitator starts a rumor but that the rumor is spread, believed, and acted upon. Moreover, the same rumors recur across widely different contexts, suggesting that an evolutionist, rather than creationist, view of them is warranted.

Again and again, the rumors are of aggressive behavior, often with but sometimes without a sexual element. In Ahmedabad (1969), a newspaper reported, falsely, that some Hindu women had been raped in public. There was also a rumor of preparations for violence being undertaken by Muslims, who had accumulated stocks of arms and murdered the custo-

---

13. Each of the enumerated functions of rumors will be discussed. In addition, on the line of action, see Carl J. Couch, "Collective Behavior: An Examination of Some Stereotypes," *Social Problems* 15, no. 3 (Winter 1968): 310–22. On the impact of rumors on ordinary people, see Basu, "When Local Riots Are Not Merely Local," pp. 2613–14. On projection, although apart from rumors, see Sudhir Kakar, "Some Unconscious Aspects of Ethnic Violence in India," in Veena Das, ed., *Mirrors of Violence: Communities, Riots and Survivors in South Asia* (Delhi: Oxford University Press, 1990), pp. 135–45, at pp. 137–38. On surrender to the most aggressive opinion as the most common mechanism of group decision-making, see Yoram Jaffe and Yoel Yinon, "Retaliatory Aggression in Individuals and Groups," *European Journal of Social Psychology* 9, no. 2 (April–June 1979): 177–86, at pp. 182–84.

14. Basu, "When Local Riots Are Not Merely Local," pp. 2613–14.

15. See Singh, *Communal Violence*, pp. 66–67.

16. Rudwick, *Race Riot at East St. Louis*, p. 28.

dian of a temple.[17] Here are other false rumors that produced Hindu-Muslim violence:

Rourkela, Orissa (1964): Refugees from East Bengal, then in Pakistan, had been vomiting after eating bread said to have been poisoned by a Muslim.

Aligarh (1978): A fight between two Muslims gave rise to a rumor that Muslims had killed a Hindu.

Moradabad (1980): Muslims, it was said, came to a religious service armed and ready for a fight; they had poisoned the drinking water, destroyed a temple, and murdered the priest.

Sambhal (1980): Hindus were rumored to have killed the local *imam*.

Biharsharif (1981): After Hindu families fled a Muslim area, some 200 Hindus were reported to have been massacred.

Bhiwandi (1984): Hindus had allegedly been massacred by Muslims.

Gujarat (1986): Muslims were said to have burned alive more than 60 Hindus traveling by bus.

Bijnor (1990): The local council had, it was whispered, allocated Hindu land to Muslims, the president of a Hindu organization had been kidnapped and killed, and a Muslim physician had abducted Hindu women.

Bombay (1992–93): Reports spread that Pakistanis and arms shipments had arrived in Bombay from the sea.[18]

After the assassination of Prime Minister Indira Gandhi by her Sikh bodyguards in 1984, rumors circulated that the Sikhs were celebrating her murder by distributing sweets and lighting lamps, that Delhi's water supply had been poisoned by Sikh extremists, that truckloads and a train full of dead Hindus had arrived from the Punjab, where Sikhs had killed them, and that Sikhs with sten guns and daggers were killing Hindus.[19]

17. Ratna Naidu, *The Communal Edge to Plural Societies: India and Malaysia* (Delhi: Vikas, 1980), p. 113; Ghosh, *Communal Riots in India*, pp. 154, 156.

18. Ghosh, *Communal Riots in India*, pp. 127–28, 151–60, 224, 228; *Sunday Observer* (Bombay), June 3, 1984; *Free Press Journal* (Bombay), June 3, 1984; Asghar Ali Engineer, "Gujarat Burns Again," *Economic and Political Weekly*, August 2, 1986, pp. 1343–46, at p. 1344; Basu, "When Local Riots Are Not Merely Local," pp. 2613–14; Suma Josson, *Bombay Blood Yatra*, a film distributed in 1993.

19. Chakravarti and Haksar, *The Delhi Riots*, pp. 237, 264, 291–92, 410, 413, 426, 451–52, 522, 577; Citizens' Committee, Delhi, *Delhi, 31 October to 4 November 1984:*

Poisoning the bread, the water, or the milk supply is a crime recurrently imputed to the future victims.[20]

Outside India, similar rumors circulate. I set them out at length to show how powerfully recurrent the main themes are:

Singapore (1950): A rumor spread that the police had killed 200 people on the *padang* (green) in the middle of the city.

Singapore (1964): According to a leaflet, "the Chinese are planning to kill Malays who walk alone in areas where the Chinese predominate." A rumor also spread that Chinese were assaulting Malays.

Nigeria (1966): Reports circulated that the eyes of Tiv students had been gouged out, that a prominent Idoma leader had been killed, that a trainload of Birom corpses had been delivered to a railway station in a Birom city.

Malaysia (1969): Chinese secret society members were said to have vandalized Malay property and beaten Malay bystanders. Thousands of Chinese were waiting to attack.

Sri Lanka (1977): Sinhalese police officers were reported killed. Bodies of Sinhalese girls had been cut up and sent back from a Tamil area in "fish boxes." Sinhalese were still being killed in that Tamil area. A Buddhist monk had been murdered by Tamils; his cut-up body had been shipped in "ice boxes" to a Sinhalese-majority city. A Sinhalese police constable had allegedly been murdered, his body "hung in a beef stall" in a Tamil city.

Ujung Pandang, Indonesia (1980): It was whispered that a woman, who actually died of kidney failure, had been raped, murdered, and chopped into small pieces by her Chinese employer.

Cairo (1981): Copts were said to have committed mass murders against Muslims.

Sri Lanka (1983): Tamil rebels were said to be battling the armed forces right in the capital and to have poisoned the water.

Report of the Citizens Commission (Delhi: Citizens' Commission, 1985), p. 36; People's Union for Democratic Rights and People's Union for Civil Liberties, *Who Are the Guilty? Report of a Joint Inquiry into the Causes and Impact of the Riots in Delhi from 31 October to 10 November 1984* (New Delhi: People's Union for Democratic Rights and People's Union for Civil Liberties, 1984), pp. 1, 2, 19, 21, 35–36.

20. See, e.g., Sudhir Kakar, *The Colors of Violence: Cultural Identities, Religion, and Conflict* (Chicago: University of Chicago Press, 1996), p. 34; Ghosh, *Communal Riots in India*, p. 211.

Sumgait, Azerbaijan (1988): A railway truck full of corpses of Azeris killed by Armenians was claimed to have arrived in Baku.

Senegal (1989): Survivors of violence in Mauritania reported that Senegalese boys and women had been sexually mutilated, the women's breasts severed.

Uzbekistan (1989): Uzbek children were alleged to have been "lifted up on pitchforks" by Meskhetian Turks, who were also said to be armed with machine guns, raping women, and killing old people.

Kyrghyzstan (1990): Uzbeks were accused of murdering Kyrghyz in other cities. Sometimes 5,000 killed was the figure given, and one of the methods reported was impalement on stakes.

Kano, Nigeria (1999): Trailer loads of bodies of Hausa killed by Yoruba were said to be on the way to Kano.[21]

The same themes recur across the centuries and across the continents. In the anti-Jewish killings that swept over Western Europe in the mid-fourteenth century, the most widely spread rumors were of well poisonings and ritual murders.[22] Before the anti-Catholic riots in London

21. Maideen, *The Nadra Tragedy*, p. 251; *Memorandum Submitted by the Government of Singapore to the Commission of Inquiry into the Disturbances in Singapore in 1964* (mimeo., March 1965), Appendix 11; Albert Lau, *A Moment of Anguish: Singapore in Malaysia and the Politics of Disengagement* (Singapore: Times Academic Press, 1998), p. 167; Ruth First, *Power in Africa* (New York: Penguin Books, 1970), pp. 329, 332; Slimming, *Malaysia*, p. 41; Tamil Refugees Rehabilitation Organization, *Communal Disturbances in Sri Lanka: Sansoni Commission, Written Submissions* (mimeo., March 28, 1980), p. 43; *Report of the Presidential Commission of Inquiry into the Incidents Which Took Place between 13th August and 15th September 1977*, pp. 77–78, 104–05, 116, 132, 137, 166, 168, 195, 204–06, 225; *Far Eastern Economic Review*, May 21, 1980, pp. 24–25; *Economist* (London), June 27, 1981, pp. 35–36; Sunil Bastian, "The Political Economy of Ethnic Violence in Sri Lanka: The July 1983 Riots," in Das, ed., *Mirrors of Violence*, pp. 286–304, at pp. 301–02; Dissanayaka, *The Agony of Sri Lanka*, pp. 91–92; Jonathan Spencer, "Collective Violence and Everyday Practice in Sri Lanka," *Modern Asian Studies* 24, no. 3 (July 1990): 603–23, at p. 618; Peter Conradi, "Riots Were Planned Genocide, Armenian Communist Paper Says," *Reuters Library Report*, November 5, 1988, p. 8; *Africa News*, May 15, 1989, p. 5; *Newswatch* (Ikeja, Nigeria), May 15, 1989, p. 38; *Krasnaya Zvezda*, June 18, 1989, p. 4; *Literaturnaya Gazeta*, June 14, 1989, p. 2, in FBIS-SOV-89-117, June 20, 1989, p. 46; *Moscow TV*, June 15, 1989, in FBIS-SOV-89-115, June 16, 1989, pp. 45–47; Valery Tishkov, "Don't Kill Me, I Am Kyrghyz: Anthropological Analysis of Violence in Osh Ethnic Conflict" (paper presented at the 13th International Congress of Anthropological and Ethnological Sciences, Mexico City, July 28–August 5, 1993), pp. 20–25; *Izvestia*, June 19, 1990, p. 2, in *Current Digest of the Soviet Press*, July 25, 1990, p. 15; *Economist*, July 31, 1999, p. 36. For another poisoned water rumor in an incipient riot situation, see Human Rights Commission of Pakistan, *Sindh Inquiry, Summer 1990* (Lahore: Human Rights Commission of Pakistan, 1990), p. 26.

22. I am indebted to the late Ivan Hannaford for this information.

(1780), there were reports of 20,000 Jesuits hidden in underground tunnels, awaiting the order from Rome to blow up the river bed and flood London, as disguised monks had already poisoned all the bread in Southwark.[23] In Northern Ireland (1969), stories of the enemy massed and poised to "swoop down" circulated, as they did in Sri Lanka (1983), when it was said that the Tamil Tigers were in Colombo to launch an invasion.[24] Mutilations and castrations performed on a kidnapped children are an old motif of interethnic apprehension.[25] Contemporary riots are more often preceded by tales of atrocities against women. Similar motifs — exaggerated casualties, attacks against women, or armies massing, or all of these — can be found as far afield in time and place as the antiblack riots in East St. Louis (1917) and Chicago (1919) and the anti-Jewish riots in Odessa (1905).[26] The Chicago riot began with the familiar refrain that a woman's breasts had been removed.[27]

In riot after riot, in other words, regardless of context or the nature of the earlier provocations, rumors of aggression inflicted *by* the target group have been involved in setting a crowd on a course of mass violence *against* the target group. The rumors are false or exaggerated. They may report violence already accomplished or merely impending. The recurrent role of such rumors in precipitating attacks indicates that belief in the hostile intentions of the target group is an important facilitator of riot activity, as it can be in international warfare.[28]

It is worth looking more closely at patterns of rumor. Rumors take several forms, depending on whether the target group has gathered en masse for a demonstration, for self-defense, or for some other purpose. If

23. Hibbert, *King Mob*, pp. 19–20.

24. Harold Jackson, *The Two Irelands — a Dual Study of Inter-Group Tensions* (London: Minority Rights Group Report no. 2, 1971), pp. 8, 15; Bastian, "The Political Economy of Ethnic Violence in Sri Lanka," pp. 300–02.

25. See Jan Harold Brunvand, *The Choking Doberman and Other "New" Urban Legends* (New York: W.W. Norton, 1984), pp. 84–88, 91–92; Florence H. Ridley, "A Tale Told Too Often," *Western Folklore* 26, no. 3 (July 1967): 153–56.

26. Rudwick, *Race Riot at East St. Louis*, p. 28; William M. Tuttle, Jr., *Race Riot: Chicago in the Red Summer of 1919* (New York: Atheneum, 1970), pp. 41–49; Robert Weinberg, "Anti-Jewish Violence and Revolution in Late Imperial Russia: Odessa, 1905" (paper presented at the Seminar on Riots and Pogroms, University of Washington, Seattle, April 1991), p. 24.

27. Tuttle, *Race Riot*, p. 49.

28. The pre–World War I mobilizations and the Soviet emplacement of missiles in Cuba in 1962 are obvious examples. See Ole R. Holsti, Richard A. Brody, and Robert C. North, "Measuring Affect and Action in International Reaction Models," *Peace Research Society Papers* 2 (1965): 170–90. Lewis F. Richardson makes the point more generally that a common precipitant of war is the expectation of attack from the other side. *Statistics of Deadly Quarrels* (Pittsburgh: Boxwood Press, 1960), p. 17.

it has, the most likely reports are that killings have already occurred. If not, then plans for killings are typically reported.

The rumors usually follow some modest violence. The riot in Jos, northern Nigeria (1945), began after a quarrel between leaders of the Hausa and Ibo trading communities. The Hausa leader was struck unconscious. The story spread that he had been killed, and Hausa proceeded to attack.[29] After a series of fights in Durban, South Africa (1949), which began when an African received a bloody cut at the hands of an Indian merchant, "the story went that the Native [African] youth had been done to death in a brutal manner by the Indians, that he had been decapitated and that the Indians had placed his head in a Mosque, whence they refused to yield it up for burial. . . . Further afield runners brought news that the Indians in Durban had 'finished off' all the Natives in the city, and Natives leapt to arms . . . ."[30] In the Indian city of Ferozabad, Uttar Pradesh (1972), after initial clashes between police and Muslims, it was represented "that a score of Rajasthani Hindu laborers had been burnt alive in their huts," although in fact it seems that the huts were burned at least a day later, not by Muslims, and only after their occupants had moved out.[31] The election riot in Zanzibar (1961) began with fights between supporters of opposing parties at the polls. A false report quickly spread among Africans that "the Arabs are killing us."[32] In Assam (1960), after two minor assaults had occurred, the rumor spread that fatal mass attacks had been made on Assamese and that atrocities had been committed on Assamese women. After police fired on students, it was reported that several students had been killed (actually, one had) and that the killing had been done by Bengalis.[33] In the anti-Ahmadi riots in the Pakistani Punjab (1953), persistent rumors circulated to the effect that the Ahmadis were driving around in cars, "shooting down people indiscriminately."[34] Burma (1930) began with a series of

29. Leonard Plotnicov, "An Early Nigerian Disturbance: The 1945 Hausa-Ibo Riot in Jos," *Journal of Modern African Studies* 9, no. 2 (August 1971): 297–305.

30. Union of South Africa, *Report of the Commission of Enquiry into Riots in Durban*, p. 4.

31. Suneet Chopra and N.K. Singh, "Ferozabad: Anatomy of a Riot," *Economic and Political Weekly*, August 15, 1972, pp. 1711–13, at p. 1713.

32. Great Britain, Colonial Office, *Report of a Commission of Inquiry into Disturbances in Zanzibar during June 1961*, Colon. No. 353 (London: H.M.S.O., 1961), p. 9.

33. Charu Chandra Bhandari, *Thoughts on Assam Disturbances* (Kashi: A.B. Sarva Seva Sangh Prakashan, 1961), pp. 37–38. Cf. K.C. Barua, *Assam: Her People and Her Language* (Shillong, Assam: Lawyers' Bookstall, 1960), pp. 15–16.

34. Government of [West] Punjab, *Report of the Court of Inquiry Constituted under Punjab Act II of 1954 to Enquire into the Punjab Disturbances of 1953* (Lahore:

fights between Telugu and Burman laborers on the Rangoon docks. Burmans who were escorted from the area by police spread reports that Burman women had been molested — and that one had had her breasts cut off — and a pagoda attacked. Actually, one woman had been injured but not sexually assaulted, and stones had been thrown at Burmans who had taken refuge near, but not in, a pagoda.[35] In Meerut (1968), false rumors also circulated that Hindu women had been molested and that Hindus had been killed and were being buried in secrecy.[36] A widely advertised Hindu procession in Ranchi (1967) brought out Muslims, some of whom brickbatted a part of the procession. Under the mistaken impression that Muslim brickbats had found a Hindu victim, part of the procession brickbatted a Muslim high school. False accounts then spread that Muslim students had been killed. From that time on, rumors of killings, true and false, in one part of town traveled to another, where violence then occurred in turn. With the exception of the first brickbatting, all of the early violence was triggered by rumors of killings in the previous violence.[37]

Often the target group is not massed at the time the attack takes place. In that case, the usual rumors portray in lurid detail the nefarious conspiracies being plotted by the target group,[38] although reports of actual aggression at some distant points may also be interspersed. Indians in Burma (1938) were credited with congregating in large numbers to attack Buddhist pagodas and conspiring with Indian shopkeepers to kill Burmans by poisoning their food.[39] The posting of a northern army company in the southern Sudan in 1955 was taken as evidence that northern

---

Superintendent of Government Printing, 1954), pp. 155–56. There, as in Guyana (1962), where a similar false story of the police killing of a small child circulated, much of the violence was directed against the police and public installations, as well as against the target group.

35. Government of Burma, *Report on the Disturbances in Rangoon during May, 1930,* in E.L.F. Andrew, *Indian Labour in Rangoon* (Bombay: Oxford University Press, 1933), p. 285; Maurice Collis, *Trials in Burma* (London: Faber and Faber, 1953), pp. 143, 147, 150.

36. Aswini K. Ray and Subhash Chakravarti, *Meerut Riots: A Case Study* (New Delhi: Sampradayikta Virodhi Committee, n.d. [1968]), pp. 10–11.

37. Government of India, *Report of the Commission of Inquiry on Communal Disturbances in Ranchi-Hatia (August 22–29, 1967)* (New Delhi: Government Printer, 1968), pp. 14–19, 79.

38. Compare the alleged Vietnamese "plan for swallowing Khmer territory and committing genocide against the Khmers." *Far Eastern Economic Review,* December 3, 1992, p. 14.

39. Government of Burma, *Final Report of the Riot Inquiry Commission* (Rangoon: Superintendent, Government Printing and Stationery, 1939), pp. 55, 86–87.

soldiers were moving in to exterminate all southerners. The belief was corroborated by fictitious tales of northern troops murdering all the southerners in the town of Juba, including patients in the local hospital.[40] The Sudan riot of 1964 began after thousands of southerners, awaiting the arrival of a southern cabinet minister at Khartoum airport, were told that his plane had been delayed. A false rumor spread that the minister had met with foul play, and the crowd spread out through the city to wreak vengeance on northerners.[41] In 1969, a Muslim protest procession marched through Ahmedabad in the Indian state of Gujarat. This demonstration, which preceded the Ahmedabad riot, was taken by Hindus as evidence of a secret Muslim plan to attack them.[42] An interlude of several days between the killing of a Hindu boy in Mauritius (1965) and the Hindu-Creole rioting which subsequently broke out was punctuated with escalating rumors of imminent mass assaults.[43] A small quarrel was converted into a riot on Pangkor Island in Malaysia (1959) when news reached Malays, assembled at their mosque for Friday prayers, "that the Chinese community was deploying itself to put the Malays in their place."[44]

A common form of violence-triggering rumor, exemplified by the Sudan (1955) stories, is the report of an impending rebellion, invasion, or takeover to be staged by the target group, sometimes accented by tales of vicious attacks already accomplished. In Meerut (1968), "a wailing woman's voice was taken to be a war cry by a neighboring area."[45] The Malaysian riots of 1945 were preceded not only by stories of outrages perpetrated by Chinese men against Malay women, but also by reports that the British, returning after the Japanese occupation, were planning to give Malaya over to the Chinese guerrilla force that had fought the Japanese.[46] In Odessa (1905), the rumor was spread that Jews aimed to set up a Danubian–Black Sea republic that they would dominate.[47] In

40. Republic of Sudan, *Report of the Commission of Inquiry into the Disturbances in Southern Sudan during August, 1955* (Khartoum: McCorquedale, 1956), pp. 35, 117–22.

41. Kenneth D.D. Henderson, *Sudan Republic* (New York: Praeger, 1966), p. 211.

42. Ghanshyam Shah, "Communal Riots in Gujarat," *Economic and Political Weekly*, Annual Number, January 1970, pp. 187–200, at p. 189.

43. Adele Smith Simmons, "Politics in Mauritius since 1934: A Study of Decolonization in a Plural Society" (D. Phil. thesis, Oxford University, 1969), p. 412.

44. Willard A. Hanna, "Pangkor Island: A Footnote to Malayan Prospects and Problems," *American Universities Field Staff Reports*, Southeast Asia Series 8, no. 14 (June 15, 1960): 2–3.

45. Ray and Chakravarti, *Meerut Riots*, p. 2.

46. Cheah Boon Kheng, *Red Star over Malaya* (Singapore: Singapore University Press, 1983), p. 225.

47. Weinberg, "Anti-Jewish Violence and Revolution," pp. 31–32.

Guyana (1962), the crowd was urged on by unfounded reports that East Indians from rural areas were marching on Georgetown to provoke violence and that a child had been killed by tear gas.[48] When Turks killed Armenians in 1915, they were convinced that they had foiled an incipient separatist rebellion.[49] The Sinhalese who fell upon Tamils in 1958 credited false rumors of a massive Tamil invasion that evoked memories of ancient wars between their two kingdoms. The rioters called themselves the "Sinhalese Army" and set themselves the task of thwarting "the Tamil hordes . . . ."[50] False accounts of Tamil atrocities — including a Sinhalese teacher whose breasts had been cut off and a child hurled from its mother's arms into a barrel of boiling tar — lent immediacy to Sinhalese fears.[51] Some Sinhalese also believed "that the Tamils had formed a secret conspiracy to take control of Colombo and the administration of the country by sinister infiltration."[52] Strikingly parallel beliefs were widely entertained in northern Nigeria (1966). A government decree ordering the unification of the civil service was believed to be the first step in the colonization of the north by Ibo civil servants. Massive Ibo migrations were anticipated. Northern rioters in Zaria referred to themselves as the "Army of the North," for an Ibo attack was regarded as imminent.[53] An army on the march, or infiltrating the city, or ready to arrive by sea or even by parachute: these are the fears that inform the crowd.[54]

These rumors provide important clues to several features of the ensuing violence. Pre-riot rumors serve channeling and justifying functions, and they also exhibit strong elements of projection and anxiety-laden perception. The reports that reach the crowd have two significant characteristics. The plans or actions to which they refer are generally violent, and the violence is of the most brutal or extreme kind. Assaults are con-

48. Government of Great Britain, *Report of a Commission of Inquiry into Disturbances in British Guiana in February 1962*, Colon. no. 354 (London: H.M.S.O., 1962), pp. 28–30, 38, 51–52.

49. Tamotsu Shibutani and Kian M. Kwan, *Ethnic Stratification: A Comparative Approach* (New York: Macmillan, 1965), pp. 392–93, 400–01. Cf. Marjorie Housepian, "The Unremembered Genocide," *Commentary*, September 1966, pp. 55–61; Helen Fein, "A Formula for Genocide: Comparison of the Turkish Genocide (1915) and the German Holocaust (1939–1945)," in Richard F. Tomasson, ed., *Comparative Studies in Sociology*, Vol. 1 (Greenwich, Conn.: JAI Press, 1978), p. 280.

50. Tarzie Vittachi, *Emergency '58: The Story of the Ceylon Race Riots* (London: André Deutsch, 1958), p. 37; see also p. 34.

51. Ibid., pp. 44–51.

52. Ibid., p. 101.

53. First, *Power in Africa*, p. 311.

54. See, e.g., Naidu, *The Communal Edge to Plural Societies*, p. 113; Kakar, *The Colors of Violence*, p. 35; Joel Williamson, *A Rage for Order: Black/White Relations in the American South since Emancipation* (New York: Oxford University Press, 1986), p. 132.

veyed as killings, one killing as many, killings as atrocities, meetings as incipient invasions. The conspiracies that are detected are portents of extermination. Poisoned bread, milk, and water, after all, kill invisibly, indiscriminately, inclusively, and cunningly. Both the violence of the incidents and their massive, outrageous, irreversible character are important in the process of triggering violence.[55]

The ostensible fact that mass aggression has already occurred or is about to occur has the effect of closing alternative channels of peaceful activity. Of what use are the ordinary processes of politics when the other side has already taken up arms? The first acts of violence provide cues for appropriate behavior in the circumstances. Inhibitions on killing are removed. If there are doubts about the propriety of murder, self-defense and retaliation are both regarded as justifiable motives. As Hans Toch concludes in his study of collective violence, it is important to create a valid "common cause," in which rioters "can see themselves individually laboring toward group ends. They can feel themselves partners of a joint enterprise. They can conceive of their own acts as defined and sanctioned by a larger effort."[56] Experimental evidence indicates that previous attacks that are regarded as unjustifiable arouse people to more aggressive responses than justified or explicable attacks do.[57] There is also a tendency for aggressors in experiments to respond with the same sort of violent act and the same strength as the act that provoked them.[58] Reports that first blood has been drawn or that an army is on the march legitimize the course advocated by the most extreme, render the fainthearted disloyal, and arouse the anger of the rest to a higher level. Rumors may, as commonly asserted, help in "collective problem-solving,"[59] but this for-

55. One riot control manual, written in the United States context, argues that, as tension mounts in crowds, rumors generally go through three chief stages: "1. They begin with tales of alleged insults and discriminations . . . . 2. Then come stories of imminent violence, of arming by the other race, of the need to protect one's home and loved ones, of invasion from another city. 3. Finally one hears the crisis rumors, the inflammatory accounts of sex assaults, beatings and murders." Raymond M. Momboisse, *Riots, Revolts and Insurrections* (Springfield, Ill.: C.C. Thomas, 1967), p. 53. Compare the sequence described by Gordon W. Allport, *The Nature of Prejudice* (Cambridge, Mass.: Addison-Wesley, 1954), pp. 63–64.

56. Hans Toch, *Violent Men: An Inquiry into the Psychology of Violence* (Chicago: Aldine, 1969), p. 203. To the same effect, see Peter Loizos, "Intercommunal Killing in Cyprus," *Man* (n.s.) 23, no. 4 (December 1988): 639–53, at p. 649.

57. Russell G. Geen, *Human Aggression* (Milton Keynes: Open University Press, 1990), p. 44.

58. Frances K. Graham et al., "Aggression as a Function of the Attack and the Attacker," *Journal of Abnormal and Social Psychology* 46, no. 4 (October 1951): 512–20.

59. Tamotsu Shibutani, *Improvised News: A Study of Rumor* (Indianapolis: Bobbs-Merrill, 1966), p. 17.

mulation may be a shade too laissez-faire if the inclinations of rioters merely await news that lifts restraints on pursuing those inclinations.

Particularly is this so where brutality is reported or where an army of ethnic opponents is said to be on the march. The mutilation, torture, and murder of women and children, plans for invasion or genocide, children impaled on stakes or pitchforks, people dropped into boiling tar, women with breasts cut off, students with eyes gouged out: these are provocations so extreme, so evocative of the malevolence, cruelty, and efficacy of the enemy that there can be no other way out than massive violence. As Ralph H. Turner has suggested, rumor defines an emerging situation, enabling people to act with confidence and unanimity that were previously lacking.[60] Rumor arises, Turner argues, when "there is a strong incentive to engage in a form of collective activity against which norms are ordinarily operative."[61] Information about the vicious plans and deeds of the target group provides direction to anger and makes violence an imperative of survival.

THE RUMOR PROCESS

The enormity of the acts depicted in rumors helps explain why ethnic riots are not more common. The usually operative restraints are overcome only by acts of this magnitude. Killing, even in a crowd, with a greatly reduced chance of later identification, is an act requiring substantial justification. The provocation, therefore, must be presented as grave. The threat is simultaneously enormous and invisible. An army is on the march but has not arrived yet. Poison has been put in the water or food, but it has not been ingested yet. Killings and mutilations have occurred, but somewhere else. The justification for countermeasures depends on the gravity of the threat but does not require direct evidence of the senses. In ordinary times, such claims of danger dire enough to justify mass killing may not be credited.

Before the rumors circulate, the particular precipitating events may arouse anger but not justify mass killing. The assassination of Indira Gandhi was such an event. The Sikhs who killed her were perceived as representatives of all Sikhs, and yet theirs was an individual criminal act. If, however, the Sikhs in general celebrated the murder, that meant they

60. Ralph H. Turner, "Collective Behavior," in Robert E.L. Faris, ed., *Handbook of Modern Sociology* (Chicago: Rand McNally, 1964), pp. 397–409.

61. Ibid., p. 405. See Patrick B. Mullen, "Modern Legend and Rumor Theory," *Journal of the Folklore Institute* 9, no. 1 (January 1972): 95–109, at p. 105 (rumor serves to clarify an ambiguous situation in a crisis).

ratified it and shared the guilt of the assassins. If, in addition, mass killings of Hindus by Sikhs were taking place and drinking water was poisoned by Sikhs, then the nature of the assassination was transformed. The Sikhs in general were deserving of punishment by death. If Sinhalese believe they are killing Tamil Tigers, rather than Tamil civilians, this is a matter of survival.[62]

In extraordinary times, such as the days following the assassination of Mrs. Gandhi, stories of atrocities and of imminent extermination find willing ears. To explain the suggestibility of those who credit rumors, descriptions of riot behavior emphasize the cohesion, excited atmosphere, and artificial unanimity that prevail in a crowd.[63] Accurate as these characterizations may be, there are additional forces at work.

The suggestibility of prospective rioters is, to begin with, attributable precisely to the need for justification. Ambiguous stimuli — a wail of a woman, a delayed plane — are accorded an aggressive overlay. The events that typically precede riots are fraught with aggressive possibilities. Selective perception operates to extract from threatening behavior the most aggressive motives. A stray assault thus becomes a harbinger of a massive attack.

Of course, these events do precede a massive attack, but in reverse: the intended victims of the rumored conspiracies become the attackers. This suggests that the expectation of aggressive behavior from the target group is properly viewed as a form of projection, the attribution of motives or emotions to others because of motives or emotions experienced by oneself. In this case, the projection may be induced by anger and fear.

The anger that has already been produced by the earlier provocations may be projected onto the target group. Rumors of atrocities seem clearly projective. They present images of what the attackers themselves would like to do and will soon in fact do. The northern Nigerian students allegedly incapacitated from studying provided a foundation for the actual incapacitation of Ibo students that was to come. The recurrent tale of dismembered females is significant in this connection. As we shall see, sexual dismemberment is common in ethnic riots: that is the projected impulse. Attacks on females are much less common than attacks on

62. See Spencer, "Collective Violence and Everyday Practice in Sri Lanka," pp. 618–19.

63. Shibutani and Kwan, *Ethnic Stratification*, pp. 391–401; Herbert Blumer, "Collective Behavior," in Alfred M. Lee, ed., *Principles of Sociology*, 3d ed. (New York: Barnes and Noble, 1969), chs. 7–9. Cf. Ted Robert Gurr, *Why Men Rebel* (Princeton: Princeton University Press, 1970), pp. 279–89; Stanley J. Tambiah, *Leveling Crowds: Ethnonationalist Conflicts and Collective Violence in South Asia* (Berkeley and Los Angeles: University of California Press, 1996), p. 299.

males, however, and dismemberment of women is much less common than dismemberment of men. Defense of women is felt to be an honorable preoccupation, and so reports of dismemberment of women furnish a justification of what will soon be done to men.

Given the element of projection, the magnitude of events depicted in rumors of aggression is often a reliable predictor of the magnitude of the aggression to follow. Rumors of invasion, extermination, and atrocity are followed by life-and-death versions of the same phenomenon. Rumors have a certain predictive utility.

Fear is also a widely prevalent emotion among ethnic groups in a conflict situation, especially pronounced among crowds assembled in the uncertain atmosphere generated by the earlier provocations. Fear is likely to prompt a complementary projection — the attribution of hostile intentions to others in order to justify and explain one's own apprehensions.[64] Both anger and fear are conducive to exaggeration of the hostility of others and ready acceptance of unverified tales of outrages. Rumors of aggression serve the function of "presenting imagery consistent with the feelings."[65]

Anxiety-laden perceptions are also in evidence in the systematic exaggeration of events that form the subjects of the rumors, particularly exaggerated estimates of the strengths and capacities of opposing groups. There was no reason to believe that the Tamils could control Sri Lanka, that the Ibo could actually occupy northern Nigeria, that Indian food vendors could poison the Burmese population, or that the northern Sudanese could apply a "final solution" to the southerners. When a radio transmitter was falsely reported to have been found in a mosque in Ferozabad, India (1972), it suggested to Hindu rioters that Muslims were loyal to Pakistan and also, of course, that Pakistan stood behind them.[66] Anxiety is conducive to the exaggeration of threats[67] and to the willing-

64. Henry A. Murray, Jr., "The Effect of Fear upon Estimates of the Maliciousness of Other Personalities," *Journal of Social Psychology* 4, no. 3 (August 1933): 310–29. Cf. Ernest Jones, *Papers in Psychoanalysis*, 5th ed. (Boston: Beacon Press, 1961), ch. 14. For more on the role of projection in ethnic conflict, see Donald L. Horowitz, *Ethnic Groups in Conflict* (Berkeley and Los Angeles: University of California Press, 1985), p. 180.

65. Turner, "Collective Behavior," p. 403.

66. See Chopra and Singh, "Ferozabad: Anatomy of a Riot," pp. 1711, 1713.

67. See Horowitz, *Ethnic Groups in Conflict*, p. 179. Cf. Colin MacLeod and Ilan Lawrence Cohen, "Anxiety and the Interpretation of Ambiguity: A Text Comprehension Study," *Journal of Abnormal Psychology* 102, no. 2 (May 1993): 238–47; Andrew Mathews, Anne Richards, and Michael Eysenck, "Interpretation of Homophones Related to Threat in Anxiety States," *Journal of Abnormal Psychology* 98, no. 1 (February 1989): 31–34; Gilian Butler and Andrew Mathews, "Cognitive Processes in Anxiety," *Advances in Behaviour Research and Therapy* 5, no. 1 (n.m. 1983): 51–62.

ness to credit exaggerated reports, no matter how fantastic they are. A degree of fear verging on panic is what Jonathan Spencer found in a remote village in Sri Lanka. The village was far from anywhere Tamil rebels might have lodged, but not so far in the imagination of Sinhalese villagers, who believed that Tamil insurgents had infiltrated the area, that Sinhalese killings of Tamils were actually Tamil killings of Sinhalese, and that the Tamils were powerful and inclined to attack anyone, anywhere, anytime.[68] The resulting bloodthirstiness Spencer refers to as "savage paranoia."[69] And paranoia does refer to a willingness to credit the incredible, in this case producing what were believed to be "defensive responses to the threat of superhuman Tamil violence . . . ."[70]

The timing of the rumored aggression is important in determining the reception of the rumor. An isolated attack reported before other precipitants have crystallized hostile sentiments may be dismissed lightly, whereas at a later stage it may be treated quite differently. Nonhostile interpretations of the behavior of antagonists become less possible as stress and, with it, conformity grow.[71]

Rumors of aggression following other precipitants enable action to proceed with confidence in its necessity: "Once a group starts to take action in a particular direction the members tend to see events in a manner which facilitates and justifies completion of the action. As the orientation toward action becomes more intense, images are favored which indicate immediate and direct rather than delayed and indirect action."[72] This is an important reason for rumors of aggression to come last in the chain of precipitants and for the increasing difficulty in preventing a riot at later stages in the development of pre-riot events. By then the rumor is indestructible, because its function is not to inform action but to help it along.

68. Jonathan Spencer, "Popular Perceptions of the Violence," in James Manor, ed., *Sri Lanka in Crisis and Change* (New York: St. Martin's Press, 1984), pp. 187–95.

69. Ibid., p. 193. Tishkov refers to "social paranoia," but generally to denote a state of hysteria. "Don't Kill Me, I Am Kyrghyz," pp. 26–28.

70. Spencer, "Collective Violence and Everyday Practice in Sri Lanka," pp. 618–19 (emphasis omitted).

71. Ole R. Holsti, "Individual Differences in the 'Definition of the Situation,'" *Journal of Conflict Resolution* 14, no. 3 (September 1970): 303–10. Compare the tendency within "securely bonded groups" to minimize threats. Ralph H. Turner, "Integrative Beliefs in Group Crisis," *Journal of Conflict Resolution* 16, no. 1 (March 1972): 25–40. Multiethnic societies with unranked groups are extremely "unbonded."

72. Turner, "Collective Behavior," p. 407. Compare the hypothesized "completion tendency" in the study of aggression. Leonard Berkowitz, *Aggression: A Social-Psychological Analysis* (New York: McGraw-Hill, 1962), pp. 198–99, 220–22.

BEFORE THE RIOT: THE LULL

Precipitants do not always evoke an immediately violent response. There is often a period, measured in several hours or a few days, during which the impact of the precipitating event is felt and forces are mobilized for the assault. This expectant interval between the last precipitant and the onset of serious violence is a lull, "an ominous quiet,"[73] "a death-like quiet,"[74] a "deadly quiet . . . that heavy atmospheric threat of something about to burst."[75] Occasionally, the period of suspended action may last as long as a week, as it did in Jerusalem (1929).[76] Before the anti-Catholic riots in London (1780), there was a "waiting week" with "a strange tension in the air, a feeling of excitement and vague expectant fear . . . ."[77] Eventually, the tension turns to violence.

The lull occurs mainly in cases where the last precipitant comes on suddenly and the question is what to make of it. If the event is both expected and significant, a lull is less likely. The passage of an ethnically lopsided language bill, long proposed, debated, and awaited, will proba-bly bring a swift violent response rather than a delayed one. This was what happened in the Pakistani province of the Sind (1972), where the passage of a bill making Sindhi the official language, over opposition demands for a compromise, promptly brought on violence.[78] If, at the other extreme, the precipitant is unexpected but is of such grave signifi-cance as to render violence the only acceptable response, then there will either be no lull or the shortest time required to assemble the fighters — typically, a very short time. This is the case where the precipitant is itself a serious violent encounter in which the ethnic contestants are inextrica-bly involved from the very beginning. The general strike that meets with resistance in enforcing the order to close shop is likely to turn violent

73. Union of South Africa, *Report of the Commission of Inquiry into Riots in Durban*, p. 4.

74. J.D. Henry, *Baku: An Eventful History* (New York: Arno Press, 1977), p. 177.

75. Jean Wakatsuki, *Farewell to Manzanar* (New York: Bantam Books, 1973), p. 53. Manzanar was not the scene of a deadly riot but of protest violence, but in this case the process was the same.

76. Roger Friedland and Richard D. Hecht, "Divisions at the Center: The Organization of Violence at Jerusalem's Temple Mount/*al-Haram al-Sharif* — 1929 and 1990" (paper presented at the Seminar on Riots and Pogroms, University of Washington, Seattle, April 23, 1991), p. 12.

77. Hibbert, *King Mob*, p. 32.

78. *Times of India*, July 10, 1972, p. 1; July 11, 1972, p. 1; July 17, 1972, p. 8; *The Statesman* (Calcutta), July 9, 1972, p. 1; July 11, 1972, p. 1; July 12, 1972, p. 7; *Far Eastern Economic Review*, July 22, 1972, pp. 16, 18; August 5, 1972, pp. 16, 19.

very rapidly, as in Penang (1967). Riots in northern Nigeria (1945) and in Burma (1930) began with fights in the Jos market and on the Rangoon docks. These could not be regarded as personal quarrels between individuals but only as ethnic violence. In these cases, the fighting immediately became more general.

The lull thus occurs in the space between these poles — when the precipitant comes by surprise, or its gravity is undetermined, or it does not necessarily commit a group to violence. From this it is not difficult to discern the general outline of what transpires during the lull. The lull is the time for assessment of the precipitant. Although the materials rarely permit a full view of what occurs during this period, there are occasional glimpses. In Durban (1949), for example, the precipitant was an assault on an African teenager by an Indian adult, which quickly developed into interethnic fights, finally broken up by the police. Sporadic fighting continued to break out in the same area. By late evening, order had been restored. A thirteen-hour lull then intervened. During this time, rumors of Indian atrocities committed against Africans were circulated, and "much discussion must have taken place," for on the next day Africans "evinced a marked change of mood. On the 13th they had been roused to sudden anger, but many had taken the occasion merely to indulge in rough horseplay. . . . [W]hen fighting broke out afresh shortly after midday on the 14th in the Central Police Area, [Africans] were generally the aggressors and they attacked with increased ferocity."[79] The lull is the time when the nature of the precipitant is interpreted, usually through the magnifying lens of rumor.[80] At the same time, the significance of the precipitant is connected to the wider ethnic situation.

If evidence from the somewhat better documented realms of lynching and ghetto protest is pertinent, a quasi-deliberative process occurs during this period. In an ambiguous situation, alternative interpretations of events are sought and advanced, and alternative courses of action are suggested.[81] This process is sometimes marked, too, by challenges from women in the area to the courage of the men engaged in the debate.[82]

79. Union of South Africa, *Report of the Commission of Inquiry into Riots in Durban*, p. 4.

80. During this period, it was reported for Durban (1949), "the 'grapevine telegraph' played a fateful role." Ibid.

81. See Ralph H. Turner and Lewis Killian, *Collective Behavior*, 2d ed. (Englewood Cliffs, N.J.: Prentice-Hall, 1972), pp. 47, 89.

82. See, e.g., Arthur F. Raper, *The Tragedy of Lynching* (Chapel Hill: University of North Carolina Press, 1933), pp. 45, 389; Toch, *Violent Men*, p. 209. See also the

Finally, a course of action is formulated, and if the decision is for violence the participants (or additional participants) must be gathered.

The lull is, therefore, not simply the calm before the inevitable storm. In the first place, it is not necessarily entirely calm; it often involves a good deal of milling about. It is a brooding or ruminating quiet. Moreover, the storm, though it may be likely, is not inevitable. In one lynching account, for example, it took three successive nights to gather enough willing participants and to marshal their sentiments and energies to proceed to action.[83] Obviously, other such intervals following provocative events have ended in inaction. Whether violence emerges seems to be a function of the evaluation of the precipitant in the light of the distribution of social support, the behavior of the potential target group, and the response of the authorities. Any of these can put a gloss on events that suggests that the precipitant is less or more significant than was at first imagined.

Take the role of displays of social support. Authoritative approval or disapproval can push incipient violence in one direction or another.[84] In Sri Lanka (1977), there had been scattered attacks on August 16 and 17. On the 18th, there was a lull, but on that evening Prime Minister J.R. Jayewardene gave a speech in which he said, "If you [Tamils] want to fight let there be a fight; if you want peace let there be peace."[85] The statement was broadcast and rebroadcast on radio, and by the 19th the anti-Tamil riots began in earnest. The lull is a critical time for the reception of such messages.

The lull highlights an important feature of precipitants. As the interpretive activity of the lull indicates, to be an effective spur to action the precipitant must be tied to the general adverse situation in which the participants see themselves. It must be typical of target-group behavior or evocative of the precarious structure of group relations. If the lull does

---

pamphlet "Challenge to the Manhood of [the] New Generation," circulated before the riot in Ranchi (1967). Government of India, *Report of the Commission of Inquiry on Communal Disturbance, Ranchi-Hatia*, pp. 149–51.

83. Raper, *The Tragedy of Lynching*, pp. 265–66. In that case, the delay appears to have resulted from inhibitions on action deriving in part from vague notions of the legitimacy of action if but only if a group of 100 were gathered to take part.

84. This is a point repeatedly made in the United States literature. For various perspectives, see ibid., passim; Ralph W. Conant, "Rioting, Insurrection, and Civil Disobedience," *American Scholar* 37, no. 3 (Summer 1968): 420–33; Joseph Boskin, "The Revolt of the Urban Ghettos, 1964–1967," *The Annals* 382 (March 1969): 1–14.

85. S. Sivanayagam, *Sri Lanka: Ten Years of Jayewardene Rule* (Madras, India: Tamil Information and Research Unit, 1987), p. 8.

not eventuate in violence, this may be because the significance of the provocation may have been interpreted in such a way that it was not the fitting occasion required or the kind of intolerable affront that brings out the angry battalions.

If provocative events continue to occur during a lull, what the lull produces will be determined with the benefit of this new information. A threshold must be reached for violence to occur, and a small increment of precipitant at a critical moment may prove decisive, particularly if it confirms malevolent intentions. In Burma (1938), a procession to protest a book insulting the Buddha occurred on July 26. When the procession attacked Indians, it was forcibly suppressed by the police. Nevertheless, July 27 and the morning of the 28th were comparatively quiet. The violence that did continue on those days mainly took the form of sporadic looting of Indian-owned shops, rather than general disorder. The violence might well have tapered off or been controlled, had it not been for an incident that occurred on the morning of July 28. Retaliating for the earlier violence, some few Indians took the offensive: in two cases monks were assaulted, and in another Burman shops were attacked. When this happened, the lull was promptly broken. Within half an hour, Burmans took to arms throughout Rangoon. These events confirmed for Burmans the hostile intentions of the Indians.[86]

During the lull, it may be possible to take action to raise the inhibitions on violence. For reasons indicated earlier, there are strong dispositions by this point to interpret information in ways that facilitate violence, and so countering rumors will be extremely difficult. Prospects for forcible control, however, are not equally slender. The lull is a time for precautions by the authorities and for organization by the initiators.[87] In Ujung Pandang, Indonesia (1980), the precipitant occurred on the evening of Day 1, Chinese shops were closed on Day 2, troops were deployed — but ineffectively — on the morning of Day 3, and violence began on the afternoon of that day.[88] The lull could have been used to avert the riot by force. In Delhi (1984), there had been a few attacks on Sikhs on the night of the precipitant, the murder of Prime Minister Indira Gandhi. The next morning:

> There was a strange hush in the city. People were clearly expecting something. Eyewitness accounts from areas on the border of Haryana testify that

86. Government of Burma, *Final Report of the Riot Inquiry Commission*, pp. 33–36.
87. For the possibilities of control by skillful deployment, see Akbar, *Riot after Riot*, pp. 116–19.
88. *Far Eastern Economic Review*, May 2, 1980.

truckloads of men were being brought into Delhi. Young men were seen going round the city on scooters and motorcycles identifying Sikh shops and homes. In some localities, houses and shops were marked with chalk. Electoral lists and information from ration shop owners were used to facilitate this process. Patrols of police and army personnel seemed to be fewer than on the previous day.[89]

By that afternoon, there were major attacks, which grew more intense the next day.

By the time the lull has set in, then, events have already taken an untoward turn. The interval is typically short: a day and a half in Burma (1938) and Ahmedabad (1969), 12 or 13 hours in Delhi (1984) and Durban (1949), one to two days in Assam (1955), Nigeria (September 1966), and Ujung Pandang (1980), and 24 hours in Malaysia (1959). The more ambiguous the precipitant, the more it requires interpretation, and therefore the longer the interval may be.

The fact that the lull is generally a very brief interval suggests that most riots are the improvised work of ephemeral leadership that rises to the occasion. A lengthier interval may also be an indication of a more organized riot in the making, as it certainly was in Jerusalem (1929), London (1780), and Singapore (1950).[90] The chance of a hostile interpretation of events is enhanced if there are leaders or organizations with a strong interest in promoting violence, but the longer it takes to organize the attack the more time there is for police deployment. Often, however, countermobilization by the authorities is difficult on the limited notice afforded by the typical lull.

Lastly, the lull may affect the locale of the riot. When the crowd does gather for action, it may assemble in a place far from where the precipitant occurred, even if the precipitant was a violent encounter.[91] In Mauritius (1965), a long lull following the first skirmishes in Port Louis resulted in an outbreak of violence in a village ten or fifteen miles to the southeast.[92] The lull in Durban changed the location of the fighting from the main area of Indian shops to areas far from the center of town and also changed the identity of the victims from middle-class Indian shopkeepers to the poorer Indians resident in the working-class areas where the postlull violence

89. Smitu Kothari and Harsh Sethi, eds., *Voices from a Scarred City: The Delhi Carnage in Perspective* (Delhi: Lokayan, 1985), p. 8.

90. See Friedland and Hecht, "Divisions at the Center"; Hibbert, *King Mob*; Maideen, *The Nadra Tragedy*.

91. For the same phenomenon in ghetto protest violence, see Conant, "Rioting, Insurrection, and Civil Disobedience," p. 425.

92. Simmons, "Politics in Mauritius since 1934," pp. 412–14.

occurred.[93] In Zanzibar (1961), a lull of less than 24 hours shifted the focal point of violence from Zanzibar Town to the countryside. The main victims there were the Manga Arabs concentrated in rural areas and uninvolved in the earlier events.[94] By changing the venue, the lull may also change the subethnic identity of the targets of the fighting.

Such a change of venue reflects, in part, the ability of riot leaders to respond to deployments made by the authorities during the quiet period. The lull does provide a chance to head off the riot by force, but success in such a venture requires not merely swift mobilization but adequate intelligence, which is not always easy to obtain in a situation fraught with what seems to be confusion.[95]

PREPARING FOR WAR, CONQUERING FEAR

It is sometimes said that collective behavior differs from organized behavior, because it lacks the force of tradition.[96] The evidence, however, is that violent episodes are suffused with traditional forms. Especially prominent are established cultural motifs conducive to warfare and to facilitation of violence in general.

THE ANALOGY TO WARFARE

Riots remind participants of long-standing methods of preparing for and making war. "All the rites of traditional tribal warfare were reenacted" in the Congo-Brazzaville riots of 1959, "beginning with the planting of a spear in front of the enemy's hut."[97] The participants wore their traditional headgear, which had the incidental benefit of making them readily identifiable in battle.[98] Preparations follow prescribed forms, often

93. Maurice Webb and Kenneth Kirkwood, *The Durban Riots and After* (Johannesburg: South African Institute of Race Relations, 1950), p. 2.

94. Government of Great Britain, *Report of a Commission to Inquire into Disturbances in Zanzibar*, pp. 8–13.

95. Sometimes intelligence is difficult to come by in urban areas, such as Singapore (see Tom Eames Hughes, *A Tangled World: The Story of Maria Hertogh* [Singapore: Institute of Southeast Asian Studies, Local History and Memoirs Monograph 1, 1980], p. 55), and easy to come by in rural areas, such as Assam (see Arun Shourie, "Assam Elections: Come What May," *India Today*, May 15, 1983, pp. 54–66, reporting a surfeit of police warnings of impending attack, none of which was acted upon).

96. Turner and Killian, *Collective Behavior*, p. 5.

97. René Gauze, *The Politics of Congo-Brazzaville*, trans., ed., and supp. Virginia Thompson and Richard Adloff (Stanford: Hoover Institution Press, 1973), p. 70.

98. Virginia Thompson and Richard Adloff, *The Emerging States of French Equatorial Africa* (Stanford: Stanford University Press, 1960), p. 490.

including feasting, ritual slaughter, and oath taking. Before the Luluabourg riots in Zaire (1959), there was naked dancing by Lulua women
and men, who had covered their "faces and bodies with paint as their
ancestors had done on days of battle."[99] When violence was apprehended
in Northern Ireland in 1969, there were traditional communal bon-
fires.[100] In Penang, Malaysia (1967), fires were also lit, goats were slaughtered for a feast, and Malays donned the black sarong of warfare.[101] In
Durban (1949), Soweto (1976), and Umbumbulu (1985), Zulu rioters
formed themselves into *impis*, traditional Zulu regiments, and shouted
Zulu war cries.[102] In Ghana (1994), Konkomba who attacked Nanumba
and Dagomba appeared in three waves, the first firing burning arrows
into their victims' huts and then poisoned arrows at the inhabitants who
emerged, the second firing gunpowder as a decoy, the third firing real
bullets. "Behind them come ululating women, cheering the men on. The
women carry pick-axes to bury their dead and they are said to attack any
cowards who try to turn back."[103] In West Kalimantan (1997), a red
bowl smeared with chicken blood, signifying war, was passed in village
rites before Dayak attacks on Madurese.[104] In such episodes, of course,
customary modes are often imagined rather than authentically uncovered. Atavism is not likely. Yet the participants' analogy to war and to the
ancestral ways felt appropriate to it is unmistakable.

BECOMING INVULNERABLE

As violence approaches, fear needs to be overcome. There are some
reports of the development of feelings of omnipotence among rioters, a
form of wish fulfillment.[105] Typically, however, assistance is needed in

---

99. Jules Chomé, *Le Drame de Luluabourg,* 3d rev. ed. (Brussels: Editions de
Remarques Congolaises, 1960), p. 5.

100. Jackson, *The Two Irelands,* p. 11.

101. Interview, George Town, Penang, February 2, 1968.

102. Union of South Africa, *Report of the Commission of Enquiry into Riots in
Durban,* p. 4; Colin Legum, ed., *Africa Contemporary Record, 1976–77* (New York:
Africana, 1977), pp. B792–93; "Umbumbulu," in Fatima Meer, ed., *Resistance in the
Townships* (Durban: Madiba, 1989), pp. 165–76. That rioters often conceptualize the
violence in terms of a recurrence of warfare, at least where there are historical enmities, is
one of the themes of the interesting novel of the Indian partition riots by Bhisham Sahni,
Tamas (New Delhi: Penguin, 1988).

103. Ruby Ofori, "Rawlings' Biggest Challenge," *Africa Report* 39, no. 3 (May–June
1994): 53–55, at p. 54.

104. *Far Eastern Economic Review,* February 20, 1997, pp. 26–27.

105. Neil Smelser, *Theory of Collective Behavior* (New York: Free Press, 1962), p. 108.

overcoming fear. In addition to being imparted by risk-reducing strategies and tactics considered later, confidence is provided by oaths and amulets. Rioters in the Punjab (1953) made a pledge in blood to die for the cause.[106] A similar oath was taken in Ahmedabad (1969).[107] Charms to provide invulnerability are more common. The specific form and function of amulets are variable. In Albania, charms were used in feuds to make assailants "light of foot," so they would not be detected until too late.[108] In Burundi (1972), Hutu who attacked Tutsi had allegedly been given a drug that made them think bullets would turn to water.[109] In Burma (1930 and 1938), tattoos, customarily used to protect against snakebite, were painted on rioters for invulnerability to swords and bullets.[110] In Malaysia (1945–46), a common method of providing invulnerability was the insertion of gold needles beneath the skin.[111] As we shall see later, certain dismembered parts of victims are also used for the purpose of conferring invulnerability in the next round of fighting.

All of these methods are also used in warfare.[112] In the Kwilu revolt of 1964 in Zaire, incisions were made in the foreheads of rebel soldiers, in which a powder was placed to render them invulnerable to bullets.[113] When Communists were attacked by the Indonesian army all over Java in 1965, it was reported that many victims had command of magic that prevented them from dying even under torture.[114]

Belief in the efficacy of these measures often crosses the boundary

106. Government of [West] Punjab, *Report of the Court of Inquiry Constituted under Punjab Act II of 1954*, p. 140.

107. Ghosh, *Communal Riots in India*, p. 152.

108. Christopher Boehm, *Blood Revenge: The Anthropology of Feuding in Montenegro and Other Tribal Societies* (Lawrence: University Press of Kansas, 1984), p. 110.

109. *New York Times*, June 8, 1972, p. 9.

110. Collis, *Trials in Burma*, p. 141; Government of Burma, *Final Report of the Riot Inquiry Commission*, pp. 75, 219.

111. Malayan Security Service, *Political Intelligence Journal*, serial no. 6 of 1946, July 15, 1946, p. 5. See also James de V. Allen, *The Malayan Union* (New Haven: Yale University Southeast Asia Studies, 1967), p. 45. For amulets implanted subcutaneously in the Philippines, see Sterling Seagrave, *The Marcos Dynasty* (New York: Harper & Row, 1988), p. 18.

112. See Collis, *Trials in Burma*, pp. 212–13; *Washington Post*, September 3, 1972, p. C5, reporting the use of charms and spells in Cambodia to ward off Communist bullets. See also J.D. Legge, *Sukarno: A Political Biography* (New York: Praeger, 1972), pp. 123, 293, 384, reporting on mystical powers attributed to Sukarno.

113. Renée C. Fox et al., "'The Second Independence': A Case Study of the Kwilu Rebellion in the Congo," *Comparative Studies in Society and History* 8, no. 1 (October 1965): 78–110, at p. 100 n. 41.

114. *Far Eastern Economic Review*, December 14, 1967, pp. 509–14.

between the groups in conflict.[115] It was reported that, in the Mauritanian riots of 1966, Moors chose to use sticks because it was known that knives would not penetrate the skin of their invulnerable Peulh victims.[116] The tactical value of perceived invulnerability across group lines can be considerable.

Religion can provide an additional source of strength. The Muslim doctrine of *sabilu'llah* connotes meritorious deeds in religious warfare. Those who die in a war of faith are assured a place in paradise. For believers in this doctrine, invulnerability might be superfluous. Nevertheless, invulnerability practices have coexisted with Islamic belief. One way of acquiring invulnerability in Malaysia (1945–46) was the repeated recitation of particular verses from the Quran after each of the five daily prayers.[117] Sufism is a form of Muslim mysticism practiced by some Malays, among many others. Certain practitioners are thought to have magical powers of endurance, transportation, and disappearance. Such beliefs feed into ethnic violence because of the strategic advantages they confer. A Malay district headman was reported to have had a vision warning him of an imminent Chinese attack. The vision revealed to him the Chinese position and line of advance. His magical powers were said to have enabled him to subdue a crowd of 200.[118] Among Philippine Muslims, charms often contain Quranic verses to protect the wearer against the penetration of knives or bullets.[119]

Invulnerability practices recur in modern riots. After violence began in Kuala Lumpur (1969), for example, stories circulated about heroes who were immune to harm, especially a Malay woman "reported to have been able to fly into burning houses as well as remaining invulnerable to bullets and knives. There was suddenly an enormous demand for *djimats*, talismans or sacred phrases rendering the wearer invulnerable.

115. One of the most powerful weapons used in the Mozambique guerrilla war of the 1980s and '90s was the belief of one side in the power of the magic employed by the other. See K.B. Wilson, "Cults of Violence and Counter-Violence in Mozambique," *Journal of Southern African Studies* 18, no. 3 (September 1992): 527–82.

116. Interview, Washington, D.C., August 5, 1971.

117. Malayan Security Service, *Political Intelligence Journal* (Singapore), serial no. 6 of 1946, July 15, 1946, p. 5. Charms were also inscribed with Quranic verses. Ibid., Supplement to no. 9 of 1947, June 15, 1947, p. 2.

118. Syed Naguib al-Attas, *Some Aspects of Sufism as Understood and Practiced among the Malays* (Singapore: Malaysian Sociological Research Institute, 1963), p. 48.

119. In spite of the many stories of men hit by bullets that did not penetrate, some Philippine Muslims deny the protective power of the amulets. Thomas M. Kiefer, *The Tausug: Violence and Law in a Philippine Muslim Society* (New York: Holt, Rinehart, and Winston, 1972), pp. 77–79.

After the violence began, some experts in the art of invulnerability, from other states, settled in Kampong Bahru [the area from which much violence emanated] in order to minister to the needs of a frightened population."[120] Paramilitary members engaged in ethnic violence in Brazzaville in the early 1990s wore bones on strings around their heads and wrists to make them invisible.[121] Jukun used amulets in anti-Tiv violence in Nigeria (1992).[122] The continuing prevalence of such beliefs reduces inhibitions on attack and renders mass violence far more likely than it would be otherwise. The commingling of invulnerability practices with doctrines of religious merit deriving from participation in righteous warfare forms a particularly potent combination in riots against nonbelievers.

Just how strong the demand for amulets can be in a conflict-prone environment can be glimpsed from intelligence reports gathered by the British Military Administration in colonial Malaya following World War II.[123] After the Japanese surrender but before the British reoccupation, Malayan Chinese, largely Communist guerrillas, emerged in control of many areas of the Malayan peninsula. They proceeded to execute Malays alleged to have collaborated with the Japanese and in a variety of ways threatened Malay villagers. In 1945 and 1946, and even into 1947, Malays seized the initiative. There were widespread attacks on Chinese. Accompanying them were invulnerability practices, generally cultivated by Malay experts from other states.

These experts often preached the need for violence at the same time as they conferred invulnerability, usually for a fee. In addition to the recitation of Quranic verses and the subcutaneous insertion of gold needles, a variety of other methods was used. In Perak state, a Sumatran was reported to have sold strips of goat's hide on which charms were inscribed. In Kedah, magic rings were sold. In Negri Sembilan, a course

120. Anthony Reid, "The Kuala Lumpur Riots and the Malaysian Political System," *Australian Outlook* 23, no. 3 (December 1969): 258–78, at p. 269.

121. Friedman and Sundberg, "Ethnic War and Ethnic Cleansing in Brazzaville," p. 3. For invisibility in Indonesian warfare, see Norman Lewis, *An Empire of the Past* (London: Picador, 1995), p. 154.

122. Ter-Rumun Avav and Mson Myegba, *The Dream to Conquer: Story of Jukun-Tiv Conflict* (Makurdi, Nigeria: Onairi, 1992), p. 23. For an example from South Africa (1990), see Heribert Adam and Kogila Moodley, "Political Violence, 'Tribalism,' and Inkatha," *Journal of Modern African Studies* 30, no. 3 (September 1992): 485–510, at p. 507.

123. The accounts that follow are drawn from Malayan Security Service, *Political Intelligence Journal*, serial no. 11 of 1946, September 30, 1946, p. 1; serial no. 2 of 1947, February 28, 1947, p. 14; serial no. 3 of 1947, March 15, 1947, p. 34; serial no. 12 of 1946, October 15, 1946, p. 1; serial no. 2 of 1948, February 28, 1948, p. 43. These cyclostyled reports are available in the Rhodes House Library, Oxford.

was offered to confer invulnerability to knife slashes; the procedure involved blessing the knives of disciples. One Malay traveled from Perak to the state of Pahang to learn the details of *ilmu garam* (salt science), a procedure by which special salt, thrown in front of the enemy, was said to give the impression of a sheet of water. That experts made money from the sale of such techniques gave them a built-in interest in fomenting violence.

There was some evidence of skepticism about such techniques. An expert who had made a substantial sum by imparting invulnerability to about 1,000 people was asked to demonstrate the efficacy of the technique. When a victim of the demonstration was wounded, the expert disappeared. Small wonder that practitioners of invulnerability often come from far away.

Even after episodes of this kind, however, the demand for invulnerability in one area of the country after another was very great. There was no shortage of products that could facilitate violence by making it less risky. The explanation for the persistent appeal of protective formulae, charms, and amulets is to be found by considering the integration of such practices with the normal life of the community. Although the market in invulnerability rises and falls with the incidence of violence, such practices typically have deeper connections with core elements in the culture and with organizations powerful in the society than might be suspected from their intermittent usage.

Take the role of the Poro Society, an array of secret West African associations that share some core ritual practices.[124] Powerfully enmeshed in the social structure of groups such as the Kpelle in Liberia and the Mende in Sierra Leone, Poro serves as an invisible sacred counterpart to secular authorities. Its power derives from its capacity to inflict sanctions on deviants, to provide a variety of medicinal products, and to augment, on appropriate occasions, the authority of local chiefs, even as it often counterbalances that authority.[125] Among the medicines dispensed are those that protect against harmful spirits, poisons, lightning, thievery, and the evil medicines of an enemy.[126]

Three specific categories of Poro medicine relate to invulnerability: (1)

124. Beryl L. Bellman, *The Language of Secrecy: Symbols and Metaphors in Poro Ritual* (New Brunswick: Rutgers University Press, 1984), p. 42.

125. See Richard M. Fulton, "The Political Structures and Functions of Poro in Kpelle Society," *American Anthropologist* 74, no. 5 (October 1972): 1218–33. See also Eugene Victor Walter, *Terror and Resistance: A Study of Political Violence* (New York: Oxford University Press, 1969), pp. 88, 91, 95, 101.

126. Beryl Larry Bellman, *Village of Curers and Assassins: On the Production of Fala Kpelle Cosmological Categories* (The Hague: Mouton, 1975), pp. 115–27.

those which allow a person to perform great feats (grow short or tall, escape from a house after being bound inside, or emerge from a knife or arrow injury without a wound); (2) those which provide the ability to kill someone in war; and (3) those which protect one "from getting shot or stabbed in war."[127] Clearly, Poro is engaged in the provision of offensive and defensive medicines, as well as in the administration of violence to compel conformity to community norms. On both counts, it is not surprising that Poro played a major role in violence directed by Mende against Temne in Sierra Leone in 1968.[128] Its prescriptions for invulnerability almost certainly were utilized during the killing.

Similar continuity between extraordinary times and ordinary practices can be observed in Malaysia, but here the connections are mainly to the Malay martial arts and the powers and protections that emerge from them. As in the case of Poro, the cultivation of superhuman powers flows from adherence to the strict personal discipline of a *guru silat*, a teacher of Malay martial arts. The *silat* master has at his disposal some ten categories of *ilmu* (science, but in this context supernatural science or the knowledge that comes from intensely cultivated discipline). Among the categories are those which render their practitioners impervious to injury or impart to them ability to perform superhuman feats, such as killing with a single blow.[129] Trance states are frequently encouraged as a prelude to fighting, and these, too, are likely to provide a sense of invulnerability.

There is no doubt that some guru silat played a leading role in Malaysian ethnic violence from at least 1945 to 1969. One prominent martial arts master, Kiyai Salleh, a Javanese who led a Sufi order in a region of Johore state heavily affected by anti-Chinese violence in 1945, was able to blend religious revelations and motivations with his reputation for invulnerability to bullets, chains, and boiling water. This potent combination and his capacity to confer invulnerability on others helped to produce a Holy War Army of the Red Scarves (Tentera Sabil Selendang Merah), which was responsible for the deaths of many Chinese.[130] Similar groups wearing red bands sprang up in the Kuala

127. Ibid., pp. 116–19. The quotation appears at page 119.

128. Walter L. Barrows, "Local Level Politics in Sierra Leone: Alliances in Kenema District" (Ph.D. diss., Yale University, 1971), pp. 334–51. I deal with Poro further in Chapter 7, below.

129. Razha Rashid, "Martial Arts and the Malay Superman," in Wazir Jahan Karim, ed., *Emotions of Culture: A Malay Perspective* (Singapore: Oxford University Press, 1990), pp. 64–95.

130. Cheah, *Red Star over Malaya*, pp. 195, 202, 207–09.

Lumpur riots of 1969.[131] Interestingly enough, disciples of Kiyai Salleh had found their way to Singapore at the time of the 1950 riots,[132] in which they probably participated.

Kiyai Salleh had earlier spent time in prison for criminal activities. The charisma of a daring leader, the lure of illicit gain, the discipline of martial arts, and the promise of invulnerability, all ostensibly mingled with religious sanction, turn out to be a potent combination. Who would not accept invulnerability in this world and paradise in the next?

In late 1967, another Holy War Army (Tentera Sabilullah) was uncovered in northern Malaysia. Among other things, it had developed some plans to attack Chinese in some areas. Its leader was a Javanese *pawang* (a specialist in spells, talismans, and medicines) who was able to work people into trances. A *lebai* (a person of some religious learning), he also sported the title of Panglima Garang (Brave Warrior) and had the ability to inspire fear as well as confidence in his magical powers. The Holy War Army, however, had another name, the Gang Duabelas Ringgit, the Twelve-Dollar Gang, so called because membership cost M$12 (then about US$4), a sum that provided protection from theft of crops and animals. In short, the organization mixed an extortion scheme, a secret society, magic, and the sale of charms with religious themes and plans for ethnic violence that were averted by police action.[133] Again, magic was not divorced from, but formed an integral part of, the ongoing features of social life.

How widespread invulnerability practices are during riots it is impossible to say, but they are far from uncommon. In the West, charms and amulets were formerly in widespread use, intermingled (as they are elsewhere) with religious verses, for countering the effects of injury, illness, and witchcraft.[134] Whether they played a prominent part in riot behavior is uncertain, but it is certain that supernatural remedies were in decline by about 1700, their obsolescence fostered by religious, philosophical, and scientific change, as well as, perhaps, a material environment more subject to human control and less in need of extrahuman intervention.[135]

This change, however, is not linear. In guerrilla warfare in Mozam-

---

131. Razha, "Martial Arts and the Malay Superman," p. 88.

132. Maideen, *The Nadra Tragedy*, p. 237.

133. I am drawing here on a series of interviews with participants and firsthand observers of the Tentera Sabilullah/Gang Duabelas Ringgit I conducted in rural Kedah in January 1968.

134. Keith Thomas, *Religion and the Decline of Magic* (New York: Charles Scribner's Sons, 1971), pp. 30, 32, 178–96, 244–52.

135. Ibid., pp. 275, 491, 643–67.

bique, "vaccination" was used to render fighters impermeable to bullets.[136] Science can operate perversely as a form of magic that encourages other forms of magic.

The fluctuating risk of participation in killing is surely one of the variables contributing to the rising and falling incidence of riots. Killings in the West — lynchings in the Jim Crow United States, genocide in Nazi Germany, bombings in Northern Ireland — have tended to take place under conditions of felt impunity. When those conditions no longer obtain, the killings cease. The decline of invulnerability should also be a force for the reduction of interethnic violence, but invulnerability is, of course, only one of several conditions responsible for creating a sense of impunity.

DISINHIBITING MANIA: AMOK AND AMOK-LIKE VIOLENCE

Frenzy is another way of conquering fear. Curiously, perhaps, building oneself into a frenetic state can be regarded as a form of self-discipline, so as to facilitate thoroughly disinhibited aggression. The deadly riot bears a certain resemblance to a species of individual violence with such characteristics. Responding to a limited class of precipitants, preceded by a lull, conducted with a furious level of energy, and occasionally featuring ethnic motives and interethnic targets, this form of violence has collective, even military, roots and has from time to time found its way into deadly ethnic riots.

Usually denominated *amok* and particularly visible in Muslim societies of Southeast Asia, this type of exclusively male violence involves a person who kills with abandon. The attack is brought on by an insult or a series of affronts to self-esteem, for which redress seems impossible. After a period of anxious brooding or depression, the *pengamok* emerges suddenly with a weapon (usually a knife or kris) and, in a burst of manic energy, kills everything and everyone in his path until he is captured or killed in turn or until, exhausted, he collapses into a state of torpor and long-lasting sleep, following which he claims amnesia about the entire event.[137]

136. Wilson, "Cults of Violence and Counter-Violence in Mozambique," pp. 527–82. Magic was widespread in the war; it included power to see into the future, disappear and reappear at will, fly, convert bullets into water, return to life after death, and turn into tall grass or anthills. Ibid., pp. 544, 552, 556.

137. For characteristic descriptions, see Justus M. van der Kroef, *Indonesian Social Evolution* (Amsterdam: C.P.J. van der Peet, 1958), pp. 33–37; Ee Heok Kua, "Amok in

What makes amok pertinent to the deadly riot are its origins in collective violence, its notably similar patterns (especially its manic fury), its continuing connections to interethnic violence, and its long-term ebbs and flows. As I suggested in Chapter 1, the various forms of violence are sometimes convertible to one another. If amok is an analogue and in some cases a source of inspiration for the deadly riot, then it offers an additional avenue for understanding patterns of riot behavior, particularly the conquest of fear.

Amok has attracted great attention from the mental health professions, concerned about how to classify it and about whether it is a culture-bound syndrome or merely a culture-specific exemplar of a disease that is universal in its incidence. If amok-like attacks have been reported in Papua–New Guinea, Trinidad, Quebec, and Japan, and from Liberia to Siberia, perhaps the correct classification is the general category of "explosive behavior disorder" or "brief reactive psychosis."[138] On the other hand, if amok is "a culturally prescribed form of violent behavior, sanctioned by tradition as an appropriate response to a highly specific set of socio-cultural conditions,"[139] then its classification as a disease is in doubt, and seemingly similar phenomena in different cultures will have different etiologies.[140] These debates need not detain us, for we can glean what we need to learn from the amok phenomenon from its

---

Nineteenth-Century British Malayan History," *History of Psychiatry* 2, pt. 4, no. 8 (December 1991): 429–36; Karl Schmidt, Lee Hill, and George Guthrie, "Running Amok," *International Journal of Social Psychiatry* 23, no. 4 (Winter 1977): 264–74.

138. Albert C. Gaw and Ruth Bernstein, "Classification of Amok in DSM-IV [*Diagnostic and Statistical Manual of Mental Disorders*, 4th ed.]," *Hospital and Community Psychiatry* 43, no. 8 (August 1992): 789–93; Charles C. Hughes, "Sudden Mass Assault Taxon," in Ronald C. Simons and Charles C. Hughes, eds., *The Culture-Bound Syndromes: Folk Illnesses of Psychiatric and Anthropological Interest* (Dordrecht: D. Reidel, 1985), pp. 263–64. See John W. Berry et al., *Cross-Cultural Psychology: Research and Applications* (Cambridge: Cambridge University Press, 1992), pp. 362–64.

139. John E. Carr, "Ethno-Behaviorism and the Culture-Bound Syndromes: The Case of *Amok*," *Culture, Medicine, and Psychiatry* 2, no. 3 (September 1978): 269–93, at p. 273.

140. For this argument in detail, see ibid. See also Raymond L.M. Lee, "Structure and Anti-Structure in the Culture-Bound Syndromes: The Malay Case," *Culture, Medicine, and Psychiatry* 5, no. 3 (September 1981): 233–48. For the other extreme, which subsumes all sudden mass murders under the same rubric, see J. Arboleda-Florez, "Amok," in Simons and Hughes, eds., *The Culture-Bound Syndromes*, pp. 251–62. Schmidt, Hill, and Guthrie, "Running Amok," found in their study of 24 *pengamok* in Sarawak that all had symptoms of one psychiatric disorder or another. See also Joseph Westermeyer, "National Differences in Psychiatric Morbidity: Methodological Issues, Scientific Interpretations, and Social Implications," *Acta Psychiatrica Scandinavica* 78, no. 344 (n.m. 1988): 23–44, at p. 27.

core culture area in the Malay peninsula and archipelago and then take note of comparable events elsewhere.

Although amok is usually described as an individual phenomenon, it derived from a form of furious warfare or, more likely, several such forms. By most accounts, amok is traceable to the Hindu empires of Southeast Asia or to India itself. Warriors were said to make a solemn vow to risk death or to work themselves into a frenzy before battle or before piracy, thus producing unusually furious, indiscriminate, and fearless attacks.[141] Slaves who found themselves abused also utilized amok as an escape, even if it meant death, and the threat of amok became a means of social control of superiors by subordinates.[142] Frenzy, then, might create war spells, so as to dissolve fear that might otherwise overtake a warrior[143] — a substitute for charms to produce invulnerability. In south India, frenzied, self-sacrificing murder was employed by a soldier to avenge the killing of a king or general in battle.[144] By the sixteenth century, amok was a military tactic, which had a spontaneous, automatic quality as a response to affront, an effort to restore dignity, an attack born of desperation in warfare. Military amok was regarded as honorable, which probably accounts for the ease of its transition to the solitary amok, the use of the same technique to resolve personal conflicts. Many observers have noted that amok appears to have continued historical sanction.[145]

In some places, individual amok appeared early,[146] and in others the collective version persisted. There was also a transition from amok as a conscious policy or a conscious reaction to provocation to amok as a dis-

141. H.B.M. Murphy, "History and the Evolution of Syndromes: The Striking Case of *Latah* and *Amok*," in Muriel Hammer, Kurt Salinger, and Samuel Sutton, eds., *Psychopathology: Contributions from the Social, Behavioral, and Biological Sciences* (New York: John Wiley & Sons, 1973), pp. 33–55.

142. Ibid., p. 35.

143. B.G. Burton-Bradley, "The Amok Syndrome in Papua and New Guinea," *Medical Journal of Australia* 1, no. 7 (February 17, 1968): 252–56, at p. 253.

144. See John C. Spores, *Running Amok: An Historical Inquiry* (Athens, Ohio: Ohio University Center for International Studies, Monographs in International Studies, Southeast Asia Series, No. 82, 1988), pp. 11–29.

145. Kua, "Amok in Nineteenth-Century British Malayan History," p. 435; Schmidt, Hill, and Guthrie, "Running Amok," p. 267; Jin-Inn Teoh, "The Changing Psychopathology of Amok," *Psychiatry* 35, no. 4 (November 1972): 345–51, at p. 347; Carr, "Ethno-Behaviorism and the Culture-Bound Syndromes," pp. 286–87. Ari Kiev, *Transcultural Psychiatry* (New York: Free Press, 1972), p. 90, points out that, even after amok has been defined as pathology, its symptomology "conforms to cultural expectations" about "how to act insane."

146. Spores, *Running Amok*, p. 14.

sociative (or less than fully conscious) reaction to distress, especially to "perceived personal abasement."[147] Pre-Islamic amok practice fused with Islamic legitimation in Philippine Muslim rebellions against the Spaniards, later against the Americans, then against the Japanese, and more recently against the Philippine army and Christian settlers.[148] Based on the belief that a righteous death brings religious merit, this form of violence approaches ritual suicide, for which the warrior in the Philippines indeed prepared.[149] Manic excitement prior to aggression simultaneously elevates the importance of the issue over which violent satisfaction is sought, thus increasing the willingness to risk death for it, and enhances the aggressive qualities of the attacker. In amok, as in riot, "hypermasculinity is expressed . . . ."[150]

There is, then, a spectrum of amok behavior, from martial and collective to martial and solitary to non-martial and solitary — and perhaps to non-martial and collective, if amok and riot have an area of overlap. What began as a conscious form of warfare had become part of a collective unconscious,[151] which undoubtedly facilitated metamorphosis, with the underlying idea of violent redress for distress intact. Until non-martial amok was defined as pathological, the various amok forms shared notions of heroism and the defense of honor against impossible odds.[152] In certain Southeast Asian societies (and some others), the heroic attack of the pengamok is a powerful cultural motif, to which people might recur in appropriately analogous conditions.[153]

Solitary amok and deadly riot have some common features. Amok is precipitated by an affront or humiliation, difficult to bear and difficult to reverse, and unusually so in Malay society, which places the highest pre-

---

147. Lee, "Structure and Anti-Structure in the Culture-Bound Syndromes," p. 239.

148. Kiefer, The Tausug, pp. 132–33.

149. Robert Winzeler, "Amok: Historical, Psychological, and Cultural Perspectives," in Wazir Jahan Karim, ed., Emotions of Culture, pp. 96–122, at p. 112; Spores, Running Amok, pp. 9, 122.

150. Lee, "Structure and Anti-Structure in the Culture-Bound Syndromes," p. 239.

151. Murphy, "History and the Evolution of Syndromes," p. 48. On the "ethnic unconscious," see George Devereux, "Normal and Abnormal: The Key Problem of Psychiatric Anthropology," in J.B. Casagrande and T. Gladwin, eds., Some Uses of Anthropology: Theoretical and Applied (Washington, D.C.: Anthropological Society of Washington, 1956), pp. 3–48, at pp. 25–33, discussed in Kiev, Transcultural Psychiatry, pp. 90–91.

152. Winzeler, "Amok," pp. 119–20.

153. For the growth of grenade amok in Laos, see Joseph Westermeyer, "Grenade-Amok in Laos: A Psychosocial Perspective," Social Psychiatry 19, no. 3/4, (Autumn–Winter 1973): 251–60.

mium on avoidance of interpersonal conflict.[154] The affront gives rise to a melancholic quiet of perhaps several days, described by the Malays as *sakit hati* (liver sickness, the equivalent of heartsickness).[155] This period of despair and rage, during which the pengamok charts his course, bears some similarity to the brooding lull that precedes riots. Stillness is then broken by a furious assault, using weapons readily available to cut down everyone in the path of the pengamok — indeed, everyone and every-thing, for, like that of some Nigerian rioters we shall soon encounter, the fury of the amok attacker is so elevated and indiscriminate that he often strikes down animals as well as people.[156] The pengamok is engaged in an utterly defiant destruction, "a self-liberation through revolt; a soul too sensitive to suggestion, humiliated by its own conscious enslavement, at last turns in upon itself, and accumulates so much energy that only the faintest pretext is needed to release it."[157]

Nevertheless, the pengamok is not without guile; his aim is to take down as many victims as possible — relatives, strangers, police sent to apprehend him — before he himself goes down. To that end, he will resort to concealment and surprise, like the Malay rioter in Kuala Lumpur (1969), who lay beside a road, feigning injury, until a Chinese physician stopped her car to assist him, whereupon he beheaded her.[158]

The targets of amok are generally the product of chance encounter, although they are likely to include "sources of criticism, frustration, or provocation."[159] Yet there is sometimes a deliberate ethnic element. Some nineteenth-century pengamoks in Malaya were known to kill Chinese and Javanese,[160] and in 1974 a Malaysian pengamok killed five Chinese at a Chinese coffee house; another killed seven Chinese.[161] Just as lynch-

154. Lee, "Structure and Anti-Structure in the Culture-Bound Syndromes"; Carr, "Ethno-Behaviorism and the Culture-Bound Syndromes."

155. Spores, *Running Amok*, p. 64; Teoh, "The Changing Psychopathology of Amok," p. 348. For amok as the functional equivalent of suicide, which is very rare among Malays, see Hugh Clifford, "The Amok of Dato Kaya Biji Derja," in Hugh Clifford, *In Court and Kampong* (London: Grant Richards, 1897), pp. 78–95. For brooding as a feature of the time preceding revenge in a feud, see Boehm, *Blood Revenge*, pp. 92–93.

156. Teoh, "The Changing Psychopathology of Amok," p. 346.

157. Henri Fauconnier, *The Soul of Malaya*, 2d ed., trans. Eric Sutton (Kuala Lumpur: Oxford University Press, 1965), pp. 226–27.

158. Slimming, *Malaysia*, p. 58.

159. John E. Carr and Eng Kong Tan, "In Search of the True Amok: Amok as Viewed within the Malay Culture," *American Journal of Psychiatry* 133, no. 11 (November 1976): 1295–99, at p. 1298.

160. John D. Gimlette, "Notes on a Case of *Amok*," *Journal of Tropical Medicine and Hygiene* 4 (June 15, 1901): 195–99.

161. Carr and Tan, "In Search of the True Amok," pp. 1297–98. The police report for the latter stated the cause of the amok to be "racial disharmony."

ing victims changed from white to black over time,[162] so is it possible to transform amok from intraethnic homicide to interethnic.

Similar phenomena have been reported from areas adjacent to the Malay archipelago. In Papua–New Guinea, where warriors enter into war spells to conquer fear, individual amoks are sometimes found among ex-warriors under conditions similar to those in Malaysia, Indonesia, and the Philippines: "the killings are envisaged as a means of deliverance from an unbearable situation."[163] (This is a formulation we might well bear in mind when we contemplate certain occasions for deadly ethnic riots.) The participation of ex-warriors makes clear the connection of collective and solitary amok.

To be sure, amok and deadly riot have some decidedly different features. The rioter generally responds to deterrence, as we shall see, whereas the pengamok, who has sometimes been thought to engage in the activity to achieve revenge and suicide in a few strokes, is not easily deterred. On the other hand, the exact susceptibility of the frenzied rioter to deterrence is not fully tested. The rioter resorts to mutilation of his victims — a theme explored later in this chapter — but such activities are alien to the pengamok, whose sense of having succeeded in turning the tables on a world that has turned against him is said to be enhanced in direct proportion to the number of victims he slays.[164] For him, the death toll is everything, and he does not pause for special efforts at dismemberment.

With those differences noted, it remains true that amok and riot share a frenzied style of violence. To an undetermined extent, solitary amok, which is a socially learned but declining form, may be transformed in the deadly riot. Because amok has been a subtly sanctioned method of escaping the most rigid restraints on the expression of interpersonal conflict, it is potentially available for infusion into deadly ethnic riots on certain occasions. Dayaks in West Kalimantan (1997), for example, participated in a trance-inducing ritual that produced a disinhibiting mania facilitating their attacks on Madurese.[165] Residual conceptions of the propriety of amok and the heroism of the pengamok, provided the cause were just, might well find their way into ethnic riot behavior, once group identifi-

162. See Chapter 1, above.

163. Burton-Bradley, "The Amok Syndrome in Papua and New Guinea," p. 254. See also Westermeyer, "Grenade-Amok in Laos."

164. For "the more you kill, the more you will be remembered." R.J. Wilkinson, *Papers on Malay Subjects* (Kuala Lumpur: Federated Malay States Government Press, 1925), p. 5.

165. *Jakarta Post*, March 2, 1997, pp. 1–2.

cation is strong and the appropriate injury is present. Such occasions may be more numerous than existing interpretations acknowledge.

One riot arguably containing identifiable amok elements is Malaysia (1969), described as a grand amok,[166] now collective but still "the external physical expression of the conflict within the Malay . . . . an overflowing of his inner bitterness."[167] Observers have used the characteristic explanation of solitary amok to interpret what they claim are the origins of the riot. Unassertive to a fault, enjoined by norms of *politesse* to restrain impulses to conflict, the Malays are abused until they can bear their restraint no more, the argument goes, and so they produce a frenzied explosion that differs from the typical amok only in its group character. Among Malays, it is said, feelings of powerlessness and dishonor trigger violence, and the Kuala Lumpur riot of 1969 probably combined the rage of amok with the discipline of Malay martial arts and religious fervor comparable to that of Philippine Muslims.[168] The Malay capacity for syncretism is formidable, and the adaptability of the heroic amok form should not be underestimated.

If the 1969 riot was a massive amok, and if other riots have been affected by the transformation of solitary amok and amok-like behavior, this has important implications for understanding the part played by overcontrolled personalities in deadly ethnic riots. Undercontrolled people are less inhibited about expressing violence. Overcontrolled personalities are those who have "excessive control of aggressive impulses. In such cases the strength of inhibition may be such that relatively minor frustrations will not be acted out. In certain circumstances, these suppressed frustrations may accumulate until the excessively high inhibitory thresholds are exceeded, and a further stimulus (perhaps relatively trivial) may trigger an act of murderous intensity."[169] Such a description captures the essence of the personality shaped by a culture that produces amok,[170] and it may be that such personalities — or such groups — are disproportionately involved in interethnic violence. This is an issue to which we shall return briefly in Chapter 7. Suffice it to say that a number of groups described as particularly averse to the expression of hostile

166. Razha, "Martial Arts and the Malay Superman," p. 64.

167. Mahathir bin Mohamad, *The Malay Dilemma* (Singapore: Donald Moore, 1970), p. 118.

168. Razha, "Martial Arts and the Malay Superman," pp. 68, 85, 88, 89, 95 n. 21.

169. Laetitia du Toit and John Duckitt, "Psychological Characteristics of Over- and Uncontrolled Violent Offenders," *Journal of Psychology* 124, no. 2 (March 1990): 125–41, at p. 125.

170. See Carr, "Ethno-Behaviorism and the Culture-Bound Syndromes."

impulses, yet suspicious of the aggressive intentions of others, have been involved in the perpetration of ethnic violence.[171]

It is important to stress the conditions of amok and similar states that facilitate violence. Amok is often described as a "disinhibited aggressive state,"[172] a disorder that produces "a desperate and furious change . . . of an individual or body of men."[173] Desperate violence is also a recurrent theme in the ethnic riot. We shall encounter it repeatedly — in precipitating events, juxtapositions of target groups and aggressors, locations of violence, and the atrocities that accompany the deadly ethnic riot.

Solitary amok has been in decline.[174] It is possible that the decline of solitary amok can coexist with the growth of collective amok as it infuses deadly ethnic riots, but such a trend is unproved. To the extent that amok is losing its legitimacy and the social sanction it long enjoyed, it may become unavailable for collective invocation as well. Like the decline of magic, the decline of a disinhibiting mania would make ethnic violence less likely. There are, however, other sources of disinhibition.

THE ATROCITY-KILLING

In late medieval Florence, before a war, there were public harangues that included insulting verses about the attributes of the enemy. After the war, there were atrocities:

> The orations on the piazza often ended in horrible tumults, in which people were torn to pieces. In 1343, after the fall of the Duke of Athens, a man was eaten on the Piazza della Signoria. Much later, after the thwarting of the Pazzi conspiracy, portions of dead bodies, according to Machiavelli, were seen borne on spears and scattered throughout the streets, and the roads around Florence were covered with fragments of human flesh. The cruelties committed in Pistoia, during the struggles of the factions, are said to have surpassed those committed in Florence, and the practice of "planting" condemned persons, that is, of burying them alive, upside down, in the soil, was general in medieval Tuscany.[175]

171. See, e.g., Melford E. Spiro, "Violence in Burmese History: A Psychocultural Explanation," in James F. Short, Jr., and Marvin E. Wolfgang, eds., *Collective Violence* (Chicago: Aldine, 1972), pp. 186–91.

172. Kiev, *Transcultural Psychiatry*, p. 87.

173. Kua, "Amok in Nineteenth-Century British Malaya," p. 429.

174. Spores, *Running Amok*, p. 7; Murphy, "History and Evolution of Syndromes," pp. 37–41; Schmidt, Hill, and Lee, "Running Amok," p. 268. Teoh, "The Changing Psychopathology of Amok," p. 346.

175. Mary McCarthy, *The Stones of Florence* (New York: Harcourt Brace Jovanovich, 1959), p. 44.

"Planting" died out, but other atrocities did not. They occur in many forms of violence, and with unusual frequency in ethnic riots. They call out for explanation.

THE PREVALENCE OF ATROCITIES

Atrocities occur in nonethnic riots, in lynchings, occasionally even in terrorist attacks. Prison hostages, rebels caught by armies, and civilians killed by secessionists are often castrated.[176] Alleged practitioners of black magic in West Java were strangled, chopped up, or buried alive in 1972.[177] Priests caught by the Viet Minh had bamboo shafts driven into their ears and nails into their heads.[178] A fairly typical lynch mob cut off a victim's "fingers and toes, joint by joint. Mob leaders carried them off as souvenirs. Next, his teeth were pulled out with wire pliers." Some further torture was followed by burning alive and simultaneous shooting.[179] South African lynchings of alleged collaborators with the apartheid regime were carried out by hacking, stoning, burning, and sexual disfigurement.[180] After arms were found at a Lebanese frontier post in the car of a well-known Nasserist, the post was attacked from the Syrian side by men who castrated and disemboweled five Christians manning it.[181] In the Liberian civil war of 1990, soldiers asked a man they stopped late at night whether he had heard a curfew was in force, and then, to emphasize his hearing deficiency, they "cut off both his ears and forced him to eat them."[182]

Even in highly organized warfare, mutilations occur. Among Afghan

---

176. For prison-hostage castrations in Britain and France, see *The Independent* (London), May 23, 1990, p. 5; *Reuters Library Report*, November 13, 1987. For castration by and of occupying soldiers, in Chechnya, Zaire, Bosnia, Mozambique, Kuwait, the southern Philippines, Peru, Liberia, Sri Lanka, see *The Times* (London), May 24, 1995, p. 1; February 9, 1993, p. 1; December 23, 1992, p. 1; British Broadcasting Corporation, *Summary of World Broadcasts*, July 24, 1992, ME/1441/B/1; *Daily Telegraph* (London), February 20, 1991, p. 3; *Reuters Library Report*, January 3, 1991; *Reuters North European Service*, June 12, 1987; *Washington Post*, March 27, 1975, p. A10; *Reuters North European Service*, February 16, 1987; October 24, 1985.

177. *Washington Post*, January 31, 1973, p. A8.

178. Thomas A. Dooley, *Deliver Us from Evil: The Story of Vietnam's Flight to Freedom* (New York: Farrar, Straus and Cudahy, 1956), pp. 175, 182.

179. Raper, *The Tragedy of Lynching*, pp. 143–44.

180. See, e.g., Allister Sparks, *The Mind of South Africa* (New York: Alfred A. Knopf, 1990), pp. 265–66; *The Times* (London), August 20, 1990, p. 1.

181. George E. Kirk, *Contemporary Arab Politics* (New York: Praeger, 1961), pp. 127–28.

182. *International Herald Tribune*, July 10, 1990, p. 6.

rebels against the Soviet-supported regime, it was common "to torture victims by first cutting off their noses, ears and genitals, then removing one slice of skin after another."[183] There, as elsewhere,[184] a frequent practice was to stuff the victim's genitals in his mouth. The boundary between atrocities in warfare and atrocities in riot is not necessarily very clear, as the boundary between the two events is not always clear to the participants. Fears of an invading "Tamil army" or "Ibo army" suggest some of the blurring.

The feud may be a different matter. Where the feud is highly regulated and its violence is closely measured, atrocities may be socially disapproved.[185] Where, on the other hand, the concept of appropriate retaliation in a feud is to raise the stakes a bit with each killing, mutilations help express contempt for the enemy. In Montenegro, it was proper to insult the victim of a feud by removing his head, so that he could not be buried properly, or by severing the "nose and upper lip of an enemy to carry home," or, in one case, by carving out pieces of the dead man's heart.[186] Mutilation can be regarded as an undesirable escalation of the feud or as part and parcel of a strategy of retrieving honor by displaying brazen indifference to the prospect of brutal revenge.

THE MEANING OF MUTILATION

In riots, there is rarely significant retaliation. Even if there is, the first attackers will probably not feel its brunt. Consequently, there is no reason for them to inhibit atrocities, which are exceedingly common in ethnic riots.[187] Certainly, the antiblack riots of the United States in the early

---

183. *Washington Post*, May 11, 1979, p. A23.

184. See, e.g., Leo Kuper, *Genocide: Its Political Use in the Twentieth Century* (New Haven: Yale University Press, 1981), p. 66. Cf. René Lemarchand, *Rwanda and Burundi* (New York: Praeger, 1970), p. 224.

185. Kiefer, *The Tausug*, p. 82.

186. Boehm, *Blood Revenge*, pp. 112, 80, 93.

187. See, e.g., Kirk, *Contemporary Arab Politics*, pp. 161–63; Chomé, *Le Drame de Luluabourg*, p. 6; Thompson and Adloff, *The Emerging States of French Equatorial Africa*, p. 490; Gauze, *The Politics of Congo-Brazzaville*, p. 70; Vittachi, *Emergency '58*, pp. 39–40; Ba Maw, *Breakthrough in Burma: Memoirs of a Revolution, 1939–1946* (New Haven: Yale University Press, 1968), pp. 187–95; Union of South Africa, *Report of the Commission of Enquiry into Riots in Durban*, p. 4; Eastern Regional Government, Federation of Nigeria, *January 15: Before and After* (Enugu: Government Printer, 1967), ch. 7; Simmons, "Politics in Mauritius since 1934," p. 477; Government of Burma, *Final Report of the Riot Inquiry Committee*, pp. 38–39; Shah, "Communal Riots in Gujarat," p. 195.

twentieth century were often accompanied by mutilations.[188] The same was true in one of the two post–World War II episodes in the United States that most nearly resembled a deadly ethnic riot: the Miami riot of 1980, in which the ears and tongues of victims were severed.[189]

Of course, the mere absence of inhibition does not explain why atrocities occur in riots, any more than it explains why they occur in other forms of violence. Nor does the existence of atrocities explain the specific mutilations that characterize ethnic riots. What we know at the outset is how few the inhibitions are, how common the atrocities are, and what characteristic forms they take. Both the incidence of atrocities and the forms they assume require explanation. Some rudimentary distinctions among atrocities are required at the outset.

A few mutilations have fairly obvious symbolic significance. Ibo students, who were thought to excel in school, sometimes lost their fingers or hands in the 1966 Nigerian violence.[190] The same happened to some Tamils in Sri Lanka (1977); among them was a typist.[191] The uncut beards and hair of Sikhs, which so intentionally distinguish them from Hindus, were, as we shall see, favorite targets of Delhi mobs in 1984, in ways that suggest the aim of obliterating the perceived arrogance of the distinction. For the rest, however, what stands out is the similarity of the atrocities across continents rather than any effort to tailor them to the supposed ethnic personality of particular classes of victim.

There is a category of what could be called functional mutilation. In societies where there are beliefs about the powers of dead people, particular mutilations occur. Certain warrior societies "are known to have practiced blood rituals on slain enemies. These involve cutting a piece of flesh from the body to subdue the dead man's spirit or tasting the victim's blood to render the spirit harmless — a spirit, it is believed, will not revenge itself on a body that has become in effect its own."[192] Christian rioters in the southern Philippines cut off the left ear of their Muslim vic-

188. See, e.g., Rudwick, *Race Riot at East St. Louis,* pp. 46–47, 50–51.

189. See Donald L. Horowitz, "Racial Violence in the United States," in Nathan Glazer and Ken Young, eds., *Ethnic Pluralism and Public Policy: Achieving Equality in the United States and Britain* (London: Heinemann, 1983), pp. 187–211, at pp. 206–08.

190. *Nigerian Pogrom: The Organized Massacre of Eastern Nigerians* (Enugu: Government Printer, 1966), p. 7.

191. *Report of the Presidential Commission of Inquiry into the Incidents Which Took Place between 13th August and 15th September 1977,* pp. 125, 127; Tamil Refugees Rehabilitation Organization, *Communal Disturbances in Sri Lanka,* p. 171.

192. Henry Kyemba, *A State of Blood: The Inside Story of Idi Amin* (New York: Ace Books, 1977), p. 109. "Such rituals," Kyemba asserts, "still exist among the Kakwa," Idi Amin's group. "If they kill a man, it is their practice to insert a knife in the body and touch

tims, in order to augment their own martial talents and provide immunity from mortal blows.[193] Dayaks who killed Chinese in West Kalimantan, Indonesia (1967), split the bodies of their victims, drank some blood, and ate the hearts and livers to ward off the avenging spirit of the corpse and transfer his strength to the killer.[194] Such mutilations depend upon a configuration of beliefs in unseen forces, invulnerability, and transubstantiation. They are not performed for torture alone. On the contrary, these mutilations occur only after death. Rather than signifying desecration, they suggest respect for the power of the victim's spirit.

Nevertheless, the line between tasting blood and eating a single vital organ required for strength or invulnerability, on the one hand, and consuming the dead enemy, on the other, is sometimes elusive. Cannibalism of the enemy is a form of complete destruction that usually partakes of hatred.[195] The contempt it entails and its connection to other mutilations are suggested by some verses of a song sung the night before an attack by the Aranda group of central Australia: "We extract their entrails and eat their fat / After we have removed the skin. / We tear their entrails."[196] There are times when cannibalism can achieve two goals at once: causing distress to survivors and absorbing the strength of the deceased.[197]

Equally consuming is fire. Fire plays a large role in ethnic riots. A common pattern is to set a house alight and burn the inhabitants to death.[198] If some emerge, they are shot, hacked to death, or soaked with gasoline and ignited.[199] In Baku (1905), an Armenian boy was dismembered while his mother was being burned to death; others were dismembered and thrown into the flames.[200] In Ahmedabad (1969), a

---

the bloody blade to their lips." Kyemba says this ritual occurred in the course of killings committed "even in the upper ranks of the government," and he describes an instance. Ibid.

193. *Le Monde* (weekly English edition), April 15–21, 1972, p. 4.

194. *Observer* (London), February 18, 1968, p. 5; *Sunday Times* (Kuala Lumpur), November 19, 1967, p. 2. See J.A.C. Mackie, "Anti-Chinese Outbreaks in Indonesia, 1959–68," in J.A.C. Mackie, ed., *The Chinese in Indonesia* (Hong Kong: Heinemann Educational Books, 1976), pp. 77–138, at pp. 126–28. For another example of drinking blood of victims for strength, see Irenäus Eibl-Eibesfeldt, *The Biology of Peace and War*, trans. Eric Mosbacher (New York: Viking Press, 1979), p. 174.

195. Eibl-Eibesfeldt, *The Biology of Peace and War*, p. 179.

196. Quoted in ibid., p. 173.

197. C.R. Hallpike, *Bloodshed and Vengeance in the Papuan Mountains* (Oxford: Clarendon Press, 1977), pp. 208–09.

198. See, e.g., Union of South Africa, *Report of the Commission of Enquiry into Riots in Durban*, p. 4; *Dawn* (Karachi), January 5, 1965; Engineer, "Meerut: The Nation's Shame," p. 970.

199. Kuper, *Genocide*, p. 65.

200. Henry, *Baku*, pp. 159, 185.

Muslim was burned alive, not inside a house but outside.[201] In Bhiwandi (1984), victims were stabbed, doused with kerosene, and then burned alive.[202] In Sumgait, Azerbaijan (1988), the main weapons against Armenians were axes and fire.[203] Sikh victims in Delhi (1984) were frequently hit on the head and then set afire, usually by their beards, occasionally having their eyes gouged out first.[204] Sometimes victims are killed first and then burned.[205] Fire, Elias Canetti remarks, is the most impressive form of destruction. "It destroys irrevocably; nothing after a fire is as it was before. A crowd setting fire to something feels irresistible; so long as the fire spreads, everyone will join it and everything hostile will be destroyed."[206] In an ethnic riot, fire is an emblem of complete hostility.

Torture in an ethnic riot is inflicted "with hilarious and joyful abandon."[207] Playful, lighthearted cruelty is common in the handling of the bodies of victims, before and after their murder. In Osh (1990), Uzbek babies were hung on meat-hooks, with labels asking "What price Uzbek meat?"[208] An exact parallel can be found in the anti-Jewish violence in Romania (1941), when signs posted next to bodies on meat-hooks announced "Kosher meat."[209] In West Kalimantan, Indonesia (1999), a "laughing man produced a severed human arm and happily posed with it for photographs," while another "displayed a severed head with a cigarette stuck up a nostril," a third offered "a lump of human heart," and a fourth "popped [human flesh] into his mouth," pronouncing it "Delicious."[210] The anti-Sikh violence of 1984 proceeded in a similar spirit of malevolent frivolity, with the "pulling out of limbs and eyes, tearing off hair, beards being set on fire, piercing of bowels and kidneys with sharp

201. Shah, "Communal Riots in Gujarat," pp. 193–95.

202. Ghosh, *Communal Riots in India*, pp. 202–03.

203. Peter Conrad, "Riots Were Planned Genocide, Armenian Communist Paper Says," *Reuters Library Report*, November 5, 1988.

204. Citizens' Committee, Delhi, *Delhi, 31 October to 4 November 1984*, p. 23.

205. See, e.g., Rabindra K. Mohanty, "Dynamics of Atrocities on Scheduled Castes in Rural India," *Indian Journal of Social Work* 49, no. 1 (January 1988): 51–66, at p. 53.

206. Elias Canetti, *Crowds and Power*, trans. Carol Stewart (New York: Viking Press, 1962), p. 20.

207. Kuper, *Genocide*, p. 104. See Tambiah, *Leveling Crowds*, pp. 279–80; Orlando Patterson, "The Feast of Blood: Race, Religion, and Human Sacrifice in the Post-Bellum South" (unpublished paper, Department of Sociology, Harvard University, 1997), pp. 11, 24; Joseph Boskin, "The Revolt of the Urban Ghettos, 1964–1967," *The Annals* 382 (March 1969): 1–14, at pp. 11–14.

208. *The Independent* (London), July 19, 1990, p. 2.

209. R.G. Waldeck, *Athene Palace* (New York: Robert M. McBride, 1942), p. 346.

210. *The Independent* (London), March 22, 1999, pp. 1, 12.

weapons . . . ."[211] It was a holiday for violence, punctuated by laughter. Laughter, Canetti points out, is an act related to the helplessness of its object, who can be treated as prey.[212]

The cruelty is ubiquitous and extreme.[213] It ranges from gouging of eyeballs to firing guns in mouths, to crucifixion, disembowelment, impalement,[214] decapitation,[215] and throwing people out of the windows of hospitals or apartments[216] or off hills (after they had been dragged along the ground, roped to horses).[217] And then there are the sex-linked atrocities: rape, the display of naked victims,[218] dismemberment of breasts,[219] removal of fetuses from pregnant women by cutting open the abdomen,[220] and — most often — dismemberment and castration of male victims,[221] sometimes in conjunction with removal of other body parts. These mutilations occur with such frequency, regardless of cultural context or riot precipitant, that they cannot be considered merely pointless or incidental features of ethnic rioting.

Part of the explanation may derive from what might be called a surfeit of hostility, more than is required for killing alone. An enormous discharge of energy occurs in the heat of mass violence. It has been sug-

211. Rajni Kothari, "The How and the Why of It All," in Kothari and Sethi, eds., *Voices from a Scarred City,* p. 14.

212. Canetti, *Crowds and Power,* p. 223.

213. "Even we, forensic experts, were overwhelmed by the savagery and sadism of the murders." Z.A. Giyasov, chief forensic expert of Uzbekistan, quoted in *Literaturnaya Gazeta,* June 14, 1989, p. 2, in FBIS-SOV-89–117, June 20, 1989, p. 45. To the same effect, see Slimming, *Malaysia,* p. 48.

214. For the list thus far, see Weinberg, "Anti-Jewish Violence and Revolution," pp. 20–21; *New York Times,* June 8, 1972, p. 9, on Burundi; Kajsa Ekholm Friedman and Anne Sundberg, "Reorganization Efforts and the Threat of Ethnic War in Congo" (unpublished paper, Department of Social Anthropology, University of Lund, 1996), p. 11.

215. Josson, *Bombay Blood Yatra; New York Times,* December 4, 1990, p. A3, on South Africa; Avav and Myegba, *The Dream to Conquer,* p. 23.

216. Engineer, "Gujarat Burns Again," p. 1346; *Times* (London), March 12, 1988, p. 1, on Sumgait; *Izvestia,* January 17, 1990, p. 6, in *Current Digest of the Soviet Press,* February 21, 1990, p. 4; Weinberg, "Anti-Jewish Violence and Revolution," p. 20.

217. Tishkov, "Don't Kill Me, I Am Kyrghyz," p. 9.

218. See ibid., p. 21; Shah, "Communal Riots in Gujarat," p. 195.

219. Slimming, *Malaysia,* p. 34; Shah, "Communal Riots in Gujarat."

220. Weinberg, "Anti-Jewish Violence and Revolution," p. 21; Avav and Myegba, *The Dream to Conquer,* p. 27; Colin Legum, "The Tragedy in Nigeria," *Africa Report* 11, no. 8 (November 1966): 23–24.

221. E.g., Northern Regional Government, Government of Nigeria, *Report on the Kano Disturbances, 16th, 17th, 18th and 19th May, 1953* (Kaduna: Government Printer, 1953), pp. 14, 16; Adam and Moodley, "Political Violence, 'Tribalism,' and Inkatha," p. 507; *Reuters North American Wire,* February 21, 1992, pp. 7–8, on Jukun-Tiv riots in Nigeria; Kakar, *The Colors of Violence,* p. 28.

gested that mutilation may be accounted for by classical frustration-aggression theory, which predicts that, all else equal, the greater the frustration, the more intense (as well as the more likely) the aggression.[222]

The bizarre incidents that occurred during the 1953 riot in Kano, northern Nigeria, lend support to the existence of a connection between mutilation and the discharge of accumulated aggressive energy. In this riot, Hausa were the aggressors, but for a short time Ibo retaliated. Mutilations, castrations, and burnings of bodies occurred. Periodically, the police were able to separate the combatants. During these intervals, there were several instances in which armed Ibo participants danced in "crocodile" formation and others in which they slaughtered with their hatchets nearby horses, donkeys, and goats, usually belonging to Hausa.[223] In the absence of human victims, the participants turned their continuing fury in other directions — ritualistic dancing and the butchering of animals that happened in the way.

Observers of collective violence have remarked that, by loosening restraints and increasing anonymity, the crowd experience increases the likelihood of brutality.[224] Experimental studies confirm that collectivities aggress more severely, sharply, and rapidly than do individuals and that anonymity and diffusion of responsibility for antisocial behavior are associated with this increased aggression.[225] The wearing of uniforms during an experiment produced more aggressive behavior by 11-year-old

222. Hubert M. Blalock, Jr., *Toward a Theory of Minority-Group Relations* (New York: John Wiley & Sons, 1967), p. 44. Blalock does not necessarily endorse this hypothesis; he merely puts it on the table for consideration.

223. Northern Regional Government, *Report on the Kano Disturbances*, pp. 14, 16, 28.

224. Ben Shalit, *The Psychology of Conflict and Combat* (New York: Praeger, 1988), p. 76; L. Festinger, A. Pepitone, and T. Newcomb, "Some Consequences of De-Individuation in a Group," *Journal of Abnormal and Social Psychology* 47, no. 2 (April 1952): 382–89; Spencer, "Collective Violence and Everyday Practice in Sri Lanka," p. 607 (in violence, people are said to lack *lajja* or shame); Kakar, "Some Unconscious Aspects of Ethnic Violence in India," pp. 142–43 (in crowds, people try to transcend their individual selves, and the need for transcendence produces brutality); Tishkov, "Don't Kill Me, I Am Kyrghyz," pp. 26–28 ("social paranoia" includes a loss of individual identification that helps account for atrocities). Cf. Susan Welch and Alan Booth, "Crowding as a Factor in Political Aggression: Theoretical Aspects and an Analysis of Some Cross-National Data," *Social Science Information* 13, no. 4/5 (August–October 1974): 151–62, on crowded living conditions.

225. Geen, *Human Aggression*, pp. 130–31; Yoram Jaffe, Nahum Sapir, and Yoel Yinon, "Aggression and Its Escalation," *Journal of Cross-Cultural Psychology* 12, no. 1 (March 1981): 21–36; Jaffe and Yinon, "Retaliatory Aggression in Individuals and Groups," pp. 177–81. Cf. Philip G. Zimbardo, "The Human Choice: Individuation, Reason, and Order versus Deindividuation, Impulse, and Chaos," in William J. Arnold and

boys.[226] The mechanism for increasing aggression may have been the sense of group identification, rather than anonymity, induced by uniforms, but in ethnic violence the two forces can operate in tandem. In another experiment, anonymity enhanced the aggression of white subjects against black targets, but not against white targets.[227] Larger lynch mobs committed more atrocities than smaller ones did, again suggesting the importance of deindividuation.[228] Anonymous subjects in experiments also suppressed perceived differences among potential targets of aggression more than identifiable subjects did.[229] Deindividuating targets facilitates aggression and atrocities and helps to explain why attacks are so random within the target-group category.[230] Deindividuation also suggests the answer to a puzzle relating to wide participation in riots, for it means that ordinary people, rather than just aggressively disposed people, can be induced in the crowd setting to do things they would not do in other settings.[231]

Once we grant the magnifying possibilities of membership in a crowd, we are still left with the insistent questions of why so much hostility is to be found in the first instance and why atrocities take the particular forms they do. Although atrocities and mutilations are occasionally present in other forms of violence, they are pervasive in the deadly ethnic riot. An appropriate explanation should be neither so particular that it has no bearing on wider phenomena nor so general as to fail to recognize the unusually high incidence of atrocities in ethnic riots. There is a strong case for turning to a cluster of relationships among sex, fear, self-esteem, domination, and violence. These elements are especially strong

David LeVine, eds., *Nebraska Symposium on Motivation* (Lincoln: University of Nebraska Press, 1969), pp. 237–307.

226. But not by girls. Jürgen Rehm, Michael Steinleitzner, and Waldemar Lilli, "Wearing Uniforms and Aggression — a Field Experiment," *European Journal of Social Psychology* 17, no. 3 (July–September 1987): 357–60. On riot participation by males but not females, see Chapter 7, below.

227. Geen, *Human Aggression*, pp. 153–58.

228. Brian Mullen, "Atrocity as Function of Lynch Mob Composition," *Personality and Social Psychology Bulletin* 12, no. 2 (June 1986): 187–97.

229. Geen, *Human Aggression*, p. 131. Cf. Stephen Worshel and Virginia Andreoli, "Facilitation of Social Interaction through Deindividuation of the Target," *Journal of Personality and Social Psychology* 36, no. 5 (May 1978): 549–56.

230. Differences of age and sex excepted, as noted above.

231. A striking instance concerns crowds that happen to find themselves at an episode of threatened suicide. Larger crowds are more likely to taunt and urge the victim to jump than smaller crowds are. See Leon Mann, "The Baiting Crowd in Episodes of Threatened Suicide," *Journal of Personality and Social Psychology* 41, no. 4 (April 1981): 703–09.

in conflict relations among ethnic groups but are not confined to those relations.

Sexuality plays a role in many intergroup conflicts. Presumed sexual attributes are often included in ethnic stereotypes.[232] As we have seen, it is not uncommon for a riot to be preceded by a rumor with a sexual component, whether it be a rape, a murder of a woman, the chopping of her body into pieces, or a severing of breasts. Once in a while, a riot is preceded by a campaign of vilification, in which images of lurid sexual practices, allegedly indulged in by the target group, are vividly (and perhaps enviously) depicted by their detractors.[233] And, very occasionally, the target group is accused of seducing women belonging to the attacking group.[234]

The symbolic significance of some mutilations seems so clear — severing the hand of a typist, for example — that perhaps castration reflects something analogous in the sexual field. Yet what stands out is how rare direct interethnic sexual competition is in severely divided societies. Very few riots are precipitated by such competition.[235] Rates of exogamy between groups with serious conflicts are typically very low,[236] and other interethnic contacts between the sexes are generally infrequent. A more indirect specification of the connections between sexuality and violence is apt to be more accurate.

There are connections between sexuality and aggression. Experimental studies have linked sexual arousal to increases in hostility.[237] Other studies have established a relation between the male hormone and aggressive

232. See, e.g., Kenelm O.L. Burridge, "Racial Relations in Johore," *Australian Journal of Politics and History* 2, no. 2 (May 1957): 162–63; Arthur Niehoff and Juanita Niehoff, *East Indians in the West Indies* (Milwaukee: Milwaukee Public Museum Publications in Anthropology, 1960), p. 100.

233. Government of [West] Punjab, *Report of the Court of Inquiry Constituted under Punjab Act II of 1954*, pp. 30, 87.

234. Government of Burma, *Final Report of the Riot Inquiry Committee*, pp. 8, 11; Union of South Africa, *Report of the Commission of Enquiry into Riots in Durban*, p. 14.

235. Malaya (1959) was one. See Hanna, "Pangkor Island." Another was the very minor Singapore riot of 1946, described in Chapter 2, note 46, above.

236. See Horowitz, *Ethnic Groups in Conflict*, pp. 61–62.

237. Andrew M. Barclay and Ralph Norman Haber, "The Relation of Aggressive to Sexual Motivation," *Journal of Personality* 33, no. 3 (September 1965): 462–75; Leonard Berkowitz, "Purposive and Impulsive Violence: Some Implications of Laboratory Studies of Aggression" (unpublished paper, Department of Psychology, University of Wisconsin–Madison, 1969), citing the work of Percy Tannenbaum. In a different study, pictures of sexually attractive females reduced levels of male anger, whereas tranquil landscapes did not. R.A. Baron, "The Aggression-Inhibiting Influence of Heightened Sexual Arousal," *Journal of Personality and Social Psychology* 30, no. 3 (September 1974): 318–22.

behavior.[238] The crowds that commit atrocities consist overwhelmingly of young men, amply supplied with the hormone. And consider the commonsense observation that some male perpetrators of violence fight in order to assert their manhood. The statement implies that those whose manhood is in doubt may be more likely to initiate aggression.

For this hypothesis, there is some support. The insults of soccer fans preceding a violent encounter consist of suggestions that the opposing team and its supporters are women or homosexuals; the resulting assault is thus related to the denigration of masculinity.[239] During the lull, as indicated previously, women sometimes taunt men gathered in crowds that later turn to violence, and the taunts question their virility. In Karachi (1984), Pathans were moved to violent action by the argument "that they would lose the rights to their own women if they did not avenge the insults to which they felt they had been subjected by the Orangis."[240] Masculinity is "recovered through murder . . . ."[241] A cross-cultural study similarly shows some relationship between physical cruelty and high levels of inhibition on sexual expression, as well as between imperfectly established masculine identity and deliberate pursuit of violence.[242]

Before some of the most serious episodes of violence, a strikingly similar idiom is employed. Members of the group that will do the attacking assert that members of the target group are "swallowing" them. The Hausa referred, in May 1966, to Ibo affronts "in Hausa by the power 'cin mutumci' (literally, *to eat someone's humanity*)."[243] In 1945, Malays thought there had been a fundamental change in intergroup relations: "Before the war we and the Chinese lived together in peace. But now they want to swallow the people (*makan orang*)."[244] At the time of the Luluabourg riot in 1959, Lulua responded to Luba political activity with a similar epigram: "One cannot ask a goat to nurse the young leopard

238. Reported in Berkowitz, *Aggression*, p. 17.

239. Peter Marsh, Elisabeth Rosser, and Rom Harré, *The Rules of Disorder* (London: Routledge & Kegan Paul, 1978), pp. 132–34.

240. Veena Das, "Communities, Riots, Survivors: The South Asian Experience" (Punitham Tiruchelvam Memorial Lecture, Sri Lanka Tamil Women's Union, Colombo, September 5, 1988; mimeo.), p. 17.

241. Ibid.

242. See John W.M. Whiting, "The Place of Aggression in Social Interaction," in Short and Wolfgang, eds., *Collective Violence*, pp. 192–97.

243. M.J. Dent, "The Military and Politics: A Study of the Relation between the Army and the Political Process in Nigeria," in Robert Melson and Howard Wolpe, eds., *Nigeria: Modernization and the Politics of Communalism* (East Lansing: Michigan State University Press, 1971), p. 398 n. 42.

244. Burridge, "Racial Relations in Johore," p. 163.

which will devour it when its teeth grow."[245] Before the Assamese riots of 1960, an Assamese had written a novel about intergroup relations. "Its theme is that the Bengalees are exploiters and they are eating up Assam."[246] The same swallowing imagery — an enemy "swallows me with his eyes"[247] — is reported for the Tausug and for other groups in violent conflict.[248]

Now there are many ways to interpret the fear of being swallowed. Much work on aggression points to explanations that rest on the use of violence in the quest for a dominant position, for control of territory, and for the restoration of a threatened self-esteem.[249] Swallowing suggests domination. As we shall see in the occasions that precipitate riots, the fear of being swallowed is often expressed in conjunction with events that connote to the participants a fear of being subordinated or degraded. If the fear of being swallowed is tantamount to the fear of being dominated, an aggressive response may be in order. After all, we have already seen that rumors before the outbreak of violence express an expectation of aggressive behavior from the targets. Even if these rumors are projective, as I have argued they are, they are effective justifications, because the targets are regarded as threatening and powerful, and so the rumor is plausible. Of course, there are fears at many levels; fear of retaliation can inhibit rather than facilitate aggression.[250] But it is well documented that generalized fear — not the sort that produces deterrence — can produce an aggressive response.[251] The fear of being swallowed is an extreme fear,

245. Henri Nicolai, "Conflits entre groupes africains et décolonisation au Kasai," *Revue de l'Université de Bruxelles*, XIIe Année (1960): 142.

246. Bhandari, *Thoughts on Assam Disturbances*, p. 28.

247. Kiefer, *The Tausug*, pp. 69, 70.

248. If Vietnamese do not stop their migration into Cambodia, "Cambodia will be swallowed by the Yuon [a derogatory term for Vietnamese] . . . ." Voice of the Great National United Front of Cambodia, February 14, 1993, in FBIS-EAS-93-030, February 17, 1993, p. 54. An Arab report is said to have stated: "The Jewish leaders are turning days into nights in order to swallow Palestine. The Jews . . . wish to swallow us alive." Quoted in Carl Gil A. Roy, ed., *Behind the Mid-East Conflict: The Real Impasse between Arab and Jew* (New York: G.P. Putnam & Sons, 1975), p. 32. A character in a Palestinian novel comments that the Jews "did eat us greedily and without pity." Another says that the Palestinians have lost "their sense of manhood." Quoted in Trevor J. LeGassick, "Some Recent War-Related Arabic Fiction," *Middle East Journal* 25, no. 4 (Autumn 1971): 491–505, at pp. 497, 495, respectively.

249. See, e.g., Eibl-Eibesfeldt, *The Biology of Peace and War*, pp. 79–87, 122–24; Shalit, *The Psychology of Conflict and Combat*, pp. 59, 66–67.

250. See Albert Bandura, *Aggression: A Social Learning Analysis* (Englewood Cliffs, N.J.: Prentice-Hall, 1973), pp. 221–25.

251. See Eibl-Eibesfeldt, *The Biology of Peace and War*, p. 106.

indeed; and it can be related to the most extreme fear, also articulated frequently by groups who do the attacking: the fear of extinction.[252] Atrocity has some appeal as an adequate response to fear at this level. Mutilation signifies complete control of the victim, even beyond killing, and serves to symbolize reversal of the discomfort of living together. The atrocity is the end of relational complexity.

Psychoanalysts have also studied the fear of being swallowed. According to Otto Fenichel, "the dread of being eaten is in practice indissolubly connected with the idea of being castrated."[253] If accurate, this interpretation fits remarkably well with the actual infliction of castration in the course of the violence.[254] Others relate the fear of being swallowed to the fear of being eaten into, robbed, and emptied.[255] Canetti, noting the strong connections of eating to power,[256] suggests that whoever wants to rule seeks "to incorporate [others] into himself and to suck the substance out of them."[257] Seizing and incorporation are therefore intimately tied to domination, and the fear of being incorporated reflects the fear of being dominated.

In primate studies, there is a phenomenon known as "phallic threatening, derived from a sexual domination gesture"[258] utilized against strangers. The relation of the male organ to domination and threats of domination is strong across cultures. Dismemberment needs to be seen as a decisive response to such threats of domination. Atrocities and desecrations can be interpreted as efforts to taunt and humiliate victims, deny

252. See Horowitz, *Ethnic Groups in Conflict*, pp. 175–78. For the linkage of swallowing to genocide, see *Far Eastern Economic Review*, December 3, 1992, p. 14. The Vietnamese, declared a publication of the Khmer People's National Liberation Front, have a "plan for swallowing Khmer territory and committing genocide against the Khmers."

253. Otto Fenichel, "The Dread of Being Eaten," *International Journal of Psycho-Analysis* 10 (n.m. 1929): 448–50, at p. 449. Fenichel also suggests that boys may fear a *vagina dentata* as retaliation for oral-sadistic impulses. Otto Fenichel, *The Psychoanalytic Theory of Neurosis* (New York: Norton, 1945), p. 79.

254. It should be noted, too, that among some groups, the knife is regarded anthropomorphically, and the blade is viewed as a penis. Razha, "Martial Arts and the Malay Superman," p. 81.

255. Erik H. Erikson, *Childhood and Society*, rev. ed. (New York: W.W. Norton, 1963), p. 411.

256. Canetti, *Crowds and Power*, p. 220.

257. Ibid., p. 210. "Underneath [power]," he says, "day in, day out, is digestion and again digestion." Ibid. Cf. Peter Loewenberg, "The Psychological Reality of Nationalism: Between Community and Fantasy," *Mind and Human Interaction* 5, no. 1 (February 1994): 6–18, at pp. 7–8, on the child's desire to swallow and incorporate all that is good in the external world.

258. Eibl-Eibesfeldt, *The Biology of Peace and War*, p. 108.

them honor, demand their subservience, demonstrate their powerlessness, and redefine them as alien and illegitimate occupants of the place
where the attack takes place.[259]

The passions that underlie atrocities make very plain the limitation of
theories that cast violence in purely instrumental terms. The more highly
regulated and calculative the violence, the less common atrocities seem to
be. Still, one can imagine some local leaders who give instructions to rioting followers that they should utilize the most brutal methods. Deadly
violence with atrocities might be a more powerful political tool than is
deadly violence without atrocities. Certain aggressors would find it
advantageous to use atrocities to deepen hatred and fear or to cultivate a
reputation for being irrational and dangerously out of control.[260]
Atrocities may keep the behavior of surviving victims more in line with
what the aggressor group deems acceptable than do killings alone. The
calculative element, therefore, cannot wholly be written out of atrocities.

Yet there are reasons to be skeptical of the general case. Calculating
rioters can usually achieve better results for themselves by more efficient
mass killing, which has the side benefit of producing refugees as a function of the overall death toll. Mutilations are labor intensive; they take
time, and they reduce the death toll. The more methodical genocides
tend to proceed with a lower overall ratio of atrocities to deaths and to
homogenize areas more completely.

Moreover, it is necessary to account, not merely for cruelty in general,
but for the particular pattern of mutilations. Why, for example, the common practice of stuffing severed genitals into the mouths of victims or
their wives? Other atrocities, which might be expected from the opportunities provided by the disorder, do not occur with what might be their
expected frequency. The bodies of men are far more often the targets of
the killers and mutilators than are the bodies of women. The lives of
women are much more often spared than are the lives of men, and
women are sometimes unmolested altogether.[261] Instrumental notions

259. For such interpretations, see Roger Jeffery and Patricia M. Jeffery, "The Bijnor
Riots, October 1990," *Economic and Political Weekly*, March 5, 1994, pp. 551–58, at p.
556; Friedland and Hecht, "Divisions at the Center," p. 46.

260. For the former, see James D. Fearon, "Ethnic War as a Commitment Problem"
(paper presented at the 1994 annual meeting of the American Political Science Association,
New York), p. 3. For the latter, see Thomas C. Schelling, *The Strategy of Conflict*
(Cambridge: Harvard University Press, 1963), p. 127. I return to the Fearon argument in
Chapter 13.

261. Absent male victims, crowds will certainly kill females, as they did in the so-called
Nellie Massacre in Assam (1983), when men were generally not present in the village being

seem ill suited to explain the recurrence of particular dismemberments and disembowelments. To judge by the infuriating effects of pre-riot rumors about the fate of women and their bodies, atrocities against women would be more likely to produce a reputation for madness, if that were the aim.

The same goes for the playful atmosphere surrounding the infliction of atrocities. The joy of collective violence seems to reflect the complete release of inner inhibition and a sense of freedom from social constraint far more than it could possibly reflect calculativeness. It represents transcendently expressive behavior; and adequate explanation cannot avoid taking account of it.

Sadism and brutality of the sort described here fit awkwardly into schema that have their origin in mechanisms framed in terms of stimulus and response, as relative deprivation theories do. The same phenomena are not likely to fit much better into theories predicated wholly on political entrepreneurship. Whatever leaders may plan, the plans would not come to fruition if the rioters did not find the festive infliction of suffering and degradation thoroughly satisfying. No hidden logic of costs and benefits can explain the violence *tout court*. For that matter, neither can it explain the prominent part played by the rioters' notions of how interethnic warfare was traditionally pursued. The problem is to deal with activity that exhibits so much affect, so much antipathy, that is a mix of prudence and passion, in order to capture the motives of the actors in violent conflict. No theory of violence has met this challenge well.

---

attacked. Similarly, it is not unknown to kill the husband and rape the wife (or in the reverse sequence) and then, as in Osh (1990) and in some Hindu-Muslim riots, parade the women naked, displaying their genitals. See, e.g., Tishkov, "Don't Kill Me, I Am Kyrghyz," p. 21. But, to take a fairly typical example, in Bhiwandi (1970), 73 people were killed in town and 86 people in the rest of the district, and six women were raped. Ghosh, *Communal Riots in India*, pp. 179, 187. Sometimes women are even treated courteously by their husbands' killers. See Veena Das, "Our Work to Cry: Your Work to Listen (The Survivor of Collective Violence)" (unpublished paper, Delhi, n.d.), pp. 23, 65.

CHAPTER 4

Selective Targeting

THERE IS A BIZARRE PARADOX of rationality in rioting. The riot is often a bestial slaughter, yet it involves elements of prudence and foresight. An orgy of killing is punctuated by interludes of detached planning. Traps may be laid for victims, who when caught will be butchered with frenzied brutality. The carefully plotted Punjab train massacres during the partition of India and Pakistan illustrate the phenomenon.[1] The East St. Louis riot of 1917 is depicted in much the same way. Despite the intense sadism of the murders and the jubilation with which they were carried out, the crowd knew what it was doing: "there was a visible coolness and premeditation about it . . . . [T]his was not the hectic and raving demonstration of men suddenly gone mad."[2] Violence of this kind is better described as lucid madness than as blind fury.

PRECISION IN TARGETING

Target selection forms part of the picture of coherent ferocity. Members of some groups are hunted down meticulously, while others escape unharmed. Some deliberate sifting of potential targets may be involved. The same crowd which a moment earlier committed atrocities on members of the target group, and will do so again when more are found, may circumspectly screen out nonmembers of the target group. The procedure described by the Commission of Inquiry into the southern Sudan riots of 1955 is representative. Northerners of all classes and occupations were killed. Nevertheless, the southern rioters "were particularly selective of

---

1. See, e.g., Penderel Moon, *Divide and Quit* (Berkeley and Los Angeles: University of California Press, 1962). See also the novel by Khushwant Singh, *Train to Pakistan* (Bombay: Chatto and Windus, 1970).

2. Elliott M. Rudwick, *Race Riot at East St. Louis, July 2, 1917* (Carbondale: Southern Illinois University Press, 1964), quoting the East St. Louis *Daily Journal*, July 5, 1917.

their victims. Foreigners' lives and property with two exceptions were untouched. In all cases, Copts, Syrians, Greeks, Egyptians, British and half-Northern-half-Southern were carefully sorted out and set free."[3] Such screening, of property as well as persons, is a recurrent feature of deadly riots. In Philadelphia (1844), an anti-Irish crowd, on its way to burn down an Irish Roman Catholic church, "passed a German Catholic church but did not harm it, underlining the anti-Irish basis for [its] actions."[4] In Sri Lanka (1977), houses owned by Tamils were burned, "while houses owned by Sinhalese and occupied by Tamils were only looted."[5] In West Kalimantan (1997), Dayaks searching for Madurese targets bypassed houses of Javanese and Malays.[6] The same discrimination, more impressive in some cases because there is a wider range of formidable and plausible potential victims, has occurred during riots in Azerbaijan, Nigeria, Burma, Zanzibar, Malaysia, Uzbekistan, Singapore, Mauritania, Mauritius, Assam, the Punjab, and the Ivory Coast, among many others. Discriminating choices are also made in laboratory settings.[7]

The mode of identification used in target selection varies with the indicia of group membership.[8] Depending on the circumstances, color, name, physiognomy, dress, grooming, bearing, facial hair, circumcision, scarification, earring holes and other bodily marks, linguistic fluency, and even familiarity with religious passages have all been employed to

3. Republic of Sudan, *Report of the Commission of Inquiry into the Disturbances in the Southern Sudan during August, 1955* (Khartoum: McCorquedale, 1956), p. 78. See also the "calculated sense of discrimination" displayed in Ahmedabad (1969). Ghanshyam Shah, "Communal Riots in Gujarat," *Economic and Political Weekly*, Annual Number, January 1970, p. 193. Cf. the discrimination displayed by a lynch mob, reported by Arthur F. Raper, *The Tragedy of Lynching* (Chapel Hill: University of North Carolina Press, 1933), pp. 289–90; and by looters in Mozambique, reported in the *Washington Post*, September 13, 1974, p. A22. Selective targeting is a long-standing and well-nigh universal practice. In the anti-Armenian killings in Turkey (1894–96), Greeks were passed over, despite the well-known hostility to Greeks. See Robert Melson, *Revolution and Genocide: On the Origins of the Armenian Genocide and the Holocaust* (Chicago: University of Chicago Press, 1992), pp. 494–95.

4. Michael Feldberg, *The Philadelphia Riots of 1844: A Study of Ethnic Conflict* (Westport, Conn.: Greenwood Press, 1975), p. 113.

5. *Report of the Presidential Commission of Inquiry into the Incidents Which Took Place between 13th August and 15th September 1977*, Sessional Paper No. VII — 1980 (Colombo: Government Publications Bureau, 1980), p. 160.

6. *Jakarta Post*, March 2, 1997, p. 1–2.

7. See, e.g., Netta Kohn Dor-Shav, Bruria Friedman, and Rachel Tcherbonogura, "Identification, Prejudice, and Aggression," *Journal of Social Psychology* 104, Second Half (April 1978): 217–22.

8. See Donald L. Horowitz, *Ethnic Groups in Conflict* (Berkeley and Los Angeles: University of California Press, 1985), pp. 46–47.

differentiate victim from attacker. None of these methods is entirely foolproof. If, for instance, dress is the primary criterion, potential targets, given sufficient warning, can assimilate temporarily.[9] By the same token, a small number of nonmembers of the target group may inadvertently be included in it.[10] But despite these mistakes, the general tendency is toward a rather high degree of accuracy in identification in the course of riots.[11] This may be surprising in view of what seems to outsiders to be the prevailing confusion. It is much less surprising when one considers that reliance is usually placed on a distinctive combination of differentiating characteristics. In Sierra Leone, for example, Temne "may be recognized by their large 'full buttoned' gowns, their fez or white cap and their forceful way of walking," while the dress of Mende is different; they bear "two or three small marks high on the cheek bone," and they are said to "lean forwards slightly when they are walking."[12] In doubtful cases, the crowd is often given extraordinary opportunities to interrogate, disrobe, and otherwise force the identifying cues from potential victims — opportunities of which it makes use when necessary.[13]

9. See, e.g., the official eastern Nigerian version of the riots in the north during September–October 1966: *Nigerian Pogrom: The Organized Massacre of Eastern Nigerians* (Enugu: Ministry of Information, 1966), pp. 15, 19 (Ibo masquerading as Yoruba); Leonard Plotnicov, "An Early Nigerian Civil Disturbance: The 1945 Hausa-Ibo Riot in Jos," *Journal of Modern African Studies* 9, no. 2 (August 1971): 297–305 (Ibo disguised as Yoruba and Hausa; *Washington Post*, April 19, 1970, p. A1 (Vietnamese wearing the sarong of Cambodian Muslims).

10. See, e.g., Tarzie Vittachi, *Emergency '58: The Story of the Ceylon Race Riots* (London: André Deutsch, 1958), p. 49 (Sinhalese misidentified as a Tamil and killed); Aswini K. Ray and Subhash Chakravarti, *Meerut Riots: A Case Study* (New Delhi: Sampradayikta Virodhi Committee, n.d. [1968 or 1969]), p. 11 (one misidentified Hindu victim); Valery Tishkov, "Don't Kill Me, I Am Kyrghyz: Anthropological Analysis of Violence in Osh Ethnic Conflict" (paper presented at the 13th International Congress of Anthropological and Ethnological Sciences, Mexico City, July 28–August 5, 1993), pp. 18–19 (only one Russian victim); Kajsa Ekholm Friedman and Anne Sundberg, "Ethnic War and Ethnic Cleansing in Brazzaville" (unpublished paper, Department of Social Anthropology, University of Lund, 1994), p. 21 (a number of misidentified Lari victims).

11. See, e.g., John Darby, *Intimidation and the Control of Conflict in Northern Ireland* (Dublin: Gill & Macmillan, 1986), p. 16, reporting no cases of mistaken identity in the riots of 1864.

12. Kenneth Little, *The Mende of Sierra Leone*, rev. ed. (London: Routledge & Kegan Paul, 1967), pp. 70, 71.

13. Compare the riot setting, at one extreme, with, at the other extreme, the lesser degree of reliability found in experiments with visual cues drawn solely from photographs. Donald N. Elliott and Bernard H. Wittenberg, "Accuracy of Identification of Jewish and Non-Jewish Photographs," *Journal of Abnormal and Social Psychology* 51, no. 2 (September 1955): 339–41; Launor F. Carter, "The Identification of 'Racial' Membership," *Journal of Abnormal and Social Psychology* 43, no. 3 (July 1948): 279–86. Between these

Precision in target selection may also be modified by the occasional killing of an alleged collaborator or a possible witness, as well as by the opportunities opened up by the riot for the settling of old scores and the acquisition of loot. Occasionally, too, selective targeting is merely a matter of emphasis, rather than perfect precision, particularly where members of one subgroup are singled out more than members of another, but not entirely to the exclusion of the other. Nevertheless, riot accounts from many sources in many countries testify to a very high degree of selectivity in the targeting process.

Few societies are so bi-ethnic as to afford no latitude in the selection of victims for violence, and many provide an abundant array of possibilities. In many states, the range of potential target groups is wide, simply by virtue of the heterogeneity of the population. Where choices are possible, choices are made. However great the anger that precedes the outburst, violence is not generally scattered among several victim groups but is instead concentrated on one or (much more rarely) two.

In consequence, some groups find themselves untouched by the violence, as others emerge battered and bloodied. The Malaysian Chinese have repeatedly been targeted, whereas Malaysian Indians generally have not. In the Ivory Coast riots of 1958, Dahomeyans and Togolese were attacked, but Upper Voltans, Lebanese, Malians, and Senegalese were undisturbed. Bengalis in Assam, rather than Marwaris or other non-Assamese, were victims of the widespread violence that overtook that Indian state in 1960. Within the targeted community, there was even further selective precision: Bengali Hindus were assaulted, but Bengali Muslims in general were not. In some 36 riots that occurred in the Punjab before World War II, 26 involved Sikhs. In 21 of these, Sikhs were arrayed against Muslims; in only two did Sikhs fight Hindus; in the remaining three, Sikhs and Hindus together opposed Muslims.[14] In the killings that accompanied the partition of the Punjab in 1947, the alignment was clearly Sikh and Hindu versus Muslim, but Sikhs and Muslims were the main antagonists. Although it was hazardous enough to be a Hindu in the Muslim-majority west Punjab, it constituted a virtual death sentence to be a Sikh — this despite the all-India context of Hindu-Muslim antipathy, of which the Punjab (being the last area to break into violence)

---

extremes is the situation of, for example, a shopkeeper able to make rough-and-ready discriminatory judgments of ascriptive affiliation on the basis of posture, gesture, clothing, and grammar, in addition to physical features. James M. Sebring, "Caste Indicators and Caste Identification of Strangers," *Human Organization* 28, no. 3 (Fall 1969): 199–207.

14. Richard D. Lambert, "Hindu-Muslim Riots" (Ph.D. diss., University of Pennsylvania, 1951), pp. 136–37.

was really a spin-off.[15] Whatever the specific ethnic environment, selective targeting is a widespread phenomenon that operates either to shield some groups completely from harm or to render some, more than others, fair game for the thrust of a dagger or the blow of a club.[16]

The reason for selective targeting and for intense violence against the targets chosen resides in an easily overlooked feature of riots. In the eyes of the participants, the violence must be justified or fitting, and the rationale for interpersonal violence resides in the antecedent conduct imputed to the target group.[17] The perpetrators and the victims must, therefore, be seen together. The victims of rioting are not merely passive recipients whose fate is determined entirely by events beyond their control or by the random behavior of those who inflict the violence. The characteristics and conduct of the target group play a prominent role in attracting violent attacks. To assert this is emphatically not to cast responsibility for the violence on those who suffer as a result. It is, rather, to reaffirm what has been observed repeatedly by students of aggression in general — that the aggressor is curiously dependent on the victim. The source of the target choice is located in their relationship and in the characteristics believed to be displayed by the targets and implicitly compared to those believed to be displayed by the aggressors. As Hans Toch says, "Psychological states or traits of one party may evoke traits or states of the other that would remain dormant elsewhere."[18]

THE AVERSION TO FALSE POSITIVES

The methods of target selection and the generally high levels of accuracy achieved point to a species of risk aversion exhibited by those who do the

15. Moon, *Divide and Quit*, passim; see, e.g., p. 262.

16. Exceptions to this rule are rare. The Bombay riot of February 1969 may be one of them. From the linguistic breakdown of those arrested, it seems that several different antipathies may have been expressed simultaneously. *Times of India*, April 16, 1969, p. 8. (I am indebted to Mary F. Katzenstein for this material.) Madagascar (1972) may have been another exception. See *New York Times*, December 15, 1972, p. 10.

17. In an experiment, subjects who believed their arousal was due to an external cause were less aggressive to a potential target than those who believed their arousal was due to the insulting behavior of the target. Mary B. Harris and Lily C. Huang, "Aggression and the Attribution Process," *Journal of Social Psychology* 92, Second Half (April 1974): 209–16. In a survey, the most common justification of violence (by far) focused on the behavior of the victim; target identity was also related to the likelihood of justification. Alan Jay Lincoln, "Preactivity Justification of Violent Behavior as a Function of Target Identity," *College Student Journal* 7, no. 4 (November 1973): 83–87.

18. Hans Toch, "The Catalytic Situation in the Violence Equation," *Journal of Applied Social Psychology* 15, no. 2 (1985): 105–23, at p. 114.

killing. Sometimes identification of prospective victims is easy. Examples include Sikhs in India, usually recognized by their uncut hair and long beards, Ahmadis in Pakistan, identified by their short beards,[19] and Uzbeks in Kyrghyzstan, distinguished by their skullcaps.[20] These features are, of course, alterable. Even without alteration, many features that identify groups are far from visible. In a substantial number of cases, it takes some effort to distinguish potential victims from members of other groups, including the attacking group. What is remarkable is how much attention the aggressors are prepared to lavish on this task when they sense the need to do so.

Prospective victims may be inspected physically and interrogated to determine their identity. If the sequence of tests devised by the leaders of the crowd is inapt for this purpose, mistakes will be made, as one was when a Sinhalese mob sought to distinguish Sinhalese from Tamil victims by requiring a prospective victim to recite Buddhist stanzas in Pali. Most Sinhalese are Buddhists. Tamils are not. As it happened, however, the particular Sinhalese being questioned was a Christian. Unable to oblige the crowd with the recitation, he was murdered.[21]

In spite of such mistakes, identifications are usually made with care. Reliability is achieved by a strategy that risks false negatives over false positives. After all, the aims of the rioters are threefold: (1) to kill members of Group B; (2) not to kill members of non-target stranger Groups C, D, and E; and (3) not to kill members of Group A, the attacking group.[22] These aims make sense if the violence really does have ethnic-group objectives, however inarticulate they may be. Where uncertainty is present in the identity of a possible victim, the desire not to risk killing a member of Group A often takes precedence over the desire to kill members of Group B. The result is that most of the identification mistakes made by rioters seem to involve false negatives rather than false positives—hence the very few cases in which members of the attacking group (or a third group) are killed in error, but the many cases in which members of the target group are not killed because of uncertainty.

If, for example, language generally differentiates the groups, the rare member of a target group who happens to be fluent in the language of

19. See *Report of the Court of Inquiry Constituted under Punjab Act II of 1954 to Enquire into the Punjab Disturbances of 1953* (Lahore: Superintendent of Government Printing, Punjab, 1954), p. 14.

20. Tishkov, "Don't Kill Me, I Am Kyrghyz," p. 18.

21. Vittachi, *Emergency '58*, p. 49; see also ibid., p. 54.

22. See, e.g., Valli Kanapathipillai, "July 1983: The Survivor's Experience," in Veena Das, ed., *Mirrors of Violence: Communities, Riots and Survivors in South Asia* (Delhi: Oxford University Press, 1990), pp. 321–44, at pp. 335–36.

the attackers can pass a language test administered by the mob and escape unscathed.[23] In ambiguous cases, the interrogation may be extensive. In Sri Lanka (1983), Sinhalese rioters suspected a man in a car of being a Tamil. Having stopped the car, they inquired about his peculiar accent in Sinhala, which he explained by his lengthy stay in England and his marriage to an English woman. Uncertain, but able to prevent his escape, the rioters went off to kill other Tamils, returning later to question the prospective victim further. Eventually, he was allowed to proceed on his way, even though the mob knew it risked making a mistake, which in fact it had: the man was a Tamil.[24]

The implication of the risk-averse strategy pursued by such crowds is that fewer people are killed in many ethnic riots than could be killed if identifications could be made more efficiently in doubtful cases. Corroboration for this conclusion is found in the common tendency of rioters who are engaged in burning houses not to burn the houses of members of the target group if that arson would risk destroying a nearby house owned by a member of the attacking group.[25] To guard against false positives, members of the perpetrator group who might be misidentified and victimized typically take precautions to distinguish themselves from members of the target group. These include posting identifying signs on structures that might be set alight.[26] Where planning is in evidence, so, frequently, is the use of maps or lists to identify target-group homes and businesses in advance. In Bombay (1984), tax lists were used to identify Muslim-owned shops; in Sri Lanka (1983), electoral lists were used to locate Tamils; and in Baku (1990), mimeographed address lists of Armenians were circulated.[27] Furthermore, as the Sudanese account

23. For such cases, see *Report of the Presidential Commission of Inquiry into the Incidents Which Took Place between 13th August and 15th September 1977*, p. 166; Tishkov, "Don't Kill Me, I Am Kyrghyz," p. 18.

24. I am drawing here on a lengthy account provided to me by the near victim, in Iowa City, Iowa, October 14, 1988.

25. For exactly this phenomenon, see Feldberg, *The Philadelphia Riots of 1844*, p. 112. The same phenomenon has been observable in anti-Roma riots in Romania. Roma houses are burned down, but not where Romanian houses might be jeopardized. I am drawing on interviews conducted at several sites of such burnings, as well as in Bucharest, between February 6 and 12, 1994. That is not to say that crowds bent on arson are always so careful. See Christopher Hibbert, *King Mob: The Story of Lord George Gordon and the Riots of 1780* (New York: Dorset Press, 1989), p. 108.

26. See, e.g., Hibbert, *King Mob*, p. 85. In Fergana, Uzbekistan (1989), Uzbek houses were marked with shreds of red cloth, to signal rioters not to touch them. So reported Moscow television, June 6, 1989, in FBIS-SOV-89-108, June 7, 1989, p. 34.

27. See, respectively, Asghar Ali Engineer, *Bhiwandi-Bombay Riots* (Bombay: Institute of Islamic Studies, 1984), pp. 15, 37; Gananath Obeyesekere, "The Origins and

quoted above states, attackers also screen out members of Groups C, D, and E, who might otherwise be plausible recipients of violence. The crowd takes its mission seriously, and it achieves accuracy at a price in the magnitude of the killing that would otherwise be possible.

TARGET SELECTION: THE STARTING POINTS

If the crowd is intent on precision in targeting, what guides its choice of target groups? It is possible for analysts to construct retrospective rationalizations for the particular choices made, but too often this is accomplished by neglecting the genuine plausibility of alternative target groups for the fury of the attackers. After the fact, target choices look too natural: they need to be rendered more problematic, so as to require explanation. One can assume, for example, that the crowd is attempting to exact retribution for some recent affront; or one can equally assume that hostility is embedded in the deep fabric of ethnic relations. The two possibilities may point to completely different target groups.

The Nigerian case is a good example of the problematic character of target choice. By the 1950s, there were rather large groups of Ibo, Yoruba, and other southerners in northern Nigerian towns. Yet, in the northern riot of 1953, as in that of 1945 as well as in the massive waves of rioting that took place in 1966, the victims were exclusively Ibo and a few other easterners. The large Yoruba community in the north was not attacked. Yoruba immunity seems particularly curious in the light of the events that culminated in the 1953 riots.

Behind this outburst lay serious differences of opinion between the dominant northern party, the Northern People's Congress (NPC), and both southern parties, the eastern (heavily Ibo) National Council of Nigerian Citizens (NCNC) and the western (that is, Yoruba) Action Group. In the weeks preceding the disturbances, the southern parties had been pressing for early self-government.[28] Reflecting northern fears of the prospect of southern hegemony and of the north's lack of prepara-

---

Institutionalization of Political Violence," in James Manor, ed., *Sri Lanka in Change and Crisis* (New York: St. Martin's Press, 1984), p. 153; *New York Times*, January 15, 1990, p. A1. Cf. Claire Mouradian, "The Mountainous Karabagh Question: An Inter-Ethnic Conflict or Decolonization Crisis?" *Armenian Review* 43, nos. 2–3 (Summer–Fall 1990): 1–34, at p. 17, reporting that, in the Sumgait riot of 1988, Armenian flats had previously been spotted and phone lines cut.

28. For the background, see James S. Coleman, *Nigeria: Background to Nationalism* (Berkeley and Los Angeles: University of California Press, 1958), pp. 396–400.

tion for competition in a self-governing Nigeria, the NPC had resisted what it regarded as the excessively rapid timetable of constitutional change advocated by the NCNC and the Action Group. A month before the Kano riots, the issue had come to a head in the Nigerian House of Representatives, meeting in Lagos.[29] Lagos was situated in the Western Region, which is Yoruba territory. During the House session, NPC leaders were heckled, and the Action Group leader made a highly pejorative and deeply resented reference to Dan Fodio, the northern culture-hero who had begun a Fulani holy war in the nineteenth century. Outside the assembly, the northern representatives were derided and reproached by angry crowds for their "reactionary" and "pro-imperialist" position. The action of these mobs was subsequently attributed by the NPC leader and the most powerful man in the north, the Sardauna of Sokoto, to the instigation of the Action Group.[30]

Following the assembly session, the NPC escalated the dispute by moving toward a northern separatist position. On their part, the Action Group and the NCNC jointly undertook a political tour of the north, intended, as an Action Group newspaper described it, "to educate the masses" of northerners to the nationalist position. The southern parties had decided to make a concerted assault on what they characterized as the retrograde attitude of British "officialdom and their stooges, the Sardauna group . . . ."[31] The Action Group's first stop was Kano. There the Hausa crowd sprang into action, beginning several days of rioting that cost at least 36 lives and hundreds of injuries.

Although Ibo were much more numerous in Kano, the city had a large and conspicuous Yoruba population.[32] At the very least, the affronts that preceded the violence were the shared responsibility of the Ibo and Yoruba parties. More likely, Yoruba would have been blamed. As noted above, the Sardauna of Sokoto, who had been the butt of the southern parties' vituperations, laid responsibility at the door of the Action Group.

---

29. See Northern Regional Government, Government of Nigeria, *Report on the Kano Disturbances, 16th, 17th, 18th and 19th May, 1953* (Kaduna: Government Printer, 1953), p. 4.

30. Alhaji Sir Ahmadu Bello, *My Life* (Cambridge: Cambridge University Press, 1962), pp. 136–37.

31. Northern Regional Government, *Report on the Kano Disturbances*, p. 6.

32. Ibo were about 59 percent of the population of the strangers' quarter of Kano; Yoruba and related groups, more than a quarter of that population. Northerners tended to see the strangers' quarter "as including three ethnic groups: Ibo, Yoruba, and 'other.'" John N. Paden, "Communal Competition, Conflict and Violence in Kano," in Robert Melson and Howard Wolpe, eds., *Modernization and the Politics of Communalism* (East Lansing: Michigan State University Press, 1971), pp. 113–44, at p. 120.

The immediate provocation for the killing was a meeting to be held by that party; the Ibo delegation had not appeared in Kano. Despite this background, not a single Yoruba was killed at Kano.[33] The southern casualties were from the Eastern Region, mainly Ibo, a fact that is puzzling not only to outside observers. The Sardauna himself later expressed surprise that, in view of the Action Group's role in the earlier provocations, the Yoruba had not been involved in the fighting.[34] For him, the target choice was problematic.

The same pattern of selective targeting was present in the northern Nigerian riots in 1945 and twice in 1966. There were then quite different sets of precipitants, in each case more clearly identified with Ibo. Still, the enemy was not defined inclusively, as it might have been, to encompass all southerners. Instead, Yoruba again were able to remain aloof from the killings and were sorted out when encountered. So immune were they from attack that some Ibo reportedly escaped injury by masquerading as Yoruba.[35]

It might be said of the Kano riots that they were in reality not brought on by the events that immediately preceded them, but by deeper, more long-range concerns. Perhaps so, but at least some research indicates that Yoruba may have been more ethnocentric than were Ibo and that Hausa in Kano (and elsewhere in the north) tended to be more favorably disposed to Ibo.[36] The "deeper" explanation will have to be more specific. It will certainly need to move beyond mere distaste.

Moreover, the opposite of a deep-fabric explanation might be argued for the Burmese riots of 1938. If the Kano rioters seemed indifferent to the identification of the precipitating events with Yoruba, Burman rioters seemed to pay close attention to the events immediately preceding the violence. In Burma, the precipitant seems more clearly connected to the targets who were chosen.

The Burmese killings have often been attributed to the growing economic hardship of the Burman masses and, to a much lesser extent, the marriage of Burman women to Indian men.[37] The difficulty with these

33. Northern Regional Government, *Report on the Kano Disturbances*, pp. 20–21.
34. Ahmadu Bello, *My Life*, pp. 136–37.
35. See note 9, above.
36. Margaret Peil, "Interethnic Contacts in Nigerian Cities" (paper presented at the annual meeting of the African Studies Association, Syracuse, N.Y., November 1973).
37. Fred R. von der Mehden, *Religion and Nationalism in Southeast Asia* (Madison: University of Wisconsin Press, 1963), pp. 167–69; Donald Eugene Smith, *Religion and Politics in Burma* (Princeton: Princeton University Press, 1965), pp. 109–11; cf. F.S.V. Donnison, *Burma* (London: Benn, 1970), pp. 119, 121.

explanations derived from underlying trends is that they point to opposite targets. The economic problem reached crisis proportions in rural areas of Lower Burma and in certain urban areas, where, during the depression of the 1930s, an extraordinarily large proportion of available land passed from Burman owners to Indian Chettiar — Hindu — moneylenders. The intermarriage problem also had serious consequences in inheritance, religion, and the status of children of mixed unions, but the men who chose Burman brides were primarily Muslims.

The precipitant of the Burmese riots, however, points in the direction of one target, and the statistics on target choice are consistent with the precipitant. In Burma, Hindus were not entirely unvictimized, as Yoruba were in Kano, for this is a case of subethnic emphasis in targeting, rather than nearly perfect ethnic selectivity. (It is not the only case of subethnic emphasis in targeting that we shall observe.) Nevertheless, a strong preference for Muslim targets was palpable and consistent across the country.

The Burmese violence was triggered by Buddhist outrage over a book by a Muslim containing unflattering references to the Buddha. During the riots, Burman crowds took special pains to search out and attack Muslims. This concentration of effort was mirrored in the official casualty figures: among the Indians, 139 Muslims, but only 25 Hindus and 13 adherents of other religions, were killed.[38] By official estimate,[39] Muslims lost some 1.6 million rupees in property, compared to Hindu losses of Rs.157,000. The degree to which this does reflect selective targeting is made abundantly plain by the fact that the 1931 census revealed an imbalance within the Indian population *in favor of Hindus*. Nearly 60 percent of the Indian population of Burma was Hindu at that time.[40] By 1938, the proportion was undoubtedly greater, for nearly all the Indian migrants to Burma in the first decades of the century were Hindu rather than Muslim.[41] If, then, targeting in the Kano riot cannot be explained without reference to the whole context of ethnic relations, in the Burmese case the further one strays from the precipitant into the broader context, the more confusing the actual target choice appears.

Clearly, selective targeting is a major problem that has not received sustained attention. As the Nigerian and Burmese cases demonstrate,

38. Government of Burma, *Final Report of the Riot Inquiry Committee* (Rangoon, 1939), p. 281.

39. Ibid., Appendix XI.

40. Ibid., p. 19.

41. Ibid.

target selection does not lend itself to obvious explanation, even in single societies; still less does it do so comparatively. To generate conclusions that have an acceptable measure of cross-cultural validity, we must attempt to identify patterns of target selection. But first it will be necessary to deal with the possibility that the only target characteristics that count are accessibility and inability to retaliate.

STRONG OR WEAK TARGETS?
THE QUESTION OF DISPLACED AGGRESSION

Fear of retribution tends to inhibit violence.[42] This basic behavioral propensity has led some psychologists and others to suggest that aggression is likely to be directed at helpless targets, because of their inability to retaliate or to persuade state authorities to retaliate in their behalf.[43] There is also much conventional wisdom arguing that victims of ethnic violence are inevitably members of weak, defenseless groups — in a word, scapegoats — and a concomitant tendency to neglect the elements of conflict between attackers and those attacked.[44]

The implications of this issue for a theory of target selection are enormous. If the victims of ethnic violence are simply helpless recipients of attacks that might, under different circumstances, be directed at others, then target characteristics may matter less than sheer availability does. If, on the other hand, victims are chosen because of characteristics they possess, it becomes necessary to specify patterns of target selection.

The issue is important for another reason as well. If the victims receive displaced aggression, it is useful to inquire into the conditions that foster the redirection of violence from one set of targets to another.

---

42. See generally Leonard Berkowitz, *Aggression: A Social-Psychological Analysis* (New York: McGraw-Hill, 1962), pp. 73–103.

43. Richard H. Walters, "Implications of Laboratory Studies of Aggression for the Control and Regulation of Violence," *The Annals* 364 (March 1966): 69–70. See also Ted Robert Gurr, *Why Men Rebel* (Princeton: Princeton University Press, 1970), p. 207; Ezra F. Vogel and Norman W. Bell, "The Emotionally Disturbed Child as the Family Scapegoat," in Norman W. Bell and Ezra F. Vogel, eds., *A Modern Introduction to the Family* (New York: Free Press, 1960), pp. 382–97. Cf. Ralph Epstein, "Aggression toward Outgroups as a Function of Authoritarianism and Imitation of Aggressive Models," *Journal of Personality and Social Psychology* 3, no. 5 (May 1966): 574–79, at p. 577, suggesting that the perception of divisions within a potential target group serves as a vulnerability cue, facilitating aggression against the divided group.

44. See Talcott Parsons, "Certain Primary Sources and Patterns of Aggression in the Social Structure of the Western World," *Psychiatry* 10, no. 2 (May 1947): 167–81.

FRUSTRATION-AGGRESSION THEORY
AND TARGET STRENGTH

The most frequently invoked — although much disputed — explanation of individual violence, the well-known frustration-aggression theory,[45] does not shed much light on patterns of target choice,[46] but it does provide insight into the displacement issue. Frustration-aggression theory postulates that aggression is the result of anger produced by the thwarting of goal-directed activity. Restraints or inhibitions may, however, channel anger into nonaggressive behavior or deflect it onto objects other than the original source of the frustration. If the source or instigator of anger is attacked, the aggression is termed *direct*. If another target is chosen, the aggression is *displaced*. Aggression is displaced if the frustrater is too remote, too inaccessible, or too powerful to be made the target of an aggressive response.

In the frustration-aggression paradigm, aggression is conceived as the outcome of a contest between anger and inhibitions on expressing that anger. Against weak targets, there may be little inhibition, but also little anger. Against strong targets, there may be great anger but also great inhibition, deriving from, among other things, fear or respect. If this were all there were to such formulations, there would be relatively little aggression, and, in a certain sense, such statements help explain the episodic character of aggression, why violence is not present all the time.

The story, however, is more complicated. As regards particular potential targets, the strength of anger and the strength of inhibitions on its expression vary separately. The further removed the potential target is from the original frustrater, the weaker are both anger and inhibitions on expressing anger. But anger and inhibitions decline at different rates, and inhibitions may decline more rapidly than anger; so that whereas inhibitions initially exceed anger, it is possible that at some distance from the frustrater, anger will exceed inhibitions. It then becomes possible to plot

---

45. Originally formulated by John Dollard et al., *Frustration and Aggression* (New Haven: Yale University Press, 1939). See also Berkowitz, *Aggression: A Social-Psychological Analysis*; Aubrey Yates, *Frustration and Conflict* (London: Methuen, 1962); and the concise statement by Berkowitz, "Aggression: Psychological Aspects," in David Sills, ed., *International Encyclopedia of the Social Sciences*, I (New York: Macmillan, 1968), pp. 168–74. Another summary is provided in Leonard Berkowitz, "Frustration-Aggression Hypothesis: Examination and Reformulation," *Psychological Bulletin* 106, no. 1 (July 1989): 59–73. This section draws on Donald L. Horowitz, "Direct, Displaced, and Cumulative Ethnic Aggression," *Comparative Politics* 6, no. 1 (October 1973): 1–16.

46. See Hubert M. Blalock, Jr., *Toward a Theory of Minority-Group Relations* (New York: John Wiley & Sons, 1967), p. 44.

the separate gradients of these two tendencies vis-à-vis targets of varying degrees of similarity to, or association with, the original frustrater. If inhibitions do indeed decline at a faster rate than anger as the injured party confronts potential targets at increasing (physical and social) distances from the frustrater, aggression becomes possible at the point when the level of anger surpasses the level of inhibitions. The strongest aggressive response occurs when the level of anger most exceeds the level of inhibitions, and that is predicted to be when the potential target retains a moderate degree of similarity to the initial frustrater.[47] If the target is too closely identified with the frustrater, the same restraints will ordinarily operate to inhibit aggression against the substitute.[48] If the potential target is too far removed, on the other hand, he or she is no longer a credible substitute to receive displaced aggression. Consequently, targets of displaced aggression are unlikely to be helpless.[49] In fact, possibly also because displaced aggression is often aimed at retrieving a wounded self-esteem, the targets tend to be moderately strong.[50] I shall soon add some further reasons for target-group strength.

CUMULATION: THE CONJUNCTION OF DIRECT AND DISPLACED AGGRESSION

Thus far the assumption has been that direct and displaced aggression are straightforward alternatives to each other, but there are reasons to think that a target may receive direct and displaced aggression simultaneously. It has long been recognized that prejudiced individuals frequently harbor hostile feelings toward more than one stranger-group.[51]

---

47. For a concise model of this process, see Berkowitz, *Aggression: A Social-Psychological Analysis*, pp. 104–31, especially the diagrams on p. 108. See also Don Fitz, "A Renewed Look at Miller's Conflict Theory of Aggression Displacement," *Journal of Personality and Social Psychology* 33, no. 6 (June 1976): 725–32.

48. For cross-cultural evidence suggesting that inhibitions on aggression tend to focus aggression on targets far out on the generalization continuum, see George O. Wright, "Projection and Displacement: A Cross-Cultural Study of Folk-Tale Aggression," *Journal of Abnormal and Social Psychology* 49, no. 4 (October 1954): 523–28. But for experimental evidence that where frustration and inhibition are both high the most similar substitute target receives more aggression than does the frustrater or an alternative, less similar target, see Lynn Stewart Hewitt, "Attack, Inhibition and Target of Aggression," *European Journal of Social Psychology* 5, no. 1 (n.m. 1975): 35–47.

49. See Berkowitz, *Aggression: A Social-Psychological Analysis*, pp. 139–40.

50. Ralph White and Ronald Lippitt, *Autocracy and Democracy: An Experimental Inquiry* (New York: Harper, 1960), p. 166.

51. Gordon W. Allport, *The Nature of Prejudice* (Cambridge, Mass.: Addison-Wesley, 1954), pp. 68–69, 404.

The same is true of groups: they may entertain multiple antipathies. If, in such cases, an initiator of aggression attacks only one target, it is reasonable to hypothesize that the single target may receive more than its share of violence. Moreover, it has been pointed out that a prior dislike for certain categories of people tends to make them more likely to become targets for displaced aggression and to receive more intense attacks than would be received by others.[52] Aggression against an already-disliked target group may not be entirely displaced; the aggression may combine direct and displaced features.

Consequently, rather than thinking in the mutually exclusive terms of direct or displaced aggression, it may be preferable to consider the possibility of cumulative aggression, attacks produced by the conjunction of different sets of frustrations or grievances but directed at fewer than all of the frustrating groups. If a target group simultaneously receives direct and displaced aggression, then it is easier to understand the intensity of certain violent outbursts, which otherwise seems inexplicable. Some initiators of violence may well be fighting what amount to wars on two fronts, but all their fire may be trained on one target.

These conflicts take two main forms, both of which exemplify the merger of direct and displaced aggression in attacks on a single target group. The first involves the inhibition of attacks against ascriptive superiors and the resulting redirection of the inhibited violence against parallel ethnic groups. The second involves a pattern of oscillation, in which conflicts against superiors alternate with conflicts against parallel groups. In both cases, when aggression is inhibited against superiors, there is reason to think that parallel groups receive it as an extra measure of violence — that is, that the aggression is not merely displaced but cumulative.

Inhibited Violence.   The Burmese riot of 1938, directed against Indian Muslims, provides a good illustration of inhibited violence that is redirected. Burma had experienced anti-Indian rioting in 1930, and it had also undergone the anticolonial Saya San rebellion of 1930–31.[53] The defeat of that uprising by a British army did not destroy the Burman

---

52. Leonard Berkowitz, *Aggression: Its Causes, Consequences, and Control* (Philadelphia: Temple University Press, 1993), pp. 77–78; Peter Marsh, Elizabeth Rosser, and Rom Harré, *The Rules of Disorder* (London: Routledge and Kegan Paul, 1978), p. 110; Berkowitz, *Aggression: A Social-Psychological Analysis*, pp. 152–60; Leonard Berkowitz and J.A. Green, "The Stimulus Qualities of the Scapegoat," *Journal of Abnormal and Social Psychology* 64, no. 4 (April 1962): 293–301.

53. See Smith, *Religion and Politics in Burma*, p. 107.

sense of oppression. Anticolonial sentiment, reflected in both the Rangoon and the provincial press, clearly played a significant part in the spread of the 1938 anti-Indian riot. That riot began with a protest procession against the book that insulted the Buddha. When the procession turned on Indian passersby, it was dispersed by the forcible action of the police, including a number of British and Eurasian sergeants. The newspapers of the following day carried outraged stories and photographs of the brutality of the colonial police against monks who, though leading a mob, were portrayed by the press as innocent victims of European barbarism. The brunt of the wrath of the Burmese press was thus directed against the British, not against Indians; but when the violence began two days later, the anger of Burmans was turned neither against the British police nor against colonial officers nor against British civilians in Burma. Despite the authoritative description of the first day's action as a prime example of British brutality, only Indians were attacked.

Recollection of the failure of the Saya San revolt may have made anti-British action seem futile. The forcible action of police officers may have inhibited further assaults on them. Neither of these restraints necessarily applied to violence against Indians. "In a sense," suggests Donald Eugene Smith, "the Indians became a scapegoat, since the Burmese extremists were not in a position to attack the British government directly."[54] It seems clear that anti-British feeling, exemplified by the hostility shown toward the European police, contributed to the occurrence and probably to the magnitude of the violence borne by the Indians.

Yet, if this was displaced aggression, as it surely was, it was also direct aggression. Antipathy toward the Indians had roots outside the sphere of Anglo-Burman relations, and the specific choice of Indian Muslims cannot be explained in terms of any special association they had with the British. Consequently, direct and displaced aggression must have merged.

The same inference can be drawn in a variety of other riots in which grievances against Europeans or against a colonial administration were channeled into violence against non-European targets.[55] The patterning of these riots supports the view that grievances against inaccessible superiors may increase the likelihood of violent action directed at parallel ethnic groups. Consider briefly several such cases.

The Durban riot of 1949 was preceded by the victory of the National

54. Ibid., p. 111.
55. For two such cases, one from Guinea and one from Indonesia, see Virginia Thompson and Richard Adloff, *French West Africa* (Stanford: Stanford University Press, 1957), p. 136; The Siauw Giap, "Group Conflict in a Plural Society," *Revue du Sud-Est Asiatique*, no. 1 (1966): 1–31, at pp. 23–24.

Party in the 1948 South African election, a victory that portended unfavorable changes in the structure of white-black relations and that was followed by the *apartheid* legislation of the 1950s. However, no whites were targeted in these riots, which were directed solely at Indians. The frustrations of the color stratification system, coupled with anticipation of its increasing rigidity, probably had something to do with the violence, displaced onto Indian targets. Yet it is also possible to interpret the Durban riot as an expression of direct aggression produced by grievances against Indians — which is how that riot has generally been interpreted.[56] The two interpretations are mutually compatible.

Violence against Fulani in Guinea in the mid-1950s probably drew added impetus from the anti-French feeling widely prevalent at the time. Favored by the French, the Fulani made especially apt targets, because they had adapted to the colonial regime. Moreover, the French displayed a preference for the more conservative party associated with the Fulani, and the riots began in connection with party rivalries. For displacement purposes, therefore, the Fulani were in several ways associated with the frustrations engendered by the colonial presence.[57] At the same time, however, there were probably independent reasons for attacking the Fulani: traditional antipathy between other groups and Fulani invaders; Fulani disaffection from the mainstream of nationalist sentiment and from the nationalist party; their separatist political tendencies; and their alleged pretensions to superiority. So, if displacement did indeed occur, it undoubtedly merged with what must be classified as direct aggression.

In a similar way, the 1958 riot next door in the Ivory Coast by Ivorians against Dahomeyans and Togolese took place against a background of Ivorian resentment at the prominence given by President Félix Houphouët-Boigny to the participation of non-Ivorians in the Ivory Coast branch of the nationalist party, the Rassemblement Démocratique Africain (RDA). In the municipal elections of 1956, for example, the RDA list for Abidjan included fifteen Ivorians, nine foreign Africans, and seven Frenchmen.[58] Yet, resentment at the overrepresentation of eth-

56. Tamotsu Shibutani and Kian M. Kwan, *Ethnic Stratification: A Comparative Approach* (New York: Macmillan, 1965), pp. 168, 197; Gwendolen M. Carter, *The Politics of Inequality: South Africa since 1948* (New York: Praeger, 1958), pp. 21, 361. Cf. Leo Kuper, *An African Bourgeoisie: Race, Class, and Politics in South Africa* (New Haven: Yale University Press, 1965), p. 301.

57. For another instance in which a group associated with the colonizers was made the object of a (probably displaced) attack as independence approached, see Thomas Turner, "Congo-Kinshasa," in Victor A. Olorunsola, ed., *The Politics of Cultural Sub-Nationalism in Africa* (Garden City, N.Y.: Anchor Books, 1972), p. 271 n. 81.

58. Gwendolen Carter, *Independence for Africa* (New York: Praeger, 1960), p. 112.

nic strangers in the party was not principally a grievance against Dahomeyans and Togolese but against Voltaics (largely Mossi) and Europeans.
Houphouët, however, had invested his prestige in ethnic harmony within
the party and in harmonious relations with France; and so, again, displacement may have occurred, with the Dahomeyans and Togolese left to
bear the brunt of Ivorian indignation. As Aristide Zolberg has pointed
out, "the level of frustration among civil servants and youth groups ran
high after the referendum [of 1958 on the French Community, in which
Houphouët successfully urged a 'yes' vote] because they had not been
allowed to vent freely their anti-European and anti-colonial feelings. It is
possible that foreign Africans constituted a convenient object for displaced aggressions."[59] But it is also true that middle-class careerist grievances existed with special strength against the Dahomeyans and
Togolese, who were also disliked for what was believed to be their arrogance and aggressiveness. Even in 1969, long after Dahomeyan and
Togolese influence and numbers had been drastically reduced, a sample
survey in the Ivory Coast showed Ivorians to be far more hostile toward
Dahomeyans and Togolese than toward Voltaics.[60] Here, too, there is the
suggestion of cumulation rather than mere scapegoating.

The 1969 survey, however, coincided with a still different set of tensions expressed in violence. Vertical strains were certainly no less pronounced than a decade before and may actually have been more pronounced. Between 1950 and 1965, the European population had trebled,
giving rise to what has aptly been called an "*éminence blanche.*"[61]
Houphouët's policy of protection remained unaltered. European employers, for their part, entertained decided ethnic preferences for certain jobs.
Mossi were often preferred to Ivorian laborers because of their presumed
reliability, steadfastness, and industry — qualities that seemed to give the
strangers the advantage in those skills required for successful competition
in a modern urban setting. To Ivorian resentment of the rewards and prerogatives enjoyed by the Europeans and their governmental allies were
added the frustrations of competing against people who seemed to start
out ahead. The violence of 1969 began in an employment exchange in a
situation that brought all of these strands together. A European employer
requested a driver, specifying Mossi. When Ivorian applicants demanded

59. Aristide Zolberg, *One-Party Government in the Ivory Coast*, rev. ed. (Princeton:
Princeton University Press, 1969), p. 247.

60. Institut Ivoirien d'Opinion Publique, *Etude Trimestrielle, Decembre 1968–Janvier
1969* (Abidjan, 1969), p. 8, cited in Michael A. Cohen, "Urban Policy and Political Conflict
in Africa: A Study of the Ivory Coast" (Ph.D. diss., University of Chicago, 1971), p. 367.

61. Ruth First, *Power in Africa* (Harmondsworth: Penguin Books, 1972), p. 72.

to know why, the European employer replied that the Mossi could be depended upon. The implication was that Ivorians could not be. The European escaped with a beating, but the Mossi who had come forward for the job reportedly lost his life.[62]

The weeks that followed were filled with expressions of Ivorian hostility, but only toward Mossi and other Voltaics. Aggression against Europeans was inhibited and presumably merged in the anti-Mossi aggression.[63] Perhaps because of the lower level of hostility felt toward the Voltaics, a fact confirmed by sample surveys,[64] the intensity of the aggression and the number of casualties in 1969 were much lower than in 1958 when the targets were Dahomeyans and Togolese. This variation tends to confirm the importance of the element of direct aggression in two riots that also involved displacement. Direct aggression was likely greater in the 1958 riot than in the 1969 riot.

Displaced aggression also characterized the anti-Chinese violence in Indonesia between 1996 and 1998. In several locations in Java (1996 and 1997), Muslim crowds, outraged by various government actions, converted antigovernment protests into violence against Chinese shops and churches. In May 1998, in Jakarta, army killings of several students produced crowd reactions that alternated between looting and anti-Chinese attacks. Many more looters were burned to death in shopping malls set ablaze than Chinese were killed, and the violence ceased abruptly upon the overthrow of the Suharto regime — a sure sign that the disorder was entangled in popular resentment against the well-defended regime, resentment redirected against the Chinese.[65]

In all of these cases, the expression of anger against superiors was inhibited. And it seems reasonable to conclude that the inhibited anger was redirected against other targets, where it merged with greater or lesser anger against them to produce a single violent outburst.

62. I am indebted to Michael A. Cohen for this description. The interpretation given it is mine. See also Efrem Sigel, "Ivory Coast: Booming Economy, Political Calm," *Africa Report* 15, no. 4 (April 1970): 18–21; J.L., "New Developments in French-speaking Africa," *Civilisations* 20, no. 2 (Second Quarter 1970): 270–78.

63. In the relatively few cases where disputes between contending ethnic labor pools have developed into ethnic riots, displacement of aggression from European employers onto ethnic antagonists is probably the rule. In addition to the Ivory Coast case, see Usha Mahajani, *The Role of Indian Minorities in Burma and Malaya* (Bombay: Vora, 1960), pp. 71–79.

64. See Michael A. Cohen, *Urban Policy and Political Conflict in Africa: A Study of the Ivory Coast* (Chicago: University of Chicago Press, 1974), p. 75.

65. I am drawing here on interviews in Jakarta, August 9–14, 1998. Subsequent rounds of violence in 1998, against the Habibie regime, followed roughly the same sequence.

Oscillating Targets.   Not all aggression against superiors is inhibited. Some conflicts oscillate, with the result that targets alternate. Around the time of independence, a number of countries experienced episodes of violence directed at Europeans and at local ethnic groups, but the two rarely occurred simultaneously. It has been remarked that the anti-European violence in Léopoldville (now Kinshasa) in early 1959 had reverberations across the Congo River in Brazzaville. But in spite of the close contacts and ethnic affinities that span the river, the rioting on the Brazzaville side was entirely between Mbochi and Bakongo.[66] Violence in Calcutta in 1945–46 passed by stages from Indian versus European to Hindu versus Muslim. According to Richard Lambert, "Indian Christians and Europeans were generally free from molestation" as the tempo of Hindu-Muslim violence quickened. "It is interesting to note the decline of anti-European feelings as communal [Hindu-Muslim] tensions increased during this period, by the decline of mob burnings of their vehicles. 'During the riots of November 1945, 46 were a total loss; in the riots of the 10th to the 14th February 1946, 35; from the 10th February to the 15th August, only 3; during the Calcutta riots from the 15th August to the 17th September, none.'"[67] In the case of Calcutta, anger against ascriptive superiors was superseded by, and probably subsumed in, much more intense anger against a parallel group.

After independence, colonialists gradually became less significant as superiors, but ascriptive stratification did not disappear. In societies doubly divided into ranked groups and unranked groups, the same oscillating conflicts can be detected.

One clear example makes the point. Conflict between Sinhalese and Tamils in Sri Lanka, which, on several occasions, erupted into serious ethnic riots and later into civil war, actually began as class conflict within the Sinhalese community.[68] Until the 1950s, undisputed elite status had been accorded to those Sinhalese who were westernized, English-speaking, and, to a lesser extent, Christian. (As mentioned earlier, the vast majority of Sinhalese are Buddhists.) For nearly a decade after indepen-

66. Virginia Thompson and Richard Adloff, *The Emerging States of French Equatorial Africa* (Stanford: Stanford University Press, 1960), p. 490.

67. Lambert, "Hindu-Muslim Riots," p. 175, quoting Sir Francis Tuker, *While Memory Serves: The Last Two Years of British Rule in India* (London: Cassell, 1950), p. 179.

68. The paragraphs which follow draw heavily on W. Howard Wriggins, *Ceylon: Dilemmas of a New Nation* (Princeton: Princeton University Press, 1960). See also Robert N. Kearney, *Communalism and Language in the Politics of Ceylon* (Durham: Duke University Press, 1967).

dence in 1948, Sri Lanka was ruled by members of this elite and the party with which they were associated. The reference models of this group were clearly British; many of its members were quite out of touch with Sinhalese culture, some even to the point of lacking fluency in Sinhala, the language of the majority of Sri Lankans.[69] In the years following independence, there was gradually mounting resentment at the power and prerogatives held by this group and generalized discomfort at the extent to which political symbolism seemed to derive from alien sources. The spearhead of this resentment was a social group whose attainments went largely unrewarded and whose elite status in the villages could not be converted into elite status on a national basis. This was the so-called vernacular-educated intelligentsia. The assault on the stratification system crystallized around the issue of *Swabasha*, the movement to displace English with the indigenous languages, Sinhala and Tamil, and the drive to restore to Buddhism its "rightful place," usurped by both Christian and secular influences.

Slowly, this intra-Sinhalese class conflict grew into conflict between the Sinhalese as a whole and the Tamils. Swabasha was construed narrowly by its proponents to include Sinhala but not Tamil, and the religious side of the movement accentuated the divide between the Buddhist Sinhalese and the Hindu Tamils. The 1956 election, in which the party of the old elite was swept from power, marked the relative decline of that group and the entrance into politics of groups previously excluded. By then, the battle had turned against what was seen as a Tamil threat.

There are many indications of this shift from vertical to horizontal conflict: the move from Swabasha to "Sinhala only" (as against Sinhala and Tamil), a move that resulted in the Sinhala-only legislation passed shortly after the 1956 election; the fact that the movement was captured for electoral purposes by a prominent, landowning member of the old elite, S. W. R. D. Bandaranaike; and, most of all, the serious anti-Tamil riots of 1956 and 1958, from which the old Sinhalese elite, however much it disapproved of the violence, emerged unscathed.

Precisely why the transformation occurred is somewhat more difficult to explain. Still, some forces seem identifiable.

For one thing, as Bandaranaike's unchallenged leadership of the

69. For examples, see Donald L. Horowitz, *Coup Theories and Officers' Motives: Sri Lanka in Comparative Perspective* (Princeton: Princeton University Press, 1980), pp. 83, 85–86; Yasmine Gooneratne, *Relative Merits: A Personal Memoir of the Bandaranaike Family of Sri Lanka* (New York: St. Martin's Press, 1986), pp. 54, 73, 75, 77, 85–86, 89, 100, 146.

Sinhalese movement showed, it was not easy to undo the bonds of respect felt in rural areas for members of his class. The entrenched Sinhalese elite could still call upon a reservoir of deference that tended to blunt frustrations or at any rate make them more legitimate and therefore more bearable. It was not a simple matter to mount a full-fledged assault on those of acknowledged high status.[70] On the other hand, the high status of ethnic strangers, whatever their social class, was less likely to receive acknowledgment in the first place.

Furthermore, the Sinhalese elite, recognizing its vulnerable minority status in the context of universal suffrage, responded to the challenge to its prerogatives by becoming increasingly accommodating. Both major Sinhalese parties attempted to bid for the Sinhalese mass vote. The Tamils, of course, could not and did not react by accommodation and outbidding. Each time it appeared that the position of the Tamil language was about to be undermined, the Tamils responded with greater solidarity. Increasingly, Sinhalese saw the Tamils as the major remaining obstacle to the attainment of Sinhalese aspirations.

Finally, there was a paradox inherent in the Sinhalese movement: the more deeply it rooted itself in the Sinhalese countryside, the more likely it was to turn against the Tamils rather than against its initial antagonists. Many of the grievances that set the Sinhala-educated intelligentsia against the English-speaking leadership were elite grievances. As such, they had much less salience among the mass of rural Sinhalese, for whom aspirations to elite status were remote, than did the relative standing of the Sinhalese and Tamil communities as a whole.

The transformation of the Sinhalese conflict is a graphic example of a process that has analogues elsewhere. It has been suggested, for example, that the virulence of Hausa attacks on Ibo in northern Nigeria was partly attributable to the tensions and frustrations engendered by the strongly hierarchical Hausa-Fulani stratification system.[71] Much the same point might be made for Guyana, where the hostility of brown and black members of the Afro-Guyanese population toward the aspirations of East Indians was especially pronounced because of the frustrating rigidities of the Creole color-class system.[72] Some Indonesian riots in the

70. See Janice Jiggins, *Caste and Family in the Politics of the Sinhalese* (Cambridge: Cambridge University Press, 1979), pp. 151–52.

71. James O'Connell, "The Anatomy of a Pogrom: An Outline Model with Special Reference to the Ibo in Northern Nigeria," *Race* 9, no. 1 (July 1967): 95–99.

72. See David Lowenthal, "Race and Color in the West Indies," *Daedalus* 96, no. 2 (Spring 1967): 580–92.

1960s involved attacks both on Chinese and on Indonesian *orang kaya baru* (nouveaux riches), suggesting connections between the two sets of grievances.[73]

Several pertinent conclusions emerge from this evidence. First, in societies containing both ranked and unranked groups, conflict tends to oscillate between the class or caste and the ethnic dimension; rarely do the two fronts receive equal emphasis simultaneously. Second, issues that initially arise in the form of class or caste antagonisms often end by assuming the character of conflicts between parallel groups and may result in violence between such groups. Third, the reverse sequence, it would seem, is rarer; that is, parallel-group conflicts do not tend to be converted into class conflicts, and such riots usually do not later turn against ascriptive superiors. Fourth, an increase in parallel tensions tends to mitigate hierarchical strains and produce greater solidarity across class or caste lines.

THE IMPLICATIONS OF CUMULATION

Aggression against superiors may thus be converted into aggression against unranked groups, and it may be hypothesized that both the likelihood and magnitude of the violence directed at parallel groups are increased by the presence of frustrations generated by ascriptive stratification. The general process is quite consistent with the theory of displacement. Most individuals learn not to antagonize those who occupy high-status roles in their community. The resulting inhibition on attacks against such superiors is a common factor in displacement. But the inhibitions that deter attacks on superiors in one's own ethnic community or subsociety do not apply with equal force to attacks on members of other groups. In this connection, the term ethnic *strangers* is especially appropriate, for it connotes the absence of ties resulting from deference and esteem, on the one hand, and fear of sanctions, on the other.

At the same time, it seems clear that more than displacement alone is involved. The incidence of ethnic riots increased greatly with the end of colonial rule and the reduction of many of the frustrations stemming from it. The targets of postcolonial aggression, even in the early period of independence, are unlikely merely to be receiving aggression intended for

73. J.A.C. Mackie, "Anti-Chinese Outbreaks in Indonesia, 1958–68," in J.A.C. Mackie, ed., *The Chinese in Indonesia* (Hong Kong: Heinemann Educational Books, 1976), pp. 101, 103.

the colonialists. Beyond this, certain groups that initiated riots, even during the colonial period, were not those that most resented the colonialists, but in some cases (for example, Lulua in Zaire, Hausa in Nigeria, and southern Sudanese) those that wanted protection from the colonial power against their domestic antagonists and were not seeking to hasten the colonial departure. The incidence and initiators of riots, as well as selectivity in targeting, tend to controvert the possibility that ethnic violence is solely the product of displacement. It seems highly probable that most ethnic riots are cases either of direct aggression alone or of the convergence of direct and displaced aggression.

The likelihood that some ethnic aggression is cumulative also draws support from the conceptualization of violence as a product of mounting tensions (which are additive), culminating in an outburst when an appropriate precipitating incident occurs.[74] Because time spans in the laboratory are necessarily more compressed, experimental studies have been able to reproduce this gradual rise in anger only most imperfectly. Yet the ability to store anger is a prerequisite to displacement, since substitute targets are not always immediately on the scene. Without that ability, the episodic quality of riots — periods of outward calm, followed by intense outbursts, followed by calm — cannot be explained adequately. If violence does in fact result from the gradual accumulation of frustrations, it is sensible to conclude that the frustrations may derive from more than one source, even though they are ultimately directed at only one of the sources. The person who feels pressed on two sides may indeed respond on only one, but with an intensity of feeling that reflects that doubly difficult situation.[75] If indeed members of Group B are receiving violence, some part of which might otherwise have been intended for other targets, the confluence of the two streams may help account for the intensity of the attacks on Group B.

It is worth repeating, however, that cumulative aggression does not constitute a full explanation for the intensity of ethnic violence. Only in some cases is there evidence of displacement. Most of the time, the explanation for violence and its intensity must be sought in the relations between the target group and the perpetrator group, a point I shall make more forcefully in a moment and repeatedly thereafter.

74. Hans Toch, *Violent Men: An Inquiry into the Psychology of Violence* (Chicago: Aldine, 1969), pp. 196–97.

75. For comments on the general notion of cumulative aggression, see Michael Billig, *Social Psychology and Intergroup Relations* (London: Academic Press, 1976), pp. 175–76.

BEYOND DISPLACEMENT:
STRONG TARGETS, WEAK MOMENTS

So far, there is not much support for the vulnerability hypothesis for target choice. Experimental data indicate that provocative targets are more likely victims of aggression than are nonprovocative targets and that aggression may be regarded as less legitimate when the victim is weak or fails to retaliate.[76] Men are attacked in riots and singled out for atrocities much more than women are, just as males are attacked more frequently than females are in experiments, and the skewing in both seems positively related to the strength of the target.[77] (In experiments, males are also more selective in their choice of targets; females distribute shocks more equally among targets. Perhaps selective targeting itself is a sex-skewed phenomenon.[78]) While target strength no doubt bolsters inhibition, the importance of normative sanctioning of violence — that is, that the violence be regarded as justifiable — also means that those who are strong and capable of retaliating may be prone to receive violence. To be sure, sometimes the strength of prospective targets is exaggerated, precisely to guarantee that the violence is seen by the participants as legitimate; but, despite the ability to exaggerate, the weakness of possible targets does not commend them to the perpetrators as appropriate victims.

Consider a riot location issue that bears on target strength. Are most deadly riots urban or rural? If a vulnerability hypothesis had validity, many violent episodes would be rural, for isolated rural minorities are especially vulnerable. Yet few such minorities are targeted. Most deadly riots are urban, even in those states where police effectiveness is much reduced in rural areas.

More than this, a surprising number of very violent riots occur in cities where the attackers are actually greatly outnumbered by members of the target group. In Kyrghyzstan (1990), Osh and Pišpek are Kyrghyz-minority cities, in which Kyrghyz nevertheless launched attacks. In Luluabourg, Zaire (1959), Lulua were outnumbered by at least two to

76. Jacquelyn Weygandt White and Kenneth J. Gruber, "Instigative Aggression as a Function of Past Experience and Target Characteristics," *Journal of Personality and Social Psychology* 42, no. 6 (June 1982): 1069–75, at p. 1073; Suresh Kanekar and Ravinder B. Ahluwalia, "Perception of an Aggressor as a Function of the Victim's Strength and Retaliation," *European Journal of Social Psychology* 7, no. 4 (1977): 505–07. (The latter findings were not statistically significant for students of one sex.)

77. Michael T. Hynan and Judith A. Esselman, "Victims and Aggression," *Bulletin of the Psychonomic Society* 18, no. 4 (October 1981): 169–72.

78. Ibid., p. 171.

one by Luba targets. In Malaysian riots — on Pangkor island (1959), in Penang (1956 and 1967), and in Kuala Lumpur (1969) — Malays were outnumbered by three or four to one by Chinese. Assamese violence has recurrently taken place in towns with Assamese minorities. Southern Sudanese attacked Arabs in Khartoum (1964), an Arab city; and in Karachi, several times in the 1980s, Pathans killed Mohajirs, although Mohajirs were at least three times more numerous. Location data thus challenge the target-vulnerability hypothesis that makes the victims simply helpless. These data reinforce experimental findings that strongly provoked subjects are deterred less by fear of retaliation than are less strongly provoked subjects.[79] The violence of desperate people may not be well inhibited by fear; the relationship of likely retribution to aggression is probably curvilinear. As we shall see, patterns of target selection challenge the target-vulnerability hypothesis even more directly, for they point to target strength, rather than weakness, as an underlying theme in targeting.

That, I should underscore, does not rule out displacement in riots. As I have argued, displaced aggression can play a role in ethnic violence. We shall soon have occasion to observe displacement at work again — and again not as an alternative to direct aggression but as a complement to it — most notably in connection with groups having certain foreign connections. But the fact that some groups may receive violence that, under other circumstances, would have been directed at other targets does not suggest that they receive this violence because of their mere availability, because they are convenient, vulnerable, and helpless, but rather because they "have appropriate stimulus characteristics."[80]

Still, there is something to the thesis that, while strong targets provoke violent impulses, the fear of retaliation from strong targets can deter violence against them. Part of the dilemma is that the inhibition formulations are excessively two-dimensional. What they omit, especially, is the dimension of time. It helps to see the issue as the initiators of violence may themselves see it. The issue for decision for a potential initiator of violence is not merely whom to attack, but when and under what conditions. Frustrations, insults, and injuries may be endured quietly at one time because conditions, including fear of retribution, do not permit

79. Russell G. Geen, *Human Aggression* (Milton Keynes: Open University Press, 1990), p. 137; Robert A. Baron, "Threatened Retaliation from the Victim as an Inhibitor of Physical Aggression," *Journal of Research in Personality* 7, no. 3 (September 1973): 103–15.

80. Berkowitz, *Aggression: A Social-Psychological Analysis*, pp. 183–84 (emphasis omitted).

(that is, do inhibit) a violent response, whereas at other times they may permit one. By the same token, certain types of affronts may be considered bearable, and others not.

If the targets of ethnic violence are seen as strong, this still does not render inhibition irrelevant to the calculus of the attackers. Strong targets may be hit at a time of momentary weakness or at a time when retribution is improbable.[81] Similarly, perpetrators of violence may attack weak or unprotected segments of strong groups.[82] To make a riot, it is necessary to have not just aggressors and targets but appropriate precipitating events and a supporting environment. *Who* needs to be aligned with *when*.

Moreover, direct retribution and official retribution may be distinguished, because the two may vary independently. Fear of official punishment may be low (due to governmental tolerance or ineffectiveness), even when the target group itself is not helpless to retaliate. In calculations of risk, this is an appreciable difference, which could conceivably push potential rioters over the threshold between not acting and acting. This is especially so if the government retains legitimacy in the view of the prospective initiators of violence, for then the unlikelihood of official sanctions may remove moral inhibitions on violence as well as those that derive from sheer physical fear.

The interrelations of target-group characteristics and other riot variables thus relieve us of the necessity to regard victims of violence as helpless bystanders.[83] On the contrary, data on riot precipitants and location both indicate that the element of threat from the targets helps to evoke violence against the targets.[84] But what kinds of threat, exactly? To answer this question will require a theory of target-group characteristics.

81. Although here there seems to be a trade-off between the magnitude of the frustration and the likelihood of escaping retribution. If the situation seems urgent enough, some initiators may not wait for a propitious moment; they may simply chance it.

82. As, perhaps, in Zanzibar (1961), where rural Arabs were attacked — although those Arabs also had a reputation for aggressiveness, as I show below. In Durban (1949), Zulu attacked periurban, largely lower-class Indians, who were certainly less well protected than those more centrally located.

83. The fact that the perpetrators see the targets as strong does not, however, contribute anything to the exoneration of the perpetrators for the killings. Compare Arthur G. Miller, "Accounting for Evil and Cruelty: Is to Explain to Condone?" *Personality and Social Psychology Review* 3, no. 3 (1999): 254–68, arguing that "situational" (as opposed to "dispositional") explanations tend toward exoneration. This reasoning is inadequate. Many people harbor grievances against others. Even when the grievances are regarded as legitimate, they do not excuse killing or torturing.

84. See Chapters 8, 10, below.

CHAPTER 5

Target-Group Characteristics

VIOLENCE EMERGES out of an ongoing relationship between groups, and target-group characteristics constitute the irritant in the relationship. Target-group characteristics tend to fall into several determinate classes. If a group has a reputation for being aggressive, if it is regarded as a long-standing enemy, if it has been a recent opponent in warfare, if it presents a political threat, if it possesses external connections that augment internal strength, or if it is thought to exhibit certain characterological traits, it is more likely to be targeted in violence than if it lacks those characteristics. Many target groups — especially those attacked with special intensity or frequency — fall into more than one of these categories.

REPUTATION FOR AGGRESSION

The most obvious threat, yet often overlooked, is the threat of physical force. Sheer physical fear may move those who are frightened to take violent action. This leads to the hypothesis that groups that are perceived as prone to aggression are likely targets.

Experimental evidence lends support to the hypothesis. Experimental subjects who believe others will attack them respond with more aggression than they direct against targets who do not elicit such a belief. They do so even when the feared attacks do not materialize; and the perception of hostile intentions produces even more aggression than do actual attacks.[1] Those who are in some way associated with fighting, such as college boxers, have also been found to elicit stronger hostility from experimental subjects than those who are not similarly associated with

---

1. Gordon W. Russell and Robert L. Arms, "False Consensus Effect, Physical Aggression, Anger, and a Willingness to Escalate a Disturbance," *Aggressive Behavior* 21, no. 5 (September–October 1995): 381–86.

violence. They are said to cue aggressive responses,[2] an explanation for the experimental results confirmed by later studies.[3] Subjects who had had experience with aggressive opponents in previous experiments were also more likely to choose aggressive responses than others were in subsequent experiments. They seemed to impute aggressive intentions more readily to potential targets.[4] For purposes of discriminating effectively among potential targets, such behavior may not be dysfunctional. One study shows a strong association between group reputations for aggressive dispositions, on the one hand, and a propensity for aggressive behavior by that group in an experimental setting, on the other.[5]

There is also some tendency for experimental subjects to respond to an instigation to aggression with the same kind of act as the one constituting the instigation. This propensity is especially pronounced where the instigation consists of physical aggression, such as slapping or hitting. Moreover, the strength of the aggressive response tends to be closely related to the strength of the instigation.[6] From this we may infer that

2. Leonard Berkowitz, "Some Aspects of Observed Aggression," *Journal of Personality and Social Psychology* 2, no. 3 (September 1965): 359–69; Leonard Berkowitz and Russell G. Geen, "Film Violence and the Cue Properties of Available Targets," *Journal of Personality and Social Psychology* 3, no. 5 (May 1966): 525–30.

3. See Michael Carlson, Amy Marcus-Newhall, and Norman Miller, "Effects of Situational Aggression Cues: A Quantitative Review," *Journal of Personality and Social Psychology* 58, no. 4 (April 1990): 622–33. Cf. W. Andrew Harrell, "The Effects of an Aggressive Model on the Magnitude of Extinction-Induced Aggression," *Journal of Social Psychology* 90, Second Half (August 1973): 311–15.

4. Stuart P. Taylor, Richard J. Shuntich, and Andrew Greenberg, "The Effects of Repeated Aggressive Encounters on Subsequent Aggressive Behavior," *Journal of Social Psychology* 107, Second Half (April 1979): 199–208. Where subjects were able to shock targets who had no ability to retaliate, they administered stronger shocks to target groups stereotyped as aggressive than they did to other targets, but they administered weaker shocks when the allegedly aggressive target group had the possibility of retaliation. Joseph Schwarzwald and Yoel Yinon, "Physical Aggression: Effects of Ethnicity of Target and Directionality of Aggression," *European Journal of Social Psychology* 8, no. 3 (May–June 1978): 367–76. Along similar lines, see Michael Hynan and Judith A. Esselman, "Victims and Aggression," *Bulletin of the Psychonomic Society* 18, no. 4 (October 1981): 169–72. Interestingly, similar results have been produced in experiments with some animal species. See Nancy W. Cain et al., "Social Responsiveness and Physical Space as Determinants of Agonistic Behavior in Betta Splendens," *Animal Learning and Behavior* 8, no. 3 (August 1980): 497–501.

5. Yoram Jaffe, Nahum Shapir, and Yoel Yinon, "Aggression and Its Escalation," *Journal of Cross-Cultural Psychology* 12, no. 1 (March 1981): 21–36. In this study, conducted in Israel, Georgian Jews, with the strongest reputation for hot-temperedness, displayed the strongest aggressive responses. Three other groups also behaved in accordance with their rank-ordered reputations.

6. Frances K. Graham et al., "Aggression as a Function of the Attack and the Attacker," *Journal of Abnormal and Social Psychology* 46, no. 4 (October 1951): 512–20, at p. 514.

anticipated physical assaults, as perhaps the strongest instigation, would give rise to the strongest response, also likely to be physical, such as riot behavior.

Criminological evidence points in the same direction. Victims of individual assaults and homicides often exhibit aggressive traits before the attack and "engage in acts with the offender which invite or excite assaultive response."[7] So frequent is the incidence of violence *by* the victim as the prelude to killing *of* the victim that criminologists speak of "victim-precipitated homicide."[8] In the experimental setting, the provocativeness of the target can be a powerful variable in accounting for the quantum of aggression expressed.[9]

Reputation for aggression is a variable trait. In a number of societies in which several targets are available, groups with a reputation for violent behavior have been targeted more frequently or more intensively than others. At least part of the reason why Sikhs and Muslims in India so regularly targeted each other through 1947 was that both had well-deserved, if only historical, reputations for martial activity.[10] The same has been noted by more than one observer in the case of the Manga Arabs, who were prominently represented among the victims of the 1961 riot in Zanzibar. Recognized as a rough group, the Manga had participated in earlier violence and were (erroneously) believed to be the nucleus of a secret military wing organized by the Arab political party.[11] Madurese, attacked in West Kalimantan (1997 and 1999), are regarded

7. LeRoy G. Schultz, "The Victim-Offender Relationship," *Crime and Delinquency* 14, no. 2 (April 1968): 135–41, at p. 139. In the hyperbole of the classic formulation, "the victim shapes and moulds the criminal." Hans von Hentig, *The Criminal and His Victim* (New Haven: Yale University Press, 1948), p. 384.

8. Marvin E. Wolfgang, "Victim-Precipitated Criminal Homicide," in Israel Drapkin and Emilio Viano, eds., *Victimology* (Lexington, Mass.: Lexington Books, 1974), pp. 79–92; Lynn Curtis, "Victim Precipitation and Violent Crime," *Social Problems* 21, no. 4 (April 1974): 594–605. See also Stephen Schafer, *Victimology: The Victim and His Criminal* (Reston, Va.: Reston, 1977), pp. 45–51. For a review of the literature, see Terance D. Miethe, "The Myth or Reality of Victim Involvement in Crime: A Review and Comment on Victim-Precipitation Research," *Sociological Focus* 18, no. 3 (August 1985): 209–20.

9. Jacquelyn Weygandt White and Kenneth J. Gruber, "Instigative Aggression as a Function of Past Experience and Target Characteristics," *Journal of Personality and Social Psychology* 42, no. 6 (June 1982): 1069–75.

10. Both Sikhs and Punjabi Muslims had been classified by the British as "martial races," and both were disproportionately represented in the British Indian Army. Stephen P. Cohen, *The Indian Army: Its Contributions to the Development of a Nation* (Berkeley and Los Angeles: University of California Press, 1971), pp. 44–56.

11. Michael Lofchie, *Zanzibar: Background to Revolution* (Princeton: Princeton University Press, 1965), pp. 78–79, 188, 204, 206; Government of Great Britain, *Report of a Commission to Inquire into Disturbances in Zanzibar during June 1961*, Colon. No. 353 (London, 1961), p. 13.

as hot-blooded.[12] Many Madurese carry a *carok*, a sickle used to settle personal disputes on Madura and occasionally used for the same purpose in Kalimantan.[13] The widespread Temne reputation for aggressive behavior is perhaps partly responsible for the violent reception Temne were accorded in Mende areas of Sierra Leone when they came there to campaign during by-elections in 1968.[14] Similar reputations probably account, in part, for the attacks on Fulani in Guinea in the late 1950s, on the "warlike" Luba in Luluabourg, Zaire (1959),[15] and on the Irish in Philadelphia (1844),[16] as well as the special attention allegedly lavished on Toucouleur by Moorish mobs in Mauritania (1966).[17] Nonetheless, group reputations for violent behavior rarely derive from a proclivity to collective violence, and in those cases where they do the reputation is historical rather than contemporary. Groups with such reputations are, after all, the targets, not the initiators, of collective violence.

Yet it is no paradox that groups viewed as especially aggressive should become recipients of aggression. Members of such groups may be disproportionately aggression-prone in individual encounters, intraethnic or interethnic. For that reason, there is probably a tendency on the part of others to interpret ambiguous behavior on their part (such as demonstrations or marches) as aggressive or threatening in intention, and their actions are more than usually likely to provide cues which arouse aggressive responses. Reputedly pugnacious groups, having a propensity for violence, may also be presumed to understand only violence, and thus, it may be felt, they must be immobilized lest they strike first.[18] Finally,

---

12. *Far Eastern Economic Review*, July 24, 1997, pp. 66–68.

13. Glenn Smith, "Carok Violence in Madura: From Historical Conditions to Contemporary Manifestations," *Folk* 39 (1997): 57–75; Human Rights Watch, "Indonesia: Communal Violence in West Kalimantan," *Human Rights Watch Reports* 9, no. 10(C) (December 1997): 6–9.

14. For the stereotype of the Temne, see John Dawson, "Race and Inter-Group Relations in Sierra Leone," part 2, *Race* 6 (January 1965): 218–21. Among Mende, there exists "some respect for the Temne on account of their well-known fighting qualities in the past." Kenneth Little, *The Mende of Sierra Leone*, rev. ed. (London: Routledge & Kegan Paul, 1967), p. 73. On a less systematic basis, Sierra Leoneans and visitors to Sierra Leone have reported the same stereotype. For a similar Bengali stereotype of the Biharis, targeted several times in Bangladesh, see A.F.A. Husain and A. Farouk, *Social Integration of Industrial Workers in Khulna* (Dacca: Bureau of Economic Research, University of Dacca, 1963), pp. 48–50.

15. See Jules Chomé, *Le Drame de Luluabourg*, 3d rev. ed. (Brussels: Editions de Remarques Congolaises, 1960), p. 9.

16. Michael Feldberg, *The Philadelphia Riots of 1844: A Study of Ethnic Conflict* (Westport, Conn.: Greenwood Press, 1975), p. 33.

17. Here I am relying on interviews with Mauritanian officials.

18. Cf. Erving Goffman, *Stigma: Notes on the Management of Spoiled Identity* (Englewood Cliffs, N.J.: Prentice-Hall, 1963), p. 70, for some precautions customarily

aggression can conquer the aggressors' fear of targets believed to be especially combative and threatening. Before the Delhi riots of 1984, Sikhs were seen as militant, aggressive, and dangerous: "a very strong and virile people."[19] After committing atrocities against them, Hindus were no longer so fearful.[20] "Now that they know that we too can do something, they'll be afraid of us; they won't be so brave now."[21] The same sort of reasoning, of course, applies to discernible subgroups reputed to be aggressive, such as the Manga. They are viewed as the advance guard, the spearhead, the fighting legions of the larger antagonist group, and they may suffer disproportionately when the riot occurs.

Many of the rumors preceding deadly riots concern aggression said to be planned or committed by the target group. Often these are tales of mass murder, threats of invasion, or poisoned water supplies. These, too, suggest that the combativeness of the target group is very much on the minds of the attackers and can move them to action.

TRADITIONAL ANTAGONISM

Contrary to conventional wisdom, relatively little ancient enmity can be found in contemporary antagonisms. Nevertheless, where it exists, long-standing enmity seems to affect target choice, even if the level of ancient enmity is sometimes vastly exaggerated. There is, of course, some overlap between pairs of traditional ethnic enemies, on the one hand, and groups stereotyped as violence-prone and those who see them that way, on the other. Often the stereotype developed in the course of repeated combat. Not surprisingly, then, traditional enemies, like groups reputed to be aggressive, tend to be targeted.

This is not just a function of selecting putative aggressors as victims but of habituation. In the course of experimental research, those involved in earlier fights, *even as victims*, tend to be attacked more strongly than others when they are identified as the source of a current frustration.[22]

---

taken against those with reputations for making trouble. For the white view in the United States south that blacks were aggressive and could understand only force, and for the connection of that view to riot behavior, see Joel Williamson, *A Rage for Order: Black/White Relations in the American South since Emancipation* (New York: Oxford University Press, 1986), pp. 119–20, 133.

19. Uma Chakravarti and Nandita Haksar, *The Delhi Riots: Three Days in the Life of a Nation* (New Delhi: Lancer International, 1987), p. 552. See also pp. 510–11.

20. Ibid., p. 533.

21. Ibid., p. 26.

22. Leonard Berkowitz, "Purposive and Impulsive Violence: Some Implications of Laboratory Studies of Aggression" (unpublished paper, Department of Psychology, University of

Similarly, targets who act provocatively in one experiment draw aggressive responses to themselves in the next, although a clear change in the behavior of targets between experiments can change the responses.[23] Together with the evidence that boxers and others associated with fighting tend to elicit hostile responses, this finding points toward some role for habitual responses in targeting.

Those who, like Bengalis in Assam, Fulani in Guinea, Vietnamese in Cambodia, Temne in Sierra Leone, Karens in Burma, Armenians in Azerbaijan, Tamils in Sri Lanka, or Muslims in north India, were battled earlier probably stand a better chance than others of being dealt with violently again, if only because they continue to evoke the same cues for aggression. The modern Assamese have not forgotten their king, "Chakradhvaj Singha, who fought for independence with the war cry, 'Better death than submit to the Bengalis.'"[24] In the post–World War II period, as politics became increasingly turbulent in Guinea, the Fulani, who had invaded in a *jihad* in the seventeenth and eighteenth centuries, pushing other peoples toward the sea, revived popular memories of their victories in war.[25] Not long after, they began to suffer victimization in riot. A similar memory of invasion infuses the relations between Khmer and Vietnamese in Cambodia. Their boundaries shrinking since the twelfth century, pushed away from what is now the Vietnamese coast during the seventeenth and eighteenth, the Khmer have continued to harbor hostile sentiments toward the expansionist Vietnamese and targeted them in the riots of 1970. The defeat of the Tamil king Elara by the Sinhalese hero Duttugemunu in the second century B.C. also became a cardinal event in the Sinhalese nationalist tradition. During the Sri Lankan riots of 1958, when rumors of an impending Tamil assault were rife, Sinhalese who

---

Wisconsin–Madison, n.d.), p. 6. Since even *victims* in earlier fighting tend to draw attacks, this finding raises the distinct possibility that what I have identified as a reputation for aggression is not a separate category but only one facet of the more inclusive category of traditional antagonists or those associated with earlier fighting. I reiterate that these categories overlap. However, the important precipitating roles played by demonstrations of strength (including the massing of people and other aspects of physical strength) and by rumors of aggression — even when the targets are not traditional adversaries — tend to negate this possibility. The point is important in practice, because of the threatening interpretation commonly put on target-group mass activity during the pre-riot period. See Chapter 8, below.

23. White and Gruber, "Instigative Aggression as a Function of Past Experience and Target Characteristics," p. 1074.

24. Hugh Tinker, *India and Pakistan: A Political Analysis*, rev. ed. (New York: Praeger, 1967), p. 15.

25. Ruth Schachter Morgenthau, *Political Parties in French-Speaking West Africa* (Oxford: Clarendon Press, 1964), pp. 220, 223.

assembled for a preemptive strike were eulogized as an army of heroes gathered to reteach the "invaders" the traditional lesson.[26] In Hindu-Muslim riots in India, similar historical images have been invoked. In Ahmedabad (1969), some Hindus "thought they could now avenge Prithvinaj against Mohamed Gazni after seven hundred years."[27] Traditional enmity may be one of several reasons why Hindu-Muslim riots were, for a long time, far more common in north India, where Muslims arrived as conquerors, than in south India, where they generally came as traders.[28] Traditional enmity also helps explain why it was Sikhs who took the major initiative in organizing the instruments of force on the non-Muslim side in 1947 and why Sikhs, even more than Hindus, were regarded by Muslim rioters as fair game.[29]

Remote though they may seem, these ancient events and relationships are not quietly forgotten. They are kept alive in oral tradition,[30] sometimes in sacred texts or modern textbooks; they may be revived by ethnic associations or political parties when the need arises. Historical memory is reflected in the creation of private armed forces ostensibly modeled on those that fought earlier invaders: the Lachit Sena of the Assamese, the Shiv Sena of the Maharashtrians, and the other *senas* (armies) that grew up in India in the 1960s;[31] the Northern Army in Nigeria, based on memories of the Dan Fodio jihad; the Sinhala Hamudawa (Sinhalese army); various paramilitary units at work in the west Punjab of 1946; the Tentera Sabil Merah (Red Scarves Holy War Army), active among Malays at the end of World War II, and a successor, the Tentera Sabilullah, organized in northern Malaysia in the 1960s. The resurrection of traditional practices during the course of rioting is supporting evidence for the role of historical memory in violent behavior.[32]

26. S. Arasaratnam, *Ceylon* (Englewood Cliffs, N.J.: Prentice-Hall, 1964), pp. 52, 60; Tarzie Vittachi, *Emergency '58: The Story of The Ceylon Race Riots* (London: André Deutsch, 1958), p. 37.

27. Ghanshyam Shah, "Communal Riots in Gujarat," *Economic and Political Weekly* Annual Number, January 1970, p. 187.

28. Cf. R. A. Schermerhorn, "The Locale of Hindu-Muslim Riots," *Indian Journal of Politics* 1, no. 1 (January–June 1971): 37–47.

29. See Penderel Moon, *Divide and Quit* (Berkeley and Los Angeles: University of California Press, 1966).

30. For Mende memory of the Temne as traditional enemies, see Little, *The Mende of Sierra Leone*, pp. 45, 70, 73, 147. On the Jukun view of the Tiv, see Kurt Maier, "Nigeria: Eternal Enmities," *Africa Report*, May–June 1992, pp. 47–48.

31. Harji Malik, "Private Armies," *Illustrated Weekly of India* (Bombay), March 15, 1970, pp. 6–13.

32. See also the apparent role of historical memory in sustaining Jurassian separatism in Switzerland. William R. Keech, "Linguistic Diversity and Political Conflict: Some

"The Turks have come," cries a Sikh lookout as Muslim crowds approach in Bhisham Sahni's novel of violence in prepartition India.[33] Of course, it is not "the Turks" who are coming, but in this fictional account Sikhs see the riot as yet another battle in a protracted war against Muslim invaders. In some societies, where the colonial experience was brief or the colonial penetration superficial, precolonial hostilities, interrupted by the arrival of the foreigner, may be especially well remembered.

The received historical account may contain the seeds of atrocities soon to be committed. In Cambodia, there was "the claim that, in the nineteenth century, a Vietnamese emperor seeking to annex Cambodian territory had his troops seek out Cambodian 'dissidents' opposed to his imperial mission. These Khmer were buried up to their necks and their heads were used to hold a large brazier on which the emperor's troops lit a fire, brewed tea and then sat around drinking it. Few Khmer educated before 1975 do not believe that things like this actually happened."[34]

None of this suggests that the history of enmity is accurate. Histories are often rewritten to emphasize the conflictual side of a relationship. Sri Lanka provides as good an example of mythologized history as any. Among the many fictitious creations of Sri Lankan popular history are the myth of Sinhalese identity unsullied by contact with Tamils and an account of Tamil entry into Sri Lanka that paints Tamils as invaders. In point of fact, Sinhalese and Tamils have exchanged words, deities, cultures, and rulers through the centuries. Their languages have mingled, as have their worship, their caste practices, and their genes.[35] Certain Sinhalese castes are largely of Indian origin; many who later became Sinhalese were Tamil-speakers; and Sinhalese kings chose Tamil queens as late as the nineteenth century. These facts do not detract from the

---

Observations Based on Four Swiss Cantons," *Comparative Politics* 4, no. 1 (April 1972): 396–402.

33. Bhisham Sahni, *Tamas*, trans. Jai Ratan (New Delhi: Penguin Books, 1988), p. 171.

34. Chou Meng Tarr, "The Vietnamese Minority in Cambodia," *Race and Class* 34, no. 2 (October–December 1992): 33–47, at p. 35. For the hostility preceding the 1970 violence, see Bernard K. Gordon, *The Dimensions of Conflict in Southeast Asia* (Englewood Cliffs, N.J.: Prentice-Hall, 1966), pp. 41–67.

35. See Stanley J. Tambiah, *Sri Lanka: Ethnic Fratricide and the Dismantling of Democracy* (Chicago: University of Chicago Press, 1986). For a subtle treatment of generational variations in popular historical memory, see Bipan Chandra, "Use of History and Growth of Communalism," in Pramod Kumar, ed., *Towards Understanding Communalism* (Chandigar: Centre for Research in Rural and Industrial Development, 1992), pp. 330–50, at pp. 336–37.

impact of the popular history, which depicts the Tamils as long-standing, dangerous enemies, who must be fought. Sudhir Kakar aptly refers to ancient defeats, embedded in the current discourse of ethnic relations, as "chosen traumas," events recalled to motivate violent assertion.[36]

The role of traditional enmity in international relations makes an interesting comparison. A crossnational stereotype study, conducted long after World War II, found that, of several possible West European choices, the French tended to name the Germans as the most difficult people to get along with; the Germans tended to name the French; and each held unfavorable images of the other.[37] It is not that long-standing animosity cannot be overcome, for Western Europe shows that it can be. Rather, a background of fighting can produce images of intransigence and hostility, which in turn can be conducive to further outbreaks. In a study of the conditions leading to war, it was found that there was "general randomness in the choice of allies and friends" — that is, randomness in international targeting — but still "the few traditional enmities are apparent . . . ."[38]

In explaining ethnically based civil wars, Barry Posen contends that potential antagonists examine the prior behavior of their opponents. If it was violent on the earlier occasion, that may indicate the need for violence against them now.[39] Experimental research likewise suggests that people with a history of doing harm are more likely to be judged as intending to do harm and are therefore more likely than others to trigger aggressive responses.[40]

The converse of traditional enmity can also be striking. Deeply embedded targeting patterns do not readily give way to new ones when the traditional targets are suddenly removed from the scene. The fact that the Punjab was partitioned in 1947 provides a case where traditional antagonists were parted, leaving traditional allies as the new antagonists

36. Sudhir Kakar, *The Colors of Violence: Cultural Identities, Religion, and Conflict* (Chicago: University of Chicago Press, 1996), p. 50.

37. Erich Reigrotski and Nels Anderson, "National Stereotypes and Foreign Contacts," *Public Opinion Quarterly* 23, no. 4 (Winter 1959–60): 515–28.

38. J. David Singer, "The 'Correlates of War' Project," *World Politics* 24, no. 2 (January 1972): 243–70, at p. 265. This, despite the significant difference that in the international system such enmities are presumably mediated by some conception of national interest, whereas in the domestic ethnic system there is somewhat greater scope for the unfettered expression of sentiment.

39. Barry Posen, "The Security Dilemma and Ethnic Conflict," *Survival* 35, no. 1 (Spring 1993): 27–47, at p. 30.

40. Russell G. Geen, *Human Aggression* (Milton Keynes: Open University Press, 1990), p. 127.

on the Indian side. It is thus a unique control case. What it shows is that traditional alliances are no inoculation against violence but that they do seem to slow down the development of violent encounters in circumstances otherwise propitious for violence.

The immediate pre-1947 period in the Punjab was filled with ethnic violence, primarily between Sikhs (or Sikhs and Hindus) on one side and Muslims on the other, culminating in the mass murders that accompanied partition. Rulers of the Punjab scarcely a century before, the Sikhs had earlier emerged as a distinct community in the course of a Hindu protest against Muslim rule. Sikhs and Muslims had fought intermittently thereafter. After partition, a new conflict alignment quickly developed on the Indian side of the border. With Muslims gone from the east Punjab, the demand for a Sikh-dominated state pitted the Sikhs against their longtime allies, Punjabi Hindus, with whom they had formerly been in very close contact, including having many family relationships. Sikh-Hindu conflict, in the context of Sikh separatism, eventually produced a second partition of the (east) Punjab 1966, dividing it into a truncated, heavily Sikh, Punjab state and a new, mainly Hindu, Haryana state, but this time both wholly within India.

Despite the growing intensity of the Sikh-Hindu conflict and the particular mode by which it was pursued on the Sikh side — by mass demonstrations and scarcely veiled threats of violence, including well-publicized attempts by Sikh leaders to evoke memories of the Sikhs' violent capacities by the public drawing of swords in a menacing manner — for many years, Sikh agitation produced very little Sikh-Hindu violence.[41] Even in the ensuing decades, when some Sikhs turned to terrorism and attempted to precipitate riots that might produce population exchanges, riot behavior was absent in the Punjab.[42]

It certainly cannot be maintained that traditional antipathy between any two groups is either a prerequisite for them to target each other or a guarantee that they will do so. If it were, it would be impossible to account for new target choices or for exemptions of traditional enemies from targeting. And intervening variables cannot be held perfectly constant. In the Punjab case, for example, the local Muslim threat was gone, but it existed just across the border, so there was a special reason to keep Sikh-Hindu relations from getting too far out of control. In the 1965 Indo-Pakistani war, Pakistanis attempted to soften the old Sikh-Muslim

41. See generally Baldev Raj Nayar, *Minority Politics in the Punjab* (Princeton: Princeton University Press, 1966), pp. 234–69.

42. I consider the Punjab nonviolence further as a negative case in Chapter 12, below.

enmity by making overtures designed to divide Sikh soldiers from Hindu. These efforts did not produce Sikh-Hindu violence, but they undoubtedly drove home to the Indian government the dangers posed by a potentially disaffected ethnic group on the border with Pakistan. The importance of maintaining the loyalty of Sikh citizens in the strategically critical Punjab, and of Sikh soldiers everywhere, probably did play a role in inducing the government to accede finally to the Sikh demand for a second partition in 1966.

Only then did Sikh-Hindu violence occur.[43] The militant Hindu party, the Jan Sangh, made a show of attempting to stop the partition of the east Punjab, in the interest of maintaining Hindu hegemony over the undivided whole. These protests led to clashes in Delhi as well as in the Punjab, between the Jan Sangh and Hindus on one side and the Sikh party, the Akali Dal, and Sikhs on the other.[44] The Jan Sangh protest was unavailing; the violence, which never approached the dimensions of Hindu-Muslim violence, was easily contained; and the second partition of the Punjab was accomplished.

Eventually, a Sikh independence movement developed in the truncated Punjab, and segments of the movement turned heavily to violence. The violence employed, however, was highly organized and strategic, falling into the category of terrorism. Only in 1984, after the assassination of Indira Gandhi, was there large-scale violence between Hindus and Sikhs; and then it took place in Delhi and a few other towns, but not in the Punjab and not between Hindu and Sikh Punjabis. As we have seen, the Sikhs' martial reputation may have helped attract aggression toward them. Yet, after the creation of Pakistan, Hindu-Sikh antipathy was slow to develop. As Bipan Chandra puts it, "People thought that in 1947 all the Hindus and Sikhs came over to this side of Punjab, hating the Muslims, and they kicked out the Muslims from Punjab and, therefore, Hindu and Sikh communalism were always allied. So people thought that now communalism was over in Punjab."[45] Delay in targeting Sikhs was related to images of traditional allies and enemies.

The same logic helped restrain Sikhs from targeting Hindus at a time

43. Herbert Feldman, "The Communal Problem in Indo-Pakistan Subcontinent: Some Current Implications," *Pacific Affairs* 42, no. 2 (Summer 1969): 150.

44. *The Times* (London), March 15, 1966, p. 9; March 17, 1966, p. 11; March 18, 1966, p. 10; *New York Times*, March 20, 1966, p. E3. This was followed a year later by a Hindu-Sikh riot across the subcontinent in Calcutta, occasioned by a dispute over access of a procession to a temple. *The Times* (London), March 30, 1967, p. 5; March 31, 1967, p. 6.

45. Bipan Chandra, "Social Roots of Communalism," in Kumar, ed., *Towards Understanding Communalism*, pp. 157–69, at p. 160.

when Sikh organizations were raising the temperature of Sikh-Hindu relations. Sikh leaders knew that the threat of violence was a more potent resource than its actual employment might have been. After 1947, they used the threat of violence to gain a variety of concessions from the central government, without risking Sikh riots against Hindus. Over the course of three centuries, the Sikh martial tradition had been developed for use against the Moghuls, and it had been invoked recently against their Muslim successors in the area.[46] It was easy enough for post-independence Sikh politicians to recall the Sikh fighting tradition without turning it, inadvertently or otherwise, against Hindus.[47]

Two different processes were at work in the post-1947 Punjab. On the one hand, the conflict alignment depends very heavily on context. Changing political and social boundaries can change conflict alignments rapidly. When the 1947 partition shrank the boundaries of the Indian Punjab, it became clear that the principal obstacle to a Sikh state was no longer Muslim but Hindu, and the lines of cleavage were accordingly contracted from Sikh and Hindu versus Muslim to Sikh versus Hindu. On the other hand, historical memory helped impede the growth of mass antipathy.

OPPOSITION IN WAR

Groups with wartime sympathies that run in opposite directions may find themselves fighting an ethnic war within an international war. The violence between Turks and Armenians during World War I makes this quite clear, for the Armenian genocide proceeded, among other things, from a Turkish sense that Armenians were in league with foreign enemies.[48] World War II also is rich with illustrations.

The Karens owed to the British their freedom from servitude to their Burman conquerors, and they expressed their gratitude by unswerving fidelity. Burmans, however, chafed under British rule. By the time of World War II, their anticolonial movement was in high gear. These opposite preferences were expressed in the fighting. The Karens stood by the British, while the Burmans harassed their retreat.[49] As the Japanese set-

46. For a concise historical summary, see Khushwant Singh, *The Sikhs Today* (Bombay: Orient Longmans, 1959), pt. I.

47. This is not to say that a fighting tradition can never be harnessed and turned in a new direction, as the Shiv Sena has done in Bombay — only that this does not happen automatically when the recent combat lines are firmly associated with tradition.

48. Robert F. Melson, *Revolution and Genocide: On the Origins of the Armenian Genocide and the Holocaust* (Chicago: University of Chicago Press, 1992), p. 248.

49. John F. Cady, "Burma," in Lennox A. Mills, ed., *The New World of Southeast Asia* (Minneapolis: University of Minnesota Press, 1949), p. 156.

tled into the occupation of Burma, armed Burman and Karen units clashed, paving the way for less organized ethnic violence. Similar events occurred, for similar reasons, between Burmans and Arakanese Muslims, aligned with the British, in 1941.[50]

For rather different reasons, Malays and Chinese were also divided by the war. Many Chinese set about to hinder the Japanese, who were the enemies of China, while the Japanese immediately perceived the Malayan Chinese as a treacherous population, to be disciplined and persecuted. Malays adapted to the occupation somewhat more easily. When Chinese guerrillas, largely Communist, attacked the Japanese from jungle bases, the guerrillas extorted food and supplies from those who lived nearby, severely punishing those who informed on them. After the Japanese departure in 1945, punitive expeditions launched by the guerrillas against Malays in several parts of the peninsula produced extensive violence directed against local Chinese.[51]

The Axis dismemberment of Yugoslavia produced even greater violence. The Germans and Italians considered the Serbs to be dangerous enemies and so favored the Croats, even to the point of creating a separate Croatia, long the aspiration of Croat nationalists. A fascist regime was installed, and it utilized the services of a Croat paramilitary force, the Ustasha. The Ustasha promptly proceeded to repay the Serbs for their earlier chauvinism — in the currency of murder. The Serbs had their own armed organization, the Chetniks, which counterattacked. Especially in the first year of the occupation, the cleavage exploited by the occupying forces generated widespread Serbo-Croat killing.[52]

Divergent wartime sympathies helped produce violence in Lithuania. The Communist Party was disproportionately Jewish, and many Jews had welcomed the Soviet occupation. When Nazi forces drove the Soviets out in 1941, Lithuanians attacked Jews.[53]

More recent wars have opened similar wounds. The Cambodian violence against Vietnamese in 1970 proceeded from the common assump-

50. See *Far Eastern Economic Review*, July 14, 1978, pp. 30–32.

51. See F. Spencer Chapman, *The Jungle Is Neutral* (London: Chatto and Windus, 1949); Chin Kee Onn, *Malaya Upside Down* (Singapore: Jitts, 1946); J.M. Gullick, *Malaya* (New York: Praeger, 1963), pp. 84–85; F.C. Jones, Hugh Borton, and B.R. Pearn, *Survey of International Affairs, 1939–1946: The Far East, 1942–1946* (London: Oxford University Press, 1955), pp. 293–94. Comparable killings of Dayaks by Communist guerrillas in West Kalimantan, Indonesia (1967), produced comparable violence by Dayaks against Chinese civilians. See *Straits Times* (Kuala Lumpur), November 21, 1967, p. 10.

52. Hugh Seton-Watson, *The East European Revolution*, 3d ed. (London: Methuen, 1956), pp. 77–82, 118–31.

53. Tomas Venclova, "Jews and Lithuanians," *Cross Currents* 8 (1989): 55–62.

tion that all or nearly all of the Vietnamese living in Cambodia had Viet Cong sympathies, and the Khmer were in the midst of a civil war in which the strongest party was actually Vietnamese.[54] Within the war that led to the independence of Bangladesh, a smaller but quite deadly war was fought between Bengalis and Biharis. Apparently convinced that their future rested with the continued existence of a united Pakistan, many Biharis opposed the Bengali movement. The West Pakistanis, in need of local assistance in Bengal, enlisted Bihari aid. As long as the Pakistanis held the upper hand, so did the Biharis. When the tide turned in the larger war, it also turned in the violence by Bengalis against Biharis.[55]

There is some circularity when we say that groups whose sympathies diverge in a larger war may, in short order, find themselves fighting their own ethnic war. One reason that the sympathies of the groups diverge is that their fundamental aspirations are also in conflict or that they are already so mutually hostile that the allegiance of one group to one side tends to push the other to the other side. But the decision is not made on those grounds alone. Warfare and the occupation that often accompanies it require a choice of sides based partially on external affinities, calculations of ethnic advantage, and the attitude of the occupying power toward the groups, as well as the reciprocal allegiance of each group's ethnic enemies. Once allegiances are fixed, displacement may also come into play, as perpetrators of violence target members of groups aligned with opposing powers when they are unable to attack the opposing powers directly. We shall see another version of this phenomenon in connection with external affinities that augment local group strength. Opposition in war may simply be a subset of this larger category.

In wartime, when so much is in flux, the choice made by each group may have consequences for the collective fortunes of the other. Restraints against violence are much lower than they were previously. Having chosen opposite sides, the groups are likely to see each other as being more dangerous than before. Typically, military forces associated with one of the antagonists condone the killing and may take part, so events are on the edge of the definition of riots in Chapter 1. In Bangladesh (1971), for example, much of the killing of Biharis was the work of the Bengali

---

54. See T.D. Allman, "The Cambodian Pogrom," *Far Eastern Economic Review,* May 7, 1970, pp. 22–23. See also *Washington Post,* April 14, 1970, p. A12; *New York Times,* February 3, 1972, p. 3.

55. See Ben Whitaker, Iain Guest, and David Ennals, *The Biharis in Bangladesh,* 4th ed. (London: Minority Rights Group Report no. 11, 1982), pp. 7–9. For a Pakistani account, see Qutubuddin Aziz, *Blood and Tears* (Karachi: United Press of Pakistan, 1974).

rebels, the Mukti Bahini. While the killing reflected intergroup hostility, much of it was not performed by civilians.

Is it wholly accurate to consider opposition in warfare a target-group *characteristic* rather than a precipitating *event*? To ask this question is to show how blurred is the line between events and characteristics. As I shall note in the treatment of precipitants, the two are difficult to separate. An event usually precipitates violence because it makes a group appear more dangerous or offensive in some way. Similarly, it can hardly be said that there are individual or group characteristics — even fictitious or misperceived characteristics — that exist abstractly, apart from behavior that points to the possession of those characteristics. A characteristic is a relational feature.

As the Burman-Karen and Khmer-Vietnamese cases suggest, there is some overlap between pairs of opponents in warfare and pairs of traditional enemies, just as there is some overlap between groups that have been traditional enemies, on the one hand, and groups with reputations for aggression and those who see them as aggressive, on the other. The three sets of behavioral attributes — reputation for aggression, traditional antagonism, opposition in warfare — comprise a cluster with a common denominator that can be expressed in a single parsimonious proposition: groups associated with violence tend to meet with violence in the deadly ethnic riot.

POLITICAL THREAT

The target-group characteristics already identified have a political aspect. Conflicting group loyalties in wartime lead to concern about relative group advantage in the peace that will follow. A presumed capacity for aggression may be a capacity for political mastery through the use of force. Traditional antipathies usually have their roots in a received history of alternating domination or waves of invasion. This is the approximate pattern of, for example, Sikh-Muslim, Sinhalese-Tamil, and Fulani-Soussou-Malinké relations over the centuries, even if it is not the whole story. The rivalries have current relevance because they evoke dreams of glory and apprehensions of defeat.[56]

There is, however, more direct evidence that groups constituting a

56. Cf. Leonard Plotnicov, "Who Owns Jos? Ethnic Ideology in Nigerian Urban Politics," *Urban Anthropology* 1, no. 1 (Spring 1972): 1–13, at p. 8: "The Hausa . . . having once experienced political control over the area in which they settled, were reluctant to relinquish that control."

political threat—by which I mean groups with an apparent intention and a plausible ability to control the state—have a greater likelihood than others do of becoming victims of violence. Political threat is, in large part, responsible for the repeated attacks on Ibo and the absence of attacks on Yoruba in northern Nigeria. The Ibo had no reputation for aggressive behavior; they and the northern Nigerians did not entertain divergent wartime sympathies; they were not traditional enemies. Yet the Ibo were repeatedly targets of northern violence.

As suggested earlier, a theory of targeting must be able to account for positive and negative cases: why the Ibo but not the Yoruba? Much of the explanation lies in their respective political strengths: the political behavior of the two groups, their comparative capacity for concerted action, their representation in politically strategic positions, and even their numerical position in the north. (Another part of the explanation is found in psychological relationships to be considered shortly.)

As the earliest and strongest pan-Nigerian nationalists, Ibo after World War II urged a swift transition to an independent, unified, and centralized Nigeria.[57] The Ibo-led nationalist movement was vigorous and assertive, sometimes too vigorous and assertive for the north. It promoted the anticolonial general strike of 1945, which caused hardship in the north and resentment against the Ibo nationalist leadership. As the strike and other events showed, the Ibo were uncompromisingly anticolonial; they tended to push northerners toward nationalist activity at a pace faster than they were inclined to move.

In all of this, the motives of the Ibo were suspect. It was believed that they sought to profit disproportionately from the quick demise of colonial rule, that they aimed to replace Europeans in the top posts and even to subjugate the north.[58] The Ibo demand for a centralized Nigeria stood in sharp contrast to the northern demand for regional autonomy and was regarded as a subterfuge for an Ibo attempt to break out of the overpopulated Eastern Region in order to seize the new opportunities available nationwide.

Seize they did. The Ibo were located in politically crucial positions, in the civil service and especially in the army officer corps, which at various

57. For the background, see James S. Coleman, *Nigeria: Background to Nationalism* (Berkeley and Los Angeles: University of California Press, 1958), chs. 16–17; Richard L. Sklar, *Nigerian Political Parties* (Princeton: Princeton University Press, 1963).

58. See, e.g., the letters and editorials reprinted in Northern Regional Government, Government of Nigeria, *Report on the Kano Disturbances, 16th, 17th, 18th and 19th May, 1953* (Kaduna: Government Printer, 1953), pp. 41–44. See also Coleman, *Nigeria,* p. 361.

times before the 1966 coups was 50 percent or more Ibo.[59] When the army made its first move in January 1966, killing leading northern politicians in the process, it did not take long for the north to see the coup "as an essentially anti-Northern, Ibo-dominated conspiracy."[60]

Perhaps most important was the sense of solidarity the Ibo projected. Often divided at home, outside their region the Ibo composed their differences and presented a politically solid front, supporting a single party and a single leader unswervingly. To non-Ibo, the Ibo conveyed the picture of an unusually cohesive, disciplined group.

The Yoruba were different. In the watershed political events of the early postwar period, the Yoruba had not been as uncompromising as the Ibo. As late as 1951, the Yoruba party, like the Hausa-Fulani leadership, had favored regional autonomy rather than the strong central government preferred by the Ibo. The Yoruba were, of course, far ahead of northerners in education and in civil service positions, but they were not heavily represented in the army. Unpopular though they, too, were in the north, the Yoruba were not viewed as conspiring to steal the state.

Like the Ibo, the Yoruba were represented by their own political party, the Action Group, but it was rife with factionalism, largely along subethnic lines. Always more divided than the Ibo, easier for northern political parties to neutralize, the Yoruba were a less potent force. After 1962, when the Action Group split, the political field was left to competition between a Hausa- and an Ibo-dominated party, each of them aligning with a different Yoruba faction. By the time of the anti-Ibo riots of 1966, the Yoruba were so badly split that they no longer constituted an obstacle to northern hegemony.[61] By contrast, the Ibo appeared politically aggressive, homogeneous, and highly dangerous.

In the north itself, as in Nigeria as a whole, the Ibo became much the more dangerous group. They, not the Yoruba, sponsored a northern political party to compete with the party of the northern emirs.[62] Attacking northern "feudalism," this Ibo-related party gave frequent

59. Ruth First, *Power in Africa* (Baltimore: Penguin Books, 1972), p. 162.

60. Paul Anber, "Modernization and Political Disintegration: Nigeria and the Ibos," *Journal of Modern African Studies* 5, no. 2 (September 1967): 163–80, at p. 163. See also Colin Legum, "The Tragedy in Nigeria," *Africa Report* 11, no. 8 (November 1966): 23.

61. For the political maneuvering of the early 1960s, see Richard Harris, "Nigeria: Crisis and Compromise," *Africa Report* 10, no. 3 (March 1965): 25–31.

62. The Yoruba party did associate itself with the opposition in the Middle Belt of the north; the Ibo affiliate, however, was based in Kano, in the "true north."

offense. By abstaining from competition in the far north, the Yoruba were able to stand aside.

In sheer numbers, too, the early Yoruba preponderance among the migrant population in the north had been outstripped by the influx of Ibo into major northern centers. By the 1950s, Ibo migration to other regions far exceeded the movement of all other ethnic groups in Nigeria.[63] In Kano, Jos, Kaduna, and Zaria, as in most of the "true north," Ibo outnumbered Yoruba by as much as two to one at the time of the 1952 census, and in some towns the Ibo population was as much as a quarter of the total.[64] Not only had this happened, but it had happened quickly, and the trend was not arrested until the 1966 riots. In Kano, for example, Yoruba had outnumbered Ibo by about five to four in 1931, but by 1952 it was nearly two to one in favor of Ibo and in 1965 probably three or four to one.[65] As Ibo preeminence in key government roles augured national hegemony, Ibo movement into the north had begun to transform the landscape and presage the prospect of Ibo control of the north itself. The Ibo presence imparted a proximate regional reality to the more abstract threat of Ibo national domination.[66]

The choice of the Ibo as targets suggests that groups that are politically threatening will tend to be attacked. Concretely, this means that (1) groups that are influential in government, (2) groups that are numerically strong, and (3) groups that are specially cohesive or well organized are more likely to receive attacks than those lacking these attributes.

Attacks on groups believed to be disproportionately represented in government service are common. Dahomeyans and Togolese in the Ivory Coast, Ahmadis in Pakistan, Bengalis in Assam, Tamils in Sri Lanka, blacks in Mauritania, Luba in Zaire, Vietnamese in Cambodia — the list is long. Sometimes this choice reflects the riot leadership of potential bureaucratic competitors. But it also reflects foreboding about the political significance of civil service domination. In terms almost identical to

---

63. Peter Kilby, *Industrialization in an Open Economy: Nigeria, 1945–1966* (Cambridge: Cambridge University Press, 1969), p. 205.

64. Federation of Nigeria, Department of Statistics, *The Population Census of the Northern Region of Nigeria, 1952* (Lagos: The Census Superintendent, n.d.), pp. 26–29.

65. See Northern Regional Government, *Report on the Kano Disturbances*, pp. 1–2; John N. Paden, "Communal Competition, Conflict and Violence in Kano," in Robert Melson and Howard Wolpe, eds., *Nigeria: Modernization and the Politics of Communalism* (East Lansing: Michigan State University Press, 1971), p. 120.

66. Only decades later, in 1999 and 2000, long after the Ibo political threat had receded and Hausa-Yoruba political rivalry had become more pronounced, was there violence between Hausa and Yoruba.

those applied to Ibo influence in the Nigerian civil service, the Tamils in Sri Lanka were said to have "formed a secret conspiracy to take control of Colombo and the administration of the country by sinister infiltration."[67] In 1958, special attention was lavished by the attackers on Tamil government employees and the Colombo suburbs where they lived. The Luba were accused by the Lulua of having "proclaimed very clearly their intention to replace the Europeans. . . . The Lulua fear that they will find themselves before a new colonial administration where the Luba have taken the place of the whites."[68] In the Sudan, in Chad, and in Congo (Brazzaville), the sending of, respectively, northern civil servants to the south, Christian civil servants to Muslim areas, and Bakongo civil servants to Mbochi areas gave rise to a violent response.[69] In each case, the appointments might have been justified by educational criteria, but they were apparently viewed instead as part of a plan by one segment of the population to colonize the other. When, for example, the Sudan civil service was "Sudanized" in 1954–55, southerners received six of the more than 800 posts available. "The results of Sudanization," wrote a southern Sudanese at the time, mean "our fellow Northerners want to colonize us for another hundred years."[70]

In the early postcolonial period, attacks on groups heavily represented in the civil service were also significant for another reason: displacement. Where displacement occurs, the most likely targets are those with some resemblance to the frustrater.[71] The most obvious point of resemblance between the colonial power and the recipients of the violence is the attribute of political power. On these grounds, there is good reason to expect the victims of displaced ethnic aggression to be credited with hav-

67. Vittachi, *Emergency '58*, p. 101.

68. Henri Nicolai, "Conflits entre groupes africains et décolonisation au Kasai," *Revue de l'Université de Bruxelles*, XIIe Année (1960), p. 138.

69. Government of Sudan, *Report of the Commission of Inquiry into Disturbances in the Southern Sudan during August, 1955* (Khartoum: McCorquedale, 1956), pp. 110–17; Virginia Thompson and Richard Adloff, *The Emerging States of French Equatorial Africa* (Stanford: Stanford University Press, 1960), p. 490.

70. Quoted in Government of Sudan, *Report of the Commission of Inquiry*, p. 114. See also Mohammed Omer Beshir, *The Southern Sudan* (London: C. Hurst, 1968), p. 72, reporting that southerners sensed an exchange "of one master for another and a new colonization by the North."

71. Leonard Berkowitz, *Aggression: A Social-Psychological Analysis* (New York: McGraw-Hill, 1962), p. 139. "If a minority, particularly an 'elite' minority, is perceived as being associated with any of the major colonial powers, the possibility of communal conflict will be increased by the displacement of anti-colonial feelings onto that minority." Margaret J. Wyszomirski, "Communal Violence: The Armenians and the Copts as Case Studies," *World Politics* 27, no. 3 (April 1975): 430–55, at p. 442.

ing entertained aspirations to political domination. Since colonial political power was exercised bureaucratically, the likely place for resemblances to the colonialists to be perceived in the immediate postcolonial context was the bureaucracy.

Decades after decolonization, the civil service still has a special, albeit declining, importance in many ex-colonial states. The colonial officer was a person of enormous power, credited with energy and ability in heroic proportions. The reverence he commanded was formidable. It is no cause for surprise, therefore, that the colonial departure should pave the way for a struggle over the position, the perquisites, and even the aura surrounding the colonial civil servant. Those who fill the shoes of their long-departed former masters are quite likely to be regarded as inheriting their mantle. They are also likely to be seen as establishing a claim to rule and to behave in ways that evoke such a claim. The quoted views of the Sinhalese in Sri Lanka, the Lulua in Zaire, and the southern Sudanese should be interpreted in this light.

In the postcolonial world, however, power is not exercised only bureaucratically. Given the importance of political threat in targeting, we would naturally expect that — all else equal — the most numerous group would also be most frequently attacked.[72] This does often, but not invariably, prove to be the case. As we have just seen, Ibo outnumbered Yoruba in northern Nigeria. Temne, apart from Mende the largest and politically most threatening group, were attacked in Sierra Leone. Chinese rather than Indians were attacked in Malaysia, where the former outnumber the latter more than three to one, just as Indians rather than Chinese were attacked in Burma, where the proportions were reversed. In Assam, in Tripura, and in Manipur, the more numerous Bengalis were attacked several times; and in Congo (Brazzaville), the Bakongo.

The importance of numbers is brought home in a variety of ways, usually connected to the political implications of numerousness. The province of Cotabato in the southern Philippines had a Muslim majority as late as the early 1960s. Ten years later it had a Christian majority and, for the first time, an elected Christian governor.[73] It also had ethnic violence. In Luluabourg, Luba migrants had become an absolute majority of the town's population by the 1950s. The outnumbered Lulua had asked for certain electoral restrictions and a program of return-migration for

72. For a suggestive treatment of the importance of numbers, see Robert M. Khoury, "The Permeability of Territorial Space: Some Evidence from Military Warfare," *Social Behavior and Personality* 12, no. 1 (n.m. 1984): 17–22.

73. *Washington Post*, August 22, 1972, p. A17.

the Luba immediately before the violence inflicted on the Luba in 1959.[74] In Assam, the large-scale migration of Muslim Bengalis from Bangladesh through the 1960s and 1970s led to concerns about their electoral impact and demands that such foreigners be purged from the electoral rolls. With general elections impending in 1980, Assamese for the first time attacked Bengali Muslims in a series of deadly riots lasting from 1979 to 1983.[75]

If numbers are important, apprehensions about numbers are equally important. Hindu chauvinists in India frequently depict Muslims as having rates of natural increase so much higher than those of Hindus that they threaten to put Hindus in a minority. The extent to which this is an anxiety-laden perception can be gauged by the Muslim share of the Indian population, currently about 12 percent.

The significance of sheer numbers, real or apprehended, should not be overestimated, however. Numbers often have something to do with political power, but not always, not everywhere, and not everything. More important are qualitative dimensions, such as the intentions imputed to ethnic groups — particularly the intention to seize control of the state. As we have seen, this was the aim attributed to the Ibo, the Luba, the Tamils, and the northern Sudanese. In this respect, it is interesting to note that the first large-scale Malay-Chinese violence occurred in 1945, after Chinese guerrillas took revenge on Malays who had cooperated with the Japanese. What this brought about, above all, was a reinterpretation of Chinese intentions. Before the war, the Chinese were unorganized, and many Malays thought "of their relations with the Chinese prior to the Japanese invasion as being reasonably satisfactory. That is, however much they may have disliked the Chinese or disapproved of them, there was no pertinent issue between them as peoples."[76] By producing a Chinese political organization bent on enforcing its will, the war gave rise to the belief among Malays that the Chinese "will not be satisfied until they have us completely in their power."[77]

Whatever its numbers, the cohesion of a group can magnify the threat it poses. The view of Ibo cohesiveness that came to be rather widely held

74. René Lemarchand, Political Awakening in the Belgian Congo (Berkeley and Los Angeles: University of California Press, 1964), pp. 206–09; Nicolai, "Conflits entre groupes africains et décolonisation au Kasai," pp. 135, 141; Chomé, Le Drame de Luluabourg, p. 16.

75. For the background, see B.G. Verghese et al., Situation in Assam (February 1980): Report of a Study Team (New Delhi: Gandhi Peace Foundation, mimeo., 1980).

76. Kenelm O.L. Burridge, "Racial Relations in Johore," Australian Journal of Politics and History 2, no. 2 (May 1957): 151–68, at p. 164.

77. Quoted in ibid.

in Nigeria was underpinned by Ibo political behavior. Like the Ibo, Bengalis in Assam, Chinese in Malaysia, Luba in Zaire, Tamils in Sri Lanka, and Indians in Guyana have all been regarded as especially cohesive and therefore especially dangerous. An ethnic group thought to be cohesive and unified is more likely to be targeted than a group riven by obvious internal differences.[78]

EXTERNAL AFFINITIES
AUGMENTING INTERNAL STRENGTH

It has sometimes been noted that numerical majorities can behave as if they were minorities — by magnifying threats from minorities and underestimating their own capacity to deal with those threats.[79] Such a statement assumes, of course, that the appropriate way to measure majority status is to count heads within accepted territorial borders. For many purposes, this may be an adequate method, but ethnic affinities commonly transcend formal territorial boundaries. Where this is the case, the majority may not be acting *as if* it were a minority — it may actually *be* a minority in the larger context.[80] At all events, the behavior of a group toward potential domestic ethnic antagonists may be conditioned by threats that appear to emanate from across a boundary — a connection dramatized during the 1992 anti-Muslim riot in Bombay, when searchlights were trained on the sea to detect the arrival of (nonexistent) forces from Pakistan.[81] International as well as interprovincial ethnic relations thus have a bearing on domestic ethnic relations.[82]

78. The hypothesis of Ralph Epstein that groups seen as less cohesive are more likely to be targeted is not borne out by the comparative evidence. See Epstein, "Aggression toward Outgroups as a Function of Authoritarianism and Imitation of Aggressive Models," *Journal of Personality and Social Psychology* 3, no. 5 (May 1966): 574–79, at p. 577.

79. Robert N. Kearney, *Communalism and Language in the Politics of Ceylon* (Durham: Duke University Press, 1967), pp. 72–73; W. Howard Wriggins, *Ceylon: Dilemmas of a New Nation* (Princeton: Princeton University Press, 1960), p. 252; Clifford Geertz, "The Integrative Revolution: Primordial Sentiments and Civil Politics in the New States," in Geertz, ed., *Old Societies and New States* (New York: Free Press, 1963), pp. 105–57, at pp. 115–16.

80. For the importance of the size of the "political field" or context in ethnic conflict, see Donald L. Horowitz, "Ethnic Identity," in Nathan Glazer and Daniel P. Moynihan, eds., *Ethnicity: Theory and Experience* (Cambridge: Harvard University Press, 1975), pp. 111–40, at pp. 132–37.

81. This event was first called to my attention by Arjun Appadurai, who mentioned it in a lecture at Duke University in 1998.

82. For an attempt to relate the two, see Myron Weiner, "The Macedonian Syndrome: An Historical Model of International Relations and Political Development," *World Politics* 23, no. 4 (July 1971): 665–83.

This has certainly been true in ethnic violence. A large number of riot targets have been border-straddling groups or groups that were thought to represent the spearhead of a foreign "invasion." The riots in Cyprus, Cambodia, Chad, Mauritania, and the Sudan reflect more than purely local tensions. They also reflect unease about the large numbers of strangers across the border. The Sinhalese fear not only the Sri Lankan Tamils but also their ties to the much larger number of Tamils in India. These fears are heightened by the lingering Sinhalese memory of ancient Tamil invasions and the occasional threats by Sri Lankan Tamil extremists to join the Tamil areas of Sri Lanka to Tamil Nadu.[83]

Some of the most serious violence in India has taken place in Assam, a state with two large Bengali neighbors: West Bengal, in India, and East Bengal, or Bangladesh. In the first instance, the Assamese were offended by the continuing links of Bengalis in Assam to West Bengal and the support that Bengali language demands received from the Calcutta press and the West Bengal government.[84] Continuing Bengali immigration, together with periodic suggestions that the heavily Bengali Cachar area of Assam be separated and transferred to West Bengal, gave the Assamese a sense of living in the shadow of the much more populous state to the west.

There was also a precedent for Bengali irredentism. In 1947, the Muslim-majority Sylhet district was detached from Assam and awarded to East Pakistan. When a similar proposal to transfer Goalpara district from Assam to West Bengal was made by Bengalis in 1955, it became the occasion for one of the periodic outbreaks of violence directed by Assamese against Bengalis.[85] A continuing grievance of the Assamese has been that "Bengali leaders in Assam . . . are in the habit of looking to West Bengal for inspiration, guidance and publicity instead of talking things out inside the State of Assam"; many Assamese fear the alleged "agents of greater Bengal residing in Assam . . . ."[86] The selection of Bengali Hindus rather than Muslims as targets in 1960 and 1972 reflected the Assamese fixation on mainly Hindu West Bengal. One of the principal points in the indictment of Bengalis in Assam was that they were "traitors,"[87] that they were loyal to West Bengal rather than to Assam.

83. W. Howard Wriggins, "Ceylon's Time of Troubles, 1956–1958," *Far Eastern Survey* 28, no. 3 (March 1959): 34.

84. Charu Chandra Bhandari, *Thoughts on Assam Disturbances* (Rajghat, India: A.B. Sarva Seva Sangh Prakashan, 1961), p. 9.

85. See the *Assam Tribune* (Gauhati), March, April, and May 1955.

86. P.C. Goswami, "Tragedy of Political Tactlessness," *Economic Weekly*, July 30, 1960, pp. 1195–98.

87. Bhandari, *Thoughts on Assam Disturbances*, p. 28.

Then, in the 1970s, alarmed by the rapid growth of Bengali Muslim population through migration from Bangladesh, Assamese students began a movement against the "foreigners." Fed by fears that ultimately a Muslim majority would "demand a referendum to join Bangladesh,"[88] four years of intermittent anti-Muslim riots began in 1979. The power of numbers combined with an external threat.

There is a strong link between targeting groups that have external affinities and targeting groups that are opposed in warfare. I referred earlier to the killings of Biharis in Bangladesh in 1971 and 1972. The Biharis were chosen, in part, because they were aligned with Pakistani forces at a time when Pakistan was at war with Bangladesh, but it would be equally true to say that they were targeted as agents of an inaccessible foreign force. The fact that the violence continued after the Pakistani army had departed reinforces the accuracy of both descriptions of the targeting choice. There are many cases in which either depiction — opposition in warfare or external affinity — is accurate. Cambodia (1970) and Lithuania (1941), both discussed earlier, are clear examples.

The thesis that some ethnic groups are "agents" of a threatening foreign power is frequently found in accounts of ethnic riots. The theme goes back centuries. In London (1780), Catholics were targeted because they were thought to be part of an international papal conspiracy involving Spain and France, two dangerous military powers.[89] In the late nineteenth century, Armenians in Turkey were regarded as harboring pro-Russian sympathies (it is important that they lived on both sides of the border). Their alleged disloyalty lay in the background to the killings that took place in the Ottoman Empire.[90] Chinese in Southeast Asia have often been cast in the role of a Fifth Column for China.[91] The connections have direct implications for violence. A protest demonstration at a Chinese consulate in Medan, Indonesia (1965), for example, soon spilled over into mass killings of Chinese residents of the city.[92] A similar event

---

88. Kuldip Nayar, "Assamese Dread of Lost Identity," *Indian Express* (New Delhi), April 16, 1980, p. 6.

89. Christopher Hibbert, *King Mob: The Story of Lord George Gordon and the Riots of 1780* (New York: Dorset Press, 1989), p. 19.

90. Melson, *Revolution and Genocide*, p. 501.

91. Cf. Guy Hunter, *South-East Asia: Race, Culture and Nation* (London: Oxford University Press, 1966), p. 10.

92. J.A.C. Mackie, "Anti-Chinese Outbreaks in Indonesia, 1959–68," in J.A.C. Mackie, ed., *The Chinese in Indonesia* (Hong Kong: Heinemann Educational Books, 1976), pp. 115.

produced many Chinese deaths in Burma (1967).[93] Especially after the Indo-Pakistani war of 1965, Indian Muslims were widely regarded as being loyal to Pakistan. These sentiments have provided the leitmotiv of anti-Muslim riots in India,[94] just as, on the Pakistan side, an accusation of disloyalty was leveled at the Ahmadis, who were targeted.[95]

"Muslims are not loyal to this country"; they are "anti-national"; they are "traitors" who should "leave India and go to Pakistan": these are frequent themes of anti-Muslim violence in India.[96] For a considerable time, Indian riots were almost completely confined to north India. Particularly after the 1965 Indo-Pakistani war, the claim that Muslims were agents of Pakistan had far more immediacy in the north than it might in the south, a thousand miles from the border. Only with the growth of Hindu nationalist organizations all across the country did recurrent, large-scale, anti-Muslim violence spread southward, mainly in the 1980s and, even then, not everywhere in the south.[97]

Just as opposition in actual warfare facilitates targeting, ideological opposition between ethnic groups is likely to produce similar results if at least one of the opposing ideologies has a dangerous foreign connection. In Iraq, Brigadier Abdul Karim Qasim, who took power in a coup d'état in 1958, set about simultaneously to contain the Communists and to ally himself with Gamal Abdel Nasser's pan-Arabist ambitions. Both efforts were anathema to the Iraqi Kurds, who hoped for Communist assistance for their aspirations and feared their submergence in a larger United Arab Republic, embracing Egypt, Syria, and Iraq.[98] By contrast, the

93. Mary F. Somers Heidhues, *Southeast Asia's Chinese Minorities* (London: Longman, 1974), pp. 96–97.

94. See, e.g., Shah, "Communal Riots in Gujarat," p. 188; Schermerhorn, "The Locale of Hindu-Muslim Riots"; Aswini K. Ray and Subhash Chakravarti, *Meerut Riots: A Case Study* (New Delhi: Sampradayikta Virodhi Committee, n.d. [1968 or 1969]), p. 7; Suneet Chopra and N.K. Singh, "Ferozabad: Anatomy of a Riot," *Economic & Political Weekly*, August 19, 1972, pp. 1711, 1713; Government of India, *Report of the Commission of Inquiry on Communal Disturbances in Ranchi-Hatia (August 22–29, 1967)* (New Delhi: Government Printer, 1968), pp. 11, 73–74.

95. Government of [West] Punjab, *Report of the Court of Inquiry Constituted under Punjab Act II of 1954 to Enquire into the Punjab Disturbances of 1953* (Lahore: Superintendent of Government Printing, Punjab, 1954), pp. 28, 40.

96. Quoted by Asghar Ali Engineer, *Bhiwandi-Bombay Riots* (Bombay: Institute of Islamic Studies, 1984), pp. 56, 80, 88–90. To the same effect, see M.J. Akbar, *Riot after Riot* (New Delhi: Penguin, 1988), p. 151.

97. The growth of a Sikh separatist movement in Punjab, with links to Pakistan, had comparable effects on Sikhs as targets. In the Delhi riots of 1984, Sikhs, like Muslims, were stigmatized as "traitors." Chakravarti and Haksar, *The Delhi Riots*, p. 198.

98. George E. Kirk, *Contemporary Arab Politics* (New York: Praeger, 1961), p. 145.

Turkomens, staunch anti-Communists, supported Qasim. They were attacked by Kurds in Kirkuk when they sought to celebrate the first anniversary of Qasim's coup.[99] No doubt, too, the Malaysian violence of 1945–46 was exacerbated by comparable divisions between pro-Communist Chinese guerrillas and anti-Communist Malay villagers. Such phenomena underscore the linkage among three target-group characteristics: opposition in warfare, political threat, and external affinities.

It would be correct, but not wholly adequate, to say simply that ethnic groups whose domestic political strength appears to be augmented by their extraterritorial ethnic affinities are more likely targets than are groups whose strength is not so augmented. What needs to be added is the element of displacement present in many, though not all, of these attacks.[100] The local targets can be proxies for their inaccessible but powerful cousins across the border or the sea. The anti-Muslim riots in India and the anti-Ahmadi riot in Pakistan bring this out most clearly, but it is also demonstrable elsewhere. If Khmer cannot reach Vietnam, they can reach local Vietnamese; if Burmans cannot target China, they can target Chinese; if Ugandans cannot attack Kenya, they can attack Kenyans in Uganda.[101]

Targeting in Assam (1968), which otherwise appears wholly idiosyncratic, can be explained on this basis.[102] Time and again, both before and since 1968, rioters in Assam have targeted Bengalis. On Republic Day 1968, however, Bengalis were not attacked, but Marwaris were. As a result of central government policies designed to assuage separatist sentiment among the hill peoples by conferring varying degrees of autonomy on them, some Assamese began to believe their state was in danger of Balkanization. Eventually, a secessionist movement emerged among Assamese themselves, demanding independence from India. The Republic Day riot began as an Assamese secessionist demonstration. The national flag was pulled down and burned. Plainly, as the occasion itself suggests, this was a demonstration directed against the central government.

Nor did the character of the proceedings change as the demonstration

99. Ibid., pp. 161–63; Arnold Hottinger, "An Eye-Witness Report on Iraq," *Swiss Review of World Affairs* 9, no. 6 (September 1959): 12–16, at p. 13. Two further episodes of Turkomen-Kurdish riots followed in 1961. *Middle East Record* (Jerusalem) 2 (1961): 283.

100. As suggested by Cynthia H. Enloe in the case of the Indonesian Chinese, *Ethnic Conflict and Political Development* (Boston: Little, Brown, 1973), p. 196 n.15.

101. For the Uganda case, see the *Washington Post*, July 14, 1976, p. A7.

102. *The Statesman* (Calcutta), February 10, 1968; "Sack of Gauhati," *Economic and Political Weekly*, February 17, 1968, pp. 318–20; "Sharpening of Carving Knives," *Economic and Political Weekly*, January 27, 1968, p. 219; Dilip Mukerjee, "Assam Reorganization," *Asian Survey* 9, no. 4 (April 1969): 297–311, at p. 308.

turned against Marwaris. Marwaris, whose ancestral home is in Rajas-than, were regarded as "Indians" rather than as local citizens. Before the riot, there were anti-Marwari posters that read "Indians go back." The Marwaris, viewed as being under the protection of the central govern-ment, thus served as surrogates for the authorities in Delhi, with whom they were believed to be in league. The occasion for the violence, the signs that preceded it, and the behavior during it all lead to the conclu-sion that the 1968 riot contained a large component of displaced aggres-sion against an inaccessible external force.[103] The anti-Marwari violence was interspersed with burnings of the national flag.[104] As in some other cases of pure displacement, the intensity of the violence was compara-tively mild, the casualties few. This is consistent with displacement the-ory — for the greater the distance between the frustrater and the target of displaced aggression, the lower the level of anger directed against that target — and it contrasts sharply with the general fury of attacks on Bengalis in Assam, before and since. Finally, as the salience of the New Delhi–Assam issue receded, old targeting patterns were resumed. In 1972 and repeatedly afterward, it was Bengalis, not Marwaris, who were attacked again.

There are thus two propositions to be stated regarding the role of external affiliations in target selection. First, ethnic groups whose domes-tic political strength appears to be augmented by their external ethnic affinities tend to be targeted. The perception of the target group's politi-cal power tends to include power ascribed to the group's external affili-ates. Second, the likelihood that such a group will be targeted depends in part on foreign relations. An exacerbation of external relations — the Indo-Pakistani war of 1965, mainland China's alleged complicity in the Indonesian Communist Party coup attempt of 1965, the increasing dis-position in New Delhi to carve up Assam, Hungarian officials urging Hungarians in Romania (1990) to regard Transylvania as "ancestral Hungarian land,"[105] or Uzbek claims on the Osh region of Kyrghyzstan (1990)[106] — tends to increase the risk that the domestic group with exter-

103. For inaccessibility of the instigator as a spur to displacement, see Berkowitz, *Aggression: A Social-Psychological Analysis*, pp. 107–08.

104. For another riot involving a foreign flag, see G. William Skinner, *Chinese Society in Thailand* (Ithaca: Cornell University Press, 1957), pp. 278–79.

105. *Reuters Library Report*, March 21, 1990.

106. Eugene Huskey, "Kyrgyzstan: The Politics of Demographic and Economic Frustration," in Ian Bremmer and Ray Taras, eds., *New States, New Politics: Building the Post-Soviet Nations* (New York: Cambridge University Press, 1997), pp. 661–62; Talant Razakov, *Osh Koogalany/Oshskie Sobytia* (The Osh Events) (Biškek, Kyrghyzstan: Renaissance, 1993).

nal affinities will indeed be targeted because of displacement.[107] Social distance studies suggest support for this conclusion.[108]

International migration has made displaced aggression against representatives of inaccessible foreign forces a more important feature of ethnic riots. In the Ivory Coast (1981 and 1985), there were deadly riots against Ghanaians. The 1985 riot followed much less serious violence against Ivorians in Ghana and was rather clearly a reprisal riot.[109] In 1989, there were reciprocal riots in Senegal and Mauritania. They began with riots in Senegal against Mauritanian Moors. When the news reached Mauritania, there were very serious riots against Senegalese. When the victims of these riots in turn reached Senegal, there were renewed, and quite deadly, riots targeting Mauritanians. Eventually, an exchange of nationals was arranged.[110]

These are, of course, hardly the first occasions for riots against foreigners. What stamps them as distinctive is the element of revenge and then further revenge, as the attackers victimize resident aliens serving as proxies for the unreachable foreigners who have attacked the attackers' cousins across the border. The growing worldwide pattern of international migration and the prospect of escalating, reverberating, reciprocal violence across borders suggests that there is room for growth in this species of targeting.[111]

PSYCHOLOGICAL STRENGTH

In referring to target-group characteristics, we are, of course, speaking about relationships between pairs of antagonists. One important rela-

---

107. Cf. Weiner, "The Macedonian Syndrome," pp. 674–75.

108. In 1962, students in India saw the Chinese as the most distant national group, with Pakistanis next. Both were then prominent external enemies. A.K.P. Sinha and O.P. Upadhyaya, "Eleven Ethnic Groups on a Social Distance Scale," *Journal of Social Psychology* 57, First Half (June 1962): 49–54. The Bangladesh war of 1971 increased the distance Hindus felt toward Muslims in India. Robert D. Meade and Labh Singh, "Changes in Social Distance during Warfare: A Study of the India/Pakistan War of 1971," *Journal of Social Psychology* 90, no. 1 (June 1973): 325–26.

109. Richard Everett, "Riots Follow Football Match," *West Africa*, September 16, 1985, p. 1932; "Goodwill Message to Ghana," ibid., September 30, 1985, p. 2064.

110. "Deep Roots of Discord," *Africa News*, May 15, 1989, pp. 5–6; Elizabeth Blunt, "In the Midst of the Madding Crowd," *Africa Events* 5, no. 6 (June 1989): 22–23; "Toughing It Out," ibid., pp. 24–25; Sulayman S. Nyang, "Fighting Cousins," ibid., pp. 28–29.

111. Cf. Marc Howard Ross, "Internal and External Conflict and Violence: Cross-Cultural Evidence and a New Analysis," *Journal of Conflict Resolution* 29, no. 4 (December 1985): 547–79, at p. 553.

tionship derives from what might be called group psychological juxtapositions. This term refers to the characterological comparisons between two groups, especially the modal personal attributes that are said to characterize them in a reciprocal way. A particularly common juxtaposition developed during colonial rule all over Asia and Africa, and grew up elsewhere under other auspices, between groups thought to be backward and those thought to be advanced.[112] So-called backward groups are generally less well represented than are advanced groups in education, the professions, and the modern sector of the economy. They are stereotyped as unenterprising, ignorant, indolent, traditional, and passive, whereas advanced groups are said to be diligent, dynamic, motivated, and intelligent, if often a bit too pushy.[113] Group identities are formed by processes of opposition and contrast, and this set of recurrent juxtapositions is a case in point.

Since this set of comparisons is invidious, in that it casts aspersions on the collective worth of the backward group, it is unusually irritating. In such cases, antipathy is fed by comparison of the targets to aggressors. The aggressors internalize the comparison and find it unflattering. Consider the Sikhs targeted in Delhi (1984). Their "Hindu counterparts" experienced what is described as "a sense of discomfort and inferiority . . . ."[114] At the same time, the Sikhs were seen as "cussed and ill-bred, vulgar and brutish."[115] The logic of this common combination is that people who are seen as undeserving are nevertheless possessed of personal attributes that place them in an advantaged position.

With very few exceptions, where such juxtapositions exist, riot behavior involves the targeting of advanced groups by backward groups. Assamese have recurrently attacked Bengalis, and not vice versa. Lulua have attacked Luba in Zaire. Sinhalese have attacked Tamils. Kurds have attacked Turkomens in Iraq. Mbochi have attacked Lari in the Congo Republic. Malays have targeted Chinese in Malaysia and Singapore.

---

112. I have dealt with the emergence and significance of such relationships at some length in Donald L. Horowitz, *Ethnic Groups in Conflict* (Berkeley and Los Angeles: University of California Press, 1985), pp. 147–84. Where such juxtapositions developed under colonial rule, the colonialists did not uniformly (or even generally) favor the "advanced" group. The French in Cambodia did favor the Vietnamese, but the Belgians disfavored the Luba, and the British did the same with the Ibo, the Malaysian Chinese, and the Burmese Indians.

113. For some surveys, see ibid., pp. 166–71.

114. Rajni Kothari, "The How and the Why of It All," in Smithu Kothari and Harsh Sethi, eds., *Voices from a Scarred City: The Delhi Carnage in Perspective* (Delhi: Lokayan, 1985), p. 17.

115. Ibid.

Pathans have attacked Mohajirs in Pakistan. Kyrghyz have attacked Uzbeks in Kyrghyzstan. Azeris have attacked Armenians in Azerbaijan. Khmer have attacked Vietnamese in Cambodia. Hausa have targeted Ibo in Nigeria. Across countries and within countries, the pattern is recurrent. Assamese attacked Bengalis in 1955, 1960, 1972, and between 1979 and 1983. Sinhalese attacked Tamils in 1956, 1958, 1977, and 1983. Malays attacked Chinese in 1945–46, 1957, 1959, 1967, and 1969 in Malaysia and twice in 1964 in Singapore. Pathans attacked Mohajirs in 1965 and recurrently after 1984. Hausa attacked Ibo in 1945, 1953, and twice in 1966. Only very rarely does a so-called advanced group attack a backward group in deadly riots.[116] This strong tendency is consistent with findings that negative social comparison can elicit aggressive responses.[117]

Occasionally, there is a plausible choice of advanced targets available, and only one is selected. Nigeria is one of these cases, and the choice of Ibo, rather than Yoruba, to receive violence sheds light again on the exact nature of the irritants.

A survey of African student attitudes, conducted in the 1960s, at roughly the time of the worst anti-Ibo riots, suggests pertinent characterological distinctions between Ibo and Yoruba.[118] Non-Yoruba provided negative-to-positive descriptions of Yoruba in roughly the same proportions as non-Ibo did of Ibo (in each case, two to one), but the typical grounds of unfavorable evaluation were quite different. According to members of other groups, the most prominent negative traits possessed by Yoruba were untrustworthiness, unreliability, shiftiness, and unpredictability. These were not the attributes imputed by outgroup members to Ibo. Rather, Ibo were said to be quarrelsome, aggressive, domineering, ethnocentric, "tribalistic," parochial, and selfish. Other

116. Two exceptions are the attacks by Mohajirs on Sindhis in 1972 and the attacks on Hausa by Ibo in Aba, Nigeria (2000), in retaliation for earlier Hausa attacks. To say that advanced groups do not generally perpetrate riots is not to say, of course, that advanced groups do not engage in violence at all. Malaysian Chinese formed the backbone of Communist guerrillas who fought from 1948 to 1960 and sporadically thereafter. Sri Lankan Tamils have mounted a terrorist insurgency of considerable dimensions. But neither has initiated deadly riots against Malays or Sinhalese, respectively.

117. See, e.g., Valerie Melburg and James T. Tedeschi, "Displaced Aggression: Frustration or Impression Management?" European Journal of Social Psychology 19, no. 2 (March–April 1989): 139–45. For the sense of powerlessness, pessimism, despair, and lack of confidence vis-à-vis Jews that animated German anti-Semitism, see P.G.J. Pulzer, The Rise of Political Anti-Semitism in Germany and Austria (New York: John Wiley, 1964), pp. 296–98.

118. Otto Klineberg and Marisa Zavalloni, Nationalism and Tribalism among African Students (Paris and The Hague: Mouton, 1969), pp. 152–53.

groups might be wary of Yoruba because of their presumed unreliability, but this was not their reason for wariness of Ibo. A majority of respondents described Ibo as "hard-working, dynamic, industrious, [and] enterprising."[119] The linkage of these traits with the allegedly aggressive, grasping, and ethnocentric character of the Ibo produces a far more dangerous combination. The positive traits suggest a competitive advantage; the negative traits suggest that that advantage will be utilized mercilessly for group purposes.

This complex of energy, control, and ethnocentrism gives rise to fear — and concomitant violence — in many countries. The more "evolved" and "enterprising"[120] the Lari became, the more dangerous they seemed to Mbochi. The more successful the Luba were in urban clerical employment, the more they were described as "haughty, arrogant, and nepotistic,"[121] as the Ibo were described, and the more they produced in Lulua a "fear of domination" and a "desire to 'catch up'" with them[122] that matched the Hausa desire to "catch up" with Ibo. The greater the capacity of the Tiv, the more the Jukun felt they might be dominated and "pushed to the corner."[123] The more culturally advantaged the Bengalis seemed, the more there was "an increase in Assamese efforts to catch up with the Bengalees by emulation."[124] The more the Khmer came to be seen as "more 'traditional'" and the Vietnamese as "more 'rational,'"[125] the more Khmer feared "being smothered"[126] by the Vietnamese and the more they imputed to them a "plan for swallowing

119. Ibid., p. 153. For a reciprocal Ibo view of Hausa as "unenterprising, lazy, backward, and feudal," see Colin Legum, "The Tragedy in Nigeria," *Africa Report* 11, no. 8 (November 1966): 23–24, at p. 23. See generally Elliott P. Skinner, "Strangers in West African Societies," *Africa* 33, no. 4 (October 1963): 307–20, at p. 314. Compare Elizabeth Nissan, "Some Thoughts on Sinhalese Justifications for the Violence," in James Manor, ed., *Sri Lanka in Change and Crisis* (New York: St. Martin's Press, 1984), p. 181: "Common but contradictory characterizations of Tamils depict them as barbarians, but with superiority in intelligence, diligence, earning power and cunning."

120. Thompson and Adloff, *The Emerging States of French Equatorial Africa*, p. 476.

121. Quoted in Crawford Young, *The Politics of Cultural Pluralism* (Madison: University of Wisconsin Press, 1976), p. 179.

122. Lemarchand, *Political Awakening in the Belgian Congo*, p. 206. This significant phrase is recurrent in such relationships. See Horowitz, *Ethnic Groups in Conflict*, pp. 171–75.

123. *Independent* (London), February 22, 1992, p. 12. See Ter-Rumun Avav and Mson Myegba, *The Dream to Conquer: Story of Tiv-Jukun Conflict* (Makurdi, Nigeria: Onairi, 1992), pp. 14–15.

124. Sajal Nag, *Roots of Ethnic Conflict* (New Delhi: Manohar, 1990), p. 83.

125. Chou, "The Vietnamese Minority in Cambodia," p. 35.

126. Quoted in Nayan Chanda, "Wounds of History: Surging Resentment of Vietnamese Could Spark New Pogroms," *Far Eastern Economic Review*, July 30, 1992, pp. 14–16, at p. 15.

Khmer territory and committing genocide against the Khmers."[127] In 1966, Hausa expressed similar sentiments about Ibo in northern Nigeria, as Malays earlier had about Chinese and Assamese had about Bengalis. In each case, the apprehension of "swallowing" was accompanied by a powerful explosion of brutality. As I have suggested, the recurrent fear of being swallowed by those who are more adept at manipulating the external environment points to the utter helplessness underpinning the violence of those who feel backward. The antipathy that follows on this common set of psychological juxtapositions is that of those who feel incapable when compared to the objects of the antipathy.[128] They project onto those others the impulses that accompany such extreme discomfort: to swallow, to smother, and to kill en masse.

The extent to which relative group positions are implicated in ethnic violence is indicated by the changing identity of the perpetrators as group positions change. In Mauritania, Moors have more than once rioted against better educated, more advanced black Africans, but in Zanzibar and in Sudan, where group positions were reversed, so were riot positions, as black Africans attacked Arabs. In Assam, Assamese have rioted and Bengalis have been victimized, but in Bangladesh, Bengalis have attacked allegedly more diligent and capable Biharis. The anti-Dahomeyan riots of 1958 in the Ivory Coast were conducted, not by the "advanced" Baoulé but by groups from the underdeveloped southwest, especially the Bété, who felt colonized by ethnic strangers and unable to compete effectively.[129] The people frequently regarded as submissive are more often the aggressors, and the allegedly aggressive people are more often the aggrieved.[130]

127. Quoted in Nayan Chanda, "Cambodia: Blood Brothers," *Far Eastern Economic Review*, December 3, 1992, pp. 14–15, at p. 14.

128. Although social comparison processes form a well-known category of social psychology and of the social psychology of intergroup relationships, invidious comparisons are not frequently cited by psychologists as a source of violent behavior. See, e.g., Michael Argyle, *The Social Psychology of Everyday Life* (New York: Routledge, 1992), pp. 173–74; Michael Billig, *Social Psychology and Intergroup Relations* (New York: Academic Press, 1976), pp. 121–80; John H. Duckitt, *Social Psychology of Prejudice* (New York: Praeger, 1992); Geen, *Human Aggression*, pp. 1–30.

129. On the Bété, see Aristide Zolberg, *One-Party Government in the Ivory Coast*, rev. ed. (Princeton: Princeton University Press, 1969), p. 246; see also pp. 199–205, 279. Of the Dahomeyan and Togolese victims, Gwendolen Carter comments that "[i]n a real sense, it was their intelligence and energy which made them subject to jealousy by the slower, less efficient people of the Ivory Coast." Gwendolen Carter, *Independence for Africa* (New York: Praeger, 1960), p. 107.

130. Obviously, I use the term *aggressive* here in a figurative sense, but it is striking that, as we have seen, groups associated with physical aggression are also targeted.

To the extent that perceived backwardness is associated with rural origins, some of this aggression may reflect hostility to urban life and urban ways. But it is more than that. There is no escaping knowledge of the greater rewards afforded by the modern economy and the status system that accompanies it for those who possess the appropriate skills. Members of backward groups understand that they do not possess these skills in adequate measure, and it is precisely a notion of inadequacy that pervades their relations with the people who become targets of violence.

All of this is compounded by a belief that the target group has and expresses a quite different sense of itself. The Bengalis of Assam were charged with possessing a "superiority complex" and being unsympathetic to other people.[131] Ibo were said to be "arrogant,"[132] as were Indians in South Africa (also said to exude an "air of superiority"),[133] and, like other advanced groups, Voltaics in the Ivory Coast clearly felt that the country's prosperity had been built on their backs,[134] for which they were rewarded with discriminatory treatment. If a great tradition overlaps a disproportionate command of modern skills, as it does for Malaysian Chinese, Sri Lankan Tamils, Bengalis in Assam, and Arab Sudanese, then ethnocentrism may be even stronger and produce greater disparagement of competing groups. If, on the other hand, the so-called backward people belong to the great tradition, their sense of humiliation may be even greater as they confront those who are advantaged although they belong to what is stigmatized as an inferior civilization. Some such sentiment was expressed by Hausa toward Ibo. Although northerners were obsessed by their own backwardness,[135] some were doubly humiliated by the Ibo, whom, lacking an Islamic background, they sometimes saw as "cannibals,"[136] "*arne* (pagans), whom they despised as unbelievers . . . and possessors of inferior culture."[137]

In a number of countries, backward groups seek, and sometimes

131. Bhandari, *Thoughts on Assam Disturbances*, p. 22; see p. 42.

132. Gretchen Dihoff, *Katsina: Profile of a Nigerian City* (New York: Praeger, 1970), p. 22.

133. Union of South Africa, *Report of the Commission of Enquiry into Riots in Durban* (Cape Town: Cape Times, 1949), p. 13.

134. Victor DuBois, "The Struggle for Stability in Upper Volta, Part IV: Foreign Reaction to the Overthrow of Maurice Yameogo," *American Universities Field Staff Reports*, West Africa Series 12, no. 4 (1969): 12.

135. Walter Schwarz, *Nigeria* (New York: Praeger, 1968), pp. 215, 253.

136. P.C. Lloyd, "The Ethnic Background to the Nigerian Crisis," in S.K. Panter-Brick, ed., *Nigerian Politics and Military Rule: Prelude to the Civil War* (London: Athlone Press, 1970), p. 3.

137. Plotnicov, "Who Owns Jos?" p. 8.

obtain, preferential arrangements to compensate for their competitive disabilities, in education, employment, and business licenses and contracts. However great the antipathy toward other groups may be, it would be a mistake to think that claims to exclude ethnic strangers from opportunities are made without a sense of self-reproach because of the violation of egalitarian norms the claims imply.[138] Moreover, the need for preferential treatment itself serves to heighten feelings of doubt among those who aim to restrict the openness of competition.[139] Far more often than not, the ground asserted to underlie the need for preferences is not the absence of fair competitive conditions but the absence of essential personal qualities: the explanation is internal, not external. If the group possessed the qualities it values, it would not need special help.

How this conflict can produce aggression has been suggested by the psychoanalyst Ernest Jones. Jones argues that hate is a common defense against apprehensiveness; and if hate brings on feelings of guilt, one way of relieving those feelings is to apply still more hate.[140] In divided societies, as I have noted, it has often been pointed out that hostile and exclusive attitudes are customarily justified by highly exaggerated descriptions of the threat posed by groups that are the objects of hostility. Sometimes the targets have responded vigorously to the hostility directed at them, thereby inadvertently confirming the perceived reasonableness of the hostility and probably facilitating the initiators' disposition to take violent action if the occasion arises. Anxiety and guilt produce hostility and the projection of hostility onto the target group.

Frustration-aggression theory takes a different route to a similar destination. It maintains that the likelihood of a violent response to frustration varies inversely with the availability of alternative channels of satisfaction.[141] Where characterological explanations for ethnic relationships prevail — where ethnic strangers are believed to have profited from innate advantages — many nonviolent channels undoubtedly seem blocked.

If backwardness implies the incapacity to attain goals to the same extent that others can attain them, violence becomes a way of wiping out all apparent differences in capacity except in the capacity to inflict harm.

138. See Horowitz, *Ethnic Groups in Conflict*, pp. 678–79.

139. For more examples of self-disparagement, see ibid., pp. 173–75.

140. Ernest Jones, "Fear, Guilt and Hate," in Ernest Jones, ed., *Papers on Psychoanalysis*, 5th ed. (Boston: Beacon Press, 1961), pp. 305–08.

141. For a convenient statement, with accompanying evidence, see Ted Gurr, "Psychological Factors in Civil Violence," *World Politics* 20, no. 2 (January 1968): 245–78.

There is probably some significance in the common phrasing of the aims of those so-called backward groups that initiate violence. The goals of the riot are sometimes described as "teaching them a lesson." This, of course, implies a satisfying reversal of roles: the group exhorted to learn the lesson of the modern world becomes the teacher of lessons to those who thought they knew them. Writing of the 1930 Rangoon riot, Usha Mahajani illustrates the point: "Undoubtedly, the 'suppressed ferocity' of the Burmese which bounced into an orgy of massacre of Indians was a manifestation of the nationalist upsurge of the hitherto downtrodden people. The average Burman on the street felt that at least once he had proved his superiority over the Indian."[142] A situation that seems to be slipping out of hand can, for the moment, be retrieved by force. In killing, at least, the group enjoined to improve its performance can demonstrate its qualities of excellence.

There is now a large body of accumulated evidence that aggressive individuals (at least those whose aggression is hot and angry rather than cool and instrumental) tend to be low on ego strength and self-esteem.[143] In experiments, subjects with low self-esteem provide more hostile reactions to insults than others do,[144] and those who suffer a blow to self-esteem display a more extreme pattern of reactions to outgroups.[145] On the other hand, some research suggests that individuals with high but unstable self-esteem are especially prone to hostility.[146] Not all the experimental results can be reconciled.

There are certainly hazards in generalizing from individual to collective violence, as well as from individual to collective self-esteem, which

142. Usha Mahajani, *The Role of Indian Minorities in Burma and Malaya* (Bombay: Vora, 1960), p. 76, quoting Maurice Collis, *Trials in Burma* (London: Faber and Faber, 1946), p. 148.

143. Berkowitz, *Aggression: A Social-Psychological Analysis*, pp. 275–80; Hans Toch, *Violent Men: An Inquiry into the Psychology of Violence* (Chicago: Aldine, 1969), pp. 143–48. For low self-esteem and ethnocentrism, see H.D. Forbes, *Nationalism, Ethnocentrism, and Personality: Social Science and Critical Theory* (Chicago: University of Chicago Press, 1985), p. 135.

144. Steven J. Kingsbury, "Self Esteem of Victim and the Intent of Third-Party Aggression in the Reduction of Hostile Aggression," *Motivation and Emotion* 2, no. 2 (June 1978): 177–89.

145. James R. Meindl and Melvin J. Lerner, "Exacerbation of Extreme Responses to an Out-Group," *Journal of Personality and Social Psychology* 47, no. 1 (July 1984): 71–84.

146. Michael H. Kernis, "The Roles of Stability and Level of Self-Esteem in Psychological Functioning," in Roy F. Baumeister, ed., *Self-Esteem: The Puzzle of Low Self-Regard* (New York: Plenum Press, 1993), pp. 171–72.

may vary independently.[147] Yet the aggregate patterns of collective target choice are consistent with the findings about individual behavior. When group positions are as disparate as are those between backward and advanced groups, and when stereotypes readily attach to each of the groups, group members are likely to act on the basis of apprehensions deriving from those positions and stereotypes — provided that the particular situation is structured so that collective behavior is called for. Needless to say, the charged situation preceding a riot is laden with cues calling forth, not just individual affect, but collective perceptions. Self-esteem thus seems to be at work in collective violence, as it is in individual violence, and it does not appear difficult to envision how group members sense that they are called upon to act as such.

To be sure, some people with low self-esteem are also high on inhibitions to aggression, which could either prevent the expression of their anger or lead them to displace it onto targets other than the frustrating agent.[148] Strong inhibitions that in the short run exceed even strong anger may lead to the accumulation of hostility over time, followed by an explosion when anger finally exceeds inhibitions on its expression. There is evidence that some people ruminate on anger-producing experiences, store their anger, and then lash out.[149] Such a propensity could help account for the recurrent but episodic — and ferocious — quality of much violence, including collective violence.

The underlying roles of self-doubt and verbal infacility in violent episodes have been singled out by Hans Toch in his study of violent men.[150] In Toch's view, a certain species of interpersonal violence reflects the desire of the "sore loser . . . not only to tear up the game but also to destroy his opponent."[151] Toch's emphasis on the person who feels "walled-in" comports with the picture I have painted here of an ethnic group experiencing similar feelings.

A number of other individual personality attributes have been linked to violence initiation. Inability to defer gratification,[152] authoritarian-

147. See Marilynn B. Brewer and Norman Miller, *Intergroup Relations* (Buckingham, England: Open University Press, 1996), p. 91; Ervin Staub, *The Roots of Evil: The Origins of Genocide and Other Group Violence* (Cambridge: Cambridge University Press, 1989), pp. 55, 104–05.

148. Berkowitz, *Aggression: A Social-Psychological Analysis*, pp. 278–79.

149. Geen, *Human Aggression*, pp. 163–64. I discuss rumination further in Chapter 13.

150. Toch, *Violent Men*, pp. 153–54.

151. Ibid.

152. Berkowitz, *Aggression: A Social Psychological Analysis*, pp. 277–78.

ism,[153] and personality development in a maternally dominant environment[154] are among the possibilities.[155] Many of these relationships are contestable, and the precise connections of self-esteem to aggression remain to be specified. But the recurrent choice of targets from among groups characterized as possessing an excess of enterprise, ambition, energy, arrogance, and achievement by those who believe themselves lacking such traits can scarcely be denied.

ANTIPATHY, SIMILARITY, AND DIFFERENCE

Just as the first three target-group characteristics — reputation for aggression, traditional antagonism, and opposition in war — comprise a cluster associated with violence, the second three — political strength, external affinities, and psychological strength — all evoke a dominance-threat dimension. (There are also strong links between the two clusters, most visible, perhaps, with respect to opposition in warfare.) The same dominance-threat element is also reflected in precipitating events, many of which involve either demonstrations of group strength by target groups or feared alterations of relative group status, to the disadvantage of the initiator group.[156]

Several questions remain about these six target-group characteristics. Are they, in any sense, cumulative — that is, additive or multiplicative? Does a larger outburst result if a target possesses more than one of them? If direct and displaced aggression conjoin to produce a larger cumulative effect where a target group receives both, it seems likely that the quantum of violence will also be greater where a target is the object of antipathy on more than one ground.[157] The massive anti-Ibo violence of 1966

153. Ted Robert Gurr, *Why Men Rebel* (Princeton: Princeton University Press, 1970), pp. 165–68.

154. Ralph Epstein, "Aggression toward Outgroups as a Function of Authoritarianism and Imitation of Aggressive Models," *Journal of Personality and Social Psychology* 3, no. 5 (May 1966): 574–79.

155. Gordon Allport, *The Nature of Prejudice* (Cambridge, Mass.: Addison-Wesley, 1954), p. 361; Toch, *Violent Men*, p. 190.

156. See Chapter 8, below.

157. Contrast with this the commonly expressed, but unproved, notion that conflict is worse if groups are divided by racial, linguistic, and religious cleavages than when they are separated by only one or two of these. See, e.g., Wyszomirski, "Communal Violence." By the same token, there is no evidence that groups differentiated by language are targeted less frequently than groups differentiated by religion, or vice versa. Either differentiation can form the basis of powerfully felt ascriptive identity. For a different view, see David D. Laitin, "Language Conflict and Violence" (paper prepared for the National Academy of

may exemplify this point; so, too, may the anti-Chinese riots in Malaysia in 1969 and the anti-Bengali riots of 1979–83 in Assam. On the other hand, a group that possesses only one target characteristic — traditional antipathy, for example — might receive less violence or receive violence less often than a group that is multiply marked. This may explain how some antagonisms based on single characteristics undergo change, as in the case of the traditional Franco-German antipathy, which looked more and more anachronistic after 1945. Still, the hypothesis needs a good test.

Equally uncertain is whether there is anything resembling a hierarchy of target-group characteristics. Surely, some attributes must be more evocative of hostility than are others. It seems plausible that political and psychological threat might be more potent in attracting violence than are other characteristics. However, some characteristics, such as reputation for aggression, may be underreported compared to others.

What happens if the characteristics point in the direction of more than one target group? There are occasional shifts in targeting over time. In the colonial period, Sinhalese leaders complained of their competitive incapacity vis-à-vis both Tamils and Moors (Muslims); in 1915 there was a serious riot against Moors.[158] With independence, the more numerous Tamils became targets. Clearly, the increasing importance of political threat accounts for the change. Some such shifts can also be explained, as I shall show in Chapter 6, by changing riot leadership and organizational rivalries. More often than not, however, the same groups are targeted again and again. Most of the time, riot leaders must cater to antipathies of their clienteles, even if they are able to alter them at the margins; and these antipathies are rooted in the enumerated target-group characteristics.

Those target-group characteristics have significance for theories of intergroup relations at higher levels of generality. In this connection, what the list of characteristics omits is every bit as interesting as what it contains. Two sets of potential target-group characteristics often invoked in everyday discussions of ethnic relations appear strikingly problematic in the light of the evidence reviewed here. One is cultural distance, and

Sciences/National Research Council Commission on Behavioral and Social Sciences and Education, Committee on International Conflict Resolution, September 13, 1998).

158. See Stanley Jeyaraja Tambiah, *Buddhism Betrayed? Religion, Politics, and Violence in Sri Lanka* (Chicago: University of Chicago Press, 1986), p. 8.

the other is economic grievance.[159] Both are frequently adduced explanations for interethnic violence.

The role of intergroup proximity or distance — or similarity and difference — in engendering hostility has a long history in studies of ethnic relations. In *Group Psychology and the Analysis of the Ego*, Freud had argued that small differences between individuals or groups in close relationships produce "feelings of aversion and hostility . . . ."[160] "Closely related races" disdain or despise each other, and "greater differences," according to Freud, ". . . lead to an almost insuperable repugnance, such as the Gallic people feel for the German, the Aryan for the Semite, and the white races for the coloured."[161] For Freud, there were thus proportional increases in hostility as "differences" — presumably cultural differences — increased. And Freud was quite clear about the mechanism underlying the relationship. Antipathy and aversion to others are a function of narcissism, love of oneself. Narcissism "behaves as though the occurrence of any divergence from [one's] own particular lines of development involved a criticism of them and a demand for their alteration."[162] Hatred of difference consequently derives from the self-preservative functions of self-love.

The narcissistic mechanism, which is remarkably consistent with later theories of social comparison,[163] does not require the proportionality of hostility to degree of difference for which Freud argued. Small differences make comparison easier and may suffice to produce hostility; large differences quickly become incomparable.

Consistent with the general Freudian view, a great deal of research confirms that, as we saw in Chapter 2, similarity (especially of belief) attracts, and dissimilarity repels. On the other hand, there is evidence of a propensity to accentuate the differences perceived between relatively similar

159. Crude associations of cultural distance with ethnic hostility are captured in currently fashionable discussions of "the Other." Equally reflexive explanations of violence in terms of "economic exploitation" can readily be found. For a survey, see Heidhues, *Southeast Asia's Chinese Minorities*.

160. Sigmund Freud, *Group Psychology and the Analysis of the Ego,* trans. and ed. James Strachey (1921; New York: W.W. Norton, 1959), p. 33.

161. Ibid.

162. Ibid., p. 34.

163. Leon Festinger, "A Theory of Social Comparison Processes," *Human Relations* 7, no. 2 (May 1954): 117–40; Henri Tajfel, "Intergroup Behavior, Social Comparison and Social Change" (Katz-Newcomb Lectures, University of Michigan, Ann Arbor, mimeo., 1974). Much of the literature was synthesized in Henri Tajfel, *Human Groups and Social Categories* (Cambridge: Cambridge University Press, 1981).

ingroups and outgroups; and, once a dimension of intergroup competitiveness is present, similarity of attitudes, values, or cultural features can actually increase the sense of rivalry.[164] Reviewing an array of studies, Rupert J. Brown concludes that in competitive situations, intergroup "similarity, because it implies an impending loss (or gain) of superiority, will enhance feelings of competitiveness and hostility still further."[165]

Of course, the psychological juxtaposition that so frequently accompanies interethnic conflict and violence is usually associated with a modicum of cultural difference, sufficient at least to support stereotypes of lesser and greater motivation, diligence, and arrogance between the antagonistic groups. But the persistence of these stereotypes requires an intensive, day-in-and-day-out process of invidious comparison that can be sustained only if the antagonists are similar enough to be within the bounds of comparability. Strong cultural difference, as I have suggested, undermines comparability and competition.

In riots, then, there is no reason to expect target choice to be associated with cultural distance, and any such expectation is, in fact, disappointed. If targeting decisions were based on the cultural distance between aggressors and targets, the Meskhetian Turks who were attacked in Uzbekistan (1989) would make poor targets indeed. Like the Uzbeks who attacked them, the Meskhetians speak a Turkic language and are also perfectly fluent in Uzbek. With considerable justice, the two groups were described as "two branches of a great [Turkic] nation."[166] If cultural distance predicted target choice, Marwaris in Assam would be more likely targets than Bengalis have been. There is much greater cultural proximity between Assamese and Bengalis than between Assamese and Marwaris.[167] The ancestral home of the Marwaris, Rajasthan (with which they continue to be in close contact and to which they send remittances),[168] is 1,000 miles from Assam. By contrast, for quite some time the British believed the rather similar Assamese and Bengali languages to be one language,[169] and

---

164. Rupert J. Brown, "The Role of Similarity in Intergroup Relations," in Henri Tajfel, ed., *The Social Dimension: European Developments in Social Psychology* (Cambridge: Cambridge University Press, 1984), pp. 603–23.

165. Ibid., p. 618.

166. Mukhammad Solikh, quoted in *Krasnaya Zvezda* (Moscow), June 17, 1989, p. 6, in FBIS-SOV-89-116, June 19, 1989, pp. 50–51, at p. 51.

167. "There are affinities between the Assamese and the Bengali people in most respects. As peoples, they are akin to each other. The Marwaris and others settled in Assam are very much distant from them as peoples." Bhandari, *Thoughts on Assam Disturbances*, p. 26.

168. See Bhawani Singh, *Politics of Alienation in Assam* (Delhi: Ajanta, 1984), p. 79.

169. Among many accounts, see ibid., p. 69.

indeed there is evidence that Assamese and the northern branch of the Bengali language had common roots.[170] Likewise, the Lulua and Luba "share the same cultural features,"[171] and the separateness of the two groups is so recent that, until World War II, Luba migrants to Lulua areas were often given land and wives by Lulua, who considered them relations.[172] Sinhalese and Tamils have exchanged, as I have noted, both DNA and culture over the centuries. Culturally more distant from the Sinhalese are the Moors, Muslim descendants of Arab traders who married locally; but, as I have just mentioned, Moors have not been targeted by Sinhalese in riots since 1915.[173] In Burma (1938), Indian Muslims, who were attacked, had been much longer resident and far more acculturated to Burmese ways than were Hindus, who were not attacked. Many Sikhs killed in Delhi (1984) had no ties to the Punjab or to the Punjabi language.[174] No doubt, culturally distant groups are sometimes attacked. During the 1970s, the Assamese, for example, turned their violent attention from long-resident Bengali Hindus of the Brahmaputra Valley to more recent, less acculturated immigrants from Bangladesh. Georg Simmel may have overstated the proposition that hostility is greater, the closer the relation is between two parties.[175] The standard really is comparability more than proximity per se. Simmel's overstatement notwithstanding, cultural distance does not emerge as a criterion for target selection.

Neither does economic grievance. As an elaborated theory of ethnic conflict, economic determinism may be dead or at least dormant,[176] but inarticulate assumptions about the destructive effects of economic competition on intergroup relations seep into treatments of violence.[177] These

---

170. Nag, *Roots of Ethnic Conflict*, p. 27.

171. Lemarchand, *Political Awakening in the Belgian Congo*, p. 206.

172. Young, *The Politics of Cultural Pluralism*, pp. 175–76.

173. For the cultural distance of the Moors, see E.F.C. Ludowyk, *Those Long Afternoons: Childhood in Colonial Ceylon* (Colombo: Lake House Bookshop, 1989), pp. 16, 78.

174. Chakravarti and Haksar, *The Delhi Riots*, pp. 72–73, 81, 267.

175. Georg Simmel, *Conflict and the Web of Group Affiliations*, trans. Kurt H. Wolff and Reinhard Bendix (Glencoe, Ill.: Free Press, 1955), pp. 43–45.

176. See Milton J. Esman, *Ethnic Politics* (Ithaca: Cornell University Press, 1994), pp. 233–34.

177. For conventional wisdom, see Tamotsu Shibutani and Kian M. Kwan, *Ethnic Stratification: A Comparative Approach* (New York: Macmillan, 1965), pp. 168, 196–97, 380–81. See also Editorial, "Race Lives," *Far Eastern Economic Review*, December 16, 1993, p. 5: ". . . the evidence suggests that prosperity remains the best balm where ethnic tensions have been rubbed raw." No evidence is cited. Compare Esman, *Ethnic Politics*, pp. 235–38.

assumptions are often unaffected even by evidence of violence in the face of growing prosperity on the part of those who engage in violence.[178] Particularly common is the assertion that so-called middleman minorities are unusually vulnerable to violence,[179] but the more general association of riot behavior with envy of material advantage is not far behind.[180]

Yet economically superior groups often escape violence. Attacking groups are typically not making the pertinent comparative judgments regarding them. In Uzbekistan (1989), rioters did not target Russians, who are both culturally distant and economically advantaged; they chose Meskhetian Turks, who occupy an economically precarious position.[181] Marwaris in Assam own rice mills, warehouses, tea marketing establishments, wholesale trading houses, and factories — indeed, nearly everything in the state not owned by foreign investors or the central government.[182] As Bhawani Singh remarks, the wealth of the Marwaris has "turned many Assamese into socialists"[183] but not into killers of Marwaris. The same has been true in other states. There were, for example, anti-Marwari riots in Orissa in 1980. Organized by students against Marwari "profiteers," the violence was, like the 1968 riot in Assam, exceedingly mild: the only people killed were two rioters shot by security forces.[184] Marwaris, it was said in Assam, were merely "exploiters," whereas Bengalis were "traitors."[185] Similar patterns are visible elsewhere. In Bombay, the targets were initially south Indians and then

178. The American protest violence of the 1960s occurred during a period of growing black prosperity, whereas the 1950s and 1970s, both decades of relative decline, were periods of quiescence. See Donald L. Horowitz, "Racial Violence in the United States," in Nathan Glazer and Ken Young, eds., *Ethnic Pluralism and Public Policy: Achieving Equality in the United States and Britain* (London: Heinemann Educational Books, 1983), pp. 193–94.

179. See Esman, *Ethnic Politics*, pp. 230–31.

180. For a cogent critique of the materialist fallacy, see Walker Connor, *Ethnonationalism: The Quest for Understanding* (Princeton: Princeton University Press, 1994), pp. 46–47, 144–64.

181. See *Krasnaya Zvesda*, June 17, 1989, in FBIS-SOV-89-116, June 19, 1989, pp. 50–51.

182. Bhandari, *Thoughts on Assam Disturbances*, p. 19. For the all-India pattern of Marwari ownership, see Thomas Timberg, *The Marwaris: From Traders to Industrialists* (Delhi: Vikas , 1978), pp. 10–11, 80–81.

183. Singh, *Politics of Alienation in Assam*, p. 79.

184. Patit Paban Misra, "Why Anti-Marwari Agitation in Orissa," *Mainstream* 19, no. 9 (November 1980): 6–9; "Orissa Town Tense after Violence," *Times of India*, September 30, 1980, p. 6.

185. Bhandari, *Thoughts on Assam Disturbances*, p. 28.

Muslims, but not the better-off Gujaratis or Parsis. In the Ivory Coast, Malian and Senegalese traders were unaffected by violence aimed at Dahomeyans and later at Voltaics. In Cambodia, the targets have been Vietnamese, but not the Chinese trading minority. There is, of course, much conventional wisdom to the contrary, and one can find some evidence of the involvement of trading rivals within the violence that takes place in particular riots,[186] but this is hardly the same as saying that crowds are moved by such jealousies. J.A.C. Mackie's conclusion for Indonesia squares with the comparative evidence: ". . . there is no simple correlation between economic hardship and anti-Sinicism, even though many Chinese believe that when the price of rice soars, they will be made the scapegoats."[187] Unfortunately for the theory and for the victims, the hostility goes deeper than the price of rice.

186. This has certainly been true in some Hindu-Muslim riots. See, e.g., P.R. Rajgopal, *Communal Violence in India* (New Delhi: Uppal, 1987), pp. 77–81; Anjoo Upadhyaya, "Recent Trends in Communal Violence: A Case Study of Varanasi" (paper presented at the Conference on Conflict and Change, sponsored by the Ethnic Studies Network, Portrush, Northern Ireland), June 9, 1992. For a fuller consideration of the part played by commercial rivals, see Chapter 6, below.

187. Mackie, "Anti-Chinese Outbreaks in Indonesia, 1959–68," pp. 135.

An Economy of Antipathy: Target Selection and the Imperatives of Violence

TARGET CHOICES ARE GENERALLY CONSISTENT with intergroup antipathy. The groups selected to receive violence are those that are disliked, feared, or felt to be threatening on any of the grounds identified in Chapter 5. Even when displacement occurs, we have seen that the victims are not chosen by chance and that displaced and direct aggression often appear to merge, producing a more intense outburst against the objects of hostility.

Nevertheless, ethnic groups can hold multiple antipathies, opening the possibility that violence may be directed at one target group or another. Although target choices tend to be consistent in successive riots, there is also a certain element of variability. Whereas Bengali Hindus were targeted in Assam in 1955, 1960, and 1972, Bengali Muslims were victimized there from 1979 onward. Whereas Dahomeyans and Togolese were targeted in the Ivory Coast in 1958, Voltaics were attacked there in 1969, and other foreigners were killed in the 1980s. Very often these shifts reflect changes in the quantum of threat produced by the respective targets, but sometimes the shifts in target choice are a function of what might be called the exigencies of violence.

Violent action, after all, has certain requirements. Even riots that are preceded by only the bare minimum of organization — those, in other words, with a heavy element of spontaneity — require efforts to insure, insofar as possible, that the rioters will not be overwhelmed by opposing force from intended victims. This simple requirement can be reflected quickly in targeting decisions. As I explained in Chapter 4, rioters follow a risk-averse strategy, in which they attempt to avoid killing members of their own group and, more important for present purposes, avoid killing members of third groups. Meticulous efforts are made to distinguish between the target group and other groups. It is not that Groups C, D, and E are not also disliked by the attacking Group A, for they often are,

and in peaceful ethnic conflict they may be excluded from the sympathetic concern of Group A, just as Group B is excluded. For example,
many Turks were not favorably disposed toward Greeks living in the
Ottoman Empire by the late nineteenth century, but Greeks were
bypassed in the killings of Armenians during 1894–96.[1] The attackers
seem to conclude that it is inefficient and may be counterproductive to
diffuse their efforts and possibly create coalitions among their enemies by
targeting all of them simultaneously. Rioters focus on those against
whom it is currently felt to be imperative to act.

The conduct of violent ventures may require a degree of precision in
targeting that is not perfectly congruent with the relative weight of prevailing ethnic sentiments — indeed, almost certainly is not. Those against
whom action is taken tend to receive more than their proportionate
share, so to speak, while others receive less or none. The fact that Yoruba
were not attacked in northern Nigeria does not mean that Hausa and
other northerners entertained no hostility toward them. It simply means
that hostility toward Ibo had a prior claim on the resources of violence.
Viewed in this way, precision in targeting, in addition to its other functions, is a mechanism to prevent the dissipation of resources and the
opening of second fronts against the perpetrators. Violence requires an
economy of antipathy.

Selective targeting is also consistent with the pressures of riot organization. It is easier for such riot leadership as emerges to focus group
anger on a single class of targets by emphasizing the significance of a set
of grievances or cues associated with those targets than it is to point that
anger at multiple targets, each of which may require evocation of somewhat different symbols and cues. In arousing and channeling anger, it is
inefficient to tap different parts of the collective memory simultaneously.
This connection between targeting and leadership directs attention to a
point which, though simple in principle, is easily forgotten in concrete
analysis. If violence is organized, then whoever organizes and leads the
riot may influence the choice of victims.[2]

At the level of the ordinary participant in violence, there is also likely

1. Robert F. Melson, *Revolution and Genocide: On the Origins of the Armenian
Genocide and the Holocaust* (Chicago: University of Chicago Press, 1992), p. 52.
2. This point was vividly brought home in the early stages of a violent protest (not a
deadly ethnic riot) in the Indian state of Bihar in 1965. Students, demonstrating against a
tuition increase and a shooting by police in a neighboring area, wished to move against the
railroad station, presumably to attack a conspicuous manifestation of government authority.
Their motive was protest. Villagers in the same crowd aimed at the town bazaar, where grain
was stored. Their motive was loot. Different goals pointed the two groups toward different

to be a target-narrowing tendency consistent with the requirements of riot leadership. It seems probable that certain cognitive mechanisms operate during the violence to expand hostility toward some ethnic groups and diminish hostility toward others. It is well established that anxiety modifies perceptions and in acute cases creates tunnel vision, a singleminded focus on a central object, operating to screen out cues from the surrounding environment.[3]

Leonard Berkowitz has also suggested the relevance of assimilation effects and contrast effects to levels of hostility.[4] In the perception of magnitudes or intensities, as we saw in Chapter 2, a relatively slight discrepancy between some object or event and an antecedent standard of measurement based on expectation tends to be assimilated to the standard and judged to be within the general range of the standard despite the discrepancy. Generally similar stimuli, in other words, tend to be perceived as more or less the same. On the other hand, a more substantial deviation tends to be contrasted with the standard and judged to be even further from it than it actually is. By this mechanism, the significance of hostile or threatening behavior (or certain group characteristics) on the part of a disliked ethnic group may be exaggerated, whereas the significance of less hostile (or different) behavior by another disliked group may be diminished in the perceptions of potential initiators of violence.[5] This cognitive mechanism, which limits the range of active hostilities, is economical for rioters, for it reduces the risks they take on at any one time. It enables rioters to conduct themselves as if they were thinking in terms of greater and lesser dangers, with the greater in need of immediate attention. In this way, certain antagonists may become targets, to the exclusion of other antagonists.

In part because of the economy and psychology of the violence

---

targets, and in the end leadership played a strong role in directing the anger of the crowd. Herbert Heidenreich, "The Anatomy of a Riot: A Case Study from Bihar 1965," *Journal of Commonwealth Political Studies* 6, no. 2 (July 1968): 107–24, at p. 112.

3. See, e.g., Ross Stagner, "The Psychology of Human Conflict," in Elton B. McNeil, ed., *The Nature of Human Conflict* (Englewood Cliffs, N.J.: Prentice-Hall, 1965), p. 56.

4. Leonard Berkowitz, *Aggression: A Social Psychological Analysis* (New York: McGraw-Hill, 1962), pp. 68–70, 146–49.

5. The opportunities for contrast effects to take hold are enhanced by the typical course of events in the immediate pre-riot period. With few exceptions — Nigeria (1953) is one of them — the events precipitating violence tend actively to involve the groups which become the targets. During this pre-riot period of mounting anger, the zeroing-in process takes place, with the group involved in the precipitating events viewed in increasingly hostile terms, while others fade into the background. As we shall soon see, this certainly was the case with Indian Muslims and Hindus, respectively, in Burma (1938).

process, selective targeting can distort the prevailing pre-riot patterns of ethnic conflict. For this reason, the violence inflicted on various groups is not necessarily reflective of the amount of hostility felt toward them in more tranquil times. This helps explain why groups that are not targeted in one riot may subsequently become targets under different riot circumstances and auspices.

If pre-riot sentiments can be skewed by the exigencies of violence, by the economy of antipathy, and by cognitive mechanisms, they can also be skewed by the nature of the event that precipitates violence, by the leadership that organizes or takes command of the riot, or by the location of the violence. No doubt, there is a certain circularity possible here that brings us back to the crucial role of pre-riot sentiments. The precipitating event may bring violence on because it implicates, in a significant way, the group thought to be the appropriate target. Likewise, riot leadership may secure a following for violence insofar as it chooses those targets against whom the greatest antipathy exists. Leadership does not always lead; it may follow group sentiment. The violence may occur in one place rather than another, simply because that is where the appropriate targets are located. Most often, therefore, these variables — precipitant, leadership, and location — are congruent with target choice based on target-group characteristics. But it would be too deterministic to think that such congruence is always present. As we shall see, sometimes these variables do skew target choice. If they were to skew it seriously and repeatedly, this would be an important challenge to a theory of targeting that rests on the quality of intergroup relations, that rests, in other words, on target-group characteristics alone.

A complete theory of targeting, therefore, must take account of group characteristics and relations *and* of the violence-related variables that can skew target choice away from antecedent patterns of conflict. And the theory must attempt to estimate how much skewing of this sort is likely. (As we shall see, not much.) Here, then, is an exploration of the possible distortions in target choice.

THE SOURCE OF THE PRECIPITANT
AND THE CHOICE OF TARGET

On the face of things, the riot in Burma (1938) seems to suggest that the precipitant itself can point the crowd toward a particular target group identified with the events which happen to precipitate the violence. In Burma, Indian Muslims, identified with a recent affront to Burmese Buddhism, were attacked. Yet, as we have seen, in Nigeria (1953), Yoruba

more than Ibo were associated with the events immediately preceding the
anti-Ibo violence in Kano. What, in fact, is the effect of the precipitant in
guiding the hand of the assailant toward one victim rather than another?

There are two ways of beginning to answer this question. First, we can
attempt to match target groups with groups associated with riot precipitants comparatively and assess the degree of identity or disparity between
the two. Second, for any given riot episode, we can look at the course of
the violence as it grows more remote from the precipitant in time and
space. Here we shall do some of each.

When we match the identity of the target group with the identity of
the group associated with the precipitating events, we find a close corre-
spondence between the two, even where there is considerable latitude in
the choice of potential targets. What we do not find, in other words, is
very much replication of Nigeria (1953), where Ibo were targeted
notwithstanding the greater association of Yoruba with the provocations
that preceded the riot in Kano. There is, to be sure, the case of Assam
(1960), in which a procession protesting language policy was a joint venture of various hill peoples and of Bengalis. Yet, in the ensuing violence,
Bengalis alone were targeted. Although the proposed policy clearly stood
to disadvantage Bengalis, still this is at least an ambiguous case, in which
one might conclude there was a divergence between precipitants and targets. Even so, this is the rare case.

Interestingly, the general tendency to attack the group associated with
the precipitant holds even for those countries in which different groups
have been targeted in recurrent riots. In Assam (1955 and 1972,
although perhaps not 1960), Bengali Hindus were identified with the
precipitating events and were attacked. In Assam (1968), as we have
observed, the occasion was Assamese discontent focused on the Indian
central government and evoked by the Republic Day celebration. The
targets of these mild riots were not Bengalis but Marwaris and other
migrant groups associated in various ways with the central government.
In Assam (1979), Bengali Muslims were attacked, after precipitants associated with them. Similarly, the rioting in Burma (1930) began with fights
between Indian Telugu dockworkers and Burman replacement workers
on the docks of Rangoon. The casualties this time, unlike those eight
years later, were not disproportionately Muslim but disproportionately
Telugu Hindu. The Ivory Coast (1969) riot was directed at Voltaics, after
precipitating events involving Voltaics. Sometimes, in recurrent riots, the
identity of the targets does broaden out, as we shall see later, but otherwise real divergence between the groups associated with precipitants and
the identity of targets is not common.

There is one repeated but only partial exception to this close corre-
spondence between groups associated with precipitants and groups later
attacked. The exception occurs in cases where there is a triangle of ethnic
groups involved in the events preceding the violence and displacement
can be identified. Burma (1938) typifies this situation, but it is present in
some other colonial and postcolonial riots. Indian Muslims were associated with conduct raising the level of Burman anger, but the British and
Eurasians, representing the colonial government, were prominently associated with conduct thwarting the first violent expression of Burman
anger. Although the British activity greatly increased the anger of the
Burmese, the resulting violence was not directed at the British, even
though it might have been appropriate to classify the British along with
the Indian Muslims as a precipitating group. The same phenomenon
occurred in the Ivory Coast (1958), when an anti-Dahomeyan protest
delegation was imprisoned. After this action was taken by the Ivorian
authorities, the attacks began, but they focused not on groups such as
the Baoulé, that were heavily associated with the government, but on
Togolese. Displacement, then, produces an easily understood exception
to the rule that groups identified with the precipitant tend also to be the
targets.

So far there are no surprises. Turning now to the second part of the
inquiry, it is possible to track the course of target selection as rioting
moves away from the precipitating events. Data that permit such an
inquiry with any specificity exist, however, for only one riot: Burma
(1938).

More than many riots, the Burmese disorders of 1938 engulfed large
parts of the country, from Tenasserim Division in the southeast all the
way to Sagaing Division in the north. In a relatively short time, the killing
spread over distances reckoned in the hundreds of miles. From end to
end, the violence spanned 500 miles or more, a fact the more remarkable
for the remoteness of some of the affected areas from major communications links. It has been suggested that as the riot moved from Rangoon,
where it began, to the hinterland, the original focus on Muslims (deriving
from the precipitating events) gave way to a more general attack on all
Indians, Hindu and Muslim alike.[6] If true, this would mean that the initial choice of target was dependent on the special character of the precipitant but that the influence of the precipitant waned with distance. If

6. Guy Hunter, *South-East Asia: Race, Culture, and Nation* (New York: Oxford
University Press, 1966), p. 54; R. Hatley, "The Overseas Indian in Southeast Asia: Burma,
Malaysia, and Singapore," in Robert O. Tilman, ed., *Man, State, and Society in
Contemporary Southeast Asia* (New York: Praeger, 1969), pp. 450–66, at p. 456.

not, this would mean either (a) that target choice was still dependent on the precipitant and that its influence did not wane (or waned only slightly, depending on the ratio of Hindus to Muslims killed) or (b) that target choice was not dependent on the association of the target group with the precipitant but on some aspect of the underlying conflict relationship between Burmans and Indian Muslims.

Fortunately, this is an issue on which we need not roam at large for long. Of all the riots for which there are casualty figures, the Burmese figures are by far the most detailed. That is not to say that they are perfectly accurate, but whatever errors exist are likely to be more or less randomly distributed by location and by subethnic identity of the Indian victims, a highly salient aspect of social life in the Burma of the 1930s. The death and injury figures are broken out by division, by district, and by town and village. To make them meaningful, I have aggregated them by division; even so, in several divisions deaths and injuries were not numerous enough to permit any inference. Since the precipitants occurred in Rangoon and the riot began there, I have also separated Pegu Division into (a) Rangoon and (b) Pegu excluding Rangoon. Table 1 depicts the differences.

It is, I think, a fair surmise, given the distances involved, that the significance of the precipitant for the choice of targets would have declined, if not dissipated altogether, as the violence fanned out from Rangoon. This judgment is reinforced by the typical determinants of the spread of violence (casualty rumors and the like), which generally make the events preceding the riot less important than the course the riot itself has already taken. The role of the press in this particular riot is additional evidence for the assumption that the precipitant, a Muslim affront to Buddhism, would have declining influence as the riot spread, for after the first protest march the press certainly emphasized the repression of the colonial authority far more than it did the substance of the protest being repressed. Rioting outside of Rangoon is said to have "started in many places almost simultaneously with . . . receipt" of the Rangoon newspapers, with their photographs depicting the brutality of the colonial police against the first Burman rioters.[7]

The part played by old scores in ethnic riots points modestly in the same direction. Although old scores may not modify the casualty figures dramatically, they may have some impact; and by definition they do not

7. Government of Burma, *Final Report of the Riot Inquiry Committee* (Rangoon: Government Printer, 1939), p. 27.

TABLE I

BURMA (1938):
CROWD-INFLICTED CASUALTIES

By Identity of Indian Subgroup and Administrative Division

	Indian Deaths			Indian Injuries		
Division	Muslim	Hindu	Percent Muslim	Muslim	Hindu	Percent Muslim
Pegu—Rangoon only	66	8	89	220	98	69
Pegu—excluding Rangoon	46	12	79	93	12	89
Irrawaddy	9	0	100	75	9	89
Magwe	10	2	83	31	7	82
Mandalay	5	2	85	80	61	57
Totals	136	24	85	499	187	73

SOURCE: Government of Burma, *Final Report of the Riot Inquiry Committee* (Rangoon: Government Printer, 1939), Appendix X.

flow from the occasion but from grievances awaiting the occasion. Of course, since these are local grievances, hence far from the place of the precipitant, there is no reason why the identity of such victims should necessarily follow the identity of the victims closer to the precipitant.[8]

These forces should push the casualty balance away from what it might be when directly affected by the identity of the group associated with the precipitant. The results of Table 1 are, therefore, all the more surprising. Rangoon, where the riot began, ranks relatively low in the percentage of Muslim injuries. Moreover, there appears to be no particular relationship between distance from Rangoon and percentage of Muslim victims. The only relationship that does appear is inverse: the more urban the locale, the fewer the Muslim victims, presumably because there were relatively fewer Muslims in the most urban populations. But this is hardly evidence for the impact of a "Muslim precipitant," which took hold in Rangoon. In point of fact, the total Muslim percentage of all deaths was 85 and of all injuries was 72. Save for the injuries in Mandalay, nowhere are the deviations from these overall figures impressive. Despite the reasons for believing that the identity of the targets would change with distance from the precipitant, the emphasis on

8. This is, of course, not the same as saying that "local grievances" might not form part of a national pattern, given the pervasiveness of the same conditions in many localities. The point is simply that old scores antedate the precipitating events and hence are a non-precipitant-related factor in target choice.

Muslim targets persisted and must, then, be attributed to factors other than the Muslim character of the precipitating events. The precipitant evoked antecedent antipathy.

One further question is raised by these figures. Overall Muslim injuries are 13 percent below Muslim deaths, and in Rangoon the difference is 20 percent (the numbers killed in Mandalay are not large enough for comparison, although the Muslim injury figure there is as low as 57 percent). What accounts for this disparity? There is no certain answer in the materials, but the question is intriguing in the context of selective targeting. A plausible possibility, for which there is no evidence either way, is that old scores had a part in rolling up a larger Muslim death toll.[9] The difference could be between street fighting, in which victims are chosen entirely at random and many might escape merely with injuries, and residential attacks, in which a particular victim or family is sought and the chances of escape are slimmer. If it is true that relatively more Muslims than Hindus were killed in this latter way, that would seem to be further evidence against the thesis that the character of the precipitant governed the choice of targets. Rather, the precipitant must have served to highlight some troublesome aspect of the underlying relations between Burmans and Indian Muslims.

The more closely we examine Burma (1938), the less it seems to contrast with Nigeria (1953), the latter being, of course, the polar case of disparity between the identity of the precipitating group and the target group. In both cases, the precipitant is not merely a chance event, but an event whose significance arises from its ability to pull together or symbolize certain underlying grievances. It may be difficult for a precipitant associated with Group A to epitomize grievances against Group B, and for that reason we generally expect to find a coincidence between the precipitating group and the target group. Yet, as Nigeria (1953) shows, it is not altogether impossible for the actions of one group to bring down an attack on members of another group.

As the Burmese data imply, it remains possible for the identification of one group as the first and appropriate target to persist even when and where the precise precipitant with which that group was associated has been forgotten or superseded by rumors of the targets' aggressive acts. This is somewhat like saying that the initial impact of the precipitant on target choice outlives the rioters' knowledge or memory of the character

9. Many old scores were, in fact, settled in Burma (1938). Government of Burma, *Final Report of the Riot Inquiry Committee*, pp. 95, 102.

and significance of the precipitating events. This possibility seems to depend on the ability of the precipitant to attach itself to some aspect of the underlying relationship.

The comparative evidence pointing to a strong relationship between precipitant and target choice can also be explained by a more systematic view of the precipitant than the view we have so far articulated. There is a distinction, insufficiently elaborated in social psychology, between a frustration — that is, a discrete thwarting event of the kind created in laboratories daily — and a frustrating situation, which is far more difficult to reconstruct experimentally. Some overlap exists between that distinction and the distinction I have roughly referred to as existing between precipitants and underlying relations. In the chapter on precipitants, I shall argue, as I have suggested here, that the significance of a precipitant — its capacity to trigger violence — lies in its evocative quality, that is, its ability to epitomize a larger conflict relationship which the initiators of violence find unsatisfactory or dangerous. Obviously, in any multiethnic society there may be more than one ethnic relationship that is susceptible to violence. Various precipitants, if they are associated with different ethnic groups, can then elicit responses directed at different targets. We need not conclude from Burma (1930 versus 1938) or the Ivory Coast (1958 versus 1969 versus 1980) or Assam (1955 and 1972 versus 1960 versus 1968 or 1979) that the precipitant *governed* the choice of target; nor need we disregard the evidence from Burma (1938) that seems to suggest that the precipitant could not have dictated target choice far from Rangoon. At any given time, a precipitating event may simply render one set of conflicts more salient than another, and so the event points the initiators of violence toward one category of target rather than another.

It is, however, somewhat more difficult to explain the locational data for Burma (1938) on this basis than to account for the comparative evidence. For if the key to understanding precipitants is their ability to evoke or elicit different aspects of unsatisfactory relationships, then why in Burma did not this ability, like the precipitant itself, wane with distance from the first violent events? To answer this, we may ultimately have to fall back upon the possibility raised a moment ago: the ability of the first identification of the appropriate targets to outlive knowledge or memory of the initial precipitating events. This still leaves open for later consideration the mechanism, the means by which the precipitant helps to set the direction of targeting, even when violence occurs at a time and place remote from the precipitating events. What we know, which is adequate for present purposes, is that the precipitant does not operate independently to skew target choice.

RIOT LEADERSHIP AND TARGET CHOICE

The potentially great role of riot leadership in target selection is well illustrated by Singapore (1950). This riot, we have already observed in Chapter 2, seems confusing because the identity of the targets varied from place to place. As I deliberately neglected to explain in that chapter, the precipitant was a judicial custody proceeding in which the teenage child of a Dutch father and Dutch or Eurasian mother (depending on how her identity was reckoned) was returned by a British court to the custody of her natural parents. The girl had apparently been adopted by a Malay woman during World War II and later married, in a hastily arranged ceremony, to a Malay man. For those riot participants who attacked British and undifferentiated European and Eurasian targets, the decision symbolized disrespect for the Islamic law of marriage and the high-handedness of the colonial authorities. Much of the riot leadership — particularly one leader whose experience of the British went back to India and Pakistan — saw the issue this way.[10] Some other leaders, however, had Indonesian origins and connections to the Indonesian nationalist movement; more than one third of those arrested were of Indonesian origin.[11] There the colonial experience was Dutch. The tendency of some crowds to target the Dutch and exempt the British, while others made opposite choices, is almost certainly attributable to these subethnic differences in riot leadership.[12] The precipitant could be interpreted in varying ways to point to alternative targets, and on this leadership was decisive.

Very often leadership in a deadly riot is not so clearly identifiable. Still, in those riots that have discernible elements of organization, it is helpful

10. See Haja Maideen, *The Nadra Tragedy: The Maria Hertogh Controversy* (Petaling Jaya, Malaysia: Pelanduk, 1989); Tom Eames Hughes, *Tangled Worlds: The Story of Maria Hertogh* (Singapore: Institute of Southeast Asian Studies, 1982).

11. Maideen, *The Nadra Tragedy*, pp. 140–41; Hughes, *Tangled Worlds*, p. 54; Statement of Andrew Howat Frew, A.S.P., to the Riot Inquiry Commission, February 27, 1951, Rhodes House Library, Oxford, MSS Ind Ocn s. 208 (mimeo.), p. 30. After World War II, the Malay Nationalist Party and the Angkatan Pemuda Insaf (API), both of them connected to radical Indonesian nationalism, were active in Singapore. The leader of the former, Dr. Burhanuddin Al-Helmy, was of Sumatran descent, and the leader of the latter, Ahmad Boestamam, was Javanese. Burhanuddin played a key role in the Hertogh protests.

12. In Singapore, *Malay* is a capacious category that can, depending on the context, embrace those of Pakistani and Indonesian background.

to distinguish among different types of leadership and the targets selected by each. In a few deadly riots, but only a few, students or others with middle-class career aspirations lead crowds and make target selections appropriate to those aspirations. Commercial rivals may do the same. Where religious leadership takes hold, target choices are skewed toward religious rivalries, which may or may not coincide with broader patterns of antipathy. Political party leadership makes target choices appropriate to party interests, of course, but since these may change over time, there is no single pattern of party-led targeting.

CAREERIST AND COMMERCIAL LEADERS

The potential importance of careerist aspirations in riot organization derives from the disproportionate importance of bureaucratic employment in conferring income, prestige, and power in many states. In view of that, it is perhaps surprising that relatively few riots have been occasioned by bureaucratic rivalries, but it is not entirely inexplicable. One reason, surely, is that ethnic leadership is frequently in the hands of political parties or extraparty organizations, both of which ordinarily cater to a mass clientele. In order to mobilize these organizations for violence, bureaucratic careerism must be tied to more general questions of ethnopolitical power. It requires a crowd to get a riot moving, and the requisite numbers are harder to mobilize when the stake of the lower classes is as tenuous as it may be in the outcome of some civil service issues. Furthermore, since the segments that are involved in careerist rivalries are heavily middle class, they are subject to all the inhibitions on direct participation in mass violence to which middle classes everywhere are heir. Although there are many cases in which bureaucratic middle classes have been in close sympathy with the violent behavior of members of their own ethnic groups, the purely careerist riot is a rare specimen.

It is, nonetheless, possible to identify riots in which the leadership, or a considerable segment of it, is assumed by ambitious middle-class elements, eager to displace ethnic opponents entrenched in the state apparatus. In such riots, the targets are, of course, members of those groups most heavily represented in the bureaucracy.

The archetype of careerist violence is the Ivory Coast riot of 1958. Its leadership was entirely careerist, and selective targeting was more clearly attributable to this leadership than in any other riot for which data are available.

The Ivory Coast ethnic configuration was an exaggerated version of one that prevailed in a large number of former colonies. During the colonial period, when the cash-crop economy expanded and intercolony migration was relatively easy, large numbers of educated Dahomeyans and Togolese entered the Ivory Coast.[13] "The French, who ran both the government and the business enterprises in the territory at the time, welcomed them because they had a justifiable reputation as being diligent workers; and, as a result, many Dahomeyans and Togolese advanced to positions of considerable responsibility in both the French colonial administration and the private sector."[14] Because Dahomeyans and Togolese were widely believed to possess "intelligence and energy which made them subject to jealousy by the [supposedly] slower, less efficient people of the Ivory Coast,"[15] the government and private companies found at independence that their ranks consisted of a large proportion of these ethnic strangers. It was rumored at the time that some 80 percent of the African personnel of some firms came from Dahomey.[16]

The "good jobs and prosperity of the 'stranger' Africans so widely employed throughout Abidjan had been a continual irritant."[17] That irritant was converted to violence by the activity of the League of Ivory Coast Natives, an organization consisting of young people of the "lower-level white-collar" stratum,[18] some of them educated in Paris. The League had planned its attack with care, designating with specificity the class of prospective victims. Unlike many riots, this one had a strongly residential focus, often a sign of organization. The leaders took pains to mark on a map the location of Dahomeyan and Togolese homes in Abidjan.[19] That they were especially concerned with the economic position of their victims is clear from the fact that in many cases the strangers were given the option to clear out or lose their lives. For the rioters, departure was as useful as death. Most victims chose to leave. Within a

13. See Ruth Schachter Morgenthau, *Political Parties in French-Speaking West Africa* (Oxford: Oxford University Press, 1964), pp. 173–76.

14. Victor D. DuBois, "Social Aspects of the Urbanization Process in Abidjan," *American Universities Field Staff Reports*, West Africa Series 10, no. 1 (November 1967): 10–11.

15. Gwendolen M. Carter, *Independence for Africa* (New York: Praeger, 1960), p. 107.

16. Ibid. Such estimates are, characteristically, much inflated and undoubtedly were in Abidjan. For another of many illustrations that could be cited, see W. Howard Wriggins, *Ceylon: Dilemmas of a New Nation* (Princeton: Princeton University Press, 1960), p. 235.

17. Carter, *Independence for Africa*, p. 108.

18. Aristide R. Zolberg, *One-Party Government in the Ivory Coast*, rev. ed. (Princeton: Princeton University Press, 1969), p. 245.

19. Carter, *Independence for Africa*, p. 113.

short time, thousands of Dahomeyans and Togolese were returned to their country of origin, their jobs taken by Ivorians.

The relation between targeting and careerist leadership in Abidjan cannot be appreciated without setting the 1958 riot in the context of the extraordinary ethnic diversity and the socioeconomic roles occupied by the various stranger-groups present at that time in the country. At least one-fourth of the Ivory Coast population in 1958 consisted of non-Ivorian Africans. As I mentioned in Chapter 5, several of these groups — Malians, Senegalese, and Guineans — as well as Lebanese, were heavily involved in trade, commerce, and crafts.[20] There was also a large contingent of Voltaics (principally Mossi), numbering nearly 10 percent of the population and concentrated in low-level wage labor, as agricultural workers, urban menials, and domestics.[21] More numerous in the capital than all but one of the Ivorian ethnic groups, the Voltaics had an extremely important political role, for President Félix Houphouët-Boigny's party had followed a policy of incorporating stranger-Africans within its ranks, and Voltaics had been disproportionately represented there. Their presence and influence in the party, and the generous allocation of candidacies to them, had been a continuing source of Ivorian complaint.[22]

Nevertheless, neither the economic position of the Lebanese, the Malians, the Senegalese, and the Guineans, nor the political position of the Voltaics gave rise to violence in 1958.[23] The League of Ivory Coast Natives singled out the Dahomeyans and Togolese for attack. This was the classic case of careerist target choice.

20. DuBois, "Social Aspects of Urbanization," pp. 9–10.

21. Victor D. DuBois, "Ahmadou's World: A Case Study of a Voltaic Immigrant to the Ivory Coast," in *The Developing World*, Vol. 1 (New York: American Universities Field Staff, 1966), pp. 108–21; Efrem Sigel, "Ivory Coast: Booming Economy, Political Calm," *Africa Report*, April 1970, pp. 18–21.

22. G.M.C. [Gwendolen M. Carter], "Trouble in French West Africa," *The World Today* 14, no. 12 (December 1958): 513–18.

23. Voltaics, however, were attacked under quite different auspices in 1969. The 1969 disturbances, which never reached the scale of the 1958 events, were led by associations of unemployed Ivorian wage laborers in Abidjan. Their competitive rivals were, of course, Voltaics. As rare as the exclusively middle-class careerist ethnic riot is, the working-class or *lumpenproletariat* ethnic riot for economic goals is even more unusual. One plausible explanation is the ethnically compartmentalized labor market that prevails in many multiethnic societies and shields the groups from direct economic competition at the working-class level. Cf. Ozay Mehmet, "Manpower Planning and Labour Markets in Developing Countries: A Case Study of West Malaysia," *Journal of Development Studies* 8, no. 2 (January 1972): 277–89. But see the exceptional circumstances that produced a dockworkers' ethnic riot in Burma in 1930. Usha Mahajani, *The Role of Indian Minorities in Burma and Malaya* (Bombay: Vora, 1960), pp. 71–79.

Bureaucratic ambitions also played an important role in Assam (1960). This riot, however, had more complex roots than the Ivory Coast riot of two years earlier, and a smaller fraction of its impetus is attributable to the ethnic employment issue.

Although still an underdeveloped state, Assam, like the Ivory Coast, underwent a significant economic expansion during the colonial era. In both cases, the expansion was due to plantation agriculture. Whereas in the Ivory Coast the crops were cocoa and coffee, in Assam the crop was tea. As in other colonies, cash-cropping resulted in diversification of the population. Tea garden laborers were recruited from Bihar, Orissa, Andhra, Uttar Pradesh, and other Indian states. Fertile soil also attracted peasant cultivators from Bengal, large numbers of them Muslims, while commercial opportunity brought Marwaris and a sprinkling of other non-Assamese traders. All of this immigration was superimposed on the preexisting heterogeneity of the state, which included, besides the Assamese, a variety of so-called tribal peoples in the hill and valley areas and Bengalis who had earlier come to serve in the British administration when Assam had been governed jointly with Bengal. Finally, the ranks of the immigrant communities swelled still further after partition, when Bengali Hindus moved across the border from Muslim East Bengal.

Due to in-migration, in the half century from 1901 to 1951 the population of Assam had a growth rate of 138 percent, compared to the all-India rate of 52 percent.[24] As in the Ivory Coast, the indigenes were compared unfavorably with virtually every group of immigrants. It was said that the Assamese were reluctant to engage in the rigorous wage labor on the tea estates that Biharis and Oriyas were prepared to undertake, that they did not possess the business acumen of Marwaris, that they were not endowed with the agricultural talents of Bengali farmers or, most pointedly of all, with the intellectual, motivational, and educational capacities of Bengali managers, technicians, and bureaucrats.

The analogy to the Ivory Coast can be pushed only to a certain point, however. The history of Assamese-Bengali interaction is both longer and deeper than the Ivorian-Dahomeyan relationship, and other aspects of ethnic relations were involved in generating the massive upsurge of anti-Bengali feeling that surfaced during the riot.[25] Yet, out of a wide range of

24. P.C. Goswami, *The Economic Development of Assam* (New York: Asia Publishing House, 1963), pp. 17–18. See also Narendra Chandra Dutta, *Land Problems and Land Reforms in Assam* (Delhi: S. Chand, 1968), p. 2.

25. See Chapter 5, above.

potential targets, Bengalis were chosen, and bureaucratic rivalries played a significant part in that selection.

The riot occurred in the midst of a campaign to make Assamese the official state language. The campaign was in large measure prompted by the conspicuous role of Bengalis in central government enterprises in Assam. Much of the state's economic expansion seemed to hinge on several such projects, most notably a new oil refinery at Gauhati. In the refinery, in the railways, and on construction sites, it appeared to Assamese that the most rewarding opportunities were being preempted by non-Assamese, mainly Bengalis. Employment at the oil refinery was a doubly sensitive issue, because it was only after great pressure to locate the refinery in Assam rather than elsewhere that the central government conceded the demand.[26] Having gained the concession, segments of the Assamese community eventually came to view it as an illusory victory. Many Assamese had assumed they would be given preference in employment at the refinery, but a Bengali was chosen to be general manager, and technical proficiency and experience as criteria for other positions precluded the hiring of Assamese.[27]

These dashed hopes fed directly into the language movement. The Assamese language was to be the key to career opportunities for the Assamese, who previously had been unable to match the educational qualifications of their Bengali rivals.[28] "It was thought that, once Assamese emerged as the official language, the Bengalis, for want of their efficiency in it, would automatically be put at bay."[29] The rioting was preceded by an assault on the Bengali manager of the oil refinery, and students were in the front ranks of the rioters.[30] Here, as in the Ivory Coast, careerist leadership produced the appropriate targets for a careerist riot: Bengalis rather than other non-Assamese, Bengali Hindus

26. Myron Weiner, "India: Two Political Cultures," in Lucian W. Pye and Sidney Verba, eds., *Political Culture and Political Development* (Princeton: Princeton University Press, 1965), p. 217.

27. P.C. Goswami, "Tragedy of Political Tactlessness," *Economic Weekly*, July 30, 1960, p. 1196.

28. See, e.g., Sushil Kumar, "Panorama of State Politics," in Iqbal Narain, ed., *State Politics in India* (Meerut, India: Meenakshi Prakashan, 1967), p. 41.

29. Ibid. To the same effect, see K.C. Chakravarti, "Bongal Kheda Again," *Economic Weekly*, July 30, 1960, p. 1193.

30. Chakravarti, "Bongal Kheda Again," p. 1193; Goswami, "Tragedy of Political Tactlessness"; K.C. Barua, *Assam: Her People and Her Language* (Shillong, Assam: Lawyers' Bookstall, 1960); Charu Chandra Bhandari, *Thoughts on Assam Disturbances* (Kashi: A.B. Sarva Seva Sangh Prakashan, 1961). Bhandari also lays a certain amount of stress on Assamese-Bengali commercial and professional rivalries in some parts of the state.

rather than Bengali Muslims. Still, it should be borne in mind that, in 1960, Bengali Hindus would have been likely targets, no matter which Assamese instigated the violence.

Although the language question was in the forefront of the events that led to the riot, selective targeting was at work even on that issue. As we have seen, some of the most vigorous opposition to exclusive official status for Assamese came from the hill peoples, who demanded the retention of English. In fact, whereas Bengalis asked only for equal official status for Bengali, the hill peoples, fearing assimilation, opposed the adoption of Assamese at all.[31] One of the most significant long-term effects of the language agitation and the riots that followed was a tremendous acceleration of separatist sentiment among the hill peoples;[32] and although reports differ about which group predominated in the anti-Assamese protest,[33] both were involved. Yet only Bengalis were singled out.

Targeting of the Bengalis also meant immunity from violence for Marwaris, who held a commanding position in the private sector in Assam. Careerist aspirations typically run to the risk-free, secure, prestigious positions found in government offices.

If middle-class sponsorship is likely to point a riot in the direction of career rivals, alternative varieties of riot leadership are equally inclined to point it in other directions. A recurrent theme of reports on riots in India is the role of business rivals in fomenting violence. Several analysts have suggested that the entry of Muslims into Hindu-dominated business niches or the increasing prosperity of Muslim competitors provoked Hindu business interests to exploit Hindu-Muslim antipathy, with the aim of undoing the competition. In Varanasi (1991), Muslim sari dealers were often targeted. Formerly, the sari trade was mainly in Hindu hands, and there is a suspicion of business motivation in these attacks.[34] In Bombay, Muslims were increasingly setting up their own power looms and participating successfully in textile production. When the 1984 riot occurred there, many of these businesses were attacked.[35] Disputes

31. Kumar, "Panorama of State Politics," p. 41; Bhandari, *Thoughts on Assam Disturbances*, p. 9.

32. Roderick A. Church, "Roots of Separatism in Assam Hill Districts," *Economic and Political Weekly*, April 26, 1969, p. 728.

33. Compare Bhandari, *Thoughts on Assam Disturbances*, p. 10, with Barua, *Assam*, p. 14.

34. Anjoo Upadhyaya, "Recent Trends in Communal Violence: A Case Study of Varanasi" (paper presented at the Conference on Conflict and Change, Ethnic Studies Network, Portrush, Northern Ireland, June 9, 1992).

35. Asghar Ali Engineer, *Bhiwandi-Bombay Riots: Analysis and Documentation* (Bombay: Institute of Islamic Studies, 1984), p. 22.

between Muslim cloth manufacturers and the Hindu traders to whom they sold cloth are also said to lie in the background of the riots in Bhiwandi (1984).[36] Likewise, Meerut, a north Indian location severely affected by Hindu-Muslim violence, is an industrial city experiencing growing Muslim prosperity. Part of that prosperity is due to the entry of Muslim power loom owners into the cloth trade, previously dominated by a few Hindu subgroups. These Hindu traders, it is inferred, used violence to strike at their new competitors in the riots of 1987.[37]

It is difficult to know how seriously to take commercial competition as a force in targeting choices. In some north Indian cities, serious competition has subsisted without any violent episodes.[38] The role that commercial competition is said to play is a covert, behind-the-scenes role, which makes proof or disproof very difficult. Although the employment of criminal gangs to pursue business rivalries by violent means is a possibility, large-scale violence directed by business rivals is much less likely, and the north Indian riots grew considerably in scale and casualties through the 1980s. The general absence of serious violence against trading minorities suggests that commercial rivalries are not likely to skew target choices in most cases. Where particular enterprises are targeted during violence, it is much more likely that business rivals have taken advantage of the cover of general disorder to strike at those they cannot harm in ordinary times. Drop out the commercial rivalries and the same group would probably have been targeted.

RELIGIOUS AND PARTY LEADERS

Religious functionaries, on the other hand, have sometimes been prominent in riot leadership. Some otherwise puzzling target choices reflect their influence.

As a result of an expansion of agriculture beginning about 1870, Burma became host to a vast influx of Indians and, to a lesser extent, Chinese, which made it a highly heterogeneous society. By 1931 there were more than a million Indians, Hindu and Muslim alike, in Burma. I have previously noted the difficulties entailed in explaining the very

36. P.R. Rajgopal, *Communal Violence in India* (New Delhi: Uppal, 1987), p. 81.

37. Dildar Khan, "Meerut Riots: An Analysis," in Pramod Kumar, ed., *Towards Understanding Communalism* (Chandigarh: Centre for Research in Rural and Industrial Development, 1992), pp. 455–70, at pp. 465–66; Asghar Ali Engineer, "Meerut: The Nation's Shame," *Economic and Political Weekly*, June 20, 1987, pp. 969–71, at p. 969.

38. Steven Ian Wilkinson, "What Large Datasets Can Tell Us about the General Explanations for Communal Riots" (unpublished paper, Harvard Academy for International and Area Studies, Cambridge, Mass., March 31, 1995), p. 27.

heavy emphasis on Muslim victims in 1938, in view of the economic and demographic setting of the riot. The choice of Muslims becomes more understandable when it is revealed that monks were in the vanguard of the rioters all over Burma. Islam is a proselytizing faith, and it was viewed as a greater challenge than was Hinduism to Buddhism and to its guardians, the monks. The challenge was a grave and visible one, because of the marriage of Burman women to Indian Muslim men, resulting in the loss of both the women and their children (called Zerbadis or Burma Muslims) to Buddhist ranks. The status of the Burman wives and Zerbadi children also had a number of disadvantageous features.[39] If the marriage consisted of cohabitation without a formal marriage ceremony preceded by conversion to Islam, the wife, when widowed, discovered that her marriage was not valid, and thus she was disinherited. If, however, she did convert, the law of inheritance was less favorable to a Muslim than to a Buddhist widow. The need for a Buddhist woman to renounce her religion to validate her marriage, her disinheritance if she failed to do so, and the discrepancy between her rights under Buddhist and Muslim law gave rise to discontent that radiated through the Burman community.

The importance of religious issues in the riot was evidenced in several ways. The precipitant was an insulting reference to the Buddha in a tract authored by a Muslim. Speeches at protest meetings preceding the violence dwelled on the intermarriage problem.[40] In the course of the riot, scores of mosques were attacked, many of them destroyed by fire. By contrast, only two Hindu temples were damaged.[41] If, as seems probable, there was also substantial animus against Hindus, the riots reflected it only to a most limited degree, considering the Hindu majority among the Indian population of Burma.[42] This fact must be attributed to the monks who, nearly everywhere, contributed their leadership to the riots and actually led many of the armed assaults.[43]

Had secular Burman nationalists taken a more active leadership role in the riots, the targets would surely have been different. The victims might

39. Government of Burma, *Interim Report of the Riot Inquiry Committee* (Rangoon: Government Printer, 1939), pp. 28–33.

40. See, e.g., Government of Burma, *Final Report of the Riot Inquiry Committee*, p. 13. See also the newspaper reports described on p. 8.

41. Ibid., Appendix XII.

42. As of 1931, Hindus comprised approximately 56 percent, Muslims approximately 39 percent, and others approximately 5 percent of the total Indian population in Burma. Government of Burma, *Interim Report of the Riot Inquiry Committee*, Appendix IV.

43. See, e.g., Government of Burma, *Final Report of the Riot Inquiry Committee* , pp. 36, 38–39.

then have been more evenly distributed between Hindus and Muslims and might also have included Chinese.[44] Target choice in Burma becomes much less mysterious when riot leadership is taken into account.

In few other riots has religious leadership had so direct a bearing on target selection as it did in Burma. In West Pakistan (1953), however, riots occurred in which the target group was determined by a combination of political party leadership and religious leadership, and probably in some small part by careerist leadership as well.

The targets of this violence were the Ahmadis, disciples of Mirza Ghulam Ahmad, a late-nineteenth-century divine who claimed to be a messiah.[45] The anti-Ahmadi movement was rooted in the general Islamic distaste for apostasy and the boldly aggressive Ahmadi program of proselytization.[46] These two were an explosive combination, ignited by the political agitation of the Ahrar political party.

The Ahrar had earlier opposed the partition of India and had cooperated politically with the Indian National Congress.[47] After the creation of Pakistan, it found itself without a following.[48] Apparently with a view to proving itself second to none in its devotion to Pakistan, the Ahrar seized on the position of the Ahmadis and began a campaign of vilification against them. Among the many accusations made against the Ahmadis

44. An inflammatory leaflet circulating in Mandalay during this period accused the Indians and Chinese of being "bloodsuckers" and called upon Burmese to go into trade. Government of Burma, *Final Report of the Riot Inquiry Committee*, p. 166.

45. See Government of [West] Punjab, *Report of the Court of Inquiry Constituted under Punjab Act II of 1954 to Enquire into the Punjab Disturbances of 1953* (Lahore: Superintendent of Government Printing, 1954), pp. 9–10.

46. "A modern sect, the Ahmadiyas, was founded in the late nineteenth century by a powerful sage in a small town of the Punjab. His followers have become more than a sectarian jati, they form a close-knit community engaged in economic activities as well as vigorous missionary work. Their center has been described as a combination of modern enterprise and fundamentalist theology; their very activism has drawn attacks from other Muslims. Like the more vigorous Hindu sects, the Isma'illis and the Ahmadiyas have developed a particularly effective internal organization. This helps bring them prosperity which in turn eventually yields respectable status in their localities . . . ." David G. Mandelbaum, *Society in India*, Vol. 2 (Berkeley and Los Angeles: University of California Press, 1970), p. 556. See also Richard S. Wheeler, *The Politics of Pakistan: A Constitutional Quest* (Ithaca: Cornell University Press, 1970), pp. 44–45. Strictly speaking, the Ahmadis were not really an ascriptive group, but, like many earlier religious movements, were probably becoming so, because of a growing sense of corporate identity, traits generally ascribed to group members, and increasing hostility to their proselytizing.

47. See Hugh Tinker, *India and Pakistan*, rev. ed. (New York: Praeger, 1968), p. 120. See also the references to sacrifices by the Ahrar for the nationalist cause in Jawaharlal Nehru, *The Discovery of India* (Bombay: Asia Publishing House, 1961), pp. 409, 417.

48. Government of Punjab, *Report of the Court of Inquiry*, pp. 10–15, 49, 254–60.

was that they were disproportionately represented in high civilian and military positions and that their loyalty in those capacities was in doubt.[49] Demands were made for the removal of Ahmadi officers, the outcasting of Ahmadis in villages (for example, by requiring them to eat with separate utensils at shops and not draw water at public wells), the official classification of the Ahmadis as a "non-Muslim minority" — a goal ultimately achieved in 1974 — and the forcible reconversion and absorption of the entire community.[50] In some speeches, it was "declared that to kill an Ahmadi was to gain the pleasure of God."[51]

The choice of the Ahmadis was deliberate. Other ethnic and sectarian cleavages were available for exploitation. Sunni-Shia and Sunni-Wahabi antagonisms had both produced sporadic violence in 1951. But the Ahmadis made singularly attractive targets for the Ahrar, for their heterodoxy transcended other differences in Punjabi Muslim society. The involvement of an Ahmadi major general in a coup attempt in March 1951 made superficially plausible the Ahrar accusation that the Ahmadis were fundamentally disloyal to Pakistan. Because of the history of Ahrar opposition to partition — ironically, the Ahmadis had taken no position on partition — a demonstration of thoroughgoing loyalty to the new state was a prerequisite to the party's regeneration. At the same time, the *maulvis* enlisted in the Ahrar cause were exceptionally sensitive to the heterodoxy of the Ahmadis and their vigorous conversion efforts.

When the campaign against the Ahmadis turned violent, individual Ahmadis, easily identified by their short beards, were murdered. The religious tack taken by the Ahrar had brought it the support of an array of Islamic organizations and a large number of Islamic functionaries. Anti-Ahmadi meetings were held in mosques, which were essentially beyond the reach of civil authority. As the riots began, *maulvis* and *mullahs*, using religious arguments, were active in inciting the crowds to violence.[52] Clearly, the potency of the movement derived from the alliance of an ambitious political party with religious functionaries. A court of inquiry later concluded that "the Ahrar gave birth to a baby and offered it to the ulama for adoption [and they] agreed to father it . . . ."[53] The

49. Ibid., pp. 28, 40. A personal campaign of abuse was also conducted against the foreign minister of Pakistan, Sir Zafrullah Khan, an Ahmadi.

50. Ibid., pp. 140, 174 (outcasting), 15 (minority status), 111, 182 (reconversion).

51. Ibid., p. 174.

52. E.g., ibid., pp. 155, 172, 173, 177, 178. In some cases, conversion was offered as an alternative to death. E.g., p. 176.

53. Ibid., p. 286. The movement really got under way only after the *ulama* had joined in. Leonard Binder, *Religion and Politics in Pakistan* (Berkeley and Los Angeles: University of California Press, 1961), pp. 262–63.

Ahmadis were targeted because of the interests and sensitivities of both parents.

Not all riots are as deliberately planned as the anti-Ahmadi riot was. But of those that are led by identifiable groups, the majority have been organized by political parties or segments of them. The predominance of parties derives from their frequent organization along ethnic lines, their capacity to mobilize crowds for specific purposes, and their interest in the tactical use of violence.

The anti-Ahmadi violence was, as we have seen, a joint venture of party and religious leadership in rioting. The party did the prompting, though it is difficult to say who played the more prominent role as the campaign gained momentum. In the Burmese case, a few politicians were also involved, but on a purely local basis. Even on that basis, there is no doubt that the monks were dominant at all stages and in most localities.

Beginning in the 1960s, similar joint leadership patterns have been discernible in violence in India. In Ahmedabad (1969), the most serious anti-Muslim riot in a half-decade of serious riots, the initiative was taken by Hindu religious leaders and leaders of the Jan Sangh, a Hindu political party. Jointly, they formed a "Committee to Defend the Hindu Religion," which held provocative public meetings and distributed inflammatory literature. These activities led directly to the riot.[54] Within a few months, riots in the Bombay area were organized by similar combinations. In Kausa (1970), it was the Shiv Sena, a local political party in the process of shifting its aggressive attention from south Indians to Muslims; in Bhiwandi (1970), it was a broad front of Shiv Sena, Jan Sangh, and a subsidiary of a Hindu extremist organization.[55] With the decline of the Jan Sangh and the rise, during the 1980s, of a more powerful Hindu party, the Bharatiya Janata Party (BJP), party organization became more common.[56]

Religious leadership points to some targets and away from others. In Bombay, the religious theme exempts south Indian Hindus who, under other conditions, might be promising targets. In other cities, conflict organized on an explicitly Hindu basis is likely to minimize intercaste violence, as it focuses on Muslims, and indeed a major problem for the BJP has been to organize support on a cross-caste basis.[57] Hindu-Muslim

54. Ghanshyam Shah, "Communal Riots in Gujarat," *Economic and Political Weekly*, Annual Number, January 1970, pp. 187–200, at pp. 191–92.

55. S.K. Ghosh, *Communal Riots in India* (New Delhi: Ashish , 1987), pp. 179–80.

56. See, e.g., Upadhyaya, "Recent Trends in Communal Violence," pp. 1–3.

57. In 1993, for example, the BJP lost the assembly elections in India's largest state, Uttar Pradesh, to a coalition of parties largely representing the very numerous so-called

rivalry presents the broadest cleavage for organization across all of India. That does not render it inevitable, for there are other choices, but it does render it attractive to those interested in a large, nationwide following.

Although the combined participation of party and religious organizations in riots is not unusual, in general ethnically based parties that organize riots take unchallenged command, because few alternative groups can compete with their organizational capacity and their legitimacy in speaking for ethnic aspirations. Selective targeting reflects their involvement. Sometimes this results in a pattern of targeting so skewed toward party purposes that it bears little relation to the general conflict situation. More often, party antipathies are so congruent with general ethnic antipathies that targeting faithfully reflects both.

Examples of both types of targeting patterns can be found in successive party-led riots within a single country: Mauritius. Mauritius is an island of considerable ethnic diversity, produced by labor migration during the colonial period.[58] Originally colonized by the Portuguese and Dutch, the island was really first settled by the French. The British captured the island in 1810 and continued the plantation economy with the same African slave labor that the French had used. The great majority of European settlers remained French, however, and so the earliest significant population groups were the so-called Franco-Mauritians and the Africans and Eurafricans, who are together called Creoles.

Following emancipation of the slaves in the 1830s, the British imported large numbers of Indians, both Hindu and Muslim, to work the sugar estates. By 1861, Indians comprised — and continue to comprise — a large majority of the population.[59] Their numbers were augmented by the migration of Indian traders, most of them Muslim, and Chinese laborers, most of whom eventually found their way into trade. There thus evolved in Mauritius a society of highly differentiated components, but with an Indian majority.

As independence approached, many of these demographic complexities were overshadowed by the fear of Hindu domination. This fear was shared by all the minorities. The main cleavage, though, was between Hindus, who alone accounted for half the population in 1962,[60] and

backward (or lower) castes and Harijans (ex-untouchables). *Far Eastern Economic Review*, December 9, 1993, pp. 18, 20.

58. Burton Benedict, *Mauritius: The Problems of a Plural Society* (London: Pall Mall Press, 1965), chs. 2–3.

59. Ibid., p. 17.

60. Ibid., p. 63.

Creoles, who made up about one-quarter but whose more solidary party organization (Hindus supported more than one party) and early participation in the affairs of the island made them formidable competitors for power.[61] The major antagonists were the Labor Party, essentially Hindu, and the Parti Mauricien, predominantly Creole. Reflecting the majority position of its Hindu constituency, the Labor Party demanded independence for Mauritius. As late as the mid-1960s, however, the Parti Mauricien opposed independence, favoring association with Britain instead.

This basic alignment was accurately reproduced in the riot of 1965, except that the Hindu participants were not drawn primarily from the Labor Party, but from the Hindu Congress, an organization appealing largely to low-caste Indians.[62] When the Parti Mauricien organized a large demonstration of support for association with Britain, Creoles and Chinese turned out in strength. Congress supporters then looted Chinese shops to retaliate for Chinese support of the demonstration. In this atmosphere, processions were held; they turned to more general violence begun by gangs affiliated with the Parti Mauricien and Hindu Congress. The 1965 violence thus mirrored the ethnic cleavage that had for decades formed the basis of political conflict. Opposing party positions, taken along the lines of ethnic interests and fears, had reinforced the cleavage.

The 1968 riot was different. With independence no longer in doubt, the major development in party competition was a strenuous effort by the Parti Mauricien to reach beyond its largely Creole — and therefore minority — clientele by bidding for Indian support.[63] The party's new emphasis on multiethnic composition resulted in the attraction of some Hindu defectors from the Labor Party, as well as some Muslims, low-caste Hindus, and Tamils.[64] The Labor Party reaction was to shore up its Indian flank by agreeing to a united front with another Hindu party and the principal Muslim party, the Comité d'Action Musulman (CAM). In 1967, this coalition produced an electoral victory for the Labor Party

61. In the 1948 election, 11 of the 19 legislators returned were Hindu, with one exception, a Franco-Mauritian; all the rest were Creole. Adele Smith Simmons, "Politics in Mauritius since 1934: A Study of Decolonization in a Plural Society" (D. Phil. thesis, Oxford University, 1969), p. 271. The following account of the Mauritian riots rests heavily on the material provided by this source. Responsibility for the conclusions is mine.

62. For the 1965 riot, see ibid., pp. 408–16.

63. Ibid., ch. 9. The Parti Mauricien also catered to a Franco-Mauritian and Chinese clientele, but none of these groups afforded a sufficient base to alleviate the problems stemming from the party's ascriptive minority position.

64. In Mauritius, as in Fiji, the Tamils have always been differentiated to some extent from the north Indian Hindus, who made their political home with the Labor Party.

and its allies. A side effect of the realignment and the consequent voting patterns was that the allegiance of the Muslims was badly divided between the two blocs. This division led directly to the 1968 violence and governed target choice.

Especially after the partition of India in 1947, Mauritian Muslims had feared the political influence of the more numerous Hindus. That fear was manifested in opposition to universal suffrage and later in opposition to independence. Although a working arrangement with the Labor Party had earlier brought the CAM tangible benefits in the form of seats in the legislature, the more far-reaching Hindu-Muslim front founded in 1967 evoked reservations on the part of many Muslims.

The intra-Muslim split was felt in the election. In a constituency where the three CAM candidates and two Chinese affiliated to the Labor Party bloc opposed two Muslims and a Chinese, all representing the Parti Mauricien, there was violence.[65] When the vote seemed to be going against the CAM, crowds affiliated to that party began to stop cars carrying Parti Mauricien voters. The Parti Mauricien retaliated, and for a time battles of Muslims against Creoles and Chinese threatened to get out of hand.

This riot was controlled, but three months later a Muslim gang responsible to the CAM leader, Razack Mohammed, and a Creole gang loyal to the Parti Mauricien began the violence again. The fighting quickly spread out beyond the gangs themselves, to the broader Muslim and Creole communities. Hindus were not targeted.

The motive for the violence is clear:

> Angered by his election defeat and by the success of the *Parti Mauricien* at attracting Muslim votes, Razack Mohammed was desperate to restore himself as leader of the Muslim community. If the Muslims had reason to fear the Creoles they would leave the *Parti Mauricien* . . . and rally behind Mohammed. This, in fact, happened. Muslim *Parti Mauricien* supporters went into hiding, and by the end of the riots [Labor Party leader and Prime Minister] Ramgoolam confidently claimed that Mohammed was the leader of the Muslims.[66]

The 1968 riot illustrates several aspects of targeting in party-led riots. The 1965 riot occurred when parties were clearly monoethnic and were thus accurate reflections of the conflict patterns of their ethnic constituencies. In 1968, the targeting process bypassed a major ethnic con-

65. Simmons, "Politics in Mauritius since 1934," pp. 468–69.
66. Ibid., p. 476.

testant, the Hindu group, because party divisions no longer entirely coincided with earlier ethnic cleavages. The Parti Mauricien's new emphasis on crossing ethnic boundaries gave rise to the riot and to this skewed pattern of targeting. In fact, the violence was initially aimed at restoring the earlier party alignments.

The two Mauritian riots were somewhat exceptional for party-led violence, in that Muslims and the Muslim party did not take part in the 1965 episode, whereas Hindus and Hindu parties were left out of the 1968 disturbances. Even in societies heterogeneous enough to afford considerable latitude in choosing target groups, the more usual pattern in successive party-led riots is for the identity of the initiators and victims to remain constant. In Congo (Brazzaville), for example, there were several major party-led ethnic riots in the late 1950s. These riots involved the Mbochi and Bakongo, the ethnic groups whose parties had been struggling for political dominance.[67] A third major group, the Vili, was left out of the violence as soon as it became clear that its party was also out of the political running. Likewise, in Guinea, riots directed against the Fulani in Conakry were products of party rivalries.[68] The Fulani were the major remaining ethnic holdout from Sékou Touré's Parti Démocratique de Guinée (PDG). Most of the violence that occurred in Guinea from 1956 to 1958 found the Soussou and Malinké, strong supporters of the PDG, on one side, and the Fulani, identified with their own parties, on the other.

As careerists seek out bureaucratic rivals and religious functionaries hunt down proselytizers, parties pursue their political competitors. Riots in Singapore (1964) were inspired by several leaders of a Malay party in Kuala Lumpur, and the violence targeted Chinese.[69] The South African rivalry between the Zulu party, Inkatha, and the multiethnic but Xhosa-led African National Congress produced a spate of riots in the Transvaal in the early 1990s, principally between Zulu and Xhosa.[70] Such riots are likely to reinforce or, as in Mauritius (1968), reestablish preexisting cleavages.

It is fair to ask whether party-instigated riots are riots within the meaning of the term introduced in Chapter 1. On a continuum from cal-

67. Carter, *Independence for Africa*, ch. 8; Virginia Thompson and Richard Adloff, *The Emerging States of French Equatorial Africa* (Stanford: Stanford University Press, 1960), ch. 25.

68. See *Le Monde*, May 7, 1958, p. 4; May 9, 1958, p. 2.

69. Michael Leifer, "Communal Violence in Singapore," *Asian Survey* 4, no. 10 (October 1964): 1115–21.

70. Donald L. Horowitz, *A Democratic South Africa? Constitutional Engineering in a Divided Society* (Berkeley and Los Angeles: University of California Press, 1991), p. 73.

culative to spontaneous, party-led riots fall closer to the calculative end. But no riot included here amounts merely to an interparty fight. As events unfold, the violence is not confined to the participating parties or their affiliated gangs. (The same is true for riots led by students or religious functionaries.) Within the targeted category, all group members are potential victims. Whatever their initial organization, these are riots between ethnic groups.

The ability of a party to organize an event in which nonparty members join and in which targeting is indifferent to the party-membership status of the victim clearly depends on the salience of group antipathies rather than of pure party goals. But, where ethnically based parties dominate politics, as they do in many severely divided societies, whole ethnic groups may be identified with particular parties. Party member or not, a person who belongs to a given group may be assumed to be in sympathy with the party that ostensibly represents the group and may be targeted accordingly. Moreover, the party behavior that precipitates the violence may be perceived as typical of the offensive behavior of the target group in general and so imputed to the whole group. That each and every opposing group member may become a victim, even in violence that begins with a high degree of organization, was graphically brought home in Mauritius. The Parti Mauricien leader, "Duval, in an effort to end the communal struggle, took one of his Muslim deputies, Abdul Carrim, to a meeting of Creoles — and Carrim came back without part of his ear."[71]

RIOT LOCATION AND TARGET CHOICE

Rioters must find proximate victims. In highly organized riots, some riot participants may be provided with transportation to enhance their tactical mobility, but most, lacking that advantage, must operate within certain geographic limits. If, therefore, potential target groups are simply not in sufficiently close proximity to attack, a riot will not materialize unless displacement occurs and appropriate targets are found.

In most cases, however, total geographic isolation of ethnic groups does not exist. (If it did, the occasions for ethnic conflict, peaceful or violent, would be greatly reduced.) Urban or semi-urban areas are the most common points of ethnic contact, and this is perhaps one of several reasons why so many riots occur in towns. But despite such points of contact, on a countrywide scale, residential segregation is the rule rather

71. Simmons, "Politics in Mauritius since 1934," p. 475.

than the exception. Patterns of population concentration can certainly affect the direction of targeting. But, rather than altering the identity of the group to be attacked, the most likely effect of skewed population distributions seems to be to point the violence toward those subgroups of the larger targeted ethnic group that are most accessible to the riot initiators.

Two illustrations can be cited. The first is, once again, the Assam riot of 1960. There the targets were Bengalis. But the Bengalis of Assam were divided by religion, region, length of residence, and degree of opposition to Assamese as the official language of Assam. In 1874, the Cachar and Sylhet areas, both largely Bengali, were added to the original territory of Assam. Sylhet subsequently became part of East Pakistan and then Bangladesh, but Cachar remained with Assam. The Bengalis of Cachar consisted largely of long-term, settled residents, with only a minority of Bengali immigrants from Pakistan. But in the Brahmaputra Valley, which comprised the Assamese heartland, the Bengali population was composed mostly of immigrants from East Bengal. When the demand arose to make Assamese the official state language, little opposition came from the valley, where Bengalis were often fluent in Assamese and some even lent their support to the Assamese demand.[72] It was in Cachar that the Bengalis formed an organization to demand, in vociferous terms, equal status for the Bengali language.[73]

The riot, however, occurred, not in Cachar, where the Bengali opposition was, but in the valley, where the Assamese rioters were. In Cachar, Assamese form an insignificant minority, and they mounted no assaults there. The Bengalis of the valley towns, moderate and accommodating though they tended to be, were targeted, largely because of the provocations of their more remote and less accessible cousins in Cachar.[74]

72. Chakravarti, "Bongal Kheda Again," p. 1194, and Goswami, "Tragedy of Political Tactlessness," p. 1195, though they agree on little else, are in accord on this point.

73. For some of the regional background, see Bhandari, *Thoughts on Assam Disturbances*, pp. 9, 22–23, 27.

74. Similarly, in Delhi (1984), the victims of anti-Sikh violence were disproportionately Labaniya Sikhs, who happened to live in the settlement colonies where the attacks occurred. Although the riot took place against the background of Sikh separatism in Punjab, the Labaniya Sikhs originated in Sind rather than Punjab, typically did not speak Punjabi, and had no connection to the separatists. The same was true for Sikhs attacked in Sultanpuri. Originating in Alwar, they spoke Rajasthani, could not communicate in Punjabi, and, as converts from Hinduism, had no ties to Punjab whatever. Uma Chakravarti and Nandita Haksar, *The Delhi Riots: Three Days in the Life of a Nation* (New Delhi: Lancer International, 1987), pp. 72, 81, 267. Location dictated the subethnic choice of targets.

Logistics also skewed targeting in Zanzibar (1961). Although that violence between Africans and Arabs arose as a direct result of ethnopolitical conflict and indeed occurred on election day, nearly all of those killed during the riot were Manga Arabs, notable for their political inactivity and even lack of interest.[75] The Manga were a subgroup of the Arab community, largely rural, relatively recent immigrants, relatively poor, and certainly relatively powerless, in contrast to the older, wealthier Arab elite, with whom they were often not on good terms. There were unquestionably reasons relating to Afro-Arab conflict for Africans to include Manga among their victims.[76] But the fact that the Manga were so disproportionately represented among the Arab casualties can also be explained in part by settlement patterns. The Manga lived in "fairly densely populated squatter areas."[77] It was easier to find and kill them, without interference from organized Arab gangs or the colonial instruments of order, than it was to hunt down other classes of Arabs.

TARGETING: REFLECTIONS AND DISTORTIONS

There are two ways to think about evidence on targeting. The first is to concentrate on targeting within an individual riot. There the evidence is of very considerable selectivity, which signifies a highly focused violence, largely explicable in terms of group characteristics. The second is to inquire into targeting across riots in the same space. Here, despite overall consistency of targets, there is somewhat greater variability, a small amount of which overall is explained by riot precipitants, leadership, or (least of all) location. In addition, I shall show later that, in successive riots conducted by members of the same perpetrator group, there is some tendency toward broadening the boundaries of the target groups, even where the core targets remain the same. The Pakistani riots of 1985 in Karachi consisted of attacks by Pathans on Biharis, but the riots of the next several years in the same city targeted not just Biharis but all Mohajirs, the designation applied to those who had migrated from north Indian states (including Bihar) and their descendants. This broadening phenomenon requires explanation.

75. Michael Lofchie, *Zanzibar: Background to Revolution* (Princeton: Princeton University Press, 1965), pp. 78–79, 188, 204, 206.

76. See Chapter 5, above.

77. Government of Great Britain, *Report of a Commission to Inquire into Disturbances in Zanzibar during June 1961*, Colon. No. 353 (London: H.M.S.O., 1961), p. 13.

Perhaps the evidence of inter-riot target variability undermines any theory of target choice. If there is hostility against several groups and a stray precipitant or a determined leadership can steer the violence in one direction or another, target choices are, by turns, capricious or strategic, but not necessarily responsive to patterns of antipathy.

The evidence we have reviewed would not support so drastic a conclusion. The frictions in intergroup relations that are manifested in violence are, to be sure, subject to the vagaries introduced by intervening variables. But close inspection reveals that there is a limit to the deflection that takes place. Displacement might be thought to alter target identity wildly and unpredictably, but it does not. The exigencies of conducting violence do introduce disproportionality but not unpredictability in the infliction of violence. Location can introduce subethnic disproportionality but not much more than that. Precipitants can point violence to one target rather than another, where there is more than one set of hostile relations, but they cannot point it where there is no antipathy. Riot leadership can skew targeting toward the concerns of particular segments or strata of the perpetrator group. But many of the cases in which leadership is clearly discernible involve ethnically based political parties, which is another way of saying that the violence is likely to be directed at targets against whom there is rather widely shared hostility.

The tendency of political leaders to follow group sentiment helps account for the somewhat greater success of careerist rivals than of commercial rivals in organizing violence: the preferred targets of the former are more likely to possess the appropriate target-group characteristics than are the preferred targets of the latter.[78] Similarly, party-organized violence does not always reinforce preexisting cleavages; but, far more often than not, it does, for those are the lines along which parties are likely to be organized in severely divided societies. The 1965 Mauritius riot is much more typical than the 1968 one. In targeting decisions, reflections far exceed distortions.

78. For a discussion of hostility toward groups in business, see Donald L. Horowitz, *Ethnic Groups in Conflict* (Berkeley and Los Angeles: University of California Press, 1985), pp. 113–24.

Organizers and Participants

THE DEAD, IT IS SAID, do not live to tell the tale, but this is not true in ethnic riots. The dead do tell the tale; it is the living who are reluctant to speak. Only because the victims are dead, injured, or displaced — and therefore identifiable — is it possible to know who is targeted in violence. To be sure, some victims are missing, some have fled, and some are in hiding. Still, the known victims constitute mute testimony to target choices. But if the dead speak eloquently because they do not move, those who do the killing are alive, on the move, and capable of concealing their identity. In ethnic riots, the casualty count is extraordinarily lopsided. With the exception of those groups that have been targets of such recurrent riots that they live in a state of readiness for violence, as they do in a few cities of India and Pakistan, rare is the target group capable of mounting a serious counterattack. Rioters thus escape unscathed and unidentified. Since arrest and prosecution are decidedly exceptional in these cases,[1] published records also tend to be unhelpful in identifying participants. For all of these reasons, it is possible to learn more about the victims of this violence than about those who victimize them.

The organization of violence is often similarly opaque. On only a few occasions are the organizers of riots eager to claim credit for their accomplishment. Publicity might provoke the authorities into prosecution, which often they are otherwise reluctant to undertake. Official and unofficial investigations of riots sometimes identify organizers and sometimes do not. When they do, there are occasionally reasons to suspect their accuracy or evenhandedness. When they do not, their silence is not conclusive. The absence of evidence pointing to the role of organizations does not necessarily mean the absence of any involvement. The organization of violence is undertaken clandestinely, and published materials

1. See Chapter 9, pp. 352–66, below.

are least informative on the events behind the events. Conspiratorial accounts that see hidden hands that may or may not actually be involved confuse matters further.

That is not to say that all riots are organized, no matter how unorganized they appear.[2] Undoubtedly, some are spontaneous, and many others are organized ad hoc by participants and leaders who improvise plans during the lull. The level of organization, the identity of the organizers, and the goals of the leaders of organized riots are all research questions. The subterranean quality of much riot organization means that there cannot be perfect confidence in the answers.[3] Still, there are glimpses of answers better than we might expect: clues from leaflets, arrests, post facto investigations, the timing of violence in relation to precipitating events, and so on.

What the evidence shows is that most riots seem to be unorganized, partially organized and partially spontaneous, or organized by ephemeral leadership that springs up to respond to events as they happen, often suddenly. Most riots, in other words, consist of angry violence. Even where riots are reasonably well organized, as in the case of party-organized riots, their main objective is to further ethnic polarization in an already polarized environment or to take advantage of a hostile mood. Those who try to organize riots in unpolarized environments do not succeed very well. Organizers are typically at work in some areas, where they enjoy certain advantages (usually a local following and sometimes access to vehicles), but not in others. There remains room, even in the most organized riots, for spontaneous action. Furthermore, where sentiments are hostile and appropriate precipitating events have occurred, strong organization may be superfluous. Certainly, as we shall see, the advantages of organization are overblown. More organization does not necessarily produce a more serious riot.

The spectrum thus runs roughly as follows:

1. A precipitating event elicits a relatively spontaneous violent response, in which leadership (if any can be identified) is assumed

---

2. Compare Paul R. Brass, *Theft of an Idol: Text and Context in the Representation of Collective Violence* (Princeton: Princeton University Press, 1997), pp. 8–9, 28, 284–85.

3. In this respect, the organization of violence resembles patterns of corruption. Both are important subjects, but the illegality of the activity makes research difficult. Cf. Jeans Christopher Andvig, "The Economics of Corruption: A Survey," *Studi Economici*, no. 43 (1991): 57–94, at p. 57; Renuka Rajkumar, "Political Corruption: A Review of the Literature," *West African Journal of Sociology and Political Science* 1, no. 2 (January 1976): 177–85, at p. 177.

more or less on the spot, usually by community toughs or others with experience in fighting. Penang (1967) is a clear exemplar.

2. A precipitating event elicits spontaneous violence, which is then escalated as leaders favoring violence seize the opportunity to expand it. Sri Lanka (1983) illustrates this pattern.

3. A precipitating event produces a hostile atmosphere, which leaders convert into a violent episode. Delhi (1984) exemplifies this sequence.

4. Organizers lead violence as a result of incidents they create or sentiments they have cultivated. This violence may be relatively contained, as in Guyana (1964), or may expand if it taps strongly hostile sentiments, as it did in Mauritius (1968).

In each category, hostility is indispensable.

No matter how spontaneous a riot may be, no event that is seen to have utility for participants will necessarily remain wholly spontaneous if it occurs on later occasions. Those who have reason subsequently to organize violence will attempt to feed off the same antipathy that produced the earlier violence. The organized riot is the tribute that organizers pay to the power of underlying ethnic sentiment to do their work for them. A certain number of riots are fomented by ethnic-extremist or paramilitary organizations. Such organizations tend to flourish in locations that have already been subject to repeated episodes of violence. Violence thus produces organization, perhaps more than vice versa, and then such organizations help to spur violence on succeeding occasions, often on the basis of precipitating events less significant than the earlier ones, thereby suggesting a lowered threshold for violence in those locations.

The degree of organization thus varies over time. In a series of riots, organization is likely to be strongly present in the later episodes or, if riots become truly endemic, organization becomes extremely visible (although in such cases riots do not really keep their shape — they turn into something approaching intergroup warfare). Short of such a state, riots run through the spectrum of organizational possibilities. Without strong underlying sentiment, however, organized crowd violence is likely to be weak violence, not invariably but generally.

The identity of participants points to the same general conclusions. As we shall see, participation in ethnic riots is remarkably open and broadly based, within certain limits of age, sex, and class. Participants do not tend to be deviants or habitual criminals, although criminals join in the disorder. To the extent that organization does not generate violence and participation is not limited to narrowly defined categories, the deadly ethnic riot is no contrived event. It is a community response to situations and events that are deemed so serious as to require violent action. This has implications for prevention that I shall touch on at the end of the chapter.

INDICATORS OF ORGANIZATION

There are some tell-tale signs of riot organization. These relate to logistics, weapons, precipitants, methods of violence, and the intensity of fighting.

If rioters arrive from very far away, this circumstance rules out spontaneity. When rioters descended upon Brazzaville from Alima, 200 miles distant, in 1959, or when they arrived in Guinea from Sierra Leone, as they did in 1956, distance alone signified organization.[4] When some rioters arrive by the truckload, as they did in Ahmedabad (1969), Kuala Lumpur (1969), northern Nigeria (1966), and Mauritania (1989), someone has been thoughtful enough to provide transportation.[5] Sometimes transportation arrangements involve planning by government officials, for often it is alleged that government vehicles are used, as they seem to have been in Sri Lanka (1956, 1958, and 1983) and Uzbekistan (1989).[6]

When the rioters have similar ordnance from one location to another, or when they use atypical weapons, that, too, evidences planning. In Dushanbe, Tajikistan (1990), the participants at several locations utilized bottles with a similar inflammable mixture and with sulphuric acid, a circumstance which gave rise to an inference of organization.[7] And in Tirgu

---

4. Jean-Michel Wagret, *Histoire et Sociologie Politiques de la République du Congo (Brazzaville)* (Paris: Librairie Générale de Droit et de Jurisprudence, 1963), pp. 84–85.

5. Ghanshyam Shah, "Communal Riots in Gujarat," *Economic and Political Weekly*, Annual Number, January 1970, pp. 187–200, at pp. 195, 197; *The Times* (London), May 27, 1969, p. 5 (Malaysia); Walter Schwarz, *Nigeria* (New York: Praeger 1968), p. 216; Human Rights Watch/Africa, *Mauritania's Campaign of Terror: State-Sponsored Repression of Black Africans* (New York: Human Rights Watch, 1994), pp. 13–14.

6. Interview with a former deputy inspector-general of police, Colombo, August 16, 1968 (1958 riots); Tarzie Vittachi, *Emergency '58: The Story of the Ceylon Race Riots* (London: André Deutsch, 1958), p. 65; Rajan Hoole et al., *The Broken Palmyra: The Tamil Crisis in Sri Lanka — an Inside Account*, rev. ed. (Claremont, Calif.: The Sri Lanka Studies Institute, 1990), pp. 63–70; Stanley Jayaraja Tambiah, *Buddhism Betrayed? Religion, Politics, and Violence in Sri Lanka* (Chicago: University of Chicago Press, 1992), p. 73; *Izvestiya*, June 10, 1989, in FBIS-SOV-89-111, June 12, 1989, pp. 35, 40.

7. *Tass*, February 15, 1990, in FBIS-SOV-90-033, February 16, 1990, p. 61.

Mures, Romania (1990), the rioters wielded identical axes and clubs, picked up from a common storage site.[8]

The more organized the riot, the less it is dependent on antecedent events that are otherwise required to arouse spontaneous sentiment. The insignificance of the precipitant may be — but is not always — an indication of organization.[9] More direct clues to organization are "the handbill and poster inciting to violence."[10] Leaflets that advocate wiping out the Chinese from Singapore (1964) or that tell the Tamils to leave Galle, in Sri Lanka (1995), demonstrate forethought.[11] Heavily residential targeting, typically using election lists, tax lists, or census lists, is another emblem of organization, as it was in the Ivory Coast (1958), Ahmedabad (1969), Sri Lanka (1983), Sumgait (1988), Mauritania (1989), Uzbekistan (1989), and Bombay (1984 and 1993).[12]

The sheer magnitude of casualties per unit of time may be a mark of strategic coordination. In Nellie, Assam (1983), in Tripura (1980), and in Meerut (1982), a high death toll in a very short period was taken as proof of planning.[13] In Nellie, the concerted character of the violence, in which some 1,383 people were killed in a string of ten villages within

8. Vladimir Socor, "Forces of Old Resurface in Romania: The Ethnic Clashes in Tirgu Mures," *Report on Eastern Europe*, April 13, 1990, pp. 36–43.

9. As it certainly was in West Bengal (1979) and in the Ivory Coast (1958). See, respectively, *Far Eastern Economic Review*, July 20, 1979, p. 32; Gwendolen Carter, *Independence for Africa* (New York: Praeger, 1960), p. 13.

10. Richard Lambert, "Hindu-Muslim Riots" (Ph.D. diss., University of Pennsylvania, 1951), p. 222.

11. Leaflet attributed to "The Singapore Malays National Struggle Organization," n.d. (mimeo. facsimile); *Ethnic Violence in Galle, June 2, 1995: A Report of the Independent Committee of Inquiry* (Colombo: ICES, 1995), p. 11. For other leaflets, see M.J. Akbar, *Riot after Riot* (Delhi: Penguin, 1988), pp. 26–27; Shah, "Communal Riots in Gujarat," p. 191; Government of India, *Report of the Commission of Inquiry on Communal Disturbances in Ranchi-Hatia (August 22–29, 1967)* (New Delhi: Government Printer, 1968), pp. 10–14.

12. Carter, *Independence for Africa*, pp. 108, 113; Shah, "Communal Riots in Gujarat," p. 193; Eric Meyer, "Seeking the Roots of the Tragedy," in James Manor, ed., *Sri Lanka in Change and Crisis* (New York: St. Martin's, 1984), p. 139; Gananath Obeyesekere, "The Origins and Institutionalisation of Political Violence," in ibid., p. 113; Tambiah, *Buddhism Betrayed?* p. 73; Claire Mouradian, "The Mountainous Karabagh Question: An Interethnic Conflict or Decolonization Crisis?" *Armenian Review* 43, nos. 2–3 (Summer/Autumn 1990): 1–34, at p. 17; Human Rights Watch/Africa, *Mauritania's Campaign of Terror*, p. 13 n.3; *Izvestiya*, June 18, 1989, p. 3, in FBIS-SOV-89-117, June 20, 1989, pp. 50–51; Asghar Ali Engineer, *Bhiwandi-Bombay Riots: Analysis and Documentation* (Bombay: Institute of Islamic Studies, 1984), p. 38; Suma Josson, *Bombay Blood Yatra*, a film (1993).

13. See, respectively, Arun Shourie, "Assam Elections: Come What May," *India Today*, May 15, 1983, p. 65; *Far Eastern Economic Review*, July 4, 1980, pp. 11, 23; *New York Times*, October 6, 1982, p. 3. Of course, the most highly organized form of ethnic violence — terrorism — generally involves fewer casualties, rather than more.

four hours, is also evidenced by the size of the attacking crowd: 12,000 people who walked from a score of villages more than ten miles away.[14] The same sort of evidence leads to the same conclusion in Nigeria (1993), where, using guns, Andoni attackers killed about 1,000 Ogoni in two towns on a single day.[15]

Often these clues signify organization but do not identify the organizers. The weapons in Nigeria may have been provided by the armed forces, the transportation in Sri Lanka may point to particular ministries and officials, and handbills and posters may give away the identity of their authors. But the distance traversed by the rioters, the size of the attacking crowd, the intensity of the killing, or the use of lists of intended victims does not, without more, point to particular organizers. And, once in a while, the clues are fallible even insofar as they merely suggest a high degree of planning. For intense affect is likely to produce many killings, sometimes fairly rapidly. This is why the enormous size of the crowd in Nellie and the unusual presence of guns in Nigeria are important additional clues that confirm the existence of organization.

ORGANIZERS

In Chapter 6, we reviewed a number of riots organized by students, career rivals, and religious functionaries. As I intimated there, relatively few riots are organized by these categories. To the extent that their interests differ from those of other potential organizers, students and career rivals typically are focused on middle-class issues that may have little resonance for the people who are needed to form attacking crowds. Students may also be more attracted to ideologically driven movements of ethnic "liberation" than to indiscriminate mass killing. On these grounds, terrorism and secessionist warfare may be more attractive to them than is the riot, although some movements — Sikh separatists and the All-Assam Students Union come to mind — have attempted some of both. Hindu-Muslim riots have had their share of inspiration, if not leadership, from religious functionaries, and Buddhist monks have, from time to time, played an organizational or contributory role.[16] Nevertheless, the vast majority of riots have not been instigated by religious functionaries.

14. Shourie, "Assam Elections," p. 65.
15. *Reuters Library Report*, September 27, 1993. See *Independent* (London), August 9, 1993, p. 8.
16. See, e.g., Government of Burma, *Final Report of the Riot Inquiry Committee* (Rangoon: Superintendent, Government Printing and Stationery, 1939), pp. 14–15, 38–39; Vittachi, *Emergency '58*, pp. 28–29.

By the same token, as I argued in Chapter 6, business rivals, often accused of fomenting violence to secure economic advantage over emerging competitors, are not likely to be effective organizers of mass violence. It seems more likely that business rivals sometimes merely take advantage of violence by looting or otherwise harming their competitors than that they are responsible for organizing riots.[17] Some good evidence for this view is provided by the anti-Muslim violence in Karamanj (1968), an Assamese town near the border with what was then East Pakistan and is now Bangladesh. In Karamanj, trading rivalries did find expression in the riot. What was missing, however, was mass sentiment. The result was a high property toll and a low death toll. Whereas more than 100 Muslim-owned houses and shops were destroyed, only seven people were killed, despite police ineffectiveness that would have permitted a much higher death toll.[18] A similarly organized anti-Tamil riot in Galle, Sri Lanka (1985), produced, remarkably enough, no deaths, presumably for the same reasons.[19] While these are not perfect tests of the organizing power of business rivals, because the precipitants were mild, they suggest that large-scale casualties are not likely where traders are among the strongest proponents of violence. Where planning is present, the organization of most serious deadly ethnic riots emanates from other sources with broader agendas. This cautions us against the most extreme hidden-hand views, for to say that an agenda with broad appeal produces the most serious violence is to concede that, when it comes to mass killing, organization cannot lead where sentiment will not go.

The principal sources of organization are divisible into four overlapping, sprawling categories: (1) political parties, factions, and individual politicians; (2) paramilitaries (sometimes linked to parties); (3) extremist organizations (sometimes linked to paramilitaries or to parties); and (4) secret societies (sometimes linked to any or all of the above). It bears repeating that these categories are identifiable only in those cases in which discernible organization is at work in the first place. Most of the time, organization seems to take a back seat to passionate killing in deadly ethnic riots.

17. See Amrita Basu, "When Local Riots Are Not Merely Local: Bringing the State Back In, Bijnor, 1988–92," *Economic and Political Weekly*, October 1, 1994, pp. 2605–21, at p. 2614; Roger Jeffery and Patricia M. Jeffery, "The Bijnor Riots, October, 1990," *Economic and Political Weekly*, March 5, 1994, pp. 551–58, at p. 556.

18. Aswini K. Ray and Subhash Chakravarti, *Karamanj Riots: A Political Study* (New Delhi: Sampradayikta Virodhi Committee, n.d.), pp. 17, 25–26, 28.

19. *Ethnic Violence in Galle.*

POLITICAL PARTIES, FACTIONS, AND LEADERS

Riots inspired or directed by political parties, factions, and leaders undoubtedly reflect the antipathies of their followers, but for the organizers the violence is also strategic. It takes place on patterned occasions (to be detailed in the next chapter) and responds to the specific predicament in which the organizers find themselves.

Party-Organized Riots.   Party-organized riots occur where ethnic relations have become thoroughly politicized and where ethnically based parties have become the vehicle for the expression of the ethnic aspirations of a large fraction of the electorate. These are the necessary but not the sufficient conditions.

The involvement of parties, factions, or individual leaders in episodes of deadly ethnic rioting can be characterized loosely as deriving from one of three sets of goals: (1) polarization, (2) the effort to counter polarization, and (3) a residual category that can be described roughly as destabilizing protest. The first embodies a desire to undo interethnic political alliances in favor of organization along ethnic lines, with the accompanying heightened conflict, from which the organizers would benefit. The second entails defensive or prophylactic operations against such a polarizing tendency. The third is a reaction to the mutually exclusive outcomes of ethnic party politics, particularly on the part of ethnically based parties that have lost elections and sense exclusion from power in perpetuity. This reaction is not necessarily strategic.

There is a paradox inherent in party-organized violence. Where party leadership inspires ethnic riots for strategic ends, its objectives are usually limited, and so is the violence. Where, on the other hand, party factions or individual leaders foster violence, their most common objective is to benefit from polarization, but their capacity to do so depends on a very significant degree of prior polarization. In no case of an ethnic riot propelled by parties, factions, or leaders could it be said that the violence was so overwhelmingly instrumental that affect played the minor role and strategy the major role.

In countries where ethnic parties dominate politics, they tend to reflect the major ethnic cleavages. In some countries, however, ethnic parties are present but do not dominate politics. These parties have a strong incentive to polarize politics by reinforcing the salience of the major cleavages. Take several disparate instances of the situation in which a multiethnic party was confronted by one or more ethnic parties on one or more flanks: South Africa (1990), Mauritius (1968), and Turkey (1978). In each case, ethnically based parties attempted to polarize the electorate, to the disadvantage of multiethnic competitors.

In South Africa (1990), the Xhosa-Zulu killings in the Transvaal paralleled the struggle between the largely Xhosa-led but multiethnic African National Congress and the Zulu party, Inkatha, for the support of Zulu outside the heartland controlled by Chief Mangosuthu Buthelezi. At the same time, the violence reflected a preexisting polarity in the views of Zulu and Xhosa.[20] The Zulu-Xhosa violence can be seen as an effort to detach Zulu support from the ANC and undercut its claim to panethnic representation.

The Mauritian riot of 1968, described in Chapter 6, had the rather clear motive of splitting Muslims from an aspiring multiethnic party, the Parti Mauricien, and driving them back to a purely Muslim party to which they had previously given their allegiance. It appears to have had that effect.

Precisely the same party motive was attributed to those who fomented Sunni-Alevi riots in Turkey (1978). The ruling Republican People's Party accused the National Action Party, supported by some Sunni, of instigating anti-Alevi violence in order to bring the government down. Alevi were heavy supporters of the left, including various Communist parties and the prime minister's own Republican People's Party (RPP). If the violence divided Sunni from Alevi, that would erode the ability of the RPP to secure support from both.[21]

One species of party-organized violence, therefore, occurs in a polarizing environment and has as its function further polarization, specifically in the form of a threat to a dominant multiethnic party or interethnic coalition.[22] What these instances suggest is that when ethnic tensions are strong, a multiethnic party that is, by definition, not aligned perfectly along ethnic fault lines is vulnerable to decomposition along those lines.

20. See Donald L. Horowitz, *A Democratic South Africa? Constitutional Engineering in a Divided Society* (Berkeley and Los Angeles: University of California Press, 1991), pp. 48–75. For another interpretation, see Heribert Adam and Kogila Moodley, "Political Violence, 'Tribalism,' and Inkatha," *Journal of Modern African Studies* 30, no. 3 (September 1992): 485–510.

21. For brief accounts of the violence, see Erik J. Zürcher, *Turkey: A Modern History* (London: I.B. Tauris, 1994), pp. 276–77; Feroz Ahmad, *The Making of Modern Turkey* (London: Routledge, 1993), pp. 172–73; George S. Harris, *Turkey: Coping with Crisis* (Boulder, Colo.: Westview Press, 1985), p. 15.

22. In India, it has been argued, the Bharatiya Janata Party has reacted violently to dangerous coalitions between backward castes and Muslims or between scheduled castes and Muslims, because it has the object of solidifying all Hindus — in other words, accomplishing polarization. See Basu, "When Local Riots Are Not Merely Local," p. 2615.

This vulnerability suggests possibilities for prophylactic violence. A multiethnic center threatened with decomposition can produce violence to counter impending polarization, as it did in Singapore (1964). The Singapore riot is unusually instructive because of the opposing functions it performed for Malay parties in Singapore and in Malaysia as a whole (of which Singapore was then a part). Leaders of both played an organizing role but for different purposes at the two levels.

The Singapore riot occurred a year after the merger of Singapore with other units to form Malaysia. During the interval, the ruling People's Action Party (PAP) of Singapore, led by Lee Kuan Yew, had entered Malaysian politics and attempted to replace the Malayan Chinese Association as the Chinese component of the multiethnic Alliance coalition that ruled Malaysia. Overtures to Malay leaders of the Alliance proved unwelcome, since a strong PAP inside the Alliance would have required reorientation of the coalition's pro-Malay balance. Any such rebalancing would risk the future stability of the Alliance, as many Malay politicians and their followers feared Lee Kuan Yew's strong appeal to the Chinese. Some Malay politicians had been skeptical from the outset of the incorporation of Singapore, more than three-quarters Chinese, into Malaysia. One of the most skeptical was also among the most active in the events that produced the riots.

The opening for violence was created by party politics in Singapore. In the 1963 Singapore elections, Malays had rejected the Malay party affiliated with the Malay component of the Alliance nationally, in favor of Lee Kuan Yew's mainly Chinese PAP. Very likely, this was a case of strategic voting that did not reflect any strong affinity of Malays for the PAP but rather a desire to avoid splitting the total vote against a Communist opposition party. The leaders of the Malay party in Singapore nevertheless felt threatened and aimed to retrieve their clientele by emphasizing Malay grievances. In this they were joined by several Malay leaders from Kuala Lumpur, who had a larger design — namely, to warn Lee Kuan Yew off efforts to undo the Alliance in Kuala Lumpur.

The speeches, by both Singaporean and Malaysian Malay leaders, were exceedingly inflammatory, focused as they were on the plight of the Singapore Malays.[23] From this, it is possible to conclude that their aims

23. See Memorandum Submitted by the Government of Singapore to the Commission of Inquiry into the Disturbances in Singapore in 1964 (mimeo., March 1965), Appendices 6 (Speech by Dato Syed Ja'afar Albar at the Malay Convention at New Star Theatre, Pasir Panjang, July 12, 1964, transcribed from tape recording) and 10 (Speech by Dato Syed Esa Almanoer, UMNO secretary-general, on the Padang, July 21, 1964, transcribed from tape recording). See also *Far Eastern Economic Review*, August 6, 1964, p. 225; *Utusan Melayu*

were mainly local.[24] But, from interviews in Singapore and Kuala Lumpur, it is clear that, whereas the Singapore Malay leaders were attempting to pull apart whatever ties might be developing between Malay and Chinese supporters of the PAP, the Kuala Lumpur Malay leaders had a quite different objective in their own larger arena: to prevent the PAP from pulling apart the Malay and Chinese parties in the Alliance.[25] Here, then, in a single party-led riot, are represented two of the most common party objectives, opposite objectives at that.

Party fission, the objective of the Malay organizers in Singapore (1964), parallels the objectives imputed to the organizers in Turkey (1978), in Mauritius (1968), and in South Africa (1990), all of which were apparently designed to separate out ethnically demarcated supporters of a broadly based party. Fusion, the objective of the fomenters of the Singapore violence who were operating from Kuala Lumpur, is undoubtedly less common, since the usual effect of ethnic violence is to polarize. In each case, party organizers are working around the edges of sentiment, to push it toward further polarization or to counter the efforts of those who want to move it that way.

Often ethnic parties restrain their followers from rioting, even when the parties may have contributed to the antecedent tension.[26] Since these are non-events, it is difficult to know just how frequent they are. When parties are involved, there is reason to believe their most common involvement is indirect. Ethnic parties benefit from at least a modicum of interethnic fear, and so they periodically keep the quantum of apprehension high. When ethnic issues arise, by no means all of them raised by ethnic parties, those parties tend to support chauvinist positions. When anger rises, ethnic parties can scarcely afford to be left too far behind,

---

(Kuala Lumpur), March 25, 1964, p. 5; July 13, 1964, p. 3; July 15, 1964, p. 4; July 18, 1964, p. 1; July 20, 1964, p. 7.

24. Michael Leifer, "Communal Violence in Singapore," *Asian Survey* 4, no. 10 (October 1964): 1115–21, at pp. 1118–19. Cf. Lee Kuan Yew, *The Singapore Story* (Singapore: Times Editions, 1998), pp. 562, 569; Albert Lau, *A Moment of Anguish: Singapore in Malaysia and the Politics of Disengagement* (Singapore: Times Academic Press, 1998), pp. 178–80.

25. Interviews, Kuala Lumpur, November 24, 1967, May 24, 1968; Singapore, December 28, 1967. For a similar view, see Lau, *A Moment of Anguish*, pp. 183–89.

26. Examples are the mild riot in Sri Lanka (1981) and the aborted riot in Malaysia (1987). See Virginia A. Leary, *Ethnic Conflict and Violence in Sri Lanka: Report of a Mission to Sri Lanka in July–August 1981 on Behalf of the International Commission of Jurists* (Geneva: International Commission of Jurists, 1981), pp. 24–25; Harold Crouch, *Government and Society in Malaysia* (Ithaca: Cornell University Press, 1996), pp. 107–12.

and party officials may then be quick to jump into the organization of violence, as they did in the anti-Sikh riot in Delhi (1984).[27]

In describing the role of parties as consisting of a mix of restraint, background agitation, and opportunistic contribution to preexisting dispositions to violence, I do not mean to say that parties never engage in the deliberate fomentation and direction of violence. In the polarizing riots I have described, they do, and they also organize preelectoral ethnic violence where they calculate that an additional increment of antipathy will aid their chances. This has been argued particularly well for India by Steven Wilkinson,[28] and it certainly seems likely that a party like the Bharatiya Janata Party, which began with a limited high-caste and north Indian base, engaged in party building by focusing on the supposed antagonism between Muslims and all Hindus. What is unclear is how general this pattern of preelectoral ethnic violence is. Ethnic parties might well be wary of inciting serious violence immediately before elections, for fear of driving support away or turnout down, or of undermining their electoral victory by prompting state repression or even a suspension of democracy, or of creating so much polarization that even they may be outflanked by yet more extreme parties. So the logic of ethnic-party politics does not point unequivocally toward the involvement of ethnic parties in ethnic violence.

Postelectoral ethnic violence by ethnically based losing parties is another matter. Party functionaries may participate in or permit it, but not necessarily because they actively wish to organize it. A significant number of such riots is associated with the crystallization of the party system along ethnic lines, not merely in the sense that these riots foster polarization but also in the sense that they confirm the polarization and constitute a hostile response to its electoral results. A series of riots in Congo (Brazzaville) in the 1950s, as party politics began to be defined along ethnic lines, makes this clear.

As we shall see at closer range in Chapter 8, the Congolese electoral contest slowly developed as a rivalry between parties associated with the Mbochi and Bakongo, respectively.[29] In this, it was similar to many other

27. People's Union for Democratic Rights, People's Union for Civil Liberties, *Who Are the Guilty? Report of a Joint Inquiry into the Causes and Impact of the Riots in Delhi from 31 October to 10 November* (Delhi: PUDR & PUCL, 1984), p. 11. For Hindu-Muslim examples, see S.K. Ghosh, *Communal Riots in India* (New Delhi: Ashish, 1987), pp. 161–70, 216–20.

28. Steven Ian Wilkinson, "The Electoral Incentives for Ethnic Violence: Hindu-Muslim Riots in India" (Ph.D. diss., M.I.T., 1998).

29. See Virginia Thompson and Richard Adloff, *The Emerging States of French Equatorial Africa* (Stanford: Stanford University Press, 1960), pp. 484–90.

bipolar ethnic-party rivalries. Along the way, each contestant sensed the crucial importance of third groups whose electoral support might prove to be pivotal. Consequently, one of the main ethnic parties used ethnic violence to solidify the support of the Batéké for itself, and later the other used violence to attempt to thwart the attachment of the Vili to its antagonist. These episodes can aptly be regarded as prophylactic and polarizing riots, in much the same way that violence in Mauritius, which had as its object the support of the Chinese (1965) or the Muslims (1968), can be seen in this way.

Once the results of these contests began to harden into a firm parliamentary majority for the Bakongo party, Mbochi responded with violence; and when the government consolidated its Bakongo character, Mbochi rioters killed large numbers of Bakongo. Violence at this juncture can scarcely be described as wholly strategic: it is the protest of those who have lost the contest. While it may have some vaguely stated aim of destabilization, it is not to be confused with the coup d'état. This violence unseats no governments, and, insofar as party leaders authorize it, their action responds mainly to anger of their followers (and their own anger) at the prospect of total exclusion. Diverse sources agree that "enraged" Mbochi party leaders gave "free rein to their militants," allowing them to "act as [they] please."[30] In fact, all of the Congolese riots were instances of very angry violence, reflecting, as they did, apprehension at the prospect of complete ethnic exclusion from power.

Faction-Led Riots. It is hardly surprising that party violence responds to party interests and widely felt sentiments, whether those interests are in peeling away supporters weakly attached to a multiethnic party or coalition or in keeping them attached, or whether those sentiments involve anger and foreboding at the consequences of an electoral loss that, because of ethnic demography, cannot be recouped. But these are merely the objectives that can be inferred when parties foment violence or create conditions that are unusually conducive to violence. When factions or individual party leaders take similar action, the problem of motivation is more complicated.

In such cases, even the involvement of particular segments of a party may be problematical, though it is often alleged. Even where their involvement is demonstrable, their motives are sometimes elusive.

---

30. The quotations derive, respectively, from Carter, *Independence for Africa*, p. 92, and René Gauze, *The Politics of Congo-Brazzaville*, trans. Virginia Thompson and Richard Adloff (Stanford: Hoover Institution Press, 1973), p. 69.

Sometimes local party leaders are involved in violence for reasons that do not differentiate them from other local participants, as local Congress Party leaders certainly were in Ferozabad (1972) and in Delhi (1984), although in the latter case there have been suggestions that their participation may have reflected the will of their superiors.[31] Mere involvement of local party officials is therefore of no special significance. But even where factions or leaders are involved as a matter of policy, it may not be possible to infer motive. The Osh city secretary of the Communist Party may have been involved in the riots in Kyrghyzstan (1990), and former Northern People's Congress politicians were thought to have been involved in the riots in northern Nigeria (1966), but the specific objectives of each remain obscure.[32] In 1969, there was a serious riot in Kuala Lumpur, preceded by the apparent loss of the Selangor state government to the Alliance. The Alliance chief minister may have been among the instigators. But since it seems unlikely that he would have thought the electoral outcome reversible by violence — and very likely that he would have thought himself subject to party discipline for creating disorder not approved by the party's top leadership — his calculations, if he actually was involved, are difficult to fathom.[33] Conceivably, as some have thought, other senior party leaders used the electoral crisis in Selangor for wider purposes, perhaps to discredit the prime minister.[34] But although Prime Minister Tunku Abdul Rahman was ultimately undone

31. Suneet Chopra and N.K. Singh, "Ferozabad: Anatomy of a Riot," *Economic and Political Weekly*, August 19, 1972, pp. 1711, 1713; Citizens' Commission, Delhi, *Delhi, 31 October to 4 November 1984: Report of the Citizens' Commission* (Delhi: Citizens' Commission, 1985), p. 27.

32. Abidin Bozdağ, "Crisis and Democracy in Kirgizia," *Aussenpolitik* 43, no. 3 (n.m. 1992): 277–86; N.J. Miners, *The Nigerian Army, 1956–1966* (London: Methuen, 1971), p. 201; James O'Connell, "The Anatomy of a Pogrom: An Outline Model with Special Reference to the Ibo in Northern Nigeria," *Race* 9, no. 1 (July 1967): 95–100, at p. 100 n. 7. In the Nigerian case, a connection has been asserted between the riots and the separatist sentiment that was then undeniably strong among northern politicians. M.J. Dent, "The Military and Politics: A Study of the Relation between the Army and the Political Process in Nigeria," in Robert Melson and Howard Wolpe, eds., *Nigeria: Modernization and the Politics of Communalism* (East Lansing: Michigan State University Press, 1971), pp. 367–99, at p. 383. But that would not explain why only Ibo and other easterners were targeted.

33. See John Slimming, *Malaysia: The Death of a Democracy* (London: John Murray, 1969), pp. 25–28.

34. Some certainly alleged afterward that the police had orders "from the top" to permit the Malay demonstration that turned violent to proceed, rather than to forbid it. Interview, Kuala Lumpur, August 18, 1975. Some believed that "the top" meant the then-deputy prime minister, Tun Abdul Razak. Interview, George Town, Penang, August 14, 1975. But even if this were true, it would not necessarily prove that Razak's motive was to topple the prime minister.

by the riot, his resignation did not come for many months, and the prospect of an opposite effect, strengthening his position, seems equally reasonable. The creation of disorder is generally cited as a motive in such cases, but rarely is disorder tied to the plausible calculations of those for whom that is said to be the motive.

If the creation of disorder hardly suffices as a motive — and, for explaining riots, is tautological — polarization is very clearly the main objective that can be imputed to factional and individual organizers, whether or not they actually think of the violence in these terms. Polarizing objectives are most obvious when factional competition can be discerned. Take the anti-Jewish riot organized by Hajj Amin al-Husayni, the Grand Mufti of Jerusalem, in 1929. The Mufti was in competition with the Nashishibi family, which was more inclined toward territorial compromise with the Zionists. In the years following his appointment by the British in 1921, the Mufti used conflict over ritual uses of the Temple Mount as a platform to gain support. This campaign culminated in the riot he organized in 1929.[35] As is often the case, intraethnic competition stretches out the spectrum of positions toward the extremes. Violence is an attractive strategy for those seeking to outflank their competitors. Hence the objective of polarization is synonymous with the pursuit of factional advantage.

Nevertheless, organizing a riot remains a more problematic undertaking for those who represent a fraction than it is for those who represent a whole. The casualties in Jerusalem (1929), like those in Kyrghyzstan (1990), northern Nigeria (twice in 1966), and Malaysia (1969), were all substantial, which suggests that factional motives can shape a riot only when people are in any event ready to fight. The party-led riots in Mauritius (1965 and 1968) and Singapore (1964) appear to have been reasonably well bounded and to have produced fewer deaths: in Singapore, about 18 in July and 15 more in a second round in September; in Mauritius, a very small number in 1965 and about 25 in 1968. Yet the image of greater control in party-led riots needs some qualification. The Mauritius killings in 1965 could not be stopped without the intervention of British troops, and in 1968 the killing went on for ten days before a curfew could be imposed. Singapore's second wave of killing, in September, was more spontaneous. Two-wave riots, which are not uncommon,[36] pose problems for explanations of violence that focus

35. Roger Friedland and Richard D. Hecht, "Divisions at the Center: The Organization of Political Violence at Jerusalem's Temple Mount/al-Haram al-Sharif — 1929 and 1990," in Paul R. Brass, ed., Riots and Pogroms (New York: New York University Press, 1996), p. 138.

36. See Chapter 2, above.

singlemindedly on organization, unless organization is present in both rounds. More often than not, the two waves suggest overflowing anger. Similarly, in party-organized violence in Turkey (1978) and in South Africa (1990), the wellsprings of antipathy were tapped in major ways. Party-inspired violence may be more limited by organizational objectives than is violence that is provoked by a faction or a leader, but this is far from an invariable rule. The opposite, in fact, is predicted by research that relates the likely duration of a violent event to the degree of its organization.[37]

The Uzbekistan riot of 1989 perhaps makes the point best. Preceded by considerable organization, since many rioters worked from address lists and used motor vehicles, the violence did not end when the Meskhetian Turks, who were its targets, were evacuated. Large and very angry crowds tried to invade refugee camps in which the Turks were housed.[38] Anger and organization are not mutually exclusive. That party-led and faction-led violence so often proves so difficult to control indicates that it cannot be explained in terms of strategic objectives alone. When parties, factions, or individual leaders incite riots, they are likely to be mobilizing growing hostility awaiting leadership. This would not be the first time leaders took people where they wanted to go anyway.

Certainly, that has been the case in the long series of anti-Tamil riots in Sri Lanka, beginning in 1956 and 1958, and moving on through 1977, 1981, and 1983.[39] Each of these riots had some leadership from Sinhalese politicians, without having the support of any party, but in none could it be said that clear-cut strategic objectives preempted the expression of mass hostility as a motive force.

In 1956, rioting occurred in Colombo and in the Gal Oya colonization area. In the latter, laborers of the Drainage and Irrigation Departments participated. The colonists were mainly loyal to the minister of lands, a man who shared the Salagama caste background of many of them, whereas the irrigation workers were loyal to the minister of agriculture, leader of a party to whose union many of the irrigation workers belonged. From this, it could be inferred that these two politicians played an organizing role, but the riot grew out of contentious language-policy

37. Samuel Vuchinich and Jay Teachman, "Influences on the Duration of Wars, Strikes, Riots, and Family Arguments," *Journal of Conflict Resolution* 37, no. 3 (September 1993): 544–68.

38. *Komsomolskaya Pravda* (Moscow), June 13, 1989, p. 2, in FBIS-SOV-89–112, June 13, 1989, p. 52.

39. In 1968, I conducted extensive interviews with politicians, former police officers, and civil servants in Sri Lanka concerning the 1956 and 1958 riots, and I did the same in 1980 concerning the 1977 riot.

issues,[40] and its organization, if any, in Colombo seems not to have involved other party leaders.

The 1958 riot had more clearly identifiable leadership in some areas. The same minister of lands may have inspired his followers in the Anuradhapura area, for some of the worst incidents of violence took place there, as well as in the Gal Oya area, where irrigation laborers perpetrated attacks.[41] Supporters of the minister of agriculture were also involved,[42] although by 1958 a new extremist organization, the Jathika Vimukthi Peramuna, was operating in one area and had a major part in the riots there.[43] Once again, laborers, perhaps responding to the minister of agriculture or perhaps to the minister of lands (opinions differ[44]), played a part in some locations. Supporters of a leftist party were responsible for killing Tamils in a southern suburb of Colombo, more than 100 miles away.[45] Organization varied from location to location.

The two ministers, C.P. de Silva (lands) and Philip Gunawardena (agriculture), had a keen rivalry,[46] reinforced by the fact that they belonged to different parties in the ruling coalition and different points on the right-left spectrum. Nevertheless, it is difficult to see what each stood to gain from violence against the Tamils.[47] Neither leader was in a position to benefit much from a polarization of party opinion, de Silva because of his minority-caste (Salagama) background, which effectively disqualified him from any higher ambitions, and Gunawardena because of his leadership of a very small Marxist party.[48] Fragmented riot leadership of this kind suggests the existence of anti-Tamil sentiments available

40. Robert N. Kearney, *Communalism and Language in the Politics of Ceylon* (Durham: Duke University Press, 1967), p. 84.

41. B.H. Farmer, *Ceylon: A Divided Nation* (London: Institute of Race Relations, 1963), p. 68.

42. Interview, Colombo, August 16, 1968.

43. Interview, Colombo, September 1–2, 1968.

44. Interviews, Colombo, August 16, 1968; August 19, 1968.

45. Interview, Colombo, August 17, 1968.

46. See Mick Moore, *The State and Peasant Politics in Sri Lanka* (Cambridge: Cambridge University Press, 1985), pp. 60, 115, 199.

47. But one of my interview respondents believed that instigation of the riots was designed to prevent the creation of district councils, which had been demanded by Tamils but which, in Sinhalese areas, might end up dominated by the left. Hence he attributed the riots to the right-wing cabinet faction associated with C.P. de Silva and assumed they were directed against Philip Gunawardena's Marxist faction. Interview, Colombo, August 3, 1968. If so, why did some associated with Gunawardena, including K.M.P. Rajaratne, leader of the JVP, allegedly play a significant role in the violence?

48. A year later, when the prime minister was assassinated, de Silva, a senior leader of the same party, was out of the country for medical treatment, which provided a reason not

for exploitation by an array of forces, more than it does the creation of violence for strategic aims. Perhaps the best explanation is that there was a demand for violence, to which leaders found it dangerous not to respond.

The 1977 anti-Tamil riot had much less conspicuous involvement of politicians. Some Sinhalese party members certainly took part, but they were clearly reacting to inflammatory events rather than participating in an organized effort.[49] A much smaller riot in 1981 involved some members of the ruling party, but the activity was confined to a few localities.[50] On the other hand, the massive anti-Tamil violence of 1983 came during a succession struggle in the ruling party. The minister of industries, Cyril Matthew, who also controlled a growing government-supported union, may have been involved; his ministry apparently provided vehicles for some of the rioters.[51]

In a climate of ethnic polarization, a leader unambiguously associated with the cause of the Sinhalese would have a clear advantage, so much so that it might be reasonable to push the polarization along, even if that meant organizing violence. Matthew was a prominent leader of a large Sinhalese minority caste, the Vahumpura.[52] Fiercely Sinhalese nationalist and devoted to Buddhism, the Vahumpura have had only limited success

---

to test his claim to the prime ministership. According to a conversation with one of my interview respondents, a group of Salagama remarked at the time that they did not see how a Salagama could become prime minister. Interview, Colombo, August 20, 1968. In the March 1960 election, de Silva led his party but then turned the leadership over to Sirimavo Bandaranaike, as it was thought electorally wiser to have a (high-caste) Goyigama leading the party. See Donald L. Horowitz, *Coup Theories and Officers' Motives: Sri Lanka in Comparative Perspective* (Princeton: Princeton University Press, 1980), pp. 34, 132. Gunawardena's party had only five seats, but it is possible that he was aiming to secure a competitive advantage with Sinhalese opinion against the other Marxist parties.

49. Interviews, Colombo, April 7, 1980, and April 8, 1980. See *Report of the Presidential Commission of Inquiry into the Incidents Which Took Place between 13th August and 15th September 1977*, Sessional Paper No. VII — 1980 (Colombo: Government Publications Bureau, 1980).

50. W. Howard Wriggins, "Sri Lanka in 1981: A Year of Austerity, Development Councils, and Communal Disorder," *Asian Survey* 22, no. 2 (February 1982): 173–79, at p. 178. Cf. Leary, *Ethnic Conflict and Violence in Sri Lanka*, pp. 20–25. Ratnapura, an area in which the minister of industries had a strong following, was heavily affected by the violence, and that minister, who had made inflammatory statements, was apparently told by President J.R. Jayewardene "to keep out of the limelight for a while." Eric Meyer, "Seeking the Roots of the Tragedy," in Manor, ed., *Sri Lanka in Change and Crisis*, p. 142.

51. Tambiah, *Buddhism Betrayed?* p. 73. For more on Matthew and the 1983 events, see Obeyesekere, "The Origins and Institutionalisation of Political Violence," pp. 161–66.

52. Janice Jiggins, *Caste and Family in the Politics of the Sinhalese* (Cambridge: Cambridge University Press, 1979), pp. 28–29, 67–68.

in converting their electoral potential into political and economic gains.[53] A significant number of Vahumpura appear to have been participants in an antigovernment insurgency in 1971.[54] Matthew cultivated a reputation as a protector of Buddhism and an antagonist of the Tamils,[55] a position consonant with that of many of his followers, who, like C.P. de Silva's Salagama, often entertained anti-Tamil sentiments. The union of which Matthew was president seems to have been involved in the 1983 violence.[56]

Even in this case, where leadership motives seem clearest, violence took place in what can only be called an explosive environment. Organization was easy because there was so much predisposition to violence. Perhaps 2,000 to 3,000 Tamils were killed in the 1983 riot,[57] a large number made comprehensible by the apprehensions of the time. "By the summer of 1983," remarks Jonathan Spencer, "Sinhalese areas were gripped by a collective panic . . . seeing [Tamil terrorists] everywhere and believing them capable of the most extraordinary feats."[58] Sinhalese villagers were so convinced of the violent proclivities of Tamils that, on hearing of the anti-Tamil violence, they assumed Tamils had perpetrated it, they believed the victims were Sinhalese, and they were even on the alert to defend themselves. The killings partook of "savagery born in terror."[59]

Here it is necessary to put back together some of what I have been assiduously taking apart. It will be recalled from Chapter 3 that riots are often preceded by (generally false) rumors of aggression committed or about to be committed by members of the target group. These rumors justify aggression against the targets as self-defense, and the possibility must be considered that they also *motivate* the violence — that the stories are believed and acted upon, that they have more than a rationalizing function. From what we know about targeting, it is clear that rioters are

53. Ibid., pp. 29, 132.
54. Thus suggesting a certain degree of alienation. Ibid., pp. 127–32.
55. Obeyesekere, "The Origins and Institutionalisation of Political Violence," pp. 161–62; Priya Samarakone (pseud.), "The Conduct of the Referendum," in Manor, ed., *Sri Lanka in Change and Crisis*, p. 115 n. 46.
56. Obeyesekere, "The Origins and Institutionalisation of Political Violence," pp. 160–66; Hoole et al., *The Broken Palmyra*, p. 64.
57. Jonathan Spencer, "Collective Violence and Everyday Practice in Sri Lanka," *Modern Asian Studies* 24, pt. 3 (July 1990): 603–23, at p. 616. More than 100,000 were made homeless.
58. Jonathan Spencer, "Popular Perceptions of the Violence: A Provincial View," in Manor, ed., *Sri Lanka in Change and Crisis*, p. 192.
59. Ibid.

inclined to attack groups they believe to be aggressive, and a long period of violent conflict can bring groups that begin with other imputed characteristics under the rubric of people prone to be cruel and violent, as the Tamils, by 1983, were certainly thought to be.

To imagine, because of the existence of organization, that the violence is wholly the *product* of organization is, then, to miss the crucial point that in these circumstances the benefits of being seen as the champion of the Sinhalese (or the Mbochi or the Assamese) and the costs of being conciliatory both increase as the predisposing mood for violence grows. Hence the most likely factional motive for organizing ethnic riots is the one that depends most heavily on preexisting proviolence affect and so cannot give rise to an inference that the violence consisted of purely instrumental action. The existence of organization is perfectly compatible with passionate violence. Leaders follow at least as often as they lead.

Moreover, the common pattern of organization in some areas and none in others, or of one set of organizers in one place and another set elsewhere, makes the idea of a single, widespread, organized riot improbable. As in Singapore (1950), which we decomposed into its constituent elements in Chapter 2, the heterogeneity of events even in a single city implies that, if overall coordination is attempted in a number of locations far from each other, it may be subject to execution that is dependent on the variable sentiments of participants who are locally oriented.

EXTREMIST ORGANIZATIONS, PARAMILITARIES, AND SECRET SOCIETIES

The more ethnic hostility is endemic and institutionalized and the more it forms part of the fabric of everyday life, the more likely it is to give rise to organizations that take as their mission the militant advancement of group interests. These organizations, often tied to ethnically based political parties, reflect and reinforce interethnic hostility through propaganda, ritual, and force. They run the gamut from civilian to proto-military organizations, operating under varying degrees of secrecy and with varying degrees of coherence and military training. Their raison d'être is the alleged danger from the ethnic enemy. The periodic occurrence of violence provides them a means to evidence their conception of the danger and to demonstrate their usefulness in warding it off by force. Ethnic riots are thus beneficial to these organizations, which participate in them with enthusiasm. Of course, the utility of violence for extremist and paramilitary organizations and the fact that they take advantage of it do not mean that all ethnic riots are coordinated by them; but in countries where violence has been so recurrent as to have become endemic, extremist and paramilitary organizers are increasingly the most likely sponsors.

Secret societies identified with a particular ethnic group also organize ethnic violence, although less frequently. As we shall see, these are not a homogeneous category. There are secret societies that are deeply entwined in the culture of particular groups, and there are societies that arise for particular purposes. The former can be mobilized for violence under appropriate circumstances, although their functions are much broader and more enduring. Most others are ephemeral. Some arise for criminal purposes. Ethnic violence may be a natural concomitant of their extortionate methods, and in situations of rising tension, ethnic violence may come to preempt their original aims.

Extremist and Paramilitary Riots.   India has an array of militant organizations available for violent activity. Most are associated with particular parties. Sometimes they act alone, sometimes in cooperation with other organizations. Perhaps the oldest is the Rashtriya Swayamsevak Sangh (RSS), founded in 1925 on a platform of Hindu nationalism and the subordination of non-Hindus.[60] The RSS has had very close relations with extreme Hindu parties, at first the Jan Sangh from its founding in 1951 and more recently the Bharatiya Janata Party (BJP).

The program of the RSS has been decidedly anti-Muslim, and the RSS has been involved in an enormous range of riots, alone, in combination with Jan Sanghis or BJP members, or in a broad coalition of extremist groups. The Meerut riot of 1968 was inspired by a combination of the Jan Sangh, the RSS, and the Hindu Mahasabha.[61] The Gujarat riots of 1969, in which more than 1,000 people were killed, were preceded by the formation of a "Committee to Defend the Hindu Religion." Organizers were Jan Sanghis and Hindu religious leaders. RSS people distributed inflammatory handbills.[62] A similar common front, the Rashtriya Ustav Mandal (RUM), was founded by the RSS, the Jan Sangh, and the Shiv Sena (a Maharashtrian paramilitary-cum-political party) before the riots in Kausa and Bhiwandi, in Maharashtra (1970). The RUM man-

60. See Geeta Puri, *Bharatiya Jana Sangh: Organization and Ideology* (New Delhi: Sterling, 1980), pp. 12–13.

61. Aswini K. Ray and Subhash Chakravarti, *Meerut Riots: A Case Study* (New Delhi: Sampradayikta Virodhi Committee, n.d. [1968 or 1969]), p. 12.

62. Shah, "Communal Riots in Gujarat," pp. 191, 199.

aged to have a Hindu procession pass in front of a mosque[63] — a time-tested provocative tactic that also produced violence in Jamshedpur (1979).[64]

From its inception, the RSS had a narrowly Brahmin orientation, but it has since widened its reach considerably. Riot coalitions, such as the one with the Shiv Sena, have been a means of broadening support for the RSS and for its affiliated party, currently the BJP. In Meerut (1982), the RSS apparently recruited ex-untouchables (in this case, Bhangis or sweepers) for anti-Muslim violence.[65] Meerut was a politically contested city, in which the BJP was attempting to capture control of the municipal council. The ascendant party, Congress (I), had allocated some tickets to Muslims, and disappointed Hindu politicians made common cause with the RSS and BJP. Bhangis were a swing vote. In addition to polarizing the situation to disadvantage Congress (I) in general, securing the participation of Bhangis in the violence presumably helped detach them from Congress (I).

As this analysis indicates, riots organized by extremist and paramilitary organizations affiliated with political parties have clear purposes. If those parties are ethnically exclusive, as Jan Sangh was and BJP is, the aims of the violence are identical to those of ethnic parties that themselves organize riots: to polarize the electoral environment, to the disadvantage of multiethnic parties, and to detach ethnically differentiated support (of what I referred to earlier as third groups) from the multiethnic party.

The precise ethnic configuration depends entirely on the local context. In Malur, Karnataka (1983), the violence was preceded by the rape of a Harijan (ex-untouchable) woman by three Muslims. Despite its historical upper-caste bias, the RSS held the inflammatory meeting that led to anti-Muslim riots.[66] The organization has also struck alliances with Amra Bengali, an organization in West Bengal — they, together with the Jan Sangh, were implicated in anti-Muslim violence in Nadia and Chapra (1979)[67] — and with various other regional militant organizations, including the All-Assam Students' Union.

63. Ghosh, *Communal Riots in India*, pp. 177–200.

64. Ibid., pp. 133–37.

65. Asgar Ali Engineer, "The Guilty Men of Meerut," *Economic and Political Weekly*, November 6, 1982, pp. 1803–05.

66. Ghosh, *Communal Riots in India*, pp. 175–76.

67. *Far Eastern Economic Review*, July 20, 1979, pp. 32–33; *New Age* (New Delhi), July 1, 1979, p. 1.

In the 1960s, a spate of senas (or armies) grew up in many states of India.[68] Typically, these paramilitaries, often poorly organized and disciplined, were dedicated to regional ethnic causes. The Shiv Sena was at first an organization of indigenes in Maharashtra, and its enemies were the mainly Hindu, south Indian migrants to Bombay.[69] Over time, Shiv Sena turned to the increasingly significant issue of relations with Muslims, questioning their loyalty and their right to live in India.[70] In the Bombay-Bhiwandi riots (1984) and the Bombay riots (1992–93), Shiv Sena took the lead.[71] Its anti-Muslim focus had the advantage of transcending parochial Bombay issues, and in the 1990s Shiv Sena was active in north Indian states far from Bombay. A comparable organization in Assam, the Lachit Sena, was involved in a mild anti-Marwari riot in 1968,[72] but the sena eventually gave way to the far more militant All-Assam Students' Union (AASU), which was involved in the massive anti-Bengali violence of 1983.[73] In the Hindu-Muslim violence following the destruction of the mosque at Ayodhya (1992), a Durga Wahini (Durga's Army) was present in north India.[74] A secessionist Tripura Sena was involved in an attack in 1980 that killed more than 2,000 Bengalis and left more than 50 times that number homeless.[75] These senas, with their varying mixes of gangsterism, violence, and party contacts, entertain political aspirations in their areas. Some have formed state governments, and most are ethnically based proto-parties.

Although the array of paramilitary organizations in India makes their activities particularly visible there, such organizations have been present in many countries: for example, the Sinhala Hamudawa in Sri Lanka and, in the 1980s, the groups associated with a union supported by the

68. For a survey, see Harji Malik, "Private Armies," *Illustrated Weekly of India* (Bombay), March 15, 1970, pp. 6–13.

69. On the formative period of Shiv Sena, see Mary Fainsod Katzenstein, *Ethnicity and Equality: The Shiv Sena Party and Preferential Policies in Bombay* (Ithaca: Cornell University Press, 1979).

70. Engineer, *Bhiwandi-Bombay Riots*, pp. 56, 93.

71. See "The Role of Shiv Sena," *Sunday Observer* (Bombay), June 3, 1984, p. 44; Josson, *Bombay Blood Yatra*; Rajdeep Sardesai, "The Great Betrayal," in Dileep Padgaonkar, ed., *When Bombay Burned* (New Delhi: UBS Publishers' Distributors, 1993), pp. 198–201.

72. Dilip Mukerjee, "Assam Reorganization," *Asian Survey* 9, no. 4 (April 1969): 297–311, at p. 308.

73. Shourie, "Assam Elections."

74. Jeffery and Jeffery, "The Bijnor Riots, October 1990," p. 552.

75. *Far Eastern Economic Review*, June 20, 1980, p. 34; July 4, 1980, pp. 11, 23.

then-ruling party; armed youth groups affiliated with ethnically based political parties in Zanzibar[76] and Lebanon; and the Grey Wolves, associated with the National Action Party in Turkey and involved in the riots of 1978.[77] In the Congo Republic, the massive violence of 1993–94 was preceded by the formation of ethnic paramilitaries.[78] Intensifying ethnic violence in Pakistan during the 1980s and 1990s was increasingly conducted by paramilitaries affiliated with political parties of the respective groups.[79] The more recurrent the violence, the more likely such organizations are to become entrenched, and the more likely there is to be further violence. When extremist and paramilitary organizations exist, riots are easier to organize and therefore more frequent than when participants must be assembled and motivated afresh for each episode. Under such conditions, the significance of the precipitants in evoking violence declines.

Secret Societies and Riots. Secret societies come in highly varied forms. Some are so firmly embedded in the surrounding society, so connected to the regulation of relationships among its members, that they perform what are virtually governmental functions. For these secret organizations, the conduct of ethnic violence constitutes one among many activities. Others are less deeply rooted and engage in a narrower range of activities, often violent, including but by no means limited to ethnic violence. Still other secret societies are essentially criminal syndicates that may from time to time employ violence against members of other groups. What all the secret societies have in common, apart from their secrecy, is the fact that they are not in business principally to conduct ethnic violence. Nevertheless, because of their secrecy, such societies have certain advantages in the conduct of violence, and sometimes they find ethnic riots to be essential to their other functions or irresistibly tempting activities in conjunction with them. Here we shall examine several types of secret societies, beginning with the deeply embedded society.

76. Great Britain, Colonial Office, *Report of a Commission of Inquiry into Disturbances in Zanzibar during June 1961*, Colon. No. 353 (London: H.M.S.O., 1961), p. 11.

77. Zürcher, *Turkey*, p. 277; Ahmad, *The Making of Modern Turkey*, p. 172.

78. Kajsa Ekholm Friedman and Anne Sundberg, "Ethnic War and Ethnic Cleansing in Brazzaville" (unpublished paper, Department of Social Anthropology, University of Lund, 1994), p. 9.

79. See, e.g., Human Rights Commission of Pakistan, *Sindh Inquiry, Summer 1990* (Lahore: Human Rights Commission of Pakistan, 1990), p. 9.

In Sierra Leone (1968), anti-Temne riots carried out by Mende involved the Poro Society.[80] Poro is a society with a secret ritual and a broad array of functions. Sanctioned by its antiquity, Poro in the Mende country historically regulated personal behavior, maintained law and order, provided a sense of the sacred, marked the boundaries of sacrilege, and — in a more mundane way — arranged for the construction of bridges and the cleaning of roads.[81] Poro has been a ubiquitous feature in the life of the Mende and of certain other people of coastal West Africa.

In some areas, the authority of Poro superseded that of chiefs; in others, the chief controlled the Poro. Poro is not necessarily one organization but "a diversity of associations that differentially share some ritual practices."[82] A society so central in the organization of a community, so legitimate in its hold on group members, and so instrumental in fostering solidarity would naturally have a part to play in collective violence. Its power could be exerted to inhibit violence or to mobilize support for it, and its routine of secrecy would be an asset in communication during times of trouble. Among the Mende, Poro played a leading role in the major Hut Tax Revolt of 1898, in the rebellion against chiefs in certain provinces of Sierra Leone in 1955–56, and in other violent episodes.[83] Poro was a natural organizer of the violence of 1968, in collaboration with the Sierra Leone People's Party, a Mende organization.

If Poro anchors the legitimate end of the spectrum of secret societies, embracing societies that exist for purposes unconnected with ethnic con-

---

80. *West Africa*, November 30, 1968, p. 1422. For an account, see Walter L. Barrows, "Local Level Politics in Sierra Leone: Alliances in Kenema District" (Ph.D. diss., Yale University, 1971), pp. 334–51. Sir Milton Margai, the Mende political leader whose party was in conflict with a party representing Temne and other northerners, was said to be an enthusiastic member of Poro. *Africa Confidential*, February 16, 1968, p. 5.

81. See Kenneth Little, *The Mende of Sierra Leone*, rev. ed. (London: Routledge & Kegan Paul, 1967), pp. 29–30, 40, 183–85, 244; W.T. Harris and Harry Sawyer, *The Springs of Mende Belief and Conduct*, rev. ed. (Freetown: Sierra Leone University Press, 1968), pp. 2, 7, 103, 124. See also Beryl L. Bellman, *The Language of Secrecy: Symbols and Metaphors in Poro Ritual* (New Brunswick: Rutgers University Press, 1984); Gilbert Herdt, "Secret Societies and Secret Collectivities," *Oceania* 60, no. 4 (June 1990): 360–81; Christian Kordt Højberg, "Beyond the Sacred and the Profane: The Poro Initiation Ritual," *Folk* 32 (n.m. 1990): 161–76.

82. Bellman, *The Language of Secrecy*, p. 42. See Kenneth Little, "The Political Function of the Poro," pt. II, *Africa* 36, no. 1 (January 1966): 62–71; Richard M. Fulton, "The Political Structures and Functions of Poro in Kpelle Society," *American Anthropologist* 74, no. 5 (October 1972): 1218–33.

83. Little, "The Political Function of the Poro," pt. I, *Africa* 35, no. 4 (October 1965): 349–65. See Martin Kilson, *Political Change in a West African State* (Cambridge: Harvard University Press, 1966), p. 256.

flict but that engage in ethnic violence on appropriate occasions, Mau Mau in Kenya occupies a different position. Less deeply rooted historically and performing a narrower range of functions, Mau Mau nevertheless could call upon evocative cultural symbols for violent ends.

Mau Mau developed in the 1950s as an armed anticolonial rebellion among Kikuyu. Divided by subethnic differences of lineage, region, and cultural practice, the Kikuyu had an incomplete sense of group identity. Mau Mau served to reinforce the emerging Kikuyu identity through, among other things, three oaths.[84] The first, subscribed by a majority of Kikuyu, was an oath of unity; it involved ritual use of a goat's intestines, goat skin, and the thorax of the carcass of a male goat, the consumption of raw goat meat, the exchange of participants' blood, and the pricking of a goat's eye and of sodom apples. The second, a warrior's oath, which committed the initiate to kill for Mau Mau, entailed the insertion of his penis through a hole in the thorax of a skinned goat. Versions of a third, more advanced oath, improvised from locality to locality, contained, variously, anal-sexual and menstrual rituals, as well as rituals of atrocity and consumption performed on the eyes, fingers, and brains of human corpses. These arcane ceremonies were creative reworkings of elements of traditional initiation rituals and of oaths used in dispute resolution by elders. Their goal was to cement the loyalty of Kikuyu to the mythical ancestors Gikuyu and Mumbi in a way that would transcend the pervasive lineage divisions of Kikuyu society and would oblige the initiate to kill for the cause.

Years after Kenyan independence, when conflict between Kikuyu and Luo became intense, Mau Mau practices were revived. The occasion was the assassination of Tom Mboya, a prominent Luo leader, in 1969. The killing both reflected and accelerated Kikuyu-Luo tension. Although significant ethnic violence did not ensue, the inflamed state of Luo opinion was manifested in attacks on police, private cars, and isolated individuals in Nairobi. Tension remained high for months, and it gave rise to a Kikuyu response to the perceived threat from Luo.

The reaction had direct connections to Mau Mau, some of whose forest fighters mobilized again. There was a renewal of oathing among Kikuyu. The oaths affirmed loyalty to the House of Mumbi. Some ver-

84. For the oaths and their functions, see Wunyabari O. Maloba, *Mau Mau and Kenya* (Bloomington: Indiana University Press, 1993), pp. 102–07; Maia Green, "Mau Mau Oathing Rituals and Political Ideology in Kenya: A Re-Analysis," *Africa* 60, no. 1 (n.m. 1990): 69–87; John Lonsdale, "Mau Maus of the Mind: Making Mau Mau and Remaking Kenya," *Journal of African History* 31, no. 3 (n.m. 1990): 393–421.

sions bound the oath taker not to permit the flag of Kenya to leave
Mumbi. The theme was the preservation of Kikuyu political dominance
by force.[85] In the event, the Kikuyu did not need to fight.[86] Yet it seems
abundantly clear that the congeries of organizations that had sprung up,
in a recrudescence of earlier patterns, to administer the oaths as a prelude
to violent activity, would have led the killing if matters had come to that.

At the opposite end of the spectrum from Poro are criminal secret
societies. These organizations, which from time to time employ violence
against members of other groups, run the gamut from tightly structured
syndicates to loosely bonded gangs loyal to charismatic individuals or to
ethnically based political parties. The Mauritian gangs, referred to earlier,
were the instruments of parties. So, too, were the Yam Mahautkata (the
"sons of madmen"), associated with the Northern People's Congress in
Nigeria in the late 1950s. They terrorized followers of competing parties
and in 1958 killed members of the Bornu Youth Movement, a Kanuri
party.[87] One step removed are the Shiv Sena gangs in Bombay, which, in
addition to doing the party's bidding, are reportedly involved in extortion, pilferage on the docks, and other criminal activities.[88] Unlike Poro
and Mau Mau, most secret societies are either criminal adjuncts of political parties or criminal syndicates that have ethnic rivals in other criminal
organizations or that stand to benefit from disorder attendant on ethnic
violence. Obviously, the line between some of these organizations and
paramilitary gangs associated with political parties can be quite unclear.

Criminal gain is sometimes a side-benefit of the political connections
of a gang, as it was in Bombay, but sometimes the criminal activities
come first and evolve into political ties and ethnic violence. In Nadia,
West Bengal (1979), Hindu-Muslim riots grew out of warfare between
gangs of smugglers. The RSS and the Jan Sangh were involved in the
buildup to the riots. So, too, were Amra Bengali (We Bengalis) and
Ananda Marg, a marginal Hindu religious organization accused of ritual
killings. The riots emerged out of this complex organizational setting,

85. For the aftermath of Mboya's assassination, see David Goldsworthy, *Tom Mboya*
(New York: Africana, 1982), pp. 282–86. For the oathing, see Colin Legum and John
Drysdale, eds., *Africa Contemporary Record, 1969–1970*, Vol. 2 (Exeter: Africa Research
Ltd., 1971), p. B123; *Africa Confidential*, November 7, 1969, pp. 1–2. For comparable
oaths among mainland Africans on Zanzibar, see John Okello, *Revolution in Zanzibar*
(Nairobi: East African Publishing House, 1967), p. 134.

86. See Chapter 12, pp. 510–11, below.

87. C.S. Whitaker, Jr., *The Politics of Tradition: Continuity and Change in Northern
Nigeria, 1946–1966* (Princeton: Princeton University Press, 1970), p. 386.

88. Engineer, *Bhiwandi-Bombay Riots*, pp. 62–63, 148.

which combined ethnic issues with smuggling, cattle theft, looting, and robbery.[89] More straightforward and more widespread was the criminal violence that turned into ethnic riots and ultimately evolved into civil war in the southern Philippines (1970).[90] Christian migrants to the south were confronted by Muslim "owners" of the land that the Christians had settled. The Muslims demanded rent or a purchase price from the settlers and sought to enforce the fraudulent demands by violence. Political organizations eventually took over where extortion gangs left off.

By now it might seem that we are so far from legitimate secret societies, such as Poro, that the term *secret society* brackets everything from quasi-governmental organizations to extortion rackets. Yet two features bind them together and are the core of what makes secret societies secret: magic and violence. Secret societies provide protective medicines, including those which promise invulnerability to certain weapons, and they deal in terror and violence. This is true of Poro,[91] and it is equally true of criminal gangs that become involved in ethnic violence. The need to protect magical formulas and the identity of participants in illegal activities forms the common underpinning for secrecy.

In Chapter 3, I described the commingling of invulnerability practices with martial arts, religion, and illegal activity in the person of Kiyai Salleh, who led Malay gangs engaged in killing Chinese at the end of World War II. A martial arts master who headed a Sufi tarekat, Salleh was said to have supernatural powers and fighting prowess which he had earlier used in straightforward criminal activity and later turned to the advantage of state political leaders.[92] As I explained, invulnerability was an integral part of the criminal scheme, for charms were sold at exorbitant prices to village people.

Invulnerability and oaths provide clues to the connection of secret societies to ethnic violence. When the targets of ethnic violence are

89. *Far Eastern Economic Review*, July 20, 1979, pp. 32–33.

90. Peter G. Gowing, "Muslim Filipinos between Integration and Secession" (paper presented at the annual meeting of the Association of Asian Studies, Chicago, March 30–April 1, 1973), pp. 5–6.

91. Beryl Larry Bellman, *Village of Curers and Assassins: On the Production of Fala Kpelle Cosmological Categories* (The Hague: Mouton, 1975), pp. 115–27; Bellman, *The Language of Secrecy*, pp. 28, 39; Eugene Victor Walter, *Terror and Resistance: A Study of Political Violence* (New York: Oxford University Press, 1969), pp. 88, 91, 95.

92. Cheah Boon Kheng, *Red Star over Malaya* (Singapore: Singapore University Press, 1983), pp. 202–30. For more detail on Salleh, see Syed Naguib al-Attas, *Some Aspects of Sufism as Understood and Practised among the Malays* (Singapore: Malaysian Sociological Research Institute, 1963), pp. 47–48.

strong, the magic and the organizational capacities that are associated with secret societies seem to be significant assets to those who would like to attack powerful enemies, whether they are Temne, Luo, or Chinese. Similarly, oaths provide solemn assurance that others will also take risks in violence, thus strengthening norms of conformity and reducing the risk borne by any one group member. (Not that secret societies necessarily succeed in their violent plans: as I shall suggest soon, they often do not.) Criminal gangs also become involved, not only because there are more illicit opportunities and less effective law enforcement in the midst of widespread disorder, but also because what they have to sell is attractive to those who contemplate participation in disorder.

Consider the Tentera Sabilullah (Holy War Army), which grew up in the northern Malaysian state of Kedah in 1967.[93] Uncovered before it engaged in ethnic violence, the Tentera was clearly a throwback to the Tentera Sabil Selendang Merah (Holy War Army of the Red Scarves), which killed Chinese at the end of World War II. The 1960s version was led by a middle-aged man of Javanese extraction, a *pawang* (magician), who sold charms to guarantee virility and held large meetings, during which he was able to induce trances among participants. Having demonstrated his powers, he persuaded or bullied villagers in a wide rural area east of the state capital to pay M$12 (US$4) in dues to join his organization, which was called the Gang Duabelas Ringgit (Twelve Dollar Gang). Operating a protection racket among *padi* farmers, the gang insured their buffalo against theft, and of course it was therefore involved in stealing the buffalo of the uninsured. For some participants, the appeal was protection; for others, the opportunity for theft. The leader was a rural character with a certain charisma and a reputation for rough tactics.

While the organization began as a straightforward extortion racket, it developed a violent political program, in the course of which it became, at least nominally, an "army" rather than a "gang" and focused on "holy war" as well as on $12. The emphasis on secrecy was accentuated. Rituals of identification were developed; these involved small details of

93. In the paragraphs that follow, I am drawing on interviews I did in Alor Setar and in villages in Kedah in January 1968, shortly after Tentera Sabilullah had been exposed, and also on a memorandum done for me by Encik Abdul Aziz Ali, "Apa Dia Tentera Sabilullah?" ["What is the Tentera Sabilullah?"] (unpublished paper, January 1968). For an early analogue to this organization — "a mixture of protection racket, gangsterism, and political intrigue" — see William R. Roff, *The Origins of Malay Nationalism* (New Haven: Yale University Press, 1967), pp. 216 n. 11, 230 n. 51.

dress, cigarette etiquette, and handshakes — practices typical of amateur-
ish conspiracies. The victims were to be Chinese — the plan was to burn
them out — and the Tentera attracted some members with histories of
anti-Chinese activity or inclinations, as well as those who relished a bit of
illegal gain. Even so, the plan was not uniform: in some areas, the gang
did not progress from the extortionate to the political. In any case, it was
exposed before it could act, and its leaders were arrested. Most members
soon received pardons from the state sultan, and the organization was
not heard from again.

THE DUBIOUS ADVANTAGE
OF STRONG ORGANIZATION

Like Mau Mau after the Mboya assassination, Tentera Sabilullah
aroused a good deal of loyalty from its members, but its plan to organize
violence did not reach fruition. Secret societies that are disconnected
from ruling authority have difficulty initiating the violence for which
they prepare. Because they are very well organized, if authority does not
support their violent ventures, their elaborate preparations may ultimately come to the notice of people with the ability to thwart them.

More generally, organization without political support rarely produces deadly ethnic riots. Of those riots having a serious organizational
element, the vast majority are organized either by political parties or by
those who have some connection to parties. Those directly organized by
parties obviously respond to party interests, as manifested by occasions
that seem to demand a violent response. The remainder, many of which
are collaboratively organized by parties and those tied to them, respond
to occasions that have raised the pitch of ethnic conflict in general and
that might have produced violence without organization. As I have suggested, even riots organized to polarize presuppose a high level of preexisting polarization. Extremist and paramilitary organizations will continue to fan the flames, but their membership will fall away if ethnic
conflict and the sentiments that accompany it begin to ebb. As the
paucity of serious riots organized by ethnically differentiated business
rivals shows with special clarity, organization, even by those with strong
motives, cannot produce significant violence when masses of people do
not share the intense preferences of the organizers.

Where, on the other hand, passion is present, it can turn what begins
as an organized riot, with limited objectives, into something quite different. In Guinea (1956), the party about to take power from the French

was controlled by Malinké; the main opposition was supported by Fulani. The Malinké-led party organized violence against its Fulani opponents, who were singled out at their homes because of party affiliation. But anti-Fulani sentiment was strong, and the violence broadened into indiscriminate lethal attacks on Fulani in general.[94] Passion can easily supply what is lacking in organization — far more easily than organization can substitute for passion. That is why so many riots are close to the spontaneous end of the continuum. Passion in response to an appropriate precipitating event can be mobilized so quickly that only the most alert authorities are able to thwart the ensuing violence. In all fighting, speed provides an important tactical advantage. Secret societies do better when, like Poro, they are entrenched in an authority structure or when they are operating in an interregnum, as Tentera Sabil Selendang Merah was before the British could reestablish control over colonial Malaya after World War II. Otherwise, their cumbersome ritual is not necessarily an asset. Sooner or later, ceremonies designed to enhance secrecy have the opposite effect: their very arcaneness attracts attention, as Mau Mau's and Tentera Sabilullah's both did.

To put the point more sharply, strong organization is an easily overrated resource in riots when other conditions conducive to violence are present — and even more when they are not. When authorities are inclined to thwart violence, organization provides a focal point for their suppression.

THE POWER OF LOOSE ORGANIZATION

Paradoxically, it is harder to thwart unorganized or loosely organized riots. Whereas Tentera Sabilullah could not produce the violence it had contemplated in Kedah for months in 1967, Malays in nearby Penang produced deadly violence without any serious organization in a matter of hours.[95] The Penang riot emerged from a protest strike by the left-wing,

94. For helpful conversations, I am indebted to certain Guinean exiles and to Donald Herdeck. For an account of the background, see Ruth Schachter Morgenthau, *Political Parties in French-Speaking West Africa* (Oxford: Clarendon Press, 1964), pp. 220–49.

95. For accounts, see Milton J. Esman, *Administration and Development in Malaysia* (Ithaca: Cornell University Press, 1972), pp. 34–36; Nancy L. Snider, "What Happened in Penang?" *Asian Survey* 8, no. 12 (December 1968): 960–75. My data on the Penang riots are drawn from interviews I conducted with participants, officials, and observers in Penang in January 1968 and from a series of contemporaneous, handwritten reports submitted to the Malaysian Chinese Association by its field liaison officers and made available to me at the time by the MCA.

largely Chinese, Labor Party against a currency devaluation in November 1967. Many shops closed in support of the protest. Small groups of party activists on motorbikes traveled from place to place to enforce shop closings on those who were reluctant. When they came to a Malay residential area in the city, a *pisang goreng* (fried banana) seller was disinclined to close. A fight developed, and the Chinese were driven off by a group of the hawker's Malay friends. Revenge was taken on two Malays, who were killed in another part of town, and Malays then mobilized for violence that took several days to put down.

The violence was concentrated along main roads leading from the city to the suburbs. There, residents of adjacent Malay and Chinese areas had previously been in conflict with each other; fights were not uncommon. (A similar point about earlier fights between Hindus and the Sikhs they later killed in the Delhi riot of 1984 is made by Veena Das.[96]) The Malay areas were politically active and had also been the scene of competition between the two major Malay political parties. The majority of riot casualties consisted of Chinese traveling roads abutted by Malay neighborhoods. Typically unaware of the untoward events, the victims were attacked by crowds drawn from these neighborhoods.

There is no evidence that either of the main Malay parties or any party leader wanted the riot to happen. In fact, there is nothing to suggest that these brutal killings were planned by anyone. On the contrary, just as a high level of organization is indicated by the presence of rioters who have traveled long distances to engage in violence, so attacks that occur this close to home signify spontaneity. There is not much room for doubt that the riot was a response to unfolding events — to the coerced shop closings and the killing of the two Malays — a response that seemed all the more natural, given the background of ethnic fights in the area. Moreover, leadership did not have to be created for this response to occur. Since the action took place neighborhood by neighborhood, preexisting local leadership was more than sufficient. Previous episodes of violence had thrown up leaders skilled in fighting, who gathered supporters quickly in the neighborhood mosque.[97]

The Penang riot is significant because the evidence is so clear. Events transpired that were violent and felt to require an even more violent response. The meaning of the events was so transparent and the feelings

96. Veena Das, "Our Work to Cry, Your Work to Listen (The Survivor of Collective Violence)" (unpublished paper, Delhi, n.d.), p. 36.
97. Interviews with two participants, George Town, January 24 and January 30, 1968.

were so widely shared that it took very little time and effort to arrange the response. This was a riot very close to the spontaneous end of the spectrum. Leadership was ephemeral, in the sense that it took charge effortlessly. The riot and its leadership were embedded in local experience and social structure. The events that brought these serious killings on were decidedly abnormal, but they occurred so close to home (literally and figuratively) that no special organization was required.

To be sure, the Penang riot of 1967 was neither as long-lived nor as destructive as the Kuala Lumpur riot of a year and a half later, and the 1969 events probably had, as we have seen, some factional leadership. But this is not evidence that more organization produces a bigger riot, for the Kuala Lumpur riot, though larger, was brought on by a much more powerful precipitant — the impending loss of political control of a very important state, coupled with publicly insulting behavior by non-Malays. A great many precipitating events, as we shall see, are of precisely the evocative sort that call forth hostile reactions requiring little or no organization to produce violence. Such obviously evocative precipitants often produce violence with minimal organization in the first of a series of riots, the ultimate effect of which is to entrench organization that then instigates recurrent riots in the same location.[98] On balance, organizations that direct violence may be more an effect than a cause of riot episodes.

A good many riots thus approximate what were called "hostile outbursts" in what is now the very unfashionable literature on collective behavior.[99] Like the Penang riot, the well-documented riot in Kyrghyzstan (1990) is one such outburst. Unlike many others, Kyrghyzstan resulted in arrests, which revealed no strong pattern of organization. The leadership, concludes Valery Tishkov, arose spontaneously.[100] The list of similar riots is long. Most of those that, like Penang, grow out of strikes, have a strong spontaneous element. Among them are Burma (1930) and Jos, Nigeria (1945).[101] Those that grow out of processions usually flow naturally from events that occur during the processions, without any

98. See Chapter 10, below.

99. See Chapter 1, pp. 35–36, above.

100. Valery Tishkov, "Don't Kill Me, I Am Kyrghyz" (paper delivered at XIII International Congress of Anthropological and Ethnological Sciences, Mexico, July 28–August 5, 1993), p. 16.

101. E.L.F. Andrews, *Indian Labour in Rangoon* (Calcutta: Oxford University Press, 1933), pp. 282–84; Leonard Plotnicov, "An Early Nigerian Civil Disturbance: The 1945 Hausa-Ibo Riot in Jos," *Journal of Modern African Studies* 9, no. 2 (August 1971): 297–305.

intervening organization, as in Sukabumi, Indonesia (1963), Ranchi, Bihar (1967), and Hyderabad, Andhra Pradesh (1981).[102] Stylized disputes that signify impending danger or evoke interethnic comparisons likewise produce violence with minimal leadership, as they did in Pangkor, Malaysia (1959), and Abidjan, Ivory Coast (1969).[103] And those riots that can be viewed as an extension of a period of unrelieved, mounting tension that increases the level of apprehensiveness also require little or no real organization. This was the case in Luluabourg, Zaire (1959), when Lulua, thoroughly intimidated by Luba in their midst, proceeded to attack them,[104] and it also describes the conditions depicted earlier for Sri Lanka (1983), which gave rise to anti-Tamil violence in which organization was in evidence in some areas but was superfluous in others and which began altogether spontaneously.[105]

It is easy to identify a significant number of lightly organized, close-to-spontaneous riots,[106] and it is easy to identify the same sort of networks of leaders and followers that could be found in Penang, sometimes inclined to political consciousness, sometimes, as in Penang, given to habitual fighting — people who may have encountered the victims on the streets previously.[107] Widespread perception of injury or threat can produce a violent reaction without the need for much organization.

102. The Siauw Giap, "Group Conflict in a Plural Society," *Revue du Sud-Est Asiatique*, no. 1 (1966): 1–31, at pp. 11–12; Government of India, *Report of the Commission of Inquiry on Communal Disturbances in Ranchi-Hatia*, pp. 10–14; "Riots in Hyderabad," *Economic and Political Weekly*, August 29, 1981, pp. 1416–17.

103. Willard A. Hanna, "Pangkor Island: A Footnote to Malayan Prospects and Problems," *American Universities Field Staff Reports*, Southeast Asia Series 8, no. 14 (June 15, 1960): 2–3; Michael Cohen, *Urban Policy and Political Conflict in Africa: A Study of the Ivory Coast* (Chicago: University of Chicago Press, 1974). A "stylized dispute" is one that evokes stereotypes relating to threatening behavior or attitudes on the part of the target group — for example, that the Chinese on Pangkor were about to take over by force or that the Mossi in Abidjan were more reliable workers.

104. Jules Chomé, *Le Drame de Luluabourg*, 3d rev. ed. (Brussels: Editions de Remarques Congolaises, 1960), pp. 5–6, 16–31.

105. See Spencer, "Popular Perceptions of the Violence."

106. See *West Africa*, July 20, 1981, p. 1630; *Agence France Presse*, November 6, 1991; *Far Eastern Economic Review*, March 11, 1993, p. 9; Government of Uganda, *Report of the Commission of Inquiry into the Recent Disturbances among the Baamba and Bakonjo People of Toro* (Entebbe: Government Printer, 1962), pp. 3–4, 6–11; *Washington Post*, December 26, 1979, p. A25; Virginia Thompson and Richard Adloff, *Conflict in Chad* (Berkeley: University of California Institute of International Studies, 1981), pp. 86–88.

107. See, e.g., Sudhir Kakar, *The Colors of Violence: Cultural Identities, Religion, and Conflict* (Chicago: University of Chicago Press, 1996), pp. 56, 59, 60, 80–86; Asghar Ali Engineer, "Gujarat Burns Again," *Economic and Political Weekly*, August 2, 1986,

The deadly ethnic riot ranges, as I said at the outset of the chapter, from relatively organized to relatively spontaneous. Strong organization is by no means a necessary feature. In a subset of relatively organized riots, organization responds to, or proceeds simultaneously with, rising levels of general antipathy that might be sufficient to carry the violence along without much leadership. In another subset, relatively strong organization confines the violence to the achievement of organizational goals and limits the casualties. A disproportionate number of high-casualty riots involve leadership that rises to the occasion, rather than leadership that creates the occasion. The paradox of organization is that, because ethnic violence is propelled by affronts, threats, and evocations of target characteristics that are all intelligible to many group members, the less organized riot may well be the more deadly. If group members need to be instigated to riot, the requisite sentiment for the worst atrocities may be lacking.

THE LEGIONS OF VIOLENCE

Hard data on the composition of the killing crowd are difficult to obtain, partly because, as noted earlier, arrests of participants in ethnic riots are rare. Nevertheless, those data that are available paint a remarkably consistent picture. Rioters are strongly skewed in terms of sex, age, and social class distribution, but otherwise quite representative of the group from which they emanate. Rioters are not generally criminals (although criminal gangs certainly join in riots), and they are not deviant in other significant ways. As the riot emerges from group sentiment, so the rioters are embedded in the group, and they return easily to the group, generally without stigma, when the violence is over. This can only be because their behavior is, in some important ways, socially approved.

Participants in deadly riots, as in violence in general, are overwhelmingly male. Forty-seven of the 48 defendants charged in Kyrghyzstan (1990) were male.[108] This is the universal pattern — in Sri Lanka (1983),[109] among Tentera Sabilullah members, all of whom were male,

---

pp. 1343–46, at p. 1345. See also John Bohstedt, *Riots and Community Politics in England and Wales, 1790–1810* (Cambridge: Harvard University Press, 1983), p. 23; S.D. Reicher, "The St. Paul's Riot: An Explanation of the Limits of Crowd Action in Terms of a Social Identity Model," *European Journal of Social Psychology* 14; no. 1 (January–March 1984): 1–21, at p. 13.

108. Tishkov, "Don't Kill Me, I Am Kyrghyz," p. 12.

109. Spencer, "Collective Violence and Everyday Practice in Sri Lanka," p. 605.

and among those arrested after the American violent protests of the 1960s and of 1992 in Los Angeles (in which only looting attracted a significant number of female participants).[110] In laboratories, male experimental subjects are far more willing to administer shocks than females are, just as they are more likely to be the targets of shocks (as they are to be the targets of deadly riots).[111] It may or may not be true that men are simply more aggressive than women;[112] but it is certainly true that they are virtually alone in committing ethnic violence, just as they are in engaging in soccer brawls and fights at work camps, both events characterized by aggressive masculinity.[113] To the extent that they participate, women are confined to an inciting role.[114]

Youth is the other overwhelmingly prevalent characteristic of the ethnic rioter. Virtually every riot report notes the youthful composition of violent crowds. Participants range from the teens to the thirties, with the median usually toward the low end of the range. In Uzbekistan (1989), the range in some locations was 16 to 30, in others 15 to 20; many participants were in their late teens.[115] In the Ivory Coast (1969), most rioters were between 16 and 30, with a few older.[116] For the 45 defendants

110. *Report of the National Advisory Commission on Civil Disorders* (New York: Bantam Books, 1968), pp. 127–35; Robert M. Fogelson, *Violence as Protest: A Study of Riots and Ghettos* (Garden City, N.Y.: Anchor Books, 1971), pp. 41–42, 81; Peter A. Morrison and Ira S. Lowry, "A Riot of Color: The Demographic Setting of Civil Disturbances in Los Angeles" (unpublished paper, RAND Corporation, Santa Monica, Calif., no. P-7819, 1993), p. 17.

111. Michael T. Hynan and Judith A. Esselman, "Victims and Aggression," *Bulletin of the Psychonomic Society* 18, no. 4 (October 1981): 169–72.

112. See R.N. Johnson, *Aggression in Men and Animals* (Philadelphia: Saunders, 1972).

113. Eric Dunning, Patrick Murphy, and John Williams, "'Casuals,' 'Terrace Crews' and 'Fighting Firms': Towards a Sociological Explanation of Football Hooliganism," in David Riches, ed., *The Anthropology of Violence* (Oxford: Basil Blackwell, 1986), pp. 164–83, at p. 173; David McKnight, "Fighting in an Australian Aboriginal Super Camp," in ibid., pp. 136–63, at p. 161. Cf. David T. Courtright, *Violent Land: Single Men and Social Disorder from the Frontier to the Inner City* (Cambridge.: Harvard University Press, 1996).

114. A point also noted by Tishkov, "Don't Kill Me, I Am Kyrghyz," p. 13; and by Ruby Ofori, "Rawlings' Biggest Challenge," *Africa Report* 39, no. 3 (May–June 1994): 53–55, at p. 54. See Hans Toch, *Violent Men: An Inquiry into the Psychology of Violence* (Chicago: Aldine, 1969), p. 209. Compare the debate over the role of women in eighteenth- and nineteenth-century food riots. E.P. Thompson, "The Moral Economy of the English Crowd in the Eighteenth Century," *Past and Present*, no. 50 (February 1971): 76–131, at pp. 115–16; Manfred Gailus, "Food Riots in Germany in the Late 1840s," *Past and Present*, no. 145 (November 1994): 157–93, at pp. 174–75.

115. Moscow Television, June 7, 1989, in FBIS-SOV-89–109, June 8, 1989, p. 24.

116. I owe these data to Michael Cohen.

arrested in the Kyrghyz (1990) riot for whom data were available, two-thirds were between 25 and 30, with half of the remainder younger and half older.[117] Sri Lankan rioters in 1977 were mainly in the 20–30 bracket.[118] In Penang (1967), the vast majority of rioters were between 18 and 25, according to a well-placed police official; another close observer put the median age at 20.[119] Of the participants in the Bombay (1969) riots who were subsequently arrested (n = 1,785), nearly three-quarters were concentrated in the 18–30 age bracket.[120] The most active participants in the Sukabumi (1963) riot were all young people, including many high school students.[121] In deadly riots, the vast majority of participants are under 30, usually well under 30, generally closer to 20 than to 30, often in their teens, sometimes as young as 12.[122]

Of course, youth is generally disproportionately represented in violent activities, including ethnic violence. The modal age of participants in the Sri Lankan insurgency of 1971 was 20, and more than three-quarters of suspected insurgents were between 17 and 26.[123] The typical participant in the United States' violent protest disturbances of the 1960s was an unmarried male between the ages of 15 and 24; very few were older than 35.[124] The same pattern holds for the lynch mobs of decades earlier. Their members were mainly in their teens, with almost none over 25; all were males, although sometimes urged on by women.[125]

If young men are the culprits, one reason may be that young people are generally unmarried. In Penang, it was remarked that the age of mar-

117. Tishkov, "Don't Kill Me, I Am Kyrghyz," p. 13.

118. Tamil Refugees Rehabilitation Organization, *Communal Disturbances in Sri Lanka: Sansoni Commission: Written Submissions* (mimeo., March 28, 1980), p. 170.

119. Interviews, George Town, January 25, 1968, and January 31, 1968.

120. *Times of India* (New Delhi), April 16, 1969.

121. Stephen A. Douglas, *Political Socialization and Student Activism in Indonesia* (Urbana: University of Illinois Press, 1970), pp. 167–68.

122. Wagret, *Histoire et Sociologie Politiques de la République du Congo (Brazzaville)*, p. 65. Many sources remark in general terms on the youth of the participants. E.g., Ter-Rumun Avav and Mson Myegba, *The Dream to Conquer: Story of Jukun-Tiv Conflict* (Makurdi, Nigeria: Onaivi, 1992), pp. 20–21; Charu Chandra Bhandari, *Thoughts on Assam Disturbances* (Rajghat, India: A.B. Sarva Seva Sangh Prakashan, 1961), p. 27. Compare Edward H. Judge, *Easter in Kishinev* (New York: New York University Press, 1992), p. 70, computing the median age of those arrested and tried as 31.

123. Gananath Obeyesekere, "Some Comments on the Social Backgrounds of the April 1971 Insurgency in Sri Lanka (Ceylon)" (paper presented at the annual meeting of the Association of Asian Studies, March 30–April 1, 1973), p. 7.

124. *Report of the National Advisory Commission on Civil Disorders*, pp. 127–35. Cf. Fogelson, *Violence as Protest*, pp. 38–39.

125. Arthur F. Raper, *The Tragedy of Lynching* (Chapel Hill: University of North Carolina Press, 1933), pp. 362, 388–89.

riage had moved up to the mid-twenties,[126] as it had in urban areas of many developing countries. Consequently, participants between 18 and 25 would rarely have the particular family entanglements that follow upon marriage and might deter engagement in violence. But the reasons, some of which may be physiological, surely go much deeper. Erik H. Erikson remarks that young people "can also be remarkably clannish, and cruel in their exclusion of all those who are 'different,' in skin color or cultural background, in tastes and gifts, and often in such petty aspects of dress and gesture as have been temporarily selected as *the* signs of an in-grouper or out-grouper."[127] They "stereotype themselves . . . and their enemies; they perversely test each other's capacity to pledge fidelity."[128] Presumably, the narrow conception of what constitutes acceptable behavior to young people would make them more ready to act on the basis of a provocative precipitating event, and the testing of each other to which Erikson refers surely includes the challenge accompanying violence. In these respects, participation of young men in ethnic violence may not require an explanation very different from the one applicable to their participation in violence in general.

There is another form of skewing that is much harder to systematize, because it so often derives from peculiar local conditions.[129] In many riots, some subethnic groups are disproportionately represented among the attackers, while others are absent. In Singapore (1950), certain Malay subgroups were arrested in disproportionate numbers; other Malays were less well represented among the rioters.[130] In Mauritania (1966 and 1989), Hartani (black Moors) attacked black Africans; so-called white Moors were much less involved in the killing.[131] Members of the Salagama and Vahumpura castes seem, at various times, to have been overrepresented among Sinhalese killing Tamils, as pointed out previously. Differential caste participation is common in Indian riots as well. In Bombay (1984), it was Hindu Marathas, not Hindus of other identi-

126. Interview, George Town, January 25, 1968.

127. Erik H. Erikson, *Childhood and Society,* 2d ed. (New York: W. W. Norton, 1963), p. 262 (emphasis in the original).

128. Ibid.

129. Here I omit the frequent participation of police or military units in the violence, since I deal with it in Chapter 9.

130. Tom Eames Hughes, *Tangled Worlds: The Story of Maria Hertogh* (Singapore: Institute of Southeast Asian Studies, 1980), pp. 54–55; Colony of Singapore, *Report of the Riots Inquiry Commission, 1951* (Singapore: Government Printer, 1951), pp. 19–20.

131. For 1966, my sources are conversations with several Mauritanians. For 1989, see Human Rights Watch/Africa, *Mauritania's Campaign of Terror*, pp. 13–14.

ties, who participated, presumably because Shiv Sena, an organization with a Maratha background, was the sponsor.[132] In Meerut (1987), Bhangis (sweepers) and Chamars (leather workers) were heavily involved in the killing of Muslims.[133] In Delhi (1984), Bhangis were also involved in killing Sikhs, as were Jats and Gujjars.[134] Dalits (scheduled castes) were the main attackers of Muslims around Ahmedabad, in Gujarat (1986),[135] but Agri, members of a middle caste, were involved around Bhiwandi (1984), whereas Dalits were not involved and sometimes aided the Muslim victims there.[136] There are no strict rules dictating subethnic participation.

Nevertheless, there are explanations. First and foremost, there is proximity. Those who kill usually are located nearby, as Bhangis were when anger against Sikhs rose in Delhi (1984).[137] Most of the time, people kill close to home, especially in riots with a large element of spontaneity, as I have pointed out in connection with Penang (1967). If, in addition, there is a background of local disputes, as there was between Dalits and Muslims in Gujarat[138] and between Gujjars and Sikhs in adjacent villages,[139] then location is an even stronger predictor of subethnic participation.

As we have seen in the Sri Lankan riots, leadership may also play a role in subethnic skewing of participants. It certainly did so in Singapore (1950), for the main leaders were Indonesian and Indian Muslim,[140] and it also did with respect to Vahumpura in 1981 and 1983. But sometimes leadership is responding to aggressive mass attitudes toward outgroups, a response also present with respect to Vahumpura and Salagama, both of them often known for anti-Tamil sentiment. (The Salagama are further divisible into subgroups, one of which has a martial tradition, which is probably pertinent to participation in all fighting, including riots.[141]) It is a much trickier matter to track the source of the differential subgroup distribution of hostile sentiments. Sometimes subgroups with a long his-

132. Engineer, *Bhiwandi-Bombay Riots*, p. 10.

133. Asghar Ali Engineer, "Meerut: The Nation's Shame," *Economic and Political Weekly*, June 20, 1987, p. 970.

134. People's Union for Democratic Rights and People's Union for Civil Liberties, *Who Are the Guilty?* pp. 3, 17, 19, 21.

135. Engineer, "Gujarat Burns Again," p. 1345.

136. Engineer, *Bhiwandi-Bombay Riots*, pp. 15, 50, 54, 56, 58.

137. Uma Chakravarti and Nandita Haksar, *The Delhi Riots: Three Days in the Life of a Nation* (New Delhi: Lancer International, 1987), p. 43.

138. Engineer, "Gujarat Burns Again," p. 1345.

139. Chakravarti and Haksar, *The Delhi Riots*, pp. 419–47.

140. See Hughes, *Tangled Worlds*, pp. 49–51.

141. On Salagama aggressiveness, see Bryce Ryan, *Caste in Modern Ceylon* (New Brunswick: Rutgers University Press, 1953), pp. 262–65.

tory of contact with the outgroup develop such sentiments, and sometimes the sentiments develop despite the absence of contact.[142] (Many
Salagama live in the far south of Sri Lanka, whereas most Tamils are concentrated in the far north.) But given differential subethnic antipathy, it is
not surprising that it is acted upon in times of violence.

Finally, one kind of subethnic skewing is interchangeable with (or a
proxy for) another. Low-status subethnic groups such as Hartani or
Dalits may be disproportionately involved in ethnic violence because
low-status people in general are disproportionately involved in this form
of violence.

This brings me to the class skewing of ethnic riot participation. In
deadly riots, by and large, elites propose, and masses dispose. Rarely
does the middle class engage in killing.[143] There are examples of middle-
class interethnic precautions against violence, even in highly polarized
atmospheres. In the Kuala Lumpur suburb of Petaling Jaya in 1969,
Malay and Chinese residents, many of them university affiliated, organized their neighborhoods to ward off violence by outsiders. Among the
Petaling Jaya residents, ethnic feelings ran high at the time, but they
agreed on their distaste for riots.[144] To note that the middle class does not
generally participate[145] is not to say that it does not play an important
legitimating role in violence by action and inaction prior to an outbreak.
When northern students demonstrated the day before anti-Ibo attacks in
Nigeria (1966), they made a major contribution to the violence carried
out by others. This is a theme to which we shall return.

There are references in the literature on deadly riots to the participation of "footloose" transients[146] and other marginal types. Despite the
well-known clichés about urban "marginals,"[147] these descriptions are
not always mere stereotypes: sometimes migrant workers or new settlers,

142. See Horowitz, *Ethnic Groups in Conflict*, p. 227.

143. For the view that middle classes also participate in crowds, but without a distinction between violent and nonviolent actions, see Carl J. Couch, "Collective Behavior: An
Examination of Some Stereotypes," *Social Problems* 15, no. 3 (Winter 1968): 310–21. See
also E.L. Quarantelli and Russell R. Dynes, "Property Norms and Looting: Their Patterns
in Community Crises," *Phylon* 31, no. 2 (Summer 1970): 168–82.

144. I am drawing here on a conversation with a participant in these efforts.

145. With the occasional exception, such as Assamese students or the private secretary
to a Sri Lankan member of parliament who participated in the 1977 riots. *Report of the
Presidential Commission of Inquiry into the Incidents Which Took Place between 13th
August and 15th September 1977*, p. 161.

146. Tambiah, *Buddhism Betrayed*, p. 52.

147. For the best demolition of the clichés, see Joan M. Nelson, *Migrants, Urban
Poverty, and Instability in Developing Nations* (Cambridge: Harvard University Center for
International Affairs, Occasional Paper no. 22, 1969).

or others who are imperfectly integrated into a community, do participate in killing.[148] And, without a doubt, conditions of disorder can attract the participation of criminals, bandits, smugglers, and gangsters, and have done so, most prominently in Karachi throughout the 1980s, Delhi (1984), and the southern Philippines in the 1970s.[149] But if occupational status is indicative, what stands out much more is the ordinariness of most participants: textile workers and manual laborers in Gujarat (1969),[150] Sinhalese subordinates attacking their Tamil supervisors and hospital staff attacking patients in Sri Lanka (1977),[151] employed high school or technical school graduates in Kyrghyzstan (1990),[152] mill hands, service workers, hawkers, artisans, odd job workers, and the unemployed in Bombay (1969)[153]—in short, something like a random sample of mainly employed young, working-class men,[154] in most cases with a bias toward unskilled rather than skilled laborers.[155] Sometimes skilled workers are more prominently represented, and sometimes unemployed workers are. But, once skewing attributable to sex, age, subethnic affiliation, and class is accounted for, there is generally nothing unusual about the composition of the crowd in the deadly ethnic riot, certainly nothing specially marginal. This conclusion parallels a similar finding for the violent protest demonstrations of the 1960s in the United States.[156]

148. See, e.g., Shah, "Communal Riots in Gujarat," p. 200 n. 13; Tamil Refugees Rehabilitation Organization, *Communal Disturbances in Sri Lanka*, p. 95; Tambiah, *Buddhism Betrayed?* p. 56.

149. For a trenchant description of how petty criminals join and encourage crowds, see Christopher Hibbert, *King Mob: The Story of Lord George Gordon and the Riots of 1780* (New York: Dorset Press, 1989), pp. 36–39, 48, 61, 81–82.

150. Shah, "Communal Riots in Gujarat," p. 197.

151. *Report of the Presidential Commission of Inquiry into the Incidents Which Took Place between 13th August and 15th September 1977*, pp. 121–23, 128, 130, 206.

152. Tishkov, "Don't Kill Me, I Am Kyrghyz," p. 14.

153. *Times of India* (New Delhi), April 16, 1969.

154. For similar interpretations, see Stanley J. Tambiah, "Reflections on Communal Violence in South Asia," *Journal of Asian Studies* 49, no. 4 (November 1990): 741–60, at pp. 747, 752; Lambert, "Hindu-Muslim Riots," p. 63; Judge, *Easter in Kishinev*, p. 70.

155. Compare, e.g., Robert Weinberg, "Anti-Jewish Violence and Revolution in Late Imperial Russia: Odessa, 1905" (paper presented at the Seminar on Riots and Pogroms, University of Washington, Seattle, April 1991), pp. 32, 40, pointing to the role of unskilled day laborers in the violence and contrasting the neutral or protective role of skilled workers, with Reed Coughlin, "Business as Usual: Ships and Riots in Nineteenth Century Belfast," *Ethnic Studies Report* 9, no. 2 (July 1991): 40–53, on shipwrights and carpenters in the violence.

156. Assertions that the American participants were disoriented recent migrants to urban areas or unemployed, uneducated members of the underclass were discredited. Participants were actually more likely than nonparticipants to be long-term residents of

Very likely, there is disproportionate participation by the most physically aggressive or undercontrolled people, but it is easy to exaggerate their participation. For several decades, in fact, psychologists and criminologists have been investigating a hypothesis that points in a different direction — namely, that the most violent, assaultive criminals are likely not to be undercontrolled but to be chronically overcontrolled and given to periodic explosive outbursts. (As we have seen, this is a hypothesis that squares with at least some riot behavior, the sort that is homologous with or derivative from amok.[157]) While some supportive evidence has been adduced, there are conflicting results, and the studies are inconclusive.[158] What is more striking in ethnic violence is the participation of ordinary people, albeit, obviously, not all or most ordinary people. Some will surely resist the temptation.[159] The frolicky atmosphere of brutal vio-

---

their cities; they were at least as well educated; and they were generally employed. For a summary of the evidence, see Donald L. Horowitz, "Racial Violence in the United States," in Nathan Glazer and Ken Young, eds., *Ethnic Pluralism and Public Policy: Achieving Equality in the United States and Britain* (Lexington, Mass.: Lexington Books, 1983), pp. 193–94. Similar patterns appear to have been present in earlier cases of ethnic violence in the United States. In the anti-Irish riot in Philadelphia in 1844, apprentices and skilled workers in their twenties were represented. Michael Feldberg, *The Philadelphia Riots of 1844: A Study of Ethnic Conflict* (Westport, Conn.: Greenwood Press, 1975), p. 67. Tenant farmers and, to a lesser extent, urban wage laborers tended to participate in lynchings. Raper, *The Tragedy of Lynching*, p. 362.

157. See Chapter 3, pp. 107–109 above.

158. See the series of studies investigating this hypothesis: Edwin I. Megargee, "Undercontrolled and Overcontrolled Personality Types in Extreme Antisocial Aggression," *Psychological Monographs* 80, no. 3, Whole No. 611 (n.m. 1966); Edwin I. Megargee, Patrick E. Cook, and Gerald A. Mendelsohn, "Development and Validation of an MMPI Scale of Assaultiveness in Overcontrolled Individuals," *Journal of Abnormal Psychology* 72, no. 6 (December 1967): 519–28; R. Blackburn, "Personality in Relation to Extreme Aggression in Psychiatric Offenders," *British Journal of Psychiatry* 114, no. 512 (July 1968): 821–28; Edwin I. Megargee, "Recent Research on Overcontrolled and Undercontrolled Personality Patterns among Violent Offenders," *Sociological Symposium*, no. 9 (Spring 1973): 37–50; Larry Arnold, Russell Fleming, and Valerie Bell, "The Man Who Became Angry Once: A Study of Overcontrolled Hostility," *Canadian Journal of Psychiatry* 24, no. 8 (December 1979): 762–66; Vernon L. Quinsey, Anne Maguire, and George W. Varney, "Assertion and Overcontrolled Hostility among Mentally Disordered Murderers," *Journal of Consulting and Clinical Psychology* 51, no. 4 (August 1983): 550–56; Ronald Blackburn, "Patterns of Personality Deviation among Violent Offenders: Replication and Extension of an Empirical Taxonomy," *British Journal of Criminology* 26, no. 3 (July 1986): 254–69; Laetitia du Toit and John Duckitt, "Psychological Characteristics of Over- and Undercontrolled Violent Offenders," *Journal of Psychology* 124, no. 2 (March 1990): 125–41.

159. On resistance to evil, see Leonard Berkowitz, "Evil Is More Than Banal: Situationism and the Concept of Evil," *Personality and Social Psychology Review* 3, no. 3 (1999): 246–53, at p. 248.

lence also indicates that riot participation will be strongly skewed toward those attracted to bullying and sadism, and certainly those local toughs who excel in violence are indispensable participants. The point is that participation is not confined entirely to bullies, sadists, and rough characters.[160] That ordinary people, rather than deviants, engage in deadly riots is probably related to the deindividuation that occurs in crowds, but it also suggests that the violence has legitimacy and social support.[161] If it did not have legitimacy and social support, otherwise respectable people would not participate and, perhaps more important, could not resume ordinary life, free of social sanction, after the fact. The ordinariness of the mob is testimony to its reflection of the norms and feelings of the group from which it springs. If the violence is seen as justifiable, then ordinary young men can and will join.

THE DEADLY RIOT AS A PICKUP GAME

The deadly ethnic riot is a pickup game with respect to both organization and participation. Elaborate organization is not essential to it and, when present, does not necessarily confer any advantage in the production of violence. Often organization responds to the demand for violence more than it shapes it. If organizers wish to polarize an environment, they do so typically when the environment is already rather well polarized. Whereas hostile sentiment without organization can produce a great deal of killing, organization without sentiment is not equally effective. In deadly riots, antipathy is the constant, and organization is the variable. This means that ethnic violence is a game that amateurs can play with ease. (Why they wish to play, rather than stand aside, is a question addressed explicitly in Chapter 13.) In this respect, the riot is quite unlike ethnic terrorism and warfare, which require specialist organization.

If, under the right conditions, anyone can organize a riot, or if no one really needs to organize the violence more than minimally once appropriate precipitants occur, and if, save for their interest in fighting, participants are close to a random sample of working-class young men of a cer-

160. It is reasonably well established that most people dislike perpetrating harm, that a minority takes pleasure in it, but that, for some initially unattracted to sadism, the pleasure can develop over time. See Roy Baumeister and W. Keith Campbell, "The Intrinsic Appeal of Evil: Sadism, Sensational Thrills, and Threatened Egotism," *Personality and Social Psychology Review* 3, no. 3 (1999): 210–21, at pp. 212–13.

161. Which is what such broad participation meant in the United States in the 1960s. Interestingly, the underlying legitimation extended precisely to the level of violence that occurred — destruction of property but not killing. For evidence, see Horowitz, "Racial Violence in the United States," pp. 195–96.

tain ethnic (and perhaps subethnic) identity, this means that riots depend on general social sanction, since most people will not engage in behavior that is authoritatively disapproved. Under these circumstances, it is appropriate to think of organization in terms that go beyond the planning of violence. In many riots, leadership ranges between general fomentation on the more active side and tacit encouragement on the less active side. A background agitation, rather than active preparation for violence, can be detected in many riots, some of which are described as highly organized.[162] Much of the time, the function of leadership in riots is probably to convey in understandable code, over a long period of time, the community's sanction for the violence, rather than to engage in strategic and tactical planning.

These organizational and participatory attributes of deadly ethnic riots have implications for riot prevention. If the very breadth of participation reflects a widely held sense of the interethnic situation and its needs, discouraging violence means discouraging what large numbers of group members feel is appropriate. Similarly, if leadership is a matter of legitimation rather than of motivating and organizing people for violence, of sending moral signals rather than dominating an environment and inducing people to do what they might prefer not to do, then leadership can accomplish its deadly goals more readily. Under these circumstances, the deadly ethnic riot is not merely a do-it-yourself, anyone-can-play event, but, for all the grotesque killing and mutilation, it also has the stamp of necessity about it. Preventive efforts may need to be concentrated on averting precipitating events that make violence seem necessary, on undermining support for the violence within the ethnic group initiating it, and — not to be neglected — on forcibly restraining outbreaks of violence.

Still, these findings about organization and participation are generally discouraging for those interested in preventive policy. They imply that ethnic riots are not quite the abnormal events we would like to believe they are. They are deep-rooted, in the sense of being regarded as justifiable. Their overall elimination — as opposed to prevention in particular cases — depends on changing such notions of justifiability. That will not be easy.

162. See, e.g., Tishkov, "Don't Kill Me, I Am Kyrghyz," pp. 16–17 (little organization but tacit encouragement from leaders of local soviets); Haja Maideen, *The Nadra Tragedy: The Maria Hertogh Controversy* (Petaling Jaya, Malaysia: Pelanduk, 1989), pp. 205–53 (buildup of inflammatory publications, speeches, and protests); Leifer, "Communal Violence in Singapore," pp. 1119–20 (speeches suggestive of need for sacrifice to preserve ethnic interests); Hibbert, *King Mob*, p. 88 (background agitation and propaganda); Judge, *Easter in Kishinev*, passim (long history of anti-Jewish propaganda).

CHAPTER 8

The Occasions for Violence

CERTAIN TARGET-GROUP ATTRIBUTES evoke hostility, and certain kinds of behavior prompt violent responses. Having identified target-group characteristics, we now need to be concerned with the actions that precipitate violence — in other words, why riots occur *when* they occur.

The precipitating event performs specific functions in the riot. Thomas C. Schelling makes the point that, in the absence of organization, the precipitant serves as a signal for a crowd to act in unison. It enables every participant to count on the participation of every other.[1] The precipitant assures each participant that a significant number of others will be as motivated to act violently as he himself is.

To accomplish this function — and this Schelling does not say — the precipitant must be anger producing. It must be threatening or transgressive. By *transgressive,* I mean that the precipitant constitutes a blatant display of what ethnic strangers are not to be allowed to do with impunity. The precipitant, therefore, may be related to the rioters' effort at risk reduction, but it can reduce risk only if it is truly inflammatory. Schelling sees the precipitant as a substitute for organization. Although organizations with an interest in violence can sometimes produce situations that make people willing to fight, the prevalence of major precipitating events before most riots is another sign that these riots have not been merely created by organizers.

There is a trade-off between the precipitant and environmental conditions supporting the use of violence.[2] What the underlying conditions may lack in conduciveness to disorder the precipitant may possess in provocativeness. If so, a highly inciting act may produce a riot even in

1. Thomas C. Schelling, *The Strategy of Conflict* (Cambridge: Harvard University Press, 1960), p. 90.
2. Cf. Stanley Lieberson and Arnold R. Silverman, "The Precipitants and Underlying Conditions of Race Riots," *American Sociological Review* 30, no. 6 (December 1965): 887–98. Underlying conditions that facilitate violence will be dealt with in Chapter 9.

what otherwise appear to be tranquil times; and in tense times or a supportive environment, a smaller incident may trigger a big riot.[3] Conversely, an unsupportive environment may be shattered by a precipitating event of such magnitude that the initiators of violence feel that they cannot let it pass unanswered. As K.O.L. Burridge says, with a simplicity that veils the subtlety of the remark, "certain things are worth fighting for"[4]— or so the participants feel.

This trade-off between the precipitant and the underlying conditions heightens the unpredictability of riots, frequently adding an element of surprise to the occurrence (or nonoccurrence) of violence when observers, looking at one factor or the other, did not expect it to occur. All precipitating events need not reach an equal intensity before they provoke violence. Disparities in provocativeness and in the duration of what might be called the incubation period do exist. A large portion of these disparities can be accounted for by offsetting disparities in the underlying conditions.

FLASHPOINTS: THE EVENTS THAT PRECIPITATE RIOTS

A precipitant is an act, event, or train of acts and events, antecedent but reasonably proximate in time and place to the outbreak of violence and causally related thereto. An alternative definition is provided by Dean G. Pruitt in the context of warfare: "Small, last-minute events that touch off war, such as the assassination of the Austrian archduke, have sometimes been called *occasions* of war in distinction to larger *causes*, such as the absence of trust or the military advantage of attacking first. Occasions involve small amounts of energy that somehow release the large amounts of energy embodied in causes . . . . Actually . . . causes and occasions are simply different kind of causes."[5] The release of energy is a suggestive

3. The Ivory Coast riot of 1958 was a highly organized, nearly provocation-free riot in a highly supportive environment, as I suggest in Chapter 9. The Singapore riot (1964) also had a considerable measure of organization, as we saw in Chapter 7, and was not really dependent on precipitating events.

4. K.O.L. Burridge, "Racial Relations in Johore," *Australian Journal of Politics and History* 2, no. 2 (May 1957): 151–68, at p. 163. Some acts constitute, in themselves, justifications for starting a fight. See Peter Marsh, Elizabeth Rosser, and Rom Harré, *The Rules of Disorder* (London: Routledge & Kegan Paul, 1978), pp. 109–10.

5. Dean G. Pruitt, "Stability and Sudden Change in Interpersonal and International Affairs," *Journal of Conflict Resolution* 13, no. 1 (March 1969): 18–38, at p. 33 n. 14 (emphasis in the original). Compare R.M. MacIver, *Social Causation* (Boston: Ginn, 1942), pp. 172–73: ". . . we mean by 'precipitant' any specific factor or condition regarded as diverting the pre-established direction of affairs, as disrupting a pre-existing equilibrium, or as releasing hitherto suppressed or latent tendencies or forces."

metaphor; many precipitating events do have this triggering quality. It is, however, not accurate to refer to such events as small, even though they may appear that way to outsiders. In the telling words of Anne Campbell, "our acceptance of the term 'trivial' indicates our inability as outsiders to interpret and make sense of the semiotic significance of opaque social events."[6]

A precipitant may seem small when it is isolated from other events that have preceded it, and it is to avoid just such artificial isolation that I have referred to the possibility of a precipitating train of acts and events.[7] Here it is useful to note the image of "crisis slides," which often precede the outbreak of international warfare.[8] In such a sequence, (1) crises come thick and fast, (2) reacting on each other and accelerating to the point where (3) international society itself seems to be collapsing and (4) policymakers see their options narrowing so that there is no longer any way out but war. There is a crisis-slide quality to some of the events that precede riots, and many of them also have the effect of backing one of the participating groups into a corner from which it senses the alternatives are violence or the prospect of an intolerable loss.

Because the warfare threshold is higher than the riot threshold, crisis slides are less common in precipitating riots than wars. Warfare is generally begun only after considerable deliberation (albeit often under stressful conditions); its consequences are likely to be enormous. The open-ended commitment and unpredictable duration of wars constitute some of the firmest foundations of peace. Riots do not entail a corporate commitment comparable to the decision to begin a war. The decision to embark on a course of ethnic violence is rarely made in an institutional-

6. Anne Campbell, "The Streets and Violence," in Anne Campbell and John J. Gibbs, eds., *Violent Transactions: The Limits of Personality* (Oxford: Basil Blackwell, 1986), p. 122.

7. The Sri Lanka riot of 1983, precipitated by a Tamil Tiger ambush of a Sri Lankan army unit, was preceded by other armed attacks by the Tigers, assaults and protest strikes at universities, and an episode of violence two months earlier. Likewise, the anti-Bengali violence in Tripura (1980) was preceded by a chain of events: Bengali opposition to a local government's measure to return tribal land that had been sold to Bengali immigrants without the approval of a district magistrate and a measure to create an autonomous tribal district covering two-thirds of the area of the state. The latter had been delayed by a judicial challenge brought by Bengalis, which in turn produced tribal boycotts of Bengali merchants and demands to expel Bengalis. In such cases, it is apt to speak of a series of precipitating events, even at the risk of blurring the distinction between precipitants and the conflicts from which they emerge.

8. Coral Bell, *The Conventions of Crisis* (London: Oxford University Press, 1971), pp. 14–18.

calculative setting and is almost never believed to entail a sustained commitment. Consequently, the inhibitions on war are generally higher than the inhibitions on riot; it requires less cumulation of precipitants to start a riot than to start a war. Here is another reason why so many riots appear to be sudden and unpredictable and why, in contrast to warfare, it is so frequently after the riot, rather than before it, that the society is perceived to be coming apart.

There is a further reason for the lower riot threshold. Ethnic contestants more often feel their vital interests threatened than do major international powers. They live at closer quarters; their daily encounters ramify more quickly and affect each other more intensively. The international system, less structured than the domestic political system, provides more buffers against confrontation, simply by virtue of the paucity of situations that seem to require a violent response in order to avert an immediate danger. Again, therefore, it may require an event of a lesser magnitude to set off ethnic violence.

Precipitants tend to fall into one or more of several categories. The categories employed here are of varying degrees of sharpness and varying levels of analysis. Some are clear-cut and obvious; others depend on identification of a unifying thread. The common criterion is the apparent significance of the pre-riot events for the participants. Most frequent among the events which seem to have the capacity to move the participants over the threshold from nonviolence to violence are (1) ethnic processions, demonstrations, and mass meetings; (2) strikes with ethnic overtones; (3) party and electoral rivalries threatening or solidifying ethnic party allegiances; (4) official or unofficial alterations of relative ethnic status; and (5) rumors of threatened or actual aggression by the target group, already examined in Chapter 3.

Many riots are precipitated by an interacting sequence of several types of event, although how and in what order they combine seem largely to be a function of local circumstances, with one significant exception: rumors of aggression repeatedly come last in the chain. Although some of these categories could be merged or reordered at a higher level of analysis, I have resisted the temptation to do so. The aim is, instead, to build the house from the bottom up, laying bare certain common themes in the flesh-and-blood form in which they are manifested and providing adequate narrative to understand the provocations as the participants probably interpreted them. One theme runs through all the events. They are evocative: they call forth threatening characteristics or behavior of the target group and support the determination that violence is required.

The analogy to certain episodes of criminal violence is compelling. Criminal violence frequently emerges out of a complex interaction between attacker and victim, in which acts by the victim that are seen as provocations provide the backdrop for escalation, producing a decisive act of aggression as the last step.[9] Murder is said to be "a situated transaction," a contest often involving rehearsals between the offender and victim on earlier occasions, with the participants attempting to hold their ground in the face of offensive gestures and challenges, until the attacker concludes that violence is required.[10] In a chain of behavior, the offense given by the victim constrains the choices the attacker believes to be available, constrains them toward violence.[11]

A PARADE OF PROCESSIONS

Processions, demonstrations, and mass meetings precipitate violence in perhaps one-third to one-half of all ethnic riots. For Hindu-Muslim riots, the proportion is probably higher because of the frequent celebration of religious festivals by public procession.[12] In a great many divided societies, however, processions provide an occasion for ethnic violence.[13]

CEREMONIAL DEMONSTRATIONS

If a demonstration commemorates a religious festival or historic event, the provocative opportunities even in an ostensibly innocuous celebration are manifold. In some cases, the extent of incitement depends upon what transpires as events unfold; in others, the significance of the demonstration itself is sufficient to call forth violence or countermeasures that lead to violence.

The celebrants may insult members of the opposing group or its sacred symbols; scuffles may develop along the way. Their importance

9. See Shlomo Shoham et al., "The Cycles of Interaction in Violence," *Israel Studies in Criminology* 2 (1973): 69–87; Rivka Banitt, Shoshana Katznelson, and Shlomit Streit, "The Situational Aspects of Violence: A Research Model," *Israel Studies in Criminology* 1 (1970): 241–58.

10. David F. Luckenbill, "Criminal Homicide as a Situated Transaction," *Social Problems* 25, no. 2 (December 1977): 176–86. The study excludes contract murder and murder committed in the course of another felony.

11. Campbell, "The Streets and Violence," p. 122.

12. For a rough estimate to the mid-1960s, see G.S. Ghurye, *Social Tensions in India* (Bombay: Popular Prakashan, 1968), pp. 304–51.

13. See, e.g., Natalie Zemon Davis, *Society and Culture in Early Modern France* (Stanford: Stanford University Press, 1975), pp. 171–72.

may be so magnified as to suggest the need for retaliation. This has repeatedly been the case on Hindu and Muslim festival days in India. Twice in 1984, in Hyderabad, Andhra Pradesh, Hindu processions were stoned by Muslims, producing violence.[14] In Ahmedabad (1969), a large march of Muslims was engaged in a celebration. As it passed a Hindu temple, a minor clash developed, in the course of which stones were thrown at the temple. This incident was picked up and exaggerated by an extremist organization and used as the basis for an inflammatory meeting, following which extensive violence was inflicted on Muslims.[15] Ritual insults that occur during religious processions are not infrequently seized upon in this way during times of tension. So recurrent have such events been in India that custom prescribes violence when certain specified events occur during a procession.[16]

Opportunities for insult and sacrilege proliferate when the faithful gather for a procession. Under such circumstances, the routing and timing of processions are important details. If a march passes a sacred spot or sensitive neighborhood,[17] or if the religious calendar dictates conflicting processions on the same day,[18] violence may ensue.

Even the scrupulous avoidance of insult may not be sufficient to avert violence. Processions often embody implicit comparisons of group worth. The scale and pomp with which a festival is commemorated may connote the status of the group that celebrates it. Anti-Chinese riots occurred in Sukabumi, Indonesia (1963), during a celebration marking the end of the Muslim fasting month. Two weeks earlier, the Chinese had held their lantern festival for the New Year. The Chinese ceremonies were on a particularly grand scale but provoked no immediate disorder.

14. S.K. Ghosh, *Communal Riots in India* (New Delhi: Ashish, 1987), pp. 123–24.

15. Ibid., pp. 151–60; Ghanshyam Shah, "Communal Riots in Gujarat," *Economic and Political Weekly*, Annual Number, January 1970, pp. 187–200.

16. Richard D. Lambert, "Hindu-Muslim Riots" (Ph.D. diss., University of Pennsylvania, 1951), p. 116.

17. More than 100 people were killed in Jamshedpur (1979) in a riot that began when Muslims objected to a Hindu procession in their neighborhood.

18. Lambert, "Hindu-Muslim Riots," p. 115. In India, the deadly collision of processions has a long history. In Benares (Varanasi) (1809), riots began when a crowd of Hindus celebrating Holi collided with a Moharram mourning procession. Sunthan Visuvalingam and Elizabeth Chalier-Visuvalingam, "Between Mecca and Benares: The Marriage of Lat-Bhairo and Ghazi Miyan" (unpublished paper, March 25, 1991), pp. 18–20. For comparable events in Palestine (1929) during reciprocal processions in the Easter-Passover–Nabi Musa holiday season, see Bernard Wasserstein, "Patterns of Communal Conflict in Palestine," in Ada Rapoport-Albert and Steven J. Zipperstein, eds., *Jewish History: Essays in Honor of Chimen Abramsky* (London: Peter Halban, 1988), pp. 611, 613, 615.

As was customary,[19] a number of Indonesians even joined in the celebration. Following the fasting month, Indonesians held several processions, also customary. One of these, unusually large, contained certain features designed to imitate the Chinese procession. Some participants were armed, and the riot began as the march approached the Chinese section. The circumstances of this procession suggested resentment at the scale of the Chinese celebration and a desire to outdo it. Clearly, some Indonesians regarded the lantern procession as a defiant gesture, especially intolerable because it occurred during the fasting month, when Muslims were required to endure the discomforts of hunger and thirst.[20]

It would be quite wrong to think of this sort of riot as culturally specific to Indonesia. In 1979, in Hyderabad, the practice began of including a large Ganesh (the Hindu elephant deity) in the Vinayak festival procession. Muslims interpreted the change as a Hindu show of strength. In 1982, a Muslim politician decided to organize a decidedly untraditional "pankah" procession a week before Vinayak, as a show of force. In subsequent years, the competing festivals became focal points of violence.[21] Both the Chinese celebration in Sukabumi and the Hindu celebration in Hyderabad had become irritants prompting competing processions of a more explicitly aggressive sort.

Both features — competition and aggression — are important. Public affirmation of relative group worth is a large part of the contest. A procession that flaunts the richness of a group's culture makes a political claim that cannot be ignored.[22] The defiant response easily leads to violence, because the counterprocession is in itself a show of strength, a proto-violent event, a massing of people capable of great destruction.

19. For an example from the mid-1930s in Jakarta (then Batavia), see R.H. Bruce Lockhart, *Return to Malaya* (New York: G. Putnam's Sons, 1936), p. 287.

20. The Siauw Giap, "Group Conflict in a Plural Society," *Revue du Sud-Est Asiatique*, no. 1 (January 1966): 10–13. For procession precipitants generally in Indonesia in the 1960s, see J.A.C. Mackie, "Anti-Chinese Outbreaks in Indonesia, 1959–68," in J.A.C. Mackie, ed., *The Chinese in Indonesia* (Hong Kong: Heinemann Educational Books, 1976), pp. 77–138, at pp. 136–37.

21. Ghosh, *Communal Riots in India*, pp. 120–24.

22. On the competition for cultural superiority, see Donald L. Horowitz, *Ethnic Groups in Conflict* (Berkeley and Los Angeles: University of California Press, 1985), pp. 166–81. For another example of how processions produce violence because of their involvement in this competition, see *Newswatch*, May 31, 1983, pp. 20–21, reporting a riot in Warri, Nigeria, between Itsekiri and Urhobo. The violence grew out of a carnival procession to mark the anniversary of the coronation of Olu of Warri. Urhobo interpreted the provocative procession as intended to affirm "the over-lordship of the Itsekiri." Ibid., p. 21.

The ethnic group, an abstraction, becomes embodied (literally) in the physical group.[23] It is no accident that march organizers who wish a procession to go off peacefully announce its peaceful character loudly and forcefully, for the march is not inherently peaceful; it derives its power from its violent possibilities. Hence, at the outset, the procession is a common precipitant of violence, because its content frequently goes to the heart of the conflict and because it is already on the edge of violence.

The intrinsic ethnic significance of the event may by itself be sufficient to provoke immediate violence. The rioting that began in Malaysia during the course of the Penang centenary celebration in 1957 provides an excellent illustration. To the later regret of many Malays, who saw the act as a surrender of Malay patrimony, Penang had been leased to the British by its Malay ruler in 1786 and had thereafter been ruled directly, rather than regarded as a "Malay State," in which deference had to be paid to the Malay sultans and the "special position" of the Malays. Symbolically, therefore, the Chinese and Indian majority in Penang owed no special obligation to the Malays. In 1857, the British devolved certain powers of local self-government to an elected Committee of Municipal Commissioners.[24] This act was the fountainhead of self-government on the island and implicitly a mark of the special (that is, non-Malay) status of Penang. When the centenary was celebrated in 1957, independence for the Federation of Malaya, including Penang, was imminent. The proposed constitution for the Federation had struck a delicate balance between Malay and non-Malay claims, but would bring a hitherto unknown degree of uniformity to all the states, including Penang, and it was being hotly debated. Opposition to joining the Federation was strongest in Penang, centering on the Straits Chinese British Association, which wanted a separate status for the island.

Because it signaled resistance to the impending uniformity, the centenary was laden with contemporary meaning. The century-old municipal council was a token of non-Malay prerogatives at the hour of the symbolic restoration of Malay sovereignty. The procession, in which Malays did not join, was seen as a demonstration of support for separatism, which some Malays still feared might succeed. It was, therefore, a formidable provocation to the Malays, producing several days of killing.

The riot in Kirkuk, Iraq (1959), began during the celebration of an

23. See Sudhir Kakar, *The Colors of Violence: Cultural Identities, Religion, and Conflict* (Chicago: University of Chicago Press, 1996), pp. 45–46.

24. See City Council of George Town, Penang, *Penang, Past and Present, 1786–1963* (George Town: Ganesh Printers, 1966), ch. 2.

event of comparable significance.[25] Turkomens and Kurds who reside in Kirkuk held quite different attitudes toward the Soviet Union. Kurds tended to be favorably disposed toward the Soviets, because the realization of Kurdish separatist aspirations seemed to depend on Soviet support. Turkomens approved the strong measures taken by the Kassem regime to contain Communist influence. When the regime prepared to celebrate Kassem's first anniversary in office, the Turkomen community joined in enthusiastically, constructing some 133 triumphal arches and parading in support of the regime. Kurds attacked both the arches and Turkomens passing under them. To Kurds, the magnitude of the celebration was evidence that the Turkomens were aligned with the enemies of the Kurds.

The Republic Day parade in Gauhati, Assam (1968), provoked riots under analogous circumstances.[26] By 1968, separatism was rife among several non-Assamese tribal groups in the state. The Indian government, which had moved to placate these movements by a state reorganization, was accused of abetting the dismemberment of Assam. Reacting to the separatist sentiments of others, Assamese students had mooted the idea of Assamese independence. Posters put up before Republic Day demanded "Indians go back," the term *Indians* referring in this case to non-Assamese migrants from other states who were associated with the central government. The celebration was therefore regarded by Assamese as a symbol of the state's impending disintegration and the role of the central government in that disintegration. An Assamese boycott of the ceremony and a counterprocession were organized. The latter rapidly degenerated into attacks, albeit relatively mild attacks, on local "Indians," mainly Marwaris, and their property.

In Penang, Kirkuk, and Gauhati, the event to be celebrated had contemporary significance. Where ethnic pluralism is the result of an earlier conquest, historic processions may be observances of engagements fought, which may suggest to marchers and onlookers alike that new battles are required.[27] Aggressive cues — weapons, uniforms, and martial

25. Arnold Hottinger, "An Eye-Witness Report on Iraq," *Swiss Review of World Affairs* 9, no. 6 (September 1959): 12–16; Johann Caspar (pseud.), "Baghdad's Year of Revolution," *Commentary*, September 1959, pp. 193–201.

26. Dilip Mukerjee, "Assam Reorganization," *Asian Survey* 9, no. 4 (April 1969): 297–311, at p. 308; "Sack of Gauhati," *Economic and Political Weekly*, February 17, 1968, pp. 318–20; *The Statesman* (Calcutta), February 10, 1968; Government of Assam, Directorate of Information and Public Relations, Press Notes No. 6 and 7, January 27, 28, 1968.

27. Such parades suggest exactly this in Northern Ireland, where the parade is a show-case in which "to display the trophies of each side's successes . . . ."Harold Jackson, *The*

symbols — may be added to other elements of provocation. But whether the commemorated event was actually a violent encounter or whether it is interpreted subsequently as a source of ethnic injury, the event is evaluated differently by the contending groups. One group's celebration is another's lamentation. Moreover, the numbers and enthusiasm of the celebrants provide a measure of its present importance for the bystanders. The commemorative occasion opens an old wound and constitutes a new test of strength.

The religious or historic procession usually provokes violence directly or provokes a counterprocession from which violence ensues. If there is something for the marchers to celebrate, there may well be something for the bystanders to fight for.

Such occasions and the ceremonial processions they prompt have also been used, albeit less frequently, by organized groups as springboards from which to launch assaults. Then the roles are reversed: bystanders become victims. This has become a common pattern in Hindu processions in India, particularly if Muslims react to them. This was also, as we have seen, a device employed in Sukabumi, where some members of the Muslim procession, their faces painted black (the Muslim *jihad* color), came prepared for violence. In the relatively organized Singapore riot of July 1964, a core group of marchers, attired in black warrior dress, picked fights with Chinese on the sidelines.[28] The demonstration that triggered the Burmese riot of 1938 was organized over a religious issue — the publication of an offensive book — and began with a meeting in a pagoda. After inflammatory speeches, the procession moved toward Indian areas, some Burmans arming themselves along the way.[29] Religious processions are especially susceptible to a first-strike mentality. In many religions, the duty to defend the faith against infidels is part of the creed. Emotional involvement with ritual and the excitement of a devoted crowd render mobilization for attack relatively easy. At the same time, the tactical advantages of the procession attack for those with an interest in violence are apparent: the assets of mass and surprise, mixed with an aggressive mood, may convince organizers of violence that so auspicious a moment may not soon return.

Two Irelands — a Dual Study of Inter-Group Tensions (London: Minority Rights Group, 1971), p. 6.

28. Michael Leifer, "Communal Violence in Singapore," *Asian Survey* 4, no. 10 (October 1964): 1115–21, at p. 1120.

29. Government of Burma, *Final Report of the Riot Inquiry Committee* (Rangoon: Superintendent of Government Printing & Stationery, 1939), ch. 8.

POLITICAL DEMONSTRATIONS

Demonstrations that express ethnic discontent, demands, or policy positions often precipitate ethnic riots. Even in the former Soviet Union, without any tradition of extragovernmental demonstrations, the political rally has led directly to ethnic violence. In Kyrghyzstan (1990), an Uzbek protest demonstration over ethnic claims to land and housing provided an occasion for serious violence.[30] An Azeri rally relating to the disputed territory of Nagorno-Karabagh produced massive anti-Armenian violence in Baku (1990).[31] The rally is designed to put a show of muscle behind a collective position, and some in the crowd may find it logical to take the next step into violence. Alternatively, the demonstration may suggest the need for countermeasures, usually counterdemonstrations. If a religious or historical procession passes without incident, the prospect of disorder has probably abated. Not so with political demonstrations, for they may begin a spiraling course of action and reaction that elevates the danger of violence. Often intended to scare antagonists off by a show of strength, they may instead egg them on by an exhibition of threat.

Three important features are recurrent in violence induced by political demonstrations. The first is the determination of crowds to redress the equivocal positions taken by politicians. The demonstrations are intended to polarize, to overcome the interethnic moderation the rioters sense in the pre-violence air. The second is the powerful role of ethnic insults. Embedded in the demonstrations are dramatizations of the most hostile and irritating aspects of ethnic relations. The third is the recapitulation of a classic escalation process familiar in international relations. It is worth taking a close look at several such riots: Assam (1960), Sri Lanka (1956 and 1958), and Malaysia (1969).

The riot in Assam (1960), discussed from a different angle in Chapter 6, is perhaps the archetype of action-reaction escalation. In 1955, Assam had already had processions and counterprocessions over issues of territory and language, and these had led to the killing of Bengalis.[32] Now,

30. *Izvestiya*, June 19, 1990, p. 2, in *Current Digest of the Soviet Press*, July 25, 1990, p. 15; *Sovetskaya Kirgizia*, June 6, 1990, p. 1, in June 6, 1990, pp. 1–2.

31. Moscow Domestic Service, January 14, 1990, in FBIS-SOV-90-010, January 16, 1990, pp. 63–64.

32. The 1955 riot arose as a result of the irredentist demand of West Bengal to absorb the heavily Bengali district of Goalpara within its borders, as well as Bengali complaints that the Assamese language was being imposed on Bengalis there and in Cachar, another large Bengali area. Over a ten-day period, these claims fused in massive demonstrations, pro and con, the demonstrators exchanging collective insults and brickbats and indulging in

however, a legislative proposal to declare Assamese the sole official language, in place of English, a proposal unanimously opposed by Bengali and tribal legislators, produced much greater violence.[33]

Militant organizations were formed to demonstrate for and against the proposal. The most provocative demonstration was a march organized by Bengalis and hill people, who saw in the demise of English in state government business an attempt by the Assamese to gain hegemony in politics and in government employment. The marchers took the offensive. Assamese, placards asserted, was "a donkey's language." Assamese signboards and posters were defaced. These actions prompted counter-demonstrations, during one of which Assamese rejoined that Bengali was "a goat's language" and took their turn at defacing Bengali signboards.[34] Isolated cases of violence were reported over the next month. When it was finally announced that a bill to make Assamese the state language would soon be introduced, Bengalis organized an all-Bengali Conference, which demanded that Bengali be made the second official language of the state. Random assaults accelerated for about ten days afterward. Then, after two Bengalis were attacked, police opened fire on a group of Assamese students, killing one of them and triggering the mass violence that engulfed the state.

The impetus for the organization of demonstrations was provided by the prospect of imminent change affecting group interests. The chief minister, an Assamese with support spanning the ethnic cleavage, had been at first reluctant to embrace the language proposal. His reluctance enraged segments of the Assamese community. Angry as they were, the demonstrations were also a form of political persuasion. Pressure from Assamese increased until, more than a month later, the state Congress Party Committee passed a resolution favoring Assamese demands. The demonstrators had undone the state government's moderation.

Disparaging references to the Assamese language — and therefore the

---

the destruction of posters and signboards printed in the language of the antagonist. These increasingly tense demonstrations were followed by arson, looting, and stabbing. *Assam Tribune* (Gauhati), March 15–April 23, 1955.

33. K.C. Chakravarti, "The State Language of Assam," *Economic Weekly*, May 7, 1960, p. 700; Chakravarti, "Bongal Kheda Again," ibid., July 30, 1960, pp. 1193–95; P.C. Goswami, "Tragedy of Political Tactlessness," ibid., pp. 1195–98; Sushil Kumar, "Panorama of State Politics," in Iqbal Narain, ed., *State Politics in India* (Meerut, U.P.: Meenakshi Prakashan, 1967), p. 40; K.C. Barua, *Assam: Her People and Her Language* (Shillong: Lawyers Book Stall, 1960), pp. 14–16; Charu Chandra Bhandari, *Thoughts on Assam Disturbances* (Rajghat: A.B. Sarva Seva Prakhashan, 1961).

34. Bhandari, *Thoughts on Assam Disturbances*, p. 38.

Assamese — were taken as a humiliating affront to a people seeking to reassert its self-respect. Language policy was an integral part of the effort of the Assamese to undo precisely the stigma the anti-Assamese demonstration had expressed. They were determined to use the political system and violence to reverse their standing as a group lagging Bengali achievement and subject to Bengali disparagement.

The Assamese riot was a long time in maturing. From the first policy announcement to the mass killings, the time was measured in months. During this time, each step of Bengali protest led to an Assamese retaliatory demonstration. This was a classic case of spiraling conflict, analogous to the mobilizations that preceded World War I, each stage investing additional prestige in the outcome and rendering retreat more difficult.

Two early Sri Lankan riots occurred as Tamils had gathered or were about to gather for demonstrations or meetings to protest a new language policy.[35] The first violence occurred in 1956, after the United National Party (UNP) was defeated by the Sri Lanka Freedom Party (SLFP)[36] of S.W.R.D. Bandaranaike, who had associated himself with the aspirations of the rural Sinhalese Buddhist majority. Before the election, there was a groundswell of support for making Sinhala the sole official language, replacing English. The SLFP rode to power on this issue and the related demand to restore to Buddhism its "rightful place" in the country. At the same time, Tamil fears of repression at the hands of the Sinhalese resulted in the overwhelming election, in Tamil areas, of candidates of the militant Federal Party. Tamils demanded parity of status for Tamil and were uncompromising in their claim that Tamil be the language of administration in the Tamil north and east.

The Bandaranaike government moved swiftly to adopt legislation declaring Sinhala the sole official language. The original bill would also have enshrined certain guarantees for Tamil, but protest meetings by

35. I am drawing here on interviews in Sri Lanka in 1968 and on the following full or partial accounts of the riots: Tarzie Vittachi, *Emergency '58: The Story of the Ceylon Race Riots* (London: André Deutsch, 1958); W. Howard Wriggins, *Ceylon: Dilemmas of a New Nation* (Princeton: Princeton University Press, 1960), pt. II; Wriggins, "Ceylon's Time of Troubles, 1956–1958," *Far Eastern Survey* 28, no. 3 (March 1959): 33–39; Robert N. Kearney, *Communalism and Language in the Politics of Ceylon* (Durham: Duke University Press, 1967), ch. 4; S. Arasaratnam, *Ceylon* (Englewood Cliffs, N.J.: Prentice-Hall, 1964), ch. 1; B.H. Farmer, *Ceylon: A Divided Nation* (London: Oxford University Press, 1963), ch. 4; *Ceylon Parliamentary Debates* (Hansard), House of Representatives, 3d Parl., 3d Sess., 1958–59, Vol. 31 (Colombo: Government Printer, 1958). For a partisan Tamil view, see S. Ponniah, *Satyagraha and the Freedom Movement of the Tamils in Ceylon* (Jaffna: A. Kandiah, 1963), ch. 4.

36. Then in coalition with some smaller parties.

Sinhalese forced the deletion of these safeguards. It then became the Tamils' turn to protest. The Federal Party began a nonviolent demonstration opposite parliament the day the House assembled to debate the Sinhala Only bill. Bands of Sinhalese attacked the demonstrators. The violence quickly spread to the streets of Colombo. In the up-country Gal Oya Valley, Sinhalese set upon and killed large numbers of Tamils.

The Sinhala Only bill was passed, but Bandaranaike promised a renewed effort to protect the status of the Tamil language. For their part, the Federalists grew increasingly intransigent, urging noncooperation with the language policy and threatening full-scale civil disobedience unless protection were given to the Tamil language.

In this atmosphere, Bandaranaike negotiated the so-called B-C Pact in 1957 with the Federalist leader, S.J.V. Chelvanayakam. The pact provided for recognition of Tamil as a minority language to be used in administration in the north and east and for the creation of regional councils, to devolve a measure of self-government to Tamil areas. The pact seemed to extreme Sinhalese opinion to be a surrender to the Tamils, and there was pressure for Bandaranaike to abandon it. The opposition UNP, hurt in the 1956 election by its failure to support Sinhalese aspirations until the last moment, saw an opportunity to recoup its losses. The UNP attacked the B-C Pact as embodying a de facto partition and circulated a map of the island with a large black footprint superimposed on the Tamil areas.[37]

As this opposition gathered momentum, the language issue assumed greater immediacy. Government buses bearing newly issued license plates had the Sinhala letter *sri* obliterated as they entered the Tamil heartland in Jaffna. Sinhalese responded by tarring Tamil signboards in Colombo and boycotting Tamil shops. Weeks later, several hundred monks and other Sinhalese gathered at the prime minister's residence to demand his repudiation of the B-C Pact. Harangued by the crowd, Bandaranaike capitulated. He renounced the pact in writing, but subsequently backtracked, declaring that he would present two bills guaranteeing "fair play" to the Tamils when parliament reconvened.

Bandaranaike's abrogation of the B-C Pact convinced the Federal Party it could not rely on his word. As the Federal Party gathered for its convention in May 1958, it had on its agenda a proposal to organize the massive noncooperation movement that had been averted by the B-C

37. The black footprint was undoubtedly meant to appeal to Sinhalese bigotry about the Tamils' generally slightly darker color.

Pact the preceding year. Many delegates traveled by train, and the first outbreak of violence occurred when Sinhalese stopped some trains and derailed others in their search for Tamils. The killings spread to Colombo and other towns. The violence far exceeded the scale of the rioting two years earlier.

In Sri Lanka, as in Assam, violence congealed around the language issue. In both, language was a symbol of group status and a gateway to career opportunities.[38] In both, too, defacement of signboards was part of the train of events that led to riot. The Sinhalese, like the Assamese, claimed sovereignty, and therefore linguistic hegemony, over the entire state, while the Tamils, like the Bengalis, demanded parity — hence equality — on a national basis. Political leaders, caught in a crossfire of incompatible demands, responded by altering their policy, thus conveying the appearance — and the reality — of inconsistency. This kept the spiral of meeting and demonstration, action and reaction, moving toward a convulsive conclusion. In both countries, the massing of members of the target groups to make ethnic demands was so threatening as to produce crowds angry enough to be bent on blood. In both, the violence made compromise outcomes impossible. In this respect, rioters may have believed they had no choice. The target groups had been exceedingly provocative, insulting the language or obliterating its script. Without violence, the target groups would have gained the moderate outcome they had sought.

The Malaysian riot that began on May 13, 1969, was directly connected to the election held on May 10, to processions and counterprocessions, and to threatening political changes.[39] As in previous elections, the ruling Alliance Party, a coalition of a Malay, a Chinese, and an Indian party, confronted at the polls several essentially Chinese and Indian parties on one flank and an explicitly Malay party on the other. The Alliance

38. For the careerist side, see, e.g., S. Arasaratnam, "Nationalism, Communalism, and National Unity in Ceylon," in Philip Mason, ed., *India and Ceylon: Unity and Diversity* (London: Oxford University Press, 1967), p. 273.

39. For two sources representing official viewpoints on the 1969 riot, see Government of Malaysia, National Operations Council, *The May 13 Tragedy* (Kuala Lumpur: n.p., 1969); and Tunku Abdul Rahman, *May 13: Before and After* (Kuala Lumpur: Utusan Melayu Press, 1969). On the antigovernment side is John Slimming, *Malaysia: The Death of a Democracy* (London: J. Murray, 1969). Less impassioned views are presented by Goh Cheng Teik, *The May Thirteenth Incident and Democracy in Malaysia* (Kuala Lumpur: Oxford University Press, 1971); and Felix V. Gagliano, *Communal Violence in Malaysia 1969: The Political Aftermath* (Athens, Ohio: Ohio University Center for International Studies, 1970). Some brief background to the riots may be found in Ozay Mehmet, "Race Riots in Malaysia," *Queen's Quarterly* 78, no. 2 (Summer 1971): 210–18.

had the problem of reconciling the conflicting political claims of Malays and non-Malays, responding to ethnic demands on both sides so as to avoid having its constituency eroded on either. As the Malays were a majority of the electorate, having also special claims to legitimacy, and the Malay coalition component faced constant competition from a single strong Malay opposition party, governmental output was weighted toward the Malay side. This in turn exacerbated Chinese (and Indian) grievances, which the Chinese in the Alliance necessarily had only a limited ability to redress.

Since before independence, the Alliance had been the dominant party. In the preceding general election, held in 1964, it had won an overwhelming majority of seats in the national parliament and most state assemblies. Several important conditions had, however, changed since 1964. First, the previous election had been held in an atmosphere of external crisis brought on by Indonesia's challenge to the formation of Malaysia, a guerrilla operation called Confrontation. This external threat presumably induced many voters to rally to the Alliance as an expression of loyalty. Now Confrontation had ended, and the overwhelming Alliance victory of 1964 was unlikely to be repeated. Second, in previous elections the non-Malay parties had been unable to arrive at a comprehensive no-contest agreement, and so their vote was split, allowing the Chinese component of the Alliance to win some seats by a plurality of the vote in those constituencies. By 1969, a no-contest pact had been reached among opposition parties, diminishing the Alliance's chance of gaining as many seats as before by mere plurality. Third, the mainly Chinese, left-wing Labor Party had decided to boycott the election, a decision that increased the relative electoral power of the remaining non-Malay opposition parties and brought the Labor Party into conflict with the government, raising the level of ethnic tension. In these altered conditions lay the seeds of a new ethnic balance of power.

Some untoward events involving the Labor Party boycott occurred shortly before the election. On April 24, a Malay supporter of the ruling party was beaten to death by Labor Party workers painting boycott signs. On May 4, a Chinese activist for the Labor Party was killed by a policeman while posting a similar notice. Taking advantage of his martyrdom, the Labor Party held a large funeral procession the day before the election. The vociferous funeral procession, another in a long series of Labor Party protests, was likely regarded by some Malays as a sign of unwarranted Chinese disaffection — the more so as the Malay funeral in Penang had been conducted quietly.

The election produced some surprising results. The Alliance majority, although still intact, was drastically reduced. The Pan-Malayan Islamic Party gained both votes and seats, rendering the Malay flank less secure than it was previously. Largely because of their no-contest agreement, the non-Malay opposition parties made even more significant gains. The Chinese component of the Alliance had its seats cut in half. The Chinese protest vote had found an effective outlet at the polls, and the claim of the Chinese component of the Alliance to represent the Chinese minority had been severely undercut.

The results produced two cabinet crises. At the national level, the Alliance's Chinese component met on May 13 and decided not to accept cabinet posts, in view of its rejection at the polls. At the state level, assembly results generally paralleled the national returns. But in three states heavily populated by non-Malays, the Alliance was hit even harder. It lost two of these to the opposition. In the third, Selangor — where the capital, Kuala Lumpur, was located — the Alliance and the opposition were in stalemate. Ultimately, by virtue of the neutrality of one of the opposition parties, the Alliance was able to form a government in Selangor, but this fact was not clearly understood when the riot broke out, and it seemed likely that Selangor would fall to the non-Malay opposition.

If the Malays seemed to be losing ground, the Chinese seemed to be gaining it. Two non-Malay opposition parties, jubilant over the results, staged separate "victory celebrations" in Kuala Lumpur. These took the form of boisterous processions that wound their way through the city, venturing into Malay areas, where ethnic insults were liberally doled out. Some supporters of the opposition drove past the residence of the Selangor chief minister, rudely demanding he abandon the residence in favor of a Chinese.

The Chinese had had their processions — three in four days, the latter two to affirm a "victory" in terms the Malays found unacceptable. They had taunted and boasted. They had flaunted their momentary success. It was time for a decisive rejoinder. As mentioned in Chapter 7, the precariously placed chief minister of Selangor apparently took a hand in planning a massive counterprocession. Malays were brought into Kuala Lumpur, a predominantly Chinese city, from rural areas. Thousands joined in the parade; some were armed, and a great many were angry. As the marchers encountered their first Chinese, the killings began. It took weeks of curfews to bring the city under control.

In this case, the provocations were substantial, their meaning clear. Malay political power was under attack. The electoral success of the

Chinese opposition meant that the brand of interethnic cooperation represented by Chinese participation in the Alliance had declining appeal. The opposition processions had been planned to offend the Malays, to challenge the rightfulness of their place in their own country. Chinese diligence in competition of all kinds was well known; unscrupulous competitors of this kind had to be resisted in strength. The day before the rioting began, the Malay-language newspaper *Utusan Melayu* alarmingly editorialized that the election results had jeopardized the future of Malay rule and suggested that prompt action was required to shore it up.

It mattered not at all that the Alliance had still won the election and that the Malay demonstrators seemed to be reaching out for defeat in the face of victory. It was the omens that counted. Anticipated deprivations can be effective spurs to aggression,[40] and the magnification of threat is a common element in anxiety-laden perceptions.

As in the Assamese and Sri Lankan cases, the crowd rejected a change in the status quo it saw as disadvantageous, although in this case a change brought about by electoral results rather than policy proposals. Each demonstration was more insulting than the previous one, until the provocations were answered with violence. The Malaysian riot is far from the only occasion when victory celebrations produced violence.[41]

DEMONSTRATIONS AND THE CONVERSION OF HOSTILITY TO VIOLENCE

Since mass violence requires crowds, and demonstrations provide crowds, it is not surprising that processions and demonstrations so frequently occasion violence. There are, however, more specific reasons.

Where there is a chain of action and reaction in the form of procession

40. See Ted Robert Gurr, "Psychological Factors in Civil Violence," *World Politics* 20, no. 2 (January 1968): 245–78, at p. 256.

41. For nonethnic riots growing out of victory celebrations, see Gary T. Marx, "Issueless Riots," *The Annals* 391 (September 1970): 31–32. Analogous instances of ethnic riots following an electoral victory procession can be found in Karachi (1965 and 1988). See *Dawn* (Karachi), January 5–7, 1965, p. 1; *Keesing's Contemporary Archives* 34, no. 10 (October 1988): 36219–20. For the background to the 1965 election, see Richard S. Wheeler, *The Politics of Pakistan: A Constitutional Quest* (Ithaca: Cornell University Press, 1970), pp. 255–58. After the mass destruction of the mosque at Ayodhya, India, in 1992, riots began during Hindu victory processions and in some cases Muslim protests in many cities. See K.L. Chanchreek and Saroj Prasad, eds., *Crisis in India* (Delhi: H.K. Publishers, 1993), pp. 112–47; Gopal Guru, "Understanding Communal Riots in Maharashtra," *Economic and Political Weekly*, May 8, 1993, pp. 903–07; Pravin Sheth, "Degeneration of a City," ibid., January 30, 1993, pp. 151–54; Asghar Ali Engineer, "Bombay Shames India," ibid., January 16–23, 1993, pp. 81–85.

and counterprocession, there is often a rise, notch by notch, in the level of hostility until some event pushes one of the parties over a threshold into violence. As we saw in Chapter 3, that final event is usually a report of actual or anticipated aggression on the part of those who become targets of violence. This process of gradually increasing hostility is difficult to reverse once it begins; people tend to feel the need to reciprocate unfriendly acts with unfriendly acts.[42] The possibilities of malevolent reciprocation are magnified by the back and forth of competing mass meetings, and the need to reciprocate is especially clearly sensed once processions are tied to a set of political demands or imminent policy changes. To fail to bring group power to bear on these issues risks losing them by default.

Processions also create a perceptual asymmetry between those who would prefer to prevent violence and those who engage in it. When action and reaction are slowly raising the pitch of conflict, it might be possible to use political methods to reverse the trend of events, but the incremental, notch-by-notch character of the escalation means that the trend of events is much more clearly seen by those in a position to use such methods after the violence has occurred than it is before. On the other hand, through selective perception, angry participants in the events are likely to connect unconnected incidents that occur along the way to produce a threatening picture, necessitating violence.[43]

Measured, balanced hostility, however, is not always the rule. Some situations develop more rapidly than others. It is possible to short-circuit the slow process of action and reaction, to skip over many of the intermediate notches and proceed quickly to violence. This usually happens when the background event is of overwhelming ethnic significance. Then, little incitement may be required to ignite large-scale violence. The May 1966 anti-Ibo riot in northern Nigeria was preceded by governmental action of inordinate ethnic importance, the federal Decree No. 34

42. See Pruitt, "Stability and Sudden Change in Interpersonal and International Affairs." See also the striking evidence on this from two international crises, provided by Ole R. Holsti, Richard A. Brody, and Robert C. North, "Measuring Affect and Action in International Reaction Models: Empirical Materials from the 1962 Cuban Missile Crisis," in Louis Kriesberg, ed., *Social Processes in International Relations* (New York: Wiley, 1968), pp. 399–400. Cf. Rosemary J. Mullick and Rosalind L. Feierabend, "Minority-Group Conflict and Conciliation: A Cross-National Study," *Proceedings*, 79th Annual Convention, American Psychological Association, 1971, pp. 313–14.

43. For a good illustration, see Government of India, *Report of the Commission of Inquiry on Communal Disturbances in Ranchi-Hatia (April 22–29, 1967)* (New Delhi: Government Printer, 1968), p. 79. On the general spiral of hostility, see Kakar, *The Colors of Violence*, pp. 41–42.

of May 24, unifying the civil service. This decree seemed to many northerners to put northern civil servants at a competitive disadvantage on a national scale, to foreshadow the colonization of the north by Ibo administrators, and to confirm that the military government was dominated by Ibo with malevolent designs. It was a short step from this decree to the violence that followed. On May 29, a Hausa student protest demonstration passed temptingly near the Ibo quarter of Kano, but went off peacefully nonetheless. The next day, a demonstration moved toward the Ibo quarter, where the fighting began.[44]

Similarly, a procession may turn rapidly to violence when the whole context of ethnic relations is so charged that any display of disagreement can mobilize the antagonists. This was the case over much of north India following the Indo-Pakistani war of 1965, when Muslims were viewed as a potential Fifth Column and the demands of Indian Muslims were interpreted as inherently separatist. In Ranchi, in the state of Bihar, rioting occurred in 1967 toward the conclusion of a Hindu procession assembled to protest an attempt to make Urdu (the language associated with Muslims) the second official language of the state. The Urdu proposal had been depicted in a Hindu extremist pamphlet circulated before the procession as a prelude to a new partition of the country.[45] During the same period, a visit by Sheikh Abdullah, former chief minister of the disputed state of Kashmir, to the town of Meerut was enough to provoke a demonstration of Hindu organizations that rapidly turned violent.[46] Suspicions of Muslim loyalties were rife. The external context by then colored all of Hindu-Muslim relations.

Violence may issue from a procession when it is preplanned or when earlier events, often earlier processions or meetings, have themselves been so provocative that any mass gathering is likely to seek victims among opponents who have engaged in that provocative behavior. The mass gathering becomes a convenient vehicle to be driven or boarded by those who are specially inclined to violence.[47] The initial decision to participate

44. John N. Paden, "Communal Competition, Conflict and Violence in Kano," in Robert Melson and Howard Wolpe, eds., *Nigeria: Modernization and the Politics of Communalism* (East Lansing: Michigan State University Press, 1971), p. 134.

45. Government of India, *Report of the Commission of Inquiry on Communal Disturbances in Ranchi-Hatia*.

46. Aswini K. Ray and Subhash Chakravarti, *Meerut Riots: A Case Study* (New Delhi: Sampradayikta Virodhi Committee, n.d. [1968 or 1969]). I am grateful to Paul R. Brass for making this document available to me.

47. For a likely example, Bombay (1974), see *Far Eastern Economic Review*, February 18, 1974, pp. 25–26.

entails no necessary intention to engage in violent behavior. For that reason, the meeting can attract a heterogeneous group of participants, only a few of whom need be favorable to violence. Once assembled, the gathering becomes susceptible to malevolent interpretations of chance events or to the spread of rumors of aggressive behavior by the opposing group, which then serve to incite violent behavior on the part of people who joined the crowd out of quite different motives.[48]

Participants in processions or demonstrations that are peaceful or only marginally disorderly may turn to violence if the procession is thwarted in its protest goals or dispersed with what the participants sense to be excessive force. The dispersal of the crowd is itself a new provocation that may symbolize or attach itself to the provocations which led to the initial demonstration.[49]

Somewhat different dynamics are at work when the demonstration is not the base from which violence issues but constitutes the precipitant that prompts violence by others against members of the demonstrating group. Such demonstrations are regarded as provocative, first and foremost, because they constitute a threatening visual display of group strength and unity. They bring together masses of people whose very numbers, as well as whose assertive demeanor, strike fear in the minds of their antagonists. The Hindu perception of the Muslim processions that preceded the Ahmedabad riot (1969) is not atypical: "Muslims took out huge processions in almost all the towns of Gujarat to protest the attack on the Al-Aqsa mosque; the one in Ahmedabad was the largest of all. Hindus interpreted the procession and some of its slogans as both a demonstration of Muslim strength and solidarity and a threat to the Hindus."[50] As we have seen in Sukabumi (1963), processions are sometimes interpreted as an ostentatious affirmation, a flaunting, of group superiority. The fact that a mass demonstration has been organized at all, or the way it is conducted, may exemplify in acute form the stereotyped traits that are particularly feared and disliked in the opposing group: troublesomeness, arrogance, recalcitrance, clannishness, ethnocentrism, the desire to dominate. The vitality of such a celebration may prove irritating to groups in competition, particularly those uncertain of their competitive capability.

48. For a clear example, Rawalpindi (1973), see ibid., April 2, 1973, pp. 13–14.

49. Contrary to what might be expected, however, police repression is rarely a precipitant of deadly ethnic riots, as I shall explain later in this chapter. Rather, for reasons explored in Chapter 9, police ineffectiveness or support for the rioters is the far more usual pattern.

50. Shah, "Communal Riots in Gujarat," p. 189.

Processions may formalize challenges to the ethnic status quo or resistance to the challenges of others. Processions sometimes implicitly claim territory by the routes they take. They may make vociferous ethnic demands regarded by other groups as unreasonable. In so doing, they magnify the symbolic importance of the political issues to which they are addressed. They may also revive memories of earlier violent conflicts. Processions provide an opportunity for indulgence in ethnic insults (Malays should "return to the village"), disparagement (a "donkey's language"), defacement (the tar-brush campaigns in Sri Lanka), or defilement (stray pigs at a mosque, a cow's head in a temple, the alleged kicking of the Quran and Ramayana during religious processions in Ahmedabad).[51] All are signals for riot. In Bhiwandi (1984), Muslims accused the leader of the Hindu extremist Shiv Sena of insulting the Prophet; in response, they pulled down the sena's saffron flag and hoisted a green Islamic flag in its place.[52] A month earlier, they had garlanded the sena leader's picture with shoes.[53] In the prelude to an ethnic fight in Namibia that is reminiscent of the insults in Assam, Ovambo described Kavambo as "dumb and womanlike." Unused to money, they allegedly spent it on drink, whereas Kavambo replied that Ovambo were "donkeys," used to working too hard and unable to enjoy life.[54] After the so-called Ibo coup of January 1966, Ibo marchers in northern Nigeria displayed photographs of coup leaders and northern leaders killed in the coup, boasted of the death of the latter, and claimed "that the Ibos' time had now come."[55] The very same behavior preceded the anti-Jewish riot in Odessa (1905) six decades earlier: in the prevailing revolutionary environment, some Jewish demonstrators carried defaced portraits of the

51. See, e.g., Lambert, "Hindu-Muslim Riots," ch. 5; P.R. Rajgopal, *Communal Violence in India* (New Delhi: Uppal , 1987), pp. 83–84; Harold A. Gould, "Religion and Politics in a U.P. Constituency," in Donald Eugene Smith, ed., *South Asian Politics and Religion* (Princeton: Princeton University Press, 1966), pp. 51–73, at p. 62; Shah, "Communal Riots in Gujarat," p. 189.

52. Asghar Ali Engineer, *Bhiwandi-Bombay Riots: Analysis and Documentation* (Bombay: Institute of Islamic Studies, 1984), p. 22.

53. Ibid., p. 57.

54. Robert Gordon, "The Celebration of Ethnicity: A 'Tribal Fight' in a Namibian Mine Compound," in Brian M. du Toit, ed., *Ethnicity in Modern Africa* (Boulder, Colo.: Westview Press, 1978), p. 225.

55. M.J. Dent, "The Military and Politics: A Study of the Relation between the Army and the Political Process in Nigeria," in Melson and Wolpe, eds., *Nigeria: Modernization and the Politics of Communalism*, p. 383. For corroboration, see N.J. Miners, *The Nigerian Army, 1956–1966* (London: Methuen, 1971), pp. 200–01. In Dent's account, only coup leaders' photographs were displayed; in Miners's account, both were. Either way, northerners felt humiliated.

tsar and attempted to force outraged Russians to doff their caps.[56] In such settings, the procession carries the dangerous implication of status reversal; it is an expression of contempt.[57] If individuals are loath to express such sentiments, the procession obliterates the inhibition for the marchers, and the objects of the insults may infer they are held in contempt at other times, too, when people are not free to say so.

Processions also give more direct evidence of aggressive designs. They may invade areas viewed as being within the territory of another group.[58] The uncompromising quality of the procession is construed as evidence of intent to coerce other groups to accede to the demands that have been made. The presence of aggressive participants, perhaps carrying weapons,[59] and the minor incidents that occur along the way constitute confirmation of the organizing group's aggressive designs. The demonstration is a challenge — a challenge often accepted. If group status or ethnic policy is at stake, there is also an instrumental reason to outdo, in scale and intensity, the antagonist's demonstration of strength, either by counterdemonstration or by violent assault. And so, finally, the procession becomes the springboard to violence.

STRIKES WITH ETHNIC OVERTONES

From Kanpur in north India (1931) to Medan in north Sumatra (1994), many riots have been preceded by strikes with ethnic overtones.[60] The overtones were present either because of the ethnic composition of the strikers or because of the segmental character of the cause they espoused. These have mainly been general strikes for purposes of politi-

56. Robert Weinberg, "Anti-Jewish Violence and Revolution in Late Imperial Russia: Odessa, 1905" (paper presented to the Seminar on Riots and Pogroms, University of Washington, Seattle, April 1991), p. 13.

57. As William Ascher remarks, attitudes conducive to violence are legitimated by the "belief that the enemy holds the ingroup in contempt." William Ascher, "The Moralism of Attitudes Supporting Intergroup Violence," *Political Psychology* 7, no. 3 (September 1986): 403–25, at p. 417.

58. See, e.g., Government of India, *Report of the Commission of Inquiry on Communal Disturbances: Jainpur and Suchetpur (District Gorakhpur-U.P.) (September 24–25, 1967)* (New Delhi: Government Printer, 1969), pp. 10–20, 31.

59. The anti-Chinese riot in Jakarta (1967) was preceded by a large, aggressive Chinese funeral procession, in which bicycle chains were waved. Mackie, "Anti-Chinese Outbreaks in Indonesia, 1959–68," p. 123.

60. See Sandra B. Freitag, *Collective Action and Community: Public Arenas and the Emergence of Communalism in North India* (Berkeley and Los Angeles: University of California Press, 1989), p. 244; *Far Eastern Economic Review*, April 28, 1994, pp. 14–15.

cal protest. Labor disputes have less frequently been involved. Strikes are the prelude to violence because of the air of expectancy they create and the participants they render available, on the one side, and the resistance they encounter and the inconvenience they generate, on the other. If the strike is effective, it is likely to move on to a new level of (usually violent) activity as the strikers sense their opportunities. If it is ineffective, the reason may well be that ethnic antagonists have been provoked to counteraction.

If a strike closes down schools and businesses, an immediate effect is to free for mass action numbers of people who might otherwise be engaged. Mass meetings are better attended than before, and extreme suggestions receive an unprecedented hearing. Success in closing down the town encourages the organizers to go one step further and puts the onus on them to do something dramatic. To participants, the closing of business enterprises is likely to appear as the beginning, rather than the end, of mass action.

This was the case in Guyana (1962), where rallies were synchronized with a general strike. The strike was effective in Georgetown, the predominantly Afro-Guyanese capital. Leaders and followers at the rallies flirted tantalizingly with the prospect of violence until the strike turned into a round of assaults, burnings, and lootings.[61]

The same sequence occurred in Ahmedabad (1969). Groups of Hindus moved from shop to shop, asking owners to close in protest at the stoning of a temple. By early afternoon most shops were closed; schools closed later, and evening movies were then canceled. "By the afternoon itself a grim atmosphere of suspense had overtaken the city."[62] The closure was seen as the forerunner of bigger things, and indeed it was.

The general strike creates an environment of abnormality. The daily routine is dramatically overthrown, and conventional norms and restraints are expected to be inoperative. The prevailing equilibrium,

61. See Government of Great Britain, *Report of the Commission of Inquiry into Disturbances in British Guiana in February 1962*, Colon. No. 354 (London, 1962), pp. 25–51. For other views and accounts, see Peter Simms, *Trouble in Guyana* (London: Allen and Unwin, 1966), ch. 19; Peter Newman, *British Guiana: Problems of Cohesion in an Immigrant Society* (London: Oxford University Press, 1964), pp. 91–95; Cheddi Jagan, *The West on Trial: My Fight for Guyana's Freedom* (London: Joseph, 1966), ch. 12; *Sunday Gleaner* (Kingston, Jamaica), March 18, 1962, p. 7; *Daily Gleaner*, March 19, 1962, p. 1; Janet Jagan, "What Happened in British Guiana?" *Sunday Gleaner*, March 11, 1962, p. 7; Peter D'Aguiar, "What Happened in B.G.: The Truth of It All," ibid., April 1, 1962, p. 4.

62. Shah, "Communal Riots in Gujarat," p. 193.

symbolized by ongoing public activity, is replaced by an exciting silence, an exceptional moment which seems to call for exceptional deeds. Such a mood is captured in the exclamation of a Guyanese rioter: "'I can dead today,' meaning that he was desperate enough to lay down his life for his cause."[63] This anticipatory atmosphere is consistent with a hypothesized "completion tendency" in aggression, a propensity for an actor who has been thwarted to carry through the response sequence to a conclusion involving the infliction of injury on the frustrating agent.[64]

The general strike makes this consummation likely by confirming the reduction of risk. If, despite all the social and internal inhibitions on the expression of anger, the crowd has succeeded in bringing business to a halt, it may also succeed in injuring its enemies. Why turn back now? Before the 1962 Guyanese riot, one of the leaders demonstrated a perceptive understanding of this logic in a speech to a night rally: "All I can tell you is this, that it is no sense taking part in this explosion which has happened at this moment if you are going to peter out or turn back halfway. You have to see it through."[65] The crowd, too, probably saw itself as having already traveled "halfway," which implied that there was unfinished business but that satisfaction was in sight.

Not all general strikes reach this stage. Many meet resistance. The Muslim *bandh* (work stoppage) organized in the Indian city of Ferozabad, Uttar Pradesh (1972), to protest the reorganization of the Aligarh Muslim University, was resented by Hindus, who planned for it in advance.[66] Hindus mobilized for action, and a small Muslim demonstration met with stern police measures, culminating in the killing of several Muslims. The same night, following the stabbing of a Hindu, the police and Hindu crowds jointly attacked Muslim areas of the city, burning, beating, and looting.

Strikes for ethnic objectives share with processions a number of provocative characteristics. First is their mass character, which constitutes an expression of the intensity of group feeling and thus of group

63. Government of Great Britain, *Report of the Commission of Inquiry into Disturbances in British Guiana*, p. 37.

64. "Inflicting injury on the anger instigator is the goal response completing the aggressive response sequence. . . . As long as the anger lasts and the individual is set to aggress, he does not obtain 'completion' until he sees that he has injured his frustrater or that someone else has done so." Leonard Berkowitz, *Aggression: A Social-Psychological Analysis* (New York: McGraw-Hill, 1962), p. 221 (emphasis omitted).

65. Government of Great Britain, *Report of the Commission of Inquiry into Disturbances in British Guiana*, p. 28.

66. Suneet Chopra and N.K. Singh, "Ferozabad: Anatomy of a Riot," *Economic and Political Weekly*, August 19, 1972, pp. 1711, 1713. The bandh was called to oppose a new

threat. Related to this is the coercive quality of strikes. Their aim is to employ pressure to affect the outcome of disputed issues. The strike may thus be viewed as an indication of a group's determination to work its will on others. The strike, like the procession, magnifies the importance of whatever ethnic issues prompt it, and its coercive aspect activates fears of group subordination. A strike for ethnic objectives therefore stands a good chance of meeting with violent resistance.

There is another reason for violent ethnic resistance to strikes. Whether or not the protest is overtly ethnic, ethnic divisions may be the basis on which approval or disapproval is conferred on the strike plan. The organizers of the strike may meet with refusals in enforcing the order to close shop. This resistance may then become the focal point for the initial violent incidents. In Ahmedabad (1985), when Muslims refused to close shop in response to a Hindu bandh protesting job reservations for backward castes, Hindus attacked.[67] In Hyderabad (1979), Hindus refused to join a Muslim strike.[68] In Assam (1972), a month of anti-Bengali rioting was begun by the refusal of shopkeepers to comply with an Assamese bandh protesting the state assembly's resolution to establish a separate Bengali university in the Bengali area of Cachar.[69] Violence occurred in Lebanon (1958) when the opposition called a general strike to protest the murder of an opposition leader. The order to close was enforced on recalcitrant Christian shopkeepers in Tripoli, producing three days of riots that accelerated Lebanon's slide into civil war.[70] Much the same sequence of resistance was repeated in Calcutta (1946), Delhi (1966), Andhra Pradesh (1979), and Mauritania (1966).[71]

The riot in Penang (1967) shows clearly why attempts to enforce a general strike commonly produce ethnic violence. The occasion, as we saw in Chapter 7, was the devaluation of the old Malayan dollar, fol-

---

federal law opening the university, traditionally a Muslim enclave, to students and teachers of all communities. Those who organized the bandh saw "the attack on the minority status of the university . . . as somehow a threat to themselves," although "their children have little or no hope of ever getting there." Ibid., p. 1711.

67. Ghosh, *Communal Riots in India*, pp. 162–65.

68. *Far Eastern Economic Review*, December 7, 1979, p. 27.

69. *Statesman* (Calcutta), October 7, 1972, p. 1.

70. See George E. Kirk, *Contemporary Arab Politics* (New York: Praeger, 1961), pp. 127–28; Fahim I. Qubain, *Crisis in Lebanon* (Washington, D.C.: Middle East Institute, 1961), ch. 5.

71. Lambert, "Hindu-Muslim Riots," ch. 6; *Keesing's Contemporary Archives*, April 30–May 7, 1966, pp. 21368–69; Ghosh, *Communal Riots in India*, pp. 119–20; Alfred G. Gerteiny, *Mauritania* (New York: Praeger, 1967), pp. 151–52.

lowing the devaluation of the British pound, to which the Malayan currency had been tied.[72] The largely Chinese Labor Party, possibly thinking it had at last found an ethnically neutral economic issue on which to attack the government, sponsored a *hartal* (work stoppage).[73] The party sought to enforce its writ by ordering shops and hawkers to close. With Chinese vendors, there was success, although coercion was necessary. But party activists ran into difficulty when they ordered Malay hawkers to stop work. Resisting the Chinese orders, Malays fought back and then started killing. In a divided society, it is not easy for a general strike to become general. The protest issue gives way to another: whether to take orders from ethnic strangers.

The ethnic division of labor also makes it difficult for any strike to cross ethnic lines. Because certain sectors of employment and certain trade unions tend to be associated with particular ethnic groups or the political parties of those groups, a strike that affects particular sectors or unions will be regarded as arising out of the concerns of the ethnic group represented in them.[74]

Ethnic specialization by trade means that the most ordinary labor dispute can result in violence. In Burma (1930), dockworkers were Indians, mainly Telugu.[75] When they struck for higher wages, Burman replace-

72. See Nancy L. Snider, "What Happened in Penang?" *Asian Survey* 8, no. 12 (December 1968): 960–75. See also Milton J. Esman, *Administration and Development in Malaysia* (Ithaca: Cornell University Press, 1972), pp. 34–36. I am also drawing here on my own interviews in Penang in early 1968.

73. The leaflet announcing this hartal gives evidence of the belief that a widespread popular grievance had been discovered. Hartal Action Committee, "Take Action, Start Hartal" (leaflet, November 23, 1967).

74. Called by some 17 unions representing workers in government departments to protest the failure of the colonial government to grant cost-of-living wage increases, the Nigerian general strike of 1945 might have appeared to transcend ethnic differences among Nigerians. James S. Coleman, *Nigeria: Background to Nationalism* (Berkeley and Los Angeles: University of California Press, 1958), pp. 258–59. Nevertheless, the unrepresentative ethnic composition of the striking unions meant that the strike produced ethnic resentments. The strike was inspired by the Ibo leader, Nnamdi Azikiwe. Few northerners were in the occupations affected, and so their participation was negligible. From their point of view, the strike was "brought about by Southerners and, more specifically, by Ibo." Leonard Plotnicov, "An Early Nigerian Civil Disturbance: The 1945 Hausa-Ibo Riot in Jos," *Journal of Modern African Studies* 9, no. 2 (August 1971): 297–305. As the strike occurred immediately following the protracted sacrifices of World War II, further shortages of essential goods created by the long strike were acutely resented. Ibid., p. 299. An anti-Ibo riot in Jos occurred three months later, and it would be stretching matters to regard the strike as a precipitant. But memories of the strike and the Ibo role in it — one of several signs of growing Ibo prominence in national politics — undoubtedly contributed to the riot.

75. See Government of Burma, *Report on the Disturbances in Rangoon during May, 1930*, reprinted in E.L.F. Andrew, *Indian Labour in Rangoon* (Calcutta: Oxford University

ments were hired. Two weeks after it began, the strike was settled. The Indians reported to work, but so did Burmans with whom no retrenchment agreement had been reached. The predictable clash quickly spread throughout Rangoon, involving Burmans and Telugus with no connection to the wharf. Most of the time, an ethnic division of labor keeps groups from impinging on each other, but in a strike it has the opposite effect.[76]

DIVISIVE ELECTIONS

As we saw in Chapter 7, political party rivalries everywhere give rise to a certain amount of interparty violence. Many riots we have already examined in this chapter, too, have had an element of party rivalry about

---

Press, 1933), pp. 279–92; Maurice Collis, *Trials in Burma*, 2d ed. (London: Faber and Faber, 1945), pp. 138–60; Usha Mahajani, *The Role of Indian Minorities in Burma and Malaya* (Bombay: Vora, 1960), pp. 72–79.

76. In Guyana, too, the division of labor and the partisan sympathies of the trade unions merged labor and ethnic issues so as to convert strikes into riots. In 1963, a strike was called by certain trade unions to protest a labor relations bill that would have conferred broad powers on the government to decide which union in a particular industry to recognize. This bill was seen by the established unions as an attempt by the governing, mainly Indian, People's Progressive Party to gain control over parts of organized labor — in particular, the sugar workers, who, although mostly Indian, had been represented by a union that consistently opposed the PPP. A well-organized, 80-day strike ensued. At various points, it threatened to deteriorate into an ethnic mêlée. Afro-Guyanese attacked Indian strikebreakers; Indians in rural areas attacked union leaders; and, at one point, after an antigovernment protest in Georgetown had resulted in police firing, Creole mobs attacked Indian passersby. The opposition parties supported the strike out of motives similar to those that moved them to mass action a year earlier. For accounts of the 1963 general strike, see Jagan, *The West on Trial*, ch. 13; Anthony Verrier, "The Need for Statesmanship in British Guiana," *The World Today*, August 1963, pp. 352–58; Trades Union Council, *The Freedom Strikers: An Account of the 1963 T.U.C. General Strike* (Georgetown, n.d.).

The strike ended in July 1963, but it was followed by another in 1964. But this time positions were reversed. The PPP-affiliated sugar workers' union began a strike for recognition as the bargaining agent on the sugar estates. A campaign was begun to prevent workers from reporting to their jobs. Although some Indian canefield workers stayed away, many of the Afro-Guyanese who staff the sugar factories continued to grind the cane and thwart the strike. This time ethnic violence grew more widespread. Bombings and burnings were common in the countryside. Incidents in one village bred reprisals in another. In all, some 15,000 people left or were forced out of villages inhabited by a majority of the opposite ethnic group. The ethnic division of labor and the ethno-political affiliations of the trade unions converted a strike into a series of riots. For accounts of the 1964 violence, see Jagan, *The West on Trial*, ch. 17; "Jagan's Bizarre Revolution," *Guiana Times News Magazine*, 3d quarter, 1964; Trades Union Council, *The Communist Martyr Makers: The Account of the Struggle for Free Trade Unionism in British Guiana in 1964* (Georgetown, n.d.).

them, whether or not parties were active organizers of violence. The initial Tamil targets in Sri Lanka (1956 and 1958) were leaders of the Federal Party. The southern parties' tour of northern Nigeria precipitated violence there in 1953. In Malaysia (1945, 1967, and 1969), the Chinese whose activities prompted violence were all identified with non-Malay political parties. Kurds who attacked Turkomens in Kirkuk (1959) were identified with the Communists; their victims were allied with their party opponents. The procession that led to violence in Singapore (1964) took place against a background of demands made by one ethnic party on a government controlled by another. Karachi (1965) followed in the wake of an electoral victory celebration, Pathans supporting one of the contestants, Urdu-speakers the other. The Karachi-Hyderabad riot (1972) found Sindhis, generally supporters of the ruling party, on one side, and Urdu-speakers, supporters of the opposition, on the other. The common tendency of different ethnic groups to support opposing political parties provides a situation conducive to the mingling of ethnic and partisan violence.

In a narrower class of cases, events connected to electoral rivalries precipitate ethnic rioting. All are the result of the identity between particular ethnic groups and party loyalties that is so common in severely divided societies. The events are significant because group fortunes, not just party futures, are affected by the conformity of electoral results to demographic facts or by their perverse failure so to conform.

Three clear patterns can be identified. In the first, identification of groups with parties makes election results predictable in advance. Group members engage in violence to enhance their chance of success, sometimes by driving ethnic strangers out in the course of the violence. In the second, a party or its following may attempt to reduce the ascriptive element of party affiliation, in order to overcome electoral disadvantages deriving from it. This produces a violent reaction. In the third, an ethnic party may try to capitalize on or render permanent its ascriptive advantages, provoking violence. The first phenomenon I call a *preemptive strike*; the second, a *breakout*; and the third, a *lock-in* (Table 2 depicts the distribution of groups and of party support that underlies breakout and lock-in violence).

THE PREEMPTIVE STRIKE

A large voting-age population consisting of members of one ethnic group promises to provide its party with victory in an impending election. If antipathies are strong, that alone may be sufficient to precipitate violence by their ethnic opponents.[77] (If it is not, further polarization may be called for, as we saw in the case of the Bharatiya Janata Party in India.) Long-standing hostilities between Tiv and Jukun in Nigeria are directly related to local electoral prospects. In the 1960s, the two neighbors adhered to different political parties, and they fought at that time. By the 1990s, they were again opposed in party politics. The serious violence of 1990 and 1991–93 concerned electoral control. Jukun had lost a 1987 election to a Tiv-Hausa coalition. In 1990 and 1991, violence directed against the more numerous Tiv, considered immigrants by the Jukun, was intended to reduce Tiv numbers in the face of impending elections, which ultimately were won by Jukun after many Tiv were displaced.[78] The Assamese riots of 1979–83 had similar origins: a growing number of Bengali Muslim immigrants who threatened to dominate the electoral rolls. Plans to hold elections without purging the rolls of immigrants infuriated Assamese, who proceeded to use their own violent methods against the Bengali Muslims.[79] By creating refugees, violence can purge the rolls.

THE BREAKOUT

Breaking out involves an effort to put the party system on a nonascriptive footing or to broaden the base of an ethnic party by expanding its clientele to include members of other groups in a new multiethnic coalition. Either way, the attempt threatens the interests of the remaining ethnic parties.

The first of these two strategies of breaking out, exemplified by Guinea (1956 and 1958) and Ghana (at various times, 1954–56),[80] may be employed by an emergent single party confronted by ethnic holdouts.

77. For the role of elections and black officeholding in precipitating antiblack riots in the United States south, see Joel Williamson, *A Rage for Order: Black/White Relations in the American South since Emancipation* (New York: Oxford University Press, 1986), pp. 127, 131, 143–44.

78. For opposing versions, see Ter-Rumun Avav and Mson Myegba, *The Dream to Conquer: Story of Jukun-Tiv Conflict* (Makurdi, Nigeria: Onaivi, 1992), pp. 9–44; Shekarau Angyu Masa-Ibi, *The Story of the Jukun/Tiv Crisis: Why and How It Happened* (n.p.: n.p., 1992), pp. 10–20, 52, 59, 64–65. See also *Daily Times* (Lagos), December 26, 1991, pp. 1, 12; *Africa Research Bulletin*, February 1–29, 1992, pp. 10471–72. For the background enmity, see Kurt Maier, "Nigeria: Eternal Enmities," *Africa Report* 37, no. 3 (May–June 1992): 47–48.

79. See Arun Shourie, "Assam Elections: Come What May," *India Today*, May 15, 1983, pp. 54–66. See also B.G. Verghese et al., *Situation in Assam (February, 1980): Report of a Study Team* (New Delhi: Gandhi Peace Foundation, mimeo., 1980), pp. 3–8.

80. On Guinea, see Ruth Schachter Morgenthau, *Political Parties in French-Speaking West Africa* (Oxford: Clarendon Press, 1964), pt. 6; Jean Suret-Canale, *La République de*

TABLE 2

PARADIGMS OF ELECTORAL VIOLENCE:
BREAKING OUT AND LOCKING IN

(Groups = A, B, C)

Type	Group Support for Ethnic Parties	Precipitant
Breakout[a]	A = 50% of voters; all support Party A B = 40% of voters; all support Party B C = 10% of voters; all support Party C	Party B tries to break out of its minority position by becoming multiethnic, provoking a violent reaction.
Pure Lock-In	A = 60% of voters; all support Party A B = 40% of voters; all support Party B	Election confirms Party A's dominance. Group B or Party B reacts violently.
Artificial Lock-In	A = 60% of voters but only two-thirds support Party A; one-third of Group A joins a coalition with Party B B = 40% of voters; all support Party B, which, coalescing with one-third of As, has 60% support	Election confirms the "illegitimate" exclusion of Party A from government. Group A or Party A reacts violently.

[a]Note that the first form of breaking out, by a multiethnic party seeking to become universal, has been omitted.

The holdouts are particular groups — actually, in Ghana and Guinea, segments of ethnic groups — who insist on expressing ethnic interests through their own party. In Guinea, the Fulani had two such parties, though some Fulani supported Sékou Touré's ruling party instead. In Ghana, Kwame Nkrumah's Convention People's Party was deprived for a time of its prized unanimity by the recalcitrance of the National Liberation Movement in Ashanti and the Northern People's Party, representing the mainly Muslim north. On several occasions in both countries, the holdout groups came into violent conflict with the panethnic uniformity sought by the ruling parties.

Guinée (Paris: Editions Sociales, 1970), ch. 3. Unfortunately, there is no complete account of the actual violence. But see Guinée Française, Ministère de l'Intérieur, *La Vérité sur les Evenements de Guinée: Livre Blanc* (mimeo., n.d. [1958?]); *Le Monde*, May 7, 1958, p. 4; May 9, 1958, p. 2. On Ghana, see Martin L. Kilson, "Authoritarian and Single-Party Tendencies in African Politics," *World Politics* 15, no. 2 (January 1963): 273–76. For the background in Ashanti, see Dennis Austin, *Politics in Ghana 1946–1960* (London: Oxford University Press, 1964), ch. 6; R.J.A.R. Rathbone, "Opposition in Ghana: The National Liberation Movement," in University of London, Institute of Commonwealth Studies, *Collected Seminar Papers on Opposition in the New African States, October 1967–March 1968* (mimeo., n.d.), pp. 29–54. For discussions on Ghana, I am also indebted to Richard Crook.

The second strategy of breaking out is really a variant of the first. It is used when an ethnic party, typically a minority party, seeks to become multiethnic by capturing the ethnic following of another party. The purpose is to escape the adverse consequences of ethnic demography by forsaking ethnic exclusivism, either for a new, nonascriptive appeal or simply a wider ethnic base. This was the precipitant in Mauritius (1968), described in Chapter 6. The mainly Creole Parti Mauricien had run some Indian Muslim candidates, defeating candidates of the acknowledged Muslim party, in the 1967 election. Violence broke out during the election and later, as Muslims affiliated with the Muslim party attacked Creoles. Sierra Leone (1968) might be described in the same terms. Mende resisted the efforts of Temne party workers to pressure them to shift their allegiance to the party identified with Temne and other northerners.[81]

Breakout violence flows from the expansive tendencies of one of the parties in the system, motivated minimally by the aim of avoiding its minority position and building a winning coalition or maximally by the aim of building a one-party state. The violence arises out of the competition of more than one party for a single ethnic clientele. More often than not, it is preelection violence, the result of coercive electoral tactics or clashes between rival party workers.

THE LOCK-IN

By contrast, locking in is a noncompetitive process. Ascriptive party allegiances propel electorally stronger ethnic groups to power, excluding others. The violence, typically postelectoral, emanates from those who are locked into a minority position.

In most polities, ethnically divided or not, there is an ascriptive element to party support. Most parties can count on a fairly stable core of adherents. Parties compete at the margins for the less committed, and from time to time erosion may also occur in the more stable sectors of a party's clientele, producing realignments. Nevertheless, much of what stability there is in political life derives, paradoxically, from the fluidity of party allegiances, in the short run at the margins and in the longer run at the core. If there are substantial numbers at the margins, for whose support parties compete, there is the prospect of alternation in office that keeps parties attached to the electoral process.

Much of the instability of ethnically divided polities derives from the

81. Walter L. Barrows, "Local Level Politics in Sierra Leone: Alliances in Kenema District" (Ph.D. diss., Yale University, 1971), pp. 334–51.

rigidity of party allegiances. As ethnic polarization takes hold, it effects fundamental alterations in the stability of party allegiances, reducing the margins, enlarging and firming up the core of adherents. Since ascriptive affiliations increasingly govern party allegiance, the election is not a mechanism of choice among competing alternatives. Voting across ethnic lines becomes uncommon. Because the system is ascriptive, the results are more permanent than those in competitive systems. Save for the generally glacial changes in the ethnic composition of the electorate stemming from ethnically differential rates of natural increase or of migration, the result of one election is likely to hold for the next. The ascriptive element of party support, present in most systems, is thus carried to an extreme. Competition becomes a chimera. As this is perceived, the loser forecasts its continuing inability to recoup its losses and ride to power. Ascription thus exaggerates party rivalry while simultaneously eliminating party competition. The prospect of exclusion from power raises the stakes of the election that produces this result and so renders the election — or its aftermath, the foreshadowing of the next — a fitting occasion to resort to violence.

Locking in can take one of two forms, which we may designate *pure* and *artificial*. The pure form refers to the results of ethnic polarization, generally where there are two major ethnic groups or blocs, each represented by its own party. Because party and ethnicity become interchangeable, the election results are a faithful, but for minorities adverse, reflection of the demographic facts. If one group wins a majority of seats, while the other can only win a minority, apparently in perpetuity, demography has produced a pure lock-in effect. The artificial variant occurs in either of two circumstances: (1) a majority group has spread its support over more than one party, thereby preventing it from gaining a majority of seats, or (2) the electoral system operates to convert a majority of votes into a minority of seats. Either way, after the election, a group finds itself locked into a minority position whereas it "ought to have" sufficient strength to enjoy a majority position. One lock-in is pure because it mirrors the numerical situation; the other is artificial because it contradicts the demographic facts. Both are seen to be illegitimate, the first by a minority group, the second by a majority group.

If the artificial lock-in is due to intraethnic party competition which effects a reduction of group strength relative to others, it may be susceptible to alteration by unifying activities solely within the locked-in group. The pure lock-in, on the other hand, may seem more difficult to escape because it results from unmitigated ascriptive voting. In practice, however, the hard work needed to reunify subgroups into a single party is less promising of success than might be imagined; and, on the other side, the purity of the pure lock-in is not always pristine: ethnic group A versus ethnic group B is less probable in real ethnic life than ethnic amalgam A versus ethnic amalgam B. These complexities make it impossible to say either that the artificial lock-in can be broken by artificial countermeasures or that the pure lock-in can never be broken because it is rooted in a clear we-they division. In the final analysis, artificial lock-ins seem more explosive because, as distortions of demography, they are seen to be less legitimate.

Several riots described earlier occurred in situations that approach the pure form of lock-in. Mauritius (1965) is one. With independence approaching, the minority Parti Mauricien was locked in and turned toward disruptive strategies, producing violence. Malaysia (1969), described earlier, may be considered the result of a local lock-in where the non-Malay majority in the state of Selangor finally seemed to have overcome its internal divisions and converted its demographic advantage into a party majority. Malays were locked in. Sierra Leone (1968), while also a product of the breakout strategy of the party of the Temne and other northerners, can also be viewed from the Mende standpoint as a case of being locked into a minority position. Likewise, Luluabourg (1959), in Zaire, can be considered as deriving from the fear of the Lulua minority that, despite its earlier electoral success, the superior numbers of the Luba majority would eventually assert themselves. In the pure lock-in, a rough congruence between the numerical strength of an ethnic group and its electoral strength places the losing party in what it regards as an intolerable and apparently permanent position.

Artificial locking in, as I have said, may result from intraethnic-party competition on only one side. This asymmetry in competition weakens the power of a group that indulges in it. Simultaneously, it opens the possibility of interethnic coalitions. If, however, such a coalition locks a majority group into a minority position, the likely result is violence.

Such an exclusion from power brought a violent response in Zanzibar (1961). Zanzibar is an overwhelmingly African territory, containing an influential Arab minority.[82] Several circumstances combined to give the

82. See generally Michael Lofchie, *Zanzibar: Background to Revolution* (Berkeley and Los Angeles: University of California Press, 1965); Lofchie, "Party Conflict in Zanzibar," *Journal of Modern African Studies* 1, no. 2 (June 1963): 185–207; Lofchie, "Zanzibar," in James S. Coleman and Carl G. Rosberg, Jr., eds., *Political Parties and National Integration in Tropical Africa* (Berkeley and Los Angeles: University of California Press, 1964); Government of Great Britain, *Report of a Commission of Inquiry into Disturbances in Zanzibar during June 1961.*

Arabs power far out of proportion to their numbers. Traditional rulers of the islands of Zanzibar and Pemba, the Arabs were landholders who could count on the political deference of African tenants. Arabs also had an early foothold in the nationalist movement, and the Arab-led Zanzibar Nationalist Party (ZNP) was the best financed and organized political party. Zanzibar Africans were divided into two, quite distinct, often hostile groups: migrants from the mainland or their descendants and Shirazis, putative indigenes of the islands. This division was reflected in party allegiances. The Afro-Shirazi Party (ASP) drew on the support of mainlanders, while the Zanzibar and Pemba People's Party (ZPPP) had Shirazi support.

The first election of 1961, held in January, produced a stalemate. With 40 percent of the vote, the ASP won ten of the twenty-two seats; the ZNP, with 36 percent of the vote, won nine seats; and the ZPPP, with 17 percent of the vote, won three. Intra-African divisions asserted themselves immediately: two of the victorious ZPPP candidates aligned with the ZNP, while the third went to the ASP. Each side thus had eleven seats, and neither could form a government. Another election was scheduled for June. To avoid a new stalemate, a twenty-third constituency was carved out.

For this election, the ZNP and ZPPP formed a coalition in advance, maximizing the strength of both parties by a no-contest agreement. Again the ASP won ten seats. Again the ZPPP won three. But this time the ZNP also won ten seats, and the combined total of the ZNP-ZPPP coalition was sufficient to form a government.

Violence began quickly. Accusations of Arab electoral fraud led to fights by gangs associated with the parties in Zanzibar Town. These outbreaks were contained during the night, but the following day, when the election results became widely known, Africans in rural areas murdered Arabs who had the misfortune to be located there.

As long as the African vote was divided, whereas the Arab vote was not, the attempt of the ASP to win a majority of seats was futile.[83] The pattern of party alignments had prevented the dominant share of power from being allocated to Africans, many of whom saw themselves as more legitimate occupants of Zanzibar than its Arab rulers. Some of them

83. A commission of inquiry into the riots later estimated that the Arab party, the ZNP, obtained as much as 70 percent of its vote in June from Africans, principally in rural areas. Government of Great Britain, *Report of a Commission of Inquiry into Disturbances in Zanzibar during June 1961*, p. 15. The spread of African votes among three parties was especially weakening and perhaps especially galling to the ASP.

undertook to rectify this situation by a coup d'état less than three years later.

A similar situation prevailed in the pre-independence Punjab, a Muslim-majority province of India.[84] As the African vote was split in Zanzibar, the Muslim vote was split in Punjab. The Muslim League emerged from the 1946 election with a plurality of 79 seats out of a total of 175. This opened the way for a coalition government of the remaining parties, consisting of the Unionists (a small party with nine Muslim seats), the Congress Party, representing Hindus, and the Akali Dal of the Sikhs. Muslim opinion was outraged.[85] Feeling cheated, the Muslim League set in motion its paramilitary force, eventually forcing the resignation of the coalition. The League was still unable to form a government, but Sikhs and Hindus, fearful that it might, demonstrated against the possibility. When they did, Muslims took the offensive, bringing with them "murder, loot and arson on a scale never witnessed before in the Punjab."[86]

In both cases, voting patterns produced multiethnic coalitions that locked party representatives of a majority ethnic group into an unacceptable minority status.[87] The split vote among Africans in Zanzibar

84. See Lambert, "Hindu-Muslim Riots," pp. 197–98; Penderel Moon, *Divide and Quit* (Berkeley and Los Angeles: University of California Press, 1962), pp. 71–81.

85. "In a united India, the wily Hindus would always succeed in this manner in attaching to themselves a section of the Muslims and using them to defeat the larger interests of the community." Moon, *Divide and Quit*, p. 72.

86. Ibid., p. 78.

87. The same phenomenon very nearly produced the same result in Trinidad (1956). For the rumors and fears prevalent at the time of the 1956 election, see the *New York Times*, September 20, 1956, p. 9; September 23, 1956, p. 17; September 26, 1956, p. 14. For the background to the election, see Ivar Oxaal, *Black Intellectuals Come to Power: The Rise of Creole Nationalism in Trinidad and Tobago* (Cambridge, Mass.: Schenkman, 1968), pp. 115–16. The election campaign of 1956 was interspersed with acts of violence and threats to the safety of leading politicians. Afro-Trinidadians formed a clear majority. The Afro-Trinidadian fear was that the newly formed People's National Movement might not attract sufficient votes to defeat the more established Indian party, the People's Democratic Party. This fear was compounded by the divisive effect of the publicly expressed opposition of the Catholic hierarchy to the PNM. Had the Afro-Trinidadian vote been badly split between the PNM and a more conservative Afro-Trinidadian party, the PDP might have won the election. But, in the event, that vote was not so badly divided, the PNM obtained seats enough to form a government, the Indians were defeated, and the threat of violence subsided in the face of a surprising degree of Afro-Trinidadian unity. In subsequent elections, similar unity was manifested, the "Indian threat" was contained, and each election was less violent than the one before. Trinidad suggests that some intraethnic divisions manifested in party competition may be easier to paper over for the sake of ethnic unity than others are.

reflected a long-standing subethnic cleavage. For many Shirazis, the traditional ties between Arabs and Africans survived the newer conflicts
between mainland Africans and Arabs, resulting in Shirazi votes not
merely for the ZPPP but for the ZNP as well. Furthermore, in both
Zanzibar and Punjab, there were leadership incentives to maintain the
split rather than forge a new unity. Ethnic arithmetic placed leaders of the
smaller African and Muslim parties in great demand by their respective
Arab and Hindu/Sikh counterparts, who needed them to be able to rule
at all. Why would such leaders give up an assured swing position for the
dubious honor of submerging their small organization in a larger homogeneous party? Hence the artificial lock-in could not be broken by an
appeal to ethnic affinities. If anything, the stubbornness of these artificial
divisions made the unfavorable position of the Zanzibar ASP and the
Punjabi Muslim League *more* intolerable, for the predicament of both
Africans and Muslims was attributable to the treachery of splitters within
their own ethnic ranks. Exactly such angry sentiments were in fact
expressed in both cases.[88]

It is not intraethnic competition per se that is important, but the asymmetry. If both sides were weakened more or less equally by intragroup
competition, the distortions produced by the election would be allevi-
ated. Nor is asymmetrical intraethnic-party competition the sole source
of electoral distortions that produce an artificial lock-in. The electoral
system itself can yield such a result, as it did in Guyana in 1961. With less
than a majority of the electorate, Indians, represented by the People's
Progressive Party, managed twice to win a majority of seats on only a
plurality of votes.[89] Afro-Guyanese were concentrated in urban areas.
This clustering permitted more PPP candidates to win more seats under
the first-past-the-post system than would have been possible had Afro-
Guyanese been more evenly distributed. In 1961, the PPP won nearly

88. The principal organizer of the coup of 1964 in Zanzibar refers to the 1961 election
with considerable bitterness. The ZPPP leadership comes in for a good deal of abuse (the
word "stooge" recurs in his account); and in planning the revolt, special pains were taken
to insure that the "troops" were overwhelmingly mainlander Africans because of the unreliability of the Shirazi. John Okello, *Revolution in Zanzibar* (Nairobi: East African
Publishing House, 1967). After the coalition government excluding the Muslim League was
formed in the Punjab, the Unionist leader, "Khizar, despite his past record and reputation,
was now represented as a traitor, clinging to power and office without regard for Muslim
interests." Moon, *Divide and Quit*, p. 72.
89. Government of British Guiana, *Report on the General Election of Members of the
Legislative Assembly* (Georgetown, 1964).

twice as many seats as the Afro-Guyanese-supported People's National Congress (PNC), on nearly the same number of votes. The feeling widely shared among Afro-Guyanese was that a majority of voters (counting PNC allies) had been shut out of power by an electoral system that permitted a minority to elect a government representing one ethnic group. The 1962 riot described earlier was in this sense a delayed response to the election of the previous year.

BREAKING OUT AND LOCKING IN:
ASPECTS OF POSITIONAL VIOLENCE

Breaking out and locking in are two sides of a coin. Activity construed as breaking out creates the risk that others will see themselves as locked in by that activity. Conversely, an ethnic party that is locked in has clear enough incentives to break out, but whether that is a feasible strategy depends on whether a new clientele is potentially available for recruitment to the expanded party. If the possibility of breaking out of a lock-in were present in a wide range of cases, then being locked in would not be so desperately provocative (and violence-producing) a fate. It is the rigidification of group and party boundaries that renders lock-in effects so commonly possible in ethnically divided polities.

The close relations of these phenomena are illustrated in textbook fashion by the sequence of rioting in the Congo Republic, within a span of three years the scene of several variations on these themes.[90] In the 1950s, Congolese politics had begun to revolve around two parties, each representing a major ethnic bloc. Each feared a lock-in by the other, and that is what developed. The road to that result was strewn with mutilated bodies.

Gradually, the main contenders became the Mbochi of the north and the Bakongo of the south. Though more numerous, the Bakongo started from behind in electoral politics, for two reasons. The first was their

90. See generally Jean-Michel Wagret, *Histoire et Sociologie Politiques de la République du Congo (Brazzaville)* (Paris: Librairie Générale de Droit et de Jurisprudence, 1963), pp. 63–100; René Gauze, *The Politics of Congo-Brazzaville,* trans. Virginia Thompson and Richard Adloff (Stanford: Hoover Institution Press, 1973), pp. 65–70; Gwendolen M. Carter, *Independence for Africa* (New York: Praeger, 1960), pp. 90–95; Virginia Thompson and Richard Adloff, *The Emerging States of French Equatorial Africa* (Stanford: Stanford University Press, 1960), pp. 477–92; John A. Ballard, "Four Equatorial States," in Gwendolen M. Carter, ed., *National Unity and Regionalism in Eight African States* (Ithaca: Cornell University Press, 1966), pp. 244–53, 314–19.

attachment to Matsouanism, a protest movement founded by a Bakongo
Christian, André Matsoua. Matsoua had died in prison in 1942, but his
followers, cultivating a belief in his divinity, refused to accept his death.
The cult of Matsoua's supernatural influence kept the Bakongo apart
from political developments. "At election times, the Bakongo voted — if
at all — for André Matsoua, writing his name on their ballots in the place
of candidates put up by the regularly constituted political parties. By
their persistence in voting for a dead man, the Bakongo left the political field open to . . . the two other main . . . groups . . . the Vili and
Mbochi."[91] The second reason for the disadvantageous position of the
Bakongo was their division into several prominent subgroups.[92] In
Brazzaville, one Bakongo subgroup, the Balali, formed a majority of the
population. Cleavages between them and their Bakongo cousins had considerable effect on party politics from 1956 to 1963 and on military politics thereafter.

With the Bakongo keeping apart from electoral politics, the territorial
assembly returned in 1952 was composed of representatives of the Vili
party and the Mbochi party. Into this milieu stepped Fulbert Youlou, a
Balali priest, for some Bakongo the heir to the Matsouanist tradition. In
1956, Youlou was opposed by candidates of the Mbochi party and of the
party identified with the Vili, a party supported in Brazzaville by the
Batéké. Confronted by a split in their own ethnic ranks, Youlou's
Bakongo forces attacked on two fronts, assaulting the remaining Mat-
souanists *and* the Batéké, with the aim of coercing both groups to support Youlou.[93] The Mbochi and the Bakongo did not attack each other;
the Mbochi party concentrated its violence, competitively, on the pivotal
group, the Batéké.

Youlou's partisans thus tried to solidify Bakongo support behind him,
to avert an artificial lock-in. With the results of this effort uncertain, they
also focused on the Batéké as part of a breakout strategy associated with
the locked-in position Youlou's followers had to assume he would
occupy.

The Brazzaville vote divided fairly evenly among the three candidates.
With Bakongo support more or less assured, Youlou's party could then

91. Thompson and Adloff, *The Emerging States of French Equatorial Africa*, p. 482.
92. See Georges Balandier, *The Sociology of Black Africa,* trans. Douglas Garman
(New York: Deutsch, 1970), pt. III.
93. Thompson and Adloff, *The Emerging States of French Equatorial Africa*, p. 484;
Wagret, *Histoire et Sociologie Politiques de la République du Congo (Brazzaville)*, p. 65.

concentrate single-mindedly on the equally painful prospect of a pure lock-in on a national scale. Again, it tried to break out by appealing to a third group.

As the Vili party began to decline, Youlou's party and the Mbochi party consolidated their power. In the territorial assembly elections of 1957, each of the two major parties won 21 of the 45 seats. Three independents won the remaining seats; two joined the Mbochi, and the other joined the Bakongo party, completing the polarization. A coalition government was formed, but it proved unstable. One source of instability was the rivalry of the Bakongo and the Mbochi for the allegiance of the Vili. In 1958, the Bakongo party chose a Vili stronghold as the site for a party conference. Its Mbochi opponents saw the choice as a Bakongo attempt to alter the equilibrium by absorbing Vili support, isolating the Mbochi in a minority position, and they resisted it with violence.

Violence stemming from a breakout strategy can involve one of two sets of players. Of course, the group associated with the party that is breaking out is a certain participant. But, on the other side, there are two possibilities. Either the swing group whose support is solicited will find itself coerced by the breakout group (Batéké in 1956) or itself respond violently to the solicitations (Muslims in Mauritius, 1967–68), or else a third group, equally interested in the support of the swing group and fearful of being locked into a minority position if the breakout succeeds, may respond violently. This last was the Mbochi position in January 1958.

The Mbochi assessment was correct. As Youlou's party consolidated its support, a lock-in effect, making the Mbochi party a permanent minority, began to develop. There was further violence in November 1958 and again, on a more massive scale, in February 1959. In each case, the precipitant was an act or series of acts solidifying Bakongo control. The Bakongo party had broken out, leaving the defeated Mbochi to respond with ethnic violence, now less calculatively than before.

The Congo violence thus ran the gamut from a preventive riot to avert an artificial lock-in, to a breakout riot to avert a pure lock-in, to a breakout riot producing a lock-in, to lock-in violence in response. The alacrity with which the groups shifted ground as their relative situation changed indicates that breakout and lock-in riots are species of a single family of violence — indeed of behavior generally — which is appropriately called *positional violence*. By that I mean simply that it is a function of the exigencies of the ethnic-party situation and that any group subject to the constraints of that system would have adequate incentives to behave in the same way.[94]

Electoral riots require elections. When one-party states and military regimes supplanted elected governments in many divided societies in the late 1960s and 1970s, often to reverse elections that locked some groups out of power,[95] breakout and lock-in riots receded around the world. It might be thought that the redemocratization of the 1990s would bring a revival of this kind of violence, but many sitting regimes, with clear memories of earlier elections, found ways to avoid free electoral tests that divided polities cleanly along ethnic-party lines.[96] One country that did experience lock-in riots again was the Congo Republic after the elections of 1993. This time they produced something close to a civil war in Brazzaville.[97] In many countries, however, the methods employed to avert such results were manipulative or overtly undemocratic, and it is possible that their results will not be durable. If there is a new wave of free elections, with ethnically based parties contesting, breakout and lock-in violence will have a bright future.

OFFICIAL OR UNOFFICIAL ALTERATIONS
OF RELATIVE ETHNIC STATUS

Policy changes impinging on ethnic interests have preceded many cases of ethnic violence. As we have seen, political demonstrations and general strikes often aim at protesting or supporting government policy altering the ethnic status quo. In Assam (1960, 1972), Sri Lanka (1956, 1958), Ranchi (1967), Mauritania (1966), Karachi-Hyderabad (1972), and

94. Erving Goffman, who has played a leading part in elaborating the implications of positional behavior, has provided evidence that persons whose roles shift dramatically but suddenly — for example, from "normal" to "stigmatized," and vice versa — "may relatively quickly experience a change in apparent personality. These perceived changes seem to be a result of the individual's being placed in a new relationship to the contingencies of acceptance in face-to-face interaction, with consequent employment of new strategies of adaptation." Erving Goffman, *Stigma: Notes on the Management of Spoiled Identity* (Englewood Cliffs, N.J.: Prentice-Hall, 1963), p. 132 (footnote omitted). The evidence adduced here suggests that ethnic actors have much the same capacity for rapid role change.

95. See Horowitz, *Ethnic Groups in Conflict*, pp. 429–37, 480–86.

96. See Donald L. Horowitz, "Democracy in Divided Societies," *Journal of Democracy* 4, no. 4 (October 1993): 18–38.

97. Kajsa Ekholm Friedman and Anne Sundberg, "Reorganization Efforts and the Threat of Ethnic War in Congo" (unpublished paper, Department of Social Anthropology, University of Lund, 1996), p. 7.

Bangalore (1994), the issue was language. In different contexts, however, other policy issues, such as claims to a "special position" for the Malays in Malaysia (1957) and Singapore (1964), have played an equally divisive role.

Several riots have involved territorial questions. In Kyrghyzstan (1990), the precipitant was a dispute over ethnic priority in housing policy and territorial boundaries. When Uzbek land was seized for housing and Kyrghyz authorities confirmed the seizures, Uzbek organizations began to demand the creation of autonomous Uzbek regions. Thereupon, Kyrghyz organizations sprang up to demand boundaries more favorable to Kyrghyz.[98] Violence followed. Assam (1955) was a response to West Bengal's claim to detach the Goalpara district. Delhi (1966) followed the decision of the central government to divide Punjab into Sikh- and Hindu-majority states. The September 1966 riots in northern Nigeria were precipitated in part by proposals to divide the regions into a larger number of smaller states.[99] An effect of such a rearrangement (later consummated) would be to narrow the range of Hausa-Fulani preeminence. The rioting in Kaa and Port Harcourt, Nigeria (1993), had strong indications of organization, but it also resulted from the fear of the Andoni that their neighbors, the Ogoni, were embarked on a campaign to create an Ogoni kingdom and to take some Andoni land for it.[100] Violence in Iran (1979) flowed from Kurdish demands for autonomy in an ethnically mixed area,[101] and violence in what was East Pakistan (1969) resulted from a demand for separate districts for non-Bengalis.[102] In these cases, most of them in federal systems, the policy issues had obvious consequences for the extent of preeminence of particular groups. At stake were fundamental alterations in the reach of ethnic status, rather than its particular attributes.

Most of these status modifications were incremental and somewhat ambiguous. They did not state in so many words that the result was to be a drastic reordering of the prevailing equilibrium. Some room was left for maneuver. In the case of language policy, it was usually intimated that

98. Eugene Huskey, "Politics and Elections in Kyrgyzstan, 1989–1990" (unpublished paper, Stetson University, De Land, Fla., n.d. [1994]), pp. 28–32.

99. The accounts of this violence are numerous. See, e.g., Ruth First, *Power in Africa* (New York: Pantheon Books, 1970), pp. 325–34. An important precipitant was also the broadcast in the north of a Radio Cotonou (Dahomey) report of the killing of Hausa in Onitsha, in what was then the Eastern Region.

100. *Reuters Library Report*, September 27, 1993.

101. *Economist*, April 28, 1979, p. 69.

102. *Washington Post*, November 23, 1969, p. F12.

members of the group to be disadvantaged by the policy might retrieve their position by compensatory effort (examinations and the like) in the newly elevated language. Moreover, the policy emanated from governments, which, to maintain stability, might be susceptible to pressure to soften the most adverse portions of the new policy. For these reasons, such policy changes generally do not bring on immediate violence, and only some of this violence can properly be seen as intended to affect policy outcomes. The violence requires a buildup, usually in the form of demonstrations or strikes. The buildup allows several things to happen: precipitants cumulate as, for example, insults occur along the way; those group members given to interpreting policy ambiguously may be displaced in leadership roles by those given to perceiving its effect starkly; and proponents of the policy change are likely to state its intended ethnic effects with increasing candor and clarity, thus rendering its adverse status implications unmistakable.

A more drastic status change does not require the mediating impact of other behavior deemed provocative. If the issue is clearly worth fighting for, the threshold for aggression may be reached very rapidly. That is the case with ethnic status changes that are extreme, sudden, unambiguous, and potentially irreversible. These tend to emanate not from government but from opposing ethnic groups, and they have the quality of maneuvers designed to steal or capture the state. For that reason, they amount to an ethnic coup d'état, although not usually a coup in the sense of a military takeover of government.[103]

Consider the contrasting cases of Fiji (1987) and the Congo Republic (1959). In Fiji, the immediate effect of a drastic reversal of ethnic fortunes in politics was a military coup; in the Congo, it was massive violence.

The Fijian election of 1987 produced an unprecedented result. A governing coalition, weighted toward the interests of Fijians, lost to a party led by a Fijian but supported almost entirely by Indians. This dramatic shift of power from one group to another might have provoked ethnic rioting; but, since the Fiji armed forces were strongly Fijian in composition, it provoked a military coup instead,[104] a not-uncommon result in a

103. Most military coups are in fact quite bloodless; rarely do they precipitate ethnic violence at all.

104. See Ralph R. Premdas, "Balance and Ethnic Conflict in Fiji," in John McGarry and Brendan O'Leary, eds., *The Politics of Ethnic Conflict Regulation* (London: Routledge, 1993), pp. 251–74, at pp. 272–74; Ralph Premdas, "General Rabuka and the Fiji Elections of 1992," *Asian Survey* 33, no. 10 (October 1993): 997–1009, at pp. 997–98.

divided society when elections point one way and officer corps composition points another.[105]

In the Congo Republic, the consolidation of Bakongo power eventually persuaded the Mbochi that the Bakongo had essentially stolen the state through the electoral process and intended to exclude Mbochi from all state power. Eventually there was a military coup to oust the Bakongo government, but it was years in coming. In the meantime, there was brutal violence. As we have seen, party rivalries between Mbochi and Bakongo had become acute by 1958.[106] As his opponents futilely demanded new elections, Youlou, the Bakongo leader, proceeded to reinforce his power, moving the capital to Brazzaville, in the Bakongo heartland. One of the most provocative things he did was to reshuffle the administration, transferring followers of his opponents and sending Bakongo civil servants to serve in Mbochi areas. In one case, a Bakongo appointed to take charge of a district in the heart of Mbochi country found destroyed bridges in his path as he traveled to his post. In February 1959, the explosion came in the Brazzaville suburb of Poto-Poto, where Mbochi hacked to death all the Bakongo they could find. The Mbochi had read the signs as an unmistakable augury of Bakongo hegemony.

Drastic reversals of ethnic fortunes also precipitated riots in Sudan (1955), Chad (1979), Burma (1942), Nigeria (May 1966), and Malaysia (1945–46). The precipitants took several forms, but all were recognized immediately as highly threatening. All brought swift, violent responses of great magnitude. In each instance, earlier behavior created the framework within which perceptions of the enormity of the threat were shaped.

Sudan experienced increasing polarization and distrust in the years preceding the riot.[107] The Anglo-Egyptian Agreement of 1953, which paved the way for Sudanese independence, was negotiated without southern Sudanese representation. This gave southerners the strong

105. See Horowitz, *Ethnic Groups in Conflict*, pp. 480–86.

106. What follows draws heavily on Thompson and Adloff, *The Emerging States of French Equatorial Africa*, pp. 488–92; Wagret, *Histoire et Sociologie Politiques de la République du Congo (Brazzaville)*, pp. 80–86; Carter, *Independence for Africa*, ch. 8; *West Africa*, February 28, 1959, p. 203.

107. The following account relies on Republic of Sudan, *Report of the Commission of Inquiry into Disturbances in the Southern Sudan during August, 1955* (Khartoum: McCorquedale, 1956); K.D.D. Henderson, *Sudan Republic* (New York: Praeger, 1965), ch. 10; Mohamed Omer Beshir, *The Southern Sudan: Background to Conflict* (New York: C. Hurst, 1968), ch. 8; Oliver Albino, *The Sudan: A Southern Viewpoint* (London: Oxford University Press, 1970), pp. 31–39.

impression that the north and the British were prepared to deal over their heads. Elections followed, in which two northern parties competed in the south. Extravagant campaign promises were made of civil service positions for southerners, despite their lack of education and seniority. When southerners received only a handful of such positions, outraged southern opinion held that "Northerners want to colonize us for another hundred years."[108]

Northern administrators in the south were not notable for their detachment: their exercise of authority had a colonial aura about it. By 1955, the intentions of the government at Khartoum were thoroughly suspect in the south, and the army stationed there was regarded as the instrument of northern domination. When, after the discovery of an alleged mutiny plot among some southern troops, 500 northern troops were flown to the south, the prevalent belief was that they would "be used for the extermination of the Southerners."[109] The coup de grâce was provided by an order to an army unit of southerners to move north to Khartoum. The troops sensed that this was an attempt to colonize the south by dissolving the last bastion of southern strength, perhaps even, in the words of an apprehensive soldier, "a trap in order that the Northern troops might have a free hand to do what they like with your wives and children, and you will be killed in Khartoum yourselves."[110] Southern troops mutinied and murdered their officers. Within a few hours, civilians joined the soldiers in the hunt for northern lives and property wherever they could be found.

Military action, rather than mutiny, precipitated the massive killing in Chad (1979)[111] but the motif was remarkably similar. The Chadian civil war had reached a turning point. The Chadian army, overwhelmingly southern and Christian, was defeated by northern, Muslim rebels. The rebel leader had demonstrated a bias against southerners in general and against the Sara in particular. When the rebels occupied the capital, Sara, fearful of forced conversion and the rumored creation of an Islamic republic, departed en masse for the south and a possible secession. Upon arrival, they expressed their sense of the catastrophe that had befallen

---

108. Republic of Sudan, *Report of the Commission of Inquiry*, p. 114.

109. Ibid., p. 120.

110. Ibid., p. 106.

111. Virginia Thompson and Richard Adloff, *Conflict in Chad* , Research Series no. 45 (Berkeley: University of California, Institute of International Studies, 1981), pp. 84–89; Samuel Decalo, "Regionalism, Political Decay, and Civil Strife in Chad," *Journal of Modern African Studies* 18, no. 1 (March 1980): 23–56, at pp. 53–54; *Africa News*, March 16, 1979, p. 2.

them by killing thousands of northerners resident in the south. The state and the southern position in it had been lost.

Military action also precipitated extensive violence in Burma (1942).[112] Both sides were led by military gangs.[113] Whereas the Sudanese mutiny and the Chadian exodus turned immediately to riot, the hostilities in Burma shaded over into the category of internal war. The participants included large numbers of civilians, and the targets were selected merely by virtue of ethnic affiliation. Whatever the precise definitional status of this violence, the precipitating events were seen as part of "a plan to rob and exterminate [the Karen] community."[114]

Beneficiaries of British protection during the colonial period, the Karen were prominently represented in the British army in Burma. When the Japanese attacked, Karen fought loyally with the British. Burman nationalists, by contrast, had sensed the opportunities the Japanese invasion might provide them to escape British rule. A few who had received military training from the Japanese became the nucleus of the Japanese-sponsored Burma Independence Army (BIA), a force that attracted more than its share of disorderly recruits. "When at last the British withdrew from Lower Burma, the disbanded Karens returned to their homes in the districts and there came face to face with the victory-flushed, race-obsessed BIA and its new, free-swinging civil administrations."[115]

After the Japanese arrival, the BIA purported to set up its own administration. The Karen had taken their weapons home with them; the BIA demanded they be surrendered. Karen villages that complied soon found themselves attacked. The Karen determined thereafter to resist. Resist they did, killing some BIA soldiers in the process, thus giving rise to reprisal raids that quickly grew into a campaign of reciprocal massacre of whole villages. As it seemed to the Karen, benign British rule was about to be supplanted by malevolent Burman rule and the decimation of their community.

The same sense of total takeover produced extensive violence in Nigeria (May 1966) and Malaysia (1945–46). In Nigeria, as we have seen, the precipitant was Decree No. 34, announcing the unification of

112. A good description of this violence appears in Ba Maw, *Breakthrough in Burma: Memoirs of a Revolution, 1939–1946* (New Haven: Yale University Press, 1968), pp. 187–95. See also Hugh Tinker, *The Union of Burma,* 4th ed. (London: Oxford University Press, 1967), pp. 9–10. For general background, see F.S.V. Donnison, *Burma* (London: Benn, 1970).

113. Ba Maw, *Breakthrough in Burma,* p. 188.

114. Ibid.

115. Ibid., p. 187.

the civil service, until then organized on regional lines. The coup of January 1966 had been welcomed in the north as providing the country with a deliverance from the machinations of politicians. As events unfolded, however, the conduct of the military government made the coup appear in retrospect to have been Ibo-inspired. An army promotion list, for example, was weighted in favor of Ibo officers.[116] By the time Decree No. 34 was promulgated, every act of government seemed part of an Ibo conspiracy. The decree "was announced in an atmosphere polluted by propaganda that behind every policy emanating from the Ironsi regime lay an Ibo plan for domination. The first step in the Ibo plan to colonize the north would be the Ibo take-over of the civil service; and the word spread that Ibo were about to migrate northwards to take over all competitive posts."[117] So seriously was the threat of colonization taken that the northern demonstrations preceding the riot had secessionist overtones.

In Malaysia, the circumstances were quite different, but they had much the same meaning.[118] As in Burma (1942), the backdrop for the violence was the war. The Japanese invasion brought with it a strong anti-Chinese policy on the part of the occupying troops. The majority of the guerrillas who fled to the jungle to fight the Japanese under the banner of the Malayan People's Anti-Japanese Army (MPAJA) were Chinese, mainly Communists. After the Japanese surrender but before the British reoccupation, the guerrillas emerged from the jungle, executed alleged collaborators, most of them Malays, seized the administration of a great many towns and villages, and announced their peremptory claim to govern. The Malays' response was swift and decisive: they took to arms, killing Chinese civilians up and down the peninsula.

Despite the diversity of the settings in which attempted ethnic takeovers have been perceived, they share several elements. They portend change that is highly unfavorable, drastic, sudden, and, because of ascription, potentially permanent. They close participatory doors with a bang. The signs of threat are clear enough. In the Congo (1959), the attempt to

116. Miners, *The Nigerian Army*, , pp. 210–11.

117. First, *Power in Africa*, p. 311. See also Miners, *The Nigerian Army*, ch. 11. As if to confirm the most malevolent interpretation of the decree, the next day the Ibo leader, Colonel Ojukwu, spoke of enhancing the scope of opportunities for civil servants of eastern origin.

118. See Cheah Boon Kheng, *Red Star over Malaya* (Singapore: Singapore University Press, 1983), pp. 195–240; Government of Malaysia, *The May 13 Tragedy*, pp. 7–8; Chin Kee Onn, *Malaya Upside Down* (Singapore: Federal Publications, 1946), ch. 24; Burridge, "Racial Relations in Johore," pp. 151–68.

rule without any opposition participation was one such signal; more potent was the dispatch of Bakongo administrators to the north in a fashion reminiscent of colonialism. Elsewhere, the intention to take over the administration was also clearly manifested — in the Sudan, by the civil service results; in Chad, by the appointment of northerners and the priority given to Arabic; in Burma, by the civilian arm of the BIA; in Nigeria, by the anticipated effects of Decree No. 34; and in Malaysia, by the control of territory and the announcements of the MPAJA. In addition, the threat of military occupation loomed large — in the Sudan as the result of troop transfers; in Chad, of the fall of the capital; in Burma, of the BIA attacks; in Nigeria, of the so-called Ibo coup and promotion patterns appearing to favor Ibo officers; and in Malaysia, of the MPAJA executions and the fact that it was the only organized armed force remaining after the Japanese surrender. The combination of impending military and civilian control by ethnic strangers is a most explosive combination, very likely to precipitate the most severe rioting.[119]

This combination is usually accompanied by the expression of contemptuous ethnic sentiments that remove any lingering ambiguity about the intentions of the target group. In this respect, too, the nakedness of these precipitating actions contrasts with the uncertainties surrounding official policy changes of lesser magnitude, rendering an instant response imperative. The Sudanese and Burmese materials are replete with expressions of ethnic chauvinism accompanying the conduct that precipitated violence. The Nigerian and Malayan data, no less graphic, provide some idea of the fears that were entertained at the time. I referred earlier to the photographs displayed by Ibo in 1966, the boasts accompanying them, and the sense among Hausa that Ibo were eating their humanity; Malays, too, felt themselves humiliated. The violence responds to a sense of degradation and an apprehension of subjugation at least, extermination at most.

Somewhere between the totality of the ethnic "coup" and the incrementalism of the policy change affecting ethnic status lies the possibility

119. There are many experimental studies relating the intensity of an aggressive response to the strength of the instigation to aggression, without prejudging the exact form the aggressive response will take. In one such study, a nearly linear relationship was obtained where the instigator-targets were siblings, friends, or inferiors, though much less steep slopes were obtained where they were parents or other authority figures. Frances K. Graham et al., "Aggression as a Function of the Attack and the Attacker," *Journal of Abnormal and Social Psychology* 46, no. 4 (October 1951): 512–20. The magnitudes of responses to the ethnic coup by unranked groups are an illustration of the same phenomenon at the societal level.

of violence arising out of threats to the value of group autonomy. Serious breaches of the norms of group autonomy, especially those which have an element of group coercion about them, are likely to lead to violence. We have seen how general strikes for ethnic objectives often provoke resistance from those who are coerced to comply. Similar violent resistance was manifested in Nigeria (1953) and Sierra Leone (1968), except that the coercion occurred in connection with an "invasion" of ethnic strangers from other regions.

The Kano riot (1953) we have already discussed from the standpoint of selective targeting in Chapter 4. As the two southern parties (one mainly Yoruba, the other mainly Ibo) grew increasingly aggressive about an early date for independence, northerners became more and more distrustful, sensing in the southern determination a scheme to take control of the north from the British before northerners were capable of doing so.[120] When one of the southern parties scheduled a rally in Kano, a northern party organized a protest, and the authorities canceled the meeting. But the damage had already been done; southerners, well known for their "domineering" behavior, were scheming to coerce northerners into subordination. Years earlier a northern leader had referred to southern migrants in the north as "invaders."[121] Now the invasion had become even more real, and northern mobs, fearful of subjugation,[122] undertook to repulse it.

A somewhat different invasion occurred in Sierra Leone (1968). There, as in Nigeria, rival regions and ethnic groups had supported rival parties, but the occasion for the violence was electoral.[123] In 1967, the northern-based, principally Temne, All People's Congress defeated the ruling Sierra Leone People's Party, largely identified with the Mende. Following a series of coups, the APC took office, but included some SLPP representatives in the cabinet. Gradually, however, the SLPP was pushed into opposition, its future cast further in doubt by judicial deci-

---

120. See Northern Regional Government, Government of Nigeria, *Report on the Kano Disturbances, 16th, 17th, 18th, and 19th May, 1953* (Kaduna: Government Printer, 1953), pp. 41–44; Coleman, *Nigeria*, pp. 361–62.

121. Abubakar Tafawa Balewa, quoted in Coleman, *Nigeria*, p. 361.

122. For these fears, see the appendices to Northern Regional Government, *Report on the Kano Disturbances*.

123. See generally Christopher Allen, "Sierra Leone Politics since Independence," *African Affairs* 67, no. 269 (October 1968): 305–29; John Cartwright, "Shifting Forces in Sierra Leone," *Africa Report*, December 1968, pp. 26–30; *West Africa*, October–December 1968; *Africa Report*, January–February 1969; Barrows, "Local Level Politics in Sierra Leone," pp. 334–51.

sions determining that its seats had been won by fraud. Mende power was on the wane. By-elections were scheduled for the SLPP seats declared vacant. As I have suggested, these elections had a lock-in quality for the Mende. But they had another dimension as well. Large groups of northern APC workers entered Mendeland to campaign for APC candidates, whereupon Poro "devils" appeared in various Mende towns and the Temne were attacked. Not only did it appear that a northern government was bent on depriving the Mende of the last vestiges of their political influence, but it also seemed that Temne had set about to coerce the Mende on their own home soil. As in Kano, ethnic strangers had bypassed acknowledged ethnic-party leaders in order to impose candidates acceptable to the north.

THE CHARACTER OF PRECIPITATING EVENTS

Precipitants are specific events to which more general meaning is attached.[124] In the view of participants, precipitants render aggression both appropriate and necessary.

Appropriate, in the sense that the event must evoke underlying conflicts and threats. Processions and mass meetings highlight the importance of the actions or issues that prompted them and alert group members to their implications for the course of relations between the contending groups. Insults and defacements constitute fighting words, because they are a challenge to group status, a denial of cultural equality and hence of collective value, and a foreshadowing of a dreaded subordination. Certain kinds of behavior — repeated demonstrations, strikes with coercive aspects — tend to arouse images of especially disliked or feared attributes, such as tendentiousness or intractability, imputed to members of the target group. Some precipitants verge on violence and likely cue violent responses.[125] Those who favor a violent response argue that the precipitating event is either the culmination of a situation already intolerable or the harbinger of a situation even worse. Either way, the event is somehow more than it seems. If violence is to ensue, "the anger

124. Stanley J. Tambiah, "Reflections on Communal Violence in South Asia," *Journal of Asian Studies* 49, no. 4 (November 1990): 741–60, at p. 750, refers to *focalization*, a process of stripping away the particulars of an event, so that it means something clear.

125. A relationship suggested by findings that the most likely victims of criminal violence are those who are themselves involved in violence. Robert J. Sampson and Janet Lauritsen, "Deviant Lifestyles, Proximity to Crime, and the Offender-Victim Link in Personal Violence," *Journal of Research in Crime and Delinquency* 27, no. 2 (May 1990): 110–39.

must attach itself to the precipitating event and must convert it into an unacceptable affront. . . . The event is interpreted as symbolically related to grievances — hence, as the occasion for action. . . . The illusion which is created converts the discrete event into a collective insult — into a deliberate provocation that is repressive and intolerable."[126] Singly or together, precipitants confirm generally hostile behavior or intentions.

Necessary, as well. The precipitant may make peaceful channels of influence and protest appear futile; it may suggest a blockage of the political process, a situation that conjures up the alternatives of violence or the risk of an intolerable loss. This view of the state of things can assume several guises. The group to be targeted is intransigent and intent on placing obstacles in the path of our aspirations; it already controls the government and will soon control us; the situation has become fluid, and the others cannot be trusted not to take advantage of it. Urgency is an important aspect of the pre-riot situation.

Within these general outlines, considerable variation is possible in the timing and intensity of precipitants. In some cases, a certain natural rhythm can be detected, as outlined for many of the procession cases. The spiral can occur over quite a long period of time. In Sierra Leone (1968), the by-election violence had something to do with coercion that took place at the general election of 1967. Then the Mende party engaged in some modest harassment of strangers in Mendeland. This impelled the Temne party a year later to import party cadres from the north on a larger scale, which in turn had the effect of mobilizing Mende in the Poro Society. But if the appropriateness and necessity for violence become apparent to the participants all at once, then the violence will be swift. Lock-in precipitants and stealing-the-state precipitants bring these two together in a dramatic fashion, producing prompt explosions quite out of proportion to the earlier rhythms.[127]

126. Hans Toch, *Violent Men: An Inquiry into the Psychology of Violence* (Chicago: Aldine, 1969), p. 204. For elaboration of "the catalytic situation," see Hans Toch, "The Catalytic Situation in the Violence Equation," *Journal of Applied Social Psychology* 15, no. 2 (n.m. 1985): 105–23. See also Lieberson and Silverman, "The Precipitants and Underlying Conditions of Race Riots," pointing out that precipitants in the antiblack riots in the United States, 1913–63, tended to be violations of strongly held mores. In the context of the feud, Thomas M. Kiefer, *The Tausug: Violence and Law in a Philippine Moslem Society* (New York: Holt, Rinehart, & Winston, 1972), pp. 53–58, points out that a public affront to self-esteem — an occasion during which "a man has been 'victimized'" — constitutes the appropriate precipitant for violence.

127. For hypotheses on why some reactions are out of harmony with earlier rhythms of action, see Pruitt, "Stability and Sudden Change in Interpersonal and International Affairs," pp. 32–33.

Precipitants thus have the capacity to unlock accumulated anger because they bear an evocative relationship to the antecedent conflict. They supply a shorthand recollection of group qualities and relations, as well as guidance for a course of action.

There is a perfect example of the amplifying interplay of events and group attributes in Mauritania (1966), which involved ethnic policy and a public-sector strike.[128] The strike was called to protest the government's decision to teach Arabic as a compulsory secondary-school subject. Previously, Arabic had been an optional subject. French was the indispensable language of education and administration. Since the educational qualifications of blacks — especially their command of French — tended to be superior to those of the Moors, upgrading the status of Arabic seemed a transparent attempt to dislodge blacks from their positions in government by imposing an artificial handicap. At the same time, the emphasis on Arabic was interpreted as a means of legitimizing Moorish domination by infusing the trappings of state power with a language associated with the north of the country and the Moorish segment of the population. Moors, on the other hand, considered blacks to be overrepresented in important positions, profiting from continuing emphasis on French and from their association with French culture. Moors grew angry at black complaints of discrimination, dismissing the complaints as so much carping. Moorish resistance to the strike was the beginning of Moorish attacks on blacks. Every antecedent event was interpreted as a manifestation of offensive group behavioral qualities. The events that elicit violence catalyze because they epitomize.

It is worth noting how rarely police action against members of the initiating group precipitates deadly violence. Every major violent protest demonstration in the United States in the 1960s was precipitated by police action.[129] In other societies characterized by ascriptive ranking, hostile police activity can provoke violence directed at symbols of authority. This was the case in the "Zhii" violence in Bulawayo, Zimbabwe (1960), when, after African nationalist demonstrators were twice dispersed, they attacked government facilities and commercial

128. I am indebted here to several Mauritanian and foreign informants, as well as to Robert Gauthier, "Mauritania — a Country of Change," *Le Monde Diplomatique*, March 1966, p. 2; Moktar Ould Daddah, "Rapport Moral," *Congrès Ordinaire du Parti du Peuple*, June 24–26, 1966 (mimeo., n.p., n.d.).

129. Harlan Hahn and Joe R. Feagin, "Riot-Precipitating Police Practices: Attitudes in Urban Ghettos," *Phylon* 31, no. 2 (Summer 1970): 183–93. The same was true in Miami (1980).

establishments, carefully avoiding attacks on people, Europeans and Africans alike.[130] If the police represent a regime deemed to be alien, then deadly violence can take place. Burma (1938), as we have seen, involved British police whose suppression of Burman crowds aggravated the violence they then directed at Indians. Taiwan (1947) involved brutality by Mainlander police of the Kuomintang regime which had installed itself on Taiwan two years earlier. The police action precipitated a combination of deadly violence against Mainlanders and violent protest demonstrations against symbols of authority. But these remain rare cases.

It is also impossible to be unimpressed by the overwhelming preponderance of political precipitants of deadly riots. Precipitating events, Mark R. Beissinger says, help create a "milieu of mistrust by signaling a fundamental shift of authority vis-à-vis a group."[131] Those who would like to prevent deadly ethnic riots would do well to focus on creating institutions to prevent zero-sum outcomes in the form of lock-in elections or drastic reversals of ethnic policy, as well as on intervening in mass public displays of group strength and strike activity that involves one group giving unacceptable orders to another. Apart from some procession-precipitated riots, the vast majority of ethnic riots are preceded in some significant way by governmental, political-party, military, or ethnic-group action that appears or promises to affect group access to the political process or the distribution of collective status by government.[132] Perhaps this seems obvious, and yet there were other plausible possibilities.

The precipitants might have centered more on group competition for material benefits. The material-competitive dimension is not entirely absent from ethnic riots, as is attested, for example, by the prominence of language issues reflecting in part elite economic interests or by the civil service strike in Mauritania (1966). But where material competition

130. Francis Nehwati, "The Social and Communal Background to 'Zhii': The African Riots in Bulawayo, Southern Rhodesia in 1960," *African Affairs* 69, no. 276 (July 1970): 250–66. *Zhii* means "devastating action" or "complete destruction."

131. Mark R. Beissinger, "Nationalist Violence and the State: Political Authority and Contentious Repertoires in the Former U.S.S.R.," *Comparative Politics* 30, no. 4 (July 1998): 401–22, at p. 414.

132. Cf. Gurr's finding of the preeminent role of political precipitants in "turmoil" generally. "A Comparative Study of Civil Strife," in Hugh Davis Graham and Ted Robert Gurr, eds., *Violence in America: Historical and Comparative Perspectives*, Vol. 2 (Washington, D.C.: Government Printing Office, 1969), pp. 455–60; and Lambert's progression, for Hindu-Muslim riots, from religious issues to identity issues to political issues. "Hindu-Muslim Riots," p. 227.

plays a role, it is a partial role, usually at the elite level. Riots require mass participation, and few riots occur without antecedent events affecting the interests and apprehensions of mass participants.

The precipitants might have been more idiosyncratic and trivial than they proved to be. As mere catalysts, they might consist of any random event. This bit of conventional wisdom, advanced repeatedly from a variety of theoretical standpoints, from rationalist to postmodernist,[133] is mistaken. Small personal quarrels, fist fights, and accidents rarely produce major episodes of violence, unless they are preceded by a lengthy buildup of hostility or unless ethnic violence is so recurrent in a given locality that it is merely punctuated by intervals of tranquility.

Cities like Karachi and Hyderabad, in Pakistan, and Meerut, in India, had been so frequently affected by ethnic violence that, by the late 1980s, personal quarrels or traffic accidents were sufficient to ignite large-scale killing.[134] Elsewhere, with the exception of Durban (1949), a riot with a significant component of displaced aggression, small personal incidents produce either no violence or violence with few or no casualties. Aligarh, India (1954), had no deaths, and riots in several Central Java towns (1980) were nonlethal except for rioters killed by soldiers.[135] Jos, Nigeria (1945), Pangkor Island, Malaysia (1959), Bukit Mertajam, Malaysia (1964), and Novyy Uzen, Kazakhstan (1989), all produced only a few fatalities.[136] All of these except Pangkor were marketplace quarrels, and in several the precipitant involved an assault or imperious behavior that evoked the reputed assertiveness of the target group. Most, moreover, took place in conducive environments. For example, earlier in the decade, Aligarh had begun its sequence of serious post-independence riots; Jos had suffered the Ibo-led general strike; and Bukit Mertajam was

133. Paul R. Brass, *Theft of an Idol: Text and Context in the Representation of Collective Violence* (Princeton: Princeton University Press, 1997), p. 96; Russell Hardin, *One for All: The Logic of Group Conflict* (Princeton: Princeton University Press, 1995), p. 155; Margaret J. Wyszomirski, "Communal Violence: The Armenians and the Copts as Case Studies," *World Politics* 27, no. 3 (April 1975): 430–55, at p. 443.

134. See Dildar Khan, "Meerut Riots: An Analysis," in Pramod Kumar, ed., *Towards Understanding Communalism* (Chandigarh: Centre for Research in Rural and Industrial Development, 1992), pp. 455–70. I deal with recurrent riot locations in Chapter 10, below.

135. Ghurye, *Social Tensions in India*, p. 317; "Small Fight with Big Results," *Far Eastern Economic Review*, December 5, 1980, pp. 10–11.

136. Plotnicov, "An Early Nigerian Disturbance"; Willard A. Hanna, "Pangkor Island: A Footnote to Malayan Prospects and Problems," *American Universities Field Staff Reports*, Southeast Asia Series 8, no. 14 (June 15, 1960): 2–3; National Operations Council, *The May 13 Tragedy*, pp. 19–20; Moscow Tass International Service, June 20, 1989, in FBIS-SOV-89-117, June 20, 1989, p. 45.

synchronized with the aggressive forays of Singapore's Lee Kuan Yew into the politics of the Malaysian mainland and with the riots in Singapore. Despite these propitious conditions, small events produced small riots.

More generally, there seems to be a rough correlation between the significance of the precipitants and the magnitude of the ensuing violence. Displays of strength by the target group tend to elicit violence directed against it. Collective activity precipitates riots because of, among other things, the mass and threatening character of coordinated group action. As we have seen, leadership in the target group sometimes sets about organizing a show of strength in order to influence the political process or to outdo or forestall action by members of the opposing ethnic camp. This course of conduct mobilizes opposition and encourages attacks against the intransigence so visibly demonstrated. Reports of assaults, invasions, and conspiracies by the target group to seize control of government; the aggressive behavior of demonstrators in processions and meetings; the uncompromising demands and threats they make; the past victories they celebrate; the coercion that accompanies strikes and the demonstration of power that accompanies electoral victories: all constitute evidence that strength provokes.

Of course, the perception of strength and cohesion is not necessarily accurate. With respect to rumors of aggression, we have seen that this is far from the case, and the same point can be made for many other precipitants as well. Acceptance of Urdu as the second official language of Bihar or a few minutes of Urdu news on television in Karnataka (1994) would not really have paved the way for a new partition, and separatism in Penang (1957) could not possibly have succeeded, any more than the fears of ethnic armies on the march or atrocities already inflicted could be validated by reference to credible evidence. But the point remains that the target groups were believed to be inordinately strong, determined to exert their strength, and threatening in the extreme if they succeeded.

Just how exaggerated are the estimates of the target group's strength can be seen from the wild — yet not atypical — claims of a leaflet distributed to "Hindu Brothers" around the time of the Bhagalpur riot (1989). On no fewer than 21 points, most demonstrably false, Muslims were said to have an advantage. "Muslim population is increasing, while that of the Hindus is decreasing"; Muslims are armed and organized, Hindus disarmed and disorganized; Muslims — an 11 percent minority — will gain political power in the next 12 to 15 years, and then will "destroy" the Hindus.[137] To be sure, the leaflet was intended to stir people up, but it could not do that unless its falsehoods had resonance with its readers. There is reason to think they did resonate: the same anxiety that credits reports of armies on the march or of entire water-supply systems poisoned facilitates belief that the behavior of the target group is enormously dangerous.

If strength provokes, there is still room for an element of target-group vulnerability in the conditions that prove conducive to violence. For it is surely true that some form of vulnerability allows for lowering inhibitions on aggression. But the mechanism for this reduction is generally a diminished fear of punishment and sense of moral restraint. These variables are more likely to be affected by the supporting social environment and conditions prevailing within the initiator group than by the behavior that precipitates violence.

PRECIPITANT-FREE RIOTS

If the precipitant has the functional importance for the resulting violence that I have attributed to it, then how to explain riots that occur in the absence of virtually any immediate provocation? What seem to be precipitant-free riots do occur once in a great while, and I suggest they fall into one or more than one of three categories.

First, the violence may be a spillover from or retaliation for violence that began elsewhere or earlier and was there or then preceded by precipitating events. Assam (1950) was really a spillover of fighting that began in East and West Bengal.[138] Like many of the two-wave riots discussed in Chapter 2, Singapore (September 1964) was a continuation of rioting that began and was suppressed the preceding July.[139] Violence of this sort is not really precipitation-free. It is provoked by reports or recollections of the earlier violence.

Revenge does not play the same highly structured role in the riot as it does in the feud, but the idea of answering violence with violence cer-

137. Quoted by Gyanendra Pandey, "In Defense of the Fragment: Writing about Hindu-Muslim Riots in India Today," *Representations*, no. 37 (Winter 1992): 27–55, at pp. 43–44.

138. *Assam Tribune*, February 10, 1950, p. 1; February 17, 1950, p. 1; February 28, 1950, p. 1; March 7, 1950, p. 1; March 14, 1950, p. 1; March 28, 1950, p. 1; March 30, 1950, p. 1. See also Richard D. Lambert, "Religion, Economics, and Violence in Bengal," *Middle East Journal* 4, no. 3 (July 1950): 307–28. The same is true of many other Hindu-Muslim riots in India.

139. Leifer, "Communal Violence in Singapore."

tainly does occur to rioters.[140] Reprisal was abundantly present in Sri
Lanka (1983), when a Tamil terrorist ambush on an army patrol produced a strong desire for vengeance,[141] and in Delhi (1984), when the
assassination of Indira Gandhi by her Sikh bodyguards led to the killing
of Sikhs in return.[142] Beginning with partition, anti-Muslim riots in India
have periodically begun as retaliation for anti-Hindu riots in Pakistan;[143]
in the 1980s, revenge riots across international boundaries took place in
West Africa. Ivorians assaulted in Ghana returned home, provoking
much more serious retaliatory violence against Ghanaians in the Ivory
Coast (1985). Four rounds took place in Mauritania and Senegal (1989).
The first was a border dispute between Mauritanian herdsmen and
Senegalese farmers. After two Senegalese were killed, Mauritanian
Moors were attacked in several Senegalese cities, whereupon more serious retaliatory attacks on Senegalese and other black Africans took place
in Mauritania. The return of Senegalese survivors to Dakar then precipitated further anti-Moor violence there.

The revenge motive is sometimes present in riots, but what is immediately noticeable is how unusual riots are as revenge for other riots. If
group A attacks group B, it is extremely rare that group B then avenges
the riot by attacking group A. Undoubtedly, what prevents such riots is
that the other conditions for violence are not generally present.
Specifically, authoritative social support or condonation is likely to
underpin the violence of group A against group B, but not the violence
of group B against group A, in the same country.[144] The conditions for
reciprocal violence are, therefore, much more likely to be present across
borders than within borders.

Second, precipitation-free violence may occur if it is very well organized. Organized groups have some latitude in creating their own occasions, and the riot that appears most unexpected may simply be the best
prepared. But major episodes of organized, precipitation-free violence
are unlikely. As we saw in Chapter 7, it takes an angry crowd to make a
good riot, and so organized groups have the problem of motivating the
participants on whom they will rely. In Guyana (1962), for example,

140. See Peter Loizos, "Intercommunal Killing in Cyprus," *Man* (n.s.) 23, no. 4
(December 1988): 639–53, at pp. 640, 648–49.

141. See James Manor, "Sri Lanka: Explaining the Disaster," *The World Today* 39, no.
11 (November 1983): 450–59, at p. 450.

142. Citizens' Commission, *Delhi: 31 October to 4 November* (Delhi: Citizens'
Commission, 1985), pp. 10–12.

143. See, e.g., Ghurye, *Social Tensions in India*, pp. 346–49.

144. See Chapter 9, below.

where the immediate precipitant was not very potent, it required considerable agitation to get the crowd moving. This took several days, and even then the magnitude of the riot was not great: some Indians were beaten, but none was killed. While an organized group may be less dependent on a particular occasion for violence, it is still dependent on a supportive environment.

Third, a riot may occur with little or no immediate provocation — although very rarely, as the limited violence growing out of personal quarrels suggests — if the supporting environment is exceptionally permissive and disinhibiting or there has been a gradual accumulation of numerous incidents that are stored up in the recollection of perpetrators. I return to the observation made at the beginning of this chapter — that underlying conditions can compensate for the insignificance of a precipitating event. Moreover, it is possible for anger to accumulate, step by imperceptible step, as the psychologist Leonard Berkowitz has observed. "Persistent thwartings can obstruct a wider and wider range of all the responses available to the individual, resulting in an increased degree of interference with the individual's total repertoire. . . . [R]epeated frustrations may increase the likelihood of an aggressive outburst, *even though the later obstructions may be seen as relatively mild*."[145] This same sequence may occur for groups as well. Many separate events can be woven together to motivate the riot.

Again, it is rare, but it can happen. Luluabourg (1959) occurred in a political context that was extremely hospitable to violence, and it was preceded by a series of small anger-generating events, each of them individually falling short of producing violence. Observers do not entirely agree on the precise spark for the violence that occurred, but it seems a few passing gibes were all the circumstances required.[146] The Lulua who attacked would undoubtedly endorse the psychologist's description of persistent thwarting as appropriate to their situation. Or they might identify more readily with the concise simplicity of Montresor in Poe's "The Cask of Amontillado": "The thousand injuries of Fortunato I had borne as I best could, but when he ventured upon insult I vowed revenge."[147]

145. Berkowitz, *Aggression: A Social-Psychological Analysis*, pp. 70–71 (emphasis supplied).

146. Jules Chomé, *Le Drame de Luluabourg*, 3d rev. ed. (Brussels: Editions de Remarques Congolaises, 1960), pp. 5–31, at p. 5.

147. Edgar Allan Poe, "The Cask of Amontillado," in Sherwin Cody, ed., *The Best Tales of Edgar Allan Poe* (New York: Modern Library, n.d.), pp. 364–71, at p. 364.

The Social Environment
for Killing

IF AN EVENT PROVOKES VIOLENCE at one place and time but not at another, perhaps group characteristics and relationships are less conflict producing in the latter than in the former. Or perhaps some facilitative condition is present in the social and political environments of the one but absent in the other. Of course, there is likely to be great indeterminacy in identifying features of the environment that support or inhibit ethnic violence. The direct antecedents of the riot are known and recorded. The same cannot be said for facilitating conditions, which are noted in some instances but not others, noted differently where noted, and problematic in their impact. The more remote from the actual violent incidents, the more questionable is the causal linkage. Yet what may be described as mere background conditions — as opposed to precipitating events — may exert a powerful inhibiting or disinhibiting influence on the commission of aggression.

Most of the conditions that facilitate violence can be grouped together under three rubrics: *uncertainty*, *impunity*, and *justification*. The vast majority of riots occur when aggressors conclude that ethnic politics is dangerously in flux, that they are likely to be able to use violence without adverse consequences to themselves, and that they are thoroughly warranted in their action.

Before we launch into a consideration of these conditions, it is necessary to push some others aside. There are several hypotheses related to the riot environment that I shall not pursue. Among the commonly cited conditions facilitating riots are periodic economic decline and rapid demographic change. Both tend to be invoked when they coincide with episodes of violence and ignored when they do not.

Among historians, there is a lively debate about the relationship of food prices to food riots in eighteenth- and nineteenth-century Western Europe. Crude notions of violence as a straightforward response to high prices and consequent hunger have been challenged by E.P. Thompson, who emphasizes, in addition to high price, a conception of "moral economy" — that is, a consensus among consumers, legitimated by others in authority, that food prices, supplies, and shipments should be regulated, by violence, if need be.[1] But Thompson, in turn, has been challenged by John Bohstedt, who provides evidence that food prices did not predict violence in Georgian England,[2] and by Manfred Gailus, who shows that riots continued in nineteenth-century Germany even though prices fell and that some food riots were motivated by straightforward theft rather than by a conception of moral economy.[3] The debate has moved from price alone to a more complex account of underlying conditions, including legitimation and the absence of effective punishment.[4] Such a progression in the food-riot debate is, in part, recapitulated in the treatment of ethnic riots. To the extent that ethnic riots have not yet yielded to more refined conceptions, they need to do so. If, after all, price alone does not predict food riots, why should we expect greater economic determinism in ethnic riots?

The assertion that economic decline is associated with interethnic violence has a long pedigree. Like food riots, European religious riots were said to be a function of the price of grain.[5] Hindu-Muslim riots, it is argued, are facilitated by economic decline.[6] Particular riots are also attributed to economic adversity. Durban (1949) occurred during a time of hardship, during which Indian shopkeepers and landlords had raised prices and rents.[7] The Ivory Coast riot (1958) took place during a reces-

1. E.P. Thompson, "The Moral Economy of the English Crowd in the Eighteenth Century," *Past and Present*, no. 50 (February 1971): 76–136.

2. John Bohstedt, *Riots and Community Politics in England and Wales, 1790–1810* (Cambridge: Harvard University Press, 1983). Bohstedt emphasizes that Thompson does not abandon the view of the riot as a response to price and to hunger but adds to it an ideological element. Ibid., pp. 15–22.

3. Manfred Gailus, "Food Riots in Germany in the Late 1840s," *Past and Present*, no. 145 (November 1994): 157–93. On theft and loot, see ibid., pp. 177–79. On falling prices, see ibid., p. 163; Bohstedt, *Riots and Community Politics in England and Wales, 1790–1810*, p. 97.

4. Gailus points to broad participation in the riots, coupled with relatively few arrests and many fewer prosecutions and punishments. "Food Riots in Germany in the Late 1840s," pp. 172–73. These are important features of ethnic riots that I shall emphasize in this chapter.

5. Natalie Zemon Davis, *Society and Culture in Early Modern France* (Stanford: Stanford University Press, 1975), p. 155. For similar arguments, see Ted Robert Gurr, *Why Men Rebel* (Princeton: Princeton University Press, 1970), pp. 312–13.

6. R.A. Schermerhorn, "The Locale of Hindu-Muslim Riots," *Indian Journal of Politics* 1, no. 1 (January–June 1971): 37–47, at p. 44.

7. Mabel Palmer, *The History of Indians in Natal* (Cape Town: Oxford University Press, 1957), p. 156.

sion, and the Burmese riot (1938) took place during a depression.[8] Anti-Chinese riots in several Indonesian cities in 1963 came during bad times, as did the Sri Lankan riots of 1956 and 1958.[9] But later Sri Lankan riots were synchronized with improvements in the economy, and the same goes for many Hindu-Muslim riots, which have coincided with periods of prosperity. Meerut (1987) occurred in the face of growing prosperity. Varanasi, a city characterized by high rates of economic growth, has had Hindu-Muslim riots repeatedly since 1966, often in good times.[10] The Jamshedpur and Ranchi belt in Bihar has had its share of Hindu-Muslim violence as well, although it is an area of relative prosperity and generally full employment.[11] For every riot in conditions of hardship, there seems to be another riot in conditions of abundance.

The last word has not been spoken on these hypotheses, but there is substantial room for doubt. Herculean efforts have been made to confirm an association between economic deprivation and the black violent protest demonstrations of the 1960s in the United States, or to confirm more complex curvilinear relationships between deprivation and the violence, but, as I pointed out in Chapter 1, the results have been inconclusive. Similar efforts to link the British violence of the early 1980s to declining economic conditions for minorities would be unavailing.[12] The price of grain, it turns out, bears no clear relation to the Protestant-Catholic violence of the late sixteenth century,[13] and efforts to distinguish riot-prone from riot-free north Indian cities on the basis of economic conditions seem futile.[14] A similar investigation of the association

8. Gwendolen Carter, *Independence for Africa* (New York: Praeger, 1960), p. 114; Government of Burma, *Interim Report of the Riot Inquiry Committee* (Rangoon: Superintendent of Government Printing & Stationery, 1939), pp. 19–20, 24.

9. The Siauw Giap, "Group Conflict in a Plural Society," *Revue du Sud-Est Asiatique*, no. 1 (January 1966): 1–31, at p. 12; Howard Wriggins, "Ceylon's Time of Troubles, 1956–1958," *Far Eastern Survey* 28, no. 3 (March 1959): 33–39, at p. 35.

10. Anjoo Upadhyaya, "Recent Trends in Communal Violence: A Case Study of Varanasi" (paper presented at the Conference on Conflict and Change, Ethnic Studies Network, Portrush, Northern Ireland, June 9, 1992). For the argument that growing Muslim prosperity attracts attacks, see Asghar Ali Engineer, "Communal Violence in Kanpur," *Economic and Political Weekly*, February 26, 1994, pp. 473–74.

11. M.A. Akbar, *Riot after Riot* (New Delhi: Penguin, 1988), p. 22.

12. See Simon Field et al., *Ethnic Minorities in Britain: A Study of Trends in Their Position since 1961*, Home Office Research Study No. 68 (London: H.M.S.O., 1981).

13. Davis, *Society and Culture in Early Modern France*, p. 155.

14. For skepticism on the oft-invoked connection between riots and competition between Hindu and Muslim artisans, see Steven Wilkinson, "Case Selection and the Study of Hindu-Muslim Violence — What Large Datasets Can Give Us" (paper presented to the Conference on Designing Social Inquiry into the Study of Ethnicity and Nationalism, Harvard

between racially motivated crime against minorities and macroeconomic conditions in New York City turned up no relationship.[15]

In-migration of ethnic strangers is also said to be associated with increases in ethnic violence. The argument is that a large influx of ethnic strangers increases competition and drives down wages; mass immigration and economic contraction together are thought to be an especially volatile combination.[16] Of course, ethnic pluralism is required for ethnic riots, and in-migration is an important source of heterogeneity. But, beyond this, the evidence is equivocal. Episodes of violence in Assam and the southern Philippines seem associated with the truly extraordinary rates of migration to those areas.[17] On the other hand, the significance of in-migration for the production of violence (where it occurs) appears far more likely to be related to politics than to economics.

Areas with large migrant populations, such as Luluabourg, Zaire, were nonviolent until the electoral implications of large numbers of ethnic strangers were recognized. The same goes for Assam and for Wukari in Nigeria, an area to which Tiv had migrated previously for centuries. Moreover, major riots can occur even in the face of large-scale out-migration of the targets or the decline of the target group as a fraction of the population owing to differential rates of natural increase. In Odessa (1905), Jews were a shrinking fraction of the population. In Burma (1938), many Indians had already returned home because of the depression. Malaysia had a massive influx of Chinese in the early decades of the twentieth century but no significant ethnic violence. By 1931, Malays were under 45 percent of the population; Chinese, 39 percent.[18] Chinese were returning to China even in the late 1920s; with the depression,

---

University Center for International Affairs, April 21–22, 1995), pp. 6–7. See also J.A.C. Mackie, "Anti-Chinese Outbreaks in Indonesia, 1959–68," in J.A.C. Mackie, ed., *The Chinese in Indonesia* (Hong Kong: Heinemann Educational Books, 1976), p. 136.

15. Donald P. Green, Dara Z. Strolovich, and Janelle S. Wong, "Defended Neighborhoods, Integration, and Racially Motivated Crime," *American Journal of Sociology* 104, no. 2 (September 1998): 372–403.

16. Susan Olzak, *The Dynamics of Ethnic Competition and Conflict* (Stanford: Stanford University Press, 1992), pp. 35–37, 179.

17. See Narendra Chandra Dutta, *Land Problems and Land Reforms in Assam* (Delhi: S. Chand, 1968), pp. 1–29; P.C. Goswami, *The Economic Development of Assam* (New York: Asia Publishing House, 1963), pp. 17, 22–32, 287–88; John H. Adkins, "Philippines 1971: Events of a Year, Trends of the Future," *Asian Survey* 12, no. 1 (January 1992): 78–87, at pp. 78–79; Peter Cook, "But Whose Law?" *Far Eastern Economic Review*, May 22, 1971, pp. 19–21.

18. Rupert Emerson, *Malaysia: A Study in Direct and Indirect Rule* (New York: Macmillan, 1937), pp. 20, 22.

there was a considerable net outflow.[19] Large-scale violence at the end of World War II followed this back-migration. By the time of independence, the Chinese fraction of the urban population had been stable for a decade.[20] Urban violence began as the Chinese share of the overall and urban population started to decline, as a result of rates of natural increase favoring Malays over Chinese and the continuing out-migration of Chinese.[21] An examination of antiblack riots in the United States from 1913 to 1963 found no association between increases in black population in a city and propensity to violence; the same negative results were found with respect to relative size of the black population.[22] Migration and the resulting competition do not seem to provide especially promising avenues of further exploration.

The timing issue can also be approached from the standpoint of seasonality. Most serious individual assaults, for example, are committed on weekends, the majority at night.[23] Violence in the United States increases in hot weather.[24] Leisure, darkness, and heat may therefore be regarded as environmental conditions propitious for violence. The calendar may have other effects as well. The 1983 Sri Lankan riots coincided with a Buddhist holiday.[25] Religious seasons, such as Easter–Passover–Nabi Musa in pre-Israel Palestine or Easter in the Russian Empire, could be recurrently dangerous.[26] Similarly, the coincidence of Idul Azah, an Islamic festival celebrated in Burma with animal sacrifices, and the Full Moon Day of Weso,

19. Ibid., p. 28.

20. Hamzah-Sendut, "Urbanisation," in Wang Gungwu, ed., *Malaysia: A Survey* (New York: Praeger, 1965), pp. 88–89.

21. See T.G. McGee, "Population: A Preliminary Analysis," in Wang, ed., *Malaysia*, pp. 77–78.

22. Stanley Lieberson and Arnold R. Silverman, "The Precipitants and Underlying Conditions of Race Riots," *American Sociological Review* 30, no. 6 (December 1965): 887–98, at pp. 893–94.

23. Leonard Berkowitz, "Some Varieties of Human Aggression: Criminal Violence as Coercion, Rule-following, Impression, Management, and Impulsive Behavior," in Anne Campbell and John J. Gibbs, eds., *Violent Transactions: The Limits of Personality* (Oxford: Basil Blackwell, 1986), pp. 87–103, at p. 96. The same was true of the 1960s violent protests in the United States. See Clark McPhail, "Civil Disorder Participation: A Critical Examination of Recent Research," *American Sociological Review* 36, no. 6 (December 1971): 1058–1073.

24. Michael Argyle, *The Social Psychology of Everyday Life* (New York: Routledge, 1992), p. 169.

25. Jonathan Spencer, "Collective Violence and Everyday Practice in Sri Lanka," *Modern Asian Studies* 24, no. 3 (July 1990): 603–23, at p. 621.

26. Bernard Wasserstein, "Patterns of Communal Conflict in Palestine," in Ada Rapoport-Albert and Steven J. Zipperstein, eds., *Jewish History: Essays in Honour of Chimen Abramsky* (London: Peter Halban, 1988), pp. 611–28.

a Buddhist Lent characterized by abstention from killing of living things, may have facilitated violence in 1988 in upcountry Burmese towns in which Muslims and Burmans are both present.[27] Several riots with Muslim participants, in widely scattered parts of the globe, have occurred during the Muslim fasting month, a time of personal discipline, abstemiousness, and, for some, short tempers. Batu Pahat, Malaysia (1945), Kano, Nigeria (1953), Malegaon, Maharashtra (1983), and Karachi (1988) took place during the fast; Sukabumi, Indonesia (1963), and Mauritius (1968) followed on the heels of the fasting month. (Many others, of course, occurred quite apart from the Islamic calendar.) Without discounting the possible influence of seasonality, I will conduct no inquiry into the regularities of the clock and the calendar.

The present subject is better described as *seasonal irregularities*, those changing conditions that create a favorable context for violence and so make it more likely. The conditions are disparate, but they seem to produce their facilitative effect through a limited number of mechanisms. Either they undermine previously stable expectations and, by rendering group prospects uncertain, make the need for violence seem exigent when an appropriate precipitant occurs, or else they lend moral sanction to violence or remove the fear that ordinarily prevents violence — or some combination of these. Particularly surprising, perhaps, will be the notion that conducive environments provide moral underpinnings for this form of violence. I shall argue, however, that this is usually the case, that the rioters are not alone in thinking that the killing is a good thing. When rioting is seen as necessary, when it can be accomplished with impunity, and when it is widely believed to be justified, there is a strong chance it will happen.

INTERREGNA

Periods of transition, say some sociologists, are the times when the potential for violence is greatest. At such times, "the situation becomes uncertain, and one cannot act out a conventional role."[28] Wags have sometimes responded to similar assertions with a cynical definition of "a time of transition": a period joining two other times of transition. Yet there are times when behavior and expectations undergo severe discontinuities, and some of these discontinuities may facilitate violence.

27. Bertil Lintner, *Outrage: Burma's Struggle for Democracy* (London: White Lotus, 1990), p. 80.

28. Tamotsu Shibutani and Kian M. Kwan, *Ethnic Stratification: A Comparative Approach* (New York: Macmillan, 1965), p. 377.

War, or certain phases of it, is one such time.[29] During most of wartime, civilian populations are subject to discipline, sacrifice, and rigorous routine. But the wheel turns in interstitial or postwar periods. In the "short period of anarchy"[30] between the Soviet withdrawal and the Nazi occupation of Lithuania (1941), Lithuanians attacked Jews. Battles between Burmans and Karens in Burma (1942) occurred after the British retreat but before effective Japanese conquest of the south of the country. Burman-Rohingya violence in Arakan occurred at roughly the same time. Violence in Malaysia (1945–46) took place in a comparable setting, in this case after the Japanese surrender but before the British reoccupation. Following the war, there were Hausa-Ibo riots in northern Nigeria (1945), Sino-Thai riots in Thailand (1945), Sino-Indonesian riots in Indonesia (1945), and Taiwanese-Mainlander riots in Taiwan (1947). The India-Pakistan war of 1965 was followed by numerous riots in north Indian cities in the second half of the decade. Immediately before and after the 1971 war for the independence of Bangladesh, there were riots between Bengalis and non-Bengalis there. Once Indian troops departed in 1972, Bengali killings of Biharis accelerated.[31] Following the victory of the insurgents, but before the new regime was consolidated, there were several riots in Ethiopia (1991), principally, but not exclusively, between Amhara and Tigray on one side and Oromo on the other — an alignment paralleling postwar military alignments.[32]

War brings the prospect of important changes in ethnic relations. Especially in the periods preceding foreign occupation or reoccupation, uncertainty pervades social life. These are times marked by an absence of authority — interregna in the strict sense of the word — and the restraints on action that derive from fear of or respect for authority are accordingly diminished. People can act on their anger in ways unthinkable at other times. Prospective targets know this and behave accordingly.[33]

The post–World War II riots had another element to them. As in peri-

---

29. Cf. Helen Fein, "Accounting for Genocide after 1945: Theories and Some Findings," *International Journal on Group Rights* 1, no. 2 (January 1993): 79–106, at pp. 84–85, arguing that war and revolution are destabilizing events that provide special opportunities for genocide.

30. Roger Petersen, "Fear, Hatred, Resentment: Toward a More Comprehensive Understanding of Ethnic Violence in Eastern Europe" (unpublished paper, Department of Political Science, Washington University, St. Louis, 1997), p. 14.

31. See Qutubuddin Aziz, *Blood and Tears* (Karachi: United Press of Pakistan, 1974).

32. See *Africa Research Bulletin*, November 1–30, 1991, pp. 10351, 10393.

33. When Hun Sen of Cambodia deposed his co–prime minister, Prince Ranariddh, in 1997, there was talk again of Vietnamese "swallowing" Cambodia. Vietnamese in Phnom Penh fled to safer areas. *International Herald Tribune*, August 9–10, 1997, p. 5.

ods between occupations, the aftermath of the war raised expectations for ethnic change, although perhaps change of a more gradual and yet more enduring sort. Then, too, power was in flux, in different ways in different countries. Taiwan, freed of Japanese occupation, found itself under Chinese occupation of a most authoritarian variety.[34] The last year of the Japanese occupation in Thailand was marked by the assumption of power by a new Thai regime, which reversed many of the anti-Chinese policies of its predecessor, greatly raising Chinese expectations of a far more favorable position in Thai society than had theretofore been enjoyed. At the same time, the Chinese Nationalist government in Chungking had stated clearly its intention to play a prominent role in Thailand's internal affairs, thus presumably giving the Thailand Chinese reason to think their political position might be altered as a result of external intervention in their behalf. The immediate precipitant of the Yaowarat riot of 1945, in which Thais attacked Chinese, reflected these transitional expectations: the Chinese flag was flown without the accompanying Thai colors.[35] Certain wartime periods thus reduce the restraining role of authority, create radically new expectations, and place power in a dramatically unstable state of flux.

The prospect of decolonization likewise made many ethnic possibilities that had once seemed remote now seem plausible. Firm instruments of control were losing their grip. A large number of ethnic riots occurred in Asia and Africa as the struggle for independence moved toward its ineluctable conclusion. Among these were India-Pakistan (1946–47), preceded by other riots at various stages of self-government; Nigeria (1953); Ghana (1954–56); Sudan (1955); Guinea (1956–58); Congo (Brazzaville) (1956–59); Malaysia (1957); the Ivory Coast (1958); Luluabourg (1959); Zanzibar (1961); Guyana (1962–64); arguably Singapore (1964); and Mauritius (1965). The list of riots on or around the threshold of self-government or independence is long, indeed.

Major regime changes in general provide opportunities for riot. Soon after the overthrow of the shah of Iran, there were riots between Sistanis and Baluch in Zahedan (1979) as well as between Kurds and Turks

34. Douglas Mendel, *The Politics of Formosan Nationalism* (Berkeley and Los Angeles: University of California Press, 1970), pp. 31–41. The Taiwan violence of 1947, it needs to be added, was actually a hybrid of a deadly riot and a violent protest demonstration, as those terms are used in Chapter 1, above. See Lai Tse-Han, Ramon H. Myers, and Wei Wou, *A Tragic Beginning: The Taiwan Uprising of February 28, 1947* (Stanford: Stanford University Press, 1991), pp. 99–140.

35. G. William Skinner, *Chinese Society in Thailand* (Ithaca: Cornell University Press, 1957), pp. 278–82.

(1979).[36] In both cases, demands for autonomy, in the face of attempts by the new regime to impose hegemony on the periphery, lay in the background. The Xhosa-Zulu killings in South Africa (1990 and following years) occurred as the transition from apartheid was set in motion.[37] An array of riots in Kyrghyzstan, Uzbekistan, Azerbaijan, and Tajikistan took place between 1988 and 1991, when the Soviet regime was losing its grip, just as anti-Jewish riots occurred in Kishinev and Odessa in the revolutionary year 1905.[38] In Indonesia, the end of the Sukarno regime in 1965 and the end of the Suharto regime in 1998 were both followed by waves of killing. A "loosening of the existing order of things,"[39] a change in authority relations, an old regime dying, or a new regime not yet born: all raise the question of who will govern once the governors are gone. One-sided outcomes become possible.

The role of instability in facilitating violence lends at least surface support to the conventional wisdom among politicians that large majorities and firm governments are necessary for stability. This makes it more difficult than it would otherwise be for constitutional engineers to design democratic regimes that provide for fluidity of political alignments and the possibility of alternation in office without engendering dangerous uncertainties and sharp reversals of fortune.

THE DECLINE OF MULTIETHNIC PARTIES AND COALITIONS

If political change and the uncertainty consequent upon it facilitate ethnic violence, then a particular kind of change is especially likely to do so: the disintegration of a multiethnic party or coalition. In most severely divided countries, party lines follow ethnic lines. In view of the incompatible demands that characterize divided polities, it takes heroic efforts or powerful electoral incentives to achieve some degree of organizational integration across ethnic lines.[40] These conditions have not been wholly

36. *Washington Post*, December 26, 1979, p. A25; April 24, 1979, p. A14.

37. Donald L. Horowitz, *A Democratic South Africa? Constitutional Engineering in a Divided Society* (Berkeley and Los Angeles: University of California Press, 1991), p. 73.

38. Edward H. Judge, *Easter in Kishinev: Anatomy of a Pogrom* (New York: New York University Press, 1992), p. 141; Robert Weinberg, "Anti-Jewish Violence and Revolution in Late Imperial Russia: Odessa, 1905" (paper presented at the Seminar on Riots and Pogroms, University of Washington, Seattle, April 1991).

39. Mark R. Beissinger, "Nationalist Violence in the Former Soviet Union, 1987–1992: An Event Analysis" (paper presented at the annual convention of the American Association for the Advancement of Slavic Studies, Washington, D.C., October 29, 1995), p. 10.

40. See Donald L. Horowitz, *Ethnic Groups in Conflict* (Berkeley and Los Angeles: University of California Press, 1985), pp. 365–426.

lacking even in the most divided polities. Some have been able to integrate antagonistic groups within a dominant ruling party for a considerable time, but these are rare. Many parties begin with multiethnic aspirations, but few endure in that form: most multiethnic parties split. The African single-party regimes that emerged after independence, claiming multiethnic coverage, were often masks for the dominance of particular groups.[41] However, coalitions of avowedly ethnic parties are more feasible. At various times, Malaysia and Fiji have had coalition arrangements purporting to be permanent, and others have had coalitions put together to contest particular elections or form governments afterward.

Whatever the organizational form, the decline of such arrangements is often the prelude to riot. Multiethnic coalitions are rightly regarded as conducive to mitigating the conflict. Hence a break in the coalition suggests a resurgence of the conflict, and it permits ethnic sentiments to be expressed and acted out in ways impossible while leaders were committed to keeping the component parties together.

Changes in the Congress Party in India have recurrently been associated with violence occurring thereafter. There were few Hindu-Muslim riots while Muslim leaders of the Khalifat were linked to the Congress following World War I, but riots resumed when the links dissolved.[42] When Congress was banned in pre-independence Hyderabad, the absence of an interethnic center was felt immediately, leaving the field to two equal and opposite organizations, one Hindu and one Muslim. Several riots followed in the state within a year and a half of the ban.[43] Riots in Meerut (1968) and Ahmedabad (1969) were preceded by Muslim shifts away from Congress candidates in the 1967 general election in these areas. Hindu-Muslim polarization increased during this time.[44] A similar change in support was noticeable in the period preceding the Delhi riot (1984), as Congress (I) reduced its dependence on minorities

41. Ibid., pp. 427–40.

42. Indian Statutory Commission, *Memoranda Submitted by the Government of India and the India Office to the Indian Statutory Commission*, Vol. IV, pt. 1 (London: H.M.S.O., 1930), pp. 95–120, at p. 99.

43. Ashutosh Varshney, "Value Rationality, Instrumental Rationality, and Ethnic Conflict: The Logic of Hindu-Muslim Relations in India" (paper presented at the annual meeting of the American Political Science Association, Chicago, August 31–September 3, 1995), p. 56. There was also a riot a few months before the ban. I shall return to the direction of causation shortly.

44. Aswini K. Ray and Subhash Chakravarti, *Meerut Riots: A Case Study* (New Delhi: Sampradayikta Virodhi Committee n.d. [1968 or 1969]), p. 5; Ghanshyam Shah, "Communal Riots in Gujarat," *Economic and Political Weekly*, Annual Number, January 1970, pp. 187–200, at p. 189.

and consolidated its base among Hindus, thus weakening restraints on anti-Sikh sentiment.[45]

Another major political system with long-standing multiethnic parties in a divided society was the Philippines before martial law was declared in 1972. Muslims and Christians had found their way into both major parties. By the time of the 1971 election, however, Christians and Muslims in the south were polarized, and many Muslims lost office when Christians who had previously voted for them ceased to do so.[46] Violence accelerated around this time.

As this discussion suggests, the relationship between ethnic riots and the decline of multiethnic parties can be reciprocal. In Hyderabad, there had actually been a riot months before the banning of the Congress; another followed soon after, and further riots took place all over the state in the following year. The withdrawal of Congress from the field removed the only organization with the ambition of interethnic conciliation. From then on, restraints were off.[47] Violence can break the multiethnic party, but a party decomposing into its constituent parts can create conditions conducive to much greater violence.

A sense of the incompatibility of ethnic interests, if not outright hostility, is what fosters the decomposition of a multiethnic party, and that decomposition then has an independent role to play. It certainly did in Sri Lanka, after the 1956 general election brought to power an all-Sinhalese government for the first time since independence, nearly a decade earlier. The previous ruling party was placed on the defensive, becoming for a time a Sinhalese-chauvinist party that sought to outbid its opponent in alienating the Tamils. For their part, as we saw in Chapter 8, the Tamils overwhelmingly elected candidates of the Federal Party, completing the polarization process. No one had an electoral reason to be moderate for some time thereafter.

The same sort of party polarization preceded violence in the Sudan (1955) and Luluabourg, Zaire (1959). Two northern Sudanese parties competed for southern votes in the election of 1954, but the Liberal Party was on the rise as a party representing southern interests. The results of

45. Rajni Kothari, "The How and Why of It All," in Smitu Kothari and Harsh Sethi, eds., *Voices from a Scarred City: The Delhi Carnage in Perspective* (Delhi: Lokayan, 1985), p. 13.

46. Peter G. Gowing, *Muslim Filipinos — Heritage and Horizon* (Quezon City: New Day, 1979), pp. 192–95.

47. I am indebted to Ashutosh Varshney for a memorandum, January 31, 1996, providing details on Hyderabad and making this point.

"Sudanization," unfavorable to southerners, gave the Liberals a boost and weakened the position of southern legislators belonging to northern parties. Resignations from those parties followed. Three months before the riot, two southern ministers left the cabinet in a dispute over southern issues. They were welcomed into the Liberal Party, and the demise of multiethnic parties was complete.[48] In Luluabourg, the 1958 election gave the ethnic association Lulua-Frères the opportunity to become a party. The Luba then formed their own Mouvement Solidaire Muluba. The two were unified under the umbrella of Patrice Lumumba's Mouvement National Congolais, but in July 1959 the MNC split into two wings: MNC/Lumumba and MNC/Kalonji. Since Albert Kalonji was a Luba, Lumumba's strategy was then to organize "an anti-Luba alliance of the Lulua, Tetela (his own ethnic group), Songye, and other peoples of Kasai."[49] The riot followed in October. Roughly similar sequences of ethnic party purification followed by ethnic violence can be identified for Guyana (1962), Mauritania (1966), and Sierra Leone (1968);[50] and, as we have seen, the uncertain continuation of the multiethnic coalition in Malaysia contributed to violence in Kuala Lumpur (1969).

Although it is not usually a precipitant of violence, the decline of a multiethnic party or coalition is a symptom and an accelerator of widening ethnic cleavages. It is associated with an upsurge in the assertiveness and sensed legitimacy of ethnic sentiments. By removing electoral restraints, it enhances the relative power of politicians inclined to extreme positions, as it simultaneously dissolves whatever early warning system might have been established as a by-product of regular contact among politicians of opposed groups. The dissolution of the multiethnic party or coalition tears the frail political bonds between groups with interests adverse to each other.

FLUCTUATIONS IN POLICY

Policy fluctuations on ethnic issues are conducive to violence. This point was made originally, with respect to colonial policy, by Robert A.

48. Republic of Sudan, *Report of the Commission of Inquiry into Disturbances in the Southern Sudan during August, 1955* (Khartoum: McCorquedale, 1956), pp. 21, 115.

49. Thomas Turner, "Congo-Kinshasa," in Victor A. Olorunsola, ed., *The Politics of Cultural Subnationalism in Africa* (Garden City, N.Y.: Anchor Books, 1972), p. 222.

50. In Guyana, a multiethnic party had split some years earlier into what became two ethnically based parties. In Mauritania, the process was far less complete: a prominent African cabinet minister had lost his position, and the government was assuming an

LeVine, who argued that a colonial policy encouraging conflicting expectations of *both* self-government *and* repression was likely to generate more anticolonial violence than a colonial policy encouraging either one expectation or the other.[51] Policy changes from authoritarian to democratic, or vice versa, were often followed by anticolonial violence. The inconsistency, rather than the nature of the policy, LeVine identified as responsible for the violence through the mechanism of conflicting expectations among the then-subject peoples.

There are many connections that could be made between the LeVine thesis and theories of collective violence. Both James Davies's well-known but unproved "J-curve hypothesis," relating revolution to periods of improvement in material conditions followed by sharp reversals, and Crane Brinton's hypotheses, relating revolution to regime liberalization following repression, share a mechanism of conflicting or dashed expectations.[52] More relevant to ethnic rioting are theoretical statements that inconsistencies in the use of force are associated with turmoil[53]— a theme to which I shall return. The LeVine view can also be assimilated to the more general propositions that relate violence to interregna and shifts from multiethnic organizations to exclusively ethnic parties. All involve uncertainty and instability. Furthermore, as already noted,[54] official alterations in group status can precipitate violence.

Virtually all ethnic riots in Sri Lanka since independence can be described in terms of fluctuation. As we saw in Chapter 8, S.W.R.D. Bandaranaike was a pristine case of vacillation.[55] Elected on a program of "Sinhala Only" in 1956, Bandaranaike brought into active political

---

increasingly Arabic flavor. In Sierra Leone, when a northern-based party finally took power after coups in 1967 and 1968, it initially included members of the Mende opposition in the government but slowly pushed them out. By the time of the 1968 by-elections, the government was identified as essentially a northern regime.

51. Robert A. LeVine, "Anti-European Violence in Africa: A Comparative Analysis," *Journal of Conflict Resolution* 3, no. 4 (December 1959): 420–29.

52. James Davies, "Toward a Theory of Revolution," *American Sociological Review* 27, no. 1 (February 1962): 5–19; Crane Brinton, *The Anatomy of Revolution* (New York: W.W. Norton, 1938), pp. 51–52. On the Davies thesis, see Abraham H. Miller, Louis H. Bolce, and Mark Halligan, "The J-Curve Theory and the Black Urban Riots: An Empirical Test of Progressive Relative Deprivation Theory," *American Political Science Review* 71, no. 3 (September 1977): 964–82.

53. Betty Nesvold, Ivo Feierabend, and Rosalind Feierabend, "Political Coerciveness and Turmoil," *Law and Society Review* 5, no. 1 (August 1970): 93–118, at pp. 114–15.

54. See Chapter 8, pp. 308–10, above.

55. See Wriggins, "Ceylon's Time of Troubles," pp. 35, 37–38.

participation Sinhala-educated Sinhalese who had been neglected under the previous regime. Committed to making Sinhala the official language, he also aimed to protect Tamils from the discrimination ardently sought by his own supporters, only to abandon detailed safeguards for the Tamil language in his language bill in response to protests by Sinhalese. The Tamil counterprotest that ensued was the occasion for the first violence (1956). Then, after Bandaranaike obtained parliamentary authorization to include protections for Tamil in the language bill, Tamils kept up the pressure. Again, Bandaranaike responded. Long negotiations produced the B-C Pact, but Tamils, now distrustful, engaged in protest activities anyway. For their part, Sinhalese, as we have seen,[56] sat down outside Bandaranaike's residence until they gained his abrogation of the pact. As the Federal Party assembled to plan its next move, the 1958 riot began. The notch-by-notch escalation that led to violence was a direct consequence of Bandaranaike's reversals of his previous positions.

The 1977 and 1983 riots also took place in the shadow of policy uncertainty. The 1977 riot coincided with a dialogue between the Tamils and the Sinhalese party about to take office after elections, following a seven-year period of anti-Tamil discrimination.[57] The 1983 riot took place during efforts to convene an all-party conference to discuss the ethnic conflict and the terrorism that had grown out of it.[58] Quite likely, those with an interest in the conflict were keen to see conciliatory efforts abandoned, and their instigation of violence was begun against a background of policy oscillation that rewarded the sort of aggressive opposition on which they embarked.[59] Very shortly, however, I shall suggest that the significance of policy oscillation is not always, or even primarily, to be found in the rewards it provides for violence.

In a field as difficult as ethnic relations, of course, completely consistent policy is improbable, but it is the radical lurch from one extreme to another that seems conducive to violence. Colonial powers often failed to follow a policy of undifferentiated neutrality toward their subjects. Some groups were openly favored in many spheres of activity; some were given

56. Chapter 8, p. 281, above. See Tarzie Vittachi, *Emergency '58: The Story of the Ceylon Race Riots* (London: André Deutsch, 1958), pp. 24–25.

57. Sunil Bastian, "The Political Economy of Ethnic Violence in Sri Lanka: The July 1983 Riots," in Veena Das, ed., *Mirrors of Violence: Communities, Riots and Survivors in South Asia* (Delhi: Oxford University Press, 1990), pp. 286–304, at pp. 297–98.

58. Ibid., p. 298.

59. As we have seen in Chapter 7, above, the 1983 riot certainly evidenced some planning, especially after the first outbreak of violence.

more limited realms of protection. Shifts in these policies have several times been followed by ethnic violence. René Lemarchand has associated the dramatic Belgian shift from support for the Tutsi to support for the Hutu in Rwanda with the subsequent Hutu uprising.[60] In Luluabourg, the Belgians similarly shifted from the earlier support of Luba to support of Lulua, the latter less sympathetic to immediate independence.[61] The British in Malaya had long followed a policy of recognizing the legitimacy of the Malays as the indigenous people and protecting them from various forms of non-Malay incursion. The Japanese occupation disrupted British control. The British then supplied and supported Chinese guerrillas in the jungle. Northern Nigerians and southern Sudanese had likewise received different forms of colonial protection from the intrusions of their countrymen. Most of this protection was tacitly abandoned in favor of vaguely articulated concepts of free competition as self-government approached. In none of these cases was the abandonment complete, and the vacillation by which the policy change was marked lay in the background to the riots in Malaysia (1945–46), Nigeria (1953), and the Sudan (1955). People who must suddenly rely on themselves, especially when their erstwhile protector seems still sympathetic, may be inclined to marshal resources for drastic action.

The impact of vacillation by authority can be viewed at closer range when it relates to particular ethnic policies. The backtracking of Assam's chief minister on the language issue in 1960 was described in the preceding chapter.[62] Following the May 1966 northern Nigerian riot, the military government also cut back severely on the purported impact of its Decree No. 34. Following the July coup, the new military regime went all the way in the opposite direction; its action was then followed by the September riots.[63] In the Sind (1972), the provincial ruling party, identified with the Sindhis, had allowed the impression to grow that it favored exclusive use of the Sindhi language for official purposes. A resolution was moved in the assembly that would have required government employees to learn Sindhi; some forms were printed only in Sindhi and English, in defiance of the interests of Urdu-speakers. These changes were then undone, but then the undoing was undone with the enactment

60. René Lemarchand, *Rwanda and Burundi* (New York: Praeger, 1970), pp. 174–77.
61. Turner, "Congo-Kinshasa," pp. 219–21.
62. See K.C. Barua, *Assam: Her People and Her Language* (Shillong, Assam: Lawyers' Bookstall, 1960), pp. 14–16.
63. N.J. Miners, *The Nigerian Army, 1956–1966* (London: Methuen, 1971), pp. 213–18.

of a bill making Sindhi the official language after all. Anti-Sindhi violence began the same day.[64] Burma (1930), it will be recalled, was a riot that grew out of a Telugu strike. Once the strike ended, the question remained of what to do with the Burmans who had temporarily taken the jobs abandoned by the Telugus. Some employers retained some Burmans; one changed his mind. The fighting broke out amidst the uncertainty.[65]

Oscillation — the alternative yielding to each of the parties in conflict — is not to be confused with compromise, which can be more or less consistent and predictable. Policy fluctuations that give alternating comfort to both sides tend to foster an auction mentality in violence. The side that raises its collective bid and inflicts the greater increment of violence stands a greater chance of winning the concession. Fluctuation reduces fear of the authorities; their responsiveness imparts legitimacy to violence that might earlier have been inhibited. In general, fluctuations seem to make possible things that previously seemed remote, and volatile swings suggest that either very good things or very bad things are possible. If fluctuation occurs after the first violence breaks out, as it did in Nigeria (May 1966), it can be interpreted as a reward for violence.

It would be inaccurate, however, to think that all riots that occur in the course of policy change can easily be placed in the instrumental category. The timing of several such episodes casts grave doubt on the calculative character of the violence. Often the fluctuation *precedes* the violence. Consider again the Sri Lankan violence of 1958. If it were designed with policy impact in mind, why did it occur after Bandaranaike's repudiation of the B-C Pact, rather than before? The pact was seen as dangerous to Sinhalese interests. Yet ethnic violence was not employed strategically to secure its abrogation. When the violence occurred subsequently, perhaps it reflected apprehension that the Tamils might somehow gain back what the pact would have given them. But the policy debate had produced a "context of communal bitterness,"[66] in which the riot took

64. Dilip Mukerjee, "Pakistan's Growing Pains: Language Riots in Sind," *Times of India* (New Delhi), July 17, 1972, p. 8; *Far Eastern Economic Review*, July 22, 1972, pp. 16, 18; August 5, 1972, pp. 16–18. The riot was actually a hybrid — part violent protest demonstration against the police, part anti-Sindhi. See *Statesman* (Calcutta), July 11, 1972, pp. 1, 7.

65. "Extracts of the Report of the Rangoon Riots Enquiry Committee," in E.L.F. Andrew, *Indian Labour in Rangoon* (Calcutta: Oxford University Press, 1933), pp. 279–92. There was also inconsistency regarding wages. One employer wanted to settle the strike at a higher figure than others, but after he did so he backed down, whereupon violence broke out.

66. S. Arasaratnam, *Ceylon* (Englewood Cliffs, N.J.: Prentice-Hall, 1964), p. 31.

place. The riot can thus be seen as a result of the policy oscillation, which reinforced the bitterness, more than as an effort to influence the policy.

The Sri Lankan riot can also be viewed as occurring during a period of reprieve from the tension the B-C Pact aroused. Comparable events can be identified elsewhere. The killing of Vietnamese in Cambodia (1970) began after the Lon Nol coup, which temporarily delivered Cambodia from Vietnamese threat.[67] Anti-Luba violence in Luluabourg (1959) also followed a policy debate about eligibility to vote and the release of Luba political leaders who had been arrested for inciting anti-Belgian feeling.[68] Issues had come and gone, and the killing took place while nothing was pending.

Even if the policy changes occur after nonviolent demonstrations, they may play into the notch-by-notch escalation process described in Chapter 8. In Assam (1972), the issue was language of instruction. The Gauhati University Council decided to make Assamese the medium of instruction, but to permit examination questions to be answered in Bengali or English. When Assamese students protested the exception, the council revoked it, producing an uproar in the overwhelmingly Bengali Cachar region of the state. The state legislature approved the council's revised decision, but provided for the creation of a new university in Cachar. Assamese saw this as the prelude to the dismemberment of Assam.[69] As in the Assamese-language controversy of a dozen years earlier, policy change produced protest, which produced another change and another protest, until one of them became violent. The Sind riot (1972) was simply a foreshortened version of the same process; in that case, the demonstrations pro and con were sometimes simultaneous, and some of the violence resulted from rival processions that met and clashed.[70]

Very shortly, it will become apparent that a certain species of inconsistency on the part of governmental authorities also proves supportive of violence, although that inconsistency also sends disinhibiting messages that policy fluctuations alone do not. What we have seen until now, from interregna and the decline of multiethnic organization as well as from policy fluctuations, is increased uncertainty, the possibility of more radical and one-sided outcomes, and the sort of polarization that puts groups on the alert for signs of danger. A pendulum swinging in a wide arc is not

67. *New York Times*, April 14, 1970, p. 1; April 16, 1970, p. 1.

68. Turner, "Congo-Kinshasa," p. 223.

69. Myron Weiner, *Sons of the Soil: Migration and Ethnic Conflict in India* (Princeton: Princeton University Press, 1978), pp. 117–24.

70. *Times of India*, July 11, 1972, p. 1.

conducive to the stability of expectations on which precariously divided polities rely for their survival.

There is another possible reason for the tendency of policy fluctuation to support resort to violence. That reason relates to the likelihood of violence designed to consolidate gains or avert losses. A substantial body of opinion holds that a loss of status is more likely to be resisted than a potential gain is to be sought, citing experimental research with dominant animals threatened with a status loss.[71] The same general idea is embraced by behavioral economists, who hold that people are less willing to risk a loss than they are to risk a gain of equivalent magnitude.[72] International relations theorists have likewise argued that "it is one of the psychological assets of the *status quo* power in crisis situations that people on the whole are more ready to take risks to keep what they have than to get something more."[73] The opposite view is not widely held, but a more subtle, limited version is available. Some theorists of collective violence have drawn on the goal-gradient hypothesis of learning theory, proposing that the impetus for violence to seek a gain increases as the distance from the goal decreases.[74] Eric Hoffer puts the point simply: "A grievance is most poignant when almost redressed."[75] Policy oscillations threaten people in both positions. They raise the prospect of a loss, including a loss of what is newly won, and they thwart the fulfillment of what is nearly attained.

AUTHORITATIVE TOLERANCE, ACQUIESCENCE, OR CONDONATION

Perhaps the most significant facilitator of rioting is authoritative social support for group violence. By *authoritative*, I mean conduct emanating from political authorities or social superiors. (I deal with police and mil-

---

71. Elton B. McNeil, "The Nature of Aggression," in Elton B. McNeil, ed., *The Nature of Human Conflict* (Englewood Cliffs, N.J.: Prentice-Hall, 1965), p. 21.

72. Amos Tversky and Daniel Kahneman, "The Framing of Decisions and the Rationality of Choice," *Science*, January 30, 1981, pp. 453–58.

73. Coral Bell, *Conventions of Crisis* (London: Oxford University Press, 1971), p. 24; Robert Jervis, "Political Implications of Loss Aversion," *Political Psychology* 13, no. 2 (June 1992): 187–204.

74. Gurr, *Why Men Rebel*, pp. 71–72; Ivo K. Feierabend, Rosalind L. Feierabend, and Betty A. Nesvold, "Social Change and Political Violence: Cross-National Patterns," in Hugh Davis Graham and Ted Robert Gurr, eds., *Violence in America: Historical and Comparative Perspectives*, Vol. 2 (Washington, D.C.: U.S. Government Printing Office, 1969), pp. 497–542, at pp. 507–08, 533 n.15.

75. Eric Hoffer, *The True Believer* (New York: Harper and Row, 1951), p. 28.

itary conduct in the next section.) *Social support* implies that this conduct is construed by the participants in violence as lending tacit or active approval to their violent behavior. (It also can make the police timid.) By *conduct*, I mean to include words as well as deeds, omission as well as commission. The conduct need only be interpreted as lending approval; it need not be so intended.

This kind of social support is very widespread, present in more than half the riots for which detailed data are available, and it may be present in others as well; the nature of the materials is such that all of the relevant symbolism may not have been picked up by those outside observers who report on violence. Social support is present, moreover, in nearly all the events in which relatively modest precipitants produce riots.

Authoritative support is so common a pattern in ethnic riots that many students of violence, from a variety of vantage points, have identified this factor as the one which makes the difference between at most a series of isolated assaults and large-scale collective violence.[76] Such a statement is too broad. There are a few riots that occur without such support and a few that occur in the face of the determined, active opposition of the authorities. Nevertheless, the recurrence of authoritative support invites several questions: What kinds of support are likely to underpin a resort to violence? What facilitating role does support play? What about instances of rioting in the face of social disapproval?

The kinds of support are easy to enumerate. In several riots occurring under colonial conditions, a green light for violence against the target group was perceived, with varying degrees of accuracy, by the initiators of violence. Burma (1930) occurred in the context of British suppression of the Indian nationalist movement and the recent arrest of Gandhi. Since Indians in Burma were closely attuned to events in their homeland, many British officials tarred them with the same brush. This the Burmans sensed keenly, taking note of the forcible dispersion of an Indian nationalist demonstration by colonial police in Rangoon some weeks before the riots. When the rioting began, a small party of colonial officials and police

76. See, e.g., Arthur Raper, *The Tragedy of Lynching* (Chapel Hill: University of North Carolina Press, 1933), pp. 277, 304–05, 362; Hadley Cantril, *The Psychology of Social Movements* (New York: John Wiley & Sons, 1941), p. 99; Elliott M. Rudwick, *Race Riot at East St. Louis, July 2, 1917* (Carbondale: Southern Illinois University Press, 1964), p. 229; Neil J. Smelser, *Theory of Collective Behavior* (New York: Free Press, 1963), pp. 231–34; Allen D. Grimshaw, "Urban Racial Violence in the United States: Changing Ecological Considerations," *American Journal of Sociology* 66, no. 2 (September 1960): 109–19, at p. 110; H. Otto Dahlke, "Race and Minority Riots — a Study in the Typology of Violence," *Social Forces* 30, no. 4 (May 1952): 419–25.

confronted and disarmed a column of perhaps 500 Burmans advancing toward the Indian quarter of Rangoon. "I didn't think," protested one of the leaders, "that there was any objection to killing Indians. The Government is against them. . . . The police let them have it . . . not long ago."[77] Sinhalese believed Britain, at war with Turkey, would welcome attacks on Muslims in Sri Lanka (1915).[78] Southern Sudanese in 1955 also mistakenly counted on colonial support and actually dispatched a request for British help.[79] Rioters in Palestine (1920) thought the British government was favorably disposed; they wrote on a public notice: "There is no punishment for killing Jews."[80] Comments Bernard Wasserstein: "Often the crowd seems to see itself as acting in some sense on behalf of the authorities in order to root an evil element out of society. The belief in the indulgent wink of government, whether or not based on reality, can be a stimulus to riot."[81]

From here on, colonial involvement gets rather more direct and malevolent. Jos (1945), we have noted, occurred against the background of the general strike led by the Ibo politician Nnamdi Azikiwe, and the Ibo were plainly in disfavor with the British for their active nationalism at this time. There is some suggestion that a local colonial official actually incited the Hausa attacks. Whether that is accurate or not, Hausa likely believed they were acting with British approval.[82] Luluabourg (1959) is a more blatant case. As in Nigeria, the colonial power supported the more gradualist of the ethnic groups in the independence movement, in this case, Lulua. Leading Luba politicians had recently been arrested for their nationalist activities, and a leaked report of a colonial official had just recommended mass deportations of Luba from Lulua areas and disenfranchisement of the remainder.[83] By the time the Lulua attacks occurred, the Luba had been virtually stripped of societal protection by the Belgians. In Guyana (1962), lack of British sympathy for the elected government of Cheddi Jagan was manifest. Most colonial

77. Quoted in Maurice Collis, *Trials in Burma,* 2d ed. (London: Faber & Faber, 1945), p. 150.
78. Stanley Tambiah, *Leveling Crowds: Ethnonationalist Conflicts and Collective Violence in South Asia* (Berkeley and Los Angeles: University of California Press, 1996), p. 289.
79. K.D.D. Henderson, *Sudan Republic* (New York: Praeger, 1965), p. 177.
80. Wasserstein, "Patterns of Communal Conflict in Palestine," p. 622.
81. Ibid., p. 620. I shall return later to the theme of the riot as a surrogate for official punishment.
82. Leonard Plotnicov, "An Early Nigerian Civil Disturbance: The 1945 Hausa-Ibo Riot in Jos," *Journal of Modern African Studies* 9, no. 2 (August 1971): 297–305.
83. Turner, "Congo-Kinshasa," pp. 222–23.

commercial firms encouraged the general strike that led to the riot, and Jagan's requests for preventive British military assistance were refused.[84] Finally, there is the unambiguous support given by Europeans to Africans in the anti-Indian riot in South Africa (1949). The anti-Indian views of South African whites, often reflected in the speeches of government ministers, were well known. When the fighting began, white civilians watched the assaults with approval or amusement. Some went further, inciting the rioters, and the official commission of inquiry credited one report that "a number of European women urged the Natives [Africans] on to 'hit the coolies [Indians]!' Thereafter they went dancing up the street with the Natives. The pictorial record shows Europeans actively inciting the Natives, or evincing all the signs of enjoyment at their excesses."[85]

There are parallels in the post-independence period. The anti-Ahmadi riot in west Punjab (1953) was, in part, the product of the tolerance by the Punjab chief minister of the long campaign of abuse that preceded the riot. The ruling Muslim League proved a willing collaborator; League branches and members often took part in the violence. Virtually no one in authority was prepared to take a firm position until after the riot was under way.[86] Attacks on Hindus by Muslims in East Bengal (1971) proceeded with the active connivance of the Pakistani military regime, which armed Muslims, partly perhaps because it regarded the Hindus as especially rebellious, partly because it wanted to convert the conflict between Bengalis and West Pakistanis to one between Muslims and Hindus.[87] The killings of Vietnamese by Khmer (1970) were "fanned by the [Cambodian] government-sanctioned campaign against the Vietcong. . . . Vietcong [was], in a sense, a code word for all Cambodia's 600,000

84. Government of Great Britain, *Report of a Commission of Inquiry into Disturbances in British Guiana in February 1962*, Colon. No. 354 (London: H.M.S.O., 1962), pp. 33, 42.

85. Union of South Africa, *Report of the Commission of Enquiry into Riots in Durban* (Cape Town: Government Printer, 1949), p. 9. To the same effect, see Maurice Webb and Kenneth Kirkwood, *The Durban Riots and After* (Johannesburg: South African Institute of Race Relations, n.d.), pp. 2, 4, 7, 9. In Soweto (1976), Zulu emerged from hostels and attacked anti-apartheid protestors belonging to other African groups. Some of the Zulu vigilantes had apparently been encouraged by white officials. As the police were slow to suppress the violence, the suspicion grew that they supported it. *New York Times*, August 25, 1976, p. 6.

86. Government of [West] Punjab, *Report of the Court of Inquiry Constituted under Punjab Act II of 1954 to Enquire into the Punjab Disturbances of 1953* (Lahore: Government Printer, 1954), pp. 93–94, 266–67; Hugh Tinker, *India and Pakistan: A Political Analysis*, rev. ed. (New York: Praeger, 1968), p. 76.

87. *Washington Post*, June 17, 1971, p. A22.

Vietnamese . . . ."[88] The riots occurred after the Lon Nol coup. Uncertain of both its external security and its internal popularity, the new regime attempted to bolster both by detaining thousands of Vietnamese in camps. Khmer read the government's conduct as signs that the Vietnamese were fair game, and indeed soldiers played a leading role in the attacks. So strong were the signs that here we are on the borderline between authoritative toleration and state sponsorship.

Misreading of authority or reading too much into expressions of hostility — these can be deadly misinterpretations. Singapore (1964) occurred less than a year after the merger of Singapore into the new Federation of Malaysia. Following the merger, the central government had demonstrated its determination to play a role in Singapore's internal security affairs, and prominent Malaysian politicians had traveled to Singapore to organize the Malays against the Chinese-dominated Singapore government. The confluence of these actions undoubtedly raised expectations among the Singapore Malays and probably gave rise to a mistaken feeling that they could act against the Chinese with greater latitude than theretofore.[89] Much the same theme was being played in Sri Lanka after the 1956 election brought Bandaranaike to power. "Sinhala Only" was the announced policy, and *apey aanduwa* ("the government is ours") was the new spirit. A friendly regime, the leniency of the authorities in dealing with earlier incidents, and the fact that, for the first time, both major Sinhalese parties appeared to be playing an anti-Tamil hand all contributed to a belief among the Sinhalese rioters that they could act with impunity.[90]

Perhaps the most unusual combination of intended and unintended approval was the Ivory Coast (1958). The violence against Dahomeyans and Togolese took place in October, soon after the death of Ouëzzin Coulibaly, a prominent advocate of panethnic unity. With Coulibaly gone and President Félix Houphouët-Boigny out of the country, the protection of ethnic strangers was left largely in the hands of officials either unsympathetic or unduly heavy-handed. Houphouët himself had not long before — and quite uncharacteristically — added to the xenophobia when he asked in a speech:

[W]ould you have us . . . accept that from frontiers near or far instructions be given to an irresponsible minority to endanger the regime we have freely

88. Ibid., April 14, 1970, p. A12.
89. Cf. Michael Leifer, "Communal Violence in Singapore," *Asian Survey* 4, no. 10 (October 1964): 1115–21, at pp. 1116, 1119.
90. Vittachi, *Emergency '58*, p. 39.

chosen? Don't count on me for this. If . . . some people, whether white or black, *originaires* of the country or *non-originaires*, men or women, want to sap the bases of indispensable co-operation by accepting the role of paid agents, I don't give them twenty-four hours to leave the Ivory Coast forever.[91]

As the riot proceeded, Houphouët sent a passionate appeal from Paris for an end to the violence. But his earlier message had been not only permissive but prophetic. "The rioters took many of the strangers to the port and shipped them out of the country. The sentiment against the strangers was so strong among the Ivory Coast population, even in the lower levels of the Government, that nothing could halt the expulsion."[92]

If leaders misspeak, violence is likely to accelerate. After anti-Senegalese violence in Mauritania (1989), the president of Senegal declared on the radio that the anger of his people was understandable. Rioters took the statement as conferring permission to kill Mauritanians.[93] After Benin accused Gabon of supporting an invasion by mercenaries, the president of Gabon announced the expulsion of 10,000 Benin nationals. The same day, Beninese were attacked in two cities of Gabon (1978).[94] J.R. Jayewardene twice contributed to a sense of official sanction for anti-Tamil killing. In a speech after violence had broken out in 1977, the Sri Lankan president suggested that if the Tamils wanted a fight, then there would be a fight. After the speech, violence accelerated and spread. Under similar circumstances in 1983, rather than commiserate with victims, he blamed Tamil separatists for precipitating the Sinhalese killing of Tamils.[95] In Dushanbe, Tajikistan (1990), in Bombay (1992), and in Bhiwandi, India (1970), authorities did not condone violence by word but by deed: they released riot leaders, thereby emboldening the rioters to do more killing.[96] When President Léon Mba of Gabon

91. Quoted by Ruth Schachter Morgenthau, *Political Parties in French-Speaking West Africa* (Oxford: Clarendon Press, 1964), p. 217.

92. Elliot P. Skinner, "Strangers in West African Societies," *Africa* 33, no. 4 (October 1963): 307–20, at p. 314.

93. *Africa News,* May 15, 1989, p. 5.

94. Jocelyn Akoumondo, "L'éxpulsion des Beninois du Gabon," *Peuples Noirs, Peuples Africains* (Paris) 1, no. 5 (September–October 1978): 60–64, at p. 62; *West Africa*, July 31, 1978, p. 1518.

95. Elizabeth Nissan, "Some Thoughts on Sinhalese Justifications for the Violence," in James Manor, ed., *Sri Lanka in Crisis and Change* (New York: St. Martin's Press, 1984), pp. 177–78.

96. Moscow TV, February 14, 1990, in FBIS-SOV-90–032, February 15, 1990, p. 70; Flavia Agnes, "Two Riots and After: A Fact-Finding Report on Bandra (East)," *Economic*

did the same in 1962, his action, "which surprised the police authorities, was interpreted as giving the green light to further aggression, with the result that the violence continued for 36 hours longer."[97] Reciprocally, the arrest of influential Bengalis in Assam (1960) seemed to confirm rumors of Bengali malevolence as well as to flash a green light.[98] The arrest of the targets sends signals similar to those sent by the release of the aggressors.

Permissive signals can be sent in many ways. Television coverage following the assassination of Indira Gandhi showed her body lying in state, with outraged crowds around her; shouts of "blood for blood" were heard in the background.[99] The transmissions contributed to a widespread atmosphere of hatred of Sikhs, in which the Delhi violence (1984) began.[100] The authorities may be permissive because they sense the popular mood, but the attackers then take aggressive cues from official behavior. The Senegalese president made his seemingly permissive radio statement after the opposition and the press had accused the government of weakness in the face of attacks in Mauritania. In Bombay-Bhiwandi (1984), Mrs. Gandhi, apparently unwilling to alienate upper-caste Maratha voters, was loath to interfere with the anti-Muslim activities of Bal Thackeray, leader of the Shiv Sena, and when the riots came the state chief minister was slow to suppress them.[101] A similar interpretation of the lethargy of the chief minister is possible in Meerut (1987), when the Provincial Armed Constabulary, which took the rioters' side in Hindu-Muslim riots, was not withdrawn.[102]

When authorities move slowly to suppress the first acts of violence, rioters sense tacit permission. They certainly did in Kyrghyzstan (1990), in Gabon (1981), and in Ahmedabad (1969).[103] After taking office in

---

and Political Weekly, February 13, 1993, pp. 265–68, at p. 267; S.K. Ghosh, *Communal Riots in India* (New Delhi: Ashish, 1987), p. 179.

97. René Gauze, *The Politics of Congo-Brazzaville*, trans., ed., and supp., Virginia Thompson and Richard Adloff (Stanford: Hoover Institution Press, 1973), p. 112.

98. Pt. Deendayal Upadhyaya, "Report on Assam Situation" (mimeo., August 25, 1960), p. 2.

99. Uma Chakravarti and Nandita Haksar, *The Delhi Riots: Three Days in the Life of a Nation* (New Delhi: Lancer International, 1987), pp. 571, 604.

100. Ibid., p. 570.

101. Asghar Ali Engineer, *Bombay-Bhiwandi Riots: Analysis and Documentation* (Bombay: Institute of Islamic Studies, 1984), p. 21.

102. Asghar Ali Engineer, "Meerut: The Nation's Shame," *Economic and Political Weekly*, June 20, 1987, pp. 969–71, at p. 971.

103. Valery Tishkov, "Don't Kill Me, I Am Kyrghyz: Anthropological Analysis of Violence in Osh Ethnic Conflict" (paper presented at the 13th International Congress of

Bihar in 1967, a new government had strongly implied that there would be no further police firing on disorderly crowds in that state. The police, moreover, had been chastened by criticisms leveled by previous judicial commissions of inquiry into their rough conduct in earlier episodes of disorder. When anti-Muslim rioting broke out in Ranchi-Hatia (1967), the combination of official permissiveness and police timidity had an encouraging effect on the rioters.[104] Even misconceived administrative rules designed to regulate the use of official force can convey to rioters a sense of license. In Bombay (1992–93), the army was believed to be authorized to shoot only if a magistrate gave the order.[105] The perverse result was to have the army on the streets but impotent to take decisive action, thus contributing inadvertently to the continuation of the violence. The Indian protocol for civilian control of the armed forces in times of disturbance derived from English law. The same effect was produced by the same rule — no firing without a magistrate's order — in London (1780). The impotence of the army heightened the brazenness of the rioters, some of whom ridiculed the soldiers.[106] And in London, too, the civil authorities, fearful of their own unpopularity, were reluctant to order firearms to be used against mobs, who were, after all, attacking Catholics allegedly aligned with the enemies of Britain. The result was condonation.[107]

For Hindu-Muslim riots occurring at and after partition, Richard Lambert has similarly found authoritative social support to be a central element in the violence, although he particularly emphasizes its role in what he terms *rural pogroms*:

> In all recent rural pogroms evidence had been found for the belief on the part of the majority community that its violence was supported, or at least condoned by the government. Removal of the censure of the government was especially marked in 1946–7. During this period, the transfer of power to indigenous political groups led to the presumption on the part of the majority community that they would be encouraged to attack the minority community by a government composed of members of their own community.

Anthropological and Ethnological Sciences, Mexico City, July 28–August 5, 1993), p. 12; *West Africa*, June 8, 1981, p. 1271; June 29, 1981, p. 1461; Shah, "Communal Riots in Gujarat," p. 193.

104. Government of India, *Report of the Commission of Inquiry on Communal Disturbances in Ranchi-Hatia (August 22–29, 1967)* (New Delhi: Government Printer, 1968), pp. 75–76.

105. *Bombay Blood Yatra*, a film by Suma Josson, 1993.

106. Christopher Hibbert, *King Mob: The Story of Lord George Gordon and the Riots of 1780* (New York: Dorset Press, 1989), pp. 63–65.

107. Ibid., p. 60.

This was especially marked in Noakhali in 1946, Bihar in the same year, and in the Punjab in 1947. Prior to the partition period, rural pogroms occurred in East Bengal during the rule of the Muslim Ministry and under the earlier smile of British encouragement of the East Bengal Muslims. In February–March 1950, the pattern was repeated in rural East Bengal, and the populace seemed genuinely surprised when the Muslim government asked them to restore the property they had taken from the Hindus.[108]

Lambert also found governmental encouragement in some urban riots. In Calcutta (1946), for example, the Muslim-dominated ministry exhibited rather clear bias, and the chief minister went so far as to order the release of some Muslim riot participants who had been arrested,[109] a move that, as we have seen, is likely to spur rioters to more violence.

Not all layers of authority need to acquiesce in violence in order to nurture it. For Kishinev (1903), Edward H. Judge has judiciously reconstructed the ingredients of toleration and encouragement. The central government, he concludes, did not want disorder and was not complicit; yet it failed to counter an impression that anti-Jewish activity was condoned. In Moldova itself, an anti-Semitic newspaper had been allowed to flourish. The provincial governor was merely ineffective, while his deputy was actively anti-Semitic. The sum of the signals left the rioters in no doubt that the riot was condoned or even authorized.[110] As in Bombay (1992–93) and London (1780), there was confusion over who was the proper authority to order troops into action against rioters[111] — the sort of confusion that seems to prevail when authorities are acquiescent or divided about the desirability of ethnic violence and that, by delaying deployment, encourages rioters to think the authorities approve. Officials in Odessa (1905), too, hinted that they "would perhaps countenance violence against Jews."[112] That was all the situation required. Even though the military attempted to suppress the riot, the mix of revolutionaries versus tsarists and of Jews versus Russians, all operating in a permissive environment, with powerful precipitants, produced considerable cruelty and killing.

Aggression, says Hubert M. Blalock, Jr., is more likely if a minority is

108. Richard Lambert, "Hindu-Muslim Riots" (Ph.D. diss., University of Pennsylvania, 1951), pp. 219–20.

109. Ibid., p. 176.

110. Judge, *Easter in Kishinev*, pp. 32–36, 45, 61, 125–33. Dahlke, "Race and Minority Riots," pp. 422–23, concurs.

111. Judge, *Easter in Kishinev*, pp. 63–65.

112. Weinberg, "Anti-Jewish Violence and Revolution," p. 13.

unprotected by the society.[113] That part of lack of protection that derives from authoritative acquiescence in or support for violence makes it possible for kerosene to be gathered with impunity from sympathetic shopkeepers, as it was in Delhi (1984), when rioters wished to burn Sikh houses, beards, and bodies; it makes it possible to anticipate that the various armed forces may not do their duty; and, as important as anything else, it makes it possible to believe that, if the authorities are tolerant or sympathetic, then the violence is permitted. What the conduct of the authorities does is twofold: it facilitates or retards forceful action against violence, and it delegitimizes or legitimizes violence. Experimental research shows that subjects in the presence of a passive observer who apparently approves of aggression behave more aggressively than when such an observer is absent.[114] Even rioters want to do the right thing.

BIASED OR INEFFECTIVE INSTRUMENTS
OF PUBLIC ORDER

In many riots, there is reason for participants to expect the lethargy, sympathy, or connivance of the instruments of public order at the outset of the violence or as the riot gets going. The incidence of police passivity or connivance with the killers is very great indeed, so much so that police or soldiers sometimes participate in the riot.[115]

Police ineffectiveness or outright bias is widespread in ethnic riots. In Tripura (1980), police, obviously alerted in advance, left their posts as the day of violence approached and were not present when the mass killing began.[116] In Sri Lanka (1977), police "constables looked on and laughed" at one violent location and did nothing at others;[117] in some,

113. Hubert M. Blalock, Jr., *Towards a Theory of Minority-Group Relations* (New York: John Wiley & Sons, 1967), pp. 43, 50.

114. Richard J. Borden, "Witnessed Aggression: Influence of an Observer's Sex and Values on Aggressive Responding," *Journal of Personality and Social Psychology* 31, no. 3 (March 1975): 567–73.

115. Compare the violent protest demonstrations in the United States in the 1960s, in which nearly every major outbreak was precipitated by police action. Harlan Hahn and Joe R. Feagin, "Riot-Precipitating Police Practices: Attitudes in Urban Ghettos," *Phylon* 31, no. 2 (Summer 1970): 183–93, at 183; Joseph Boskin, "The Revolt of the Urban Ghettos, 1964–1967," *The Annals* 382 (March 1969): 1–14, at p. 10. By contrast, interpersonal ethnic riots, including antiblack riots at East St. Louis, Detroit, and Chicago earlier in the century, were typically accompanied by police who were friendly to the rioters. See, e.g., Rudwick, *Race Riot at East St. Louis*, pp. 31–32, 229.

116. *Far Eastern Economic Review*, June 20, 1980, p. 34.

117. Government of Sri Lanka, *Report of the Presidential Commission of Inquiry into the Incidents Which Took Place between 13th August and 15th September 1977*, Sessional

police or soldiers joined in assault and arson.[118] Six years later, the record of the police was more mixed, but again police and military forces sometimes participated on the side of the rioters.[119] Riots in India are frequently facilitated by police ineffectiveness or bias against Muslims.[120] In the colonial period, police were sometimes outnumbered and incapable of intervening.[121] During the partition riots, police were often half-hearted about suppressing violent crowds consisting of members of the same group as the police.[122] In many post-independence riots — among them, Varanasi (1991), Delhi (1986 and 1987), Meerut (1987), Moradabad (1980), Bhiwandi (1970), Ahmedabad (1969), Karamanj (1968), and Calcutta (1967) — the police and the Provincial Armed Constabulary (PAC) were either absent or biased or disinclined to intervene.[123] In many others, the police, the PAC, or the State Reserve Police (SRP) participated in the riots, inciting, shooting, or looting — for example, in Bijnor (1990), east Delhi (1990), Ahmedabad (1985), Delhi (1984), Meerut (1982), and Ferozabad (1972).[124] The same propensities are found around the world.

Paper No. VII — 1980 (Colombo: Government Publications Bureau, 1980), pp. 132, 139, 140, 147, 149–53, 162, 164, 167, 170, 171, 203, 206, 210, 230, 236.

118. Ibid., pp. 181, 188–91.

119. T.D.S.A. Dissanyaka, *The Agony of Sri Lanka: An In-Depth Account of the Racial Riots of 1983* (Colombo: Swastika Press, 1983), p. 81; Manor, "Sri Lanka," pp. 456–57; Bastian, "The Political Economy of Ethnic Violence in Sri Lanka," p. 298; Valli Kanapathipillai, "July 1983: The Survivor's Experience," in Das, ed., *Mirrors of Violence*, p. 330.

120. See generally V.V. Singh, *Communal Violence* (Jaipur: Rawat, 1993), pp. 142–65. Indian writers on the police, including former officers, often despair about declining standards of neutrality, discipline, and diligence in keeping order. See, e.g., K.F. Rustomji, "Law, Policing and Communalism," in Pramod Kumar, ed., *Towards Understanding Communalism* (Chandigarh: Centre for Research in Rural and Industrial Development, 1992), pp. 496–503; Engineer, *Bombay-Bhiwandi Riots*, pp. 18–19.

121. See, e.g., Sandra B. Freitag, *Collective Action and Community Public Arenas and the Emergence of Communalism in North India* (Berkeley and Los Angeles: University of California Press, 1989), p. 245. In others, they failed to act impartially. See, e.g., Lambert, "Hindu-Muslim Riots," p. 159, on Dacca (1941).

122. See, e.g., Penderel Moon, *Divide and Quit* (Berkeley and Los Angeles: University of California Press, 1962), p. 80.

123. See Upadhyaya, "Recent Trends in Communal Violence," p. 4; "Communal Riots: Role of the Police," *Economic and Political Weekly*, June 6, 1987, p. 864; Dildar Khan, "Meerut Riots: An Analysis," in Kumar, ed., *Towards Understanding Communalism*, pp. 455–70, at pp. 457–58; Akbar, *Riot after Riot*, pp. 36–37; Ghosh, *Communal Riots in India*, p. 189; Shah, "Communal Riots in Gujarat," p. 193; Aswini K. Ray and Subhash Chakravarti, *Karamanj Riots: A Political Study* (New Delhi: Sampradayikta Virodhi Committee, 1968?), p. 27; *Times of India*, March 31, 1967, p. 6.

124. Roger Jeffery and Patricia M. Jeffery, "The Bijnor Riots, October 1990," *Economic and Political Weekly*, March 5, 1994, pp. 551–58, at p. 554; Shalini D'Souza

In Nigeria (1991–92), police were said to have been ineffective or to have sided with Jukun against Tiv.[125] They looked the other way in Burma (1988).[126] Police lost control of the riot in Dushanbe, Tajikistan (1990).[127] An ineffective police chief was dilatory in taking action in Mauritania (1966).[128] Indonesian soldiers were accused of watching Dayak crowds kill Chinese in Kalimantan (1967) and were slow to act in Bandung (1963) and Sukabumi (1963).[129] Iranian army units, consisting heavily of Azeris, favored Turks over Kurds in 1979, indeed helped to kill Kurds; a Kurdish unit sent to Kirkuk, Iraq (1959), on the other hand, promptly took the Kurdish side and attacked Turkomens.[130] Southern Sudanese troops and police joined civilians in killing northerners in 1955; northern Nigerian soldiers helped kill Ibo in 1966; Khmer soldiers took part in anti-Vietnamese violence in 1970; Interior Ministry forces and the militia both contributed to the violence against Meskhetian Turks in Uzbekistan (1989).[131] Troops supported violence in Thailand (1945) and Burma (1942); police stood aside in Singapore (1950) and in Gabon (1981); and soldiers were accused of lacking neutrality in Kuala Lumpur (1969).[132]

---

and Arundhuti Roy Choudhury, "The Riots and the Perception of the People: Notes from the Field," *Social Action* 44, no. 1 (January 1994): 114–25; Ghosh, *Communal Riots in India*, p. 165; Citizens' Commission, Delhi, *Delhi, 31 October to 4 November 1984, Report of the Citizens' Commission* (New Delhi: Citizens' Commission, 1985): pp. 18–21, 25–26; Asghar Ali Engineer, "The Guilty Men of Meerut," *Economic and Political Weekly*, November 6, 1982, pp. 1803–05; Suneet Chopra and N.K. Singh, "Ferozabad: Anatomy of a Riot," *Economic and Political Weekly*, August 19, 1972, pp. 1711, 1713.

125. Ter-Rumun Avav and Mson Myegba, *The Dream to Conquer: Story of Jukun-Tiv Conflict* (Makurdi, Nigeria: Onaivi, 1992), pp. 36–37.

126. Lintner, *Outrage*, p. 81.

127. Moscow TV, February 14, 1990, in FBIS-SOV-90–032, February 15, 1990, p. 70.

128. Interview, Washington, D.C., September 13, 1971.

129. *Straits Times* (Kuala Lumpur), November 21, 1967, p. 10; Mackie, "Anti-Chinese Outbreaks in Indonesia, 1959–68," pp. 101, 103–06, 126–28.

130. *Washington Post*, April 26, 1979, p. A29; Johann Caspar (pseud.), "Baghdad's Year of Revolution," *Commentary*, September 1959, pp. 193–201, at pp. 198–99.

131. Republic of Sudan, *Report of the Commission of Inquiry into the Disturbances in the Southern Sudan during August, 1955*, pp. 32–77; "The Cambodian Pogrom," *Far Eastern Economic Review*, May 7, 1970, pp. 22–23; Walter Schwarz, *Nigeria* (New York: Praeger, 1968), pp. 215–16; *Izvestiya*, June 18, 1989, p. 3, in FBIS-SOV-89–117, June 20, 1989, p. 50.

132. Skinner, *Chinese Society in Thailand*, pp. 278–80; Ba Maw, *Breakthrough in Burma: Memoirs of a Revolution* (New Haven: Yale University Press, 1968), pp. 187–95; Tom Eames Hughes, *Tangled Worlds: The Story of Maria Hertogh* (Singapore: Institute of Southeast Asian Studies, 1980), pp. 54–55; *West Africa*, June 29, 1981, pp. 1461–62; John Slimming, *Malaysia: The Death of a Democracy* (London: John Murray, 1969), p. 31.

None of this is new.[133] Police participated in Odessa (1905) and Jerusalem (1920, 1921, and 1929); police and soldiers were passive in Baku (1905) and Kishinev (1903).[134] The conception of the police and armed forces as ethnically neutral representatives of the law is itself relatively new, accepted only shallowly in many societies, difficult to implant in forces without superior training, and, even where accepted, difficult to act on in the heat of the passions that spread through divided societies in their worst moments.[135] All this looks doubly difficult when it is considered that most police and armed forces in such societies are ethnically skewed in their composition, for reasons that generally relate to the authorities' view of tasks they may be called on to perform.[136]

The problem is compounded by the circumstances surrounding riots. In some cases, police and army officers are targeted to receive propaganda from extremist parties that may support violence.[137] In Meerut (1982), there had been a visit by a prominent Hindu extremist leader; he received a public salute from a senior police officer and a district magistrate, who were said to have ordered the police firing during the riot later that year that killed 29 Muslims.[138] In any case, officers are not likely to be neutral and detached but to partake of sentiments common to group members.[139] In many countries, politicians have pressured police to be lenient toward offenders who have political influence. Such a chastening will likely make police officers wary of using decisive force unless they are certain that the rioters lack political protection.[140] Quite possibly,

133. For the United States, see Gary T. Marx, "Civil Disorder and the Agents of Social Control," *Journal of Social Issues* 26, no. 1 (Winter 1970): 19–57.

134. Weinberg, "Anti-Jewish Violence and Revolution," pp. 20–21; Wasserstein, "Patterns of Communal Conflict in Palestine," pp. 618–19; J.D. Henry, *Baku: An Eventful History* (New York: Arno Press, 1977), p. 153; Judge, *Easter in Kishinev*, pp. 138–39.

135. See generally David H. Bayley, *Patterns of Policing: A Comparative International Analysis* (Princeton: Princeton University Press, 1985); Ajay K. Mehra, *Police in Changing India* (New Delhi: Usha Jain, 1985); David H. Bayley, *The Police and Political Development in India* (Princeton: Princeton University Press, 1969).

136. For skewed composition, see Horowitz, *Ethnic Groups in Conflict*, pp. 445–57.

137. See, e.g., Amrita Basu, "When Local Riots Are Not Merely Local: Bringing the State Back In, Bijnor, 1988–92," *Economic and Political Weekly*, October 1, 1994, p. 2618; "A Man Called Moinuddin," *Far Eastern Economic Review*, February 14, 1974, pp. 25–26.

138. Engineer, "The Guilty Men of Meerut," p. 1804.

139. See, e.g., the description of the "fierce nationalism" of the police in Kyrghyzstan (1990). *Pravda*, August 6, 1990, p. 3, in *Current Digest of the Soviet Press*, September 5, 1990, pp. 29–30.

140. See, e.g., Stanley Jeyaraja Tambiah, *Buddhism Betrayed? Religion, Politics and Violence in Sri Lanka* (Chicago: University of Chicago Press, 1992), pp. 49–50; Tamil

particular events preceding the riot have affected the interests or sympathies of the police or army. In Sri Lanka, as separatist terrorism began in the 1970s, police officers were often murdered.[141] This hardly disposed police to protect Tamils during the 1977 riot. The precipitant of the 1983 riot was a Tamil Tiger ambush of an army patrol. As Tamil houses and factories burned, the army "looked on nonchalantly."[142]

If there is a long history of ethnic conflict, it may take some twists and turns that are inimical to neutral police behavior. In Nigeria (1992), mobile police were accused of colluding with the Jukun, to the disadvantage of their Tiv victims. "The Tivs played a large role in the Federal forces in the war against Biafra, and the mobile police are mostly Ibos. They hate the Tivs," according to a local government official.[143] The lower ranks of police in Delhi consist disproportionately of Haryana Jats, who are frequently anti-Sikh[144] (Haryana is the Hindu-majority rump of the Punjab, which was divided in 1966 to meet demands for a Sikh state). Severely divided societies produce just such coincidences. On the other hand, if there is no recent history of ethnic disorder, as there was not in much of the former Soviet Union, the first major riot will probably find the instruments of force "simply unprepared to act in such a complex situation."[145]

Finally, there is the police understanding of the violent event in the context of what political authorities expect. It is difficult to generalize about how this understanding can foster inertia, but there is an unparalleled example in what has come to be called the Nellie massacre, which took place in Assam on February 18, 1983. For reasons of her own, Prime Minister Indira Gandhi had decided to hold state elections in Assam without purging the electoral rolls of numerous noncitizens, mainly Bengali immigrants. Such a decision was certain to inflame Assamese opinion. Mrs. Gandhi's Congress (I) could expect considerable Muslim support, and most recent Bengali immigrants were Muslim. Hundreds of small violent incidents occurred during the election campaign. Assamese police

Refugees Rehabilitation Organization, *Communal Disturbances in Sri Lanka: Sansoni Commission: Written Submissions* (mimeo., March 28, 1980), p. 365.

141. Government of Sri Lanka, *Report of the Presidential Commission of Inquiry into the Incidents Which Took Place between 13th August and 15th September 1977*, p. 45.

142. Dissanyaka, *The Agony of Sri Lanka*, p. 81.

143. Quoted in *The Independent* (London), February 22, 1992, p. 12.

144. Kothari, "The How and Why of It All," p. 16.

145. Lieutenant General V.K. Pankin on the militia response to the riot in Uzbekistan (1989), quoted in *Sovetskaya Rossiya*, June 15, 1989, p. 4, in FBIS-SOV-89-115, June 16, 1989, p. 48.

came to believe the central government had betrayed the Assamese and put the police in an untenable position. Nationally recruited, the Central Reserve Police Force was not Assamese in composition; there was tension between it and the local police. Cooperation was therefore minimal. The army was kept out. The police had been told to insure that the balloting was conducted with a minimum of disturbance and, to that end, been instructed to protect election officials. Arun Shourie, who studied police dispatches, found abundant warnings about the 12,000 attackers who came from villages 18–20 kilometers from Nellie. The police, however, apparently reasoned (or were content to believe) that they could not simultaneously protect election officials and the villages around Nellie. They chose to protect only the officials. Despite specific messages describing violence in progress, no police patrol arrived in the Nellie area until three hours after the killing, by which time some 1,383 people, in ten villages, were dead.[146]

It can make a substantial difference to the victims whether it is the police or the army that is partisan or ineffective in suppressing the riot. The military typically arrives after the police have been unwilling or unable to control the violence. Generally, the police have had greater training in riot control. Yet regulations typically provide for military supersession of civilian authority when the army is called in. If the army fails in its backup role, the scale and scope of the violence are likely to be magnified several times over. There have been various combinations of police-military behavior, ranging from lax police and army, at one end, to firm police and army, at the other, and lax police–firm army or vice versa, in the middle. Clearly, however, it is more dangerous to employ an ethnically partisan or ineffectual army than a partisan or ineffectual police force, since the army is the force of last resort. As we have seen, much of the disorder in Burma (1942), Punjab (1947), Kirkuk (1959), Nigeria (1966), Cambodia (1970), and Iran (1979) can be attributed to military participation in the killing. There are also differences among military units. Whereas the army was generally permissive of violence in Sri Lanka (1977), the navy and air force were not.[147] The Malay Regiment apparently behaved in a partisan fashion in Malaysia (1967 and 1969), but the Sarawak Rangers were firm.[148] Perhaps the worst combination is

146. Arun Shourie, "Assam Elections: Come What May," *India Today*, May 15, 1983, pp. 54–66.

147. Interviews, Colombo, April 7, 1980; April 8, 1980.

148. Slimming, *Malaysia*, p. 31; interviews, George Town, Penang, January 23, 1968; January 29, 1968.

one in which police and army personnel are both partisan, but on opposite sides, as seems to have been the case in Sind (1990).[149]

More often than not, extensive riots that threaten to get completely out of hand, once the police show indifference to or support for the violence, are ultimately controlled by military intervention: Singapore (1950), Assam (1960), Mauritania (1966), Ranchi (1967), Sierra Leone (1968), Ahmedabad (1969), Karachi (1972), Jamshedpur (1979), Meerut (1982), Delhi (1984), Bombay-Bhiwandi (1984), Ahmedabad (1985), Sumgait (1988), and Kyrghyzstan (1990), among others.[150] In some cases, calling in the army, or particular units, is synonymous with changing the ethnic identity of those responsible for order; in others, the military is simply more professional and detached. In Singapore (1950), Gurkha soldiers did what Malay police failed to do; in Karachi (1972), Pathan troops supplanted Sindhi police who had fired on Mohajir demonstrators. Moktar Ould Daddah, the president of Mauritania, was overseas when the riot of 1966 began; on his return, he called in paratroopers, who promptly suppressed the violence. In large federations, such as India or the-then Soviet Union, army units can be called from regions removed from the state-level or republic-level ethnic conflict. In India, the police, the Provincial Armed Constabulary, and the State Reserve Police often take the side of the rioters; the army, the Border Security Force, and the Central Reserve Police generally do not. The same was often true of com-

---

149. The police were said to be pro-Sindhi, the army pro-Mohajir. Human Rights Commission of Pakistan, *Sindh Inquiry, Summer 1990* (Lahore: Human Rights Commission of Pakistan, 1990), p. 65.

150. Statement of Andrew Howat Frew, ASP, to the [Singapore] Riot Inquiry Committee, February 27, 1951 (mimeo.), p. 27, in Rhodes House Library, Oxford, MSS Ind. Ocn. s. 208; K.C. Chakravarti, "Bongal Kheda Again," *Economic Weekly*, July 30, 1960, pp. 1193–95, at p. 1194; interview, Washington, D.C., September 13, 1971; Government of India, *Report of the Commission of Inquiry on Communal Disturbances in Ranchi-Hatia*, pp. 52–61; *Times of India*, July 15, 1972, p. 1; Akbar, *Riot after Riot*, p. 28; Engineer, "The Guilty Men of Meerut," p. 971; Chakravarti and Haksar, *The Delhi Riots*, pp. 46–47; Engineer, *Bombay-Bhiwandi Riots*, pp. 18–19; Ghosh, *Communal Riots in India*, p. 165; *Times* (London), March 5, 1988, p. 1; Tishkov, "Don't Kill Me, I Am Kyrghyz," p. 12. In Mandatory Palestine, the British army typically created order after Arab police had joined the rioters. Wasserstein, "Patterns of Communal Conflict in Palestine," pp. 616, 618–19. Likewise, in antiblack riots in the United States, the National Guard was typically firm in dealing with rioters after police had been lenient or encouraging. See, e.g., Rudwick, *Race Riot in East St. Louis*, pp. 31–32. In Delhi (1984), the police were either absent, passive, or participating in the violence, and the army got little or no help from the police when it was called in. People's Union for Democratic Rights and People's Union for Civil Liberties, *Who Are the Guilty? Report of a Joint Inquiry into the Causes and Impact of the Riots in Delhi from 31 October to 10 November* (Delhi: PUDR & PUCL, 1984), pp. 4, 9.

parable units in the Soviet Union. Friction between police and army units is common,[151] but if the army is dependable, the riot will end as a riot. If it is not, it may become something much worse.[152]

INHIBITION AND DISINHIBITION

A multiethnic society held together by the fragile notion that it is impermissible to alter distasteful arrangements by force can begin to crack when doubts arise about the illegitimacy of violence. Given the common human propensity to abdicate conscience functions to authority, the approval or disinterest signaled by authorities can unleash hostility previously well hidden from view, creating precisely those occasions when strong targets can be hit at weak moments, when they are unprotected. The difference between isolated assaults and large-scale riots can often be accounted for by the perceived legitimacy conferred on the violence.[153] One way to view the riot is as a form of thuggery that has been sanctioned and sometimes even glorified as a contribution to the welfare of the group, so that those who might otherwise see themselves as criminals are able to see themselves as warriors.

To the moral support that derives from condonation must be added the physical support that derives from impunity. As fear of punishment tends to inhibit aggression, increases in general permissiveness may be followed by increases in aggression.[154] The causal relation between police inability or unwillingness to act and the boldness of crowds bent on violence is brought out in many riot sources. In Sri Lanka (1958), "rioters had arranged signals — one peal of a temple bell to signify police, two to signify army and so on. They also had a simple system of hand signals to give their associates in the distance such information as which way a police patrol went."[155] Those who agitated for violence in Singapore (1950) astutely anticipated and relied on the disaffection of the Malay

151. People's Union for Democratic Rights and People's Union for Civil Liberties, *Who Are the Guilty?* p. 9; Government of India, *Report of the Commission of Inquiry on Communal Disturbances in Ranchi-Hatia,* pt. IV.

152. See, e.g., René Lemarchand, *Burundi: Ethnocide as Discourse and Practice* (Cambridge: Woodrow Wilson Center Press and Cambridge University Press, 1994), pp. 156–57.

153. See Dahlke, "Race and Minority Riots"; Grimshaw, "Urban Racial Violence in the United States," p. 110.

154. Leonard Berkowitz, *Aggression: A Social-Psychological Analysis* (New York: McGraw-Hill, 1962), pp. 75–76, 87–88.

155. Vittachi, *Emergency '58,* pp. 37–38.

police. A speech during the prelude to the riot which cleverly touched on the possibility of violence as a "last resort" included a pointed reference to the police: ". . . I may be frank in telling you that the [ethnic] feeling today is not confined to the Muslim civilians, but also to the members of the police."[156] The anticipation of the organizers was subsequently confirmed, and it quickly emboldened their followers. Ultimately, as we have seen, Gurkha troops ended the riot, but in the early stages, when there was still a question of tactics to avert violence, a Gurkha riot squad was brought up and then withdrawn, in order to avoid provocation. The crowd saw this as weakness: as the Gurkhas withdrew, shouts of "*takut*" (afraid) were heard, and the violence accelerated thereafter.[157]

If we bear in mind that social support serves to reduce inhibitions by conveying a sense of *both* legitimation and impunity to potential rioters, we may begin to explain some of the exceptional cases of rioting in the face of opposing force. Often these cases involve a division of authority. In Durban (1949), the police were forceful, but social and governmental disdain for the Indian targets had been manifested frequently, severely, and recently. Similar divisions between the police and social superiors can be identified clearly in west Punjab (1953) and Guyana (1962), and arguably in Assam (1960), although in Assam it was rumored that Assamese students had been fired on by *Bengali* policemen,[158] while subsequently Assamese police appear to have been passive in the face of Assamese disorders.[159] In these cases — except for Assam — the police and army were firm despite strong social support for the violence. The police, rather than the rioters, might then be regarded as the deviants. What these riot episodes show is that legitimation can sometimes outweigh lack of impunity in overcoming inhibitions on violence. To put the point in the language of frustration-aggression theory, police repression of violence believed to be legitimate may increase the initial level of anger by an increment greater than the degree by which it raises inhibitions deriving from fear. Such a bifurcation of might and right, as perceived by the rioters, helps to explain why violence can occur even when it is clear that the instruments of public order are determined to prevent it. The felt legitimacy of the action is a powerful motivator of violence.

156. Abdul Karim Ghani, quoted in Colony of Singapore, *Report of the Riots Inquiry Commission, 1951* (Singapore: Government Printer, 1951), p. 13.

157. Ibid., p. 17.

158. Charu Chandra Bhandari, *Thoughts on Assam Disturbances* (Rajghat, India: A.B. Sarva Seva Sangh Prakashan, 1961), p. 38; Barua, *Assam*, pp. 15–16.

159. Chakravarti, "Bongal Kheda Again," p. 1194.

Consider the results of two studies of international warfare relating the initiation of war to the balance of national strength and weakness. In one of these studies, Melvin Small and J. David Singer found that the initiators were victorious in 34 of 49 wars and lost fewer soldiers than their adversaries in 36 of the 49. Initiation of international violence was, in other words, generally related to the prospect of success.[160] In the second study, Ole R. Holsti and Robert C. North found that perception of its own inferior capability might deter a state from attacking, but they also concluded that if the perception of "injury, threat or frustration" is sufficient, a state may attack even though it is significantly weaker than the state it attacks.[161] These formulations highlight the existence of two conditions in which an attack might be expected to occur: first, when the prospects of success are good and, second, when the prospects of success are poor but the threat from the target is so great as to override inhibitions deriving from fear of the consequences.

For riots, the first of these situations relates, as I have indicated, to the presence of authoritative social support, for that generally seems to enhance the chance of inflicting injury with relative impunity. Social support of this kind may be especially necessary where the targets are perceived as possessing certain kinds of strength. Then, as I have argued, the initiators may wish to attack at a moment of special vulnerability, which is provided when the authorities signal or seem to signal that they will look the other way or when the police do in fact look the other way.

The second situation may be reformulated as follows. In practice, moderate weakness may deter the weak party from attacking, but severe weakness, if it is seen as a danger (and in ethnic relations it certainly is), may actually *incite* the weak party to attack. This possibility roughly coincides with occasions when groups have attacked in the face of authoritative opposition, including the forcible opposition of the police and army, as indeed they did in Burma (1938), Sierra Leone (1968), Burundi (1988), and Taiwan (1947).[162] On these occasions, the initiating

160. Melvin Small and J. David Singer, "Patterns in International Warfare," *The Annals* 391 (September 1970): 145–55, at pp. 153–54.

161. Ole R. Holsti and Robert C. North, "The History of Human Conflict," in McNeil, ed., *The Nature of Human Conflict*, p. 169.

162. Taiwan (1947), however, was a hybrid, involving attacks on cars and buildings associated with the regime, as well as attacks on Mainlanders. In the conditions specified, it is not surprising that a violent protest demonstration is at least an equal possibility. The violence I refer to in Burundi is not the genocide of Hutu but the prior attacks by Hutu on Tutsi, which were provoked by the movement of Tutsi *gendarmes*. See Lemarchand, *Burundi*, pp. 124–27.

groups perceived their situation to be especially desperate and their opponents to be especially oppressive and alien. While tolerant authorities are a powerful facilitator of violence by those who sense their approval, oppressive authorities may also, although more rarely, abet violence by those who perceive them as creating a hopeless situation. As Holsti and North say of warfare, "Perceptions of inferior capability, if perceptions of anxiety, fear, threat, or injury are great enough, will fail to deter a nation from going to war."[163] This, however, is the exceptional case. Ordinarily, clear and consistent disapproval of violence deters ethnic riots.

When the authorities do not provide support, when they manifest their intolerance for violence, even in the face of strong popular sentiment and provocative precipitants, there may still be violence, but it is not likely to take the form of riot. Antipathy between Copts and Muslims in Egypt grew through the 1970s, culminating in restrictions on construction of churches and the state's commitment to an Islamic legal system in 1980. In 1981, a dispute over land for a church or a mosque, inflamed by rumors of mass murder by Copts, produced a Muslim attack on Copts. Police quickly made 260 arrests. President Anwar Sadat announced his determination that there would be no more rioting. Over the next months, disturbances occurred sporadically, and Sadat announced more arrests. The violence did not end, but, without authoritative support, it turned into something closer to terrorism than to riot.[164] Similarly, while the authority of the Soviet Union was crumbling, Moscow evinced some determination to punish riot behavior and prevent recurrence. After the first incidents in Tuva (1990), law enforcement was strengthened. In spite of intense anti-Russian feeling and the election of a Tuvinian nationalist government in 1990, no full-scale riot occurred. Instead, there were many small incidents: houses burned, shots fired, petrol bombs thrown. Still, few Russians were killed. Even after several people who had thrown bottles of combustible fluid at Russian houses were sentenced to lengthy prison terms, the violence did not abate completely, but mass violence was averted in what were otherwise most pro-

163. Holsti and North, "The History of Human Conflict," p. 169.

164. See *African Recorder*, July 16–29, 1981, pp. 5682–83; October 8–21, 1981, pp. 5746–47. For the background, see Sharon Lefevre, "From a Coptic Leader: A Recipe for Moslem-Coptic Accord," *Monday Morning* (Beirut), August 10, 1981, pp. 50–55, at pp. 52, 53; J.D. Pennington, "The Copts in Modern Egypt," *Middle Eastern Studies* 18, no. 2 (April 1982): 158–79, at pp. 170–74; Abd al-Monein Said Aly and Manfred W. Wenner, "Modern Islamic Reform Movements: The Muslim Brotherhood in Contemporary Egypt," *Middle East Journal* 36, no. 3 (Summer 1982): 336–61, at pp. 358–59. By the 1990s, terrorism and organized gang violence were still the main threats to the Copts. See, e.g., *Africa Confidential*, January 22, 1993, pp. 2–3.

pitious conditions.[165] In addition to arresting rioters, the Soviet regime typically removed officials in the republics who were complicit with or sympathetic to rioters.[166] No doubt many of the removals were intended merely for cosmetic effect. Where central authorities themselves were complicit in the violence, as in North Ossetia (1992), there were neither prosecutions nor removals.[167] Yet, where action was taken, repeat riots were rare. Recurrence was averted after 50 people were convicted following the riot in Kyrghyzstan (1990).[168] On the return of President Moktar to Mauritania after the 1966 riot, arrests were made, the cabinet was reshuffled, and the violence was condemned at a party congress. For quite some time, there was no further mass violence in Mauritania, a very deeply divided society.

Force seems generally to deter. As police hesitation reduces inhibitions in a crowd, early, determined police action can avert what might have been a very serious riot.[169] Perhaps most telling are examples of effective police action in a few locations among many others in which police inaction had allowed mass violence to proceed. There was much less violence in Sind at the time of partition in 1947 than in Punjab, because the police were firmer and more neutral in the former than in the latter.[170] There are also instances of police who were willing to use weapons facing down angry crowds in Sri Lanka (1977) and Delhi (1984), in the midst of serious riots in other locations.[171] The disposition of the crowds to engage in violence was plainly present, and the inter-

165. *Tass*, August 4, 1990, in FBIS-SOV-90-151, August 6, 1990, pp. 71–72; Moscow Television Service, August 3, 1990, in FBIS-SOV-90-151, August 6, 1990, p. 71. Cf. Toomas Alatalu, "Tuva — a State Reawakens," *Soviet Studies* 44, no. 5 (n.m. 1992): 881–95, at p. 890.

166. After the riot in Dushanbe, Tajikistan (1990), for example, several high party and government leaders were removed from their positions. *Pravda*, February 17, 1990, p. 3, in FBIS-SOV-90-034, February 20, 1990, pp. 64–65; *Keesing's Contemporary Archives*, March 1990, p. 37323. The same happened after the violence in Sumgait (1988), where the party leader, mayor, and police chief were all sacked. *New York Times*, August 31, 1988, p. A1.

167. Valery Tishkov, *Ethnicity, Nationalism and Conflict in and after the Soviet Union* (London: Sage, 1997), pp. 155–82.

168. Tishkov, "Don't Kill Me, I Am Kyrghyz," p. 5. Compare Baku (1988), in which no criminal charges were filed, and Dushanbe, Tajikistan (1990), in which 58 rioters were arrested but many leading participants were later released.

169. See, e.g., Ghosh, *Communal Riots in India*, p. 195.

170. I am indebted to Steven Wilkinson for calling this contrast to my attention.

171. Tamil Refugees Rehabilitation Organization, *Communal Disturbances in Sri Lanka: Sansoni Commission: Written Submissions*, p. 363; Chakravarti and Haksar, *The Delhi Riots*, p. 163. A very well informed Sri Lankan Tamil source points to specific locations near Kurunegala, Anuradhapura, and Weligama where the leadership of firm police inspectors averted or ended violence. Interview, Colombo, April 8, 1980.

vening variable was the use or threat of force. There are, however, relatively few such documented instances once rioters have assembled, because police bias, indifference, or ineffectiveness is so widespread and the rioters' assembly usually takes place in anticipation (typically well founded) of police inaction.

Punishment after the event is also unusual. If the police are biased and make arrests, the arrests will reflect the bias. In Bhiwandi (1970), Hindu processionists arrived armed with staves, and they behaved abusively toward Muslims along the way. The police failed to respond. After processionists began the anti-Muslim riot, the police opened fire on a number of occasions, but they killed only Muslims. Arrests followed the same pattern: more than seven Muslims were arrested for every Hindu.[172] The same pattern was reported for Bhiwandi (1984), a riot in which the vast majority of the dead were Muslims and in which the vast majority of those arrested were Muslims as well.[173] As we shall see presently, this skewed pattern of arrests eventuates in few convictions.

If the authorities are supportive or tolerant of violence, careful investigation is also unlikely. After Delhi (1984), a riot in which at least 1,000 people were killed, only 80 cases were registered by the police,[174] and the first convictions were obtained eleven years later.[175] By 1963, a Hutu regime in Rwanda had become so tolerant of (if not complicit in) anti-Tutsi violence that it rejected the findings of its own investigation, which had resulted in 89 convictions, and subsequently prosecuted only a few people, most of whom received light sentences.[176] But even where central authorities are ill disposed to violence, the results of the criminal justice process may be meager. Kishinev (1903) was one such case. There were trials after the violence, but they produced some acquittals, light sentences for those convicted, and few awards for restitution. Unsurprisingly, two years later, Kishinev experienced another anti-Jewish riot.[177]

There are good figures on arrests, prosecutions, and convictions after some riots in India. They suggest a startlingly low probability of punishment. Of those arrested after Bhiwandi (1984), fewer than one-third were prosecuted; fewer than one-third of these in turn went to trial; of these,

172. Ghosh, *Communal Riots in India*, pp. 188–90.
173. Engineer, *Bhiwandi-Bombay Riots*, p. 163.
174. People's Union for Democratic Rights and People's Union for Civil Liberties, *Who Are the Guilty?* p. 29.
175. *New York Times*, September 16, 1996, p. A4.
176. Lemarchand, *Rwanda and Burundi*, p. 226.
177. Judge, *Easter in Kishinev*, pp. 119, 125–33, 141.

more than 60 percent were acquitted. Despite a large number of arrests (more than 2,100), there had been, as of one and a half years later, only four convictions, while only 65 cases (under 3 percent of the total arrests) were still pending.[178] Once the police have abdicated their responsibilities, it is harder to build cases, even if there is later a desire to do so.

Colonial authorities do not seem to have done very much better. Singapore (1950) was a riot the British were keen to punish. A Riot Investigation Unit detained 778 people, of whom it released 403 unconditionally and 106 conditionally on good behavior and observance of curfew and reporting requirements. Charges of rioting were brought against 200 people, but only 100 were convicted. Seven people were convicted of taking part in killing; all received death sentences that were commuted, some to seven years and some to life in prison. Most of the remainder were sentenced for lesser crimes to between six months and seven years in prison.[179] The majority of rioters, very likely including the majority of those who committed homicide, escaped unpunished. Although the number of defendants convicted is much higher, most escaped punishment in Burma (1938) as well. More than 4,300 people were arrested, but by 1939 fully 2,453 cases had been closed on grounds of mistake, insufficient evidence, or similar inadequacies; 808 defendants were acquitted or discharged; and only 900, or 21 percent of arrestees, had been convicted of anything.[180] This, after riots that produced considerable loss of life and property at no fewer than 111 towns up and down the country.

Research by Steven Wilkinson on the criminal process in India following six riot episodes in the colonial period and eleven riots in the independence period reveals conviction rates as low as 9 percent of cases tried in some colonial riots and 2 percent in Hyderabad (September 1983). Only twice did the conviction rate rise to 50 percent of cases tried, and these figures include convictions for minor offenses. In Moradabad (1980), 141 people died, and about 2,000 people were arrested. As of six years later, there had been only six convictions. Six, in fact, is the median number of convictions for the eleven post-independence riots studied. While the British did no better in the conviction-to-trial ratio, many

178. P.R. Rajgopal, *Communal Violence in India* (New Delhi: Uppal, 1987), pp. 91–93.

179. Haja Maideen, *The Nadra Tragedy: The Maria Hertogh Controversy* (Petaling Jaya, Malaysia: Pelanduk, 1989), pp. 283–90.

180. Government of Burma, *Final Report of the Riot Inquiry Committee* (Rangoon: Superintendent of Government Printing and Stationery, 1939), Appendix VII, p. xxix.

fewer people were killed, on average, in colonial Indian ethnic riots, and the ratio of convictions to riot deaths appears decidedly higher.[181]

Results elsewhere are also generally unimpressive. Kano (1953) produced a fair number of arrests and 120 criminal cases that were adjudicated. Of the defendants, 59 — about half — were found not guilty, and 18 were found guilty only of unlawful possession of a weapon. Of the remaining 43 found guilty of rioting, two were discharged altogether and 41 were sentenced to between one and three months in prison, with the median below two months.[182] Zanzibar had even more impressive arrest figures — nearly 1,400 — but 300 to 400 were released uncharged, for want of an adequate evidentiary case; and by the time the riot inquiry commission began its hearings, there had been only 183 convictions: 50 for curfew offenses, 78 for carrying weapons, 28 for looting, 27 for rioting, and none for homicide.[183] The more serious the riot, the more likely army units will be brought in, and the more likely it will be that, as in Zanzibar, prosecutions will have to be abandoned because of their lack of training in gathering evidence.

These are the results when the authorities showed some determination to put the violence down and punish the culprits.[184] The results are far less significant elsewhere. Most of the time, no prosecutions ensue. One reason ethnic riots are so widespread is that the activity is so rarely punished.

ABSENCE OF REMORSE: THE MORAL MASS MURDER

An important, neglected reason for the frequency of riots is that the activity is so commonly approved in the wider society of which the riot-

181. Steven Wilkinson, "Riot Prosecutions and Convictions in India" (unpublished typescript, n.d. [1997]). One of what I have described as the six colonial riot "episodes" actually is the aggregate of data from the whole of the United Provinces for the year 1927. The others are all specific riots.

182. Northern Regional Government, Government of Nigeria, *Report on the Kano Disturbances, 16th, 17th, 18th, and 19th May, 1953* (Kaduna: Government Printer, 1953), p. 21.

183. Great Britain, Colonial Office, *Report of a Commission of Inquiry into Disturbances in Zanzibar during June 1961*, Colon. no. 353 (London: H.M.S.O., 1961), p. 12. It is possible that there were a few more convictions after that date, but unlikely that there was a change in the pattern of acquittals and convictions.

184. For a variety of reasons, such determination is rarely manifested with respect to police misbehavior in riots. See, e.g., N.S. Saksena, *Communal Riots in India* (Noida, India: Trishul, 1990), pp. 94–96. Low rates of arrest and prosecution were also prevalent in nineteenth-century European food riots. See Gailus, "Food Riots in Germany in the Late 1840s," p. 172.

ers are a part. This is a point easily missed by anyone who assumes that all right-thinking people condemn violence.

In describing the posture of the civil authorities, the police, and the armed forces, I have attempted to explain the effect of their support in overcoming the fear and the moral inhibitions felt by potential rioters. Many actions and events that precede the riot feed into the calculations of the rioters about the prudence and permissibility of the course on which they are about to embark. Efforts to achieve invulnerability obviously relate to the conquest of fear. Disinhibiting mania is, by definition, in the same category. Rumors of aggression by the target group serve generally to underscore the gravity of the situation and to justify the riot as self-defense. Precipitating events also embody a large element of threat, convincing rioters that a response is necessary and appropriate. As we have already seen, both necessity and appropriateness are plainly on the minds of the rioters.

Justification, it needs to be underscored, is as much a major theme of these events as is impunity.[185] An utter absence of remorse pervades the typical post-riot atmosphere. To be sure, in some countries, most notably India, small but vocal groups of intellectuals and professionals speak up, investigate the violence, demand punishment, and deplore the likelihood of further violence. But, across countries and centuries, what stands out is the general absence of such sentiments or actions taken on the basis of them.[186]

There may be some shame, particularly if the attention of international bodies or the press has been attracted to the events, for outsiders rarely find the killing justifiable. And so occasionally it is said that the riot, which had drawn condemnation from outside, was perhaps not a good thing but had turned out to be "a blessing in disguise,"[187] since it produced effects of which group members approved. For some years after Durban (1949), the Zulu Hlanganani Association "commemo-

185. Here I mean *justification* precisely in the sense of an evaluation of the act as (at least) not blameworthy, as opposed to *excuse*, which evaluates the act as wrong but the actor as exempt from responsibility. See Joram Graf Haber, *Forgiveness* (Savage, Md.: Rowman & Littlefield, 1991), p. 33; Donald L. Horowitz, "Justification and Excuse in the Program of the Criminal Law," *Law and Contemporary Problems* 49, no. 3 (Summer 1986): 109–26.

186. See Davis, *Society and Culture in Early Modern France*, pp. 165–66.

187. I am quoting from a number of interviews with civil servants in Malaysia in 1975, referring to the riot of May 1969. Compare Halinah Bamadhaj, "The Impact of the Japanese Occupation of Malaya on Malay Society and Politics (1941–1945)" (M.A. thesis, University of Auckland, 1975), p. 236.

rate[d] the 1949 riots in an annual celebration."[188] An African National Congress leader who attended the 1951 celebration remarked that the riots "had focused the attention" of the South African government on the problems of Africans, particularly in trade.[189] "The average Burman on the street," it was reported after the 1930 anti-Indian riot, "felt content that at least once he proved his superiority over the Indian. As for the Burmese elite, the Indians, in close touch with them on social levels, sensed a lurking undercurrent of satisfaction only marred by a sense of revulsion at the methods resorted to by the masses."[190] That is about as far as regret goes in these cases. It is not very far.

Much more often insiders find the killing justifiable, not half-apologetically, as in the blessing-in-disguise formulation, but wholeheartedly.[191] They justify the killing, even if they themselves would not engage in it, and they justify it in strikingly similar terms. Just as the Russian minister of the interior said after Kishinev (1903) that the Jews had become "conceited" and needed to be "taught a lesson,"[192] black victims were said in Chicago (1919), Detroit (1943), and East St. Louis (1917) to have grown "arrogant" and to "deserve what they get."[193] Sikhs were also described in Delhi (1984) as having become "arrogant" and needing to be "taught a lesson"; "they deserved it"; they "brought it on themselves."[194] Sikhs, after all, were "regarded as extremely successful and cocky. The riot was regarded by many in Delhi as an act of pruning and also a judicious whittling down of the Sikh ego."[195] Even some Hindus who risked their lives to save Sikh friends and neighbors declared that Sikhs deserved what they got.[196] The violence in Sri Lanka (1983) was

188. Leo Kuper, *An African Bourgeoisie: Race, Class, and Politics in South Africa* (New Haven: Yale University Press, 1965), p. 304.

189. Ibid.

190. Usha Mahajani, *The Role of Indian Minorities in Burma and Malaya* (Bombay: Vora, 1960), p. 76.

191. "I met teachers, civil servants and tourist guides, all of them actively in sympathy with the killings" of Madurese in West Kalimantan, Indonesia (1999). *The Independent* (London), March 22, 1999, p. 12.

192. Judge, *Easter in Kishinev*, p. 123.

193. Rudwick, *Race Riot in East St. Louis*, p. 228.

194. Chakravarti and Haksar, *The Delhi Riots*, pp. 214–15, 506–07, 552, 567.

195. Shiv Vishwanathan, "The Spectator as Witness," in Kothari and Sethi, eds., *Voices from a Scarred City*, pp. 47–52, at p. 50.

196. Chakravarti and Haksar, *The Delhi Riots*, pp. 214–15. Precisely the same ambivalent behavior was reported by an Ibo cleric who gave shelter to ten Hausa during the riot in Aba, Nigeria (2000). On the first morning of the violence, he was present at an attack but did not participate. Yet he acknowledged being "happy these things were being done" to the Hausa victims. "In my heart I was saying, 'Yes, do that to them.'" Quoted in the *New York Times*, March 26, 2000, p. A22.

deemed justified in order to "teach the Tamils a lesson."[197] In the Nigerian riots (1966), the Ibo, it was said, "had it coming to them":[198] they "deserved what they got."[199] Muslims in Bijnor (1990), in Ahmedabad (1969), and in Surat (1992) "either started the trouble, or deserved what they got."[200] As the Sikhs were "arrogant" and "cocky," the Bengalis in Assam (1960) were said to be condescending; the violence was justified because of their "complex of superiority," their false pride about their culture and intelligence.[201] There was no remorse on the part of those who engaged in anti-Chinese violence in Sukabumi (1963); they felt they were being patriotic.[202] In Malaysia, at the end of World War II, the Malay elite defended the anti-Chinese violence, pointing to the severity of the provocations.[203] "'This is a lesson the Muslims needed to be taught! We should have put them in their places long ago!' was the general consensus" among civil servants and their families who, "in a gay mood," watched from a distance as Hindus killed Muslims in Rohtak, near Delhi (1947).[204] The festive mood during the violence implies lack of remorse afterward, for that mood is based on the pent-up desire to take what is seen as rightful action.[205]

The crowd has lessons to teach; the victims have lessons to learn; and respectable bystanders are, on this point, generally closer to the crowd than to the victims. The image of teachers and pupils is not so much a metaphor as it is the depiction of a role reversal, for the complaint of the aggressors is that, in social life, the Sikhs, the Ibo, the Bengalis, and the Chinese, among many others, are doing the teaching, altogether too

197. Spencer, "Collective Violence and Everyday Practice in Sri Lanka," p. 620. To the same effect, see Tambiah, *Leveling Crowds*, p. 97.

198. K. Whiteman, "Enugu: The Psychology of Secession, 20 July 1966 to 30 May 1967," in S.K. Panter-Brick, ed., *Nigerian Politics and Military Rule: Prelude to the Civil War* (London: Athlone Press, 1970), p. 116.

199. S. Aluko, "Displaced Nigerians," pt. II, *West Africa*, April 15, 1967, pp. 495–98, at p. 497.

200. Jeffery and Jeffery, "The Bijnor Riots, October 1990," p. 555; Ratna Naidu, *The Communal Edge to Plural Societies* (Delhi: Vikas, 1980), p. 103; Asghar Ali Engineer, *Lifting the Veil: Communal Violence and Communal Harmony in Contemporary India* (Hyderabad: Sangam Books, 1995), p. 216.

201. Bhandari, *Thoughts on Assam Disturbances*, pp. 22, 42.

202. Giap, "Group Conflict in a Plural Society," p. 14.

203. Bamadhaj, "The Impact of the Japanese Occupation of Malaya on Malay Society and Politics (1941–1945)," p. 236.

204. Sudhir Kakar, *The Colors of Violence: Cultural Identities, Religion, and Conflict* (Chicago: University of Chicago Press, 1996), p. 33.

205. See Tambiah, *Leveling Crowds*, pp. 279–80. Cf. Joseph Boskin, "The Revolt of the Urban Ghettos, 1964–1967," *The Annals*, no. 382 (March 1969): 1–14, on the connection between exultation and justification.

much teaching, sometimes of unwanted lessons. Teaching lessons to the arrogant teachers: this is no accidental formulation but one that goes to the nature of the violence as an expression of anger on the part of those who have felt vulnerable to threats to their collective sense of well-being.

The targets are those who provide the threat, and the justification of violence is focused on the behavior of those who become its victims.[206] Actually, it is said, they brought it on themselves.[207] Without justification in these terms, there would be much less need for rumors confirming the malicious intentions and actions of the targets and less need for specific precipitating events as well.

Once justification takes hold, it is difficult to dislodge. One reason rioters are infrequently punished is that authorities understand the popularity of the event among members of the attacking group. The lack of punishment then confirms the justification, perhaps laying the groundwork for the next event.

In Chapter 12, when we deal with negative cases — with non-riots, as it were — we shall see that when justification of killing is not widely forthcoming, the deadly ethnic riot is a much less common event. Nonlethal violent protest demonstrations remain possible, and terrorist killings can persist in the face of social disapproval. In the absence of justification, however, the deadly ethnic riot is likely to die out.

Remorse may thus be an important element in riot prevention. Absence of remorse implicitly justifies the preexisting moral choice.[208] Since justification is important to the rioters, the conduct of the authorities with respect to previous riots clearly bears on riot prospects as well. But the magnitude of the preventive task should not be underestimated — and not merely because the riot is a popular event. Even where punishment can be expected, the riot may proceed. In Durban (1949), there was the usual lack of remorse following the violence: some of those who were punished declared that they fully expected punishment but had acted violently to settle what they regarded as their account with the Indian targets, adding "that they would welcome an opportunity in the future to liquidate the debt."[209] The conduct of the state may affect the

---

206. See Chapter 4, note 17, above.

207. Nissan, "Some Thoughts on Sinhalese Justifications for the Violence," pp. 175–76.

208. Janet Landman, *Regret: The Persistence of the Possible* (New York: Oxford University Press, 1993), p. 36. See generally pp. 33–36.

209. Union of South Africa, *Report of the Commission of Enquiry into Riots in Durban,* p. 10. To the same effect, see Maurice Webb and Kenneth Kirkwood, *The Durban*

conduct of the rioters, but a strong sense of justification may even outweigh fear of punishment.

A fundamental problem is the absence of moral community between members of one ethnic group and another in a severely divided society. The literature on fights and feuds makes very clear that, in this respect, there is a great difference between intragroup and intergroup violence. Within a group, violence tends to be less lethal. To make sure that remains so, the choice of weapons in intragroup fighting is different.[210] In societies with strong ideas about revenge, conventional forms of revenge do not apply when intragroup homicide occurs.[211] Intragroup murder, when it occurs, is punished quite differently from intergroup murder. The crime is regarded as more dangerous to group solidarity and is often characterized as a sin.[212] No such clear stigma attaches to intergroup killing.

One of the striking findings of Sudhir Kakar's interviews with 20 Hindus and 20 Muslims in Hyderabad is the absence of a consensus on either side that killing males in a riot is wrong.[213] The respondents justified such acts as retaliation or likened "the situation to a time of war," when killing and being killed are normal events.[214] In Hyderabad, empathy is not wholly absent, despite profound deterioration in Hindu-Muslim relations. Neither side yet considers members of the other group "less than human and therefore . . . deserving prey for every imaginable brutality."[215] One might describe the situation as involving badly frayed interethnic empathy. Still, this minimal degree of empathy is not sufficient to provide unequivocal condemnation of killing during a riot. Hyderabad has been the setting for a significant number of Hindu-Muslim riots since the 1930s. The periodic occurrence and growing routinization of riots probably render the warfare analogy plausible to those

Riots and After (Johannesburg: Institute of Race Relations, 1949), p. 5; Kuper, *An African Bourgeoisie*, p. 302.

210. Emanuel Marx, "Some Social Contexts of Personal Violence," in Max Gluckman, ed., *The Allocation of Responsibility* (Manchester: Manchester University Press, 1972), pp. 281–321, at p. 287; Edward Evans-Pritchard, *The Nuer* (Oxford: Oxford University Press, 1940), pp. 121, 151.

211. Christopher Boehm, *Blood Revenge: The Anthropology of Feuding in Montenegro and Other Tribal Societies* (Lawrence: University Press of Kansas, 1984), pp. 105, 208, 212.

212. Jacob Black-Michaud, *Feuding Societies*, 2d ed. (Oxford: Basil Blackwell, 1980), pp. 228–34.

213. Kakar, *The Colors of Violence*, pp. 136, 141. Females, it was thought, should be exempt from riot victimization.

214. Ibid., p. 139.

215. Ibid., p. 141.

who invoke it. Certainly, as Kakar's findings suggest, even this minimal sense of fellow-feeling could deteriorate further.

None of this makes it completely impossible to change norms about intergroup killing. Such norms can change and, in some places, have changed.[216] Yet the absence of moral community is a profoundly important feature of severely divided societies. Where community across group lines is utterly absent, where even the minimal empathy of Hyderabad has not taken root or has died, it becomes possible to consider that lives on the other side of the boundary are of trivial value.[217]

There is an interesting contrast to be drawn between two varieties of intergroup conflict: interclan or interlineage conflict, on the one hand, and interethnic conflict, on the other. Ritualized conciliation and pacification are possible in the former, and highly stylized homage ceremonies are available to accomplish these ends. Typically, killers or, in the case of long-standing hostilities, those who are ahead in the death count display extreme humility toward relatives of those lost to the violence. Sometimes with hands tied behind their back or walking upon their knees, they beg forgiveness and make a gesture of compensation.[218]

216. A point I shall make in Chapter 12.

217. This is not well captured by survey research on ethnic relations, which tends to measure social distance and hostile attitudes. Social scientists have not been brash enough to ask about the felt propriety of killing. Cf. Daniel Jonah Goldhagen, *Hitler's Willing Executioners: Ordinary Germans and the Holocaust* (New York: Alfred A. Knopf, 1996). Nevertheless, keen observers have long been struck by this feature of ethnicity. For observations by one of the very keenest, see Hugh Clifford, "The Wages of Sin," in Hugh Clifford, *In a Corner of Asia* (New York: Robert M. McBride, 1926), pp. 183–84. Many of the attitudinal studies are collected in Donald L. Horowitz, "Self-Determination: Politics, Philosophy, and Law," *Nomos* 39 (1997): 421–63, at p. 457 n31. For a sense of social distance studies, see Harry C. Triandis and Leigh Minturn Triandis, "A Cross Cultural Study of Social Distance," *Psychological Monographs* 76, no. 21 (1962).

218. Keith M. Brown, *Bloodfeud in Scotland, 1573–1625* (Edinburgh: John Donald, 1986), pp. 49, 54; Black-Michaud, *Feuding Societies*, pp. 52, 89–93; Boehm, *Blood Revenge*, pp. 134–36. That is not to say that this is the invariable practice. Compare, e.g., Frederik Barth, *Political Leadership among Swat Pathans*, 2d ed. (London: Athlone Press, 1965), pp. 97–98; Thomas M. Kiefer, *The Tausug: Violence and Law in a Philippine Moslem Society* (New York: Holt, Rinehart, and Winston, 1972), p. 102. But stylized contrition ceremonies are not uncommon as ways to end such conflict. Even where the ceremony is decidedly less ritualized, admission of guilt is a common accompaniment of reconciliation. See, e.g., Monica Wilson, *Good Company: A Study of Nyakusa Age-Villages* (Boston: Beacon Press, 1963), pp. 101, 107. And, whatever the method of reconciliation, it embodies an acknowledgment of moral community between the two sides, by, for example, an exchange of goods or food. See, e.g., C.R. Hallpike, *Bloodshed and Vengeance in the Papuan Mountains* (Oxford: Clarendon Press, 1977), p. 205. For surrender on hands and knees in warfare, see John Keegan, *The Face of Battle* (New York: Viking Press, 1976), p. 194.

Reconciliation is then based on contrition. Ethnic riots, however, do not end this way. When interethnic violent episodes end, they usually do so because the remaining victims have fled, the instruments of force have restored order, the attackers are exhausted or satisfied, or some combination of these. In the very rare case where hostilities end by agreement, there are no conciliation ceremonies, no pleas for forgiveness, no gestures of humiliation. Rather, what occurs is more likely to be a loosely structured, fragile, blameless, perhaps insincere or even fraudulent, truce arranged by a third party.[219] In these conditions, remorse is the last thing on anyone's mind, precisely because moral community is lacking.[220]

219. For an example, see Cheah Boon Kheng, *Red Star over Malaya* (Singapore: Singapore University Press, 1983), pp. 227–30.

220. For a fine explication of the reasons for lack of community, see Kenelm O.L. Burridge, "Racial Relations in Johore," *Australian Journal of Politics and History* 2, no. 2 (May 1957): 151–68, at p. 167.

Location, Diffusion,
and Recurrence

COMPARED TO WHAT CAN BE SAID with reasonable certainty about social support for violence, about justification, absence of remorse, ineffective police, and inadequate prosecution — or about patterns of precipitants and target choices, for that matter — compared to these, explaining the locations (and nonlocations) of violence within a country can be a complicated assignment.

Consider the poor results achieved in comparable exercises with more complete data. Herculean efforts have been devoted to distinguishing cities affected by racial protest violence in the United States in the 1960s from those that were unaffected. Whether hypothesized explanations were grounded in patterns of minority disadvantage, or changes in those patterns, or minority dissatisfaction, or police practices and precipitants, cities experiencing violence were, as it turned out, not significantly different from those not experiencing it.[1] The same inability to discriminate was the result of a study embracing violent episodes between blacks and whites in the United States from 1913 to 1965.[2] Thus far, similar inconclusiveness characterizes efforts to distinguish violent from nonviolent cities in India. In a study of Hindu-Muslim riots from 1960 to 1993, it

1. The evidence is summarized in Donald L. Horowitz, "Racial Violence in the United States," in Nathan Glazer and Ken Young, eds., *Ethnic Pluralism and Public Policy: Achieving Equality in the United States and Britain* (London: Heinemann Educational Books, 1983), pp. 192–94. For an example of the continued puzzlement, see Gregg Lee Carter, "Black Attitudes and the 1960s Black Riots: An Aggregate-Level Analysis of the Kenner Commission's '15 Cities' Data," *Sociological Quarterly* 31, no. 2 (Summer 1990): 269–86.

2. Stanley Lieberson and Arnold R. Silverman, "The Precipitants and Underlying Conditions of Race Riots," *American Sociological Review* 30, no. 6 (December 1965): 887–98. Milton Bloombaum, "The Conditions Underlying Race Riots as Portrayed by Multidimensional Scalogram Analysis: A Reanalysis of Lieberson and Silverman's Data," *American Sociological Review* 33, no. 1 (February 1968): 76–91, suggests that nine variables, taken together, discriminate between riot and non-riot cities between 1913 and 1965.

was found that 24 towns, representing only 19 percent of India's urban population, accounted for half the riots and nearly two-thirds of the deaths; in some states, the concentration of violence in one or two towns was even greater.[3] In another study of 68 towns in the large state of Uttar Pradesh, 36 of the 65 towns for which full data were available experienced no riots between 1950 and 1990; and, when the most frequently hypothesized explanations for riots are arrayed alongside the cities with and without riots, no clear pattern emerges.[4] In both studies, there was skewed distribution: a few cities experienced many riots, some experienced some riots, and most cities experienced none or at most a single riot. "Communal violence in India," concludes the author of the 1960–93 study, is "town-specific."[5] The determinants of the skewed patterns remain obscure.

The incidence of riots from place to place is only one of several questions pertaining to the distribution of violence over space. Three general categories of spatial question present themselves: (1) location, (2) diffusion, and (3) recurrence.[6] Under the rubric of location, one can ask why one city is affected while another is not, or why certain types of location are affected but others are not, and it is equally pertinent to investigate the specific sites chosen by rioters within given locations. Under diffusion, it needs to be noted that some riots spread quickly and widely, while others spread not at all. For some, it is plausible to suggest that something like a process of contagion is at work, where the stimulus to violence is simply not site-specific. For others, violence is kept at home. In-between, there are processes of selective spread at work that remain to be uncovered. Finally, some locations are repetitiously violent, to the

3. Ashutosh Varshney, "Religion, Nationalism, and Violence: Hindus and Muslims in India" (unpublished manuscript, Harvard University Center for International Affairs, 1996).
4. Steven Ian Wilkinson, "What Large Datasets Can Tell Us about the General Explanations for Communal Riots" (paper presented at the annual meeting of the Association for Asian Studies, March 31, 1995), pp. 20–22. The literature on India contains a certain number of standard explanations, most of them pertaining to economic competition within particular cities. Competition between ethnically differentiated groups of artisans, or between manufacturers and traders, or between workers and moneylenders are among the commonly cited factors said to be "behind" the riots. See, e.g., P.R. Rajgopal, *Communal Violence in India* (New Delhi: Uppal, 1987), pp. 77, 81–82; Dildar Khan, "Meerut Riots: An Analysis," in Pramod Kumar, ed., *Towards Understanding Communalism* (Chandigarh: Centre for Research in Rural and Industrial Development, 1992), pp. 464–65; Akhilesh Kumar, *Communal Riots in India* (New Delhi: Commonwealth Publishers, 1991), pp. 72–90.
5. Varshney, "Religion, Nationalism, and Violence," p. 1 (emphasis omitted).
6. Recurrence may seem at first glance as a question of distribution over *time*, but I mean here to ask why riots return at later times to the same place.

point where they become riot-prone areas. It would be useful to learn what distinguishes these from other locations and what features characterize a recurrent riot area once such a tendency is established.

Within a single country, the layers of location range from regional variations to variations between locations and types of location, even within the same region, and to specific sites within what might be thought of as a single location. Location reveals quite a bit about the way rioters conceive of the venture on which they are embarked. It shows, for example, how much the riot depends on conditions that assure its safety for those who pursue the violence. At bottom, rioters are risk-averse actors. Location also illustrates the part played by learning in violence. In the first instance, learned behavior tends to be repeated, so that locations appear to be habitual. As violence proceeds, rioters seem to learn broader lessons, and these can open the way to more frequent, more intense, and more widely distributed violence.

LOCATION: DIFFERENTIALS IN THE FUNDAMENTALS

If the question is which locations within a given country are likely to experience riots, then there is already a clue. If a few cities experience many riots, while others experience none, then one reason for the location of a riot may be simply that earlier riots were located there. (Perhaps not so simply, because the earlier riots still need to be accounted for.) Suffice it to say for the moment that riots do return to the same place, sometimes again and again.

It is important not to overlook the obvious in differentiating riot locations from non-riot locations. If riots occur more frequently in a certain place, that may be evidence that intergroup hostility is greater there than in others, that authoritative social support for violence is greater there, that precipitants have occurred there, that organizers are based there, or that subgroup cleavages follow particular geographic lines.

Levels of intergroup hostility certainly can vary from place to place within the same country,[7] just as they vary between groups and between countries. William Crowther has found large variations from one city to another in Romanian attitudes toward Hungarians, Roma (Gypsies), and Jews; his findings control for education and social class, so location

---

7. Herbert Feldman, "The Communal Problem in the Indo-Pakistan Subcontinent: Some Current Implications," *Pacific Affairs* 42, no. 2 (Summer 1969): 145–63, at p. 152, points out that Hindu-Muslim antagonism "varies in intensity from place to place and from time to time." To my knowledge, no one has pursued this insight in Indian studies.

is not a proxy for these variables.[8] In a study of social distance in the Philippines, Rodolfo A. Bulatao also found locational differences: in some cities, familiarity with a group bred acceptance of it, while in others it bred rejection.[9] These findings pertain to relations among Filipino Christians. City-by-city variations were also found in measures of hostility toward Philippine Muslims and Chinese.[10] With regionally concentrated groups, such as Hungarians in Romania or Muslims in the Philippines, perhaps proximity drives hostility. That is true with respect to Hungarians in Romania, but there was a much less clear-cut association of proximity with hostile Filipino Christian attitudes toward Muslims; and location differentials in hostility persist with respect to the Roma in Romania and Chinese in the Philippines, both groups present in many areas of their countries. Both Crowther and Bulatao speculate that something like city-specific historical events are at work, for some locations seem to be persistently hostile, regardless of intensity of current contact.[11]

The linkage of locational variations in hostility to the incidence of violence has not really been studied explicitly. Yet there is occasionally a powerful demonstration of the relationship. In Burundi (1988), Hutu attacks on Tutsi precipitated a slaughter of Hutu in turn.[12] The attacks, however, were confined entirely to only two communes. Adjacent to

8. Crowther's findings on Romania (and on Moldova) are as yet unpublished, but he has been kind enough to share the data with me, and they are available in my files. See also William Crowther, "Defining Attitudes toward Minorities in Romania" (paper presented at the Conference on Ethnic Conflict in Bulgaria and Romania, Duke University, September 20–21, 1996), pp. 6–7, 11–12.

9. Rodolfo A. Bulatao, *Ethnic Attitudes in Five Philippine Cities* (Quezon City: University of the Philippines, 1973), pp. 104–06. On the relationship between contact and hostility, see H.D. Forbes, *Ethnic Conflict: Commerce, Culture, and the Contact Hypothesis* (New Haven: Yale University Press, 1997).

10. Bulatao, *Ethnic Attitudes in Five Philippine Cities*, pp. 86–99. Occasionally, the phenomenon has been noted elsewhere; hostility differentials from place to place have sometimes been attributed to subethnic differences within the group entertaining the variable hostility. See, e.g., Gary Alan Fine, "The Pinkston Settlement: An Historical and Social Psychological Investigation of the Contact Hypothesis," *Phylon* 40, no. 3 (September 1979): 229–42.

11. Crowther, "Defining Attitudes toward Minorities in Romania," pp. 5–7; Bulatao, *Ethnic Attitudes in Five Philippine Cities*, p. 88. Crowther notes in such locations that newcomers do not generally share the same strong antipathies. While Bulatao (*Ethnic Attitudes in Five Philippine Cities*, p. 96) found that acceptance of Muslims "does not follow a simple gradient of distance from Muslim areas," nevertheless hostility rankings by location suggest "the greater immediacy and perhaps the greater threat of the Muslim problems in Cebu, Tacloban and Davao as opposed to Manila and Naga."

12. René Lemarchand, *Burundi: Ethnocide as Discourse and Practice* (Cambridge: Cambridge University Press, 1994), pp. 118–27.

Rwanda, these communes had experienced an influx of Tutsi refugees after the Hutu revolution of 1959 in Rwanda. Those Tutsi refugees were hostile to Hutu. Across the border were Hutu exiles from Burundi, harboring equal but opposite hostility and communicating regularly with Hutu in the two Burundian communes. Here, then, the location of violence is explained by the location of strong intergroup antipathies.[13]

The relationship between local variations in hostility and local variations in violence needs exploration, but there is no doubt of such a relationship when we compare whole regions within countries. With some quite notable exceptions, such as Hyderabad, Hindu-Muslim riots have been far more frequent in north India than in south India. Patterns of group relations and hostility explain much of the regional disparity. In the north, it is far easier for Hindus to regard Muslims as agents of Pakistan — witness, for example, the apprehension in Ranchi-Hatia (1967) that making Urdu a second official state language was the prelude to another partition of the country.[14] In much of the south, no such emphasis on the external attachments of Muslims is possible. In addition, caste grievances were historically so great among Hindus in the south that they preempted some of the hostility that might have been directed against Muslims.[15] Such disparities in hostility exist in many countries and are likely to be related to the differential incidence of ethnic violence between regions[16] — and, if between regions, then quite possibly, too, between cities in the same region.

An equally obvious locational variable, from the discussion in Chapter 9, pertains to social support and police bias or ineffectiveness. In some countries, to be sure, these conditions may be more or less uniformly distributed, but this need not be the case. For example, we have seen that the riot in Penang (1967) began when Malays resisted Chinese

13. A similar point has been made for north Indian cities with substantial numbers of Hindu and Sikh refugees from Pakistan, who tend to be anti-Muslim.

14. See Government of India, *Report of the Commission of Inquiry on Communal Disturbances in Ranchi-Hatia (August 22–29, 1967)* (New Delhi: Government Printer, 1968), pp. 10–12.

15. Varshney, "Religion, Nationalism, and Violence," pp. 155–76.

16. Some of the variation may be subgroup-related, as in the case of Africans' special hostility toward Manga Arabs in Zanzibar, or Vahumpura and Salagama hostility to Tamils in Sri Lanka. For further thoughts on the geography of hostility, see Donald L. Horowitz, *Ethnic Groups in Conflict* (Berkeley and Los Angeles: University of California Press, 1985), pp. 227–28. In the United States in the 1960s, there was a great regional disparity in the incidence of black protest violence: the south was left out of the violence for reasons having to do with the way the civil rights movement developed there and not in the north. See the interesting analysis of Howard Hubbard, "Five Long Hot Summers and How They Grew," *The Public Interest*, no. 12 (Summer 1968): 3–24.

enforcement of a hartal. The police seemed unprepared, and the chief police officer of Penang was later transferred. At about the same time, the Labor Party, admittedly less strong in Kuala Lumpur, urged a hartal in the capital, too, but the police there took steps to neutralize the hartal demand.[17] No riot developed in Kuala Lumpur in 1967. Police effectiveness was not the entire explanation, but it surely contributed.

Later in this chapter, we shall review evidence that rioters are extremely cautious in site selection within cities. It seems likely that the same unwillingness to assume undue risk accounts for their indisposition to riot at all in certain cities, and so microconditions, such as police preparations, likely account for some such choices. The panoply of conditions that discriminates across countries ought generally to discriminate between cities within countries as well.

Precipitating events are a variable not generally considered in studies of location. If precipitants are events evoking violence, rather than merely providing convenient excuses for its commission, then riots should generally be located where precipitants occur and not located where they do not occur. (Whether they then spread beyond those locations is a different question.) The Delhi riot (1984) occurred where Mrs. Gandhi was assassinated, rather than in a major center of Sikh separatism. The capricious result was that the main victims in Delhi were Sikh immigrants from Sind, Rajasthan, and other places outside Punjab; often they were not Punjabi-speaking and not supporters of Punjabi separatism.[18] Sri Lanka (1983) began at the Colombo cemetery where the bodies of soldiers ambushed by Tamil separatists were to be buried.[19] As in Delhi, the location involved targets not especially sympathetic to separatism. The Sierra Leone (1968) violence occurred in Bo and Kenema, where Temne politicians had come to campaign,[20] just as the Nigerian riot (1953) occurred in Kano, where Action Group politicians had come to hold a rally.[21] Kano was a more homogeneously Hausa city than Kaduna or Jos, cities that might have been expected to experience vio-

17. Nancy L. Snider, "What Happened in Penang?" *Asian Survey* 8, no. 12 (December 1968): 960–75, at pp. 965–66. I was in Kuala Lumpur at the time, and my own observations of December 3, 1967, recorded in my field notes, are in accord with Snider's account.

18. Uma Chakravarti and Nandita Haksar, *The Delhi Riots: Three Days in the Life of a Nation* (New Delhi: Lancer International, 1987), pp. 72, 81, 259, 267.

19. Sunil Bastian, "The Political Economy of Ethnic Violence in Sri Lanka: The July 1983 Riots," in Veena Das, ed., *Mirrors of Violence: Communities, Riots and Survivors in South Asia* (Delhi: Oxford University Press, 1990), p. 300.

20. *West Africa*, December 14, 1968, p. 1463.

21. Northern Regional Government, Government of Nigeria, *Report on the Kano Disturbances, 16th, 17th, 18th and 19th May 1953* (Kaduna: Government Printer, 1953). The

lence (as Jos had in 1945). That Kano, rather than the others, experienced the riot attests to the role of the precipitant in evoking violence. The Malaysian riots of 1957 and 1967 were both Penang affairs, because the precipitants occurred there and had peculiarly local content, while the riot of 1969 was a Kuala Lumpur event, for the same reason (among others already discussed).[22] Since precipitating events are often locally evocative, the reaction — at least the first reaction and perhaps the entire reaction — is usually situated accordingly. In the Malaysian case, federalism reinforced the local character of the precipitant, but federalism is not necessary for this purpose. People generally react locally in the first instance.

The locally evocative character of precipitating events has a species of conditionality attached to it. Peace is conditioned on a view of what is seen to be tolerable behavior on the part of the target group. This conditionality helps account not merely for the initial localization of violence, but also for its episodic character.

To the extent the riot is organized, location reflects patterns of organizational support. The most serious incidents in west Punjab (1953) occurred where the Ahrar party was strongest; it had taken the most hostile position against Ahmadi, who became targets.[23] There was a discernible tendency for the Delhi riot (1984) to be concentrated in areas where local Congress (I) supporters were numerous,[24] just as, in Sri Lanka (1956 and 1958), the Gal Oya and Padavia areas, where followers of particular politicians had been settled, were riot sites.[25] The involvement of Shiv Sena in Bombay-Bhiwandi (1984) focused the riots on areas

---

riot took place in Kano, and only in Kano, despite the fact that the precipitating agent, the Action Group, was a Yoruba party, whereas the targets were Ibo, against whom there was hostility in many northern cities.

22. As we saw in Chapter 8, the 1957 precipitant involved the loss of Penang's special status, and the 1967 precipitant involved an effort by the Labor Party, especially strong in Penang, to enforce a hartal there. The 1969 precipitant involved the formation of a post-election government in the state of Selangor, where Kuala Lumpur was located; there was a deep feeling about that issue and about the processions that followed the elections in that state. It is also true, however, that the Penang riot did not spread to Kuala Lumpur because of police precautions, as I have indicated, and the Kuala Lumpur riot did not spread for other reasons explained below.

23. Government of Punjab, *Report of the Court of Inquiry Constituted under Punjab Act II of 1954 to Enquire into the Punjab Disturbances of 1953* (Lahore: Superintendent of Government Printing, Punjab, 1954), pp. 151–82.

24. People's Union for Democratic Rights and People's Union for Civil Liberties, *Who Are the Guilty? Report of a Joint Inquiry into the Causes and Impact of the Riots in Delhi from 31 October to 10 November* (Delhi: PUDR & PUCL, 1984), p. 3.

25. Tarzie Vittachi, *Emergency '58: The Story of the Ceylon Race Riots* (London: André Deutsch, 1958), pp. 20, 23–24, 96.

where the sena's following was strong and on castes and subgroups that tended to support the organization.[26] In 1937–38, the shift in frequency of Hindu-Muslim riots from Punjab to the United Provinces was related to the sharp competition there between Congress and the Muslim League.[27] Where organization is manifest, the killings follow the footsteps of the organizers. Supporters of other organizations, located elsewhere, are likely to remain aloof.

Likewise, if the riot grows out of a conflict that does not embrace whole groups, location is limited accordingly. Early Sri Lankan riots were the product of a conflict defined mainly as a quarrel between Tamils and Sinhalese Buddhists, rather than all Sinhalese. Accordingly, the 1956, 1958, and 1977 riots generally did not involve areas inhabited by Sinhalese Catholics.[28] The 1965 riot in Mauritius was between Creoles and Hindus, whereas the 1968 riot was between Creoles and Muslims. Not surprisingly, the violence in 1965 began in Trois Boutiques, the site of adjacent Hindu and Creole villages, while the 1968 violence occurred in Port Louis.[29] In neither case was the other place involved. Location follows cleavage lines more or less precisely.[30]

PROPINQUITY AND URBAN BIAS

The vast majority of ethnic riots occur in urban areas. Rural riots are conspicuous mainly by their relative paucity. The southern Philippines (1971) is a contrary example, but the violence there tended to be relatively well organized.[31] It also involved land disputes, as did two other prominent rural riots: Rwanda (1963) and Nellie (1983).[32] From 1960 to 1993, 90 percent of the riots and 95 percent of the deaths in India occurred in cities

26. Asghar Ali Engineer, *Bhiwandi-Bombay Riots: Analysis and Documentation* (Bombay: Institute of Islamic Studies, 1984), pp. 10–11, 27.

27. Richard D. Lambert, "Hindu-Muslim Riots" (Ph.D. diss., University of Pennsylvania, 1951), p. 137.

28. For a 1977 exception, see Tamil Refugees Rehabilitation Organization, *Communal Disturbances in Sri Lanka: Sansoni Commission, Written Submissions* (mimeo., March 28, 1980), p. 171.

29. Adele Smith Simmons, "Politics in Mauritius since 1934: A Study of Decolonization in a Plural Society" (D.Phil thesis, Oxford University, 1969), pp. 408–16, 476.

30. Lucknow has generally been a conspicuous exception in Uttar Pradesh, a state prone to Hindu-Muslim violence, for there the Sunni-Shiite cleavage has been more salient than the Hindu-Muslim cleavage. Ashutosh Varshney, "Value Rationality, Instrumental Rationality, and Ethnic Conflict" (paper presented at the annual meeting of the American Political Science Association, Chicago, August 31–September 3, 1995), p. 28.

31. See *Far Eastern Economic Review*, September 11, 1971, pp. 10–11.

32. René Lemarchand, *Rwanda and Burundi* (New York: Praeger, 1970), pp. 482–83; Nellie (1983) is described in Chapter 9, above.

and towns.[33] To be sure, riots can spread from towns to villages, and rural violence can be extremely lethal. The rural violence in Burma (1942), Malaysia (1945–46), Punjab (1947), and Chad (1979) — none of which, with the exception created by the Punjab partition, involved land issues — took many thousands of lives. Kamrup (1980) and Nellie (1983), both in Assam, took fewer, though the numbers were still large.

Riots are initiated in urban areas because, first of all, the public, threatening character of many precipitants brings with it an urban bias: processions, strikes, protests, demonstrations of strength and of mass are all more likely where population is concentrated. Urban areas are also more heterogeneous, facilitating reciprocal insult, sacrilege, and cheek-by-jowl confrontation. Furthermore, attackers, as we have seen, target those who are threatening. Since it is often difficult for two groups with divergent cultures and land-use patterns to live together in the same village[34] — even ethnic subgroups are often spatially separated in villages[35] — the result is that village heterogeneity is usually limited to isolated minorities. Such minorities are likely neither to attack nor to be threatening enough to receive attacks. Of course, as in Nellie (1983), the aggressors may come from some distance to attack a village majority — and this, as we have seen, is a sure sign of strong organization. (Very much the same kind of organized attacks became common in rural Sind by 1990,[36] but they are not the norm.) Finally, as Nellie (1983) ironically suggests, police intelligence is frequently more easily obtained in rural than in urban areas. The Nellie riot occurred despite a flood of intelligence, not because of any dearth of it.[37] Riot prevention thus becomes more challenging in cities, where force may be available to the authorities but intelligence may not. If, however, prevention fails in rural areas, the available force is rarely adequate to stop the violence promptly.[38] Rural violence lasts longer, is more sporadic, and is more difficult to end.

33. I am indebted to Ashutosh Varshney for these data.

34. For an explanation, see Leo A. Despres, *Cultural Pluralism and Nationalist Politics in British Guiana* (Chicago: Rand McNally, 1967), pp. 92–93, 113–18.

35. See, e.g., Peter J. Wilson, *A Malay Village and Malaysia* (New Haven, Conn.: HRAF Press, 1967), pp. 18–24.

36. Human Rights Commission of Pakistan, *Sindh Inquiry, Summer 1990* (Lahore: Human Rights Commission of Pakistan, 1990), pp. 15–16, 21.

37. Compare Haja Maideen, *The Nadra Tragedy: The Maria Hartog Controversy* (Petaling Jaya, Malaysia: Pelanduk, 1989), pp. 230–31, on the difficulty of the Singapore authorities in gathering accurate information, despite the lengthy buildup to the riots.

38. Here I am drawing on a field trip to sites of anti-Roma violence in rural Romania in February 1994. Local police posts were well informed about rising anti-Roma sentiment in each pre-violence period, but at the village level they were badly understaffed, underequipped, and immobile, so that outbreaks of violence proved difficult to contain.

All of these considerations create a strong impetus for ethnic violence to be an urban phenomenon.[39] Whether it then spreads to rural areas is a different matter: most violence does not. In general, too, the location of the violence is in close propinquity to the location of the attackers' homes. In Singapore (1950), Geylang was the worst-affected area; it was the area of the rioters' residence.[40] In Bhiwandi (1984), the attackers came from merely one to one and a half kilometers away.[41] These are typical cases: absent strong organization, rioters do not commute long distances to engage in violence.[42] They will, of course, go where the target group is, and sometimes that means a bit of travel.[43] Sometimes, too, if ethnic groups are unevenly distributed, so that the targets are concentrated in urban areas and the aggressors in rural areas, the latter may invade the precincts of the town from villages that surround it, as Hindus did to Bhiwandi (1984) and Kyrghyz did to Osh (1990).[44] This was also part of the pattern in Kuala Lumpur (1969), and there was some such movement in Burma (1938), although most participants in both of those riots came from the vicinity of the violence.[45] In the midst of disorder, it can be dangerous for rioters to stray too far from home.

39. There is a similar tendency of terrorist violence to be urban. See Michael Poole, "The Geographical Location of Political Violence in Northern Ireland," in John Darby, Nicholas Dodge, and A.C. Hepburn, eds., *Political Violence: Ireland in a Comparative Perspective* (Belfast: Appletree Press, 1990), p. 67. For the city as the major site of ethnic confrontation, see Fred Riggs, "Inter-Ethnic Relations: Change and Stability" (paper presented at a UNESCO conference, Ottawa, Canada, December 11–14, 1993; mimeo.), pp. 3–4.

40. Maideen, *The Nadra Tragedy*, p. 264.

41. Engineer, *Bhiwandi-Bombay Riots*, p. 24.

42. Kano (1953), for example, was a riot that came on rather quickly, with participants drawn almost entirely from Kano itself. Northern Regional Government, *Report on the Kano Disturbances*, p. 22.

43. An automobile economy facilitates such moves. In Los Angeles (1992), a hybrid deadly riot cum violent protest demonstration, most of the attacks on Korean persons and property were apparently committed by people living in adjacent neighborhoods — the usual pattern — but some rioters drove to Koreatown from south-central Los Angeles, about three miles away. Peter A. Morrison and Isa S. Lowry, "A Riot of Color: The Demographic Setting of Civil Disturbance in Los Angeles" (unpublished paper no. P-7819, the RAND Corporation, Santa Monica, Calif., 1993), pp. 13, 15, 33.

44. In 1970, by contrast, Bhiwandi Hindus fanned out from the Muslim-majority town to kill Muslims on the periphery. S.K. Ghosh, *Communal Riots in India* (New Delhi: Ashish, 1987), p. 202. For Kyrghyzstan (1990), see *Izvestia*, June 6, 1990, p. 2, in *Current Digest of the Soviet Press*, July 11, 1990, p. 2.

45. See Government of Burma, *Final Report of the Riot Inquiry Committee* (Rangoon: Superintendent of Government Printing & Stationery, 1939), pp. 201–05; Karl von Vorys, *Democracy without Consensus: Communalism and Political Stability in Malaysia* (Princeton: Princeton University Press, 1975), pp. 323–38.

SITE SELECTION AND RISK AVERSION

The *exact* location of riots is not foreordained by precipitants, organizations, cleavages, or even urban bias. In specific site selection, rioters tend to be opportunistic and risk averse. Possible sites can be evaluated from the standpoint of the probable safety of those attacking. Rarely do they choose the least safe areas to do their killing, even if the payoff to them there might be great; and when they do choose risky locations, they are readily dissuaded by displays of force. Generally, however, they do not choose the areas safest to themselves. They tend to take some risk, but typically a moderate one, and they can be moved quickly from greater to less risk.

The initial choice of locale is shaped by the rioters' desire to avoid target-group defenses and police deployment, provided the police are not known in advance to be favorably disposed or indifferent to the prospect of violence. On the rare occasions when they ignore these precautions, they pay a steep price in casualties, as they did in Kano (1953) during an attack in the heart of the targets' residential area and in Durban (1949) when the police did their duty.[46]

Adaptability is generally in evidence among rioters. In Burma (1938), Indian victims organized a bit of retaliatory violence after the first incidents, and the police were decidedly unfavorable to rioters. Burmans solved the first problem with superior force, attacking Indians even in the same areas where Indian retaliation had taken place, and handled the second by avoiding the police. The police were deployed on main streets, and so Burmans attacked in side streets and remote areas.[47] Indian resistance evaporated, and Burman crowds controlled Rangoon for several days, until police began firing on them.[48] More determined targets or

46. For the Kano and Durban casualty figures, see note 54, below. There was also durable resistance to anti-Chinese violence in Singapore (1964). This unusual behavior by a target group is accounted for by the existence of well-organized Chinese secret societies that fought back, producing a somewhat more equal Malay-Chinese casualty count than might otherwise have been expected. See Lee Kuan Yew, *The Singapore Story* (Singapore: Times Editions, 1998), pp. 558, 567; Albert Lau, *A Moment of Anguish: Singapore in Malaysia and the Politics of Disengagement* (Singapore: Times Academic Press, 1998), pp. 168, 171.

47. Government of Burma, *Final Report of the Riot Inquiry Committee*, pp. 35–37. The adaptability of rioters in these conditions is well demonstrated. In Biharsharif (1981), a curfew was imposed in the town center after the first incidents. Rioters promptly shifted their attention, on successive nights, to areas where the curfew had not been imposed. Ghosh, *Communal Riots in India*, pp. 128–29.

48. Government of Burma, *Final Report of the Riot Inquiry Committee*, pp. 37–41.

more effective police, however, can serve to deflect attacks. Karachi (1965) arose out of an electoral victory procession that had been heavily guarded by police, so, at its conclusion, processionists moved to outlying areas to attack their electoral-cum-ethnic enemies.[49] When British armed forces finally regained control in Shahabad district of the then United Provinces, India (1917), violence shifted to adjacent areas of the next district.[50] If the first incidents occur in an area unfavorable to the attackers and a lull follows, there may well be a change of venue when the attacks resume, as there was in Durban (1949), Zanzibar (1961), and Mauritius (1965).[51] In all three, the violence shifted from town centers before the lull to periurban areas after. The tactical advantage of the shift is suggested by a passage in an official report on Durban (1949) describing the new locations as containing the houses of Indian targets, scattered over a wide area.[52] To put the point succinctly, attackers respond to the balance of force and extricate themselves when necessary. They are not merely attacking strong targets at weak *moments* but at weak *points*, too.

The risk aversion of rioters is well reflected in the balance of casualties, which is generally overwhelmingly favorable to the aggressors. The overall figures for India during the 1960s are typical, reflecting as they do the fact that, in such riots, Hindus nearly always attacked Muslims. According to a reasonably comprehensive count, Muslims accounted for 89.5 percent of the deaths in those riots.[53] There can be a fair amount of variation around such numbers, but, as a rule of thumb, 85–95 percent

49. *Dawn* (Karachi), January 5, 1965, p. 1; January 7, 1965, p. 4.

50. Indian Statutory Commission, *Memoranda Submitted by the Government of India and the India Office to the Indian Statutory Commission,* Vol. IV, pt. 1 (London: H.M.S.O., 1930), p. 98.

51. Maurice Webb and Kenneth Kirkwood, *The Durban Riots and After* (Johannesburg: South African Institute of Race Relations, n.d.), p. 2; Great Britain, Colonial Office, *Report of a Commission of Inquiry into Disturbances in Zanzibar during June 1961,* Colon. no. 353 (London: H.M.S.O., 1961), pp. 8–12; Simmons, "Politics in Mauritius since 1934," pp. 412–14.

52. Union of South Africa, *Report of the Commission of Enquiry into Riots in Durban* (Cape Town: Cape Times, Ltd., 1949), p. 7.

53. Gopal Krishna, "Communal Violence in India: A Study of Communal Disturbance in Delhi," pt. I, *Economic and Political Weekly,* January 12, 1985, pp. 61–74, at p. 73. Krishna counts 2,397 Muslims killed in the 1960s, of a total dead of 2,679, and finds also that more than 90 percent of the property damage related to Muslim-owned property. Veena Das states that in Indian riots from 1954 to 1960, 86 percent of those killed were Muslim. Veena Das, "Communities, Riots, Survivors: The South Asian Experience" (Punitham Tiruchelvam Memorial Lecture, Sri Lanka Tamil Women's Union, Colombo, September 5, 1988, mimeo.), p. 15. By another count, based on riots from 1968 through 1978, Muslim deaths outnumbered Hindu deaths by more than three to one. S.K. Ghosh, *Violence in the Streets* (New Delhi: Light and Life, 1981), p. 114.

is a reasonable estimate, absent considerable police vigilance or unusual target-group retaliation.[54]

Such relative death tolls say as much about the strong tactical advantage of initiative, arms, momentum, and mass in fighting as they do about the risk aversion of the attackers per se. Still, this is an impressive number. When we put it together with the great accuracy of rioters in choosing individual targets — as manifested in their aversion to false positives — the total result reads as follows: Since rioters attack in force, *and* they do not generally make mistakes about the identity of their targets, *and* they do not generally miscalculate police response or target resis-

---

54. Official figures on deaths are notoriously unreliable, but here are a few examples from relatively reliable official and unofficial reports, with some notable caveats appended:

Ahmedabad (1969): Hindus, 24; Muslims, 430; undetermined, 58
Bhiwandi (1970): Hindus, 17; Muslims, 59; undetermined, 2
Bombay-Bhiwandi (1984): Hindus, 8; Muslims, 243
Durban (1949): Africans, 87; Europeans, 1; Indians, 50; undetermined, 4
Jalgaon (1970): Muslims, 42; other, 1
Kano (1953): northerners, 15; southerners, 21
Kosheh, Egypt (2000): Christians, 19; Muslims, 1
Kyrghyzstan (1990): Kyrghyz, 50; Russians, 1; Uzbeks, 120
Kuala Lumpur (1969): Chinese, 143; Malays, 25
Meerut (1969): Hindus, 1; Muslims, 16
Moradabad (1980): Hindus, 28; Muslims, 134
Ranchi-Hatia (1967): Hindus, 19; Muslims, 135; undetermined, 1
Sambhal (1980): Hindus, 23; others, 2
Sudan (1955): northerners, 36; southerners, 20 (excludes 55 southerners who
         drowned during the course of the riots)
Zanzibar (1961): Africans, 3; Arabs, 64; other, 1

Several of these require comment. The aggressors in Kano were northerners, but in this riot, unlike most, the targets organized counterattacks. This, plus the fact that the local police generally did their duty, accounts for the relatively large number of northern deaths. See Northern Regional Government, *Report on the Kano Disturbances*, pp. 13–20. Africans were the aggressors in Durban. Once the riot got going, the targets were, unlike the targets in Kano, mainly passive. The large number of African deaths is accounted for mainly by the action of the security forces. Webb and Kirkwood, *The Durban Riots and After*, p. 4. For Kuala Lumpur, most unofficial observers believe "that the number of Chinese killed was much higher." Harold Crouch, *Government and Society in Malaysia* (Ithaca: Cornell University Press, 1996), p. 24. The Kyrghyzstan figures, provided by Valery Tishkov, "Don't Kill Me, I Am Kyrghyz: Anthropological Analysis of Violence in Osh Ethnic Conflict" (paper presented at the 13th International Congress of Anthropological and Ethnological Sciences, July 28–August 5, 1993), are far lower than other sources provided. See, e.g., *The Independent* (London), July 19, 1990, p. 10, estimating 1,000 killed in Uzgen alone. Abidin Bozdağ, "Crisis and Democracy in Kirgizia," *Aussenpolitik* 43, no. 3 (1992): 277–86, at p. 278, reports an Uzbek organization's figure of 5,000 killed, including 4,500 Uzbeks. The Kyrghyz fraction of the total reported by Tishkov may also be too high, but if Kyrghyz deaths exceed 10 or 20 percent of the total, that would surely be because the police acted, where possible, to disperse crowds. As in Durban, therefore, most of the casualties inflicted on the attackers were probably not inflicted by the target group.

tance, *and* they are generally free of serious criminal sanction afterward, they do not generally get themselves killed. The risk-reward ratio of the deadly ethnic riot makes it a promising venture.

Rioters may attack in areas of a town where members of the target group are concentrated or where they are isolated, where the neighborhoods occupied by groups are relatively homogeneous or where they are relatively heterogeneous. The choices of the rioters again reveal a strong sense of self-protection.

Rioters may try to attack the targets squarely in the targets' home area, as Hausa did in the Ibo *sabon gari* (strangers' quarter) of Kano (1953), but this risks encountering strong defenses or even counterattacks.[55] As we have seen, the Ibo, unlike most target groups, did organize themselves for battle in Kano.[56] In Penang (1967), when rioters encountered large crowds of the target group, violence was avoided — this in the midst of ferocious killing elsewhere.[57] Given the risks, a successful attack on the targets' homogeneous home area, while possible when rioters have overwhelming force,[58] is rarely the preferred course. If rioters move in this direction and encounter serious resistance, as they did in the early phases of Kuala Lumpur (1969), they will usually do what the Kuala Lumpur rioters did: disengage and relocate their attacks.[59] This, of course, is the same strategy followed after the lull by those who experience an unfavorable situation in fighting before the lull. Usually, however, prospective rioters anticipate danger. "Some of us took up our *parangs* [long knives]," reported a Malay in connection with anti-Chinese violence in Johore (1945–46). "But just here we are only a few — the Chinese outnumber us greatly. So there was no killing. But we were very angry."[60] Action based on anger will still be sited carefully.

If the target group's homogeneous neighborhood poses unacceptable

55. See R.A. Schermerhorn, "The Locale of Hindu-Muslim Riots," *Indian Journal of Political Science* 1, no. 1 (January–June 1971): 37–47, at p. 44.

56. Northern Regional Government, *Report on the Kano Disturbances*, p. 13.

57. Interview, Batu Ferringhi, Penang, February 2, 1968.

58. See, e.g., Engineer, *Bhiwandi-Bombay Riots*, p. 23. Asghar Ali Engineer, "Bastion of Communal Amity Crumbles," *Economic and Political Weekly*, February 13, 1993, pp. 262–64, at p. 263; Paul R. Brass, *Theft of an Idol: Text and Context in the Representation of Collective Violence* (Princeton: Princeton University Press, 1997), p. 220.

59. See von Vorys, *Democracy without Consensus*, pp. 328, 332–33.

60. Quoted in Kenelm O.L. Burridge, "Racial Relations in Johore," *Australian Journal of Politics and History* 2, no. 2 (May 1957): 151–68, at p. 164 (footnote omitted). In East St. Louis (1917), even after black resistance collapsed once the killing got going, white rioters did not venture into heavily black areas. Elliott M. Rudwick, *Race Riot at East St. Louis, July 2, 1917* (Carbondale: Southern Illinois University Press, 1964), p. 56. Such restraint is the norm.

risks, then it is possible for attackers to reduce risk by moving to areas
that are more thoroughly heterogeneous or even to those controlled by
majorities of the attacking group. I have already argued that urban riots
are facilitated by the propinquity of groups in a common space and that
rural riots are much less frequent because of insufficient village heterogeneity: riots are most likely where groups are in close contact. Once
locations where the balance of force is unfavorable to the attacking
group are ruled out, the most common locations should be characterized
by a strong presence of the target group, but still short of a majority.

There is much evidence that supports this prediction. Ever since the
seminal work of Richard D. Lambert on Hindu-Muslim riots, two types
of urban area have been identified. The most common venues for Indian
urban riots were "the mixed areas where one community was in a distinct minority, and the borderline area between strongholds of opposing
communities."[61] Lambert's work was followed by the attempt of Allen
D. Grimshaw to specify neighborhood types in which black-white violence in the United States was most likely to be found.[62] In major race
riots — interpersonal violence, not protest violence — the most active violence took place in black lower-class areas in which white-owned businesses were also located and, especially, in downtown business districts
and at transportation transfer points where white majorities encountered
black minorities. "Contested areas," residential neighborhoods resisting
change from white to black, were relatively quiet during major episodes
of violence.[63] Like Lambert, Grimshaw found the heterogeneous locations claimed by no one group, as well as a majority area with a strong
minority presence, to be most vulnerable to mass violence.

Heterogeneous market areas of central cities are indeed common sites
of ethnic riots, in India as in America,[64] and in many other countries, too.
Borderline locations are also likely to experience violence.[65] A residential
area belonging mainly to one group is often the base for attacks on
nearby heterogeneous market areas, boundary areas, and mixed residen-

61. Lambert, "Hindu-Muslim Riots," p. 218. See ibid., pp. 123, 130, 155–56, 174.
62. Allen D. Grimshaw, "Urban Racial Violence in the United States," *American
Journal of Sociology* 66, no. 2 (September 1960): 109–19.
63. Ibid., pp. 110–17.
64. V.V. Singh, *Communal Violence* (Jaipur: Rawat, 1993), p. 105 (Aligarh and
Moradabad); Ghosh, *Communal Riots in India*, pp. 216–20 (Meerut); Rudwick, *Race
Riot at East St. Louis*, p. 56; William M. Tuttle, Jr., *Race Riot: Chicago in the Red Summer
of 1919* (New York: Atheneum, 1978), p. 65.
65. This was the case also in Natal (1989), where violence between those aligned with
Inkatha and those with the UDF-ANC took place. Wherever housing areas predominantly
of one group overlap or touch those of another, there was "persistent violence." Stavros

tial areas. Penang (1967) is a classic example. Not many Malays left their home areas to attack Chinese elsewhere. Rather, the attacks came from Malay settlements adjacent to Chinese neighborhoods and to main roads. Victims were generally found along the boundary or traveling along a road.[66] With the exception of the initial procession, which involved some rural Malays, Kuala Lumpur (1969) followed the same pattern. Inhabitants of Malay settlements ventured out to kill Chinese along nearby streets and highways.[67] Sri Lanka (1977) combined the two patterns: some Sinhalese attacks took place in localities where Tamils were clearly in the minority, while others occurred in mixed areas, such as Trincomalee town.[68] Attacks in mixed areas, of course, are safer than attacks in the target group's heartland.

What Grimshaw calls contested areas — mixed residential areas without an established ethnic identity or areas undergoing change in identity — are also common sites for violence outside the United States. It is sometimes hard to distinguish a contested area from a merely mixed one, but violence certainly does occur in planned industrial towns, where groups are thrown together in a new setting in which none can claim a superior attachment to the territory. A good example is Jamshedpur, Bihar (1979), a new city designed around a steel plant.[69] Kirkuk, Iraq (1959), is an oil city on the edge of a Kurdish area, but in which Kurds are more recent inhabitants than are Turkomens[70] — a perfect contested area. Sumgait (1988) is a new petrochemical city in Azerbaijan, housing Armenians as well as Azeris.[71] The colonization areas of Sri Lanka, prominent locations of rioting in 1956, 1958, and 1977, were mainly in

---

Stavrou and Lwazi Shongwe, "Violence on the Periphery: The Greater Edendale Complex," *Indicator SA* 7, no. 1 (Summer 1989): 53–57. Although these were political groups, they were also very often aligned along clan or ascriptive subethnic boundaries as well. See Stavros Stavrou and Andrew Crouch, "Molweni: Violence on the Periphery," ibid., 6, no. 3 (Winter 1989): 46–50. As in much other rural violence, land issues between migrants and earlier-settled populations played a part.

66. Interviews, George Town, Penang, January 23, 1968; January 25, 1968; February 2, 1968.

67. Von Vorys, *Democracy without Consensus*, pp. 332–33.

68. *Report of the Presidential Commission of Inquiry into the Incidents Which Took Place between 13th August and 15th September 1977*, Sessional Paper No. VII-1980 (Colombo: Government Publications Bureau, 1980), pp. 238–53. An exception was Vavuniya, where Sinhalese were a minority, but there was rather strong evidence of police complicity in those killings. See Tamil Refugees Rehabilitation Organization, *Communal Disturbances in Sri Lanka*, pp. 96–100.

69. For a good description, see *New York Times*, September 26, 1979, p. 2.

70. See Arnold Hottinger, "An Eye-Witness Report on Iraq," *Swiss Review of World Affairs* 9, no. 6 (September 1959): 12–16.

71. See *New York Times*, August 31, 1988, pp. A1, A8.

the borderlands between established Sinhalese and Tamil zones, but most of the colonists were Sinhalese, and there was a sense that the effective boundary of Sinhalese settlement was being pushed outward and resentment at the prospect that Tamils might also be settled there.[72]

Contested neighborhoods, as well as cities and towns, are riot sites. The violence in Jerusalem (1929) began near holy places and spread out to adjacent mixed neighborhoods at a time of demographic change.[73] Ranchi (1967) was largely confined to the workers' colony of an engineering complex[74]—a location like Jamshedpur. Northern Ireland (1969) took place along the points at which Catholic and Protestant neighborhoods meet, in west Belfast, and virtually nowhere else in that city; it featured house burnings more than direct fighting, as might be expected in a contested area.[75] It was the continuation of a pattern of riots throughout the nineteenth century, when violence was used in precisely the same neighborhoods "to establish . . . territorial dominance." In that period, ethnic shares of the population rose and declined, the composition of neighborhoods was in doubt, and "house-wrecking" was a means of enforcing ethnic homogeneity.[76] Almost all the affected neighborhoods in Penang (1967) were old Malay settlements, typically inhabited by descendants of the original owners but surrounded by newer Chinese residences. In some of them, Chinese who had bought land at the edge of a Malay settlement were living in the original Malay-style houses.[77] Such areas have very much the flavor of the endangered neighborhood described by Grimshaw.[78]

Perhaps a parsimonious conception of location does not require a category for contested areas. Contested or not, riot areas tend to be heterogeneous. Two features conduce to rioting in border areas. Targets can be

72. Vittachi, *Emergency '58*, pp. 20–24.

73. Bernard Wasserstein, "Patterns of Communal Conflict in Palestine," in Ada Rapoport-Albert and Steven J. Zipperstein, eds., *Jewish History: Essays in Honour of Chimen Abramsky* (London: Peter Halban, 1988), p. 66.

74. Feldman, "The Communal Problem in the Indo-Pakistan Subcontinent," p. 151.

75. *Violence and Civil Disturbances in Northern Ireland in 1969: Report of Tribunal of Inquiry*, Cmd. 566 (Belfast: H.M.S.O., 1972), pp. 133, 137, 225.

76. See the illuminating treatment of Sybil E. Baker, "Orange and Green: Belfast, 1832–1912," in H.J. Dyos and Michael Wolff, eds., *The Victorian City* (London: Routledge & Kegan Paul, 1973), pp. 789–814. The quotation appears on p. 792.

77. Interviews, George Town, January 25, 1968; February 2, 1968.

78. Of course, the contested-area category carries some baggage in the United States that is unlikely to be present in some other countries, for it relates to the assumed undesirability of living in close proximity to ranked subordinates. Even so, there are similar phobias elsewhere, and in any case, attachment to neighborhood territory can give rise to a sense of contest as neighborhood demography begins to change.

found along the boundary, and safety can be found by retreat to the attackers' home area.

Safer still are attacks where the rioters' ethnic group comprises the majority. A substantial body of writing on Indian riots argues that towns with a Muslim population of 10 to 30 percent, or in some formulations, 20 to 50 percent, are most likely to experience Hindu-Muslim riots, and there is some evidence to support the argument.[79] On the other hand, in India and elsewhere, a recurrent pattern has the overall riot occurring in a town where as much as 50 percent of the population — or more — consists of members of the target group, but has the specific attack occurring in local areas where the targets are at a disadvantage because, in those neighborhoods, the target group is in the minority. This was the case, for instance, in Biharsharif (1993) and Bhiwandi (1970 and 1984).[80] In all of those instances, crowds took care where they sought out victims.[81] The byword in target-majority towns is conservatism in killing.

On the other hand, the attackers do not follow the very safest strategy. They attack in heterogeneous cities, such as the ones just mentioned and many others, but they do not seek complete impunity by opting for truly homogeneous towns or villages where helpless, stranded minority victims can be found in small numbers and safely dispatched.

It is important not to paint the rioters as excessively averse to risk taking. For there is a clear-cut class of riot towns in which rioters who might expect to be outnumbered attack the urban majority. In Chapter 9, I referred to this as desperate violence. It occurs where a town or an area is inhabited principally by people categorized as immigrant and when the indigenes see themselves as subject to unfavorable comparisons that stigmatize them as backward in relation to those they see as having seized

79. Krishna, "Communal Violence in India," p. 65; Wilkinson, "What Large Datasets Can Tell Us about the General Explanations for Communal Riots," pp. 18, 23, 26. For race riots in the United States, 1913–63, however, no association was found between the black percentage of an urban population and the propensity of such cities for violence. Lieberson and Silverman, "The Precipitants and Underlying Conditions of Race Riots," p. 894.

80. For a particularly helpful account of Biharsharif, see Ghosh, *Communal Riots in India*, pp. 126–30. See also Government of India, *Report of the Commission of Inquiry on Communal Disturbances in Ranchi-Hatia*, pp. 14–15; Kajsa Ekholm Friedman and Anne Sundberg, "Reorganization Efforts and the Threat of Ethnic War in Congo" (unpublished paper, Department of Social Anthropology, University of Lund, 1996), p. 11; Engineer, *Bombay-Bhiwandi Riots*, p. 13.

81. Failure to take care can produce battles between opposing crowds, as it did in Malegaon, Maharashtra (1983), a town with a two-thirds Muslim majority, rather than producing the typical, one-sided riot — which is why such care is so often taken. Asghar Ali Engineer, "From Nationalism to Communalism: Transformation of Malegaon," *Economic and Political Weekly*, July 16, 1983, pp. 1259–61.

control of the area. We have seen the furious violence this juxtaposition can generate in Chapter 5.

When such violence occurs, the rioters are undeterred by their relatively small numbers. Osh and Pišpek are both Kyrghyz-minority cities, but in 1990 Kyrghyz attacks took place there nonetheless.[82] Luluabourg (1959) was a town where the Lulua, for whom it was named, were outnumbered more than two to one by their Luba targets.[83] Ivory Coast riots have typically been initiated by groups (often Bété) indigenous to a region but in towns controlled by immigrants.[84] Many towns in the Assam Valley fit the same description,[85] but Assamese attacked Bengalis there anyway. Neighboring Tripura is a state that had a 70 percent "tribal" majority at Indian independence, reduced to 48 percent by 1951 as a result of refugee flows from East Bengal, and by the 1971 census to only 29 percent tribals.[86] Despite declining proportions, tribals attacked Bengalis there in 1980. Tuvinians are a minority in their capital, Kyzyl, but Russians were attacked there, rather than outside the city, where Tuvinians are in the vast majority.[87] So prominent was the Indian majority in Rangoon in the 1930s that Hindustani had become the lingua franca.[88] Still, Burmans attacked Indians there in 1930 and 1938. Singapore (1964) was the location of a riot by Malays against Chinese, who at the time comprised more than three-quarters of the city's population, compared to about one-seventh for Malays.[89] Every Malaysian riot in the postwar period has begun in a location where Malays were greatly outnumbered and felt displaced by Chinese — Penang (1957 and 1967), Pangkor (1959), and Kuala Lumpur (1969) — and none has taken place

82. Bozdağ, "Crisis and Democracy in Kirgizia," pp. 277–86.

83. Jules Chomé, *Le Drame de Luluabourg*, 3d rev. ed. (Brussels: Editions de Remarques Congolaises, 1960), p. 16; Henri Nicolai, "Conflits entre groupes africains et décolonisation au Kasai," *Revue de l'Université de Bruxelles*, XIIe Année (1960): 131–44, at p. 135.

84. Aristide Zolberg, *One-Party Government in the Ivory Coast*, rev. ed. (Princeton: Princeton University Press, 1969), pp. 45–46.

85. See Myron Weiner, *Sons of the Soil: Migration and Ethnic Conflict in India* (Princeton: Princeton University Press, 1978), pp. 94–95. See also R.C. Muirhead Thomson, *Assam Valley: Beliefs and Customs of the Assamese Hindus* (London: Luzac, 1948), p. 91.

86. *Far Eastern Economic Review*, June 20, 1980, p. 34.

87. Toomas Alatalu, "Tuva — a State Reawakens," *Soviet Studies* 44, no. 5 (1992): 881–95. As I have noted previously, however, the violence in Tuva never quite became massive enough to be a riot; it consisted of killings of individual or small groups of Russians, over an extended period, largely because of law enforcement.

88. Guy Hunter, *South-East Asia: Race, Culture, and Nation* (London: Oxford University Press, 1966), pp. 19, 120.

89. Ibid., p. 15.

on the east coast of Malaysia, where Malays vastly outnumber Chinese. The sentiments of the attackers in all of these areas were well captured by a member of a crowd in Kuala Lumpur (1969), who would not be dissuaded from violence. "We cannot bear this any more," he shouted.[90]

Desperation is a theme that runs through a great deal of ethnic violence.[91] A good many groups are convinced that they are or soon will be swamped, dominated, and dispossessed by their neighbors, perhaps even rendered extinct.[92] The more numerous the neighbors, the more immediate the danger. The conduciveness of these apprehensions to violence ought to be obvious, and such a state of mind helps explain why rioters might be willing to risk very serious danger to themselves by attacking in cities where they are badly outnumbered.

Even under these circumstances, however, desperation does not give way to imprudence. We have already observed that Malays, outnumbered in overwhelmingly Chinese areas of Kuala Lumpur, retreated to more advantageous locations in which to conduct attacks. In Luluabourg (1959), Lulua attacked Luba in peripheral areas, where the targets were much more vulnerable.[93] The impulse to choose specific sites with an eye to population composition does not desert even desperate rioters in desperate cities.

The proof of the proposition lies in the balance of death. In every case of desperation demography, the target group suffered not merely a preponderance of casualties but the overwhelming brunt of them. For example, despite their strong majority in the state, perhaps 2,000 Bengalis were killed in Tripura in early June 1980, and when Bengalis organized a bit of retaliation at the end of the month, it was met with more powerful counterattacks on Bengalis.[94] In no case was the target group able to turn the tables, regardless of the population balance.[95]

Furthermore, by every other indicator of the immediate success or

90. Government of Malaysia, National Operations Council, *The May 13 Tragedy* (Kuala Lumpur: n.p., 1969), p. 51.

91. For a nice explication of this theme, characterized as "persecution anxiety," based on group rhetoric, see Sudhir Kakar, *The Colors of Violence: Cultural Identities, Religion, and Conflict* (Chicago: University of Chicago Press, 1996), pp. 162–69. For a sample, see Bhawani Singh, *Politics of Alienation in Assam* (Delhi: Ajunta, 1984), pp. 76–78. Tishkov, "Don't Kill Me, I Am Kyrghyz," pp. 26–28, describes a condition he calls "social paranoia," consisting of suspicion, anxiety, fear, hatred, and infringed self-esteem.

92. "If we Malays do not oppose the PAP Government [of Lee Kuan Yew] from now, within 20 years there will be no more Malays in Malaysia . . . ." Pre-riot leaflet, quoted in Lau, *A Moment of Anguish*, p. 162.

93. Chomé, *Le Drame de Luluabourg*, p. 5.

94. *Keesing's Contemporary Archives*, November 21, 1980, p. 30576.

95. But see Singapore (1964), discussed in note 46, above.

failure of the attacks, the perpetrators came out ahead. Some 50,000 Luba had left Luluabourg within two months of the Lulua attacks, and the number grew inordinately in succeeding months.[96] Some 20,000 Telugus fled Burma soon after the 1930 riot; many more Indians left after the 1938 riot.[97] The war that came to Burma soon after brought further killings "and a huge exodus of Indians from Burma — it is thought that about 500,000 left,"[98] though no doubt many would have stayed where they were had the Japanese done the same. Tiv, the largest group in Wukari in Taraba state, Nigeria, were attacked in 1990 by Jukun, who, feeling "they had been pushed to the wall,"[99] succeeded in displacing so many Tiv that, after the attacks, Tiv were unrepresented on the traditional council. Russians left Tuva steadily through 1990, and tens of thousands of Uzbeks departed Kyrghyzstan after the violence of the same year. Perhaps 200,000 Bengalis lost their homes in Tripura (1980). There was no comparison in the balance of suffering.

It is not difficult to identify adverse effects of the riots for the initiator group after the event. Rioting is not always profitable in the long term, indeed may be very unprofitable.[100] But so far as the rioters' limited objectives are concerned — to kill without being killed — the violence succeeds even in cities where it might have been thought dangerous. This appears to be due, largely, to specific site selection within those cities, as well as to the usual tactical advantages favoring aggressors over unarmed civilians.

To summarize, then, areas of attack within cities can be scaled from those most dangerous to rioters to those least dangerous, as follows:

1. Attack targets in the targets' own, relatively homogeneous areas;

2. Attack targets in heterogeneous areas or along the borderline between areas occupied by the target group and the attacker group;

3. Attack targets in mixed areas, in which the targets are in a minority;

4. Attack targets in the attackers' own, relatively homogeneous areas.

96. Thomas Turner, "Congo-Kinshasa," in Victor A. Olorunsola, ed., *The Politics of Cultural Sub-Nationalism in Africa* (New York: Anchor Books, 1972), p. 223.

97. E.L.F. Andrew, *Indian Labour Rangoon* (Calcutta: Oxford University Press, 1933), p. 286; Virginia Thompson and Richard Adloff, *Minority Problems in Southeast Asia* (Stanford: Stanford University Press, 1955), pp. 69–75.

98. Hunter, *South-East Asia*, p. 19.

99. Ter-Rumun Avav and Mson Myegba, *The Dream to Conquer: Story of Jukun-Tiv Conflict* (Makurdi, Nigeria: Onaivi, 1992), p. 12.

100. For an assessment of riot effects, see Chapter 11, below.

Attackers, as I have shown, generally avoid both extremes, in the first case because the targets' own areas are too dangerous, and in the fourth despite the fact that attacks in the attackers' own homogeneous areas are safe.[101] Rather, they attack in areas 2 and 3, borderline or heterogeneous areas of various kinds, making certain they will not be badly outnumbered. Even when they attack in target-majority cities and towns, they choose sites that do not subject them to undue risk. The lack of peril for rioters helps explain why riots are so common and also suggests why a town that has had one such riot may then have another, while so many towns have not had any riot at all: success breeds success, while uncertainty breeds caution.

THE DIFFUSION OF VIOLENCE

Some riots spread from one town to another or to outlying areas, while other riots do not spread at all. Some spread very quickly, some more slowly. When riots spread, the violence sometimes moves smoothly to contiguous areas, whereas spreading violence in others is characterized by radical noncontiguity. The diffusion of violence therefore embraces three questions: whether, how fast, and where—and, incidentally, how intensely. I shall have something to say about all of these questions, although what I say about the speed at which violence diffuses is limited and, at that, often indirect.

WAVES AND CLUSTERS: CONTAGION AND IMITATION

In some cases, it is fair to say that a wave of riots has occurred, so rapid and seamless is the movement of violence from one place to another. Consider the following examples:

1. In Rwanda (1959), a rumor of an attack on a Hutu subchief precipitated a Hutu attack on an aggressive Tutsi subchief and some others. The violence spread instantly all over the country, "triggered off by the force of example,"[102] in René Lemarchand's reveal-

---

101. See M.N. Buch, "Urban Growth Accentuates Communal Tensions," in Kumar, *Towards Understanding Communalism*, p. 221, noting pointedly that ethnic rioters in Moradabad did not carry the violence to villages a short distance away, although Muslim victims were readily available there. Cf. Ratna Naidu, *Old Cities, New Predicaments: A Study of Hyderabad* (New Delhi: Sage, 1990), pp. 140–41.

102. Lemarchand, *Rwanda and Burundi*, p. 163.

ing phrase. The violence was, as he describes it, "unstructured, amorphous . . . ."[103] Another wave of violence occurred with similar speed in Rwanda (1963).[104]

2. India and Pakistan (1946–47) also had such waves around the time of partition, although there was, at the same time, a pattern of alternating and reciprocal violence, in which killings on one side of the border then stimulated killings on the other.

3. India has had at least three waves since then. In 1980, violence in Moradabad spread rapidly to other Uttar Pradesh cities: Sambhal, Meerut, Bareilly, Rampur, Pilibhit, Aligarh, Agra, Allahabad, and Lucknow. Within a fortnight, violence had spread to five north Indian states. A decade later (1990), when Hindu crowds were turned away from the Babri mosque at Ayodhya, and then much more severely after crowds destroyed the mosque (1992), anti-Muslim riots spread promptly all over the north of India.

4. In Indonesia (1963), anti-Chinese violence swept several major urban areas of West Java, embracing no fewer than nine cities and towns in close succession.[105] The riots seemed to proceed from the same originating conditions and to be conducted in the same spirit. Each piece of the violence appeared as another act in a single play, raising again the question that was raised in Chapter 2, about where one riot ends and another begins. In the wake of the 1965 coup, another wave washed over Java, this one targeting both Communists and Chinese, the latter identified as supporters of both Communism and China. Yet a third wave struck Indonesia in the last two months of 1980. Unlike the 1965 violence in Java, this was regionally confined; unlike the 1963 violence, it spread quickly from one city to another in Central and East Java, rather than West Java. As in West Java (1963), the precipitants in most individual towns were not serious, and the casualties in each were not numerous.[106] Again, there is the sense that the incidents formed small parts of a single event. And, if this is so, the distinctive characteristics of a given place may be submerged in the overall event or event sequence.

103. Ibid., p. 164.

104. Ibid., pp. 223–27.

105. Stephen A. Douglas, *Political Socialization and Student Activism in Indonesia* (Urbana: University of Illinois Press, 1970), pp. 167–68.

106. See *Far Eastern Economic Review*, December 5, 1980, pp. 10–12; *Le Devoir* (Montreal), December 10, 1980, p. 1.

Certain ethnic issues are of such high saliency across a whole territory that a single precipitating event at one place can produce violent reactions at many locations almost simultaneously. The Ayodhya incidents of both 1990 and 1992 are of this character, but most precipitants are not. When, however, such conditions do obtain, what we have really is something like a single riot in many locations, rather than a case of spreading violence. The 1980 Javanese violence, on the other hand, was certainly not based on any such single major precipitant — or even on any major precipitant at any of the individual locations — and it is better described in terms of imitative behavior from one location to another. In fact, news of the initial violence apparently spread via the bus route from Surakarta to Semarang, producing violence at the latter.[107]

These are perhaps two species of contagion: imitation, on the one hand; common responses to a single precipitant, on the other. Contagion is possible where hostility is strong and where motifs of intergroup relations are relatively homogeneous across the relevant territory, so that the initial precipitant readily evokes imitative patterns. Rwanda (1959 and 1963), India-Pakistan (1946–47), India (1980), and Indonesia (1963 and 1980) fit this description. Contagious violence can be said to be present when behavior spreads "as the result of a prototype or model" that facilitates the repetition of the behavior.[108] Contagion does not require a separate set of precipitants at the subsequent locations.[109] As indicated, India (1990 and 1992) also did not require a separate set of precipitants — the Ayodhya events were sufficient — but the riots in various locations were, as I have argued, not so much imitations of events at the earlier locations as they were common responses to the single precipitant.

Imitation or, at the very least, learning takes place when violence at one place is followed swiftly by violence at another, and so the mechanisms underlying contagion must be at work in such sequences. In this sense, the distinctions between India (1990 and 1992) and the riot waves just discussed cannot be regarded as absolute; neither, for that matter, can the distinction between contagion and other forms of diffusion.

Nevertheless, there is a need for great caution in utilizing contagion as the universal solvent for puzzles about the spread of violence. *Contagion* is a term the very etymology of which suggests the absence of a need for

107. *Far Eastern Economic Review*, December 5, 1980, at p. 10.

108. Manus Midlarsky, "Analyzing Diffusion and Contagion Effects: The Urban Disorders of the 1960s," *American Political Science Review* 72, no. 3 (September 1978): 996–1008, at p. 1006.

109. Ibid., pp. 1002–5.

explanation. One catches violence as one catches a virus; in some countries, indeed, it is common to speak of the ethnic or communal "virus."[110] Such locutions are not helpful, because they assume the conclusion. Still, a carefully limited place for contagion seems warranted when violence spreads quickly from place to place without the usual antecedents, as in the Javanese and Rwandan riots, and therefore an inference of imitation is inescapable.[111]

To be sure, episodes of violence often cluster in time. Clustering suggests that elements of contagion may be present. Rioters, as I have said, are undoubtedly inspired by similar deeds elsewhere. But contagion is rarely the whole explanation, and it certainly cannot explain the failure of violence to spread to "immune" locations. A general change toward conditions conducive to violence may be at work when violence spreads. This change may affect many locations. Yet a contagion explanation would miss it. For example, the Hindu-Muslim riots in India in the years immediately following the 1965 India-Pakistan War resulted from accentuated hostility to Muslims that the war produced, but the riots also, of course, followed knowingly upon each other.[112]

Increases in hostility and imitation of aggression elsewhere are alternative explanations for violent events, but they are not mutually exclusive and probably were not so in India at this time. Anti-Bengali rioters in Tripura (1980) no doubt took a leaf out of the book of anti-Bengali aggressors in neighboring Assam, Manipur, and Mizoram.[113] Violence does not occur in isolation; it derives intellectual impetus and succor from events regarded as comparable elsewhere. Actors judge the plausibility of their conduct by the fact that others have carried out similar plans.[114] Sheer prudence requires as much, and rioters are, in such respects, prudent, as their site selection shows. The possibility of diffusion is a major reason for concern about the first acts of violence. But the Tripura rioters also had their own passionately held reasons for the violence they committed.

110. See, e.g., Nissim Ezekiel, "The Communal Virus," *Monthly Commentary on Indian Economic Conditions* 22, no. 2 (September 1980): 9–10.

111. Neil J. Smelser, *Theory of Collective Behavior* (New York: Free Press, 1962), p. 251; Leonard Berkowitz, "Studies in the Contagion of Violence," in Herbert Hirsch and David C. Perry, eds., *Violence as Politics* (New York: Harper & Row, 1969), pp. 41–45.

112. Feldman, "The Communal Problem in the Indo-Pakistan Subcontinent," pp. 145–63.

113. See *Far Eastern Economic Review*, June 20, 1980, p. 34.

114. Cf. Stuart Hill and Donald Rothchild, "The Contagion of Political Conflict in Africa and the World," *Journal of Conflict Resolution* 30, no. 4 (December 1986): 716–35.

Much experimental evidence shows that observation of an aggressive model increases the frequency and magnitude of aggression.[115] Interestingly enough, far more aggression is produced by the conjunction of anger and the observation of an aggressive model than the mere addition of the two would predict.[116] Anger and contagion are a powerful combination. One view, based on conditioning, is that aggressive stimuli cue behavior associated with them, thereby producing more aggression in aggression-prone people than would be produced without those stimuli.[117] Alternatively, contagion may operate by the reduction of inhibition that accompanies observation of the seemingly successful aggression elsewhere.[118] Inhibition, of course, can be based on fear or on belief in the illegitimacy of violence, among other things. As I shall argue, one powerful determinant of diffusion is justification. This may suggest that a function of aggressive models is to provide justification for later aggressors.

Contagion rarely explains entire waves of violence, because it adds to, rather than substitutes for, aggressive impulses. The mildness of the violence in Indonesia (1980) may be accounted for by a shortfall of special reasons for anti-Chinese aggression at that time.[119] Contagion does, however, help explain why violence can spread from one place to another when precipitants at the subsequent location are far less significant than they were at the first. Contagion, in the sense of imitation of an aggressive model, functions as something like a precipitant-substitute where hostility is present.

PATTERNS OF DIFFUSION

As I have suggested, contagion does not explain the extent to which violence spreads. Contagion does likely account for the location of the first spread of violence, which is often to contiguous areas or to the nearest urban areas. But not all of the early diffusion of violence occurs contiguously: there are many episodes of noncontiguous spread.[120] Such patterns are difficult to account for in full, but some of the main determinants are identifiable.

115. Ladd Wheeler and Anthony R. Caggiula, "The Contagion of Aggression," *Journal of Experimental Social Psychology* 2, no. 1 (January 1966): 1–10.

116. Ibid., p. 8.

117. Berkowitz, "Studies in the Contagion of Violence," pp. 45–46.

118. Wheeler and Caggiula, "The Contagion of Aggression," p. 9.

119. See Chapter 12, below, pp. 489, 490, below.

120. See Margaret J. Abudu Stark et al., "Some Empirical Patterns in a Riot Process," *American Sociological Review* 39, no. 6 (December 1974): 865–76, at pp. 873–74.

If there is a bit of organization, the chance for smooth spread to mainly contiguous areas (or at least the main cities) is enhanced. This was the case in Punjab (1947), when attacks began in Lahore and spread to other major cities,[121] and it was also the pattern in Kyrghyzstan (1990), when the riot spread within a day from Osh to the republic's second city, Uzgen.[122] The anti-Sikh violence (1984) was mainly a Delhi event. To the extent it spread, diffusion occurred within the same region, mainly in Uttar Pradesh cities such as Kanpur,[123] although there are large Sikh populations elsewhere, most notably Calcutta. The anti-Ahmadi riots in Pakistan (1953) were more strongly organized, and they spread across Punjab quite smoothly.[124] When this happens, however, the first location often has higher-intensity violence and violence of longer duration than later locations do,[125] because of the more significant precipitants and other propitious conditions out of which the riot began. A perfect example is the violence against Meskhetian Turks in Uzbekistan (1989), which began in Fergana and spread first to Kokand before moving on to nearly all the urban centers of the republic. Fergana and Kokand proved the most difficult areas to stabilize; the Fergana rioting lasted a full week.[126] Imitation without anger produces weak violence.

Contiguity prevails, even if there are alternative, plausible possibilities for diffusion. The 1921 riots in Palestine spread from Jaffa up and down the coastal plain but not inland to Jerusalem, whereas those in 1929 spread from Jerusalem south to Hebron and north to Sefad but not to the coast.[127] These were surely two completely different communications networks — each the sort that dictates diffusion to nearby areas. If word-of-mouth is the method, violence will be limited to proximate areas.[128]

When word-of-mouth is the method, even if two or more noncontigu-

121. Penderel Moon, *Divide and Quit* (Berkeley and Los Angeles: University of California Press, 1962), p. 66.

122. Tishkov, "Don't Kill Me, I Am Kyrghyz," pp. 1–6.

123. Harsh Sethi, "The Citizen's Response: A Glimmer of Possibilities?" in Smitu Kothari and Harsh Sethi, eds., *Voices from a Scarred City: The Delhi Carnage in Perspective* (Delhi: Lokayan, 1985), pp. 59–73, at pp. 69–70.

124. Albeit especially where the Ahrar were strong. See generally Government of Punjab, *Report of the Court of Inquiry Constituted under Punjab Act II of 1954 to Enquire into the Punjab Disturbances of 1953*, pp. 151–212.

125. A point also made by Abudu Stark et al., "Some Empirical Patterns in a Riot Process," p. 874.

126. *Izvestiya*, June 9, 1989, p. 12, in FBIS-SOV-89-111, June 12, 1989, p. 34; *Tass*, June 12, 1989, in ibid., p. 37.

127. Wasserstein, "Patterns of Communal Conflict in Palestine," p. 616.

128. As the Malegaon, Maharashtra (1983), riot spread by word-of-mouth to the neighboring towns of Dabhori and Satna. Engineer, "From Nationalism to Communalism," p. 1260.

ous locations are involved at an early stage — usually because of separate precipitants — diffusion contiguous to those areas is the most likely pattern. Sri Lanka's three most serious riots all exemplify the pattern. In 1958 and 1977, Colombo and the colonization areas of the North Central Province were affected initially, and the first wave of diffusion occurred in those very areas.[129] The 1983 violence began in Colombo, spread first to other areas of the city, to the southern suburbs, and then to Kalutara, further south. At almost the same time, violence began in Kandy, which spread to nearby Gampola and other upcountry areas. As the days wore on, the violence radiated out from those two core areas, with occasional outliers.[130] Absent intervening variables, contiguity is the rule in diffusion.

Noncontiguous spread appears to be accounted for by either (1) what is essentially a new precipitant arising out of the earlier violence but occurring in the new location, or (2) authoritative ratification of the violence, or (3) mass media methods of communication of the first violent events. In the first case, the violence may be contained; in the latter two, it is likely to spread very widely. Moreover, the susceptibility of a new location to spreading violence is conditioned by the previous experience of similar violence, for some locations are habitual sites.

Evidence of prior aggression or rumors of prior aggression by the target group are common precipitants of noncontiguously spreading violence, just as they are of the initial violence. Corpses are a major stimulus to the spread of violence.[131] The Sri Lankan riot of 1983 began at the Colombo cemetery where soldiers killed by Tamil separatists were to be buried,[132] but it spread — noncontiguously, as I have mentioned — to Kandy after the cremation of three of the soldiers there. The 1977 violence in Sri Lanka spread wherever Sinhalese, evacuated from the north, told tales of their alleged abuse by Tamils.[133] The transportation of the body of a dead rioter in Assam (1960) spread the violence all along the 230-mile path of its procession,[134] and in Penang (1967) the return of the

129. Vittachi, Emergency '58, pp. 23–24, 63–68, 96; interview, Colombo, April 8, 1980.

130. T.D.S.A. Dissanyaka, The Agony of Sri Lanka: An In-Depth Account of the Racial Riots of 1983 (Colombo: Swastika Press, 1983), pp. 74–79, 84, 92–93.

131. See, e.g., Indian Statutory Commission, Memoranda Submitted by the Government of India and the India Office to the Indian Statutory Commission, Vol. IV, pt. 1, p. 106.

132. Bastian, "The Political Economy of Ethnic Violence in Sri Lanka," p. 300.

133. Interview, Colombo, April 7, 1980. Cf. Report of the Presidential Commission of Inquiry into the Incidents Which Took Place between 13th August and 15th September 1977, p. 116.

134. K.C. Chakravarti, "Bongal Kheda Again," Economic Weekly, July 30, 1960, pp. 1193–95, at p. 1194; Deendayal Upadhyaya, "Report of Assam Situation," placed before

bodies of two innocent bystanders to their homes on the mainland threatened to spread the riot there. By then, however, the armed forces were deployed.[135]

Obviously, the sight of corpses seen as victims is inciting and gives rise to thoughts of revenge. Prospective rioters in the new location seem to work on the basis of a scorecard mentality: they wish to even the score, if it is uneven. This might lead to the conclusion that violence can spread only if the identity of attackers and targets is reversed at the new location, but this assumes that the news from the initial location about who has killed whom is accurate. The news, however, is often false. Burma (1938) spread, as we have seen,[136] far upcountry from Rangoon, on the basis of reports that seemed to suggest that Burmans were the victims of colonial police rather than that Burmans were actually the killers of Indians. The killings in northern Nigeria (1966) spread on the basis of a false report, carried by Radio Cotonou in Benin and relayed by stations in Kaduna, that northerners had been killed in the Eastern Region.[137] In Sri Lanka (1977), the stories of mistreatment brought by students from Jaffna were also gravely exaggerated, and the rioter killed in Assam (1960) was not killed by a Bengali crowd but by the police. Noncontiguous spread does not rule out the same attackers and targets.

Despite this, however, the desire to square accounts furnishes a special impetus for the spread of violence. Rumors that the majority of the dead thus far at Ranchi (1967) were Hindu led Hindus to attack Muslims, in an effort to redress the balance.[138] Conversely, an accurate report of the balance of casualties can impede the spread of violence. When the Kuala Lumpur riot (1969) was in progress, Malays in adjacent states south of Selangor were making preparations to attack Chinese but were mollified when they learned that few Malays but many Chinese had been killed in Kuala Lumpur.[139]

Since revenge is a motive and since prospective rioters count casualties, reversal of attacker and target roles can occur. Within individual

---

the Bharatiya Karya Samiti of the Jan Sangh party, August 25, 1960, Hyderabad, p. 4 (mimeo.). This report predictably emphasizes the malevolent role of Muslims but is otherwise a reasonable account.

135. Interview, Bukit Mertajam, January 11, 1968; interview, George Town, January 25, 1968.

136. See Chapter 6, p. 200, above.

137. *West Africa*, October 8, 1966, p. 1140.

138. Government of India, *Report of the Commission of Inquiry on Communal Disturbances in Ranchi-Hatia*, p. 79.

139. I owe this account to a Malay researcher who was traveling in these areas at the time and took soundings along the way.

countries, however, it occurs only very rarely, because other conditions are not present.[140] If, after all, the police are biased in favor of the initial attackers, then they are unlikely later to be biased in favor of the initial target group, if it should be inclined to turn the tables and attack. Similarly, if political authorities have given a green light to the initial attackers, the target group is unlikely to sense a green light for *it* to attack at a different location. Hence the consistency in the ethnic identity of casualties in most episodes of violence, even after the targets in other locations have had plenty of time to formulate a response. The response is precluded by unfavorable conditions.

There is, however, a large category of exceptions: riots that, sooner or later, cross international boundaries or, less often, state boundaries in a federal system.[141] Here the spread of violence coincides with a reversal of roles.

The classic case is the partition violence in India-Pakistan (1946–47). The violence spread back and forth, between Calcutta and Dacca, and then to Bihar, even before partition. Before and after partition, a new front for reciprocal riots was opened in Punjab, as Muslim refugees and corpses arrived in Pakistan and Hindu refugees and corpses arrived in India, each wave with its evidence of atrocities to be avenged.[142] This pattern continued in East and West Bengal long after 1947. In 1950, the harassment of Hindu evacuees on the Pakistani side generated violent incidents in Calcutta, then larger reprisals in Dacca, which were answered in Calcutta and as far away as Uttar Pradesh.[143] In 1964, refugees carried reports of outrages from Khulna and Jessore in East Bengal to Nadia and Calcutta in West Bengal, then back to the east

140. If it does occur, the retaliatory riot is likely to be on a small scale and to conclude quickly. This describes the retaliatory riot in Suchetpur, Uttar Pradesh (1967). In Jainpur, a completely local dispute over a cemetery had produced a Muslim attack, inflicting three deaths, on a Hindu funeral party. In neighboring Suchetpur, Hindus then killed eleven Muslims. With the exception of Hindu looting in villages surrounding Suchetpur (interestingly, the rural violence was completely nonlethal), the matter was then at an end. Even this degree of reciprocal violence in the same general area is rather unusual. See *Report of the Commission of Inquiry on Communal Disturbances: Jainpur and Suchetpur (District Gorakhpur-U.P.) (September 24–25, 1967)*, Vol. 2 (New Delhi: Government of India, 1969).

141. See, e.g., *Far Eastern Economic Review*, December 24, 1973, p. 21, on reciprocal riots in Maharashtra and Karnataka; *Economist*, July 31, 1999, p. 36, on reciprocal riots in Sagamu and Kano, Nigeria. And, most notably, see the serious violence of February 2000 in the southeastern Nigerian city of Aba, in retaliation for the violence of a week earlier in the northern city of Kaduna. Killings began in Aba after corpses arrived from Kaduna. *New York Times*, March 26, 2000, p. A22.

142. See, e.g., Moon, *Divide and Quit*, pp. 58, 66, 116, 138.

143. Richard D. Lambert, "Religion, Economics, and Violence in Bengal," *Middle East Journal* 4, no. 3 (July 1950): 307–28, at pp. 321–23.

again, and finally to West Bengal and Bihar, before a nearly three-month period of killing ended.[144] Only the departure of millions of Hindus from East Bengal at the time of the independence of Bangladesh in 1971 ended these sequences,[145] just as the extremely painful homogenization of west and east Punjab had in 1947.

The dissolution of the Soviet Union made possible the same sort of reciprocal violence. Sumgait (1988) and Baku (1990) were both direct products of the arrival of Azeri refugees from Armenia bearing tales of killings there.[146] Kyrghyzstan (1990) spread briefly into adjacent districts of Uzbekistan, where Uzbeks took revenge, provoking additional attacks on them in Kyrghyzstan and threatening interrepublic warfare.[147]

Africa has had much reciprocal ethnic violence across borders. After attacks on Gabonese in the Congo Republic (1962), followed by attacks on Congolese in Gabon, Congolese were expelled from Gabon. Their arrival in the Congo Republic produced new violence against Gabonese.[148] In the Ivory Coast (1985), a riot against Ghanaians constituted a reprisal for a riot against Ivorians in Ghana.[149] In 1989, riots in Senegal began with violence against Mauritanian Moors. When news of the violence reached Mauritania, there were riots against Senegalese. When the victims arrived in Senegal, Mauritanians were attacked again.[150] Eventually, there was an exchange of nationals by the two countries, so again the violence ended with homogenization.

If we look at noncontiguous spread in light of this evidence, it is, as I said, produced by what is essentially a new precipitant, but of a special sort. The precipitant is the report of the earlier violence, especially if made vivid by the arrival of victims, living or dead. Noncontiguous violence is very likely to be more tempting for members of the target group, but they are inhibited from initiating it unless they are outside the boundaries of the state in which the violence that provokes them is located. Outside those boundaries, they are much less inhibited. One of the disruptive consequences of partition and state proliferation is the enhanced

144. Ghosh, *Communal Riots in India*, pp. 13–37, 210–12; Feldman, "The Communal Problem in the Indo-Pakistan Subcontinent," p. 148.

145. Even so, there was a near miss in 1979. See *Far Eastern Economic Review*, July 20, 1979, p. 32.

146. See, e.g., *New York Times*, August 31, 1988, pp. A1, A8.

147. Bozdağ, "Crisis and Democracy in Kirgizia."

148. René Gauze, *The Politics of Congo-Brazzaville*, trans. Virginia Thompson and Richard Adloff (Stanford: Hoover Institution Press, 1973), p. 112.

149. *West Africa*, September 16, 1985, p. 1932; September 30, 1985, p. 2064.

150. *Africa Events*, June 1989, p. 22; *Africa News*, May 15, 1989, p. 15.

possibility for reciprocal violence, with attendant danger of escalation into international warfare.[151]

Authoritative ratification that occurs in the midst of the violence also produces noncontiguous spread. Richard D. Lambert points out that rural Hindu-Muslim violence up to 1950 was usually contained. On those occasions when a rural riot became a major episode, it typically took the form of a "rural pogrom" against the local minority, and he identifies two conditions that produce such episodes. First, they are generally reciprocal riots, aimed at revenge for what was said to have happened elsewhere.[152] Second, in "rural pogroms evidence had been found for the belief on the part of the majority community that its violence was supported, or at least condoned, by the government."[153] This was particularly true in 1946–47, when the presumption gained currency, in both India and Pakistan, that the majority could attack the minority with impunity. The growth of such ideas greatly facilitates noncontiguous diffusion of violence.

There is a fine illustration of this in Sri Lanka (1977). As mentioned, the early violence was confined to Colombo, Kandy, and a few other towns. Then, however, Prime Minister Jayewardene gave his ill-starred and frequently rebroadcast radio address, in which, far from condemning the rioting outright, he laid responsibility at the door of the Tamils. The violence, which had spread very little during the previous day, promptly spread over most of the country and intensified in areas where it had already begun.[154] In the diffusion of violence, as in its inception, apparent condonation or authoritative social support, now in the form of ratification, is a force to be reckoned with.

The means of communication affect the pattern of diffusion. As the Jayewardene broadcast spread the riot broadly, so newspaper reports can achieve the same result. From Ahmedabad (1969), the violence spread quickly through Gujarat, first north and south, and then much further afield to the southwest. Proximate locations mainly received their information face to face or along rail lines, whereas more distant loca-

151. An argument I have made in Donald L. Horowitz, "Self-Determination: Politics, Philosophy, and Law," *NOMOS* 39 (1997): 421–63, at p. 436.

152. Lambert, "Hindu-Muslim Riots," p. 219.

153. Ibid.

154. Interview, Colombo, April 8, 1980. In 1958, then prime minister S.W.R.D. Bandaranaike had made a speech in which he mentioned the killing of D.A. Seneviratne, presumably — but, as it turned out, falsely — by Tamils as the cause of the riot. The immediate result was an escalation of the violence but not its diffusion through substantially the whole country. Vittachi, *Emergency '58*, pp. 44–51.

tions relied on newspaper reports.[155] Affected at most for only two or three days, none of the outlying areas approached the magnitude or duration of the violence in Ahmedabad itself. There the violence reached its peak within two days, with more than 400 killed within 18 hours, and trailed off slowly over the next ten days. Bhiwandi (1970) is a clearer case for diffusion to towns as far away as Jalgaon, 200 miles distant; there and in Mahad, 100 miles south of Bhiwandi, radio and newspapers were the sources.[156] The nearer to the starting point at Bhiwandi, however, the greater were the casualties,[157] a general pattern we have already noticed specifically in Uzbekistan (1989). With the same aggressors and targets, intensity wanes with distance.

The official report rendered for Burma (1938) is rich in data on location and intensity.[158] The violence spread principally by means of inflammatory newspaper reports, so it is not surprising that diffusion was not wholly contiguous. By the third day, there was violence in Mandalay, far to the north, as there was in areas much closer to Rangoon. But it took nine days for the last area to be affected by violence; and, despite the relatively rapid spread to Mandalay and other noncontiguous locations, the later-affected areas were, on the whole, more distant from Rangoon than the earlier locations were. Despite the impact of the mass media, which facilitate noncontiguous spread, there are still elements of contiguity evident. Contiguity was associated with the intensity of the violence. Without doubt, the violence was predicated on underlying antipathies, as I have argued in Chapter 6, but those were apparently more significant at and near the point of first impact. Imitation, on the whole, produces less passionate violence.

Rangoon, where the violence began, was the scene of more than half the total number of deaths. Outside Rangoon, there were five or more deaths in only four towns. Of these Pegu (five deaths) is 50 miles from Rangoon, Letpadan (seventeen deaths) is 85 miles, and Nyaungwaing (nine deaths) is about 60 miles; only Yenangyaung (six deaths) is as much as 270 miles away, in the context of violence that spread more than 400

155. Commission of Inquiry into the Communal Disturbances at Ahmedabad and at Various Places in the State of Gujarat on and after 18th September 1969, *Report* (Gandhinagar, Gujarat, India: Government Central Press, 1970), pp. 233–307.

156. D.P. Madon, *Report of the Commission of Inquiry into the Communal Disturbances at Bhiwandi, Jalgaon, and Mahad in May 1970* (Bombay: Government Central Press, 1975), Vol. 4, p. 373; Vol. 5, p. 246.

157. Hence Bhiwandi, Khoni, and Thana suffered many more deaths than did Jalgaon and Mahad, where the riots were also more short-lived.

158. Government of Burma, *Final Report of the Riot Inquiry Committee* (Rangoon: Superintendent of Government Printing and Stationery, 1939), pp. 45–222, Appendix X.

miles from Rangoon. Mandalay, the second largest city, 375 miles from Rangoon, had only four deaths among its target-group population. (Of course, number of deaths is only a crude indicator of intensity and is subject to intervening variables, such as police effectiveness, which was unusually low at Letpadan.[159]) Elsewhere, in individual locations, the deaths were scattered, mainly in the ones and twos, but they tended to be somewhat more concentrated the closer they were to Rangoon; and this tendency is stronger at the higher level of the administrative division, where, regardless of the day on which the violence arrived, it was (with few exceptions) more intense, as measured by deaths inflicted, the closer the affected division was to Rangoon.[160] Consequently, even where diffusion was accomplished by mass communication and was not dependent on face-to-face accounts, proximity still counted for a great deal in the casualty count.

RECIDIVIST LOCATIONS

I said earlier that there are some habitual sites of violence within countries, and I noted that research on India showed that a minority of towns had produced the majority of deaths. Of 65 Uttar Pradesh urban areas for which riot data are available, 35 had no riots between 1950 and 1990, 13 had only one, seven had two, and ten more had more than two. The six cities with the greatest incidence of riots accounted for 63 percent of the 115 riots in those 40 years, and the top two alone accounted for more than one-third of the 115.[161] From this, it is clear that (1) non-riot locations are abundant and need serious consideration, (2) there is some modest tendency for riot locations to repeat, and (3) there is a class of locations severely affected by recurrent episodes.[162]

We have also seen how violence strikes the same regions more than

159. Ibid., p. 195.

160. So Pegu, surrounding Rangoon, was second in target-group deaths, with 58 to Rangoon's 74, and Irrawaddy and Magwe outdid more distant Sagaing and Tenasserim.

161. Calculated from Wilkinson, "What Large Datasets Can Tell Us about the General Explanations for Communal Riots," pp. 20–22.

162. For the view that violence (often ethnic riots) increases the likelihood of further episodes, see Stanley Tambiah, "Reflections on Communal Violence in South Asia," *Journal of Asian Studies* 49, no. 4 (November 1990): 741–60; Donald G. Morrison and Hugh Michael Stevenson, "Political Instability in Independent Black Africa: More Dimensions of Conflict Behavior within Nations," *Journal of Conflict Resolution* 15, no. 3 (September 1971): 347–68; Michael C. Hudson, "Conditions of Political Violence and Instability: A Preliminary Test of Three Hypotheses," *Sage Professional Papers in Comparative Politics* 1, no. 5 (1970): 243–94, at pp. 278–81; Ted Gurr, "Psychological Factors in Civil Violence," *World Politics* 20, no. 2 (January 1968): 245–78, at p. 301.

once, just as it tends to avoid others. North India has been far more affected than south since colonial times.[163] Sri Lankan riots have occurred repeatedly in the North Central Province and in Colombo. Ethnic violence occurred in Zanzibar in 1961 and again in 1964, but on neither occasion did it spread to adjoining Pemba.[164] Cities, too, recidivate. Bombay and Bhiwandi experienced violence in 1970 and again in 1984.[165] Kano, scene of the 1953 anti-Ibo riot, was the location of the first 1966 anti-Ibo riot. Nablus, often a center of anti-Christian riots in the nineteenth century, became a center for anti-Jewish riots in the twentieth.[166] Durban, South Africa, sustained anti-Indian violence in 1949, 1953, and again in 1985;[167] it suffered anti-Pondo riots at the end of 1985.[168] Even the same neighborhoods are affected repeatedly. Treichville in Abidjan was the center of the Ivory Coast riots of 1949, 1958, and 1969. The same areas of Dacca were affected in 1930 and in 1941, as the same areas of Penang were in 1957 and 1967.[169]

Certain recidivist locations may be places that are violent in more than one direction. Recall the convertibility of forms of violence from Chapter 1. Kirkuk, scene of the 1959 Kurdish-Turkomen riot and of two more such riots in 1961, had experienced a violent oil strike in 1946 and food riots in 1948.[170] Perhaps when violence finds a place in such an environment, the norms that impede ethnic violence fall more readily by the wayside than they do in generally less violent locations. As there are some people who are systematically more aggressive than others,[171] per-

163. Indian Statutory Commission, *Memoranda Submitted by the Government of India and the India Office to the Indian Statutory Commission*, Vol. IV, pt. 1, p. 107.

164. Great Britain, Colonial Office, *Report of a Commission of Inquiry into Disturbances in Zanzibar during June 1961*, pp. 8–9; John Okello, *Revolution in Zanzibar* (Nairobi: East African Publishing House, 1967), pp. 154, 175.

165. Ghosh, *Communal Riots in India*, pp. 180, 185, 190–91.

166. Wasserstein, "Patterns of Communal Conflict in Palestine," p. 613.

167. Webb and Kirkwood, *The Durban Riots and After*; Leo Kuper, *An African Bourgeoisie: Race, Class, and Politics in South Africa* (New Haven: Yale University Press, 1965), pp. 302, 305; Fatima Meer and Alan Reynolds, "Sample Survey of Perceptions of the Durban Unrest — August 1985," in Fatima Meer, ed., *Resistance in the Townships* (Durban: Madiba, 1989), pp. 259–74.

168. "Umbumbulu," in Meer, ed., *Resistance in the Townships*, pp. 165–76.

169. Lambert, "Hindu-Muslim Riots," pp. 148, 155, 156, 161; interview, George Town, January 25, 1968.

170. Stephen Hemsley Longrigg, *Iraq, 1900 to 1950: A Political, Social and Economic History* (London: Oxford University Press, 1953), pp. 338, 352.

171. Leonard Berkowitz, *Aggression: Its Causes, Consequences, and Control* (Philadelphia: Temple University Press, 1993), p. 125; Russell G. Geen, *Human Aggression* (Milton Keynes: Open University Press, 1990), pp. 159–63.

haps there are similar group dispositions that make the recurrence of violence more likely in some places than in others.

Aggression can become habitual.[172] The modest but significant part played by traditional enmities and martial backgrounds in ethnic violence, not to mention the role of traditional paraphernalia and ritual in rioting and the attempts to create fighting organizations modeled on the exploits of historical ethnic heroes, suggests a role for habit and memory. But habit alone is liable to tautology as an explanation: where violence recurs, it has become habitual; where violence is habitual, it will recur. The phenomenon is difficult to distinguish from the explanation. If there is a role for habit — and I think there is — then mechanisms need to be specified, but this turns out to be difficult.

Several candidates are available. First of all, experience of earlier violence may convince ingroup members that they are dealing with outgroup members who entertain aggressive intentions and so must be dealt with violently again. A second possibility is that prior experience cues or channels responses in an aggressive direction. A third is that earlier aggression may be subject to reinforcement, either because the infliction of harm is itself satisfying or because it is rewarded subsequently.

Where the targets are associated with earlier violence, cueing may be involved, but so may reinforcement from satisfaction.[173] In an interesting experiment, subjects who had experienced two previous aggressive opponents tended to attack a third (nonaggressive) opponent more intensely than did subjects without such experience.[174] Furthermore, even observation of the prior attacks, without experience of them as a participant, was sufficient to elicit greater aggression in the third round. Observers as well as participants in the first two rounds set shocks higher when they became subjects in the third round than did subjects who had observed two previous rounds that did not involve aggressive opponents. Clearly, the prior rounds had an effect, but whether it was due to reinforcement

172. Elvin Staub, *The Roots of Evil: The Origins of Genocide and Other Group Violence* (Cambridge: Cambridge University Press, 1989), p. 52; Gordon Allport, "The Role of Expectancy," in Hadley Cantril, ed., *Tensions That Cause Wars* (Urbana: University of Illinois Press, 1952), p. 52.

173. See Leonard Berkowitz, *Aggression: A Social-Psychological Analysis* (New York: McGraw-Hill, 1962), pp. 201–28. See also George Wada and James C. Davies, "Riots and Rioters," *Western Political Quarterly* 10, no. 4 (December 1957): 864–74, at p. 864.

174. Stuart P. Taylor, Richard J. Shuntich, and Andrew Greenberg, "The Effects of Repeated Aggressive Encounters on Subsequent Aggressive Behavior," *Journal of Social Psychology* 107, no. 2 (April 1979): 199–208.

from observing the earlier pain of the victims or the attribution of aggressive intent to them is unclear.[175]

Both seem important. The part played by the imputation of aggressive intentions to target groups is beyond dispute. We have seen it at work in selective targeting and even more pervasively in rumors of aggression preceding violence. Equally, reinforcement is probably at work. Since aggression induced by anger tends to be a satisfying outlet for that anger, it can be quelled when the participants obtain a degree of satisfaction. The reinforcement effect of such satisfactions may make it a more likely course of action under comparable future conditions.[176] Experimental subjects with strong histories of aggression report that aggression produces positive affect, particularly because it allows the aggressors to achieve domination of the target.[177]

Observation of nonaggressive behavior may reduce aggressive responses, just as observation of aggressive behavior tends to increase them; sometimes the target's response to aggression conditions the subject's subsequent behavior, but sometimes not.[178] In certain animals, early exposure to aggressive exchanges between adult animals increases later aggressive behavior toward unfamiliar animals introduced into the environment.[179] Other experiments seem to confirm the independent effects of prior learning and assessment of the provocative character of the targets.[180]

The importance of learning implies that absence of disapproval after the event makes aggressive outcomes more likely.[181] If a sudden outburst of serious violence shocks authorities into a realization that "something

175. Although the experimenters are inclined to the view that attribution of aggressive intent is the more likely mechanism, since the observers of the first two rounds had not themselves had the satisfaction of inflicting the earlier pain. Ibid., pp. 205–06.

176. Berkowitz, *Aggression: A Social-Psychological Analysis*, p. 227.

177. James M. Driscoll, Bonita J. Jarman, and Pamela A. Yankeelov, "Effects of a Person's History of Aggression on Attributions of Affect to Aggressors," *Journal of Social Behavior and Personality* 9, no. 4 (December 1994): 685–700.

178. Marcia Donnerstein and Edward Donnerstein, "Variables in Interracial Aggression: Exposure to Aggressive Interracial Interactions," *Journal of Social Psychology* 100, First Half (October 1976): 111–21.

179. R. Lore and D. Meyerson, "Early Exposures to Intermale Aggression Increases the Adult Aggression of Male Rats," *Behavioural Processes* 16, nos. 1–2 (March 1988): 57–66.

180. Jacquelyn Weygandt White and Kenneth J. Gruber, "Instigative Aggression as a Function of Past Experience and Target Characteristics," *Journal of Personality and Social Psychology* 42, no. 6 (June 1982): 1069–75. Contextual variables can mediate these effects.

181. "When people respond approvingly or even indifferently to the actions of assailants, they convey the impression that aggression is not only acceptable but expected in certain situations." Albert Bandura, *Aggression: A Social Learning Analysis* (Englewood Cliffs, N.J.: Prentice-Hall, 1973), p. 129.

must be done" to alleviate the grievances alleged to have given rise to the violence, and if that something takes the form of policy concessions that effectively reward the violence, the rewarding effects of the violence may convince future participants that violence pays. The direct effects of the riot are significant, and so is the authoritative interpretation of the event, in determining whether rioting is rewarded.[182]

This is not a point to be pushed too far. There is no evidence that rioters are alert to the negative secondary consequences of the violence that occur significantly after the riot is concluded — such as the discouragement of investment that might have increased prosperity. There is equally little reason to think rioters will see all the benefits that the violence brings them afterward. In any case, the violence alone cannot produce benefits; politicians and other agenda setters who interpret and use the violence for this purpose are indispensable. They claim credit for policy changes, and they are unlikely to share credit with rioters. Still, at least the immediate reception and policy results of a riot may be elements in its likely recurrence. Consequently, it is not surprising that subsequent episodes may have a somewhat more instrumental aspect than earlier episodes do — or that they may be better organized.

RECURRENT RIOTS

If one riot does lead to another, and if that happens yet again within a short span of time, then a location can be transformed into a scene of recurrent violence. If that transformation takes place, then many of the rules of riot behavior are modified. This is what has occurred in a number of locations, but especially in Assam, in northeast Ghana, in Taraba state in Nigeria, in several Indian cities (most notably, Meerut, Aligarh, Allahabad, Moradabad, and Hyderabad), increasingly in West Kalimantan and the Moluccan islands of Indonesia, and, perhaps above all, in Karachi.

Riots vary in the degree to which they are independent of antecedent riots.[183] In many cases, earlier episodes are sui generis, but very often the memory of these events persists and attaches itself to new issues. Decades

---

182. Particularly, the search for "root causes" that can be redressed. It goes without saying that the interpretation of an individual event is hardly obvious and is subject to an intensely political process. Paul R. Brass is right to emphasize that process, albeit not to the exclusion of the event itself. See Brass, *Theft of an Idol.*

183. Veena Das makes a similar point when she says that some riots are repetitions of earlier ones, whereas others move into new areas and therefore say something new about group relations. Das, "Communities, Riots, Survivors: The South Asian Experience," p. 6.

may pass, but the same patterns are renewed. Certainly, that is the only inference that can be drawn from a careful study of Northern Ireland riots of the nineteenth century, which, after a very long lapse, were renewed in nearly identical form.[184] If the earlier episodes formed a pattern often repeated, as in Northern Ireland, or were cataclysmic, as in the Burundi genocide of 1972, the influence of the earlier on the later can scarcely be doubted. In Burundi (1988), Hutu, recalling the 1972 genocide, interpreted movements of the virtually entirely Tutsi *gendarmerie* as an augury of recurrence, whereupon they began killing Tutsi civilians.[185] It must be presumed that important episodes of violence form part of the leitmotiv of memory.[186] When episodes of violence form a closely ordered sequence, one riot following a few years after another, as in so many north Indian cities, then the recollections and the consequences — structural and attitudinal — of the earlier episodes form part of the machinery in place for the later ones. If every riot were truly an independent event, recurrent riots would not have the distinctive characteristics that they do. Their distinctiveness derives from the cumulative deposits of the earlier events in the series.

In locations with recurrent riots, especially those that come fast upon each other, the nature of the violence changes. Precipitants become more trivial as rioting becomes more routine. Eventually, precipitants become unnecessary. Targets, initially chosen highly selectively, broaden out significantly. Locations of violence also proliferate. The episodic character of the riot event gives way to something less discrete and more incessant. The violence becomes more organized and less spontaneous. There are tendencies to greater severity and to more casualties over time. The distinctions among types of violence begin to break down, as the same ethnic groups engage in different types of violence. With its more indiscriminate character, greater organization, and increased intensity, violence begins to partake of some features of warfare. The recurrent riot is best conceived in terms of a transition to warfare, with its specialized functionaries, its interplay of strategy and tactics, and its degradation of the security environment.

Take some of the more noteworthy cases mentioned earlier. Assam, it will be recalled, had ethnic riots in 1950, 1955, 1960, 1968, and 1972,

---

184. Baker, "Orange and Green."

185. Lemarchand, *Burundi: Ethnocide as Discourse and Practice,* pp. 118–30.

186. Here I have in mind, for example, the influence of the Bhiwandi (1970) riot on Bhiwandi (1984), since both flowed, in different ways, from the Shivaji Jayanti procession in the city. Ghosh, *Communal Riots in India,* pp. 201–05.

and then intermittently but much more severely from 1979 into the 1980s. By 1968, non-Bengali victims (especially Marwaris) were targeted, although very mildly, and later that year Bengali Muslims were targeted (also mildly). In 1972, the victims were again Bengali Hindus,[187] but later in the decade there was a strong shift to Bengali Muslim targets. Organizations came into being to pursue the violence, and they were alert to threats from many directions. Specific events were less necessary to start the violence. By the end of the 1980s, not only Assamese but tribals, who had been heavily involved as aggressors in 1950,[188] again took the lead in killing Bengalis. As late as 1993 and 1994, the violence was far from ended. There were Bodo raids on several districts of the state, and they seemed increasingly to have the quality of organized warfare designed to drive Bengalis (and Nepalese, too) from Assam.[189] Tightly defined episodes of violence had broadened out into a war of various indigenes against various immigrants at various times — and even beyond, as Bodo attacked Santhal (also classified as "tribal") in 1996.

There was a broadening of aggressors and targets in northeast Ghana, too, and the development of warfare over the years was unmistakable. In the Nanumba district, Konkomba, originally migrants from Togo, are landless laborers who work in a clientage relationship, contributing crops and services to their Nanumba, Gonja, and Dagomba hosts. Controlled by their hosts' traditional authorities, Konkomba began to demand their own chieftaincy. In 1981, Konkomba attacks on Nanumba in the district capital of Bimbilla and then in the village of Wulensi left more than 2,000 dead and at least 30,000 homeless.[190] This violence had only a semblance of organization, and it responded to precipitating events. A series of Konkomba attacks in 1991, 1992, 1994, and 1995 grew increasingly organized. Again, there were claims for group autonomy, now emanating from Nawuri as well as Konkomba.[191] The targets in 1991 and 1992 were mainly Gonja, and the main location was close to

187. M.S. Prabhakar, "The 'Bongal' Bogey," *Economic and Political Weekly*, October 21, 1972, p. 2142.

188. *Assam Tribune*, March 7, 1950, p. 1; March 28, 1950, p. 1.

189. *Reuters Library Report*, October 10, 1993 (BC Cycle); *Reuters World Service*, July 27, 1994 (BC Cycle).

190. Youri Petchenkine, *Ghana: In Search of Stability, 1957–1992* (Westport, Conn.: Praeger, 1992), p. 105; *Africa Contemporary Record, 1981–82* (New York: Africana, 1982), p. B421; *Africa Research Bulletin*, June 15, 1981, p. 6049; *West Africa*, July 20, 1981, pp. 162–30; June 1, 1981, p. 1260; May 4, 1981, p. 1001.

191. The Nawuri live just north of Lake Volta, near the border with Togo. The Konkomba live further north and are not generally considered a very closely related group.

Bimbilla. In 1994, Dagomba were involved in what appeared to be a pre-emptive strike against Konkomba, but Konkomba quickly organized killings of Dagomba, Nanumba, and Gonja, in episodes that extended over a three-month period.[192] The 1994 violence spread out from Bimbilla to affect seven districts, with perhaps 2,000 dead. A smaller outbreak in 1995 spread quickly again. This time automatic weapons replaced the bows and arrows that had been used in the previous year.[193] The Northern Region was in something like a state of war.

The evolution of violence from riot to warfare occurred swiftly in Wukari, in Taraba, Nigeria. There, the Jukun minority, ever fearful of Tiv power and numbers, began to fight Tiv in 1977. There were further attacks in 1987 and 1990. By 1991, the attacks were more extensive and more organized. There were more than ten violent episodes in 1990 and 1991. Some of these encounters lasted for weeks. Villages all over the Wukari area were affected. Tiv then counterattacked, and by 1992 tit-for-tat battles were being fought. The violence went on into 1993, and, while the targets did not broaden out as much as elsewhere, some other groups in the area were targeted if they seemed aligned with one or the other group. Thousands were killed.[194]

For the sheer repetition of violence, hardly any location approaches Karachi. The postelection riots (1965) involved, as we have seen, attacks by Pathans on Mohajirs, but another set of cleavages, between Sindhis and Mohajirs, became violent in 1970[195] and then, more seriously, in 1972, when it was proposed to promote Sindhi, apparently at the expense of Urdu (the language familiar to most Mohajirs), for official purposes in Sind province. Both cleavages have flourished violently ever since.

In 1985, Mohajirs (largely Biharis) killed Pathans in Orangi, a Karachi squatter area in which the two groups were present in roughly equal numbers. Orangi was the prototypical heterogeneous location. In mid-October 1986, there were two days of relatively mild Pathan-

192. Rubi Ofori, "Rawlings' Biggest Challenge," *Africa Report*, May–June 1994, pp. 53–55; *West Africa*, February 20–26, 1995, p. 261; *Reuters World Service*, March 16, 1995 (BC Cycle).

193. *Reuters World Service*, March 16, 1995 (BC Cycle); *Agence France Press*, March 21, 1995.

194. The two main partisan accounts do not disagree on these general outlines. See Avav and Myegba, *The Dream to Conquer*, pp. 9, 12, 22–34, 44; Shekarau Angyu Masa-Ibi, *The Story of the Jukun/Tiv Crisis: Why and How It Happened* (n.p.: n.p., 1992), pp. 14, 22–32. See also *Daily Times* (Lagos), December 26, 1991, pp. 11, 12; *Africa Research Bulletin*, February 1–29, 1992, pp. 10471–72.

195. *Washington Post*, January 28, 1970, p. A17.

Mohajir rioting, followed at the end of the month by violence on both sides, but more by Pathans, who climaxed several days of killing by driving jeeps into Bihari areas of Orangi, machine-gunning people, and burning houses.[196] These episodes merely set the stage for December 1986, when police tried to evict Pathans (and related Afghans) from an area where they allegedly dominated the drug trade. Apparently sensing a Mohajir hand behind the police action — the apprehension was that there was a Mohajir plot to remove Pathans from Karachi — Pathans burned a nearby Mohajir area and attacked Biharis in Orangi.[197] Revenge was then taken on Pathans on Karachi streets, and in January 1987 Mohajirs, who had had little police protection in the December violence, attacked the police. In April, July, and August, three separate episodes of Pathan-Mohajir violence occurred, each with gun battles between militants of the two groups. The April and July fighting spread from Karachi to nearby Hyderabad. By then, it had a highly organized quality. In January, February, and March 1988, Mohajirs and Pathans fought again, and in May major battles erupted between the two groups. The fighting, which spread widely, involved gangs arriving in cars, trucks, minibuses, and jeeps and, in well-coordinated attacks, employing Kalashnikovs imported from the Afghan war.[198]

The Pathan-Bihari conflict had grown into a broader Pathan-Mohajir conflict, and it had solidified because of a considerable flow of Pathan refugees from Afghanistan, who lived in a milieu of criminal gangs in Karachi. The Pathan influx complicated the efforts of Mohajirs, the majority in Karachi and the largest minority in the Sind,[199] to establish themselves as a recognized, fifth main ethnic group in Pakistan and to counter policies recognizing Sindhis as the indigenous (and preferred) people of the province.

No sooner had the violence between Pathans and Mohajirs reached its

196. Farida Shaheed, "Pathan-Muhajir Conflicts in Pakistan, 1985–1986: A National Perspective," *Ethnic Studies Report* (Colombo) 5, no. 1 (January 1987): 19–31.

197. Ibid.; Akmal Hussain, "The Karachi Riots of December 1986: Crisis of State and Civil Society in Pakistan," in Das, ed., *Mirrors of Violence*, pp. 185–93; Akbar S. Ahmed, "The Approach of Anarchy," *Far Eastern Economic Review*, February 19, 1987, pp. 40–41.

198. *Dawn*, January 10, 1988, p. 5; January 18, 1988, p. 1; February 6, 1988, p. 1; February 7, 1988, p. 1; May 8, 1988, p. 1; May 9, 1988, p. 1; May 10, 1988, p. 1; May 11, 1988, p. 1; May 13, 1988, p. 1.

199. See Abbas Rashid and Farida Shaheed, *Pakistan: Ethno-Politics and Contending Elites* (Geneva: United Nations Research Institute for Social Development Discussion Paper no. 45, 1993), p. 12; Theodore P. Wright, "Center-Periphery Relations and Ethnic Conflict in Pakistan: Sindhis, Muhajirs, and Punjabis," *Comparative Politics* 23, no. 3 (April 1991): 299–312.

apogee in May 1988 than it was transformed in July into Mohajir-Sindhi violence. As if to start a new sequence, an assassination attempt on the Mohajir mayor of Hyderabad produced an escalating series of attacks over the next several months, with deaths for each episode generally in single digits, until, on September 30, Sindhis machine-gunned a large number of Mohajirs in Hyderabad.[200] The next day, Mohajirs took extensive revenge in Karachi, using the usual sophisticated weapons and organization.[201] In these exchanges, hundreds were killed. This pattern of attack and revenge attack continued into the 1990s,[202] relieved only by a shift to Sunni-Shiite violence in 1995.[203]

Housing, as they do, the dual conflicts of Sindhis and Mohajirs (sometimes Sindhis on one side and Mohajirs and Punjabis on the other) and of Mohajirs and Pathans, Karachi and Hyderabad are cities hospitable to ethnic violence. Mohajirs are seen by Sindhis as capable, arrogant people inclined to take over their homeland, in which Sindhis feel "left out" and in danger of becoming "American Indians."[204] Mohajirs feel unprotected

---

200. *Dawn*, July 18, 1988, p. 1; July 19, 1988, p. 1; July 22, 1988, p. 1; September 9, 1988, p. 1; October 1, 1988, p. 1.

201. Ibid., October 2, 1988, p. 1.

202. See, e.g., Human Rights Commission of Pakistan, *Sindh Inquiry, Summer 1990*, pp. 33–34; *Far Eastern Economic Review*, August 31, 1994, p. 23.

203. Sunni-Shiite violence punctuated the entire period, with notable episodes in 1984 and 1988.

204. For background, see Rashid and Shaheed, *Pakistan*, pp. 11–14, 18, 45, 48; Tahir Amin, *Ethno-National Movements of Pakistan* (Islamabad: Institute of Policy Studies, 1988), pp. 82–93, 125–26; Shaheed, "Pathan-Muhajir Conflicts in Pakistan, 1985–1986," pp. 19–21; Iftikhar H. Malik, "The Politics of Ethnic Conflict in Sind: Nation, Regions and Community in Pakistan," in Subrata K. Mitra and R. Alison Lewis, eds., *Subnational Movements in South Asia* (Boulder, Colo.: Westview Press, 1996), pp. 76, 80. Some of the flavor of everyday contacts is captured in a report in the Indian press:

> Karachi and Hyderabad have an extremely mixed demography. In terms of voting strength, as the 1988 election showed, Urdu speaking Mohajirs continue dominating the two largest cities of the province. But economically they are divorced from both industry and large-scale commerce, the perceptions of Sindhi nationalists notwithstanding. Large-scale trade and commerce still has a share in the hands of Gujrati [*sic*] speakers, though a diminishing one. Much of the new industries and the newer companies of large-scale trade and commerce, including inter-provincial transport, is in Punjabi hands. Karachi houses the money market of the country, with banks dominating. But the pure Sindhi share is next to nil, while Mohajirs still have a large share among the clerks and chaprasis, while all senior posts are held by migrants from the north. The Pathans are the second largest ethnic group in Karachi and the third largest in Hyderabad in terms of sheer numbers. But they are concentrated in unskilled jobs that few want and are competitors with virtually no one.
>
> It is this picture in Karachi that is not exactly replicated in Hyderabad (because in the latter city, the second largest ethnic group comprises ethnic Sindhis) that is

and "besieged"[205] by Sindhis as well as Pathans, and they see Pathans as aggressive people (dominating the transport business and not averse to running down pedestrians), perhaps in need of tough treatment. These, we know, are familiar conflictual patterns.

As early as the 1960s, Pathans and Mohajirs supported different parties, as did Sindhis and Mohajirs. Sindhis formed a militant, occasionally separatist Jeeya Sind movement. Mohajirs in turn formed a Mohajir Qaumi Mahaz (Mohajir National Movement) in 1984. Both became active in electoral politics and in gang warfare. Pathans then organized a Pukhtun Mutahida Mahaz (United Pathan Front). In provincewide politics, the Sindhi-led People's Progressive Party disappointed the MQM in appointments and influence, while in Karachi and Hyderabad politics the Mohajir electoral success, particularly in the 1988 and 1990 elections, produced resentment among both Sindhis and Pathans. No interethnic coalitions proved durable.[206]

What helped convert areas of high-violence propensity to areas of endemic violence was the high level of organization of each group in an environment suffused with criminality and access to arms. Traditional dacoits or bandits were co-opted by the ethnic groups to which they belonged to perform paramilitary duty. Karachi is a gun and drug distribution center, and the activity is organized along ethnic lines. As early as the 1986 violence, criminal gangs were in the vanguard of the protagonists.

As the violence proceeded, all the rules of ethnic rioting were broken. Targeting broadened out, from Biharis alone to Mohajirs inclusively. Precipitants occurred intermittently but were unnecessary for violent episodes to begin. Several aggressor-target alignments alternated: Sunni-Shiite, Pathan-Mohajir, and Sindhi-Mohajir, but also, from time to time,

---

responsible for political mayhem of the last four years. Sindhi nationalist opinion had more or less reconciled itself to the loss of Karachi. But the upsurge of the new political movement among the Urdu speakers after 1986, known as Muhajir Qaumi Movement (MQM), has frightened and alienated the Sindhis. They feel that Hyderabad too has all but been lost. They mean to fight it out. Loss of Hyderabad is simply not acceptable to any Sindhi nationalist and the Mohajir control of the Hyderabad Municipal Committee has been the chief bone of contention since 1985.

M.B. Naqvi, "Why Sindhis Are Better in Pakistan," *Indian Express*, April 3, 1990, p. 1. For the "Red Indian" theme of extinction in ethnic relations, see Horowitz, *Ethnic Groups in Conflict*, pp. 175–78.

205. Rashid and Shaheed, *Pakistan*, p. 28.

206. See Charles H. Kennedy, "Managing Ethnic Conflict: The Case of Pakistan," in John Coakley, ed., *The Territorial Management of Ethnic Conflict* (London: Frank Cass, 1993), pp. 123–43.

Punjabi-Mohajir as well. Although Pathans and Sindhis targeted Mohajirs more frequently than they were targeted by Mohajirs, the violence was reciprocal. Retaliatory violence became the norm, once attacks began. As each wave of episodes accelerated, the violence became more severe and more organized, until a great massacre occurred. Even the rules of location did not hold. With mobility and automatic weapons, lightning attacks deep in the home areas of the targets became possible. Aggressors were not confined to mixed areas or areas adjacent to their own home location. Atrocities were not absent, but the need for speed in target-group areas and the use of modern weapons meant that the infliction of atrocities was frequently sacrificed. The basic goal of killing the ethnic enemy, especially the main ethnic enemy in each case, was not abandoned, but, as the dispute became paramilitarized, the coherence, the high definition of the riot event, began to be lost. There was just too much of a good thing.

Something like this, but typically less extreme, is the pattern wherever rioting becomes recurrent. In major Indian cities subject to recurrent riots, such as Aligarh or Ahmedabad, thresholds for violence are lower with each riot.[207] A few ritualized signals (a cow's head in a temple, a pig's head in a mosque) suffice. Organization substitutes for precipitants in a location of high hostility and recurrent violence.[208] Broadened targeting appears in two different ways. In some cases, flushed with relatively recent success, rioters go on to inflict violence, usually of lesser seriousness, against third groups they had formerly abjured as targets. A month after the anti-Chinese riot in Malaysia (1969), Malays killed, for the first time, a few Indians.[209] In 1971, a small number of Yoruba were killed in northern Nigeria.[210] Elsewhere, precision is lost, particularly in excluding certain groups and subgroups as targets. Sri Lanka (1977) involved, for the first time, Indian Tamils as well as Sri Lankan Tamils as targets, and they were then included in 1981 and 1983 as well.[211] In the

207. Ghosh, *Communal Riots in India*, pp. 213–15; Rajgopal, *Communal Violence in India*, pp. 84–89.

208. Varshney, for example, notes that, in Aligarh, great preparations precede violent events, and criminal gangs are to be found on both sides. Varshney, "Religion, Nationalism and Violence," pp. 190, 194. René Lemarchand's description of anti-Tutsi riots in Rwanda (1959, 1960, and 1963) shows each of them to have been a bit more organized than the previous one. Lemarchand, *Rwanda and Burundi*, pp. 162–64, 179–80, 223–27.

209. John Slimming, *Malaysia: The Death of a Democracy* (London: John Murray, 1969), p. 64.

210. Said one observer: "I think the Hausa has realized what he can do by chopping off a few heads." *Christian Science Monitor*, October 20, 1971, p. 9.

211. *Report of the Presidential Commission of Inquiry into the Incidents Which Took Place between 13th August and 15th September 1977*, pp. 136, 136, 137, 142, 206;

latter stages of the riots in Nigeria (1966), other easterners, as well as Ibo, were targeted.[212] Locations broaden out. By 1977, Sri Lankan violence, formerly confined to specific areas, was widespread across the country.[213] In 1999, Christian-Muslim violence spread from Ambon to other Moluccan islands in Indonesia; by 2000, it had moved west to Lombok, near Bali. Participants sometimes broaden out, too. By September 1966, Birom, Idoma, and Tiv joined Hausa in killing Ibo in Nigeria, as Malays joined Dayaks in killing Madurese in West Kalimantan (1999), in contrast to five earlier episodes between 1977 and 1997.[214] Gangs begin to participate, as they did in the Moluccas and West Kalimantan. Despite the absence of serious precipitants, the violence becomes more severe over time. Middle-class areas may no longer be protected by the police.[215] Partly because experience crowds out rioters' fear, partly because new weapons are introduced, the deaths inflicted in successive riots increase in number.[216] Varanasi's deaths roughly doubled as violence recurred in each of the four years following 1987.[217] And a violent episode may go on for weeks or even months.[218]

I have described recurrent riots as verging on warfare. In their organization, reciprocal character, tactics, professionalization of personnel, and extended duration, that is not an inaccurate description, but in one respect it does not fit. The forces often do not fight each other. Rather, as in riots, they attack civilian targets, generally preserving their own impunity. These attacks, in turn, keep the violence going, because each

---

Virginia A. Leary, *Ethnic Conflict and Violence in Sri Lanka: Report of a Mission to Sri Lanka in July–August 1981 on Behalf of the International Commission of Jurists* (Geneva: ICJ, 1981), p. 22; W. Howard Wriggins, "Sri Lanka in 1981: Year of Austerity, Development Councils, and Communal Disorders," *Asian Survey* 22, no. 2 (February 1982): 171–79, at p. 178; *Far Eastern Economic Review*, August 11, 1983, p. 16.

212. Leonard Plotnicov, "Who Owns Jos? Ethnic Ideology in Nigerian Urban Politics," *Urban Anthropology* 1, no. 1 (Spring 1972): 1–13, at p. 5.

213. *Report of the Presidential Commission of Inquiry into the Incidents Which Took Place between 13th August and 15th September 1977*, p. 335.

214. Ruth First, *Power in Africa* (New York: Pantheon Books, 1970), p. 329; James O'Connell, "The Anatomy of a Pogrom: An Outline Model with Special Reference to the Ibo in Northern Nigeria," *Race* 9, no. 1 (July 1967): 95–99; Plotnicov, "Who Owns Jos?" pp. 5, 10; *The Independent* (London), March 22, 1999, p. 1.

215. Valli Kanapathipillai, "July 1983: The Survivor's Experience," in Das, ed., *Mirrors of Violence*, pp. 338, 341.

216. See, e.g., Lambert, "Hindu-Muslim Riots," p. 227; *South China Morning Post* (Hong Kong), July 29, 1999, p. 11, reporting gunshot wounds in Ambon.

217. Anjoo Upadhyaya, "Recent Trends in Communal Violence: A Case Study of Varanasi" (paper presented at the Conference on Conflict and Change, Ethnic Studies Network, Portrush, Northern Ireland, June 9, 1992).

218. E.g., Rajgopal, *Communal Violence in India*, p. 84.

episode creates a community desire for revenge, which is then inflicted, yet again, on civilians.[219] The recurrent and reciprocal character of the violence does not, therefore, enhance the vulnerability of those who engage in violence. As they are not victims of revenge, their risk aversion can coexist with a greatly elevated level of violence.[220] The combination of targeting that is selective by group but random by individual member creates an enticing ratio of reward to risk. "Since retribution seldom fell on the guilty, aggressive men had little reason to fear for their lives, while the relatives of the harmless victims had every reason to retaliate in kind."[221]

It would almost be apt to describe a tacit agreement whereby the A paramilitary attacks B civilians, the B paramilitary attacks A civilians, and the A and B paramilitaries do not attack each other. Such conditions differ enormously from the archetypical deadly ethnic riot, in which civilians attack civilians and, at the time of the violence — although not later — need to worry about whether they will be vulnerable to counterattack.

I mentioned the Mohajir attack on the Karachi police in January 1987, an event that signaled the decline of distinctions among types of violence in the course of recurrent riots. In Turkey, a series of Sunni-Alevi riots between 1978 and 1980 later gave way to assassination attempts, terrorist attacks (in one of which 37 Alevi were killed in a set hotel fire), and police firings on Alevi protesters.[222] If the police force is biased to begin with, recurrent riots will soon test its restraint, likely beyond the breaking point.[223]

219. For the role of grudge killings in sustaining terrorism over protracted periods, see Robert Clark, *The Basque Insurgents: ETA, 1952–80* (Madison: University of Wisconsin Press, 1984), p. 278.

220. Compare C.R. Hallpike, *Bloodshed and Vengeance in the Papuan Mountains* (Oxford: Clarendon Press, 1977), p. 211: "One of the principal factors in the generation of warfare has been the inability of the tribes effectively to control the aggression of their individual members, while at the same time vengeance for their acts is liable to fall on *any* member of their tribe — a state of affairs combining the minimum of social control with the maximum opportunity for extending the network of conflict."

221. Ibid., p. 229.

222. For two of the riots, see C.H. Dodd, *The Crisis of Turkish Democracy* (Beverly, England: Eothen Press, 1983), pp. 17, 20. For the assassination attempt and arson, see *Mideast Mirror*, July 5, 1993, p. 1; July 7, 1993, p. 1. For the police killings, see *Turkish Daily News*, March 14, 1995, p. 1; March 15, 1995, p. 1; March 27, 1995, p. B1.

223. See, e.g., *Far Eastern Economic Review*, July 11, 1987, p. 52, describing police roundups of Muslims for killing as well as active police participation in anti-Muslim riots in Meerut (1987); ibid., May 30, 1985, p. 24, describing attacks by soldiers and civilians on Tamils in Anuradhapura, Sri Lanka, and again in Delft and Jaffna. Many such examples could be cited.

The persistence of violence also opens the way for other ethnic conflicts in the same environment to become violent. Around the time of the most severe violence in northeast Ghana (1994), at least two other interethnic disputes produced riots in other parts of the country.[224] In Sri Lanka, Sinhalese-Moor violence was sandwiched between the 1981 and 1983 anti-Tamil riots.[225] As riots recur, everyone is learning: aggressors, victims, third groups. Confident crowds discover they need be less afraid of countervailing force and so can broaden the class of targets and even take on new enemies. Victim groups finally borrow the organizational strategies and tactics of aggressors and ultimately turn the violence around. By the force of example, bystander groups are enabled to overcome their own initial inhibitions on the use of violence.

There is no doubt that the first riot or two breaches an important barrier pertaining to inhibitions (and perhaps also to the pleasure obtained by harming others).[226] Ongoing events thereafter provide feedback about the absence of adverse consequences to the rioters. To the arsenal earlier utilized to overcome inhibition — amulets, oathing, manic enthusiasm, religious sanction, and false rumors that leave rioters no choice but to kill — is added the evidence of the senses. The location unlucky enough to experience several riots in a short period is then likely — especially in an environment with a significant admixture of criminality and police ineffectiveness — to experience the militarization of the conflict. Prevention strategies focused on drawing bright lines against mass violence have much to commend them.

An altogether curious cognitive brew of the magical and the empirical is served up to rioters. Mechanisms such as wish fulfillment and projec-

224. *Reuters World Service*, April 7, 1994 (BC Cycle); *Reuters Textline* (BBC Monitoring Service: Africa), February 1, 1994.

225. Even after the 1958 riot, there was a brief Tamil-Moor riot. Government of Ceylon, *Administration Report of the Inspector-General of Police for 1958*, pt. III (Colombo: Government Press, 1960), pp. A154–56.

226. A point implicit in Midlarsky's distinction between diffusion and contagion. Midlarsky, "Analyzing Diffusion and Contagion Effects," pp. 1002–05; Manus I. Midlarsky, Martha Crenshaw, and Fumihiko Yoshida, "Why Violence Spreads: The Contagion of International Terrorism," *International Studies Quarterly* 24, no. 2 (June 1980): 262–98. For the likely connection between conquest of fear and recurrent violence with broadened targeting, see Don Fitz, "A Renewed Look at Miller's Conflict Theory of Aggression Displacement," *Journal of Personality and Social Psychology* 33, no. 6 (June 1976): 725–32. For evidence suggesting that perpetrators who are not initially inclined to cruelty may develop a taste for it, see Roy F. Baumeister and W. Keith Campbell, "The Intrinsic Appeal of Evil: Sadism, Sensational Thrills, and Threatened Egotism," *Personality and Social Psychology Review* 3, no. 3 (1999): 210–21, at pp. 212–13. See also the story of two habitual fighters in Ambon, Indonesia, in the *New York Times*, February 19, 2000, p. A4.

tion facilitate participation in individual riots, the former to defeat fear and the latter to justify the violence as necessary. These are the conditions that obtain when the threshold of participation in violence is still high. What cognition is present at later stages when the threshold is being lowered? Verification of impunity, the most important condition necessary to transform episodic into endemic violence.

CHAPTER II

Aims, Effects, and Functions

THE INFLICTION OF PAIN AND DEATH are undoubtedly satisfying to aggressors. That satisfaction alone could explain the deadly ethnic riot, but even in the most spontaneous specimens of such an episode there is room for a slightly enlarged, if not fully consciously formulated, agenda on the part of rioters. If the riot flows from the discomforts and apprehensions of intergroup relations, then it is reasonable to ask how the rioters mean to alleviate their situation. A separate question pertains to the results the rioters produce, and still farther afield one can inquire into the implications of their action — its functions — for the affected populations.

Of course, to describe rioters as harboring intentions or pursuing an agenda is to entertain a capacious conception of intentionality and to assume what ought not to be assumed — that rioters have a plan that extends beyond killing. A stripped-down understanding of what rioters do casts doubt on such enlarged conceptions. They kill members of other groups and commit atrocities upon them, angrily yet playfully, when and where those groups have displayed threatening behavior toward them and when and where it is reasonably safe to do the killing. None of this evidences much of a plan beyond killing. Take the matter of selective targeting and its meaning for riot objectives. Ethnic terrorists, using bombs that cannot identify all victims in advance or discriminate (except very crudely and probabilistically) among victims, display a willingness to kill some members of their own ethnic group. For them, it is part of the cost of doing business. That is because terrorists act in accordance with at least fragments of a plan. Rioters, however, are completely unwilling to kill members of their own group and go out of their way to avoid doing so. Just as they are risk averse as individual participants in violence, so, too, are they unwilling to pay a price in the lives of their own group members to achieve an objective beyond killing. That is because they do not need to do so to achieve a further objective. Ironically, the terrorist's sloppiness in this respect is strategic: killing is a means to an end, and if the means entail inadvertently killing members of one's own group, the end prevails. Conversely, the rioter's precision is merely tactical: he kills in order to kill.

Or very nearly so. There are, I shall argue, only two general riot aims that can be ascertained, beyond the killing and infliction of hurt.[1] The first is to engage in a demonstration of dishonor or degradation of the victims and is captured in part by the phrase "teach them a lesson," which we encountered in Chapter 9. The second aim, which can sometimes be inferred from the explicit statements and behavior of rioters but also from its sheer foreseeability and pervasiveness as a direct consequence of the violence, is the reduction of ethnic heterogeneity. Both of these aims are close to the very act of killing itself. After all, for the victims to be murdered ignominiously is to be devalued in a radical way, and to lose population through murder and the flight that is bound to follow is to contribute to a reduction of heterogeneity at the site of the killing.

For the rest, there are well-known dangers to inferring intentions from consequences — dangers that need especially to be heeded when the behavior is angry. Furthermore, even if the rioters surely entertained intentions far beyond killing, it would be safe to surmise that any such intentions would generally be deflected by the usual forces that create unanticipated consequences. Varied adaptations to the violence on the part of multiple actors — victims in several categories, those who purport to speak for various categories of victim, interpreters of the event (official and unofficial), policymakers — as well as the interrelations among those adaptations, all mean that the precise effects of the riot lie beyond the control of those who commit the violence.

It cannot be claimed, of course, that all violence, even violence with certain similarities to the deadly riot, has few aims beyond the violence itself. It has been argued that British food riots in the late eighteenth and early nineteenth centuries were designed to make threats of violence more credible in general, so as to secure price and supply concessions from merchants.[2] Some of the evidence for these intentions is, unfortu-

---

1. For present purposes, I leave aside some of the specific aims that were identified in Chapter 7 in cases where the violence has a significant measure of organization.

2. Statements about food riots in this paragraph are derived from John Bohstedt, *Riots and Community Politics in England and Wales, 1790–1810* (Cambridge: Harvard University Press, 1983), pp. 36, 40, 54; E.P. Thompson, "The Moral Economy of the English Crowd in the Eighteenth Century," *Past and Present*, no. 50 (February 1971): 76–136, at pp. 78, 111, 120–26.

nately, derived from the effects of the riots, but that need not detain us. Food riots were generally motivated by hunger and by indignation about price and supply. It is hardly surprising to find strategic intentions, given these motivating conditions. Moreover, food riots entailed sales of grain stocks at forced prices; the riots were not so much destructive as they were appropriative. By contrast, ethnic riots are characterized by great destruction, even of valuable property that rioters might have chosen to seize instead. Outside the most organized ethnic riots, none of the instrumental aims sometimes imputed to rioters (policy changes, expropriation of property, and the like) is verifiable, and some are refuted by the statements and behavior of the rioters, as we shall see — for example, when they urge fellow rioters to kill rather than loot and when they burn with abandon. The deadly ethnic riot partakes of violence mixed with little else.

NARROW AIMS, BROAD EFFECTS

In spite of their own limited intentions, focused on killing and its most direct effects, the rioters achieve more, often much more. Sri Lanka (1983) is a riot with unusually well documented effects at various levels. One can examine what the Sri Lankan Tamils did following the riot, what the Indian Tamils did, what the organizations who spoke for both subgroups did, what the Sri Lankan government did, what Tamils abroad did, and what the Indian government did. From these observations, it is easy to see the range of consequences and the areas in which they operate.

Start with Indian Tamils, also called "estate Tamils," largely descendants of laborers brought from Tamil Nadu to work the tea estates in upcountry areas, surrounded, not by Sri Lankan Tamils, who are concentrated in the north and east and scattered in the south as well, but by Sinhalese, with whom they lived, more or less in peace, until 1977. Indian Tamils are divisible into estate laborers and shopkeepers. After 1983, small shopkeepers who suffered financial loss tended to recover their insurance claims and move elsewhere. Larger shopkeepers tended to expand, to some extent at the expense of their neighbors' destroyed premises, but now with Sinhalese business partners for protection. Others chose to stay open but on a scaled-down basis, in order to reduce risk; and one effect of this in turn was to open opportunities for Sinhalese or Muslim traders to fill the gap. Salaried Tamils mainly stayed in their positions but sent their families elsewhere for safety. Estate laborers tried to move to more secure estates, at higher elevations, or to become wage laborers in homogeneous Tamil areas, or to emigrate to India or the Middle East.[3] The Ceylon Workers Congress, representing Indian Tamils, attempted to straddle these multiple adaptations, eschewing separatism (an implausible course, given the noncontiguity of Indian and Sri Lankan Tamil areas) and conciliating the ruling Sinhalese party while urging a moderate course upon it.

For Sri Lankan Tamils, the problems and adaptations were at least as various. Some families moved out of the areas in which they were attacked, leaving those Tamils who remained more isolated. In some cases, family members had to disperse. Some Tamils with ties to Jaffna moved northward. Many Tamils in the south, however, had no ties to Jaffna, disliked the idea of territorial separatism being mooted by Tamil organizations, and were well integrated with neighbors in Colombo and other towns. After the riots, significant numbers of these began to think about emigration. A very few others began to work at assimilation, fruitlessly, given the elevated level of Sinhalese hostility and distrust. In one poignant account, a Tamil mother advises her children to marry non-Tamils; the family even begins to speak Sinhala at home.[4] Children urge their parents to change their names (in Sri Lanka, names are usually a reliable clue to identity), and they use Sinhala in public.[5] For individual Tamil actors, Indian and Sri Lankan alike, there were crosscurrents of internal and external migration and attempts to come to terms with Sinhalese in situ as well.

At the collective level, responses were less variable. The government felt obliged to appease Sinhalese militant sentiment by proscribing separatist political parties from sitting in parliament. In the face of the riot, the Tamil United Liberation Front (TULF) could scarcely concede and abjure separatism, whereupon it lost its parliamentary representation. On the other hand, the effect of the riot on Sri Lankan Tamil opinion was to give a fillip to the several armed separatist organizations, which were able to recruit with alacrity and obtain weapons and training, aided by resources furnished by émigré Tamil communities in the West.[6]

3. R.P. Slater, "Hill Country Tamils in the Aftermath of the Violence," in James Manor, ed., *Sri Lanka in Change and Crisis* (New York: St. Martin's Press, 1984), pp. 214–18.

4. The inefficacy of any such strategy in the short run is a demonstration of the failure of participants in the violence to embrace constructivist views of ethnic identity. Their view of group boundaries, historically inaccurate though it is, is far more rigid and deterministic.

5. Valli Kanapathipillai, "July 1983: The Survivors' Experience," in Veena Das, ed., *Mirrors of Violence: Communities, Riots and Survivors in South Asia* (Delhi: Oxford University Press, 1990), pp. 321–44.

6. See *Far Eastern Economic Review*, December 22, 1983, pp. 40–41.

Government security forces collaborated unwittingly in these efforts. Each time the separatists attacked and the security forces retaliated against civilians, Tamils saw fewer alternatives to separatism. Rebuffed by government, the TULF was put in an impossible position; it was largely superseded as a negotiating partner by the armed Tamil organizations. A series of peace plans, advanced by government with a view to resolving the major issues through devolution to Tamil regional authorities, was repeatedly thwarted by the opposition of Sinhalese politicians and Buddhist monks, as many similar plans had been since 1957. India, which housed Tamil separatist headquarters and many refugees, attempted unsuccessfully to mediate in 1984–85 and then, equally unsuccessfully, to intervene militarily in 1987. The armed Tamil organizations fought each other militarily, leaving one, the Tamil Tigers, triumphant. The armed forces and the separatists faced each other starkly on the battlefield, while civilians fell victim to reciprocal atrocities, and more Tamils found themselves having to relocate out of harm's way or be herded into refugee camps.[7]

Increasingly, Sinhalese came to define relations with the Tamils in terms of the paradigm of an indigenous group confronted by much later immigrants who demand a disproportionate share: the familiar image of the guest who takes over the house. Armed Tamil separatists, on the other hand, having made contacts with comparable groups around the world, developed a left-wing ideology with intragroup as well as intergroup conflict components. They seemed bent on abolition of the Tamil caste hierarchy. The Tigers were representative of a range of Tamil castes but were led by a member of the Karaiyu (fisher) caste distrusted by the land-owning Vellala who dominated Tamil civilian politics; he was probably distrustful of Vellala in turn.[8] Since normal politics might restore the political leadership of higher-caste Tamils, intra-Tamil caste rivalry may explain some of the tenacity of the armed movement that was so greatly reinforced by the 1983 violence. The riot, then, interacted with cleavages within the target community as well as those between it and the initiators of violence.

Some of these effects of the 1983 riot are actually effects of the

7. See, e.g., ibid., February 7, 1985, p. 9.
8. Dagmar Hellmann-Rajanayagam, "The Tamil Militants — before the Accord and After," *Pacific Affairs* 61, no. 4 (Winter 1988–89): 603–19. For Tamil caste cleavages more generally, see Bryan Pfaffenberger, "The Political Construction of Defensive Nationalism: The 1968 Temple Entry Crisis in Sri Lanka," in Chelvadurai Manugaran and Bryan Pfaffenberger, eds., *The Sri Lankan Tamils: Ethnicity and Identity* (Boulder, Colo.: Westview Press, 1994), pp. 143–68.

effects — that is, secondary or even tertiary effects and, at that, in combination with the effects of other forces and events. Furthermore, some of these are effects of the 1983 riot in conjunction with effects of the 1977 riot, just as the effects of the 1977 violence had connections to what followed the 1958 violence. For example, one Tamil village lost population to migration after the 1958 riot; feeling insecure, the remainder of its inhabitants left after the next riot, 19 years later.[9] Similar adaptations tend to follow each riot and to be cumulative. In 1977, Indian Tamils on estates sought employment on other estates, more secure because the latter had more Tamil than Sinhalese employees,[10] just as they did six years later. It is not only the example of the earlier behavior that inspires the later reaction but also the demographic effect of the earlier behavior, the first movement out having already made those left behind less secure by the time of the later riot. One of the hazards of studying events conceived as discrete is that behavior falls into grooves cut by earlier behavior. No sooner is a phenomenon isolated in time than its connections to other phenomena across time become apparent. Here is yet another warning of the dangers of individuating events.

With such qualifications, it is fair to identify these as the main results of the 1983 riot: Indian Tamils migrating locally, interregionally, and internationally; Sri Lankan Tamils migrating interregionally and internationally; large numbers of refugees, ultimately in the hundreds of thousands; some traders adapting one way, some another; a growing sense among Tamils that it would be difficult to live as Tamils alongside Sinhalese; a hardening of Sinhalese positions on intergroup relations (recall that even Sinhalese Christian areas were now involved in the violence); formerly mixed areas becoming more Sinhalese; and an increased militarization of the interethnic conflict. Nearly all of these effects had been in evidence, but more modestly, after the 1977 violence.[11]

These effects can be categorized generically and parsimoniously. First, there was growing ethnic homogenization of regions and of localities.[12] Second, between groups, a powerful polarization occurred, rendering

9. Tamil Refugees Rehabilitation Commission, *Communal Disturbances in Sri Lanka: Sansoni Commission: Written Submissions* (mimeo., March 28, 1980), p. 150.

10. *Report of the Presidential Commission of Inquiry into the Incidents Which Took Place between 13th August and 15th September 1977*, Sessional Paper No. VII — 1980 (Colombo: Government Publications Bureau, 1980), p. 208.

11. See ibid., pp. 123–24, 130, 144, 215–16, 261.

12. An exception applies with respect to the Eastern Region, where the Sinhalese share of the population was growing, but some of this was attributable to the same forces, notably Tamil migration to more secure areas.

compromise difficult, agents of compromise redundant, and warfare more likely. Third, within groups, there was a tendency to compress differences, such as those between Indian and Sri Lankan Tamils and between Sinhalese Buddhists and Christians. Fourth, and following naturally from the second and third effects, conciliatory policy on interethnic relations was retarded. Fifth, efforts to control the armed forces and prevent them from attacking civilians proved ineffective, thereby feeding back to increase insecurity, homogenization, polarization, and warfare. Altogether, this is a dark picture. None of the effects benefited the target group.

Not everywhere will the picture be equally dark. In identifying these effects, I mean to claim the categories as subjects for investigation, but not to presuppose the outcomes for each category to be invariable across riots. Many of the Sri Lankan elements are common effects of ethnic riots, but the precise configuration, with the exception of spatial homogenization, varies from country to country. Although I shall argue that some outcomes are more likely than others, the effects of violence run the gamut from constructive policies of interethnic accommodation to governmental repression and ethnic bias, to the proliferation of armed groups, followed by more and better organized episodes of violence. The very serious Malaysian riot of 1969 and the equally serious Mauritian riot of 1968 were not followed by further episodes of violence. Comparable events in Chad and Nigeria, as well as Sri Lanka, however, produced spirals of increasing violence and, ultimately, warfare with international ramifications. Whether an ethnic riot will produce an impetus to compromise; whether it will produce policy changes favorable to one or another of the ethnic contestants, upsetting delicate policy balances and generating new grievances that legitimize organized resistance; or whether it will produce augmented armed forces that are provocative or unduly nervous and repressive — whether a riot will generate any of these common reactions is a question to which there is, at present, no answer. In a study of the effects of terrorist violence, Christopher Hewitt found a few consistent effects — chronic violence had, for example, a negative impact on the economy, particularly on tourism — but most results were inconsistent across countries. In some, politics became polarized, but this was not the result everywhere. A tendency to harsher security measures and military authoritarianism was evident, but democratic reforms were initiated, too.[13] In these divergent conditions, identifying the intervening

13. Christopher Hewitt, *Consequences of Political Violence* (Aldershot, England: Dartmouth, 1993), pp. 21–28, 97–109, 110–27.

variables that move a riot to produce one effect rather than another becomes a critical task.

DEGRADATION

Well within the ambit of aims that may be inferred from conduct is a cluster of goals involving humiliation, punishment, revenge, and dishonor. We know from the infliction of atrocities how important humiliation is to rioters. We know from reciprocal riots, initiated by target-group members in response to attacks on them elsewhere, and from riots that respond to guerrilla attacks, such as Malaysia (1945–46) and Sri Lanka (1983), or to the assassination of Indira Gandhi in Delhi (1984), that revenge is a frequent aim.[14] The matter goes beyond revenge for an act and can extend to revenge for a whole course of conduct or for an imputed manner or way of being — for Sikhs who were said to have gotten "too big for their boots"[15] — or (more remotely) for a series of defeats, massacres, tortures, and rebellions, in the case of traditional enemies.[16] We have also seen that revenge in these senses overlaps a vernacular notion of punishment, in which rioters act as if they are surrogates or unofficial state agents when the state has defaulted on its obligation to sanction transgressions by ethnic strangers.[17]

The retrieval of lost or endangered honor relates, of course, to the desire to impose domination on others or resist the domination of others.[18] In this respect, as in the quest for revenge, the riot and the feud have a great deal in common. In anti-Muslim riots in India, contend Roger Jeffery and Patricia M. Jeffery, the aim of taunting and humiliating is to reduce the victims' honor (*izzat*) "and demand their subservience."[19] The

14. For that matter, Delhi (1984) also had an element of revenge against Sikhs for the bad treatment being meted out against Hindus in Punjab. See Uma Chakravarti and Nandita Haksar, *The Delhi Riots: Three Days in the Life of a Nation* (New Delhi: Lancer International, 1987), p. 207.

15. Ibid., p. 216.

16. Sudhir Kakar, *The Colors of Violence: Cultural Identities, Religion, and Conflict* (Chicago: University of Chicago Press, 1996), pp. 48–51; Peter Loizos, "Intercommunal Killing in Cyprus," *Man* (n.s.) 23, no. 4 (December 1988): 639–53, at pp. 640, 648–49.

17. On the paragovernmental quality of feuding violence, see Christopher Boehm, *Blood Revenge: The Anthropology of Feuding in Montenegro and Other Tribal Societies* (Lawrence: University Press of Kansas, 1984), p. 183.

18. For the argument that honor is the prize of aggression, where aggression is not the means to other goals, see Jacob Black-Michaud, *Feuding Societies* (1975; Oxford: Basil Blackwell, 1980), pp. 25, 179, 186–88, 190.

19. Roger Jeffery and Patricia M. Jeffery, "The Bijnor Riots, October 1990," *Economic and Political Weekly*, March 5, 1994, pp. 551–58, at p. 556.

anti-Ahmadi riots in West Pakistan (1953) clearly had such a purpose, for the demand was that Ahmadis be declared non-Muslims. A second riot in 1974 achieved precisely that goal: an amendment to the Pakistan Constitution declaring Ahmadis to be non-Muslims.[20] Thereafter, Ahmadis were subject to an array of humiliations suggestive of downward caste mobility in the South Asian context, such as prohibitions on the use of common wells to obtain water.[21] A good many people dream of achieving such results — of dealing with strong neighbors by converting them into ranked subordinates or people outside the community.[22] Every so often, the opportunity to realize the dream arises, as it did in Nazi Germany. There, before the genocide, it was made clear to the Jews, by state policy and by social behavior, that they were dominated and dishonored.[23] In the absence of a state willing to participate actively in genocide, the riot can serve as an emblem of utter rejection by the community.

Violence, it is said, is useful for its perpetrators in "dramatizing the importance of key social ideas."[24] The reversal of invidious comparisons, the retrieval of imperiled respect, and the redistribution of honor are among the central purposive ideas embedded in the dramaturgy of the ethnic riot. The fact that fleeing refugees are often attacked, even as their flight helps reduce heterogeneity, suggests that degradation can be an aim independent of homogenization, not merely a second-best choice.

Many relationships, of course, are permeated with indignity, and all societies have their specified rituals of degradation. When everyday forms of contempt, mainly silent and silently borne, are transformed into public displays of collective humiliation, the injury is magnified manyfold. The ability to move from quiet contempt to dramatic humiliation

20. *Washington Post*, September 23, 1974, p. 1. See Constitution of the Islamic Republic of Pakistan, 1973, art. 106, cl. 3, as amended by Constitution (Second Amendment) Act 1974, Act No. 49 of 1974, § 2, and P.O. No. 14 of 1985, art. 2.

21. The analogy to racial pollution in the Jim Crow south of the United States would not be amiss.

22. See Roger Petersen, "Fear, Hatred, Resentment: Toward a More Comprehensive Understanding of Ethnic Violence in Eastern Europe" (unpublished paper, Department of Political Science, Washington University, St. Louis, 1997), p. 9.

23. Daniel Jonah Goldhagen, *Hitler's Willing Executioners: Ordinary Germans and the Holocaust* (New York: Alfred A. Knopf, 1996), p. 135. Following the terminology of Orlando Patterson, *Slavery and Social Death: A Comparative Study* (Cambridge: Harvard University Press, 1982), Goldhagen says the Jews were made to feel "socially dead." Nazi discourse was suffused with "teach-them-a-lesson" rhetoric. The Jews were said to be "impudent" and "to have grown too big." Goldhagen, *Hitler's Willing Executioners*, pp. 105, 107.

24. David Riches, "The Phenomenon of Violence," in David Riches, ed., *The Anthropology of Violence* (Oxford: Basil Blackwell, 1986), p. 11.

implies a correlative inability of the victim to respond.[25] The demonstration of the ability and inability of the perpetrator and victim, respectively, constitutes the essence of the transaction. When, in addition, the demonstration is ceremonious, it can effect "a changed social identity," an affirmation or reaffirmation that the targets, temporarily subject to total control, are "of a lower species," placed outside the moral order.[26]

That people who ordinarily elude mastery by others, because they are aggressive or politically or psychologically powerful, can be mastered and degraded, that the ability to commit atrocities on them can turn them into playthings — recall the playful atmosphere surrounding atrocities: these are the ultimate reversals of honor. It matters, then, that Jews in Kaunas, Lithuania (1941), were forced to clean manure by hand from a garage floor and that their bodies were filled with water from hoses placed in their mouths before they were beaten to death, that Sikhs in Delhi (1984) had their beards shaved or burned, and that, after their death, the unidentified, decaying bodies were dug up by pigs.[27] These are not regarded by anyone as heroic deaths — the victims, after all, attempt to flee for their lives, sometimes in disguise — but as the deaths of people whose manner of dying is chosen to show that they no longer count.

Viewed this way, the deadly ethnic riot embodies physical destruction combined with degradation and the implicit threat of genocide. That the victims need the protection of the authorities or, worse, that the rioters kill with abandon until their thirst for killing is slaked reinforces the message that there is power to destroy the targets.

The measurement of honor is a difficult enterprise, and so it is uncertain just how much long-term success rioters achieve in this domain. Sometimes, however, explicit recognition, even certification, of their success can follow. The Ahmadis, clearly, were cast into a status far more degraded than the one they previously enjoyed. After riots, many aggressors are left to infer their success from policies that do not pertain explicitly to the contested issue of group honor but that implicitly decree a victory. (Of these, we shall speak later in the chapter.) Many target groups begin to lie low after such riots, to speak only among themselves of mat-

25. See James C. Scott, *Domination and the Acts of Resistance: Hidden Transcripts* (New Haven: Yale University Press, 1990), pp. 112–15.

26. Harold Garfinkel, "Conditions of Successful Degradation Ceremonies," *American Journal of Sociology* 61, no. 5 (March 1956): 420–24, at p. 421.

27. Petersen, "Fear, Hatred, Resentment," p. 14; Veena Das, "Our Work to Cry: Your Work to Listen (The Survivor of Collective Violence)" (unpublished paper, Delhi, n.d.), pp. 15, 64.

ters that could previously have been discussed openly or did not need to be discussed at all, and to develop their own forms of coded communication and underground humor. Aggressors, on the other hand — including those who approve of the violence but would not themselves engage in it — signal in a variety of ways that continued peace is conditioned on the targets' acceptance of the new terms, on their good behavior, so to speak. Conceived as a warning, degradation reduces the threat from the targets. The tendency of the targets to restrain challenges they might otherwise have advanced, in conjunction with the departure of large numbers of people from their homes, to which some will never return, the infrequency of revenge riots (those initiated by victims of previous riots) in the same space, and the commonplace acquiescence of victims in a new status quo unfavorable to them, indicates that dishonor is a goal frequently attained.

Save, of course, for those target groups that have their own territory, a homeland to which they can repair following the riot. For them, the riot is very often a new beginning, either of reciprocal revenge violence or of secessionist warfare (about which, more later). Consequently, within groups, one can identify bifurcated reactions. In Sinhalese areas, Tamils try to blend in or become Sinhalese, while, in Tamil areas, some Tamils become Tigers who kill Sinhalese. In the Brahmaputra Valley, Bengalis take care to speak Assamese, but, in Bengali-dominated Cachar, Bengalis speak of Cachar's leaving Assam. Between groups, too, something turns on possession of a territorially demarcated portion of a state. When Ibo were killed in large numbers in northern Nigeria (1966), more than one million of them returned to the Eastern Region of Nigeria to pursue the establishment of Biafra; when Chinese were killed in Malaysia (1969), they had nowhere to go. Demography may not be destiny, but whether rioters achieve their goals in general depends, unsurprisingly, on the territorial resources available to the targets following the violence.

HOMOGENIZATION

If degradation constitutes a form of proto-genocidal intention, then homogenization approaches genocidal aims more closely. There is abundant evidence that rioters want members of the target group to disappear: to die, to leave, or, occasionally, to renounce their identity and assume the identity of the aggressor group, restoring what is usually an idealized homogeneous status quo ante. If, in a severely divided society, group members do not generally relish the company of those across the ethnic boundary, then it is to be expected that, when conditions conduce to disorder, a major aim will be to reverse the circumstances that led to unwanted contact.

Rioters themselves proclaim homogenizing intentions. Slogans, leaflets, and warnings before the violence are explicit and abundant:

1. "Bongal Kheda!" [Drive out the Bengalis!]. A slogan in Assam (1960).

2. "Ceylon for the Sinhalese!" and "Sinhala from Point Pedro to Dondra Head!" [from one end of the country to the other]. Slogans in Sri Lanka (1958).

3. "Drive out the Chinese!" A leaflet in Sukabumi, Indonesia (1963).

4. "We must kill all Vietnamese in Cambodia." A rioter in Cambodia (1970).

5. "Russians get out . . . a war has begun." A notice posted in Tuva (1990).

6. "Indians go back." "Assam for the Assamese." Posters in Assam (1968).

7. "All Muslims — Leave our Country!" Leaflets in Burma (1988).

8. "Do not loot, but kill, the Tamils!" Wall slogans outside Colombo, Sri Lanka (1977).

9. "All non-tribals to leave by June 26"; those who did not would be "exterminated." Posters, Tripura (1980).

10. "East St. Louis must remain a white man's town." Slogan, East St. Louis (1917).

11. Muslims "quit India!" Leaflets, Meerut (1968); posters, Ahmedabad (1969).

12. "[S]end this damnable lot [the Coast Moors] out of the country." Newspaper, Sri Lanka (1915).

13. "The Kasaians [Luba] have looked after themselves; they have done nothing for us; so they must go. They must get out and if they don't we will make them pay." Shaba's governor, Kyungu wa-Kumwanza, Zaire (1993).

14. ". . . Bankim Chakma saw a decapitated chicken and its severed head hanging from a pole near his house. To the retired state-government employee, the message was clear: Clear out, or the fate of the chicken will be yours." Arunachal Pradesh, India (1994).

15. "[Y]ou prepare the ships, we will see to it that they embark — in two

days there will not be a single Indian left in the country." African rioters in Durban (1949) to the police.

16. "Get rid of the Mossi." Sign posted in Ivory Coast (1958).

17. "Madurese out." Graffiti, West Kalimantan, Indonesia (1997).

18. "We just don't want Madurese. All of the Madurese must leave." Rioter in West Kalimantan, wearing a recently severed human ear on a string around his neck (1999).

19. "Death to Uzbeks, safety for the Kirgiz." Kyrghyzstan (1990).[28]

Behavior speaks just as loudly. When people are forced across borders, as Rohingya have been repeatedly in Burma, or as whole villages of black Africans were in Mauritania (1989),[29] and as Bangladeshis were after Bombay (1992), when they are encouraged to leave cities or when their homes, rebuilt after violence, are then destroyed again,[30] and when they

28. Sources, by number, are as follows: (1) K.C. Barua, *Assam: Her People and Her Language* (Shillong, Assam: Lawyers' Book Stall, 1960), pp. 16–17; (2) Tarzie Vittachi, *Emergency '58: The Story of the Ceylon Race Riots* (London: André Deutsch, 1958), p. 33; (3) The Siauw Giap, "Group Conflict in a Plural Society," *Revue du Sud-Est Asiatique*, no. 1 (January 1966): 1–31, at p. 7; (4) *Washington Post*, April 14, 1970, p. A12; (5) *Los Angeles Times*, November 13, 1990, p. 2; (6) Memorandum from K.P. Tripathy, Assam minister of finance and labor, to prime minister, deputy prime minister, and home minister, undated, 1968, p. 1; (7) Bentil Lintner, *Outrage: Burma's Struggle for Democracy* (London: White Lotus, 1990), p. 80; (8) *Economic and Political Weekly*, September 10, 1977, pp. 1603–05, at p. 1605; (9) *Keesing's Contemporary Archives*, November 21, 1980, p. 30576; (10) Elliott M. Rudwick, *Race Riot at East St. Louis, July 2, 1917* (Carbondale: Southern Illinois University Press, 1964), p. 28; see ibid., p. 44; (11) Aswini K. Ray and Subhash Chakravarti, *Meerut Riots: A Case Study* (New Delhi: Sampradayikta Virodhi Committee, 1968), p. 4; Ghanshyam Shah, "Communal Riots in Gujarat," *Economic and Political Weekly* Annual Number, January 1970, pp. 187–200, at p. 188; (12) Stanley J. Tambiah, *Leveling Crowds: Ethnonationalist Conflicts and Collective Violence in South Asia* (Berkeley and Los Angeles: University of California Press, 1996), p. 58; (13) *The Guardian*, January 4, 1993, p. 6; (14) *Far Eastern Economic Review*, November 17, 1994, p. 20; (15) Union of South Africa, *Report of the Commission of Enquiry into Riots in Durban* (Cape Town: Cape Times, 1949), p. 4; (16) Efrem Siegel, "Ivory Coast: Booming Economy, Political Calm," *Africa Report*, April 1970, pp. 18–21; (17) *Jakarta Post*, March 2, 1997, p. 1; (18) *Independent* (London), March 22, 1999, p. 11; (19) Valery Tishkov, *Ethnicity, Nationalism and Conflict in and after the Soviet Union* (London: Sage, 1997), p. 151.

29. E.g., *Far Eastern Economic Review*, May 19, 1978, pp. 36–37; Human Rights Watch, *Mauritania's Campaign of Terror: State-Sponsored Repression of Black Africans* (New York: Human Rights Watch, 1994), pp. 13–17.

30. Amrita Basu, "When Local Riots Are Not Merely Local: Bringing the State Back In, Bijnor, 1988–92," *Economic and Political Weekly*, October 1, 1994, pp. 2605–21, at pp. 2612–13; Gunbir Singh, "Hindutva's Low-Intensity War against Bombay's Riot Victims," ibid., May 8, 1993, pp. 908–10.

are forced to abandon distinctive dress and other badges of identity as the price of safety, as they were in Assam (1960),[31] the inference is inescapable that rioters aim to create a homogeneous environment.[32] If the differentiation is religious, a rare but not unknown practice is to afford a victim the option of conversion or death;[33] but, if group boundaries are not deemed porous, conversion does not avail, as it did not for most Sikhs in Delhi (1984).[34] If the targets are defined not merely as strangers but as foreigners with an alternative homeland, the choice between expulsion and death may be offered to some of the victims, as it was for many Dahomeyans in the Ivory Coast (1958), for some Hindus in west Punjab (1947), and even for Ibo in certain northern Nigerian towns (1966) and some Armenians in Baku (1990).[35] When some victims are killed and others are put on boats, it seems clear that rioters are intent on creating a society purged of the irritating presence of the targets.[36]

There are times, in the most organized riots, when the rioters have obvious pecuniary motives for removing the targets physically. They may covet a certain class of position in which the targets are heavily represented,[37] or aspire to succeed to their property.[38] But most rioters and riot instigators are not in a position to compete for such positions; and, as I have suggested, killing people and burning property are far more prevalent than are looting or seizing property. Land sometimes is a motive, but it is particularly so in reciprocal riots, in which the earlier targets, driven from their homes, need shelter across the border for themselves and for

31. Charu Chandra Bhandari, *Thoughts on Assam Disturbances* (Rajghat: A.B. Sarva Seva Prakhashan, 1961), pp. 20–23, 36.

32. Revealingly, in Nigeria, where there was no international boundary dividing the north from the Ibo homeland, northerners aspired to create one in May 1966, for the slogan of the rioters was the secessionist "Araba" (Let us part). Ruth First, *Power in Africa* (New York: Pantheon Books, 1970), p. 311.

33. See, e.g., Penderel Moon, *Divide and Quit* (Berkeley and Los Angeles: University of California Press, 1962), pp. 125–26; Government of [West] Punjab, *Report of the Court of Inquiry Constituted under Punjab Act II of 1954 to Enquire into the Punjab Disturbance of 1953* (Lahore: Superintendent of Government Printing, 1954), p. 176.

34. Citizens' Commission, Delhi, *Delhi, 31 October to 4 November 1984, Report of the Citizens' Commission* (New Delhi: Citizens' Commission, 1985), p. 25.

35. Gwendolen M. Carter, *Independence for Africa* (New York: Praeger, 1960), p. 113; Moon, *Divide and Quit*, pp. 193–200, 223; N.J. Miners, *The Nigerian Army, 1956–1966* (London: Methuen, 1971), p. 203; *Washington Post*, January 24, 1990, p. 34.

36. For the view that this was the aim of rioters, see Walter Schwarz, *Nigeria* (New York: Praeger, 1968), pp. 215–16; First, *Power in Africa*, pp. 328–29.

37. See, e.g., Elliott P. Skinner, "Strangers in West African Societies," *Africa* 33, no. 4 (1963): 307–20, at p. 314; *Report of the Presidential Commission of Inquiry into the Incidents Which Took Place between 13th August and 15th September 1977*, p. 207.

38. P.R. Ragjopal, *Communal Violence in India* (New Delhi: Uppal, 1987), p. 85.

other refugees. While this helps to explain motives in later riots — and helps to explain an accelerating spiral of violence, once refugees have crossed borders en masse, as in Punjab (1947)[39] — it helps not at all in explaining the earlier riots. Moreover, succession to property is not always recognized:

> One of the recent trends in communal riots is the motivation of communal elements who engineer the riots with a view to making what are presently mixed localities into homogeneous ones. . . . They expect the minorities in the respective pockets to make distress sale of their properties at throwaway prices in their anxiety to move to areas in which the majority of their community live. During the Ahmedabad communal riots of 1985 it was alleged that there was a deep seated political-police-underworld nexus, which was interested in such sales. The government responded to this very effectively by refusing to recognise the transactions relating to the transfer of property which had taken place after a particular date.[40]

The same policy of lack of recognition was followed after Guyana (1964).[41] Still, the riots occur; indeed, Ahmedabad itself had one a year later. There does not seem to be any way around recognition of the aim to homogenize as such and for itself, more than as a means to another aim.

Homogeneity is valued because, as we have observed, the capacities of and dangers posed by target groups are exaggerated and their negative impact on the fulfillment of the aggressors is emphasized. Very often it is thought, generally erroneously, that the society was homogeneous in the past and that homogeneity contributed to happiness and self-expression, to being at home in one's own land and being free of invidious comparisons constantly generated by the presence of ethnic strangers.

As an aim, homogeneity may seem to be at odds with (mere) degradation, but it is not. After all, if it is possible to remove the targets by a combination of extermination and expulsion, why bother to humiliate them? Simply because, for the aggressors, living in an environment with a controlled and degraded target group is a good second-best to living in

---

39. Moon, *Divide and Quit*, pp. 263–64, 280–82. Moon explains that, because Sikhs would otherwise be divided between a Muslim west Punjab and Hindu east Punjab, they were determined to concentrate all Sikhs on the Indian side. The combination of their revenge for Muslim killings in the west and their need for space in the east created special aggressiveness by Sikhs toward Muslims, thereby provoking further Muslim killing of Sikhs on the Pakistan side.

40. P.R. Rajgopal, *Communal Violence in India* (New Delhi: Uppal, 1987), p. 85.

41. For the recommendation, see Government of British Guiana, *Report of the National Rehabilitation Committee* (Georgetown: The Government Printery, mimeo., 1965), pp. 23–24.

a homogeneous environment. In any case, the deadly riot, while it deals in humiliation rather than complete removal, is a rather obvious portent, an installment along the way. And homogenization is not an all-or-nothing proposition: it is quantitative and therefore altogether relative. Some is better than none.

Homogeneity is what rioters want, and growing homogeneity is what they get. (As we shall soon see, homogenization makes possible some other outcomes of violence that rioters assuredly do not want.) By far the most common consequence of the riot, apart from death, is the production of refugees. Sometimes they return quickly, as 20,000 Indian Muslims returned from Bangladesh within two weeks of the riot in Nadia, West Bengal (1979).[42] But many refugees never return. A severe episode of killing can produce a stark change in population composition. In Equatorial Guinea (1978), almost half the population, nearly all non-Fang, was said to have fled repeated violence (not all of it riots).[43] After Sri Lanka (1983), there were nearly a million internal refugees in the country. The Eastern Province lost a substantial portion of its Tamil population. Formerly a very mixed province in undivided India, Punjab became remarkably homogeneous on each side of the border after 1947, attesting to one of the great refugee flows of the twentieth century. If there is somewhere else to go — and there is not always somewhere else — riot victims will go there, unless the police and home government take prompt steps to assure their safety.

From what we know of retaliatory violence across borders, it seems reasonable to assume that target groups with ties to other countries will be more likely to flee in the first instance and not to return later than will those who are not identified with a homeland elsewhere. Some 200,000 or more Vietnamese, at least 40 percent of the Vietnamese population, left Cambodia in the wake of violence there in 1970.[44] The various mass repatriations in Africa — from the Ivory Coast (1958), from Gabon (1981), from Mauritania and Senegal (1989) — suggest that target groups see themselves as especially vulnerable if they are found on the wrong side of a border. Some 220,000 Armenians left Baku in 1988. Before long, their place was taken by 130,000 Azeris fleeing Armenia. After the 1990 riot in Baku, the reciprocal exodus was nearly complete in the two republics. Russians in Tuva, Uzbeks in Kyrghyzstan, Tajiks and Meshketian Turks in Uzbekistan, Armenians and Russians in Tajikistan —

42. *Far Eastern Economic Review*, July 20, 1979, pp. 32–33.
43. *Washington Post*, January 25, 1978, p. A15.
44. Ibid., August 3, 1970, p. A12.

all fled after violence against them.[45] In Tuva, a cobalt mine nearly stopped functioning once its Russian director and skilled workers left, and the departure of Russian specialists also hurt a variety of Tajik industries. Rohingyas fled Burma for Bangladesh in the hundreds of thousands every time there was violence against them, and some 20,000 Telugus returned to India after the riot in Burma (1930).[46] Two hundred thousand people were displaced in northern Ghana (1994); half of them fled to Togo.[47] The other side of a border means safety.

State and provincial borders can serve the same purpose — witness the flight of Ibo to the former Eastern Region (1966) and Tiv refugee flows from Taraba state to Benue state (1990–93), where Tiv are in a stronger position, or the flow of Bengalis to West Bengal after each riot in Assam, or the enormous exodus of Luba from Luluabourg to south Kasai (1959) and from Shaba to east and west Kasai (1993), or the repeated departures of Tamils to the north of Sri Lanka. With each episode of violence, more members of the target group flee. How many ultimately return to the location of the violence is uncertain, but it seems clear that a smaller fraction returns after each successive riot. Fears for safety grow as violent events can no longer be described as idiosyncratic.

Not only do target groups flee, reducing heterogeneity as they go, but third groups — groups not targeted — sometimes also decide to leave. Many Punjabis left Sind after Sindhis targeted Mohajirs (1972),[48] just as Russians fled Kyrghyzstan after Kyrghyz killed Uzbeks (1990).[49] In Baku (1990), the suppression of anti-Armenian riots by Soviet troops produced revenge violence against Russians, and the result was the same: two streams of refugees, Armenian and Russian, rather than just one. One flight may not be enough, however, if there is no homeland to which to flee. Many Chakma fled Bangladesh (then East Pakistan) in 1964, set-

---

45. So, too, did Ingush flee North Ossetia, although the violence directed against them took more than one form. Some of it was highly organized and militarized; some was riot behavior. See Tishkov, *Ethnicity, Nationalism and Conflict in and after the Soviet Union,* ch. 9. A large number of Slavs and Germans also left Kyrghyzstan after the anti-Uzbek violence. Eugene Huskey, "Kyrgyzstan: The Politics of Demographic and Economic Frustration," in Ian Bremmer and Ray Taras, eds., *New States, New Politics: Building the Post-Soviet Nations* (Cambridge: Cambridge University Press, 1997), p. 663.

46. E.L.F. Andrew, *Indian Labour in Rangoon* (Calcutta: Oxford University Press, 1933), p. 286.

47. Ruby Ofori, "Rawlings' Biggest Challenge," *Africa Report* 39, no. 3 (May–June 1994): 53–55, at p. 54.

48. *Far Eastern Economic Review,* August 5, 1972, p. 16.

49. Abidin Bozdağ, "Crisis and Democracy in Kirgizia," *Aussenpolitik* 43, no. 3 (n.m., 1992): 277–86.

tling mainly in Assam and moving ultimately to what became Arunachal Pradesh in 1987.[50] There they were threatened with violence in 1994, whereupon some moved, and others contemplated moving, yet again. Precisely the same fate awaited many Meskhetian Turks, attacked in Uzbekistan (1989) and relocated in Krasnodar, where they were threatened again.[51] The price of homogenization in the original home area is not, in such a case, reconcentration elsewhere, but dispersion, for the new hosts may be as unfriendly as the old.

As I have said, it is difficult to know how many refugees fail to return, especially since the fraction changes with ethnic relations in the riot zone. After the riot in Delhi (1984), a count in one housing area found that 30 percent of Sikhs formerly residing there had resettled in Punjab.[52] (Many Sikhs who did this had had no former contact with Punjab; they simply sought safety.[53]) Where target-group fractions of the population are smaller to begin with and insecurity is accordingly greater, it seems probable that larger percentages resettle. Again, one cannot judge by the initial number of refugees alone, but it is suggestive that in Kanpur, where many fewer Sikhs were killed in 1984 but where many fewer lived, a number approaching half the Sikh population departed.[54]

The result of all such movements is a growing separation of populations, not just in the large but at the regional and local levels as well. Following the anti-Chinese riot in West Kalimantan, Indonesia (1967), Chinese fled rural areas for the main towns, depleting the rural economy.[55] A similar effect was achieved in Malaysia (1945–46), when violence pushed Chinese toward towns, leaving many rural areas entirely Malay.[56] Non-Sindhis fled the interior of Sind after the anti-Mohajir riot

---

50. Other Chakma are in Assam, Tripura, and Mizoram, while still others have returned to Bangladesh or migrated elsewhere in India.

51. *Forced Migration Monitor* (New York), no. 22 (March 1998): 6–7.

52. Chakravarti and Haksar, *The Delhi Riots*, p. 583.

53. Ibid., pp. 119–22.

54. Harsh Sethi, "The Citizens' Response: A Glimmer of Possibilities," in Smitu Kothari and Harsh Sethi, eds., *Voices from a Scarred City: The Delhi Carnage in Perspective* (Delhi: Lokayan, 1985), pp. 69–70. Basu, "When Local Riots Are Not Merely Local," pp. 2612–13, reports a much-reduced Muslim presence in Bijnor after the 1992 violence. Before the riot, Muslims comprised 48 percent of the population, and the aim, claims Basu, was to make all space in Bijnor unsafe for Muslims. Caste Hindus were, she says, obsessively fearful of the growing size and power of the Muslim population in the city.

55. Hugh Mabbett and Ping-Ching Mabbett, "The Chinese Community in Indonesia," in *The Chinese in Indonesia, the Philippines and Malaysia* (London: Minority Rights Group, 1972), p. 10.

56. Halinah Bamadhaj, "The Impact of the Japanese Occupation of Malaya on Malay Society and Politics (1941–1945)" (M.A. thesis, University of Auckland, 1975), pp. 22–23.

of 1972, and the tendency for rural Sind to become homogeneously Sindhi accelerated after later violent episodes.[57]

The same process affects neighborhoods.[58] The matter has been studied most closely with respect to housing intimidation in Northern Ireland. Every study finds that, with each outbreak of violence, the affected locality became more segregated.[59] Nor is this surprising. The violence generally occurred along the boundary where the two groups met. The parades that usually precipitated violence were intended partly to delimit territory claimed by each group. Once the violence began, houses of the target group were generally set alight, in a none-too-subtle hint that their occupants should leave; and, once group members evacuated an area and moved to a more homogeneous area of their own, the influx created pressure in the reception area, thus leading (as we have seen in the large in Punjab and elsewhere) to reciprocal intimidation of the minority in the reception area, finally making both the sending and receiving areas more homogeneous.[60]

Everywhere group members seek safer neighborhoods. After the riot in Jos (1945), Ibo shifted their population concentration from the native town to the township, and the process accelerated after the riot in Kano (1953).[61] Guyanese violence in 1964 led local minorities to leave their villages for the safety of homogeneous squatter areas.[62] Creoles fled Muslim

57. Tahir Amin, *Ethno-National Movements of Pakistan* (Islamabad: Institute of Policy Studies, 1988), pp. 125–26; Human Rights Commission of Pakistan, *Sindh Inquiry, Summer 1990* (Lahore: HRCP, 1990), pp. 15, 29, 41, 48, 61–62, 65.

58. See Ratna Naidu, *Old Cities, New Predicaments: A Study of Hyderabad* (New Delhi: Sage, 1990), pp. 121–22; Nancy Crawshaw, "Cyprus after Kophinou," *The World Today* 24, no. 10 (October 1968): 428–35; at p. 434; Shah, "Communal Riots in Gujarat," p. 187; K.C. Chakravarti, "Bongal Kheda Again," *Economic Weekly*, July 30, 1960, pp. 1193–95.

59. See John Darby, "Intimidation and Interaction in a Small Belfast Community: The Water and the Fish," in John Darby, Nicholas Dodge, and A.C. Hepburn, eds., *Political Violence: Ireland in a Comparative Perspective* (Belfast: Appletree Press, 1990), pp. 84, 85, 87; Michael Poole, "The Demography of Violence," in John Darby, ed., *Northern Ireland: The Background to the Conflict* (Belfast: Appletree Press, 1983), p. 154; Harold Jackson, *The Two Irelands — a Dual Study of Inter-Group Tensions* (London: Minority Rights Group, 1971), p. 11; *Violence and Civil Disturbances in Northern Ireland in 1969: Report of Tribunal of Inquiry*, Cmd. 566 (London: H.M.S.O., 1972), Vol. 1, p. 248.

60. See *Violence and Civil Disturbances in Northern Ireland in 1969*, Vol. 1, pp. 9, 133, 137; Jackson, *The Two Irelands*, p. 6; John Darby, *Intimidation and the Control of Conflict in Northern Ireland* (Dublin: Gill and Macmillan, 1986), pp. 88–89.

61. Leonard Plotnicov, "An Early Nigerian Civil Disturbance: The 1945 Hausa-Ibo Riot in Jos," *Journal of Modern African Studies* 9, no. 2 (August 1971): 297–305, at p. 304.

62. Government of British Guiana, *Report of the National Rehabilitation Committee* (Georgetown: Government Printery, mimeo., 1965), pp. 5–6.

areas after the violence in Mauritius (1968).[63] The Hindu-Muslim riot in Hyderabad (1990) induced Hindu members of the Pardis caste to relocate. Those who remained became "an embattled enclave in the walled city . . . ."[64] Following the recurrent violence of the 1990s in the Congo Republic, Brazzaville became a city divided into ethnic zones, and it was dangerous to move from one to another.[65] The violence in Karachi and Hyderabad of the 1980s and 1990s produced strong tendencies for Sindhis, Mohajirs, and Pathans to segregate themselves,[66] as the 1964 riots in Singapore did for Malays and Chinese.[67] In peaceful times, people migrate and mingle;[68] in violent times, they migrate and separate.

Members of the target group also seek safety at work. Sometimes, as in Mauritania (1989),[69] it is made clear that it is unsafe to stay; at other times, the targets choose to separate. They demanded segregated labor gangs on plantations after Guyana (1964).[70] In Sri Lanka (1977), as we have seen, plantation laborers sought employment on estates with overwhelmingly Tamil work forces, while salaried employees applied for transfers to safer locales.[71] In Karachi, institutions such as the bar and hospitals became completely divided by ethnic group, so that, just as there developed a sense that certain residential areas now belonged to one group or another,[72] so, too, did occupational space come to be divided.[73]

63. Thomas Hylland Eriksen, "A Future-Oriented, Non-Ethnic Nationalism? Mauritius as an Exemplary Case," *Ethnos* 58, nos. 3–4 (1993): 197–221, at p. 214.

64. Kakar, *The Colors of Violence*, p. 105. For the same result in east Delhi (1990), see Shalini D'Souza and Arundhuti Roy Choudhury, "The Riots and the Perception of the People: Notes from the Field," *Social Action* 44, no. 1 (January 1994): 114–25, at p. 123.

65. Kajsa Ekholm Friedman and Anne Sundberg, "Reorganization Efforts and the Threat of Ethnic War in Congo" (unpublished paper, Department of Social Anthropology, University of Lund, 1996), pp. 11–12.

66. Abbas Rashid and Farida Shahid, *Pakistan: Ethno-Politics and Contending Elites* (Geneva: U.N. Research Institute for Social Development, Discussion Paper no. 45, 1993), p. 25.

67. Lee Kuan Yew, *The Singapore Story* (Singapore: Times Editions, 1998), p. 563.

68. See generally Thomas Sowell, *Migrations and Cultures: A World View* (New York: Basic Books, 1996).

69. See *Africa Events*, June 1989, p. 23.

70. Here I am drawing on field interviews I conducted with Guyanese plantation managers in the mid-1960s.

71. Respectively, *Report of the Presidential Commission of Inquiry into the Incidents Which Took Place between 13th August and 15th September 1977*, p. 208; interview, Colombo, April 7, 1980.

72. Human Rights Commission of Pakistan, *Sindh Inquiry, Summer 1990*, pp. 39–41, 52.

73. Ibid., pp. 42, 44.

As it is no longer necessary to live near ethnic strangers, it no longer seems necessary or worth the risk to cooperate with them at work. Spatial separation and occupational separation are both products of the riot.

POLARIZATION

Even in the rare cases in which violence produces impulses to reconciliation among leaders, it produces more general polarization. Richard D. Lambert puts the effect succinctly: "When one is subject to stray assault or mob attack upon the basis of his association with a religious community, he is quickly impressed with the significance of that membership. Thus the accumulating nature of social violence in turn broadens and intensifies the basic tension upon which it feeds."[74] Polarization encompasses outgroup aversion and ingroup solidarity.

As groups are divided from each other, narrower definitions of identity take hold. Before the 1986 Karachi riot, Mohajirs were content to be called "Pakistanis." The situation changed after the riot, and Mohajirs began to be more serious about their demand for "fifth nationality" status.[75] The 1989 violence in Mauritania "destroyed what fragile understanding there was between the Moors and black African sections of the population, leaving fear and mistrust on both sides."[76] Once Moorish refugees returned from Senegal "with stories of their sufferings, Moorish opinion in Mauritania turned very hostile towards any black African. People began to say openly that Mauritania meant the country of the Moors, and that black Africans were not really Mauritanians, whatever their official nationality."[77] Hindu and Sikh refugees from the 1947 partition violence in Pakistan who settled in north India had poor relations with their Muslim neighbors, who tended to dislike them in turn.[78]

The polarizing effects of violence are visible in the one study that depicts interethnic attitudes before and after riots: a study of Mohajirs'

74. Richard D. Lambert, "Hindu-Muslim Riots" (Ph.D. diss., University of Pennsylvania, 1951), p. 17.

75. Charles H. Kennedy, "Managing Ethnic Conflict: The Case of Pakistan," in John Coakley, ed., *The Territorial Management of Ethnic Conflict* (London: Frank Cass, 1993), pp. 131–33.

76. *Africa Events*, June 1989, p. 23.

77. Ibid.

78. Steven I. Wilkinson, "The Electoral Incentives for Ethnic Violence: Hindu-Muslim Riots in India" (Ph.D. diss., M.I.T., 1998), p. 214. See Raghuraj Gupta, *Hindu-Muslim Relations* (Lucknow: Ethnographic and Folk Culture Society, 1976), p. 171.

images of Sindhis in 1970 and 1988.[79] In 1970, right at the outset of a long series of Sindhi-Mohajir riots, Mohajirs saw Sindhis as possessing character traits only slightly more negative than those Mohajirs imputed to themselves, and on some dimensions Mohajirs were marginally more positive toward Sindhis than toward themselves. By 1988, at the height of the violence, Mohajirs were somewhat more flattering toward themselves than before and far less flattering toward Sindhis, whom they painted almost uniformly in negative terms. In 1970, the overall mean rating differential on a scale of one to seven was very small (one-eighth of the scale), and Mohajir evaluations of both groups clustered near the midpoint. By 1988, the overall mean differential had grown fivefold, Mohajir mean ratings of Sindhis had declined to well under two (one was the most negative rating), and Mohajir mean ratings of Mohajirs had increased to a point just above six (seven being the most positive). It is a fair inference that the violence and events associated with it had led Mohajirs to widen the gap between their evaluations of themselves and Sindhis.

Of course, extreme changes of this kind are likely to be ephemeral if the violence subsides, but attitudes are unlikely to return to anything like the earlier friendliness. The violence in Soweto, South Africa, in 1976 was not a deadly ethnic riot, but rather a violent protest demonstration that met with deadly repression. Nevertheless, it appears to have had a durable negative effect on interethnic attitudes. White attitudes toward Africans hardened after 1976, and African attitudes toward Afrikaners (but, interestingly, not toward English-speaking whites) grew decidedly less favorable.[80]

Hostile behavior follows hostile attitudes. There was an African boycott of Indian traders after the Durban riot (1949)[81] and considerable reluctance on the part of Chinese to deal with Malays after Kuala Lumpur (1969).[82] I have recounted previously how a riot in Burundi

79. Abdul Haque, "Generational Changes in Ethnic Stereotypes Held by Second and Third Generations of Urdu-Speaking Youth toward Sindhi-Speaking in Pakistan," *Pakistan Journal of Psychological Research* 4, nos. 1–2 (Summer 1989): 17–25. The respondents were students, and the instrument was a semantic differential test.

80. J.M. Nieuwoudt and C. Plug, "South African Ethnic Attitudes: 1973 to 1978," *Journal of Social Psychology* 121, Second Half (December 1983): 163–71. For later studies, see Donald L. Horowitz, *A Democratic South Africa? Constitutional Engineering in a Divided Society* (Berkeley and Los Angeles: University of California Press, 1991), p. 43 n.3.

81. Leo Kuper, *An African Bourgeoisie: Race, Class and Politics in South Africa* (New Haven: Yale University Press, 1965), p. 301.

82. Here I am drawing on conversations with Malaysian Chinese in the period following the riot.

(1988) by Hutu led directly to genocide and how riots have led to recurrent violence in certain north Indian cities, in Assam, in northeast Ghana, in West Kalimantan, in Wukari in Nigeria, and in Karachi.[83] Many of these episodes were accompanied by a growing paramilitarization of ethnic relations.[84]

Violent organizations and parties making extreme demands quite generally benefit from support proffered after riots. The Hindu Rashtriya Swayamsevak Sangh (RSS) was founded as a paramilitary "self-defense" organization after the performance of Hindus in the Nagpur (1923) riot was seen to be deficient.[85] The Tamil Tigers were identifiable by 1976, but they really grew up in response to the 1977 riot and profited further from the 1983 Sri Lankan violence. Earlier, polarization had followed the 1958 riot, when the Federal Party took support from the less militant Tamil Congress and the United National Party became increasingly anti-Tamil in order to stay competitive with the Sri Lanka Freedom Party. This is a standard pattern.[86]

If intergroup cleavages widen after riots, intragroup cleavages are likely to narrow. Both occurred in Mauritius (1968), a riot precipitated by efforts of a Creole party to break out of its minority status by attracting Hindus and Muslims.[87] Following Muslim-Creole violence, the two groups, which "had learned to live with each other, became terrified of each other. The Muslims turned to the Hindus for support."[88] Eventually, Indians, regardless of religious identity, ended up on one side, while Creoles were on the other. Enhanced intragroup solidarity was also the effect of repeated violent episodes in India during much of the twentieth century.[89] Early in the century, it would scarcely have been possible to regard Hindus and Muslims as cohesive entities, given India's fragmented

83. See Chapter 10, above.

84. Which also afflicted the Congo Republic. Anne Sundberg, "When Is the Party Over? The Problem of Change in an African One-Party System" (unpublished paper, Department of Social Anthropology, University of Lund, March 1997), p. 19.

85. D.V. Kelkar, "The R.S.S.," *Economic Weekly*, February 4, 1950, p. 133.

86. See, e.g., Michael Feldberg, *The Philadelphia Riots of 1844: A Study of Ethnic Conflict* (Westport, Conn.: Greenwood Press, 1975), pp. 133-38, reporting that a nativist party gained support after the riot. See generally Tambiah, *Leveling Crowds*, pp. 223, 255-56.

87. See Chapter 6, pp. 217-19, above.

88. Adele Smith Simmons, "Politics in Mauritius since 1934: A Study of Decolonization in a Plural Society" (D. Phil. thesis, Oxford University, 1969), p. 477.

89. See Jeffery and Jeffery, "The Bijnor Riots, October 1990," p. 556; Anthony Parel, "The Political Symbolism of the Cow in India," *Journal of Commonwealth Political Studies* 7, no. 3 (November 1969): 179-203, at pp. 192-93.

social structure, but violence diminished internal disjunctions. The partition riots in Punjab, for example, reduced divisions among Muslims and brought Hindus and Sikhs together as well.[90] The anti-Sikh riot in Delhi (1984) accelerated the rupture of Hindu-Sikh ties that had been solidified in 1947, and it also enhanced pan-Sikh unity.[91] Sikhs who had originated in Sind, rather than Punjab, began to participate in traditions unknown to them formerly, after the violence drove home their common identity with Sikhs elsewhere.[92] A similarly ironic result followed Sri Lanka (1983). Many Colombo Tamils, without ties to Jaffna and hostile to the separatism that began to flourish there, were brought closer by the violence to the Jaffna Tamils; but some chose emigration instead.[93] The violence of the 1980s in Assam also brought a newfound emphasis on the links of the Assamese, an amalgamated group, to related peoples in neighboring states in which Bengalis could also be seen as the enemy: Meghalaya, Mizoram, Arunachal Pradesh, and Tripura.[94] Post-riot tendencies to solidarity are strong.[95]

CIVIL AND SECESSIONIST WARFARE

A common effect of the deadly ethnic riot is further violence, often in the form of organized warfare. This is not surprising, given the growth of

90. Lambert, "Hindu-Muslim Riots," pp. 198, 204.

91. Chakravarti and Haksar, The Delhi Riots, pp. 169, 172, 188–89, 201, 239.

92. Ibid., pp. 79, 81 n.5.

93. Kanapathipillai, "July 1983: The Survivor's Experience," p. 334.

94. Sanjib Barua, "'Ethnic' Conflict as State-Society Struggle: The Poetics and Politics of Assamese Micro-Nationalism," Modern Asian Studies 28, no. 3 (July 1994): 649–71, at p. 659.

95. As interethnic divergence can have organizational manifestations, so can intraethnic convergence. After the 1969 riot in Kuala Lumpur, Malaysian Chinese political parties held discussions among themselves, and a "Chinese Unity Movement" was launched, just as similar conversations were being held among Malays. See Heng Pek Koon, Chinese Politics in Malaysia: A History of the Malaysian Chinese Association (Singapore: Oxford University Press, 1988), p. 265; N.J. Funston, Malay Politics in Malaysia: A Study of the United Malays National Organisation and Party Islam (Kuala Lumpur: Heinemann Educational Books, 1980), p. 226. Ultimately, to be sure, it was possible for much of the Chinese and Malay opposition to join the government, in coalition with parties they had fought for the votes of their respective groups. See Karl von Vorys, Democracy without Consensus: Communalism and Political Stability in Malaysia (Princeton: Princeton University Press, 1975), p. 428. That the 1969 Malaysian riot at first increased the felt distance between Malays and Chinese, but that the increased distance did not preclude a broadened Malay-Chinese coalition, suggests not merely growing intraethnic solidarity but the existence of forces operating to counter Malay-Chinese polarization. Similarly, the strong impetus to polarization that followed Mauritius (1968) also gave way to conciliatory impulses. It needs to be underlined, however, that these are extraordinary. The usual

armed organizations as a result of riots and the diffusion of doubt about whether it is possible to live together after the killing. The additional violence can take the form of civil war if the groups are territorially intermixed or of secessionist movements if they are territorially separated.

Civil war is the less likely event, but it is not impossible. The riot in Sumgait (1988) precipitated a flow of refugees not only from Azerbaijan proper but also from Stepanakert and Shusha, the main towns of Nagorno-Karabagh, leaving them homogeneous and paving the way for the Armenian-Azeri battle for the *oblast*. The Malaysian violence of 1945–46 probably also contributed to the determination of Chinese guerrillas who had fought the Japanese to begin an insurrection against the British colonial government. The 1929 riot in Palestine was the prelude to a rebellion that pitted Arab forces against Jewish forces and both against British forces. The party-based ethnic violence in the Congo Republic (1993) also turned into something approaching civil war in Brazzaville. Civil war is certainly a danger.

What is noteworthy, however, is how unusual these instances are and how tenuous are the causal linkages even in these instances. Before the Sumgait violence, the Karabagh soviet had actually resolved that the region be transferred to Armenia.[96] The armed struggle did not begin until 1991, and it was made possible by the dissolution of the Soviet Union and by the weapons the Red Army left behind. The violence by Malays undoubtedly hardened the resistance of the Chinese guerrillas, but the insurrection owed more to foreign Communist direction, to British abandonment of the Malayan Union scheme that would have made the Chinese equal citizens, and to British suppression of Communist-affiliated trade unions than it did to the earlier Malay attacks.[97] The Palestinian rebellion began in 1936, seven years after the riot, and was very much a result of Arab factional outbidding, Jewish land purchases, and inconsistent British immigration policies that

---

effect of violence is polarization, a continuation of the growing bipolarity that precedes the riot and is also fostered by the need for an economy of antipathy in conducting violence.

96. Claude Mutafian, "The Struggle for Unification: 1988 Onwards," in Christopher J. Walker, ed., *Armenia and Karabagh: The Struggle for Unity* (London: Minority Rights Publications, 1991), pp. 123–24.

97. For varying assessments, see John Coates, *Suppressing Insurgency: An Analysis of the Malayan Emergency, 1948–1954* (Boulder, Colo.: Westview Press, 1992), pp. 12–18; Richard Stubbs, *Hearts and Minds: The Malayan Emergency 1948–1960* (Singapore: Oxford University Press, 1989), pp. 46–62; Michael Stenson, *Class, Race and Colonialism in West Malaysia* (St. Lucia, Queensland: University of Queensland Press, 1980), pp. 122–30; Gordon P. Means, *Malaysian Politics,* 1st ed. (New York: New York University Press, 1970), pp. 75–78.

restricted and then facilitated the influx of Jewish settlers in the wake of the Nazi seizure of power in Germany.[98] Finally, the Brazzaville situation was as much a stalemate as an active civil war.[99]

In many other riots where groups are intermixed, including other riots in several of these countries, civil war did not follow. There are interests in peace, as there are interests in civil war. I refer here not to the general interest in prosperity, which is rarely sufficient to dissuade actors from jeopardizing it by violent means — witness Lebanon, Cyprus, and Sri Lanka — but the concrete interests of whole groups and of political leaders. The peace that followed the riots in Mauritius (1968) and Malaysia (1969) will be examined when we explain negative cases in the next chapter. Suffice it to say briefly here that group interests and leadership interests need to be analyzed separately.

Take first the situation of target groups that are territorially intermixed with those who have attacked them. They will be reluctant to proceed from riot to warfare. Although a group victimized in the riot may wish to seek revenge, or to overthrow the conditions that gave rise to its victimization, or to punish the authorities who failed to protect it, the group is vulnerable to further victimization if it attempts to use violence for these purposes. The post-riot atmosphere, as we have observed, is hardly likely to be filled with contrition on the part of the perpetrators. Recurrence cannot be ruled out if the targets give offense. There is, to my knowledge, no instance of an intermixed target group that turned the tables without precipitating yet another set of attacks on it, and there are more than a few cases, including India-Pakistan (1946–47) and the episodes reviewed in the recurrent riots section of Chapter 10, in which such tactics produced extensive rioting back and forth. The inclination of the perpetrators to use violence in conditions favorable to them generally deters the targets, who are, therefore, inclined to lie low after a riot.

The situation of territorially separate groups may be different. The existence of a territorial base gives the victims a destination to which to flee. No such escape is possible for target groups lacking a home region. Contrast post-riot conditions in Malaysia (1969) with those in Sri Lanka (1983). Whereas the vast majority of Chinese lived within striking distance of Malays, this was not true of those Sri Lankan Tamils who inhabit the homogeneous Jaffna peninsula. Tamil separatists had a base

98. Yehoshua Porath, *The Palestinian Arab National Movement: From Riots to Rebellion* (London: Frank Cass, 1977), Vol. 2, pp. 49–161.

99. Friedman and Sundberg, "Reorganization Efforts and the Threat of Ethnic War in Congo," p. 7.

of operations and could be ruthless about the interests of Tamils remaining in Sinhalese or heterogeneous areas, not all of whom had connections to Jaffna. To be sure, had the Communist insurrection been ongoing in Malaysia at the time of the 1969 riot, the outcome there might have been different, for there would have been preexisting jungle bases to which to repair. Without such bases, territorially intermixed targets are likely to propitiate the group whose members have attacked them — which is to say that an ethnic riot in conditions of territorial intermixture will almost surely aggravate an ongoing insurrection but will not likely lead to one. Sequencing is extraordinarily important in such matters.

The interests of politicians of the target group are also different where groups are territorially separate.[100] If political leaders of a territorially intermixed target group countenance resort to arms, the maximal gain they are likely to achieve is a share of power, perhaps a modest share, once they have shown their strength. This much they might have been able to achieve without applying force. If they lose, they stand to lose everything. On the other hand, the potential gains of leaders of territorially separate groups are inestimably greater, while their potential losses may be smaller. Even if they lose, they may wring some concessions from the center, whose reach they may still be beyond. If, however, separatist warfare succeeds, separatist leaders, previously small fish in a big pond, stand to become big fish in a small pond. Typically, they have been ethnic-minority leaders unable to expand their clientele beyond their own group. With the success of secessionism, or even the grant of a generous measure of regional autonomy, they become leaders of a state or of a region in a larger state. They, therefore, begin with incentives to choose separatism. Once the riot makes the calculus of their followers congruent with their own, separatist warfare may begin in earnest.[101]

Among target groups with a homeland, therefore, separatism frequently follows the deadly riot. The Bihar riot (1946) apparently hardened Mohammed Ali Jinnah's determination to pursue the creation of Pakistan.[102] Among Sikhs, support for an independent Khalistan increased dramatically after Delhi (1984),[103] and the Punjab insurgency assumed

100. I discuss the interests of leaders of the initiator group in Chapter 12, below.

101. I have elaborated such arguments in Donald L. Horowitz, "Self-Determination: Politics, Philosophy, and Law," NOMOS 39 (1997): 421–63; and Horowitz, "Irredentas and Secessions: Adjacent Phenomena, Neglected Connections," in Naomi Chazan, ed., Irredentism and International Relations (Boulder, Colo.: Lynne Rienner, 1991), pp. 9–22.

102. Herbert Feldman, "The Communal Problem in the Indo-Pakistan Subcontinent: Some Current Implications," Pacific Affairs 42, no. 2 (Summer 1969): 145–63, at p. 155.

103. Chakravarti and Haksar, The Delhi Riots, pp. 526–27.

considerably greater proportions. The killing of Muslim Rohingyas by Burmans in 1942 led to the flight of 80,000 of them to Bengal and to a Mujaheed rebellion after World War II. These watershed events could scarcely have been forgotten when widespread anti-Rohingya riots began in Burma (1983). Within a short time, they produced the same effects: refugees and a Kawthoolei Muslim Liberation Front.[104] The secessionist movements in Nigeria after 1966 and Sri Lanka after 1977 (and especially 1983) were also, of course, produced by riots against targets who then became separatist. Separatist leaders no longer had to deal with so many reluctant followers.

Indispensable to target-group secessionism is the back-migration of group members who are outside the home region. If they remain outside in their previous numbers, they continue to be exposed to attack, and yet they probably still believe it is possible to live in an undivided state. Very likely, they are outside the region for a reason: they are in positions that produce earnings, significant portions of which are probably being remitted to the home region. If secessionism grows strong while a large fraction of group members is not in the separatist territory, the home region stands to lose remittances and some of its population, often the most talented part of the population. The dispersion of group members is, therefore, inimical to separatism. All of this changes when members of the target group return home, typically bearing accounts of the outrages they have suffered. When a million Ibo returned to the Eastern Region of Nigeria in 1966–67, a million Luba moved to South Kasai in Zaire after 1959; and when tens, if not hundreds, of thousands of Sri Lankan Tamils went north to Jaffna after 1983, secessionist movements soon followed, or those that already existed became energized by a change in mass sentiment and by what in Sri Lanka was described as "a flood of recruits into the militant groups."[105] Similar migrations of Sikhs from Delhi and other north Indian areas to Punjab after 1984, albeit on a relatively smaller scale,[106] fed the Khalistan movement.

Separatism, however, is not confined to the victims: the perpetrators often pursue it as well. The logic is easy to fathom. Riot violence is

---

104. *Far Eastern Economic Review*, February 9, 1984, p. 23; April 26, 1984, pp. 33–34.

105. Rajan Hoole et al., *The Broken Palmyra: The Tamil Crisis in Sri Lanka — an Inside Account*, rev. ed. (Claremont, Calif.: The Sri Lanka Studies Institute, 1990), p. 71.

106. By way of example, Chakravarti and Haksar, *The Delhi Riots*, p. 583, estimate that in one Delhi housing block affected by the riot, about 30 percent of Sikh residents left for Punjab. For migration to Punjab of Sikhs from Bihar who had no connections with Punjab, see ibid., pp. 119–22.

employed against targets who are dangerous, intractable, aggressive. Often the target groups have migrated to the initiators' area, where they encounter the hostility of their hosts. After the riot, the felt danger from the targets may endure. There may be a sense that the only way to deal with the ethnic strangers is to be free of them altogether. Genocide is one way to achieve this end, but — tempting though it is — it has its problematic aspects. More attractive is the attainment of sovereignty, coupled with the ability to control, disfranchise, or expel the immigrants.

Such desires lie behind a number of separatist movements.[107] They are especially powerful where the regional immigrants control the central government. Such sentiments animated the northern Nigerian separatist slogan "Araba" (Let us part) that was the "cry of the killings" of Ibo in May 1966.[108] The same sense of futility prevailed in southern Chad, in the southern Philippines, in the Ivory Coast, and in Assam as well. When a Christian-led government was replaced in Chad by a Muslim-led regime in 1979, southerners killed northern Muslims by the thousands in southern towns, and a United Front of the South embarked on a separatist course.[109] Rioting also preceded the growth of the Moro separatist insurgency in the southern Philippines. The riots and the separatism both emerged from the difficulty Muslims saw in controlling large numbers of Christian settlers.[110] On a much smaller scale, Bété separatists in the Ivory Coast (1970) killed Baoulé in Gagnoa, the main town of the Bété area, as they also declared an independence that was quickly suppressed.[111] The killings and the separatism were expressions of despair at dealing with Baoulé, who largely controlled the central government. After anti-Bengali violence (1960) did not alter Assamese-Bengali relations, Assamese began to demand an independent state under the slogan "Assam for the Assamese."[112] The same impulse animated the separatism

107. Horowitz, "Self-Determination," pp. 425–32.

108. First, *Power in Africa*, p. 311. The separatism was short-lived only because of serious intranorthern differences; it yielded to Ibo separatism after the replacement of an Ibo-dominated government by a northern one in July, followed by the further killings of Ibo in August–September of the same year.

109. Virginia Thompson and Richard Adloff, *Conflict in Chad* (Berkeley: University of California Institute of International Studies, 1981), pp. 76–89.

110. See John H. Adkins, "Philippines 1972: We'll Wait and See," *Asian Survey* 13, no. 1 (January 1973): 140–50.

111. Michael Cohen, *Urban Policy and Political Conflict in Africa* (Chicago: University of Chicago Press, 1974), pp. 178–79.

112. Bhawani Singh, *Politics of Alienation in Assam* (Delhi: Ajanta, 1984), pp. 134–35.

as had animated the riot. That impulse was to be rid of the strangers, who were numerous in the region.

If targets are often propelled toward separatist violence once refugee flows reduce their numbers outside the home region, and if riot initiators can also turn to separatism once they sense their region remains over-populated with members of the target group, third groups, who are nei-ther attackers nor targets, can be similarly affected by riots. The 1960 and 1972 anti-Bengali riots in Assam helped convince various hill and plains tribal groups that it would be impossible to live with the Assamese. An array of peripheral states ultimately emerged from Assam as a result of tribal separatism. Within truncated Assam itself, as Assamese anti-Bengali violence persisted into the 1980s, a new sepa-ratism emerged among the Bodo, a group that comprised a minority in its own areas of Assam and engaged in anti-Bengali violence on its own. The Bodo wished to be free of Assamese and Bengalis alike.[113] If civil war among intermixed groups is a rare result of riots, there are possibilities for secessionist warfare even in heterogeneous areas. This secessionism is, however, not likely to be pursued in such areas by riot targets, who, as I have said, are likely to apprehend even worse to come if they engage in further conflict behavior.

Post-riot separatism, then, can come from target groups whose mem-bers return in large numbers to their home region after a riot occurs out-side that region or from perpetrators of the riot who want to complete the job of controlling or removing the threat from the target group. What the riot does that makes separatism more probable is to align the inter-ests of leaders and followers among the putative separatist group.

Political leaders of territorially separate groups are often inclined to secessionism, for the reasons I have indicated, but they are generally restrained by the interests group members have outside the home region. For the targets, the riot can destroy many of those interests. For the ini-tiators, the riot that meets with impunity can provide a sense of group power. If it nonetheless fails to control the target group adequately from the standpoint of the initiators, a violently separatist course may appear to be the next logical step.

For intermixed groups, there is also a distinctive post-riot logic. As the targets tend to be fearful of further violence of any kind, leaders and fol-lowers are both likely to be strongly inhibited. The perpetrators are not

113. See *Far Eastern Economic Review*, March 9, 1989, p. 23. Cf. Sudhir Jacob George, "The Bodo Movement in Assam," *Asian Survey* 34, no. 10 (October 1994): 878–83.

necessarily disinclined to further violence, but they are likely to respond favorably to the quiescence of the targets. (Interestingly enough, the Bengali targets in the Assam Valley were unable to control their own group's post-riot demeanor, because the more homogeneously Bengali Cachar region of Assam and the overwhelmingly Bengali West Bengal state were vociferous about Bengali interests in Assam, thereby provoking the Assamese despite Bengali quiescence in the valley.) Moreover, leaders of the initiator group may have special reasons for post-riot restraint, particularly if, as is often the case, they are in control of government and wish to capitalize on the new, post-riot political status quo. The net is that a riot can abet separatism from either side, but the result is far from invariable.

CONTINGENT EFFECTS

Up to this point, we have progressed almost imperceptibly from effects that follow virtually automatically from the violence to those that depend in part on the response of leaders and followers, albeit a response that has a large measure of predictability. From here on out, the response is less predictable — or at least not wholly predictable from a study of riots — and the effects are even more variable. Much depends on whether non-rioters (usually elites) use the violence that has occurred for one purpose or another.

Take the question of order and disorder. The general loosening of restraints that follows rioting can upset the balance of force in a polity. In India in the 1960s, the southern Philippines in the 1970s, Pakistan in the 1980s, and the Congo Republic in the 1990s, the effect was to entrench militant organizations that engaged in further violence. In such conditions, the line between the criminal and the political becomes blurred, and opportunities are created for vigilantes to pursue extortion, larceny, and land grabbing alongside ethnic violence. These opportunities are greater in rural areas, where gangs may engage in ethnic expulsion,[114] but the gangs may also become available to group leaders operating in towns. By the same token, if the police were biased in the riot, the bias may be expressed again after the riot, now in the form of raids or assaults on members of the target group.[115]

114. See Human Rights Commission of Pakistan, *Sindh Inquiry, Summer 1990*, pp. 61–62, 65. Cf. Richard S. Wheeler, *The Politics of Pakistan: A Constitutional Quest* (Ithaca: Cornell University Press, 1970), p. 300.
115. Human Rights Commission of Pakistan, *Sindh Inquiry, Summer 1990*, p. 30.

For the most part, then, the violence produces further insecurity. This, however, is not the invariable result. In the five years following the 1969 riot in Kuala Lumpur, the Malaysian government, intolerant of disorder, increased its armed forces by more than 50 percent,[116] and it cracked down on individual episodes of violence.[117] Many regimes would be tempted to move in the same direction if they could muster the material and political resources, since violence can prove threatening and unpredictable for incumbent elites. Malaysian leaders had a special reason to do so, for they developed a policy agenda from the riots, and its success would have been undermined by further violence. Apart from that, Malaysia had limited tolerance for disorder to begin with; unlike Pakistan, for instance, the writ of its government has been effective just about everywhere since the end of the postwar Communist insurgency. More effective governments are likely to respond to riots by increasing security. Since less effective governments cannot do so, decreased security is at least equally likely. Although opposites, both are effects of riots.

The impact of riots on the political system is also equivocal. In Chapter 8, we discussed riots begun by groups locked into an electoral minority position. Groups experiencing electoral lock-ins, having rioted to no avail, have subsequently broken the lock-in by ethnically related coups. Failing twice at the ballot box and once on the streets, Zanzibar's Africans executed a coup in 1964.[118] In stages, the same occurred in the Congo Republic, where, in 1968, a coup finally brought Mbochi and other northerners to power.[119] Unfavorable experiences with controlling riots and coping with political pressures during periods of violence can also inspire military officers to thoughts of displacing politicians.[120]

If military officers do not respond to riots by turning the political system in an authoritarian direction, civilian politicians like Ferdinand Marcos in the Philippines may do so. Repeatedly, the impulse is to respond to disorder by increasing control, with consequences inimical to democracy. Like Marcos, the Turkish government proclaimed martial

116. Cynthia H. Enloe, "Civilian Control of the Military: Implications in the Plural Societies of Guyana and Malaysia," in Claude E. Welch, Jr., ed., *Civilian Control of the Military* (Albany: State University of New York Press, 1976), pp. 78–79.

117. For an example, see Donald L. Horowitz, "Cause and Consequence in Public Policy Theory: Ethnic Policy and System Transformation in Malaysia," *Policy Sciences* 22, nos. 3–4 (November 1989): 249–87, at p. 261.

118. See John Okello, *Revolution in Zanzibar* (Nairobi: East African Publishing House, 1967).

119. See Samuel Decalo, *Coups and Army Rule in Africa* (New Haven: Yale University Press, 1976), pp. 136–55.

120. See Donald L. Horowitz, *Coup Theories and Officers' Motives: Sri Lanka in Comparative Perspective* (Princeton: Princeton University Press, 1980), pp. 125–29.

law after the riot of 1978; the Malaysian government suspended parliament for 21 months following the Kuala Lumpur riot of 1969; the Sri Lankan government, as we have seen, outlawed separatism and expelled the Tamil opposition from parliament when it refused to abjure separatism after the 1983 riot; and the Senegal River Valley of Mauritania became an occupied area after the antiblack violence of 1989.[121] There is no doubt that riots create a risk for democracy.

Still, the unpredictability of the results stands out. The response of the Sri Lankan government to the 1981 riot was completely different from its response two years later. In 1981, it disciplined extremist politicians, transferred police officers tolerant of the violence, and began a dialogue with the Tamil opposition.[122] In Kyrghyzstan (1990), the riot strengthened democratic forces. The Communist first secretary of the republic was forced out of office, and the new regime was, for a time, significantly more tolerant of opposition.[123] The Mauritanian riot (1966) produced no democratization, but it did result in a cabinet reorganization, in which politicians favorable to the violence were removed; some were then imprisoned, and a more evenhanded policy toward Africans was pursued.[124] All of these effects, however, proved ephemeral. Rarely does the target group gain anything durable after the riot.

Although the outcomes are unpredictable, the violence often does counter preexisting policy immobility and make action possible that seemed impossible previously.[125] Everywhere, the riot gives way to a struggle to interpret the event, a struggle that occurs at multiple levels and can produce conflicting results.[126] The Palestine riot (1929) simulta-

121. *Economist*, December 30, 1978, pp. 25–26; von Vorys, *Democracy without Consensus*, p. 416; Sunil Bastian, "The Political Economy of Ethnic Violence in Sri Lanka: The July 1983 Riots," in Das, ed., *Mirrors of Violence*, p. 302; Human Rights Watch/Africa, *Mauritania's Campaign of Terror: State-Sponsored Repression of Black Africans* (New York: Human Rights Watch, 1994), pp. 134–46.

122. W. Howard Wriggins, "Sri Lanka in 1981: A Year of Austerity, Development Councils, and Communal Disorders," *Asian Survey* 22, no. 2 (February 1982): 173–79; Council for Communal Harmony through the Media, "The Press and the Racial Violence of August 1981" (mimeo., Colombo, February 1982), p. 11.

123. Huskey, "Kyrgyzstan," pp. 663–69.

124. Here I am drawing on several conversations with Mauritanian and foreign observers of the violence and its aftermath.

125. See Ralph H. Turner, "Collective Behavior," in Robert E.L. Faris, ed., *Handbook of Modern Sociology* (Chicago: Rand McNally, 1964), p. 422.

126. Ibid., p. 420; Paul R. Brass, "Introduction: Discourses of Ethnicity, Communalism, and Violence," in Paul R. Brass, ed., *Riots and Pogroms* (New York: New York University Press, 1996), pp. 1–55; Gyanendra Pandey, "In Defense of the Fragment: Writing about Hindu-Muslim Riots in India Today," *Economic and Political Weekly*, Annual Number, 1991, pp. 559–72.

neously "provided pro-Zionist opinion within the British government with a powerful argument against a Palestinian legislative council" and Palestinians with a cause that converted the local conflict "into a pan-Islamic issue."[127] If the riot is precipitated by a change in ethnic policy, there is a good chance that a compromise will follow or that implementation of the policy will be postponed for a time. A year after the Assam riot (1960), there was an Assamese-English compromise policy adopted, just as after Sind (1972) a Sindhi-Urdu compromise was reached, and after Mauritania (1966) the exclusive use of Arabic in the schools was delayed.

Sometimes, however, a dominant interpretation of the violent event takes hold, and that makes bold policy initiatives possible. After Kuala Lumpur (1969), Malaysian agenda setters were able to persuade policymakers that the riot was rooted in Malay economic deprivation. This view, dubious though it was, was not seriously contested by non-Malays, and it led to the adoption of a New Economic Policy, a comprehensive set of ethnic preferences designed to boost Malay participation in the economy.[128] The riot can thus produce an altogether new policy equilibrium.

Preferential results, if not policies, are not uncommon after riots. Once Dahomeyans left the Ivory Coast (1958), Ivorians moved into their vacated positions. After the anti-Voltaic violence (1969), the Ivory Coast government apparently agreed to give Ivorians preference in filling positions, even in the private sector.[129] After violence in Jakarta (1974) directed against Japanese and Indonesian Chinese firms, the Indonesian government became more serious about channeling bank credit and government contracts to indigenous business,[130] as it did again after anti-Chinese violence in 1998. Following Durban (1949), African traders moved into market areas where Indian business had been disrupted by the riot, and they were allocated more transport licenses as well.[131] A *Zondizitha* (Hate the Enemies) Buying Club, composed of African shopkeepers, sprang up; it lobbied for trading licenses and facilities to be

127. Roger Friedland and Richard D. Hecht, "Divisions at the Center: The Organization of Political Violence at Jerusalem's Temple Mount/*al-haram al-sharif*—1929 and 1990," in Brass, ed., *Riots and Pogroms*, p. 138.

128. Horowitz, "Cause and Consequence in Public Policy Theory," pp. 255–57.

129. J.L., "New Developments in French-speaking Africa," *Civilisations* 20, no. 2 (1970): 270–78, at p. 278.

130. *Far Eastern Economic Review*, September 21, 1979, pp. 113–19.

131. Kuper, *An African Bourgeoisie*, pp. 301–03; Maurice Webb and Kenneth Kirkwood, *The Durban Riots and After* (Johannesburg: South African Institute of Race Relations, n.d.), p. 9.

accorded Africans in preference to Indians.[132] The distributive outcomes of riots are variable, but they often include demands for ethnic quotas.[133]

If policy changes result from the violence, the perpetrator group is more likely to gain a distributive advantage over the target group, although this result is not a sure thing.[134] It would be a mistake to read these probable effects back into riot objectives. Not a single riot was precipitated by an issue regarding preferential policies, and none has been shown to have been organized by those who aimed to institute such policies after the violence. Preferential policies are, after all, matters of concern to elites, not to the people who must be energized to do the killing. After the violence, however, elites certainly may, and sometimes do, capture the riot for their own purposes, among which preferential policies rank highly.

What all this uncertainty suggests is that riots have consequences, but their direction depends on the use that leaders are inclined and able to make of the violence after the fact. It is sometimes asserted that the desire to avoid further violence constitutes a motive among elites for interethnic conciliation after violence has occurred.[135] This may be true, but it is a minority tendency. A major reason is that elites in severely divided societies do not customarily enjoy the freedom that is sometimes imputed to them.[136] After the riot, constraints are especially strong, for even if the riot chastens elites, it also degrades victims, creates refugees, disrupts residential arrangements, polarizes populations, and sometimes leads to more organized forms of warfare. In such conditions, the odds against conciliation are long.

Finally, the riot often has negative effects on economic development,

132. Kuper, *An African Bourgeoisie*, p. 304.

133. Compare Charles H. Kennedy, "Managing Ethnic Conflict: The Case of Pakistan," *Regional Politics and Policy* 3, no. 1 (Spring 1993): 123–43, at p. 132, with Jules Chomé, *Le Drame de Luluabourg*, 3d rev. ed. (Brussels: Editions de Remarques Congolaises, 1960), p. 54. For the argument that ethnic riots do not lead to policy change, see Gary T. Marx, "Issueless Riots," *The Annals* 391 (December 1970): 21–33, at p. 29.

134. After Nigeria (1966), the principal beneficiaries of the departure of Ibo from the north were not Hausa-Fulani but Birom and Idoma; and, in the federation as a whole, Yoruba and Edo benefited. In all of these cases, the beneficiary group was well positioned, by dint of education, to step into positions vacated by Ibo.

135. Eric A. Nordlinger, *Conflict Regulation in Divided Societies* (Cambridge: Harvard University Center for International Affairs, Occasional Paper no. 29, 1972), p. 51. Cf. Arend Lijphart, *Democracy in Plural Societies* (New Haven: Yale University Press, 1977), pp. 100, 165–66.

136. For reasons I have enumerated in Donald L. Horowitz, *Ethnic Groups in Conflict* (Berkeley and Los Angeles: University of California Press, 1985), pp. 573–74; Horowitz, "Self-Determination," pp. 439–40.

job creation, foreign investment, and tourism. Many of these effects redound to the disadvantage of rioters. It is difficult to know whether the prospect of such consequences has ever deterred rioters, but rioters behave as if they are oblivious of such concerns. In this respect, ethnic riots are no different from other forms of violence. Civil and secessionist warfare, violent protest demonstrations, and terrorism have produced comparable economic effects in a good many countries, sometimes deliberately. Just as rioters generally fail to benefit from preferential policies, they often ultimately incur economic loss. But, then, rioters do not generally riot for profit, and they do not riot to avoid economic loss either. Their satisfactions lie in other realms.

THE PUTATIVE FUNCTIONS OF VIOLENCE

If we have correctly identified the aims and effects of ethnic riots, it is possible to go a step further and ask whether this form of violence serves any social functions. Of course, the term *function* is notoriously slippery. At one level, to serve a function is simply to fill a need; but, if so, whose need? At a much higher level, it is possible to ask whether the violence provides biological benefits, even an increase in inclusive fitness.

Assuredly, ethnic violence fills certain needs for the rioters, but this is merely to identify their gratification after the event with their aims before the event. The riot may also perform a function frequently associated with conflict in general, by increasing the internal cohesion of each of the combatant groups.[137] This result, as we have seen, is common but not uniform.[138]

The question becomes far more complex when one asks whether the riot has any utility for the society as a whole. Georg Simmel was concerned to assert the functions of conflict in binding antagonists together, resolving tensions between opposed positions, and maintaining a balance of power between antagonists,[139] but these suppositions seem far-fetched

137. See, e.g., Lewis Coser, *The Functions of Social Conflict* (Glencoe, Ill.: Free Press, 1956), pp. 87–110.

138. Violence does generally reduce subethnic divisions, as it did, for example, for Muslims in Mauritius (1968); but it did not do this for Indians in Burma (1938), where, following the anti-Indian riot, divisions between Hindus and Muslims grew. Some Hindus undertook to propitiate Burmans, rather than cement their ties to Muslims. See Usha Mahajani, *The Role of Indian Minorities in Burma and Malaya* (Bombay: Vora, 1960), pp. 79–80.

139. The arguments are concisely stated by Coser, *The Functions of Social Conflict*, pp. 33–38, 72–85, 121–37.

with respect to so extreme an expression of conflict as deadly ethnic riots. As we have seen, polarization, not binding together, usually follows the riot.

Some other functional possibilities at the societal level are not quite so easily dismissed. Certain forms of aggression are said to obviate the need for even more destructive forms of violence, or to limit future conflict by creating dominance hierarchies, or to facilitate exploitation of an environment by spreading populations out.

Conflict in general, it is argued, serves to regulate relationships by expressing hostile dispositions, thereby warning of the possibility of even more disruptive behavior that might terminate the relationship between antagonists.[140] Can this also be true of ethnic violence, which is already an extreme form of conflict behavior? If the deadly riot is the prelude to warfare, those who wish to avert warfare could see the riot as a cautionary event. Furthermore, the random, brutal killing of targets based merely on their ascriptive identity has, I have argued, a proto-genocidal quality about it; it is an augury of extermination. Certainly, the targets usually interpret the warning in this way, whether they flee to safer areas or attempt to become inconspicuous where they remain, hoping to avert further violence. Primate studies emphasize the role of limited violence in controlling intraspecific aggression. Aggressive displays, on the one hand, and submissive gestures, on the other, serve to limit serious violence.[141] The same has been noticed in certain forms of human aggression, in which fights end with the first sign of submission.[142] In both cases, such violence as occurs is calibrated to minimize the incidence of serious injury, and the explanation usually advanced is that there is an effort to prevent more damaging forms of aggression.[143] But the deadly ethnic riot can scarcely be depicted as merely an aggressive display, and it does not end with the first sign of submission.

The use of display and submission in order to minimize further violence is closely related to attempts to establish hierarchies. Significantly,

140. See ibid., pp. 39–48.

141. See, e.g., Irwin S. Bernstein and Thomas P. Gordon, "The Function of Aggression in Primate Societies," *American Scientist* 62, no. 3 (May 1974): 304–11, at pp. 306–07.

142. Peter Marsh, Elizabeth Rosser, and Rom Harré, *The Rules of Disorder* (London: Routledge & Kegan Paul, 1978), pp. 104, 126–28.

143. This is not to say, of course, that there are always limits to aggression. On the contrary, animals and humans can and do kill conspecifics with abandon. See Edward O. Wilson, *On Human Nature* (Cambridge: Harvard University Press, 1978), pp. 100–01, 103–05. The question here pertains to the relationship between forms of violence at varying levels of severity.

"the greater the social rank disparity between two animals, the less frequently we see aggressive encounters."[144] Limited violence, it is suggested, begets or reinforces hierarchy, which, by restraining further violence, reduces threats to both parties to the first violent transaction.[145] And, of course, opportunities for cooperation increase as the danger of aggression within a social unit declines. Ethological studies show a tendency for members of the same species to regard strangers with hostility and to direct aggression against them.[146] Much of this aggression seems to relate to dominance and subordination. Once dominance is achieved, within some species in as short a period as 48 hours, vigorous fighting may stop.[147] Perhaps the recurrent desire of unranked ethnic groups to establish dominance hierarchies — that is, to turn unranked into ranked relationships — is expressed in fighting and derives from similar impulses to limit competition and reduce threat.[148]

Fighting is also said by ethologists to space out members of the same species who would otherwise compete for resources.[149] It has long been known that crowding increases aggression among animals,[150] and similar

144. Bernstein and Gordon, "The Functions of Aggression in Primate Societies," p. 308.

145. Intraspecific role diversification performs the same function as interspecific niche diversification: both limit competition. Peter H. Klopfer, *Behavioral Aspects of Ecology*, 2d ed. (Englewood Cliffs, N.J.: Prentice-Hall, 1973), p. 139.

146. See, e.g., Peter Marler, "On Animal Aggression: The Roles of Strangeness and Familiarity," *American Psychologist* 31, no. 3 (March 1976): 239–46. Cf. Wilson, *On Human Nature*, p. 119.

147. G.B. Messe and R. Ewbank, "The Establishment and Nature of the Dominance Hierarchy in the Domesticated Pig," *Animal Behaviour* 21, no. 2 (May 1973): 326–34.

148. Gaetano Mosca, *The Ruling Class*, ed. Arthur Livingston; trans. Hannah D. Kahn (New York: McGraw-Hill, 1939), pp. 29, 103, observed the tendency of nations and ethnic groups to impose their own type of civilization on those they conquer, and he derived from this an impulse to dominate rather than destroy. Cf. David H. Marlowe, "In the Mosaic: The Cognitive and Structural Aspects of Karen-Other Relationships," in Charles F. Keyes, ed., *Ethnic Adaptation and Identity: The Karen on the Thai Frontier with Burma* (Philadelphia: Institute for the Study of Human Issues, 1979), pp. 207–08. Marlowe points out that hierarchical societies are premised on ecological complementarity. For the ranked-unranked distinction, see Horowitz, *Ethnic Groups in Conflict*, pp. 21–36.

149. Javier Salgado-Ortiz and Russell Greenberg, "Interspecific Defense of Trees by Wintering Yellow Warblers," *Auk* 111, no. 3 (July 1994): 672–82; Andrew R. Blaustein and Arthur C. Risser, "Interspecific Interactions between Three Sympatric Species of Kangaroo Rats (Dipodomys)," *Animal Behaviour* 24, no. 2 (May 1976): 381–85; Irenäus Eibl-Eibesfeldt, "The Fighting Behavior of Animals," in Thomas Eisner and Edward O. Wilson, eds., *Animal Behavior* (San Francisco: W.H. Freeman, 1975), pp. 278–84.

150. Lee C. Drickhamer and Stephen H. Vessey, *Animal Behavior: Concepts, Processes, and Methods* (Boston: Willard Grant Press, 1982), p. 421; Eugene P. Odum, *Fundamentals of Ecology* (Philadelphia: W.B. Saunders, 1953), pp. 150, 349; Miranda L. Dyson and Neville I. Passmore, "Inter-Male Spacing and Aggression in African Painted Reed

claims have been made for a relationship between proximity and enmity among humans.[151] In Papua, groups located on opposite sides of mountains had the friendliest relations, particularly if there was virgin forest between them, whereas groups separated merely by a river had less friendly relations.[152] Papuan groups defeated in warfare sometimes relocated out of the enemy's range.[153] On the other hand, it has also been suggested that a permissive ecology — one with just this kind of room for expansion — may foster warfare, because it allows the disputants the geographical mobility to avoid the full effects of defeat by reorganizing themselves after defeat and finding refuge beyond the reach of their enemies.[154]

Ethnic groups certainly exhibit strong territorial propensities, when, for example, they make political claims based on prior occupation, as animals also do when resources are concentrated.[155] Within groups, fission may occur after a fight if a lineage has become "too large to exploit its home territory and must divide or perish."[156] If warfare is conceived as "a ritualized form of territorial demarcation,"[157] then perhaps the deadly ethnic riot, with its numerous refugees and the growing conviction that it is impossible to live together, serves the same function of limiting niche competition.

These, at all events, are the strongest hypotheses that a functionalist view of ethnic riots might entertain. Their application to human aggression overall cannot be dismissed a priori. To be sure, the ecological foundation of ethnic group behavior is sometimes challenged on the ground that it reflects "pseudospeciation," the maladaptive treatment of other groups as if they were separate species.[158] The idiom of ethnic relations is

---

Frogs, Hyperolius Marmoratus," *Ethology* 91, no. 3 (July 1992): 237–47; Nancy Cain, Cynthia Jessen, and Michael Flanagan, "Social Responsiveness and Physical Space as Determinants of Agonistic Behavior in Betta Splendens," *Animal Learning and Behavior* 8, no. 3 (August 1980): 497–501; Robert H. Elton and Brian V. Anderson, "The Social Behavior of a Group of Baboons (Papio Anubis) under Artificial Crowding," *Primates* 18, no. 1 (January 1977): 225–34.

151. C.R. Hallpike, *Bloodshed and Vengeance in the Papuan Mountains* (Oxford: Clarendon Press, 1977), p. 202.

152. Ibid., pp. 203–04.

153. Ibid., p. 204.

154. Riches, "The Phenomenon of Violence," p. 24.

155. See Klopfer, *Behavioral Aspects of Ecology*, pp. 54–55.

156. David H. Marlowe, "Commitment, Contract, Group Boundaries, and Conflict," *Science and Psychoanalysis* 6, no. 1 (1963): 43–55, at pp. 54–55.

157. Irenäus Eibl-Eibesfeldt, *The Biology of Peace and War*, trans. Eric Mosbacher (New York: Viking Press, 1979), p. 179.

158. Edmund Leach, "The Integration of Minorities" (Second Annual Minority Rights Group Lecture, London, December 12, 1973; mimeo.), p. 3; Erik H. Erikson, "The

rife with specious species discourse, replete, as it is, with false dogmas about "mixed breeds" and references to "zebras among horses."[159] The pseudospeciation objection is not dispositive, however, for ethnic distinctions might be viewed as analogous to subspecies differences throughout the animal world. At the moment, analogy is the strongest term that could be used for these relationships, since there is no basis for concluding that prominent similarities between ethnic behavior and subspecies behavior are explained by a common underlying mechanism.

Nevertheless, two aspects of the analogy are intriguing. First, well-documented patterns of intraspecific competition are related to and in some ways similar to patterns of interspecific competition. Second, certain resemblances between intraspecific and interethnic competition are marked.

Animal subspecies are often called "races" or "varieties." Yet the basis of subspeciation is usually as thin (or nearly so) as the basis of ethnic dif-

---

Concept of Identity in Race Relations: Notes and Queries," *Daedalus* 95, no. 1 (Winter 1966): 145–71, at pp. 152–53. Cf. Mary Midgley, *Beast and Man: The Roots of Human Nature* (New York: New American Library, 1978), pp. 305–06.

159. In the early years of African slavery in the Western Hemisphere, it was thought that whites and blacks were different species, incapable of interbreeding; when experience disproved this notion, it was replaced by talk about "mixed breeds," including the belief that mulattoes possessed the vices of both white and black, but not the virtues. Charles R. Boxer, *The Golden Age of Brazil, 1695–1750* (Berkeley and Los Angeles: University of California Press, 1962), pp. 17–18. The Sinhalese words *jatiya* and *vargaya*, meaning physical type or species, are also used for ethnic group, as are related Sanskritic terms in India. Robert N. Kearney, "Language and the Rise of Tamil Separatism in Sri Lanka," *Asian Survey* 18, no. 5 (May 1978): 521–34, at pp. 524–25; Hugh Tinker, *India and Pakistan: A Political Analysis*, rev. ed. (New York: Praeger, 1967), p. 131. A boast about Trinidad's ethnic relations declares that the "cat and dog can live together." Quoted by Ivar Oxaal, *Black Intellectuals Come to Power: The Rise of Creole Nationalism in Trinidad and Tobago* (Cambridge, Mass.: Schenkman, 1968), p. 23. Europeans in a Chinese crowd in Singapore were said to be "like zebras among horses." Johnny Ong, *Sugar and Salt* (Kuala Lumpur: Eastern Universities Press, 1975), p. 179. When a Malay woman married a Chinese in Malaysia, a Malay observer referred to the disapproved match as "marrying a cat to a mouse." Douglas Raybeck, "Ethnicity and Accommodation: Malay-Chinese Relations in Kelantan, Malaysia," *Ethnic Groups* 2, no. 3 (January 1980): 241–68, at p. 255. That ethnic groups tend to be endogamous and may develop somewhat differentiated genetic inventories, often reflected in phenotype, makes the species analogy plausible. Consider the case of Afghans in Bengal: "A couple of Kabulis, holding their long staffs, pushed contemptuously through the crowd . . . ; we could not help admiring their height and swagger, their hooked noses and blue-black bobbed hair under the huge floppy turbans, their loose white trousers and dark embroidered waistcoats; among the slim white-clad Bengalis they looked as decorative and arrogant as a pair of peacocks among a flock of sparrows." Jon Godden and Rumer Godden, *Two under the Indian Sun* (New York: Alfred A. Knopf, 1966), p. 81.

ferentiation. Typically, a subspecies is a geographically defined group of populations which differs in color, size, or other taxonomic characteristics from other populations in the same species but which breeds with them where their ranges come into contact.[160]

The insubstantiality of intraspecific differences — and yet the importance of the distinctions — is illustrated by bullfrogs and the sounds they make.[161] The call of a single species of bullfrog is slightly different from one region to another. Frogs respond more vigorously to their own local dialect, showing greatest agitation when they hear calls of frogs from their home district. In mating, a frog can hear only the call of a member of the same species, but it discriminates within its own species, so as to prefer, from among the sounds it hears, those emanating from frogs of the same locality. Much the same is true of birds and bird dialects.[162] Birds are able to discriminate between the songs of their neighbors and those of conspecific strangers to the area. The diversity of the environment affects the range and significance of these distinctions,[163] just as context affects the tendency for ethnic-group distinctions to emerge.[164]

Intraspecific competition is most severe, because members of the same species have identical requirements for food, mates, and other sources of sustenance.[165] Unrestrained, each variety, like each species that competes for the same niche, presses on those species or those varieties that are most closely related and "tends to exterminate them."[166] According to Gause's Law, the principle of competitive exclusion, if two noninterbreeding populations occupy the same ecological niche and one multiplies slightly faster, the other will become extinct.[167] Competition, however, is not always unrestrained. Often, social hierarchy, territoriality, or differentiation of function serve to limit competition.

160. S. Charles Kendeigh, *Animal Ecology* (Englewood Cliffs, N.J.: Prentice-Hall, 1961), p. 257. Generally, subspecies exhibit at least some clinical differences in the frequency of particular genes, even if these are only statistically detectable. Ethnic groups need not exhibit such differences, although they often do.

161. John Tyler Bonner, *The Evolution of Culture in Animals* (Princeton: Princeton University Press, 1980), p. 111.

162. Drickhamer and Vessey, *Animal Behavior*, p. 309.

163. Klopfer, *Behavioral Aspects of Ecology*, pp. 131–37.

164. Horowitz, *Ethnic Groups in Conflict*, pp. 64–70.

165. Kendeigh, *Animal Ecology*, p. 183.

166. Garrett Hardin, "The Competitive Exclusion Principle," *Science*, April 29, 1960, pp. 1292–97.

167. Ibid., p. 1292. See G.F. Gause, *The Struggle for Existence* (Baltimore: Williams and Wilkins, 1934).

The overall tendency of sympatric subspecies to be sharply competitive is suggestive for studies of ethnicity. The severity of competition between varieties that are closest in characteristics is reminiscent of Freud's "narcissism of small differences,"[168] meaning that competitive comparisons tend to be made between those who are most nearly alike — a notion that has been applied to ethnic relations.[169] In view of the resemblances between interspecific and intraspecific competition, as well as between intraspecific competition in general and interethnic competition in particular, it is much too early to dismiss ethnic aggression as pseudospeciation, a form of Darwinian false consciousness.

It is also too early to succumb to the appeal of ecological explanations. Still less would it be justified to suggest that, since aggression is "natural," ethnic violence and the special forms it takes are inevitable. No doubt hostility and warfare have provided advantage to those who engaged in them over hundreds of thousands of years, but the expression of aggression is highly variable across closely related species.[170] There is a danger of functional teleology in studying aggression, the danger of inferring overarching social utility from the pursuit of utility at much lower levels, not to mention the danger of inferring the adaptiveness of a practice from its survival thus far.[171] Human aggressors can and sometimes do behave dysfunctionally. Such behavior is common, because circumstances in the past may have favored adaptations that are now inappropriate.

If, for example, the infliction of degradation is aimed at the creation and maintenance of a status hierarchy, what stands out in the ethnic riot is the proclivity to carry the matter so much further, to degradation by torture and mutilation. Animals do kill conspecifics, but rarely, if ever, do they appear to do so in quite this way.

Likewise, the aim of homogenization may have a spacing effect when large numbers of target-group members flee the riot location for more hospitable territory. But, more often than not, the departure of target-

168. Sigmund Freud, *Civilization and Its Discontents* (London: Hogarth Press, 1946), p. 114.

169. Gordon Allport, *The Nature of Prejudice* (Garden City, N.Y.: Anchor Books, 1958), p. 132. For the relationship between closeness and conflict intensity, see Coser, *The Functions of Social Conflict*, pp. 67–72.

170. Wilson, *On Human Nature*, pp. 100–03, 111–14, 119.

171. See J.R. Durant, "The Beast in Man: An Historical Perspective on the Biology of Human Aggression" (unpublished paper, University College of Swansea, n.d. [ca. 1982]), p. 42. See also C.R. Hallpike, "Functionalist Interpretations of Primitive Warfare," *Man* 8, no. 3 (September 1973): 451–70, at pp. 465, 468. For a refutation of functionalist interpretations of feud violence, see Jon Elster, "Norms of Revenge," *Ethics* 100, no. 4 (July 1990): 862–85, at pp. 871–83.

group refugees does not contribute to the efficient utilization of resources at the sending site, where the victims previously performed valuable functions, but rather incurs costs there and produces unsustainable crowding at the receiving site.[172]

Finally, to what extent is the riot an analogue of the aggressive display or relatively harmless fight that averts more serious violence? As I have observed, the riot can be seen as an intimation of genocide. The "taught-them-a-lesson" language of gloating aggressors can be interpreted as reflecting the rioters' view that the violence is a warning of worse to come if the targets do not become suitably compliant. If so, perhaps the riot helps to avert warfare by coercing the target group into less threatening behavior. This function of the riot, however, needs to be viewed in the context of counterconsequences. Not only does the killing constitute far more serious violence to begin with than does the animal display or harmless fight, but rioters are unable to control the escalation of violence to higher and higher levels in locations such as Karachi, where actual warfare was increasingly approached rather than averted. Still less can they dictate a response in accordance with their intentions when the target group decides to embark on a course of secessionist warfare rather than conciliatory or deferential behavior. Such cases, which are not infrequent, make it difficult to claim that the riot is a warning that settles things down. More often than it settles them down, it stirs them up. The riot is destabilizing in precisely the sense that it makes possible a range of unpredictable outcomes.

In all of these ways, ethnic riots appear to involve — quite literally — overkill. This signals a problem common to the ecology of human aggression: that a disposition to behavior, such as aggression, can be explained by phylogenetic evolution does not mean that the behavior cannot be carried too far or carried out in maladaptive ways.[173]

Nor is it clear what role culture plays. Some species fight irrespective of rearing method, whereas the level of aggression of others can be affected by rearing. Some such differences may be related to differences in ecology, but some animals fight despite differences in both ecology and rearing.[174] Merely because culture may ultimately feed back upon genes does not preclude cultural adaptations that occur without genetic feedback. There is a tendency toward promiscuity in finding adaptive signif-

---

172. Cf. Hallpike's strongly worded conclusion that Papuan violence was not adaptive in this sense at all. *Bloodshed and Violence in the Papuan Mountains*, pp. 230–31.

173. For a helpful analysis, see Eibl-Eibesfeldt, *The Biology of Peace and War*, p. 168.

174. I am indebted to Peter H. Klopfer for these observations.

icance in every corner of human behavior, including, prominently, various forms of aggression and warfare.[175] Even if apparently similar acts across species have similar aims, that does not suffice to identify the underlying mechanism: analogy is not homology.[176]

More proximate, more demonstrable explanations may be more useful than overarching functionalist explanations are. There are those who insist on understanding aggression in terms of the social relations of those involved — and not moving beyond them.[177] Non-state-directed warfare, contends C.R. Hallpike, provides gratification to those who engage in it, because it is a "definitive means of proving one's superiority over an enemy,"[178] and it persists "because there is no way to stop it, not because it is performing some vital function for that society."[179]

As Hallpike ironically suggests, the problem of control is not necessarily easier if aggression is not instinctual. In Papuan society, with its lack of central direction, the problem is assuredly intractable. Moreover, what I have described as overkill appears to be an excess of violence to achieve the functions asserted for it and the actual attainment, in many cases, of escalation rather than limitation. So it is inaccurate to correlate the adaptiveness of violence with its most extreme expressions. On the contrary, ethological studies suggest a tendency toward strict economy in the employment of intraspecific aggression, as we have seen with respect to display and submission. Nonfunctionalists more often emphasize the beastly quality of human violence than do those who trace the violence to the beast in the human species.

The controversy about the innate quality of aggression and its functions need not be settled here. Even if ethnic violence served the functions that have been claimed, it would be quite wrong to think these functions could not be fulfilled in alternative ways that do not entail comparable cruelty. Humans possess, as animals do not, problem-solving and policy-making capabilities that can attempt to reduce threat, enhance cooperation, and regulate the contest for superiority.

175. Not even excluding the military coup. See R. Paul Shaw and Yuwa Wong, *Genetic Seeds of Warfare: Evolution, Nationalism, and Patriotism* (Boston: Unwin Hyman, 1989).

176. Peter H. Klopfer and Lisa Klopfer, "On 'Human Ethology,'" *Semiotica* 39, nos. 1–2 (February 1982): 175–85.

177. Durant, "The Beast in Man," p. 39.

178. Hallpike, "Functionalist Interpretations of Primitive Warfare," p. 459.

179. Ibid., p. 455. For an interesting effort to investigate the utility of evolutionary theory in explaining ethnic politics, see Robert Hislope, "Can Evolutionary Theory Explain Nationalist Violence? Czechoslovak and Bosnian Illustrations," *Nations and Nationalism* 4, pt. 4 (October 1998): 463–82.

Violence and Quiescence

THERE ARE MANY RIOTS, but there is much more antipathy than there is violence. One might wonder why people who nourish antipathy do not kill each other even more often. In India, it has been observed, if a town is violent, every condition present tends to be viewed as a cause of violence; if a town is peaceful, then every condition present there tends to be viewed as a cause of peace.[1] Although I shall soon argue that an undifferentiated quest for the sources of civic peace is an unprofitable enterprise, there is a need to contrast violent episodes with instances of nonviolence.[2]

In the study of events, two types of question need to be distinguished. One relates to the *incidence* of an event, its occurrence contrasted with its nonoccurrence. The other involves the *characteristics* of an event, those features that are displayed when the event occurs. If the issue is event incidence — in this case, the conditions in which riots occur — it is impossible to determine this without examining instances in which the phenomenon did not occur. If, on the other hand, the issue is the characteristics of a deadly riot, then it may be superfluous, although not altogether fruitless,[3] to include non-riots.

Throughout this book, I have been concerned with both categories. I

1. Steven I. Wilkinson, "U.P.'s 'Riot-Prone' Towns," *Seminar*, no. 432 (August 1995): 27–34.

2. See Valery Tishkov, *Ethnicity, Nationalism and Conflict in and after the Soviet Union* (London: Sage, 1997), p. 296; Mark R. Beissinger, "Nationalist Violence in the Former Soviet Union, 1987–1992: An Event Analysis" (paper presented at the annual meeting of the American Association for the Advancement of Slavic Studies, Washington, D.C., October 29, 1995), pp. 6–8; Ian Lustick, "Stability in Deeply Divided Societies: Consociationalism versus Control," *World Politics* 31, no. 3 (April 1979): 325–44, at p. 333.

3. Compare David Collier and James Mahoney, "Insights and Pitfalls: Selection Bias in Qualitative Research," *World Politics* 49, no. 1 (October 1996): 51–91, at pp. 63–64, with David Collier, "Translating Quantitative Methods for Qualitative Researchers: The Case of Selection Bias," *American Political Science Review* 89, no. 2 (June 1995): 461–66, at p. 465.

have asked when, where, and why deadly riots occur, and also how riot-ers behave in the course of rioting: who participates, what methods are used, what aims are pursued. In delineating riot characteristics, it has hardly been necessary to contrast them explicitly with the characteristics of more tranquil times. More often, I have made comparisons with other forms of violence. In ascertaining the conditions in which deadly riots occur, however, I have introduced negative evidence at various levels of generality: across regions, across episodes, and within episodes. For example, I tried to explain why violence occurred in Penang (1967) but not in Kuala Lumpur, why violence occurred in Kuala Lumpur (1969) but not in Penang, and why Hindu-Muslim violence has been more com-mon in north India than in south India.[4] In Tuva (1990), conditions for the deadly riot seemed propitious, but it did not materialize; it was nec-essary to explain the anomaly.[5] I noted that when trading rivals instigated violence in an environment lacking mass hostility, as in Karamanj (1968), there was more property damage than killing.[6] I looked at the effect of police action where force was deployed in a few locations within very serious riots and produced outcomes different from those in the majority of locations, where the police were inert.[7] And I have used Mill's method of elimination to infer, for instance, that cultural distance does not pre-dict target choice and that personal quarrels rarely produce deadly ethnic riots and very rarely produce severe riots.[8]

For the propositions I have advanced that pertain to the sources, rather than the characteristics, of violence, a more systematic confrontation with negative cases is warranted, so that we avoid selecting on the dependent variable. The frequent existence of quiescence or of other forms of violence in the face of the conditions I have associated with riots would require modification of the explanation, and a better understanding of quiescence in such conditions might also point toward paths to riot prevention.

PROOF POSITIVE AND PROOF NEGATIVE: THE PROBLEM OF VARIANCE

The task of connecting explanations for the incidence of violence with explanations for its absence is more problematic than might be imagined.

4. Chapter 10, pp. 378–79, 380; Chapter 5, p. 175.
5. Chapter 9, pp. 362–63.
6. Chapter 7, p. 230.
7. Chapter 9, pp. 363–64.
8. Chapter 5, pp. 188–91; Chapter 8, pp. 321–22. See John Stuart Mill, *A System of Logic* (Toronto: University of Toronto Press, 1974), p. 392. The argument is that even uncontrolled comparisons can eliminate hypothesized explanations not found to be present.

Nonviolence is a capacious category, to say the least. Standard injunctions about the need to study negative as well as positive cases are difficult to apply, partly because the outer boundary of the negative phenomenon is indeterminate. Is it, for example, all of nonviolence, all of nonviolence in severely divided societies, or all of nonviolence only when violence might have been expected? Such quandaries evoke sympathy with the cynic who declaimed that methodology is medicine we prescribe for others but avoid for ourselves. Still, a brief excursion into issues of method points to ways of coping with the question of nonviolence.

Following rather stern criticism of selection bias[9] — choosing cases on the dependent variable — some thoughtful qualifications have emerged. It has been pointed out, as I have above, that negative cases may not be required if the aim is simply to rule out hypothesized causes that are not found in the phenomena studied or to explain variance within a domain rather than between it and a larger universe.[10] The unit of selection has also been questioned: is each study an isolate, vulnerable to selection bias, or is it preferable to think of the community of investigators, each of whom chooses "observations based upon knowledge of cases from parallel studies"?[11] Even no-variance designs can provide explanations based on cumulative knowledge acquired in the course of "a larger research cycle" of comparative studies.[12] Some uncompromising foes of selection bias concede that, even if a single study selects on the dependent variable, that study, used in conjunction with prior studies, may produce "a valid causal inference."[13] No research begins on a truly blank slate. Investigators who seem to be selecting on the dependent variable are usually working in the context of prior findings and implicitly contrasting the findings of the new study with those. The deficiency of many comparative studies may not be selection bias so much as it is the failure to be explicit, in order to make visible the relation of the new findings to the old. As I shall show shortly, however, this line of attack is not especially helpful in the study of ethnic violence.

9. Gary King, Robert O. Keohane, and Sidney Verba, *Designing Social Inquiry: Scientific Inference in Qualitative Research* (Princeton: Princeton University Press, 1994), pp. 129–31; Barbara Geddes, "How the Cases You Choose Affect the Answers You Get: Selection Bias in Comparative Politics," in James A. Stimson, ed., *Political Analysis*, Vol. 2 (Ann Arbor: University of Michigan Press, 1990), pp. 131–50.

10. Collier, "Translating Quantitative Methods for Qualitative Researchers," pp. 464–65.

11. David D. Laitin, "Disciplining Political Science," *American Political Science Review* 89, no. 2 (June 1995): 454–56, at p. 456.

12. Collier and Mahoney, "Insights and Pitfalls," p. 74.

13. King, Keohane, and Verba, *Designing Social Inquiry*, p. 147.

Another selection issue pertains to the units within studies. Variation may be spatial or temporal, although the latter is rarely acknowledged except in studies explicitly labeled diachronic. If a study examines a phenomenon at two proximate time points, before and after the phenomenon occurs, this is a study of two observations, one negative and one positive, for each case. This may help explain the common resistance of historians to analyzing negative cases separately. I shall attempt to make further use of variation across time as well as space.

Sometimes selection on the dependent variable is preferable to a controlled study. If, for example, the effort to avoid selection bias requires comparison across cases that would likely introduce an unmanageable number of variables or require excessive conceptual stretching,[14] a more homogeneous data base may be the better choice.[15] This is a common problem when the case units are large and complex, as states are. Where such constraints impinge on the research design, negative variance can be introduced by the analysis of counterfactuals, speculation about possible outcomes had certain conditions been different from what they were in the cases investigated.[16] This is the enterprise many studies are already engaged in *sub silentio*. It has the advantage of permitting the analyst to imagine that all else (apart from the hypothesized causal condition) is equal, whereas in real cases all else may not be equal.[17] On the other hand, the statement of many counterfactuals — though phrased in negative form — is tantamount to the statement of the positive proposition.[18] If so, the variance they introduce is illusory.

These, then, are three possible solutions to the problem of introducing variance in an environment plagued by heterogeneity and noncomparability: the aggregation of parallel studies, specifically those that deal with the sources of quiescence vis-à-vis the sources of violence; the use of variance over time rather than space; and the invocation of counterfactuals.

14. Cf. Giovanni Sartori, "Comparing and Miscomparing," *Journal of Theoretical Politics* 3, no. 3 (July 1991): 243–58.

15. Collier and Mahoney, "Insights and Pitfalls," pp. 68–69.

16. Collier, "Translating Quantitative Methods for Qualitative Researchers," p. 464. See James D. Fearon, "Counterfactuals and Hypothesis Testing in Political Science," *World Politics* 43, no. 2 (January 1991): 169–95.

17. Fearon, "Counterfactuals and Hypothesis Testing in Political Science," p. 173.

18. For example: "If the United States had not dropped atomic bombs on two Japanese cities in August 1945, the Japanese would still have surrendered roughly when they did." This statement, taken from the editors' introduction to Philip E. Tetlock and Aaron Belkin, eds., *Counterfactual Thought Experiments in World Politics* (Princeton: Princeton University Press, 1996), p. 4, does no more than reverse the proposition that the atomic bombs ended the war. Pursuing the statement would scarcely test the proposition.

Some surprises await those who try to use these strategies to introduce variance between riots and the inchoate class of non-riots. "Parallel studies" are less helpful than might be imagined. Variance over time proves easy to locate but difficult to explain. Counterfactuals should be a strategy of last resort, to be used when data really are not available. Here they seem less promising than is the close examination of some non-riots that are not so far removed from conditions of actual violence.

The fundamental problem is to cope with the boundless quality of what might constitute a non-riot. While we might be interested in all instances in which riots did not occur, it would not be illuminating to study all of civil peace, in order to verify the conditions that produce violence, for that would be to investigate everything in social life apart from the riot. Even a more bounded study of all severely divided societies that did not experience riots would introduce too many variables.[19] This is the problem that leads David Collier and James Mahoney to urge a focus on the appropriate "frame of comparison" and to caution against making "comparisons across contexts that may . . . encompass heterogeneous causal relations."[20] Consequently, my inevitably imperfect solution to the problem will entail narrowing the frame of comparison.

THEORIES OF QUIESCENCE FROM THE LARGER RESEARCH CYCLE

There is ongoing dialogue among investigators about the sources of violence and the sources of quiescence. It is embodied in parallel studies that comprise a larger research cycle. Unfortunately, it is difficult to match up the two sets of findings. Although those who study quiescence aim explicitly to redress the balance favoring studies of violence, often they resort, ironically enough, to a parallel strategy of studying peace separately from violence. The observation that if a town is violent, every condition present is identified as a cause of violence, whereas if a town is peaceful, every condition present *there* is identified as a cause of peace embraces not one but two equal defects in reasoning. One can select on

19. Compare the positive and negative cases discussed in Joseph V. Montville, ed., *Conflict and Peacemaking in Multiethnic Societies* (Lexington, Mass.: Lexington Books, 1990), pp. 1, 131–447. Another effort at whole-state-level comparisons is described by Steven I. Wilkinson, "High Conflict/Low Conflict: Six Case Studies of Ethnic Politics: Report of a Workshop Held at the Woodrow Wilson International Center for Scholars" (Washington, D.C., October 1993).

20. Collier and Mahoney, "Insights and Pitfalls," p. 68.

the dependent variable of quiescence as easily as on the dependent variable of violence.

Explanations for an absence of violence have been offered at every level. Changes for the better in the international environment allegedly affected group relations.[21] Political leaders suddenly found an interest in cooperation across group lines.[22] Extremist organizations, with an interest in violence, were absent.[23] Group members practiced mutual avoidance, or their relations somehow became less antagonistic.[24] Cleavages other than ethnicity preempted ethnic violence.[25] Economic competition along ethnic lines, present in violent towns, was absent in peaceful ones.[26] The killing in earlier riots provided sufficient satisfaction to enable potential rioters to avoid a repetition.[27] Mutually profitable intergroup interactions,[28] or growing general prosperity,[29] or various forms of "civic engagement"[30] across group lines, or intragroup policing and sanctioning

21. Feliks Gross, *Ethnics in a Borderland: An Inquiry into the Nature of Ethnicity in a One-Time Genocide Area* (Westport, Conn.: Greenwood Press, 1978), p. 114. The antecedent violence Gross contrasts with the peace he seeks to explain did not consist entirely of riots; there were also highly organized mass killings.

22. Ibid., p. 115.

23. Aswini K. Ray and Subhash Chakravarti, *Karamanj Riots: A Political Study* (New Delhi: Sampradayikta Virodhi Committee, n.d.), p. 17; V.V. Singh, *Communal Violence* (Jaipur: Rawat, 1993), pp. 102–03.

24. Gross, *Ethnics in a Borderland*, pp. 116, 122–27; Kathleen A. Cavanaugh, "Interpretations of Political Violence in Ethnically Divided Societies" (paper presented at the annual meeting of the American Political Science Association, San Francisco, August 29–September 1, 1996), pp. 8–10.

25. Arun R. Swamy, "Sense, Sentiment, and Popular Coalitions: The Strange Career of Cultural Nationalism in Tamil Nadu," in Subrata K. Mitra and R. Alison Lewis, eds., *Subnational Movements in South Asia* (Boulder, Colo.: Westview Press, 1996), pp. 191–236, at pp. 209, 219; Ashutosh Varshney, "Religion, Nationalism and Violence: Hindus and Muslims in India" (unpublished manuscript, Harvard University, January 1996), pp. 158–64, 197–98. Cf. Crawford Young, *The Politics of Cultural Pluralism* (Madison: University of Wisconsin Press, 1976), pp. 360–61.

26. Singh, *Communal Violence*, pp. 102–03.

27. Amrita Basu, "When Local Riots Are Not Merely Local: Bringing the State Back In, Bijnor, 1988–92," *Economic and Political Weekly*, October 1, 1994, pp. 2605–21, at pp. 2619–20.

28. Ashutosh Varshney, "Structure of Civic Life and Communal Violence: Hindus and Muslims in India" (unpublished manuscript, Harvard University, 1997), p. 9. Cf. Hillel Frisch, "Explaining Variation in the Intensity of Violence in the West Bank/Judea and Samaria during the Intifada" (unpublished paper, Department of Political Science, Hebrew University, Jerusalem, July 3, 1991).

29. Diane Mauzy, "Malaysia: Political Hegemony and 'Coercive Consociationalism,'" in John McGarry and Brendan O'Leary, eds., *The Politics of Ethnic Conflict Regulation* (London: Routledge, 1993), p. 126.

30. Varshney, "Structure of Civic Life and Communal Violence," p. 1.

of those who cause trouble[31] contained violence. These are merely some of the sources of intergroup quiescence that have been postulated.

Some of these explanations, it will be observed, contradict others. Some rely on unexplained changes as the mechanism, thereby replacing one unknown with another. Some are circular. Most would benefit from closer proximity of the explanation for tranquility with the phenomenon of violence whose absence is being explained.[32] The explanations are not necessarily wrong — and we shall return to some of them — but they are difficult to verify by themselves.

First, the contradictions. Intergroup avoidance may promote peace, as may intergroup interaction and engagement, but both cannot do so without some mediating principle: they are mutually exclusive courses. Moreover, economic contacts are a form of intergroup interaction, asserted to be conducive to violence in some places but to violence prevention in others.[33]

Second, the unexplained changes. If group leaders move toward cooperation or if underlying intergroup relations become less antagonistic, these conditions can hardly be invoked without explaining how they came to pass. Parachuting cooperation in constitutes a form of explanatory smuggling.

Third, circularity. Is there no violence because of effective intragroup policing, or are intragroup controls visible because there is no significant violence, which, if it occurred, would swamp efforts to keep group members in line? Likewise, if there is no violence because other cleavages have preempted ethnic cleavages, why are those others the stronger cleavages? Perhaps those alternative cleavages have become important because the ethnic cleavage is already insignificant — in which case the absence of ethnic violence could hardly be attributed to the presence of alternative cleavages.

There is a need for closer connections of such explanations with violence. If the benign actions of external forces are responsible, then it

31. James D. Fearon and David D. Laitin, "Explaining Interethnic Cooperation," *American Political Science Review* 90, no. 4 (December 1996): 715–35.

32. It should be said that not all the works cited explicitly undertake to explain the absence of violence. Some aim to explain the lack of conflict in general. Still, their utility for present purposes is limited by their lack of connection to violence.

33. Although business rivalries between Hindu traders and Muslim artisans are frequently cited sources of violence in India, it was reported in Varanasi that Hindu traders worked to prevent violence following the destruction of the Babri mosque in 1992, lest their business relations with Muslims be disrupted. Wilkinson, "U.P.'s 'Riot-Prone' Towns," pp. 28–29.

might be expected that many riots would respond to changes in external relations. In the case of target groups with external affinities or those who find themselves on opposite sides of an international war, changes in external conditions will likely reduce violence; but external conditions are not the source of violence in the majority of cases that turn violent. With respect to prosperity, we have witnessed a good deal of violence in relatively prosperous cities, regions, and countries. Quiescence in the face of declining prosperity is also not uncommon. The prosperity explanation has been advanced specifically for post-1969 Malaysia,[34] but Malaysia was just as quiet in the hard recession years of the mid-1980s and the late 1990s; and its closest encounter with another riot, the near-miss of November 1987, occurred during the early period of recovery from the mid-'80s recession.[35] Similar assertions about the association of economic decline and either lynching or other acts of bigotry have proved to be unsustainable.[36] The satisfaction of bloodlust in 1990, which supposedly inhibited further violence in Bijnor two years later,[37] after the demolition of the mosque at Ayodhya, failed to do so in scores of other Indian cities, which had serious riots at both times.[38] The absence of extremist organizations has been said to explain the dearth of violence in some Indian locations, but the presence of those same organizations has also been adduced to explain quiescence: a Hindu extremist state government appointed local officials who, it is said, took preventive measures against violence.[39] A great many riots are not organized

34. Mauzy, "Malaysia," p. 126.

35. In 1987, Malaysia's gross domestic product grew dramatically. The growth accelerated as the year went on. *Economist Country Report: Malaysia*, June 14, 1988, available in *Lexis*, Asiapc Library: Malay File. More refined arguments, concerning the economic welfare of the specific groups that engage in ethnic violence, also have conspicuous problems. In the United States, the quiescent 1970s were a time of declining relative black prosperity compared with the rising black prosperity of the 1960s; and the same was true for Britain, where the improving conditions of minorities in the early 1980s coincided with violence that was absent in the stagnant 1970s. See Donald L. Horowitz, "Racial Violence in the United States," in Nathan Glazer and Ken Young, eds., *Ethnic Pluralism and Public Policy: Achieving Equality in the United States and Britain* (London: Heinemann Educational Books, 1983), p. 206.

36. Donald P. Green, Jack Glaser, and Andrew Rich, "From Lynching to Gay Bashing: The Elusive Connection between Economic Conditions and Hate Crime," *Journal of Personality and Social Psychology* 75, no. 1 (July 1998): 82–92.

37. See Basu, "When Local Riots Are Not Merely Local," pp. 2619–20.

38. Among the many cities affected in both years were Ahmedabad, Aligarh, and Kanpur. I am grateful to Steven Wilkinson for sharing some data with me on the repeat riots of 1990 and 1992.

39. Compare Ray and Chakravarti, *Karamanj Riots*, p. 17, and Singh, *Communal Violence*, pp. 102–03, with Basu, "When Local Riots Are Not Merely Local," pp. 2619–20.

by extremist groups, and many are not well organized at all: the positive cases alone tell us that.

Some of the hazards of explaining quiescence without examining violence are evident in James D. Fearon and David D. Laitin's original attempt to account for the absence of interethnic violence in terms of restraints imposed on group members to prevent them from triggering an escalation of conflict.[40] Fearon and Laitin begin with the common propensity of people to engage in antisocial behavior ("cheating, shirking, malfeasance, fraud, exploitation, embezzlement, extortion, robbery, and rape"[41]), if left to their own devices. To this problem, a number of solutions are possible, including the growth of networks of trust and cooperation founded on expectations of future interdependence and supported by reputations for reliability. Since interethnic relations are characterized by distrust and an absence of reputational information, sanctioning and deterrence of individual misbehavior across groups lines are difficult: "interethnic conflict has a high propensity to spiral . . . ."[42] To prevent the spiral, intragroup policing is practiced. Expectations develop that anyone who disturbs interethnic relations by antisocial behavior directed against an ethnic stranger "will be identified and sanctioned by members of his or her own group."[43] The growth of such expectations is a principal support of interethnic peace, contend Fearon and Laitin, and a breach of those expectations results in interethnic violence for the purpose of deterring future misbehavior.

No doubt, intraethnic policing of this kind occurs on occasion, and it may restrain a very limited species of interethnic conflict escalation. Group leaders certainly have a part to play in violence prevention, especially in view of the strong role of authoritative social support in facilitating riots. But the claim that such policing, *on such occasions and for such purposes*, is a major reason for peace in severely divided societies is not sustainable. Here is where connective tissue between mechanisms of peace and occasions for violence would be helpful.[44] The vast majority of ethnic riots are precipitated by events with a notably collective and polit-

40. Fearon and Laitin, "Explaining Interethnic Cooperation." In challenging the view that ethnic conflict is widespread, Fearon and Laitin appear to mean that ethnic *violence* is not widespread. There is good reason to treat conflict and violence separately.

41. Ibid., p. 717.

42. Ibid., p. 730.

43. Ibid.

44. The empirical illustrations provided by Fearon and Laitin pertain almost exclusively to policing mechanisms rather than violence mechanisms. "Explaining Interethnic Cooperation," pp. 727–30.

ical, rather than individual and personal, flavor — events originating at the group-competitive level rather than the level of the individual miscreant. Negative cases are not needed to prove this point. Microlevel conflicts between members of different groups sometimes get out of hand, but when they escalate they usually produce interethnic violence of a very modest sort.[45]

If individual misbehavior were a major source of interethnic violence, then a great fraction of quiescence might be accounted for by intragroup policing. But if group-level precipitants produce violence, efforts of intraethnic leaders to police individual miscreants and mediate personal quarrels will be inadequate to prevent violence, and their conflict-limiting efforts will be brushed aside as irrelevant to the larger issues that divide groups.[46] Embedded in the policing explanation is a theory of the origins of the riot that is not supportable.

The form of the violence that occurs when policing is alleged to fail bears on the cogency of the policing explanation. Fearon and Laitin speak of "indiscriminate retribution,"[47] attacks on randomly identified ethnic strangers — just what we have been considering under the rubric of riot. But if the violence is for deterrent purposes, random attacks of this kind would appear dysfunctional. Indiscriminate retribution would make it possible for the miscreants who are said to trigger the retribution to engage in antisocial behavior without significant risk that they themselves or those closest to them will bear the brunt of retaliation. That is

45. Note that I do not make the claim that because personal quarrels do not precipitate violence, intraethnic policing must be insignificant. Such an argument could easily be turned around: because policing is successful, personal quarrels do not precipitate violence. My claim is rather that even when policing of antisocial behavior fails and personal quarrels produce violence, the violence is rarely of great magnitude. Such policing thus cannot account for the prevention of serious episodes of ethnic violence.

A good example of violence produced by what was probably seen as a failure of intragroup policing is the violence that followed the elopement of a Mohajir man and a Pathan woman in Karachi in February 1998. After police failed to find the couple, Pathans "went on a rampage," attacking police and killing two innocent bystanders, but conspicuously failing to turn the matter into an interethnic issue. After the couple was found, several members of the bride's family took revenge on the groom, critically injuring him. *Durham Herald-Sun* (N.C.), February 12, 1998, p. A6; March 5, 1998, p. A5. The few casualties inflicted in the public rampage and the subsequent revenge taken on a family-to-family basis both suggest that, even in highly charged Karachi, where ethnic violence is commonplace, deadly ethnic riots do not issue from serious and uncontrolled family quarrels, which are more likely to produce feudlike behavior.

46. For an example of Hindu and Muslim leaders whose joint efforts to avert violence were swept aside, see S.K. Ghosh, *Communal Riots in India* (New Delhi: Ashish, 1987), pp. 131–32.

47. Fearon and Laitin, "Explaining Interethnic Cooperation," p. 728.

the meaning of *indiscriminate*.[48] To foster miscreant accountability, the measured, discriminate violence of the feud or the lynching would seem more apt than is the indiscriminate violence of the riot.[49] In fact, those are the forms of violence utilized for such purposes. Moreover, it is difficult to square the atrocities that occur in ethnic riots with the aim of restoring a cooperative status quo ante. Atrocities break the ties between antagonists, as the polarizing effects of riots show repeatedly. In truth, indiscriminate violence is not generally unleashed in this way at all. As we saw in Chapter 7, organized riots typically have aims other than preservation of a peaceful equilibrium.[50]

A major price in explanatory power is paid by theories that reduce collective behavior to individual grievance or individual antisocial behavior and that deal with quiescence alongside violence without connecting the two. The latter is the mirror image of focusing on violence without attending to the sources of quiescence.

NEAR-MISS STRATEGIES

If studies of quiescence usually fail to meet the adversary — violence — and so produce free-standing explanations for the absence of violence, the gap they leave suggests a way to narrow the frame of comparison, by

48. The classic treatment of reprisal, emphasizing its calculated, measured quality, is Thomas C. Schelling, *Arms and Influence* (New Haven: Yale University Press, 1966), pp. 129, 141–51, 168–69. "Reprisals," says Schelling, in terms reminiscent of Fearon and Laitin's vocabulary, "often have the function of policing qualitative limits against violation . . . ." Ibid., p. 169. But, he argues, "the idea of *reprisal* involves potential restraint — ruptured restraint to be sure, with damages exacted for some violation or excess — but the essence of reprisal is an action that had been withheld, and could continue to be withheld if the other had not violated the bargain." Ibid., p. 129 (emphasis in the original). It is the antithesis of indiscriminate violence.

49. Indeed, that is what the literature indicates. Christopher Boehm, cited by Fearon and Laitin, notes that intragroup feuding is far more amenable to efforts to control it than is intergroup feuding. Christopher Boehm, *Blood Revenge: The Anthropology of Feuding in Montenegro and Other Tribal Societies* (Lawrence: University Press of Kansas, 1984), p. 106. To the same effect, see David McKnight, "Fighting in an Australian Aboriginal Supercamp," in David Riches, ed., *The Anthropology of Violence* (Oxford: Basil Blackwell, 1986), pp. 136–63, at pp. 159–60. See also the Karachi example in note 45, above. Here again, we are back to the importance of disaggregating the forms of violence, which I emphasized in Chapter 1.

50. The only example I can think of in which indiscriminate violence was organized for deterrent purposes is Fiji (1987), discussed below. The Fijian violence, however, concerned large political issues dividing the groups in conflict, rather than individual instances of antisocial behavior, and yet was carefully calibrated to get the message across. It was unusually mild, consisting of completely nonlethal attacks.

employing what I call, loosely, *near-miss strategies*. These involve focusing on instances of quiescence or of non-riot violence that occur in what
seem to be the most fertile conditions for riots. Suppose, for example,
there is evidence of strong ethnic conflict, and non-riot violence, such as
terrorism or lynching, occurs. Why did this form of violence, rather than
a riot, emerge? Alternatively, imagine that a deadly riot occurs, but it is
conspicuously lacking in severity, or events occur that participants fear
will produce a riot, but the riot does not materialize. Why the mild event
or the non-event? Or suppose there is a long history of deadly riots, but
then, for many years, riots have abated. The change calls out for explanation. All of these configurations create opportunities for inference
within a narrower band than the undifferentiated field of civil peace. The
hunt for the missing variable that, if present, would have produced a riot,
or for the additional variable that propelled the violence toward a different form, should be easier than dealing with the imponderables of quiescence in general.[51]

To focus on non-riot ethnic violence, low-intensity riots, near-riots,
and unrepeated riots is to select a considerable range of values on the
dependent variable,[52] turning a dichotomous (riot or no-riot) variable
into a continuous one.[53] Furthermore, in the case of nonrecurring violence, there are three observations over time: the period before the riots,
the riots, and the subsequent quiescent period. If it is possible to ascertain
how action develops or fails to develop, it should be possible to discriminate among the conditions that sustain the various violent or nonviolent
outcomes — indirectly, then, the conditions sustaining deadly riots.

Even in this more limited frame of comparison, however, the proof of
positives by the proof of negatives is not easy. It is difficult, as we shall
see, to explain sustained periods of nonrecurrence after a violent event
and particularly challenging to account for non-riots in seemingly propi-

51. For a similar problem of defining the relevant universe and an analogous limiting
solution, see Christopher H. Achen and Duncan Snidal, "Rational Deterrence Theory
and Comparative Case Studies," *World Politics* 41, no. 2 (January 1989): 143–69, at pp.
162–63.

52. See King, Keohane, and Verba, *Designing Social Inquiry*, pp. 141–42. Non-riot ethnic violence is perhaps not quite on the same axis, but it is worth examining in the same cluster on the grounds that it is generally less intense or extensive than the deadly ethnic riot.

53. In addition, since near-miss cases begin with conditions apparently propitious for
deadly riots, the strategy loads the dice, as it were, in favor of riots and so highlights for
explanation the fact that riots nevertheless did not occur. Hence it provides a better test of
riot theories than would a broader explanation of nonviolence in general. For the logic
underlying such an approach, see ibid., pp. 209–12. Cf. Harry Eckstein, "Case Study and
Theory in Political Science," in Fred I. Greenstein and Nelson W. Polsby, eds., *Handbook of
Political Science*, Vol. 7 (Reading, Mass.: Addison-Wesley, 1975), pp. 79–137.

tious conditions. The closer we come to purely negative cases, the more uncertain are the results. Hence the utility of the borderline episode, in which *ceteris paribus* logic can be employed.

Nevertheless, alternative forms of ethnic violence, mild riots, near-riots, and nonrecurring riots are generally explicable in terms of the absence of one or more of the following: appropriate precipitants, appropriate targets, police indifference or condonation, or social support for violence. The loss of social support may follow from an underlying change in ethnic antipathy or from a change in the disposition to sanction interpersonal violence against civilians. Overall, the evidence suggests that deadly ethnic riots result from the confluence of specific conditions, the absence of any one of which renders riots decidedly less probable. There is, therefore, an asymmetry between the positive and negative cases. The control cases look more different from each other than the riot cases do, because the same general conditions concatenate again and again to produce a riot, whereas a riot can fail to materialize for want of any of these conditions.

ALTERNATIVES TO RIOTS:
LYNCHING AND BURNING

From 1990 to 1997, Romania experienced more than two dozen episodes of arson perpetrated in separate villages against Roma (Gypsies) resident there. These were crowd attacks against at least several houses, often many houses; in several, individual Roma were lynched or burned to death inside houses. Each event, organized spontaneously, lasted no longer than a day or a night; it was preceded by a theft, murder, rape, insult, or trespass attributed to a Gypsy or a fight between Roma and Romanians. Characteristically, Romanians complained that the police had done nothing to prevent Roma from misbehaving. Few Romanians were punished after the fact, although some lax police officers were. Many Roma were intimidated from returning to or rebuilding their homes, in some cases for months afterward. In the damp winter of 1993–94, some exiled villagers were bundled up in holes in the ground on a muddy hillside.[54]

54. In February 1994, I visited all the major sites of this violence in rural Romania that had occurred to that point, in the course of an investigation of anti-Roma events. I conducted interviews with victims, participants, police officers, group leaders, and government officials. The account contained in this section is based on these interviews, on unpublished governmental and nongovernmental papers and reports, and on Romanian newspaper accounts.

These events are recognizable as near-riots — against property, rather than people — coupled with lynchings of putative offenders. There was little attempt at stealth. Crowds were gathered on the spur of the moment using church bells, thus allowing most Roma to flee, and damage was often, but not always, confined to the houses of those regarded as troublemakers. In the affected villages, there was great support for the violence. Crowds often numbered in the hundreds, sometimes including nearly the whole village; in a few cases, even local Roma, differentiated by subgroup, joined in the arson.[55] As in lynchings in the United States south, Roma who were regarded as uninvolved in antisocial behavior were often conspicuously left unharmed.[56] Similar episodes occurred during the same period in other East European countries after comparable precipitants.[57]

Why did the violence take this form rather than that of deadly ethnic riots? Not for want of hostility. Antipathy to Roma in Romania is exceedingly powerful. The vast majority of survey respondents confess to entertaining very strongly negative feelings toward Roma.[58] The police, delegitimized after the fall of the Ceauşescu regime in 1989, were demoralized, outnumbered, sometimes sympathetic to the crowds, and rarely effective in stopping the violence. In accounts provided after the events, government officials blamed the Roma for precipitating the violence,[59] and the government, feeling local sentiment, was cautious about prosecuting offenders. On every count, crowds might have been encouraged to

55. Nicolae Gheorghe, "Prosecuting and Preventing Violence and Intolerance against Romanies (Gypsies) in the CSCE Countries: The Case of Romania" (paper presented at the CSCE Seminar on the Human Dimension of Tolerance, Warsaw, November 16–20, 1992, mimeo.), p. 7.

56. "Report of the Committee on Human Rights, Religious Affairs and National Minorities of the Chamber of Deputies of the Romanian Parliament on the Events at Hadareni (Mures)" (mimeo.; November 19, 1993), p. 3. The same omission was as notable in Constanta as in Hadareni.

57. See Anna Giza, "Prevention of Anti-Roma Violence: A Polish Case Study" (paper presented at the conference entitled "Warning: Road under Construction," Warsaw, March 17–19, 1991).

58. I am drawing here on the extensive survey data of William Crowther, who used "thermometers" to measure intergroup hostility. In his subsample of midsized cities, some of them near the locations of anti-Roma violence, a clear majority of respondents chose the most hostile point at which to locate their feelings toward Roma — that is, 1.0 on a scale of 1.0 to 10.00. In Baia Mare, not far from some of the violence, 90 percent chose the 1.0 point on the scale, and no respondent chose a location beyond 2.0!

59. "Statement of the Romanian Government Regarding the Events in the Village of Hadareni-Chetani, County of Mures, September 20–21, 1993" (mimeo.; September 23, 1993), p. 1; Ministry of Interior, General Inspectorate of Police, "Note about the Activities Developed by Police Unities [sic] for Preventing and Controlling Ethnic Conflicts" (unpublished memorandum, typescript, n.d. [ca. 1994]), pp. 1–2.

do what crowds elsewhere have done to their enemies: kill them indiscriminately.

Clearly, they aimed to harm identified miscreants and to expel alleged troublemakers from their villages.[60] This was more or less discriminate, not indiscriminate, violence, precisely the sort that occurs when ethnically differentiated individual offenders engage in antisocial behavior. Many Roma had special reasons to engage in petty offenses in post-Communist Romania. Habitually landless, they did not qualify for the return of state land to its former owners and were sometimes reduced to stealing potatoes or chopping wood on their neighbors' land.[61] For a group stereotyped as inclined to crime,[62] this was dangerous indeed. In some villages, Romanians demanded that Roma leaders control — or "police" — their followers.[63] *Police* is indeed an appropriate term, for villagers complained, as those engaged in lynching have always complained, that they were performing a police function. Since the police and Roma leaders could not control the Roma, the crowd was obliged to do so.[64]

Notably absent in the face of antipathy, police ineffectiveness, and governmental sympathy for the Romanian side is an appropriate precipitant for deadly ethnic riots or a relationship of aggressors and targets conducive to that form of violence. These were mainly trivial precipitants: a theft, a personal quarrel, a fight in a bar. Roma are despised, but

60. Manuela Stefanescu and Vera Cîmpeanu, "Report on the Apador-Ch Fact Finding Mission to Hadareni and Tîrgu Mures (October 5–7, 1993)" (mimeo.; 1993), p. 3. Roma were told, in some cases explicitly, that they would not be permitted to return, and in some they were attacked when they did return. This was the case in Boletin Deal, where the initial arson and flight occurred in April 1991. By the time of my visit in February 1994 Roma were not able to return. In Hadareni as well, four months after the violence, those who had been burned out were still not back, and Romanian villagers made it quite clear that they were vociferously opposed to their return.

61. These were common infractions cited against Roma. See, e.g., ibid., p. 4.

62. For the stereotype of Roma as uneducated beggars and thieves, poor, dirty, but musical, see Giza, "Prevention of Anti-Roma Violence." See also Ian Hancock, "Anti-Gypsyism in the New Europe" (unpublished paper, University of Texas at Austin, 1992).

63. My field notes are replete with Romanian remarks about the need for the Roma group to put its house in order, for Roma leaders to impose order on the Roma, or "to give Roma a period of time to see if they can behave in a civilized way."

64. "The absence of a permanent police station in the village tempted people into taking justice in their own hands." "Report of the Committee on Human Rights, Religious Affairs and National Minorities of the Romanian Parliament," p. 2. "One of Hadareni peasants who spoke at the meeting . . . declared: 'We are not proud of what we did on 20 September, but we had to do it!' He insisted that the authorities — the police and the D.A. office — did not do anything to solve previous complaints regarding antisocial behavior of the Gypsies in Hadareni." Stefanescu and Cîmpeanu, "Report on the Apador-Ch Fact Finding Mission to Hadareni and Tîrgu Mures," p. 4.

they make no serious political claims (they are, in fact, significantly divided), they engage in no strikes, demonstrations, or polarizing elections, and they create no serious apprehension about their abilities as social competitors. Unlike Hungarians in Romania, they have no dangerous external affinities. When the claim is, as it recurrently was in Romania, that individual miscreants are causing trouble or that personal quarrels have turned violent, the indiscriminate violence of the deadly ethnic riot does not follow. Rather, milder violence that takes the form of burning — the sort of violence that attracts crowds who might not be attracted to mass face-to-face killing — is what follows a mere failure of day-to-day social controls.

ALTERNATIVES TO RIOTS: ETHNIC TERRORISM

Firmly in the category of discriminate violence is ethnic terrorism. The conditions that are sufficient for ethnic terrorism are not the same as those that are required for ethnic riots. Ethnic terrorism is rarely accompanied by deadly riots.

If ever ethnic terrorism and the events surrounding it were of a magnitude to provoke deadly ethnic riots, those conditions were present in the Indian Punjab from 1984 to 1994. Yet the riots did not materialize, providing a negative case worthy of close scrutiny. I pointed out in Chapter 5 that the configuration of traditional enmities and alliances may have shielded Punjab from Hindu-Sikh riots. Just how strong a shield Punjab had is evident from an examination of the incidence of riots contrasted with the available precipitants and the scale and deadliness of the terrorism.

There have been some Hindu-Sikh riots in India, but their scale has always been far greater outside Punjab than inside. In Calcutta (1967), eleven were killed.[65] In Delhi (1984), Sikh deaths ran to the thousands. Yet, in 1966, when a highly contentious decision was made to divide the Indian Punjab into two states, Punjab and Haryana, in order to satisfy demands for a Sikh-majority state, only four people were killed in a total of six locations, not all of them in Punjab.[66] Nor did anti-Hindu riots follow Operation Bluestar in 1984, when Indian troops entered the Sikhs' most sacred temple at Amritsar, killing large numbers of Sikh militants

65. Herbert Feldman, "The Communal Problem in the Indo-Pakistan Subcontinent: Some Current Implications," *Pacific Affairs* 42, no. 2 (Summer 1969): 145–63, at p. 151.
66. Ibid., p. 150.

and their charismatic leader. Revenge took the form of the assassination of Prime Minister Indira Gandhi, rather than mass violence. When that assassination produced the anti-Sikh riot in Delhi and a flow of Sikh refugees to Punjab, the rioters were not Punjabi Hindus, and reciprocal revenge did not take the form of Sikh riots against Hindus in Punjab. Instead, there was a strong acceleration of the violent movement for an independent Sikh state, Khalistan.

Not that Hindu-Sikh relations were tension-free. There were some confrontations in 1982–83 and small population movements from 1984 onward, as the Khalistan terrorism accelerated in Punjab.[67] But, in spite of the substantial Hindu minority in Punjab, the substantial Sikh minority in neighboring Haryana, and decades of Sikh separatist agitation, in the post-independence period both states had some of the lowest rates of riots and riot deaths in all of India. Serious provocations on the part of Sikh militants — attacks on Hindus in buses, attacks on RSS members engaged in martial exercises, the placing of cigarettes in Sikh *gurdwaras* and of cows' heads in front of Hindu temples — failed to produce significant ethnic violence.[68] No intraethnic policing could account for the absence of riots. The militants were not policed; they did all they could to provoke riots.[69]

The separatists had good reason to try to ignite riots, for they undoubtedly wished to generate an exodus of Hindus, about 40 percent of the Punjab population, and, even more important, a migration of Sikhs to Punjab from the many areas of India where they lived comfortably. Riots in Punjab might be met with retaliatory riots against Sikhs outside Punjab, bringing about a two-way migration and making independent Khalistan more realistic than it would be while large numbers of Sikhs remained outside its borders.[70] There was sufficient disorder in Punjab to provide abundant opportunities for riot. By the time the sepa-

67. M.J. Akbar, *Riot after Riot* (New Delhi: Penguin, 1988), p. 123; Pravin Patel, "Violent Protest in India: The Punjab Movement," *Journal of International Affairs* 40, no. 2 (Winter/Spring 1987): 271–85. The small incidents of 1982–83 that occurred in several towns were generally nonlethal and easily controlled by curfews.

68. Robin Jeffrey, *What's Happening to India: Punjab, Ethnic Conflict and the Test for Federalism*, 2d ed. (New York: Holmes & Meier, 1994), pp. 161–62; S.C. Arora, *Turmoil in Punjab Politics* (New Delhi: Mittal, 1990), pp. 194–95, 212. Observant Sikhs are enjoined not to smoke, as caste Hindus are enjoined not to kill cows.

69. A perfect contrast is provided by the extremely violent Sinhalese riot in response to a Tamil Tiger attack on an army unit in Sri Lanka (1983).

70. On the importance of back-migration to the home region as a condition of secession, see Donald L. Horowitz, *Ethnic Groups in Conflict* (Berkeley and Los Angeles: University of California Press, 1985), p. 247.

ratists were defeated in 1994, some 25,000 people had been killed, the vast majority of them Sikhs, mainly alleged informers, members of competing separatist organizations, or terrorists and guerrillas killed by the police.[71]

It is not necessary to understand the precise etiology of the terrorism to explain the absence of Hindu-Sikh violence in Punjab and Haryana. The separatist movement was the product of a complex interplay of Sikh religious revival, anxieties about assimilation, strong regional, caste, factional, and party cleavages among Sikhs, and serious failures and inconsistencies on the part of the central government.[72] The one thing not implicated was hostility between Sikhs and Hindus in Punjab. When riots affected Punjab in 1978, the attackers were Sikhs, and the 16 who were killed were also Sikhs, of the heterodox Nirankari persuasion.[73] Among the other things this attack makes clear is the limited Sikh support enjoyed by the militants.[74] Support tended to be confined to some sections of some castes and to certain regions of Punjab.

On the other hand, ties between Sikhs and Hindus persisted. In Haryana, although high rates of Hindu-Sikh intermarriage ended

71. See Stanley J. Tambiah, *Leveling Crowds: Ethnonationalist Conflicts and Collective Violence in South Asia* (Berkeley and Los Angeles: University of California Press, 1996), p. 148; Arora, *Turmoil in Punjab Politics*, pp. 196–97, 210.

72. See Tambiah, *Leveling Crowds*, pp. 145–50; Paul Wallace, "Political Violence and Terrorism in India: The Crisis of Identity," in Martha Crenshaw, ed., *Terrorism in Context* (University Park: Pennsylvania State University Press, 1995), pp. 352–410; Sucha Singh Gill, "The Punjab Accord of 1985 and Its Failure," in K.M. de Silva, ed., *Peace Accords and Ethnic Conflict* (London: Pinter, 1993), pp. 99–111; Surindar S. Suri, *Anomie, Violence and Peace in Punjab* (New Delhi: Voluntary Health Association of India, 1993), pp. 15–16; Gurharpal Singh, "Ethnic Conflict in India: A Case Study of Punjab," in John McGarry and Brendan O'Leary, eds., *The Politics of Ethnic Conflict Regulation: Case Studies of Protracted Ethnic Conflicts* (London: Routledge, 1992), pp. 84–105; Hamish Telford, "The Political Economy of Punjab: Creating Space for Sikh Militancy," *Asian Survey* 32, no. 11 (November 1992): 969–87; Surjit Hans, "From Sedition to Riots," in Pramod Kumar, ed., *Towards Understanding Communalism* (Chandigarh: Centre for Research in Rural and Industrial Development, 1992), pp. 471–81; Carl H. Yaeger, "Sikh Terrorism and the Struggle for Khalistan," *Terrorism* 14, no. 4 (October/December 1991): 221–32; Surendra Chopra, "Ethnicity, Revivalism and Politics in Punjab," in Paul Wallace and Surendra Chopra, eds., *Political Dynamics and Crisis in Punjab* (Amritsar: Guru Nanak Dev University, 1988), pp. 465–501; Paul Wallace, "Religious and Secular Politics in Punjab: The Sikh Dilemma in Competing Political Systems," in Wallace and Chopra, eds., *Political Dynamics and Crisis in Punjab*, pp. 1–44; Patel, "Violent Protest in India: The Punjab Movement," pp. 276–79.

73. Telford, "The Political Economy of Punjab," pp. 975–76.

74. Gurharpal Singh, "Understanding the 'Punjab Problem,'" *Asian Survey* 27, no. 12 (December 1987): 1268–77, at p. 1276; Yaeger, "Sikh Terrorism in the Struggle for Khalistan," p. 221.

decades before, Hindus still practiced Sikh death rites; in Punjab villages where terrorists shot Hindus, Sikhs cared for their families, and Sikh police guarded them, averting panic-induced migration.[75] Caste affinities span the Hindu-Sikh boundary, particularly among landowning Jats of the two groups.[76] No amount of effort by Sikh religious extremists sufficed to harden the intergroup boundary altogether. Hindus and Sikhs still enjoyed a diluted version of the old "*Beti-Roti* relationship," one that permitted intermarriage and interdining.[77] Typically, intra-Sikh caste divisions were stronger than Sikh-Hindu divisions between members of comparable castes. To the extent the Khalistan movement had general appeal, it was a struggle between Punjab and Sikhs, on one side, and the Indian central government and Hindus beyond Punjab, and even beyond Haryana, on the other side.

The extraordinary degree to which preexisting group relations survived is attested by residential patterns in Punjab villages after a decade of terrorism. Hindus and Sikhs were commonly able to live intermixed, whereas the few Muslims often lived on the edge of the village.[78] There could be no more graphic demonstration of felt conflict alignments. If Romania had the requisite antipathy but inadequate precipitants and inapt target-group characteristics, Punjab had the precipitants in abundance. What makes it a negative case is the absence of serious antipathy and the social support for riot violence that can (but does not always) flow from antipathy.

MILD RIOTS AND NEAR-RIOTS

The deadly ethnic riot is characterized by its brutality: large-scale killing and atrocities. As the Romanian arson-lynchings attest, however, not every violent interpersonal episode runs true to form. There are events in which crowds attack ethnically differentiated targets but in which there is a marked lack of intensity. Beating may occur without killing, or few

75. I am drawing here on presentations made to a conference on Punjab terrorism and its suppression that I attended in Chandigarh, June 7–11, 1994, particularly on the remarks of H.S. Mehta, Jagtar Singh, P.P.S. Gill, Harish Puri, and K.P.S. Gill.

76. D.R. Chaudhry, "Politics of Haryana," in T.R. Sharma, ed., *New Challenges of Politics in Indian States* (New Delhi: Uppal, 1986), pp. 174–75.

77. Jitendra Narayan, *Communal Riots in India* (Delhi: Ashish, 1992), p. 16.

78. I am drawing here on brief visits to such villages in June 1994, including the village of Beant Singh, Sikh assassin of Mrs. Gandhi. After her assassination, Sikh villagers feared an attack from Hindus in neighboring villages — significantly, not from within their own — but no such attack materialized. Calm prevailed.

deaths may result. Examples include Palacode, Tamil Nadu (1979), in which large-scale violence produced four deaths, two of them the result of police fire; Moldova (1990), in which Moldovan crowds attacked Russians in Kishinev but did not engage in mass killing;[79] Fiji (1987), in which Fijian crowds attacked Indians but killed none; Madagascar (1972 and 1973), in which thousands of Merina fled the coast to the highlands but no deaths were reported; and a veritable array of anti-Chinese episodes in Java (repeatedly in 1980, 1984, 1996, 1997, and 1998) and Sulawesi (1997) that, in the aggregate, resulted in a handful of deaths.[80] I have collected materials on about 30 such events (not counting separately each Indonesian outbreak when events occur in multiple locations). Since mild violence is surely underreported, there must be a very large number of such episodes. In none that I have examined has a confluence of all the elements that appear to produce full-blown deadly riots been present.

Some episodes edge over into non-riot forms. The violence in Burma (1988) had elements of lynching and arson, as well as mild riot. The precipitant was a personal incident, a fight at a Muslim-owned tea shop in Taunggyi that Burmans later burned down, as they then did others. The trivial character of the precipitant did not prevent the spread of the violence to Prome, where a personal insult produced more violence. Despite police ineffectiveness, the main attacks targeted Muslim-owned property, with specific emphasis on property of alleged culprits,[81] in a way that resembles the events in Romania. The violence in Jakarta (1974) had elements of a protest demonstration (against Chinese, against Japanese investors, and against the Indonesian regime) as much as it did an ethnic riot.[82] Hence the low level of casualties. The events in Medan, Indonesia

79. Daria Fane, "Moldova: Breaking Loose from Moscow," in Ian Bremmer and Roy Taras, eds., *Nations and Politics in the Soviet Successor States* (Cambridge: Cambridge University Press, 1993), pp. 121–53.

80. See, respectively, Government of India, *Third Annual Report of the Minorities Commission (for the Year Ending 31st December, 1980)* (New Delhi: Government Printer, 1981), pp. 78–83; *Far Eastern Economic Review*, June 4, 1987, p. 40; *Africa Research Bulletin*, December 1–31, 1972, pp. 2692–97; Colin Legum, ed., *Africa Contemporary Record, 1972–1973* (New York: Africana, 1973), pp. B4, B200; ibid., *1973–1974* (New York: Africana, 1974), p. B199; *Far Eastern Economic Review*, December 5, 1980, pp. 10–12; October 18, 1984, pp. 18–19; March 13, 1997, pp. 42–47; *New York Times*, April 8, 1997, pp. A1, A7.

81. Bertil Lintner, *Outrage: Burma's Struggle for Democracy* (London and Bangkok: White Lotus, 1990), pp. 80–82. In 1997, an alleged assault on a Burman girl by a Muslim in Mandalay produced a spate of desecration and destruction of mosques and Muslim homes and cars; people were apparently not targeted. Associated Press report, March 20, 1997, 1997 WL 4858397.

82. *Far Eastern Economic Review*, June 3, 1974, p. 15.

(1994), were a mix of anti-Chinese violence and labor violence.[83] There was much arson but only one death. The Madagascar (1972 and 1973) events combined beating of Merina with burnings of public buildings and records.[84] There are, then, some hybrid events among those that might be categorized as mild riots, and the outcomes are therefore influenced by the variables that govern those alternative phenomena. But, even if we eliminate these hybrids, there are many low-intensity riots to explain.

INAPPROPRIATE TARGETS

Among the most powerful explanations for the low intensity of some riots are inappropriate target-group characteristics, in the sense in which those are depicted in Chapter 5. India furnishes clear evidence. Assam, a state filled with large-scale anti-Bengali riots from the 1950s into the 1990s, experienced very mild anti-Marwari riots in Gauhati and nearby towns in 1968, in conjunction with Republic Day celebrations. Assamese separatism had been growing; Marwaris, identified as "Indians," based on their origins outside Assam, were, as I have argued,[85] targeted as surrogates for the central government. Despite considerable property damage and police passivity, no one was killed.[86] Once the political protest passed, Assamese went back to targeting Bengalis in deadly episodes of the more usual, extravagant magnitude. Marwaris have occasionally been targeted elsewhere in India, but always mildly. Despite its very small Muslim population, Orissa can generate a significant Hindu-Muslim riot on occasion, notably Rourkela (1964), in which at least 62 were killed, and Rourkela (1991), in which at least 15 died. The Orissa violence of 1980, which affected a number of towns over the course of a week, produced only arson and plunder of Marwari-owned shops and godowns. Hundreds of Marwari homes were destroyed, but no one was killed, save arsonists shot by the police.[87] The contrast in casualties between

---

83. Ibid., April 28, 1994, pp. 14–15; Ariel Heryanto, "A Class Act," ibid., June 16, 1994, p. 30.

84. See Legum, ed., *Africa Contemporary Record*, 1972–73, pp. B174–75, B200; ibid., 1973–74, p. B199; *Africa Research Bulletin*, December 1–31, 1972, pp. 2696–97.

85. See Chapter 5, above.

86. "Sack of Gauhati," *Economic and Political Weekly*, February 17, 1968, pp. 318–20; *Statesman*, February 10, 1968. There was suspicion that the state government may actually have encouraged the rioters, in which case the absence of deaths stands out even more prominently.

87. *Times of India*, September 30, 1980, p. 6; October 6, 1980, p. 1; October 7, 1980, p. 7; *Deccan Herald* (Bangalore), October 1, 1980, p. 1; October 4, 1980, p. 7. See Patit Paban Misra, "Why Anti-Marwari Agitation in Orissa?" *Mainstream* 19, no. 9 (November 1980): 6, 9.

Indian riots in which Muslims (or, in Assam, Bengalis) are targeted and those in which Marwaris are victimized speaks eloquently to the depth of antipathy against some groups and its shallowness against others.[88]

Similar contrasts can be observed in Sri Lanka when Tamils are targeted by Sinhalese and when Muslims are: in Galle (1982), Sinhalese-Muslim violence claimed two lives.[89] A year later, anti-Tamil violence claimed at least several hundred. The 1982 violence involved a landlord-tenant dispute, furnishing more evidence that individual quarrels, even when unpoliced, do not produce major riots. For this reason, the 1982 events could just as easily be analyzed under the rubric of trivial precipitants as under the rubric of inappropriate targets. For obvious reasons, the two tend to covary. Or compare Singapore (1950) with Singapore (1964), the former violence directed variously against Dutch, European, or Eurasian targets, the latter unequivocally against Chinese. Although police bias in favor of the 1950 rioters was evident early on, rioters mainly beat, rather than killed, their victims.[90] The force of a reasonably provocative precipitant was, in this case, blunted by the unusual difficulty of identifying the culpable target category. No such difficulty was presented in 1964, when rioters killed two to three times as many victims as in 1950, despite police firmness.[91] Variable anger against target groups seems closely related to the intensity of the violence.

INADEQUATE PRECIPITANTS

Trivial precipitants explain some episodes of mild violence. The Ivory Coast experienced riots against Mauritanians (1980), after increases in the price of bread sold by Mauritanian traders; about 30 were injured, but few or none died.[92] In 1985, after the Ivory Coast team won a soccer game in Ghana, there were assaults on Ghanaians in Abidjan, whereupon Ghanaians took revenge on Ivorians in Ghana, injuring several and possibly killing two.[93] Similarly, Gabon experienced anti-Cameroonian

88. For another mild anti-Marwari riot, see Ghosh, *Communal Riots in India,* pp. 206–09.

89. *Far Eastern Economic Review*, August 6, 1982, p. 26.

90. "Statement of Andrew Howat Frew, ASP, to the Riot Inquiry Commission," Singapore, February 27, 1951 (mimeo.), copy in the Rhodes House Library, Oxford.

91. Michael Leifer, "Communal Violence in Singapore," *Asian Survey* 4, no. 10 (October 1964): 1115–21.

92. *West Africa*, March 16, 1981, p. 596; FBIS, Daily Reports, West Africa, April 21, 1980, p. T2.

93. *West Africa*, September 30, 1985, p. 2064.

riots in (1981) after a soccer defeat, but few or no Cameroonians were killed;[94] and, in the same year, Sinhalese killed Indian Tamils following a sports meet between Sinhalese and Tamil students, but, in contrast to the usual casualties in Sinhalese-Tamil riots, fewer than ten were killed, despite the indifference of police and army observers.[95] Several anti-Chinese episodes in Indonesia had trivial precipitants and limited violence. In Muncar, East Java (1994), Madurese fishermen gathered to demand that new fishing nets introduced by local Chinese be destroyed. They assaulted a local leader associated with the Chinese fishermen and then destroyed the new equipment and the homes and storage sheds of several Chinese.[96] In Ujung Pandang, Sulawesi (1997), a double murder by a Chinese produced an easily controlled attempt to lynch the culprit, but nothing more.[97] In West Java (1997), a late-night quarrel produced a good bit of anti-Chinese arson but little face-to-face violence,[98] in a familiar pattern of a small dispute gone awry. Again, we are back to wondering whether these events are really ethnic *riots* at all.

FIRM POLICE

If the instruments of public order are capable and determined, they may not be able to prevent all forms of violence, but they can have a profound effect on the course it takes. In Tuva (1990), discussed in Chapter 9, what would certainly have been serious riots were transformed into a much smaller number of individual murders by strict law enforcement and punishment of offenders. Anti-Muslim violence in Kanpur (1994), in which four died, was rendered less lethal than it might have been because of a trivial precipitant and the prompt deployment of the army.[99] Palacode (1979) and Malegaon (1983) were riots cut short by police fir-

94. Colin Legum, ed., *Africa Contemporary Record, 1981–82* (New York: Africana, 1982), p. 366.

95. Virginia A. Leary, *Ethnic Conflict and Violence in Sri Lanka: Report of a Mission to Sri Lanka in July–August 1981 on Behalf of the International Commission of Jurists* (Geneva: ICJ, 1981), pp. 20–21.

96. Donald K. Emmerson, "Orders of Meaning: Understanding Political Change in a Fishing Community in Indonesia," in Benedict Anderson and Audrey Kahin, eds., *Interpreting Indonesian Politics: Thirteen Contributions to the Debate* (Ithaca: Cornell Modern Indonesia Project, 1982), pp. 157–59.

97. Interview, Jakarta, August 13, 1998. It helped that the police were determined to protect the murderer from being lynched.

98. *New York Times*, April 8, 1997, pp. A1, A7.

99. See Paul R. Brass, *Theft of an Idol: Text and Context in the Representation of Collective Violence* (Princeton: Princeton University Press, 1997), pp. 240–59.

ing on rioters.[100] The riots that spread through Central and East Java in 1980 were perhaps easy to control, because the precipitant was just a fight, but the determination of the army to suppress the violence probably also limited its intensity. For the most part, only property was attacked.[101]

When this evidence is placed side by side with the inhibiting effects when police at some riot locations use force,[102] contrasted with the disinhibiting results at other locations where they fail to act decisively, a strong case can be made for explaining riot severity, in significant part, by reference to police demeanor. What we know of the risk aversion of rioters from the study of riot site selection reinforces the conclusion that crowds are often engaged in a tentative endeavor, which, if all — including the police response — goes well for the rioters, will be escalated, to the detriment of the targets.

AUTHORITATIVE SOCIAL DISAPPROVAL

The close relationship of police behavior to authoritative social support suggests that unequivocally expressed social disapproval may account for the low intensity of some mild riots. The covariance is not perfect. If a central government firmly disapproves of violence, but local police favor it, the police may not always do their duty. But if control over the police is effective, lack of authoritative social support will have greater impact in reducing levels of violence. An anti-Jewish riot in Warsaw (1790) that took place in otherwise propitious conditions produced no deaths. Local authorities did not encourage the violence, armed forces did not hesitate to fight the crowds, and convictions and imprisonment followed the violence.[103] The nonlethal anti-Marwari riots in Orissa (1980) spread widely, but the chief minister issued shoot-to-kill orders to the police, who, as we have seen, did fire on rioters. The combination of inappropriate targets, firm police, and authoritative disapproval was powerfully

100. Government of India, *Third Annual Report of the Minorities Commission (for the Year Ending 31st December, 1980)*, pp. 78–83; P.R. Rajgopal, *Communal Violence in India* (New Delhi: Uppal, 1987), p. 82.

101. The army's determination may also explain why, in 1984, anti-Chinese violence in Jakarta took the form of two bombings of banks owned by a prominent Chinese businessman. See *Far Eastern Economic Review*, October 18, 1984, pp. 18–19.

102. See Chapter 9, pp. 363–64, above.

103. Krystyna Zienkowska, "'The Jews Have Killed a Tailor': The Socio-Political Background of a Riot in Warsaw in 1790," *Polin* 3 (1988): 78–101. Much the same restraint, imposed by Hausa civilian and military leaders on rioters, greatly limited anti-Yoruba violence in northern Nigeria (1971).

restraining on the rioters. Underlying the inhibiting effect of the combination of an insignificant precipitant and forcible army action in Kanpur (1994) was the prompt response of the state government to the anti-Muslim attacks. On the other hand, the aversion of local leaders to violence may be inadequate by itself, especially if they do not control the police. In Hazaribagh (1983), Hindu and Muslim elders agreed on a new route for a provocative Hindu procession, but procession leaders disregarded the compromise, precipitating violence.[104]

Authoritative social approval or disapproval embraces not only the attitudes and action of political leaders but the more diffuse sentiments that can slowly reshape community attitudes toward violence, even if they do not transform interethnic antipathy. I pointed out in Chapter 1 that ethnic riots are now much more common outside the Western world than inside it, although this was not always the case and although the West is far from free of ethnic terrorism and violent protest demonstrations. Underlying this change is a considerable rethinking about the legitimacy of interethnic killing.

This change is evident in Britain, a country that has historically had its fair share of collective, deadly violence.[105] During the course of the twentieth century in Britain, however, there has been a sharp, secular reduction in every form of collective violence, with the single exception of football violence.[106] This change is reflected in violent ethnic encounters, ranging from the white attacks on West Indians in Nottingham and Notting Hill (1958) to the mainly black, violent protest demonstrations in Bristol (1980), Brixton (1981), and Toxteth (1981), the black-white fights in Southall (1981), and the violent protests in Handsworth, Brixton, Toxteth, and Broadwater Farm Estate (all 1985) and in six separate locations in England and Wales in 1991.[107] In spite of the signifi-

104. Ghosh, *Communal Riots in India*, pp. 131–32.

105. See Simon Field, "Urban Disorders in Britain and America," in Simon Field and Peter Southgate, *Public Disorder: A Review of Research and a Study in One Inner City Area,* Home Office Research Study No. 72 (London: H.M.S.O., 1982), pp. 4–5.

106. See Michael Argyle, *The Social Psychology of Everyday Life* (New York: Routledge, 1992), p. 179.

107. See Edward Pilkington, *Beyond the Mother Country: West Indians and the Notting Hill White Riots* (London: I.B. Taurus, 1988), pp. 106–23; S.D. Reicher, "The St. Paul's Riot: An Explanation of the Limits of Crowd Action in Terms of a Social Identity Model," *European Journal of Social Psychology* 14, no. 1 (January–March 1984): 1–21; John Rex, "The 1981 Urban Riots in Britain," *International Journal of Urban and Regional Research* 6, no. 1 (March 1982): 99–113; Akwe Amosu, "Inner Cities Boil Over," *West Africa*, October 21, 1985, pp. 2202–03; Gerry Northam, *Shooting in the Dark: Riot Police in Britain* (London: Faber & Faber, 1988), p. 7; *Keesing's Record of World Events* 37, no. 1 (London: Longman, 1991): 38404, 38445.

cant scale of some of these events and the ethnic antipathy and social support especially evident in Notting Hill (1958),[108] not one became a deadly riot, and the death toll in all of them together can be counted on the fingers of one hand.[109]

Only a sea change in views about collective killing of ethnic enemies could explain so much violence with so little lethality. Evidence of similar changes will be apparent in our later consideration of certain riots that do not recur, but it is worth underscoring here that the participants, enthusiastic about the violence, nevertheless entertained a precisely focused view of what was appropriate. In St. Paul's, Bristol (1980), there was a keen sense of the rightness of the undertaking but a limitation of weapons to bricks and stones against police, arson against police cars. There was stern disapproval of harm inflicted on anyone other than the police.[110] The same focus was in evidence in Handsworth (1985), where bricks, bottles, and petrol bombs were used against the police and fire brigade, and arson and looting of shops soon followed — these limitations despite widespread support for violence among blacks, whether they participated or not, and the presence in the area of many whites and Asians who might have become targets.[111] Conspicuous self-restraint was at work in episodes of quite angry violence.

A survey conducted at the height of the 1981 violence suggests rather considerable acceptance of minorities by whites and, consistent with this finding, a powerful sense on the part of minority respondents that their relations with the police were worse than their relations with whites in general.[112] These findings help explain the precise focus in virtually all of the 1980s violence on police targets, which places them in the category of violent protest demonstrations.

STRONG ORGANIZATION

Mild riots very often have an above-average level of planning and organization to them. Contrary to the intuition that mass killing requires significant instigation, deliberate arousal, and mobilization, these characteris-

---

108. See Pilkington, *Beyond the Mother Country*, pp. 116–20.

109. Two killed accidentally by fires, a rioter killed by a police officer, and a police officer stabbed to death. These are casualties characteristic of violent protest demonstrations — and rather fewer than the number typical of the genre.

110. Reicher, "The St. Paul's Riot," p. 11.

111. See Dervla Murphy, *Tales from Two Cities* (London: Penguin, 1989), pp. 278–84.

112. "Race Relations in 1981: An Attitude Survey" (mimeo. report of the Commission for Racial Equality, London, November 1981), pp. 16–17 and 11, respectively. Other

tics, on the whole, appear to be inversely related to the intensity of deadly riots. Organization may be needed to compensate, but usually inadequately, for the lack of passion or to restrain the expression of passion when an excess of violence would not be in the interest of the organizers.

Fiji (1987) is a case of organized restraint. Fiji is a severely divided society that for decades had a multiethnic but generally pro-Fijian government. The election of mid-April 1987 brought to power a new coalition, weighted toward Indian rather than Fijian representation, although the new prime minister was a Fijian. There were Fijian protests, but by the end of April the new government seemed to be consolidating its position.[113] The response of Fijians in the military was the coup described in Chapter 8, in which the civilian prime minister was arrested. When he was subsequently released, his Indian supporters held a rally of welcome, which was attacked by Fijians in a display of violence remarkable for its studied restraint. "No one was reported critically injured, and it often seemed," according to an eyewitness, "that the attacks, although brutal, were short of murderous. The mobs usually let their bloodied victims run off, or the attackers themselves ran on after landing a few blows."[114] Police arrested some attackers, and troops prevented further violence the following day.

This degree of choreography suggests high levels of organization, particularly in a society in which Fijian hostility to Indian political claims runs deep. The coup, after all, took place under the slogan "Fiji for Fijians."[115] When the prime minister was released, the new military regime had seemed to be losing momentum. Fijian civilian leaders were divided in their enthusiasm for it, and alternatives were being mooted. The violence, nonlethal though it was, sufficed to provide a taste of the

---

sources are consistent. In Brixton, for example, the focus of both the violence and the grievances was the police. See *The Brixton Disorders, 10–12 April 1981*, Report of an Inquiry by the Rt. Hon. the Lord Scarman, O.B.E., Cmnd. 8427 (London: H.M.S.O., 1981), pp. 44–45, 59–61. Surveys conducted in several locations after antipolice violence revealed, strikingly, that nearly two-thirds of respondents — and, in some cases, more minority than white respondents — were satisfied with life in their area. See Peter Southgate, "The Disturbances of July 1981 in Handsworth, Birmingham: A Survey of the Views and Experiences of Male Respondents," in Field and Southgate, *Public Disorder*, pp. 47–48.

113. Stephanie Lawson, *The Failure of Democratic Politics in Fiji* (Oxford: Clarendon Press, 1991), pp. 255–59.

114. *New York Times*, May 21, 1987, p. A6. See *Far Eastern Economic Review*, June 4, 1987, p. 40.

115. Ralph Premdas, "Balance and Ethnic Conflict in Fiji," in John McGarry and Brendan O'Leary, eds., *The Politics of Ethnic Conflict Regulation* (London: Routledge, 1993), pp. 272–73.

disorder that was possible and so to strengthen the hand of the coup leader against the governor general, who was as yet uncommitted to the new regime. Following the violence, a new Council of Advisors was appointed, which legitimized the coup.[116] The degree of violence had been finely calibrated to underscore Fijian hostility without risking the regime's precarious position by resorting to a bloodbath. Mild violence was exactly what this extraordinary situation demanded. Unlike some organized riots, this one did not get out of hand.

If violence is used tactically, the strategic objective may limit its intensity. Similarly, if crowds are not keen to kill, organization will not compensate for their lack of enthusiasm. A general strike of Afro-Guyanese workers in Guyana (1962) was designed to weaken or depose an Indian-dominated government.[117] On "Black Friday," February 16, 1962, the strike reached its apogee, when crowds looted shops, at first only those owned by Indians. When police intervened, the rioters set fire to much of downtown Georgetown. But what became an angry crowd began reluctantly, very likely because of lack of an apt precipitant. It took several days of incitement to produce the requisite numbers, and, while five people died, no civilians were killed by the rioters.[118] Tellingly, when disorder resumed in the following year, it took the form of distance killing, bombings and burnings, again with a considerable measure of organization.

Here, then, are two ways in which organization is likely to be associated with less, rather than more, intense violence. Although there are times when organized violence has so much resonance with those who do the attacking that it gets out of hand, organizers often have a keen interest in inflicting only mild violence.[119] Passion often wants to kill, in order to teach a major lesson in ethnic relations. Strategy usually wants to

116. Robert T. Robertson and Akosita Tamanisau, *Fiji: Shattered Coups* (Leichhardt, New South Wales: Pluto Press, 1988), pp. 79–80.

117. As an official inquiry correctly concluded. *Report of a Commission of Inquiry into Disturbances in British Guinea in 1962*, Colon. no. 354 (London: H.M.S.O., 1962), p. 18.

118. Personal violence was secondary to property damage. Four of the five dead were rioters; the fifth was a policeman. Ibid., pp. 49, 61. It might be appropriate to categorize this event as a hybrid violent protest demonstration against the government and a very mild anti-Indian riot. Many of the shops that were burned were Indian-owned. Ibid., p. 50. For another account, see Peter Simms, *Trouble in Guyana* (London: George Allen & Unwin, 1966), pp. 155–63.

119. See, e.g., Pramod Kumar, "Communal Riots in Mau Nath Bhanjan," in Kumar, ed., *Towards Understanding Communalism*, pp. 427–54, especially pp. 449, 451; Government of India, *Third Annual Report of the Minorities Commission (for the Year Ending 31st December, 1980)*, p. 82; Leary, *Ethnic Conflict and Violence in Sri Lanka*, pp. 21–22. Organization also accounts for the mild anti-Tamil violence in Galle, Sri Lanka (1995). Posters and warnings to Tamils preceded the violence by several days. In the face of police

teach a more specific, limited lesson, which requires only a modicum of violence.

Naturally, there are times when a surfeit of violence is in the interest of the organizer. When government is the organizer in such conditions, violence will be anything but mild. Kenya (1992) involved deadly riots instigated by the heavily Kalenjin regime of Daniel arap Moi against Luo, Kikuyu, and Luhya, three groups presumed to support Moi's opposition in an abortive process of democratization. The aim seems to have been to underscore the costs of civic participation and electoral democracy. Those costs were high: between 1992 and 1993, more than 1,000 died, and 250,000 became homeless.[120] As the record of genocides shows, given ethnic antipathy, government may be the one organization with the capacity and the incentive to engage in killing without restraint.

ETHNIC FIGHTS

What I called in Chapter 1 the ethnic fight constitutes a form of controlled ethnic violence. These are ethnically defined fights that usually do not produce death. In an analysis of what they lack may lie some explanation of what the deadly riot possesses.

Typically, such fights are precipitated by a personal quarrel in an environment of intergroup hostility. Fights of this kind tend to develop in ethnically differentiated mines and work camps, environments where the threshold for violence is low, where fighting may be a frequent social activity, and so where the participants cannot afford to permit the violence to get out of hand. There is precision in targeting, as in deadly riots, but often there are tacit limits on acceptable weapons and on rules of engagement. These latter sometimes include termination of a fight by gestures of submission, precisely the sort of gesture that is utterly unavailing in a deadly ethnic riot. Over long periods of time, remarkably few deaths result, but there may be serious injuries.[121]

---

inaction, Tamil shops were looted and burned, their inhabitants often allowed to escape, only to be assaulted at their homes. In contrast to the usual intensity of anti-Tamil violence, this episode produced not a single death. *Ethnic Violence in Galle, June 2, 1995,* A Report of the Independent Committee of Inquiry (Colombo: International Centre for Ethnic Studies, 1995). I am grateful to K. M. de Silva for making a copy of this report available to me.

120. Makau wa Mutua, "Kenya: The Politics of Doom," *Africa Report,* May–June 1992, pp. 13–16; *Africa Research Bulletin,* April 1–30, 1993, pp. 10977–78.

121. For fine treatments, see Robert Gordon, "The Celebration of Ethnicity: A 'Tribal Fight' in a Namibian Mine Compound," in Brian M. du Toit, ed., *Ethnicity in Modern Africa* (Boulder, Colo.: Westview Press, 1978), pp. 213–31; McKnight, "Fighting in an Australian Aboriginal Supercamp."

A characteristic of ethnic fights that is assuredly not shared with deadly riots is the balance of force between sides. Whereas aggressors in deadly riots easily overpower their targets and avoid encounters with massed opponents in conditions that might render the outcome uncertain, participants in ethnic fights are gathered en masse on both sides. These are not attacks at clear moments of weakness. Participants also tend to consist of people who may need to encounter each other again and again. Both conditions would seem to inhibit impulses to engage in the most lethal forms of violence.

Even where a more serious precipitant produces what looks like an emerging deadly riot, violence may be more muted when crowds gather on both sides than it would be if there were an imbalance between aggressors and targets. What seems at first glance like a set of circumstances ripe for all-out warfare turns out to be exactly the opposite. An example is the aptly titled "almost race riot" that occurred when a crowd of whites and Lumbee Indians gathered to attack African Americans in Baltimore (1968).[122] Once a black crowd also gathered, what began as a menacing event, with echoes of the deadly antiblack riots of the first third of the century, was converted into a much more limited fight, with no weapons more lethal than bottles and rocks. The fight was easily ended by the National Guard. The metamorphosis was a function of the higher-than-expected likely costs of serious violence.[123] Effective target-group response, very rare in deadly riots, is likely to be a significant force for limiting violence.[124]

Undoubtedly, too, there is a reciprocal relationship between willingness to defend oneself and assessment of the likely risks. Crowds of targets turn out to fight, because they sense in the situation, as riot targets do not, that, come what may, they are unlikely to be killed. The aggressors may not be up to killing, because, living or working at close quarters, they may be vulnerable to revenge, or because there has been a change in attitudes about interethnic killing, or because both sides surmise the police will intervene before the violence becomes lethal. In the pre–World War II period, black targets did not generally appear on the

---

122. Richard A. Berk, "The Emergence of Muted Violence in Crowd Behavior: A Case Study of an Almost Race Riot," in James F. Short, Jr., and Marvin E. Wolfgang, eds., *Collective Violence* (Chicago: Aldine-Atherton, 1972), pp. 309–28.

123. Ibid., pp. 327–28.

124. In Notting Hill, Britain (1958), the growing willingness of West Indians to fight back, after three days of attacks on them, reduced the interest of whites in continuing the attacks. Pilkington, *Beyond the Mother Country*, pp. 123–26.

scene to confront white aggressors bent on riot, presumably because they had no such expectation of a nonlethal outcome. By contrast, prior episodes of fighting in mines and work camps provide a common expectation that there are indeed limits to the violence.

One feature that does not differ between the deadly ethnic riot and the ethnic fight is interethnic disdain, present in both.[125] What is different in the fight is that fear of immediate retaliation inhibits the most severe aggression. The deadly ethnic riot is unusually free of such fear. The relative mildness of ethnic fights testifies once again to the aversion of rioters to excessive risk.[126]

CHANGES OVER TIME: NONRECURRING RIOTS

Some countries that formerly experienced ethnic riots have not experienced them for a long time.[127] In some cases, the same cleavages persist, but ethnic violence takes other forms. In others, the cleavages are present but so diminished in saliency as to make rioting more or less unimaginable. In still others, the cleavages remain powerful, but changes in the ethnic balance of power have undermined conditions conducive to violence. As we shall observe from an examination of six cases in which riots have not recurred for at least 30 years, more enduring changes in cleavage lines and attitudes take place over longer time periods than do changes in other riot-inhibiting conditions.

ATTITUDINAL CHANGE AND DECLINING SOCIAL SUPPORT

An example of nonrecurring riots that calls out for explanation is Northern Ireland, which, from 1857 to 1935, experienced a long series of Protestant-Catholic riots. There had been no repetition until 1969, when confrontations in Belfast and a couple of other towns produced ten deaths.[128] No further riots of any seriousness ensued. Instead, there was an extended period in the early 1970s during which Catholics and Protestants in some locations were intimidated into leaving their homes

---

125. See Gordon, "The Celebration of Ethnicity," p. 214.

126. Even as it shows the willingness of targets to hazard moderate risks.

127. Within India, a number of formerly violent cities have grown quiescent. Steven Ian Wilkinson, "The Electoral Incentives for Ethnic Violence: Hindu-Muslim Riots in India" (Ph.D. diss., M.I.T., 1998), Table II-4, pp. 88–89.

128. *Violence and Civil Disturbances in Northern Ireland in 1969: Report of the Tribunal of Inquiry*, Cmd. 566 (London: H.M.S.O., 1972), Vol. 1, pp. 5–14, 241.

in mixed areas for the safety of more homogeneous neighborhoods.[129] There was also an increase in terrorist activity by paramilitaries, resulting in about 3,100 deaths from 1969 to 1993. Casualties peaked in 1972 and have declined since. Civilian deaths have declined faster than casualties overall. The "true enigma," observed an anthropologist early in this period, "is not why so many have died; rather, it is why so few have been killed."[130]

Neither intimidation nor terrorism requires mass involvement. Intimidation requires only anonymous threats and attacks on those who fail to heed them. Terrorism is also a small-group phenomenon. Remarkably, paramilitaries behave in accordance with their understanding that mass violence is unacceptable, and the public declares that this understanding is correct.

The Irish Republican Army, in particular, has been constrained to develop a restrictive doctrine of legitimate targets, generally abjuring attacks on civilians except as part of its campaign against economic targets.[131] Although Catholics tend to see police and military personnel as "engaged in a war,"[132] neither Catholics nor Protestants condone violence against civilians.[133] To the contrary: in 1979, 61 percent of Ulster Catholics thought the Irish Republic government ought to pursue a harder policy against the IRA, and 64 percent wished the Republic were willing to extradite to the North those accused of political crimes.[134] John McGarry and Brendan O'Leary estimate that IRA violence is supported by "at most 10 percent of the voters in Northern Ireland."[135]

Under these conditions, there would be no support for deadly ethnic riots. This is a marked change from the conditions that fed violence in

129. John Darby, *Intimidation and the Control of Conflict in Northern Ireland* (Dublin: Gill and Macmillan, 1986), pp. 52–60.

130. Elliot Leyton, "Opposition and Integration in Ulster," *Man* (n.s.) 9, no. 2 (June 1974): 185–98, at p. 194.

131. John Darby, "Legitimate Targets: A Control on Violence?" in Adrian Guelke, ed., *New Perspectives on the Northern Ireland Conflict* (Aldershot: Avebury, Ashgate, 1994), pp. 46–64.

132. Darby, *Intimidation and the Control of Conflict in Northern Ireland*, p. 137.

133. Ibid., pp. 157–58; Graham McFarlane, "Violence in Rural Northern Ireland: Social Scientific Models, Folk Explanations and Local Variation," in Riches, ed., *The Anthropology of Violence*, pp. 184–203; Christopher Hewitt, *Consequences of Political Violence* (Aldershot: Dartmouth, 1993), p. 58.

134. Ken Heskin, *Northern Ireland: A Psychological Analysis* (Dublin: Gill and Macmillan, 1980), p. 45.

135. John McGarry and Brendan O'Leary, *Explaining Northern Ireland* (Cambridge: Blackwell, 1995), p. 53.

the nineteenth and early twentieth centuries, a period characterized by "middle-class tolerance for the violence of the rioters," when "ethnocentrism dulled Belfast's public conscience," and each side "knew 'the other sort' only as stereotypes — alien, if not suspect."[136] Now, strong majorities of both groups favor increased contact at school and in residential neighborhoods.[137] Intermarriage, although still somewhat controversial, has doubled, from 6 percent of all marriages in 1969 to more than 11 percent in 1991, including fully 20 percent of marriages in Belfast.[138] Asked for opinions about the other side, each group describes the other as "about the same" as itself, and the phrase "ordinary people" is frequently invoked.[139] People seeking increasing contact with each other and empathizing as individuals are not likely to be interested in the degradation and homogenization that form the core aims of ethnic riots. When two-thirds or more of each group wishes to live in mixed neighborhoods, "Drive out the Bengalis!" is not the sort of slogan that appeals. In terms of tacit coordination, a person disposed to riot would, in these circumstances, be foolish to count on the simultaneous action of others.[140]

That is not to say that the underlying conflict has wholly abated. Strongly asymmetric views are held by the respective groups about the political system;[141] and, as late as 1986, large minorities of Protestants and Catholics alike had positive images of their respective paramilitaries,[142] even as they disapproved of violence against civilians. (There are suggestions of similar views in the Basque country, where there has also been no mass interethnic violence, despite a major influx of non-Basques.[143]) As some Catholics see the IRA engaged in a war against

136. Sybil E. Baker, "Orange and Green: Belfast, 1832–1912," in H.J. Dyos and Michael Wolff, eds., *The Victorian City* (London: Routledge & Kegan Paul, 1973), p. 804.

137. John Darby, *Northern Ireland: Managing Difference* (London: Minority Rights Group, 1995), pp. 15, 25.

138. Ibid., pp. 15, 24–25; Valerie Morgan et al., *Mixed Marriages in Northern Ireland* (Coleraine: University of Ulster Centre for the Study of Conflict, 1996), pp. 4, 15–18.

139. Heskin, *Northern Ireland*, pp. 32–37, 43. It is worth noting how such views cast doubt on facile formulations such as "the Other" and "otherization," which assume the stereotypes that groups in conflict have of each other.

140. See Thomas C. Schelling, *The Strategy of Conflict* (Cambridge: Harvard University Press, 1960), p. 90.

141. John E. Finn, "Public Support for Emergency Anti-Terrorist Legislation in Northern Ireland: A Preliminary Analysis," *Terrorism* 10, no. 2 (n.m. 1987), pp. 113–24, at p. 119.

142. Hewitt, *Consequences of Political Violence*, p. 58.

143. See ibid., showing low support for violence but a positive image of ETA.

British occupation, some Protestants see Loyalist paramilitaries in a war against the IRA. However, unlike Sudhir Kakar's respondents in Hyderabad, who were unwilling to condemn collective violence against male civilians,[144] people in Northern Ireland draw the line to exclude such targets. Despite the presence of many elements conducive to riots, social support has been missing.

The United States also has a long history of several forms of ethnic violence.[145] In the mid–nineteenth century, there were deadly riots against immigrants, particularly German and Irish.[146] From about 1880 to the late 1930s, lynching was a common and brutal form of antiblack — and sometimes anti-Italian[147] — violence, mainly in the south. Overlapping lynching in time, but not coinciding with it — and occurring in different parts of the country — was the deadly ethnic riot again, now not directed against immigrants but against blacks, beginning with the draft riot in New York (1863).[148] Crowds attacked random black victims, in cities such as Detroit, Chicago, and East St. Louis. Antiblack riots reached their apogee early in the twentieth century, declined in the 1920s, and ended in the 1940s. Following the antiblack riots was black protest violence. This variety became familiar in the 1960s, but it actually began in Harlem three decades earlier. Generally, it took the form of attacks on property owned by whites and on symbols of public authority, rather than attacks on people.[149] Few whites were killed. There were reprises in Miami (1980 and 1982) and Los Angeles (1992), albeit with some emphasis in these cities on interpersonal attacks as well, on Cubans and Koreans, respectively.[150]

144. Sudhir Kakar, *The Colors of Violence: Cultural Identities, Religion, and Conflict* (Chicago: University of Chicago Press, 1996), pp. 136–41.

145. For a survey, see Richard Wade, "Violence in the Cities: A Historical View," in Roger Lane and John J. Turner, Jr., *Riot, Rout and Tumult* (Westport, Conn.: Greenwood Press, 1978), pp. 349–63.

146. See, e.g., Michael Feldberg, *The Philadelphia Riots of 1844: A Study of Ethnic Conflict* (Westport, Conn.: Greenwood Press, 1975); George H. Yater, *Two Hundred Years at the Falls of the Ohio: A History of Louisville and Jefferson County* (Louisville: Heritage Corp., 1979), pp. 661–71.

147. See John Higham, *Strangers in the Land: Patterns of American Nativism 1860–1925*, 2d ed. (New York: Atheneum, 1963), pp. 90–91, 169, 184–85.

148. In the paragraphs that follow, I am drawing on Horowitz, "Racial Violence in the United States," pp. 187–211.

149. For deliberate restraint in this respect, see Robert M. Fogelson, *Violence as Protest: A Study of Riots and Ghettos* (Garden City, N.Y.: Anchor Books, 1971), p. 16.

150. On Miami, see Horowitz, "Racial Violence in the United States," pp. 207–08. On Los Angeles, see Ivan Light, Hadas Har-Chvi, and Kenneth Kan, "Black/Korean Conflict in Los Angeles" (paper presented at the Fulbright Colloquium, "Managing Divided Cities," Magee College, Derry City, Northern Ireland, September 6–8, 1993; mimeo.).

The shift to violent protest demonstrations signals a much lower death count and a change in attitudes about violence. Despite enormous property damage, in more than 500 such events between 1963 and 1970, fewer than 300 people in toto were killed — about the same as the number lynched in the worst single year of the 1890s. Indeed, in only a small number of cases was anyone killed at all, and most of the deaths were inflicted by authorities seeking to control the violence. Long after the violence subsided, substantial fractions of ghetto residents — in some cities, even small majorities — believed violence to be justified.[151] Killing, however, was not justified. Black survey respondents believed the protest violence was useful in calling attention to grievances, but there was "little approval given the sniping and firebombing that took place."[152] Themes of revenge, violence as an end, or "teach them a lesson" were absent.[153] Instead, the theme was "our grievances have been highlighted."[154]

Like the Northern Ireland terrorism, this violence lacked the approval or condonation of killing of civilian members of a target group that is required for deadly riots. However different they were in their goals and methods, in these events the underlying attitudes of supporters constrained the participants to adopt a more circumscribed view of appropriate targets that turns the events into fundamentally different phenomena from deadly riots.

In Northern Ireland and the United States, marked changes in interethnic attitudes were also evident. With continuing immigration into the United States, yesterday's immigrants became today's natives, the former conflicts abated, and group boundaries sometimes dissolved.[155] But neither Protestant-Catholic conflict in Northern Ireland nor black-white conflict in the United States ended altogether, despite those attitudinal changes.[156] There are gradations of mutability. Yet the experience of both countries suggests that ethnic conflict does not need to subside for the

151. See Horowitz, "Racial Violence in the United States," p. 195.

152. Joel D. Aberbach and Jack L. Walker, *Race in the City* (Boston: Little, Brown, 1973), p. 218, reporting results from Detroit, which otherwise had levels of sympathy for the violence.

153. See Gary T. Marx, *Protest and Prejudice: A Study of Belief in the Black Community* (New York: Harper & Row, 1967), p. 33.

154. Despite the fact that whites did not interpret the violence in this way. See Horowitz, "Racial Violence in the United States," p. 195.

155. See Richard Alba, *Ethnic Identity: The Transformation of White America* (New Haven: Yale University Press, 1990).

156. For the United States, see Paul M. Sniderman and Thomas Piazza, *The Scar of Race* (Cambridge: Harvard University Press, 1993); Howard Schuman, Charlotte Steeh, and Lawrence Bobo, *Racial Attitudes in America* (Cambridge: Harvard University Press, 1985). For Northern Ireland, see notes 141–42, above.

deadly riot to become obsolete — a point that provides some reason for optimism about ethnic violence in general. However, it remains unclear what produced the attitudinal changes that deny legitimacy to the killing of civilians even where conflict persists.

These changes coincide with more general declines in deaths from domestic collective violence throughout most of the West in the twentieth century, particularly in the period following World War II.[157] For many Western countries, the United States included, the period from the 1830s to the 1930s was filled with more domestic deadly collective violence than was the subsequent period.[158] Noting the tendency for minority-majority relations in the West generally to have become more peaceful than those relations elsewhere, Ted Robert Gurr calls attention to the absence of severe discrimination and repression in Western countries, resulting in less intensely felt grievances, as well as public approval of "accommodation of contending interests" and concomitant disapproval of violence.[159] In a sense, this is to restate the question, rather than to answer it. The question, as I said at the very outset of the book, looms over the materials: why has the deadly ethnic riot virtually died out in the Western world, a world that knew the phenomenon only decades ago? In the final chapter, I shall take more precise aim at the question. For the moment, a first look at one or two hypotheses is worthwhile, but to dwell on them excessively would be to neglect some equally interesting changes in patterns of ethnic violence outside the West.

The absence or moderation of ethnic violence in some Western countries may be evidence of the growth of civic identity that competes with ethnic identities. Certainly, that has been true for many European immigrant groups in the United States, France, and Australia and for English, Welsh, Scots, and Irish in Britain. In others, such as Switzerland, Canada, and Belgium, group identities are strong, but other cleavages (religion,

---

157. Among countries exhibiting the most benign "political violence profiles" from 1948 to 1965, the vast majority were Western countries. See Ivo K. Feierabend, Rosalind L. Feierabend, and Betty Nesvold, "Social Change and Political Violence: Cross-National Patterns," in Hugh Davis Graham and Ted Robert Gurr, eds., Violence in America: Historical and Comparative Perspectives, Vol. 2 (Washington, D.C.: Government Printing Office, 1969), p. 513. For the period from 1948 to 1977, see Ekkart Zimmermann, "Political Unrest in Western Europe: Trends and Prospects," Western European Politics 12, no. 3 (July 1989): 179–96.

158. For the United States, see Roger Lane, "Criminal Violence in America: The First Hundred Years," The Annals 423 (January 1976): 1–13, at pp. 9–12.

159. Ted Robert Gurr, Minorities at Risk: A Global View of Ethnopolitical Conflicts (Washington: United States Institute of Peace Press, 1993), pp. 139–40.

class, often region) compete for attention with ethnicity, and ethnic issues emerged late in relation to the development of parties, so that party politics is not a perfect reflection of ethnic conflict.[160] These conditions would account for a generally low level of violence in the ethnic conflicts of the West, but they would not be sufficient to account for the changes in Northern Ireland or in black-white violence in the United States.

Professionalization of the police may also have something to do with these underlying trends. Even in the United States and Northern Ireland, where police bias has been a serious issue, the performance of the police in the 1960s violence was markedly more detached than it was in the white-black violence of the first third of the twentieth century and the Catholic-Protestant violence of the nineteenth and early twentieth centuries, respectively, when police bias was the rule. The unwillingness of increasingly equality-minded liberal states to permit or assist their citizens to kill each other (the domestic analogue to the theory of no war between liberal states) may be hypothesized as well, although, again, that leaves open the sources of public support for egalitarian states.

ATTITUDINAL CHANGE AND DECLINING CONFLICT

Transitions from violence to quiescence are not limited to the West. Attitudinal change is also at the root of some of these transitions, in some cases more far-reaching attitudinal change than in Northern Ireland and the United States. Ethnic conflict is often intractable, but not necessarily permanent. Like those that divided natives from immigrant Irish and Germans in the nineteenth-century United States, some conflicts may be extinguished, while others may lapse into desuetude. Taiwan and Thailand provide examples of violent conflicts that have become sharply subdued.

Taiwan experienced serious attacks by Mainlanders against Taiwanese in 1947.[161] Thousands died. The violence had a profoundly alienating effect that might ultimately have caused rebellion against the oligarchy that fled to Taiwan from the Mainland from 1945 to 1949. Genocidal

160. These are points I have elaborated in "Democracy in Divided Societies," *Journal of Democracy* 4, no. 4 (October 1993): 18–38, at p. 20; and in "Immigration and Group Relations in France and America," in Donald L. Horowitz and Gérard Noiriel, eds., *Immigrants in Two Democracies: French and American Experience* (New York: New York University Press, 1992), pp. 10–13. Cf. Dan Deudney and John Ikenberry, "The Logic of the West," *World Policy Journal* 10, no. 4 (Winter 1993–94): 17–25.

161. Lai Tse-Han, Ramon H. Myers, and Wei Wou, *A Tragic Beginning: The Taiwan Uprising of February 28, 1947* (Stanford: Stanford University Press, 1991).

retaliation might have followed, along the lines of Rwanda or Burundi. In the event, however, there was no recurrence of the violence. Instead, there was gradual interethnic reconciliation, spurred in the first instance by Taiwan's precarious security situation and ultimately by its loss of international legitimacy.[162] While many Taiwanese lean toward independence and many Mainlanders lean toward reunification, the threat of China makes both goals unattainable and pushes extreme political positions toward the center.[163] What would otherwise have been profound dissensus about the legitimate boundaries of the state, as exists in Northern Ireland, was muted. The desire of the Taiwan government to recapture political legitimacy led to an extremely successful democratization, beginning in the 1980s and characterized most prominently by the Taiwanization of the ruling Kuomintang. Meanwhile, Mainlanders, recognizing the improbability of a return to China, began serious social integration with Taiwanese. By the mid-1970s, rates of intermarriage were well in excess of 20 percent, and they have grown since. In ethnic identity, about 20 percent of the population declares itself exclusively Taiwanese, another 20 percent Chinese, and more than half considers itself to be both Taiwanese and Chinese. Ethnic conflict has not disappeared, but it has declined in salience, largely as a result of the fortuitous external threat.

Not all external threats are integrative, however. Thailand's threat from China at the end of World War II was clearly disintegrative. The danger of China's designs on Thailand and the presumed allegiance of the Chinese minority in Thailand to China helped precipitate the anti-Chinese riot of 1945.[164] In the postwar period, controlling Chinese immigration and controlling the Chinese were pervasive themes in a Thai politics dominated by the military.[165] Partly because of the fear of Chinese-oriented political parties, bureaucratic and military elites delayed the legalization of parties.[166] As in Taiwan, this meant that social

162. See John Fuh-sheng Hsieh, "Politics of Ethnicity and National Identity" (paper presented at the Woodrow Wilson Center Conference on High Conflict/Low Conflict Areas, Washington, D.C., June 28–29, 1993).

163. See Wu Naiteh, "National-Identity Conflict and Democratic Consolidation in Taiwan" (Working Paper, American Political Science Association, Conference Group on Taiwan Studies, 1996).

164. See G. William Skinner, *Chinese Society in Thailand* (Ithaca: Cornell University Press, 1957), pp. 278–80.

165. Kenneth P. Landon, "Siam," in Lennox A. Mills, ed., *The New World of Southeast Asia* (Minneapolis: University of Minnesota Press, 1949), p. 253.

166. Chai-Anan Samudavanija and Sukhumbhand Paribatra, "Political Contestation in Thailand," in Norma Mahmood and Zakaria Haji Ahmad, eds., *Political Contestation: Case Studies from Asia* (Singapore: Heinemann Asia, 1990), p. 77.

integration had a chance to precede democratization, subduing the political significance of ethnicity.

Sino-Thai integration had had a good start. The external threat of 1945 was, in some sense, an aberration. For a variety of reasons, Chinese had identified with Thais and the Thai state early on.[167] Chinese had long cultivated ties with military and civilian officials. These ties included intermarriage, to which there were no serious religious obstacles.[168] Yet, by the time the authoritarian regime began to crumble in the 1970s, the Chinese were no longer closely identified with it. They had begun to emancipate themselves from clientelistic dependence, preferring to be free of its exactions, and were supportive of democratic forces in the struggle against the army and civil service.[169] The growth of significant Chinese political influence and officeholding after 1988 was not well received by the military, but it was no longer controversial in the society at large.[170] Nowhere else in Southeast Asia had a Chinese minority managed to integrate itself so thoroughly. As in Taiwan, the effect was a great reduction of the underlying ethnic conflict. In both cases, an inclusive democracy began to emerge as a result of the need to align against powerful military threats, one external and the other internal.

ETHNIC HEGEMONY AND DECLINING SOCIAL SUPPORT

In the four cases discussed thus far, significant attitudinal changes took place over at least several decades. In this time, attitudes toward deadly violence against civilians changed in Northern Ireland and the United States, and ethnic relations themselves underwent substantial change in Taiwan and Thailand. In the shorter time available since the last ethnic riot in Malaysia (1969), no such attitudinal changes are yet visible. Inter-

167. For identification with Thais, see J.A.C. Mackie, "Changing Economic Roles and Ethnic Identities of the Southeast Asian Chinese: A Comparison of Indonesia and Thailand," in Jennifer W. Cushman and Wang Gungwu, eds., *Changing Identities of the Southeast Asian Chinese since World War II* (Hong Kong: Hong Kong University Press, 1988), p. 228. For the tradition of service to the Thai state, see Jennifer W. Cushman, "The Chinese in Thailand," in Leo Suryadinata, ed., *The Ethnic Chinese in the ASEAN States: Bibliographic Essays* (Singapore: Institute of Southeast Asian Studies, 1989), p. 226.

168. Catherine E. Dalpino, "Political Corruption: Thailand's Search for Accountability," *Journal of Democracy* 2, no. 4 (Fall 1991): 61–71, at p. 63; Cushman, "The Chinese in Thailand," pp. 227, 240.

169. Chai-Anan Samadavanija, "Thailand: A Stable Semi-Democracy," in Larry Diamond, Juan J. Linz, and Seymour Martin Lipset, eds., *Democracy in Developing Countries: Asia* (Boulder, Colo.: Lynne Rienner, 1989), pp. 304–46; Mackie, "Changing Economic Roles and Ethnic Identities of the Southeast Asian Chinese," p. 249.

170. In this paragraph I have drawn on conversations in Bangkok in January 1993.

ethnic reconciliation did not precede democratic politics in Malaysia, as
it did in Thailand and Taiwan. Electoral institutions, adopted before
independence, raised issues of ethnic power that were often seen in zero-
sum terms. Yet the series of postwar riots (1945–46, 1957, 1959, 1967,
and 1969) shows every sign of having abated.

Although the 1969 riot increased ethnic polarization, it also induced
Chinese to behave with great political circumspection, and it convinced
Malay leaders of the ruling party to restructure the coalition so as to
reduce Chinese influence and the chance that Chinese electoral discontent
could thwart the coalition's reelection,[171] thus reducing the electoral occasions for violence. Interpreting the 1969 riot as motivated by Malay economic frustration, the regime adopted a far-reaching series of preferential
policies favoring Malays in business, education, and employment. To
adopt the policies without creating resistance required an unthreatening
formulation, one that did not appear to upset the delicate interethnic bargain reached at independence. Hence the rather radical post-riot program
was framed to assuage the fears of Chinese, already chastened by the violence.[172] Many Chinese leaders were convinced that the policies went to
the root of ethnic conflict and so afforded some assurance of future stability.[173] While actual implementation of the policies increased Chinese
grievances, the policies and the reduction of Chinese influence heightened
Malay satisfaction. The Malaysian system increasingly tilted toward
Malay political hegemony. As Chinese political threats receded, so did the
occasions for Malay violence. Moreover, the regime, with its augmented
armed forces, seemed determined to defeat attempts to interfere with the
stability required for the success of its ethnic-economic restructuring plan,
dependent as it was on growth as well as redistribution.

The plausibility of this interpretation of Malaysian post-1969 quies-

171. Among other things, constituencies were realigned for the 1974 election, to the
further disadvantage of parties supported by Chinese voters. See Sothi Rachagan, "The
Development of the Electoral System," in Harold Crouch, Lee Kam Hing, and Michael
Ong, eds., *Malaysian Politics and the 1978 Election* (Kuala Lumpur: Oxford University
Press, 1980), pp. 276–79. On the expansion of the coalition, see Harold Crouch, "From
Alliance to Barisan Nasional," in ibid., pp. 1–10.

172. Thus, the prime minister, Tun Abdul Razak, wrote in his foreword to the Second
Malaysia Plan, the definitive document initiating preferential policies, that the program
would be implemented in such a way so that "no one will experience any loss or feel any
sense of deprivation of his rights, privileges, income, job or opportunity." Government of
Malaysia, *Second Malaysia Plan 1971–1975* (Kuala Lumpur: Government Press, 1971),
p. 3.

173. I am drawing here on interviews I conducted with Chinese political leaders in
Kuala Lumpur in 1975. The interviews displayed a remarkable degree of acceptance of the
need for the policies.

cence is enhanced by the near-miss of 1987, an episode in which several ethnic issues had provoked Chinese protest and Malay counterprotest, explicitly threatening anti-Chinese violence on the 1969 model. A Malay political rally that would almost certainly have turned violent was canceled by the prime minister, and many arrests were ordered. These issues arose at a time of intra-Malay political competition, and they may have been permitted to simmer accordingly.[174] Nevertheless, all the elements of a riot were in place, save authoritative social support and police indifference.

PERSISTENT MULTIPOLARITY

The change in Mauritius to a decidedly more peaceful politics after 1968 has a rather different explanation. Ethnic differences in Mauritius were significant but not as deeply felt as those in the other divided societies under discussion. Although Creoles arrived about a century before Indians, no claim to indigenousness was advanced in their behalf, as it was in many other divided societies. Group identities were politically important, but so were subgroup identities, along color lines among Creoles and along religious, caste, and linguistic lines among Indians. These multiple identities mitigated the bifurcation between Indians and Creoles to which Mauritius was also periodically subject. Although the 1968 riot at first drew Muslims and Hindus closer together, it could not still Muslim fears of Hindu domination. Nor could the Hindu Labor Party count on the undivided loyalty of all Hindus, since Hindi speakers were socially divided from speakers of Marathi, Tamil, and Telugu. The result was not bifurcation between Indians and Creoles, with its mutually exclusive outcome, but social fluidity, paralleled by party fluidity: changing alignments and coalitions, unstable though they might be. On all these counts, Mauritius began in an advantageous position; and, as we have seen in the case of Thailand, small tendencies to integration can develop further.

The 1968 riot reflected this fluidity, for, it will be recalled, it was a response to fears of Muslim political leaders that Muslim support could be cultivated by a Creole political party, an unlikely possibility elsewhere. Like the 1965 riot, which responded to Creole party fears about inde-

---

174. For the manipulation argument, see Mauzy, "Malaysia," pp. 114–16. For the official version, see *Towards Preserving National Security*, Parliamentary White Paper no. 14 of 1988 (Kuala Lumpur: Ministry of Home Affairs, March 14, 1988). A balanced account is provided by Harold Crouch, *Government and Society in Malaysia* (Ithaca: Cornell University Press, 1996), pp. 107–12.

pendence, the 1968 riot fell well toward the organized end of the spectrum. Once the specific anxieties that produced each violent episode passed, so did impulses to riot.[175] Less organized violence is far more likely to be produced by recurrent general apprehensions about intergroup relations than by the ephemeral concerns of political parties, even if those relate to ethnic politics. If strategic violence succeeds in its objectives, it is unlikely to be recurrent.

Following the Mauritian violence, there was room for coalition politics. This periodically suited the interests of Creole leaders, who would otherwise be relegated to a permanent minority position, and of Indian leaders, who were eager to prove that the violence would not make it impossible to govern.[176] A new multiethnic party was even able to form a government in 1982, although it subsequently dissolved along ethnic lines. The pattern of fluid politics was conducive to a growing sense that no one was permanently excluded from the Mauritian political community, a sense reflected in the growth of an ideology of multiethnicity and increased rates of intermarriage.[177]

JOURNEYS TOWARD QUIESCENCE

As I noted earlier, mild riot cases seem more different from each other than riot cases do, because they are characterized by the absence of any

175. Mauritius has been riot-free but not altogether violence-free. In 1999, protest demonstrations by Creoles against an apparent police killing turned decidedly violent, but they were directed against the police, not against members of other groups. See Deborah Bräutigam, "Mauritius: Rethinking the Miracle," *Current History* 98, no. 628 (May 1999): 228–31, at p. 229.

176. A similar reason is advanced by Adele Smith Simmons for the Labor Party restraint that prevented the riot of 1965 from turning into civil war. Whereas the Creole opposition had an interest in disorder, the ruling party had the opposite interest. Adele Smith Simmons, "Politics in Mauritius since 1934: A Study of Decolonization in a Plural Society" (D.Phil. thesis, Oxford University, 1969), pp. 406–07.

177. I have drawn these conclusions from several sources, none of which puts the matter in exactly these terms: A.R. Mannick, *Mauritius: The Politics of Change* (Mayfield, East Sussex: Dodo Books, 1989), pp. 28–95; William F.S. Miles, "The Mauritius Enigma," *Journal of Democracy* 10, no. 2 (April 1999): 91–104; Terrance Carroll, "Owners, Immigrants and Ethnic Conflict in Fiji and Mauritius," *Ethnic and Racial Studies* 17, no. 2 (April 1994): 301–24; Eliphas G. Mukonoweshuro, "Containing Political Instability in a Poly-Ethnic Society: The Case of Mauritius," *Ethnic and Racial Studies* 14, no. 2 (April 1991): 199–224; Thomas Hylland Eriksen, "A Future-Oriented, Non-Ethnic Nationalism?: Mauritius as an Exemplary Case," *Ethnos* 58, nos. 3–4 (n.m. 1993): 197–221; Amédée Darga, "Social Dynamics and the Competitive Model of a Multi-Party System: A Case Study of Mauritius," in Peter Myens and Dani Wadada Nabudere, eds., *Democracy and the One-Party State in Africa* (Hamburg: Institut für Afrika Kunde, 1989), pp. 291–303. I have also benefited from the helpful remarks of Thomas Hylland Eriksen and Lynn Hempel.

one or more conditions that combine to produce violence. The same is true of nonrecurring riots. Nonetheless, the apparent heterogeneity of conditions in these six countries can be reduced. Long-term changes in interethnic attitudes were apparent in several cases, facilitated by waves of immigration in the United States, common external struggles in Taiwan, and internal struggles in Thailand. Changing attitudes toward violence, more than the still-significant changes in interethnic attitudes, played important parts in transforming black-white violence in the United States and Protestant-Catholic violence in Northern Ireland. Multiethnic coalitions helped mitigate bifurcation in Malaysia and Mauritius, but in other respects their journeys toward nonviolence differed. Malaysia's was characterized by changing political balances that undercut the sources of Malay violence as they underscored police determination to thwart it. Mauritius's path to peace was built on intragroup fragmentation and the nonrecurring character of the earlier precipitants of violence. In all, a mix of attitudinal changes, some deeper than others, produced decreasing support for riot behavior. In Mauritius, Taiwan, and Thailand, there were, as well, no longer appropriate precipitating events. In the United States, Northern Ireland, and Malaysia, there were such events, but they did not produce deadly riots.

Although nonrecurrence is generally associated with increasing ethnic inclusion and establishing cooperative equilibria, not every case is explicable in these terms. As Malaysia suggests, arrangements for inclusion in severely divided societies are often precarious, because they generate anger on the part of those who wish to exclude others. As the Malaysian regime grew more ethnically slanted, it actually became easier to avert violence. There are, in short, several paths to quiescence, for there are several ways in which the conditions that support violence can be undermined.

NON-RIOTS

The further out we move into purely negative cases, into true non-events, the more uncertain the explanation is. Explaining the nonrecurrence of riots is a bit more problematic than explaining mild riots or violence that takes non-riot forms. Non-riots are most difficult to explain.

The best place to begin is with some plausible cases, involving particular group juxtapositions that might be thought ripe for violence. Why do not other Christian Filipinos target Ilocano or other Ghanaians target Ewe? Both Ilocano and Ewe fit the profile of psychologically strong and, periodically, politically powerful groups. Why have Kerala and Tamil Nadu been so notably free of Hindu-Muslim violence, even though ethnicity is the main motif of politics in Kerala? Why, in the face of strong anti-Russian sentiment and violent protest demonstrations in 1986 and 1989, have there been no significant attacks on Russians in Kazakhstan, in contrast to the events in Tuva and Tajikistan? These are broad negatives to explain. Only for some are satisfying answers available.

Economy of antipathy is surely a major part of the Filipino answer. Antipathy is directed at Chinese and Moros, and Ilocano receive favorable social distance and attitudinal evaluations from other Filipino Christians.[178] No such explanation, however, could be adduced for the Ghanaian case, for Ewe evoke considerable social distance on the part of other Ghanaians.[179] The very fluid system of coalition politics in Kerala, which evolved under the influence of certain idiosyncratic conditions, proved unusually hospitable to ethnic inclusion,[180] but there may be other reasons as well.[181] The logical explanation to be inferred from the literature on Tamil Nadu rests heavily on the prevalence of intra-Hindu caste conflict in that state, to the exclusion of Hindu-Muslim conflict.[182] An interesting alternative highlights the party-led growth of a Dravidian populism sufficiently inclusive to embrace even Tamil Muslims.[183] But, of course, caste conflict is not unique to Tamil Nadu, and competing political parties in other states have abetted Hindu-Muslim conflict rather than muted it, so one needs to get behind these explanations. Kazakhstan and Ghana's quiescence still await a cogent theory.[184]

Non-riots in especially fertile ground are not necessarily easier to fathom. When the Luo politician Tom Mboya was assassinated in Kenya

178. Rodolfo Bulatao, *Ethnic Attitudes in Five Philippine Cities* (Quezon City: University of the Philippines Social Research Laboratory, 1973), pp. 38–168; Chester L. Hunt, "Social Distance in the Philippines," *Sociology and Social Research* 40, no. 4 (March/April 1955–56): 253–60; Daniel F. Doeppers, "'Ethnic Urbanism' and Philippine Cities," *Annals of the Association of American Geographers* 64, no. 4 (December 1974): 549–59.

179. David R. Smock and Audrey C. Smock, *The Politics of Pluralism: A Comparative Study of Lebanon and Ghana* (New York: Elsevier, 1975), pp. 206–07.

180. See Horowitz, "Democracy in Divided Societies," pp. 33–34.

181. See Varshney, "Religion, Nationalism and Violence," pp. 197–98.

182. See, e.g., Swamy, "Sense, Sentiment and Populist Coalitions: The Strange Career of Cultural Nationalism in Tamil Nadu."

183. Narendra Subramanian, "Ethnicity and Pluralism: An Explanation with Reference to Indian Cases" (unpublished paper, Department of Political Science, McGill University, ca. 1996).

184. Compare Martha Brill Olcott, "Kazakhstan: Pushing for Eurasia," in Ian Bremmer and Ray Taras, eds., *New States, New Politics: Building the Post-Soviet Nations* (Cambridge: Cambridge University Press, 1997), pp. 547–70; Smock and Smock, *The Politics of Pluralism*, pp. 226–303.

in 1969, there were massive Luo protests. Twice, President Jomo Kenyatta's car was threatened by angry crowds of Luo. Police fired on them and ultimately arrested leaders of the mainly Luo Kenya People's Union. The KPU felt desperate, as indeed Luo in general did,[185] and it threatened violence.[186] Yet, in spite of what must be considered the ripest conditions, no riots materialized, probably because of the great danger signified by a powerful Kikuyu regime, hostile police, who certainly would have suppressed Luo violence, and the recrudescence of Mau Mau oathing.[187]

Some other non-riots are more comprehensible. The Gang Duabelas Ringgit, discussed in Chapter 7, never was able to consummate anti-Chinese violence it planned in the Malaysian state of Kedah. There was no precipitant available, and neither police sympathy nor more general social support could be mustered for a disreputable enterprise that extorted money from Malay villagers it claimed to protect against the Chinese. Bhanauli, a very heterogeneous village in Uttar Pradesh, was visited in 1985 by a Hindu crowd eager to attack Muslims who had fled a nearby village attacked immediately previously. The attackers were urged on by the police, but Hindu villagers declared firmly that they would not permit Muslims to be hurt, and the riot was thwarted.[188] In Lithuania (1941), Jews were attacked brutally in Kaunas but not in Vilnius. The Soviet occupation of Kaunas of 1940 had placed Jewish functionaries in powerful positions, much to the resentment of Lithuanians. In Vilnius, by contrast, Poles, rather than Jews, were in political control, and Jews were untouched.[189] Again, non-riots that are amenable to explanation are explicable in terms of the absence of necessary conditions: precipitant, police indifference, and social support in Kedah; antipathy in Bhanauli; appropriate targets in Vilnius. Explaining them is easier if the non-riots are in close spatial and temporal proximity to riots, to which they can be compared, as they could in Malaysia and Lithuania. This seems to vindicate the utility of near-miss strategies.

---

185. Marc Howard Ross speaks of a Luo fear of being exterminated. See Ross, "Political Alienation, Participation, and Ethnicity: An African Case," *American Journal of Political Science* 19, no. 2 (May 1975): 291–311, at p. 307.

186. Colin Legum, ed., *Africa Contemporary Record, 1969–70* (New York: Africana, 1970), pp. B125–26.

187. See Chapter 7, pp. 249–50, above.

188. Akbar, *Riot after Riot*, pp. 132–33.

189. Roger Petersen, "Fear, Hatred, Resentment: Toward a More Comprehensive Understanding of Ethnic Violence in Eastern Europe" (unpublished manuscript, Department of Political Science, Washington University, St. Louis, ca. 1997), pp. 20, 24.

THE HUNT FOR THE MISSING VARIABLES

The negative cases, however enlightening they are as contrasts to deadly riots, do not confirm perfectly what an examination of riots suggests. Not every negative case has a clear explanation. There also remain some explanatory variables that themselves still need explanation, most notably changes in attitudes toward ethnic groups that were former targets and changes in attitudes toward deadly violence. Some, such as the attitudinal changes in Taiwan, Thailand, and the United States (with respect to white natives and immigrants), seem adequately explained already. Other attitudinal changes do not, and I shall give them further attention in the concluding chapter.

Nevertheless, if we ask whether there are non-riots that display all the causal conditions I have associated with deadly riots or whether there are riots that fail to exhibit those conditions, the answer is generally that there are not. But, despite the strong relationships, no one can explain all the variance. Particular causal conditions identified in positive cases are also found in some cases that do not eventuate in violence. For example, in severely divided societies, violent or not, it is common for the police to be biased or for powerful group juxtapositions to produce antipathy. The claim is that, where riots occur, certain combinations of conditions are highly likely to be present. The presence of these conditions without the ensuing violence would not mean that the conditions are not causes of violence. Although we have not identified a single negative case possessing the full combination of conditions, I would not be prepared to warrant that the combination of conditions identified here is *always* sufficient to produce deadly riots. There is just too much to know about the indeterminate world of non-riots in the large to make such a statement.

Social support, appropriate targets, and precipitants appear to come close to being necessary conditions, in the sense that very, very few riots happen without them.[190] Police indifference or condonation approaches the status of necessary condition more distantly, since rioters sometimes defy police determined to stop them. An uncertain political environment, as we saw in Chapter 9, is also at least a highly facilitative condition. Nothing we have learned from alternatives to riots, mild riots, near-riots, ethnic fights, nonrecurring riots, and non-riots contradicts, in a significant way, what the examination of riots has disclosed.

Several other observations drawn from negative cases bear highlight-

190. Cf. King, Keohane, and Verba, *Designing Social Inquiry*, p. 87 n. 10.

ing. First, the fact that ethnic terrorism and riots do not tend to occur in the same general space at the same general time confirms that, although both are species of ethnic violence, they have different configurations of determinants. Second, because a combination of conditions produces deadly ethnic riots, those riots can fail to materialize for any of many reasons, not merely for any single, overarching reason, whether that is the absence of extremist organizations, or satisfaction from earlier killing, or intragroup policing. Indeed, the three reasons just mentioned seem especially unpromising explanations for quiescence, since extremist organizations are present in some negative cases and absent in others, some rioters indulge a lust for killing in repeated episodes, and not a single negative case examined here can be attributed to evidence of intragroup policing. For understandable reasons, attitudinal change seems more prevalent in explaining failures of recurrence than in explaining mild riots, where a wider range of inhibiting conditions seems operative.

Finally, there are surprising, even paradoxical, findings. Where large numbers of people mass on both sides, the intensity of violence is likely to be reduced, rather than increased, because the probability of impunity is reduced. Where riots are mild, they may nevertheless spread widely, as in Orissa (1980), in Indonesia (1980), and in the Romanian arson-lynchings of the early 1990s. The determinants of spread are different from the determinants of intensity. Where riots are strongly organized, violence is often mild and, even if not mild, as in Mauritius (1968) and Singapore (1964), may well be nonrecurrent, for strategy usually implies limited objectives. These are conclusions that may seem obvious in retrospect, but volumes of casual assertions speculate otherwise.

PATHS TO PREVENTION

If the absence of suitable targets, or appropriate precipitants, or social support, or biased police tends to thwart the occurrence of riots, then those who are interested in prevention can find openings for intervention. Riots can be discouraged by making them riskier, by undermining their justification, or by controlling the provocations that precipitate them. Unfortunately, most of these conditions are not easy to alter, at least over the short term, and other prescriptions are even more difficult to implement. If we wish Assam's structure of cleavages to resemble Belgium's, all we need do is wait some decades for an industrial revolution to produce class cleavages that mitigate the starkness of Assamese-Bengali divisions. If our aim is to turn Assam into Taiwan, then we simply require a threatening and proximate China to claim the people and the territory as its own, thereby heightening affinities among those in Assam. If we prefer Assam to resemble Kerala, all that is necessary is the construction of a fluid party system and two competing multiethnic coalitions. But if that recipe could be followed with ease, cookbooks on interethnic harmony would resemble each other far more than they do. Likewise, if we assume that the path to peace is strewn with measures to increase intergroup contacts, create superordinate goals, or provide inter-cultural training[191] — in spite of H.D. Forbes's brilliantly skeptical evalu-ations of the scientific status of several of these popular formulas[192] — it is easy to show that the disposition to engage in such activities is the result, rather than the cause, of a conflict already gone soft.[193]

There are undoubtedly structures and techniques to ameliorate inter-group conflict, some less fanciful than others. Democracy might be thought to reduce the incidence of deadly riots, as people use peaceful channels to express discontent.[194] Helen Fein is right that stable democra-cies do not perpetrate genocide against their citizens,[195] but if it takes sta-ble democracies or inclusive polities to eradicate ethnic riots — and India and several other riot-prone countries would be conspicuous exceptions — the future of deadly riots in much of the world is bright. Furthermore, in severely divided societies, democracy can easily contribute to riots by facil-itating the permanent inclusion of some groups and the exclusion of oth-ers, as lock-in, breakout, and other riots related to elections show. If "changing . . . central values" of whole populations is required,[196] many people will die as they wait for value change. Measures such as territorial autonomy, recognition of minority languages, and various forms of power sharing have all been recommended, mainly in a hortatory way, as if, regardless of their own interests, political leaders would respond favorably to these proposals, once they saw their violence-reducing possibilities.[197] A

191. Argyle, *The Social Psychology of Everyday Life*, pp. 184–89.

192. H.D. Forbes, *Ethnic Conflict: Commerce, Culture, and the Contact Hypothesis* (New Haven: Yale University Press, 1997), pp. 42–139.

193. The analogy to Kenneth Waltz's well-known analysis of prescriptions to end war is too strong to ignore. Kenneth Waltz, *Man, the State, and War* (New York: Columbia University Press, 1959).

194. Demet Yalcin, "Ethnic Identity, Democracy, and Political Violence" (paper pre-sented at the annual meeting of the American Political Science Association, San Francisco, August 29–September 1, 1996), p. 25.

195. Helen Fein, "Accounting for Genocide after 1945: Theories and Some Findings," *International Journal on Group Rights* 1, no. 1 (January 1993): 79–106, at p. 92.

196. Natalie Zemon Davis, *Society and Culture in Early Modern France* (Stanford: Stanford University Press, 1975), p. 186.

197. Arend Lijphart, *Democracy in Plural Societies* (New Haven: Yale University Press, 1977); Gurr, *Minorities at Risk*, pp. 290–313; Joseph R. Rudolph, Jr., and Robert J.

more promising long-term approach is to create a strong, consistent set of political incentives to interethnic accommodation, but this, too, usually founders on two difficulties: creating incentives for political leaders to adopt the incentives and finding a process conducive, as bargaining and negotiation are not, to the adoption of a strong and coherent package of such conciliatory institutions.[198] It is too soon to give up hope on such approaches but also too soon to count on them to eliminate ethnic riots.[199]

There is no doubt that explanations for violence have implications for the regulation of violence,[200] but there is a need to be discriminating in the choice of measures. A narrower focus may be more effective than an emphasis on systemic change or accommodative policies, for politicians who find the latter two unpalatable may still sense the desirability of reducing violence; and high-ranking police officers, who dislike losing control to crowds, may have their own distinctive reasons for thwarting violence, even if they dislike the targets.

Two strategies of riot prevention follow from the analysis of negative cases. First, all else equal, it is preferable to attack variables that are closest to being truly necessary conditions, for the obvious reason that, if they are necessary, their removal obviates the violence. Second, it is essential to seize on conditions that have strong elements of manipulability. There is some tension between the two strategies, since those conditions closest to necessary may be less manipulable. Yet the two approaches, taken together, point toward reducing the incidence of certain precipitants, changing environmental conditions supporting violence, and focusing on police strategy and tactics.

None of these approaches assumes the sudden appearance of concilia-

---

Thompson, "Ethno-territorial Movements and the Policy Process: Accommodating Nationalist Demands in the Developed World," *Comparative Politics* 17, no. 3 (April 1985): 291–311, at p. 297.

198. I have discussed the appropriate institutions and the difficulty of adopting them in *Ethnic Groups in Conflict*, pp. 563–652; *A Democratic South Africa? Constitutional Engineering in a Divided Society* (Berkeley and Los Angeles: University of California Press, 1991), pp. 163–226; "Democracy in Divided Societies," pp. 31–37; "Encouraging Electoral Accommodation in Divided Societies," in Brij Lal and Peter Larmour, eds., *Electoral Systems in Divided Societies: The Fiji Constitution Review* (Canberra: National Centre for Development Studies, Australian National University, 1997), pp. 21–37; and "Constitutional Design: An Oxymoron?" *NOMOS* 40 (2000): 253–84.

199. Moreover, as Raphael Zariski has shrewdly observed, some concessions in the direction of accommodation can escalate the demands of ethnic militants rather than reduce conflict. Timing may be a decisive intervening variable; early is far better than late. Raphael Zariski, "Ethnic Extremism among Ethno-territorial Minorities in Western Europe," *Comparative Politics* 21, no. 3 (April 1989): 253–72, at p. 264.

200. Marc Howard Ross and Jay Rothman, *The Conflict Management Implications of Major Theories of Ethnic Conflict* (Colombo: International Centre for Ethnic Studies, 1996).

tory desires that transform a society into something other than a severely divided one. For riot prevention, it is not profitable to attempt a change in relations between aggressors and targets, as this is a core, nonmanipulable element of the conflict in the short run. On the other hand, some measures require no commitment from political leaders to what they see as impossible and, very likely, undesirable for their standing in a conflicted polity. These measures include reducing the uncertainty and the policy oscillation that are conducive to violence, or reducing authoritative social support for violence, even without signaling a change in ethnic relations that might produce a swift withdrawal of popular support, and altering police behavior and the likelihood of punishment for rioters. Of course, these approaches are not cost-free in severely divided societies, but none is as costly politically as the maximalist, systemic-transformation measures that are so often prescribed.

The criterion of manipulability points to some distinctions among precipitants. Preventive action can be taken to control processions, demonstrations, and ethnically defined strikes that have a high probability of precipitating riots. If simply any spark does not suffice to set off a riot, if precipitants are meaningful events for rioters and not just excuses for violence, then by controlling precipitants it is possible to reduce violence. The demand for violence in a severely divided society is not inelastic.

In spite of this, some categories of precipitant do not lend themselves to ready alteration. Consider the recurrent role of false rumors preceding riots. If false rumors could be countered, innumerable observers tell us, the killing could be averted. This might indicate, in policy terms, an emphasis on the media of communication and their part in disseminating accurate information promptly. But a careful study of rumors shows that they serve such deeply important functions in riots, especially legitimating the desired violence as self-defense, that crowds are exceedingly unlikely to attend to more reliable information falsifying the rumors. More promising would be use of the time provided by the lull after the precipitant to deploy force that would deter the violence.[201]

Or take what I called in Chapter 8 breakout and lock-in riots in connection with elections that produce rigid outcomes because of ascriptive party alignments. Elections lacking in competition for clientele portend permanent minority status and can be viewed as something other than real elections. The major means of averting this form of ethnic violence

201. See Akbar, *Riot after Riot*, p. 118.

consists of policies to preserve a measure of fluidity in the party system —
and a very important element in interethnic accommodation that is[202]—
but such policies go to the heart of ethnic conflict relations in a way that
puts them in the category of measures difficult, if not always impossible,
to adopt.

Some common electoral prescriptions, if not appropriately refined,
can actually worsen the effects of an anticipated lock-in. The exhortation
to break the ascriptive basis of party affiliation by fostering intraethnic
party competition (more than one party per group) is medicine best not
taken in half doses. If one side has intraethnic party competition — and it
usually does so as a result of genuine subethnic cleavages — whereas the
other side is unified behind one party, the former may be artificially
locked in. That is, it may comprise an electoral majority whose divisions
have made it a parliamentary minority. The antimajoritarian character of
this kind of lock-in renders it especially illegitimate. The same can be said
of the advice to form a multiethnic coalition. If the coalition inclines
toward the interests of a minority or a group otherwise seen as illegitimate (such as an immigrant group in a state claimed by indigenes), the
excluded parties will tend to resist the arrangements violently — witness
both the military coup and ethnic assaults in Fiji (1987). Policy pertaining to electoral politics needs to be calibrated carefully, and even then it
can produce capricious results.

There are some striking examples of clear withdrawal of authoritative
social support for violence that had the intended effect. In some cases
where extremist parties controlled Indian states and wished to thwart
Hindu-Muslim violence, it was thwarted.[203] Stanley J. Tambiah has
argued that the absence of serious Sinhalese riots against Tamils since
1983 can be attributed to the firm antiriot position taken by three Sri
Lankan presidents serving since that time. Pacification of separatist-dom-
inated areas would be retarded by a sense that the regime was complicit
in killing Tamil civilians.[204] Similarly, in the post-1969 period, for reasons
discussed above, the Malaysian government has had a keen interest in
tranquility. Whatever cause it has given Chinese for grievance, the regime
has protected Chinese lives. Threats of violence have been treated as

202. See Horowitz, A Democratic South Africa? pp. 163–203.

203. Basu, "When Local Riots Are Not Merely Local," pp. 2619–20; Jayati
Chaturvedi and Gyaneshwar Chaturvedi, "Dharma Yudh: Communal Violence, Riots and
Public Space in Ayodhya and Agra City: 1990 and 1992," in Paul R. Brass, ed., Riots and
Pogroms (New York: New York University Press, 1996), pp. 187–90.

204. Tambiah, Leveling Crowds, p. 332.

"trouble cases," to be dealt with urgently.[205] When some off-duty Malay soldiers killed several Chinese civilians in 1984, it was made quite clear that the armed forces were not above the prohibition on all forms of interethnic killing. It will not escape notice, however, that the Sri Lankan and Malaysian examples exhibit idiosyncratic motivations, and both cases involve regimes that have already satisfied one ethnic constituency at the expense of another. One wonders whether the same firmness could be expected of regimes less ethnically slanted, in circumstances of exactly the sort of uncertainty and policy oscillation that we know from Chapter 9 are conducive to deadly ethnic riots.

Enforcing a flat prohibition on interethnic killing would be particularly efficacious if the prohibition were pursued early in a sequence of riots. In a series of recurrent riots, we have seen that precipitants seem to become less and less grave. In such circumstances, riots are more abundant, more severe, and more difficult to anticipate. They also foster the growth of extremist organizations. It is worthwhile keeping the threshold for violence high. Some riots, we saw in Chapter 2, proceed in two waves, with a mild anticipatory riot that precedes a more severe outbreak. The anticipatory riot provides a warning that ought not be ignored. Within emerging riot episodes in which precipitants grow notch by notch, there will also be many points for intervention, as Malaysia's near-miss of 1987 shows. When there is a prospect that violence that is occurring in one location can spread to another, there are opportunities for quarantine.[206] Likewise, when precipitants have occurred in location A that might produce violence in location B, there are ways to prevent the spread. The effects of the transportation of bodies from A to B, or of the movement of survivors who bring home tales of atrocities, are well enough known, so that their interdiction or delay until precautions are taken is feasible.

The political costs of prevention are lower than those of punishment. Both have the same animating idea: to prevent potential rioters from thinking that violence is permitted or approved. The disposition to engage in criminal activity is, in part, a function of expectations about the stigma attached to crime and about the likely behavior of others. A sound policy of deterrence prevents an increase in just such expectations

205. See Donald L. Horowitz, "Cause and Consequence in Public Policy Theory: Ethnic Policy and System Transformation in Malaysia," *Policy Sciences* 22, nos. 3–4 (November 1989): 249–88, at pp. 260–61.

206. For example, police prevented the spread of violence from Penang (1967) and from Kuala Lumpur (1969).

that other people will engage in forbidden behavior.[207] Punishment can diminish those expectations, but punishment of rioters is difficult for reasons already explored: identification of crowd members is imperfect, and evidence gathered in the course of collective violence, by police or military units not trained for criminal-detective work, may not meet the standards of proof in criminal cases. Punishment of rioters belonging to groups identified with a regime, especially in the further polarized environment the riot has helped to foster, becomes politically costly. The failure to punish signals tacit permission for recurrence.[208] On every count, prevention is the superior strategy. Even so, we are talking about preventing and, often, suppressing action widely felt to be necessary and justifiable. Small wonder that so many politicians and police officers fail the test.

The presence of police who do nothing frequently accelerates the scale of violence, as the apprehensions of participants decline,[209] just as police who use excessive force at an early stage increase levels of crowd anger. There is no doubt that there would be a substantial payoff in riot prevention from professionalization and neutrality of the police.[210] But police recruitment is often ethnically skewed, and so ethnic neutrality is difficult to obtain. Beyond this, there are subtle issues involving the organization of the instruments of order that affect their ability to prevent and suppress deadly riots.

Perhaps most fundamental are the incompatible demands of crime control and riot control. Whereas crime control demands a dispersed force, so that police have a chance of being somewhere in the vicinity of criminal activity, riot control demands a concentrated force, so that police can be present in adequate numbers where rioters gather.[211] The difficulty of concentrating forces in far-flung rural areas is a principal

207. See Dan M. Kahan, "Social Influence, Social Meaning, and Deterrence," *Virginia Law Review* 83, no. 2 (March 1997): 349–95.

208. See Edward H. Judge, *Easter in Kishinev: Anatomy of a Pogrom* (New York: New York University Press, 1992), pp. 119, 133.

209. For a good example, see Andrew Sullivan, "What a Riot," *New Republic*, May 27, 1991, pp. 10–11.

210. Brass, *Theft of an Idol*, shows that the police in India, far from adhering to any norms of professional neutrality, are subject to control by local politicians, assuredly subject to local biases, and entangled in affairs far beyond those in which a professionalized force would be involved.

211. See James Q. Wilson, *Varieties of Police Behavior* (Cambridge: Harvard University Press, 1968), p. 81 n. 26. For a subtle, street-level exposition of a similar theme, by a young black resident of Handsworth shortly after the 1985 violence, see Murphy, *Tales from Two Cities*, p. 296.

reason why rural riots, although rarer than urban ones, can quickly become more intense.[212]

The response to the dilemma of concentration versus dispersion is typically the provision of backup forces — police, paramilitary, reserve military, or regular military — to handle serious collective violence. At the outset, therefore, multiple units must be properly recruited, trained, and deployed for riot duty. By the same token, crime prevention often emphasizes neighborhood policing, with its advantages of recognition and familiarity between officers and residents — characteristics that are utterly dysfunctional when the forces of public order need to convince rioters that they are prepared to shoot them, if need be.[213] For this reason, regimes that are serious about violence control typically import backup units from distant, peripheral regions, or sometimes from abroad, to make the threat of force more credible.

Add to these issues the difficulties of historical memory and logistics. In Northern Ireland (1969), police, faced with serious crowd violence for the first time since 1935, believed that they were dealing instead with an IRA insurrection. Quite apart from issues of bias, their tactics suffered from this misapprehension. So did their ordnance, for in some locations they utilized Browning machine-guns mounted on tanks, which had a great capacity for killing bystanders.[214] The proliferation of missions is (literally) deadly for riot control.

This is not to imply that the police cannot avert and control riots. In close consultation with political leaders, they can be skillful in adopting and altering flexible tactics that discourage crowds.[215] But if politicians signal their fear of a backlash from the group from which the crowd is drawn, few police officers will risk appropriately severe action, particularly when their ethnic composition matches that of the crowd.

For all these reasons, it is unsafe to rely on police alone. Paramilitary

---

212. In Romania in the early 1990s, rural anti-Roma violence was greatly facilitated by the usual presence of only one police officer in a village. The officer had the disadvantage of being outnumbered and being familiar with the people he was obliged to suppress, and in addition he did not have adequate communications with other villages or with regional police headquarters to call in prompt reinforcements.

213. For the tacit threat, communicated by crowds to police called in to restrain them, that the police will no longer be able to live among them if they use force, see Schelling, *The Strategy of Conflict*, p. 146.

214. *Violence and Civil Disturbances in Northern Ireland in 1969*, Vol. 1, pp. 16, 172–75.

215. For an account of interesting police responses to a different type of disorder, see Uriel Rosenthal and Paul T. Hart, "Riots without Killings," *Contemporary Crises* 14, no. 4 (December 1990): 357–76.

or military backup units are indispensable. Yet the experience of many countries shows that these units may recapitulate the problems that make riot control by the police so difficult. In India, various backup units behave with widely varying degrees of bias and neutrality in Hindu-Muslim riots. In Sri Lanka, the army has often been utterly unsympathetic to the mission of protecting Tamil targets, but in 1977 the navy and air force, somewhat differently composed and led, suppressed anti-Tamil riots. Moreover, multiple missions confound the armed forces. In most Asian and African countries, the external mission of the armed forces (fighting wars against foreign armies) has been subordinated to internal missions, but the internal missions are themselves differentiated. Many regimes regard military coups as a much greater threat to themselves than they do ethnic riots, in which they are not the targets. The skewed ethnic composition of palace guards and special mobile units whose mission is coup-proofing may be completely inapt for deadly ethnic riots, depending on the identity of the aggressors and the targets. Such units are trained to deter and fight units of the regular army whose commanders may aspire to displace the regime.[216] They are inappropriately trained and equipped for riot duty. This means that yet another set of units must be prepared properly for this specialized task. Some regimes have taken the necessary steps, but many have failed to differentiate functions adequately and make the requisite preparations.

In most countries, there are incremental possibilities for preventing ethnic riots, but few deliberate paths to prevention. Discouragingly, there is often a trade-off between the creation of an inclusive multiethnic polity and the prevention of riots.[217] Arrangements for inclusion in severely divided societies are generally precarious, and they generate anger on the part of those who wish to exclude others; hence, ironically, the greater capacity of ethnically slanted regimes to avert violence when they have reason to do so. Although it requires only the absence of a single causal condition to avert a riot, many such conditions are difficult to manipulate, barring attitudinal changes that may develop over decades. The result of all this is that deadly ethnic riots can certainly be prevented or controlled at an early stage of their development, but many are not, and perhaps many never will be.

216. I have dealt with many of these issues of military politics in Horowitz, *Ethnic Groups in Conflict*, pp. 532–56.

217. For an analogous trade-off between two strategies of prevention of ethnically based coups, see ibid., p. 559.

CHAPTER 13

The Calculus of Passion

A THEORY OF THE RIOT EPISODE ought to explain the occurrence of the phenomenon in general and its distinctive features: its scale, explosiveness, and apparently disproportionate character; its brutality and gore; its selectivity between groups and indiscriminateness within groups; its ability to attract participants, in spite of the apparent benefits of sitting on the sidelines; and its mix of impulsive and instrumental elements. The riot produces many more casualties than do violent protest demonstrations, lynchings, and terrorist attacks, indeed more casualties than any form of ethnic violence short of outright warfare or genocide. In their indiscriminate targeting of outgroup members, riots contrast with lynchings and with terrorist killings, which have a more focused approach, and with feuds, in which violence is trained on narrow circles of targets. Participation is also broader in riots. Those who kill in feuds hold a personal or familial grievance. Those who kill in riots act out of a more widely shared or vicarious grievance. Unlike terrorism, which is the prerogative of specialists, riots are the work of large numbers of casual participants. Riots mix impulsive and instrumental elements, but not necessarily in the same proportions as other forms of violence. Riots have a distinctive profile.

The scale and explosiveness of the riot are among its most prominent features. The violence in Rwanda (1959) was, according to Hutu participants, "*muyaga* — the wind, something that comes you know not whence, and goes you know not whither."[1] The wind is a powerful metaphor for the fury that appears suddenly, sweeps people up, and swiftly cuts down those in its path.[2] Impressing as they do even those who

1. René Lemarchand, *Rwanda and Burundi* (New York: Praeger, 1970), p. 164, quoting a British missionary.
2. The same image was used in Hyderabad, India, where participants spoke of locations where "the wind is to be spread (*hava phailana*)," meaning where killings will occur. Sudhir

have seen it before, the startling intensity of the violence and its sheer brutality require specific explanation, some of which has already been provided in the analysis of atrocities. I shall provide more in this chapter.

Selectivity in targeting between groups has received sustained attention in Chapters 4 through 6, but little has been said about lack of selectivity among possible victims belonging to the target group. The riot is
almost as indiscriminate within the targeted category as it is discriminate
among possible target categories.[3] This inclusive conception of appropriate targets is matched by the broad appeal of the riot in attracting masses
of participants and the high pitch of destructive enthusiasm rioters bring
to the task. The riot reaches heights of disinhibition.

With these observations, we return to the overarching issues raised in
Chapter 1. In earlier chapters, I answered specific questions about the riot
process, targeting, participants, location, and the like. In Chapter 12, I
showed that the absence of an appropriate target group or adequate precipitants or social approval, among other things, would likely thwart the
emergence of a riot of significant magnitude. Each of these elements performs certain functions that make the violence possible. Some perform
more than one function; social approval, for example, contributes to both
impunity and justification. From these specific answers, we can piece
together a causal account of the riot in general. With some additional
causal elements provided along the way, we can also answer questions
about the distinctive features of the riot. Then we can match our account
against alternative approaches, draw some conclusions about passion and
calculation in an episode that partakes of both, and, finally, speculate
about why deadly ethnic riots seem to have died out in the Western world.

CONVENING THE KILLING CROWD:
A CAUSAL ACCOUNT

The deadly ethnic riot defies a great many theories and proto-theories:

1. The riot is not an unstructured frenzy, made possible by a gap in
   public order.
2. It is not a random shock, set off by some spark in group relations.

Kakar, *The Colors of Violence: Cultural Identities, Religion, and Conflict* (Chicago: University of Chicago Press, 1996), p. 80.

3. I say *almost* as indiscriminate mainly because of the greater emphasis of crowds on
male victims than on female.

3. It is not the product of a failure in social control, a deviant act for which the wider community bears no responsibility.

4. It is not the result of an escalated personal quarrel that was mishandled at the point of origin.

5. It is not an envy riot, aimed at pulling down (or confiscating property of) those who are better off.

6. It is not a cynically organized plot to gain for manipulative leaders through force what they could not gain otherwise.

7. It is not simply an effort to gain a clear policy objective or redress specific grievances.

8. It is not motivated by straightforward hatred of "difference" or "otherness." (Perceptions of similarity form part of what makes groups cohere, but difference alone is not what makes them kill. Many types of "otherness" produce, at worst, indifference.)

At times, the riot can veer toward one or another of these descriptions (some far more than others), but it is synonymous with none of them, singly or in combination. Its violence is structured, nonrandom, socially sanctioned, destructive rather than appropriative, relatively spontaneous, uncalibrated, and yet precisely focused on certain groups.

The concatenation of four underlying variables best explains the deadly ethnic riot:

1. a hostile relationship between two ethnic groups;

2. a response to events that engages the emotions of one of these collectivities, a response usually denominated as anger but perhaps more accurately rendered as arousal, rage, outrage, or wrath;[4]

3. a keenly felt sense of justification for killing; and

4. an assessment of the reduced risks of violence that facilitates disinhibition.

These are the indispensable elements of this form of violence to which the precipitants, targets, and various features of the social environment all contribute. A theory of the violent episode that tries to specify mechanisms requires an understanding of how these causal conditions are activated.

---

4. Jon Elster, *Alchemies of the Mind: Rationality and the Emotions* (Cambridge: Cambridge University Press, 1999), p. 282, proposes *wrath* as the term expressing a wish not merely that its object suffer but that the agent experiencing the emotion must be the instrumentality that inflicts the suffering.

The riot is underpinned by hostility directed against target groups believed to possess certain threatening characteristics. Arousal is produced by an occasion deemed suitable for violence, believed to present one or more of a limited class of threats in intergroup relations; the riot is event-driven. Justification is a function of beliefs about the propriety of violence against ethnic strangers and about the transgressive conduct of those strangers. Reduced inhibitions are produced by environmental conditions and actions taken by the rioters themselves that affect the rioters' calculations of risk. These components, which I shall unpack in inverse order in the four subsections that follow, conjoin to produce the violent episode. They also help to explain some of the salient features of the riot, but a full explanation of its characteristics requires a wider range of variables that I shall introduce as we proceed.

A parsimonious syllogism:

1. If risks are few and restraints are removed, we can do as we please to our adversaries.

2. If our adversaries' actions are aggressive and dangerous to us, we are justified in taking action against them.

3. If our adversaries' actions threaten an unstable status quo in intergroup relations, they will arouse us to action against them.

4. If we entertain strong antipathy toward our adversaries, and we are apprehensive about them, their characteristics, and their presence in the polity, our method of dealing with them when conditions one through three are satisfied will consist of killing them.

Underlying each step in the syllogism that leads to violence is a distinctive set of conditions, subjective states through which the external world is assessed, that combine to produce violence. On some matters, such as risk, rioters are quite circumspect, acting only when inhibitions on acting are drastically reduced, while on others, such as the evaluation of the danger posed by the targets, they are hypervigilant, magnifying threats and producing a disproportionate quantum of violence. This odd combination of circumspection and hypervigilance is a central feature of the rioters' repertoire.

RISK REDUCTION AND DISINHIBITION

A major theme of the violent enterprise is risk reduction. Angry or aroused people are not necessarily heedless of risk. An impressively wide range of variables affects the rioters' calculation of risk. Among these are supernatural beliefs in invulnerability, lack of credible opposing force or possible retaliation, societal condonation (confirmed by the action and inaction of the state), inadequate police deployment, and a variety of risk-averting tactical decisions taken by the rioters themselves.

The precipitant that inadvertently coordinates action by signaling the willingness of fellow group members to fight, the creation of over-whelming mass, the use of (usually bladed) weapons against unarmed civilians, and the leadership of local figures skilled in fighting all provide an initial advantage for the aggressors. (Small, unarmed crowds do not kill large numbers of victims.) Although selective targeting derives from other sources, it operates to reduce the prospect that multiple opponents will combine against the attackers. The care with which rioters go about choosing victims is also designed to avert the possibility that the attack-ers will accidentally kill a member of their own group. (Such a killing would, among other things, reduce intraethnic support for the violence.[5]) Crowds generally stay close to home, attack in locales where they have the tactical advantage, and retreat or relocate the attack when they encounter unexpected resistance. Crowds choose moments when their targets are unprotected by the police and by social and political authori-ties, when they have little fear of retaliation or criminal punishment, and when compunctions about killing are inoperative. As I have said, they attack strong targets at weak moments.

Not all the means employed are perfectly adapted to the goal of reduc-ing risk. Inhibitions on violent behavior are overcome by a number of methods, some of dubious efficacy: oaths and war spells, as well as charms, religious passages, and amulets that are supposed to impart invisibility or invulnerability to those who use them. If these induce aggressors to believe they are protected in battle, they may either reduce or enhance the aggressors' chance of survival. The chance of survival will be enhanced if belief in these methods transcends group lines, as it very often does; magic is a matter on which there is generally a fair amount of interethnic consensus.[6] Frenzy, disinhibiting mania, and amok-like

5. Even under cover of the disorder attending the riot, individual perpetrators do not take advantage of the opportunity to kill or settle old scores against disliked members of their own group.

6. For the effects on violence of intergroup consensus about the efficacy of claims to invulnerability, see K.B. Wilson, "Cults of Violence and Counter-Violence in Mozam-bique," *Journal of Southern African Studies* 18, no. 3 (September 1992): 527–82, at pp. 575, 579.

behavior are also recognizable in riots. Their furious quality may have the effect of maximizing the advantages enjoyed by the aggressors, but it may also convince them, to their fatal detriment, that risks do not exist.[7] Amok, after all, is the paradigm instance of emotion-laden violence involving the utter disregard of risk, often resulting in the death of the pengamok. Collectively, however, uninhibited fury may contribute to the success of the perpetrators, provided that the targets sense that the aggressors are heedless of risk. While the fearless person may ultimately be brought down, his irrationality may well contribute to the collective effort, particularly if his apparent obliviousness to risk inspires fear and immobilizes the opponent.

When all of these efforts at risk reduction are added up, it becomes clear just how great are the precautions that rioters take. That these precautions do, in the aggregate, reduce risk is demonstrated by the lopsided casualty count, heavily in favor of the attackers. There is not a single riot considered in this book in which rioters miscalculated their own tactics and power, the intentions of the police, or the response of their targets, such that the rioters suffered more casualties than the targets did.[8] The multifaceted character of the precautions shows how tactically cautious rioters are and how likely it is that if risk were increased prospective rioters would be dissuaded from turning to violence. Powerful reduction of inhibition is a necessary condition for a riot.

None of this tells us yet what gratification the riot brings for the perpetrator. Nor does it mean that rioters never trade off risk reduction against other values. They do. Rioters, for example, choose relatively safe sites at which to attack, but they do not always choose the safest sites. And some rioters do die in ethnic riots. What the precautions indicate, however, is the great concern rioters exhibit for the safety of the enter-

7. To be sure, inducing rioters to take extraordinary risks by persuading them that they will be invulnerable or will have a place in paradise may be rational for the leaders, although leaders may well fear retribution by family members if someone said to be invulnerable dies while attacking. But there is no evidence that leaders initiate such transactions except when there is already a brisk market for the benefits afforded by oaths, charms, and amulets, a market created by an atmosphere ripe for killing.

8. Only one arguable exception comes to mind. In Jakarta (May 1998), the majority of those killed were not Chinese but Indonesian looters, trapped in burning shopping malls that had been set afire by other Indonesians. But the Jakarta violence was a hybrid of a deadly riot and a violent protest demonstration (as we have seen, looting is rare in deadly ethnic riots); and the Indonesian casualties were inflicted neither by Chinese nor, for the most part, by security forces trying to repress the violence. Interviews, Jakarta, August 10–14, 1998.

prise. The riot is not wholly risk-free, but it is a low-risk enterprise. Passion has its calculus.

RIGHTFUL VIOLENCE:
JUSTIFICATION AND THE RIOTERS' ONTOLOGY

To see the riot only in terms of passion or in terms of instrumental activity makes it easy to miss the riot conceived as rightful violence. Recall from Chapter 9 how uniformly rioters act on the basis of broad social approval of the violence and how remorse is virtually never encountered after the riot. As a departure from norms, violence is greatly facilitated by a sense of justification that can bring the activity within the normative framework. We have earlier reviewed experimental studies showing that unwarranted attacks arouse more aggressive responses than warranted ones do and that the presence of approving observers induces more aggressive responses than are provided in the absence of approval. People gauge the appropriateness of their responses to provocation by reference to justification, they seek signals of justification, and they reason about justification, however cursory and faulty their reasoning may be. Justification motivates violence: it frees up otherwise inhibited participants for violence, as it simultaneously gives the upper hand in a crowd to aggressive personalities whose following would otherwise be limited. The sadism of the riot would be difficult to sustain without a belief among the crowd and beyond it that the victims deserve their fate.

It is useful to distinguish between thresholds and motifs of justification. I shall note later that the threshold for attacking ethnic antagonists is lower than it is for attacking ingroup members or members of outgroups toward whom there is indifference or only modest antipathy. But, even so, justification is required. Motifs, however, are generic; the same justifications recur in intergroup as in intragroup violence, and they are grounds for legitimating action that transcends cultures and centuries.

There are several motifs of justification employed in riots and a cognitive mechanism utilized by rioters and their supporters to bring justifying principles to bear. These justifications appear even in circumstances propitious for the rioters, providing all the more reason to credit their motivating force.

Justification typically relates to what are seen as the specific offenses of the target group that proximately produce the violence, but it can extend beyond those offenses as well. Rioters articulate justification based on the enormity of the danger they face, and this is usually cast in terms of self-defense or, less often, retribution for the targets' transgressions. Either way, the threatening character of the actions of the target group justifies the violence. If we ask what allows people to kill others without feeling remorse, we see that precipitating events are interpreted as posing grave, often physical threats to those who initiate the riots. Those events convert the violence into self-defense, and self-defense is everywhere a justification for killing. The rioters commonly see themselves as repelling mass aggression from the target group, which is to say that they can easily see themselves as involved in a species of defensive warfare. It is clear from rumors of aggression and armies on the march, from pre-riot military rituals, and from traditional martial practices in the course of the riot that the attackers view themselves as participating in something akin to military operations.[9] If the riot is analogous to an episode in protracted warfare, killing in battle is permissible and may even become a duty.

Another view of the riot sometimes entertained by participants justifies it in punitive terms. Retribution may be present in riots,[10] and it is often linked to a view of violence as intended to inflict punishment for group wrongdoing that government should have inflicted but has failed to inflict.[11] This is a conception of the function of violence pervasive in

9. For such a conception, see Kakar, The Colors of Violence, p. 70. See also Tamotsu Shibutani and Kian M. Kwan, Ethnic Stratification: A Comparative Approach (New York: Macmillan, 1965), pp. 400–01; Jonathan Spencer, "Popular Perceptions of the Violence: A Provincial View," in James Manor, ed., Sri Lanka in Change and Crisis (New York: St. Martin's Press, 1984), pp. 187–95, at p. 193; Christopher Boehm, Blood Revenge: The Anthropology of Feuding in Montenegro and Other Tribal Societies (Lawrence: University Press of Kansas, 1984), p. 89.

10. In addition to Delhi (1984), discussed in these terms in Chapter 3, see, e.g., Alnur B. Elebayeva, "The Osh Incident: Problems for Research," Post-Soviet Geography 33, no. 2 (February 1992): 78–88, at p. 83; Mark R. Beissinger, "Nationalist Violence and the State: Political Authority and Contentious Repertoires in the Former U.S.S.R.," Comparative Politics 30, no. 4 (July 1998): 401–22. For the distinction between retribution and revenge, see Robert Nozick, Philosophical Explorations (Cambridge: Harvard University Press, 1981), pp. 366–68. Nozick claims that retribution is proportionate to the offense, whereas revenge may not be, and that the agent of retribution, unlike the agent of revenge, need have no personal tie to the victim of the wrong for which he or she exacts retribution. He also asserts that revenge involves pleasure at inflicting suffering, while retribution entails pleasure in doing justice, for retribution involves commitment to some general principles that frame the offense. On this view, insofar as the riot has a punitive dimension, it would seem to be a hybrid.

11. Lemarchand, Rwanda and Burundi, p. 164; Natalie Zemon Davis, Society and Culture in Early Modern France (Stanford: Stanford University Press, 1975), pp. 154, 166–67; Bernard Wasserstein, "Patterns of Communal Conflict in Palestine," in Ada Rapoport-Albert and Steven J. Zipperstein, eds., Jewish History: Essays in Honour of Chimen Abramsky (London: Peter Halban, 1988), pp. 611–28, at p. 620; Paul R. Brass, Theft of an Idol: Text and Context in the Representation of Collective Violence (Princeton: Princeton University Press, 1997), p. 257.

lynchings (and not just in the United States[12]) and common in feuds.[13] The riot constitutes a form of shadow legal redress, a kind of collective lynching — but, of course, without exemption for individual targets not identified as miscreants; the whole target group is miscreant. Social approval of the violence means that superiors agree with the rioters that the target group has committed something like a collective offense. Justification then attaches easily.

However different they are in other respects, the common core of self-defense, warfare, and punishment for wrongdoing is that each killing is not considered singly but as part of an extended transaction, in which victims and perpetrators change places.[14] The person who kills under these circumstances is relieved of responsibility for the killing by virtue of the connection established between that killing and the conduct that precedes it. The killing is not subject to moral judgment apart from the entire sequence of events.

The riot provides an opportunity to assess how ordinary people think about events and causation. In Chapter 2, when we considered the riot as a bounded episode, we saw that the individuation of events and actions is not self-evident. That is as true for killers as it is for philosophers. Rioters do not define a riot episode as beginning sometime after the precipitant. As practicing ontologists, they do not individuate each event in the sequence; they string together chains of events. For them, the violence inflicted *on* the target group is indissolubly linked to the antecedent behavior *of* the target group, as a soldier sees today's attack as inextricably bound up with last week's attack by the opposing army, or even bound up with last year's declaration of war, and as the criminal justice system sees today's punishment as related to — indeed, unintelligible without reference to — yesterday's crime. The tight compression of the riot with precipitating events and target-group behavior in general into what rioters construe as a single transaction is essential to externalizing responsibility for the violence.[15] The perpetrators' failure to individuate ele-

---

12. See, e.g., *South China Morning Post* (Hong Kong), July 10, 1998, p. 12.

13. See Keith M. Brown, *Bloodfeud in Scotland, 1573–1625* (Edinburgh: John Donald, 1986), p. 33; Boehm, *Blood Revenge*, p. 183.

14. On justification and self-defense, see Robert C. Brown, Jr., and James T. Tedeschi, "Determinants of Perceived Aggression," *Journal of Social Psychology* 100, First Half (October 1976): 77–87; on revenge, see Peter Loizos, "Intercommunal Killing in Cyprus," *Man* (n.s.) 23, no. 4 (December 1988): 639–53, at pp. 640, 648–50.

15. From this standpoint, precipitating events have three functions. They are emblematic of the danger posed by the target group and so motivate the perpetrators to action; their severity, as I said earlier, signals participants that they will not be alone when they act; and their character as breaches of the formula for living together contributes to the justification for violence.

ments in the sequence constitutes the mechanism that makes it possible to justify the killing. This is exactly the kind of linkage between provocations and criminal acts that legal systems are especially wary of, lest, by legitimizing it, they acquit defendants who are guilty of murder. Self-defense is a carefully circumscribed justification in most legal systems.[16] That does not, however, prevent people from interpreting their aggressive acts as acts committed in the course of self-defense. Rioters assuredly do.

Intergroup attribution studies support this cognitive view of the matter. Ingroup members commonly attribute negative outgroup behavior (including violence) to the inherent characteristics of outgroup members, such as their "bloodlust," whereas ingroup members attribute negative ingroup behavior (including violence) to external causes, such as the need to retaliate or the fear of attack from the outgroup. The ingroup's justification of violence by means of external attributions and projections is tantamount to a belief "that it is really the out-group . . . which is *causing*" the violence perpetrated by the ingroup.[17]

There is also support in attribution research for the tight linkage of one event to another. An important study of autobiographical accounts of conflict reveals a tendency for people who are provoked to anger by the conduct of others to place the most recent provocations "in a longer time frame." They "describe a series of provocations or grievances," rather than a single, discrete incident.[18] There is a tendency to interpret a precipitating incident not only in the light of the imputed characteristics of the target group but in the light of instances of the targets' prior conduct. Rioters' judgments of justification take account of the whole series of events, not just the most recent, according a cumulative weight to the series. As ontologists, rioters are radical unifiers; they resist the individuation of their own conduct and that of the targets as well. This cognitive propensity to act on the basis of chains of events greatly facilitates justification of the resulting violence.

16. In particular, the law typically requires that, to constitute self-defense, the defendant's conduct respond to a threat that is not merely grave but imminent — that is, temporally proximate to the defendant's response. The criminal law could scarcely function without a strong tendency to individuate the defendant's actions from those that preceded them. It is precisely this individuation that rioters reject. Cf. Donald L. Horowitz, "Justification and Excuse in the Program of the Criminal Law," *Law and Contemporary Problems* 49, no. 3 (Summer 1986): 109–26.

17. J.A. Hunter, M. Stringer, and R.P. Watson, "Intergroup Violence and Intergroup Attributions," *British Journal of Social Psychology* 30, no. 3 (September 1991): 261–66, at pp. 264, 265 (emphasis in the original).

18. Roy F. Baumeister, Arlene Stillwell, and Sara R. Wotman, "Victim and Perpetrator Accounts of Interpersonal Conduct: Autobiographical Narratives about Anger," *Journal of Personality and Social Psychology* 59, no. 4 (October 1990): 994–1005, at p. 1001.

AROUSAL AND THE MAGNITUDE
AND SATISFACTIONS OF VIOLENCE

The line between anger or arousal and justification is slightly elusive, for anger is greater if it is felt to be justified. Nevertheless, riot violence cannot be understood without separate consideration of the emotional state that accompanies it. That emotional state and its specific properties help explain several features of the violence, especially its magnitude and explosive character and its ability to attract participants.

The deadly ethnic riot is, indisputably, angry violence. Although individual dispositions to anger vary, anger is an emotion evoked by a stimulus external to the person who feels it. We take note of those we call "angry people," but only because the durability of this emotion in them deviates from its normally fluctuating, externally induced character. The external stimulus may be a wrong that has been committed, an affront, a thwarting, or a threat from an identifiable source. The stimulus arouses people to counter it. In this sense, anger is based, however loosely, on reason. But, as a hot response to what may be a cold threat, anger can call up an emotional repertoire far wider than is necessary to meet the demands of the moment. Visceral as it is, anger always raises the prospect of action that outruns its cause.

Such disproportionate responses characterize the deadly ethnic riot. In the first instance, the violence responds to information about danger, and it is possible to discern the outlines of purposes at the core of the violence, but the violence then goes well beyond the danger.

Behind the anger of the perpetrators lies apprehension about impending consequences. Anger, as Aristotle explained in the classic treatment of the emotions,[19] can ultimately be reduced to fear, especially fear of those who entertain ill will and have the capacity to inflict harm, for they must be presumed to be planning to act on their intentions. Severely divided societies are filled with feelings of wrong produced by ingroup bias and discrimination, the desire of groups to reap disproportionate shares of rewards, and the wish to place the status of ethnic strangers at sufferance and, if possible, to establish an ethnic hierarchy. When one group claims to dominate a whole state, while another merely claims equal treatment in it, both can feel wronged if the political equilibrium is not at either of the preferred points.

19. Aristotle, *The Rhetoric*, trans. Lane Cooper (New York: D. Appleton, 1932), Bk, II, § 4, pp. 107–10.

Generalized apprehension, however, is not sufficient to arouse people to violence. People seek information about the aims of their adversaries. For rioters, the precipitating event constitutes the most recent source of information about the intentions of the target group. Virtually every precipitant of a deadly ethnic riot is interpreted as a challenge to domination, an augury of subordination, a confirmation of hostile intentions, a demonstration of target-group cohesion, strength, and intransigence, or an indication that ethnic politics has become uncertain. Precipitants are the proximate behavioral manifestations of target-group inclinations, and they convey a strong sense of danger. In some cases, such as lock-in elections, the danger of political subordination is immediate; in others, such as changes in ethnic policy, the danger is merely foreshadowed by the implicit alteration in group status; while, in still others, such as strikes begun by one group and resisted by another, the danger is signified by the demand that the resisters should take orders from the ethnic strangers who are striking. Ethnic groups are on the lookout for clues, and theirs is an early-warning watch.

Why this is so is easy to discern. The human experience with alien rule has been a decidedly unhappy one. The magnitude of the possible consequences requires close attention to the symbolic meaning of actions, in rather the same way that states in the international system attend to and act preemptively to forestall grave but less-than-immediate dangers that, if permitted to be consummated, might produce a cumulative, adverse effect. To wait is to permit the balance of power to become less favorable.

None of this means, however, that the rioters' arousal is proportionate to the danger or that violence is the only apt response. The targets are imagined to be very dangerous, but they produce no mass violence before or after the riot. It is a short step from apprehension to the imputation of hostile intentions to the targets. In experimental settings, perceptions of hostile intentions on the part of others produce more aggression against them than is produced even by actual attacks by those others.[20] These perceptions may be inaccurate or projective, and they often involve anxiety-induced exaggerations of the dangers posed by the targets — all of which we have observed in great measure, beginning with the rumors enumerated in Chapter 3. The term *fear*, which conventionally implies realistic apprehension, may be misplaced, as I shall explain later in this

20. Gordon W. Russell and Robert L. Arms, "False Consensus Effect, Physical Aggression, Anger, and a Willingness to Escalate a Disturbance," *Aggressive Behavior* 21, no. 5 (September–October 1995): 381–86, at p. 384.

chapter, when I assess alternative approaches to ethnic violence. One of the most striking features of the riot data consists of the contrast between the risk aversion and circumspection with which rioters conduct their violent enterprise and the promiscuous evaluation of danger that leads them to violent action in the first place.

To those who analyze aggression, this comes as no surprise. Experimental studies of the phenomenon are replete with examples of variable aggressive responses to the same aversive stimuli. These responses may be more or less severe, depending on the relationship of the experimental subjects to the targets, the identity of the targets, and the emotional state of the subjects. But nothing in the laboratory quite matches the extreme hypervigilance of ethnic rioters.

The discharge of aggression is a satisfying experience. Studies of the cathartic effects of aggression are numerous. They uniformly show a decrease in arousal after aggression, whether arousal is measured behaviorally, by reduced iterations of aggression after the event, or physiologically, by declines in systolic blood pressure.[21] The satisfying quality of aggression explains the ability of the riot to attract participants from among those who are aroused.[22] The participation of rioters can hardly be explained, in fact, by any objectives beyond the violence itself. To the extent that property is implicated, destruction is the theme. Theft is decidedly secondary. Looting is usually discouraged in killing crowds, in favor of arson. Even an objective as draconian as homogenization encounters a free-rider problem, for it is assuredly an indivisible benefit. Like all the other changes in group relations that might follow ethnic violence, non-rioters, too, will enjoy it if it materializes.[23] Risks have been

21. See, e.g., Vladimir J. Konečni and Ebbe B. Ebbeson, "Disinhibition versus the Cathartic Effect: Artifact and Substance," *Journal of Personality and Social Psychology* 34, no. 3 (September 1976): 352–65; Vladimir J. Konečni, "Self-Arousal, Dissipation of Anger, and Aggression," *Proceedings of the Division of Personality and Social Psychology* (American Psychological Association, mimeo., 1974); Anthony N. Doob and Lorraine E. Wood, "Catharsis and Aggression: Effects of Annoyance and Retaliation on Aggressive Behavior," *Journal of Personality and Social Psychology* 22, no. 2 (August 1972): 156–62.

22. Even in nonlethal violent protest demonstrations, there is a certain warm feeling, even joy, engendered by the sense of a community acting without restraint. See S.D. Reicher, "The St. Paul's Riot: An Explanation of the Limits of Crowd Action in Terms of a Social Identity Model," *European Journal of Social Psychology* 14, no. 1 (January–March 1984): 1–21, at p. 16.

23. The same goes for reduction of fear. For members of the perpetrator group, if the only question is whether to support the violence, the asserted danger from the other side might constitute an adequate reason for general support. Fear of the other side, however, is insufficient to induce active participation in the violence. In fact, the more acutely realistic the fear, the more reluctant a prospective participant might be.

dramatically reduced for riot participants, but they are scarcely negligible (especially if the police are misjudged), and the most serious risk that can materialize is catastrophic: an unpleasant death. Under these conditions, the temptation to let others do the rioting should be overwhelming, unless, of course, participation *is* the benefit. I have argued that killing and degrading constitute a large part of the satisfaction generated by the riot. No free rider can secure these benefits.[24] Aggressive subjects in experiments, it will be recalled, enjoy the aggression, especially the experience of domination it provides.

Crowd composition suggests that the violence is valued for itself but that the taste for violence is not evenly distributed. If it were, others might join in with the same enthusiasm that is displayed by the fractional cohorts of young males who comprise the bulk of the participants. A central component of riot gratification presumably relates to hormonal elements that pertain to all fighting.

If the violence is an emotional response to events, it also has an exemplary character, embodied in the phrase "teach them a lesson." The perpetrators might have refrained from killing had the targets behaved in accordance with the rioters' understanding of an appropriate regime of interethnic political relations. Hence, again, the motivating importance of precipitants — they are not mere sparks. Hence, too, local precipitants usually meet with a local response, and violence generally declines in intensity as it spreads. Peace is conditioned upon tolerable political behavior by the target group, and the rioters, fearful of change, act to restore a tolerable status quo ante. Rioters are sometimes mollified when such a reversion — or, better, regression to terms even more favorable to them — takes place, as in Malaysia after 1969.

The exemplary message is consonant with that part of the perpetrators' behavior that relates to the *incidence* of violence, but not to all aspects of its *conduct*. Some specific features of the riot can be explained only by the emotional character of the episode and some additional conditions, soon to be highlighted, that are associated with its emotional features. Rioters will, if necessary, coexist with a thoroughly humbled target group that has learned its "lesson." Nevertheless, rioters generally prefer a homogeneous environment, rather than settling for the mere humiliation of the targets. Politicians use the riot after the fact and sometimes try

24. Note that the targets have their own version of the free-rider problem, and they choose to ride free. For them, safety might be obtained either by fighting back or by hiding. Overwhelmingly, they choose not to fight. Since their action would be defensive, they have no consummatory satisfaction in fighting.

to organize it in advance to send a clear message of conditional coexistence, but the behavior of the rioters renders the text of the message murky, ambiguous, hard to read, and blurred by much harsher messages, usually auguring genocide. The ferocity of the violence induces many target groups in possession of the appropriate territorial or human resources to resort to secession or other forcible means, such as the military coup, to assert themselves; and so the riot becomes dysfunctional to the goal of conditional coexistence on terms favorable to the perpetrator group. Politicians who try to use the riot for specific objectives usually find that the crowd will not act in an appropriately calibrated way.

The future-oriented, behavior-shaping, instrumental features of the riot never preempt the pleasure of the violent act. Riots may begin by being exemplary, but they end by being euphoric. Atrocities and mutilations, which might be interpreted as intended to communicate with the target group in an even more terrorizing way than can be accomplished by killing alone, are performed with such sadistic glee at the degradation and the gore that no imputation of merely instrumental motive can supplant the obvious affect of these events. Rioters do not permit male victims to escape so that they may communicate the message of the rioters' terror to others more effectively. When one family member is forced to watch the dismemberment of another and then is killed in turn, no elaborate argument is needed to conclude that, for the rioter, the pleasure is in the doing and the overdoing, rather than in any communication with other members of the target group that the violence manages to achieve.

The characteristic strength of the target group implies that the riot has utility for the group that inflicts the violence. But the violence that aims to thwart domination, particularly the violence of so-called backward groups, is suffused with affect born of humiliation. Much of the pleasure that violence brings springs from the mastery that reverses dishonor. The euphoria of the rioters derives from breaking loose and doing what needed to be done and ought to have been done sooner, from being, for once, deliberately unmeasured and out of control. That rioters behave this way even when the riot has been relatively well organized, as in Mauritius (1968) or Delhi (1984), is telling evidence of the generous measure of reactivity and impulsivity that overcomes the participants.[25]

In its response to affront and in its experience of "the ecstasy of mortal combat,"[26] the riot resembles amok and performs the same function

25. The nonlethal violence in Fiji (1987), described in Chapter 12, is the best counterexample of self-restraint deriving from organization and limited goals.

26. Henri Fauconnier, The Soul of Malaya, trans. Eric Sutton, 2d ed. (Kuala Lumpur: Oxford University Press, 1965), p. 225.

for the aggressor, redeeming him from painful restraint.[27] In many ways, but not in the pengamok's resignation to his own death, amok-like impulses pervade the riot;[28] and amok, however calculative in its methods, is the polar opposite of instrumental violence. There is no way to convert the riot into a wholly instrumental activity.

For a few riot leaders, those who excel in brutality, there is an instrumental benefit not yet identified, but it lies in intraethnic, rather than interethnic, relations. The violent criminal, according to Jack Katz, enjoys the violence: he is "in control of the meaning of the situation"; he "rules the moment"; he delights in generating "dread."[29] Gratuitous violence — more than the occasion demands — what Katz calls "recreational violence,"[30] a phrase apt for the gleeful flavor of the riot,[31] is good for the reputation of the practitioner of violence, for it establishes him as a person never to be trifled with.[32] Yet such a person is not acting only out of reputational self-interest but also out of "commitment to the transcendence of a hard will."[33] The man who emerges as a riot leader will become an ethnic hero as tales of his brutality spread within his group. A good example is Kiyai Salleh, whom we encountered in Chapters 3 and 7. Still, whatever the reputational rewards, the hard-willed killer — and most communities harbor such aggressive people[34] — will also bask in the consuming gratification that killing an enemy can provide. This, again, is a benefit that cannot be enjoyed by sitting on the sidelines.

From all of this it should be obvious that, while danger gives rise to anger, there is an overflow. A specific precipitant or series of precipitants produces a generalized response, an outpouring of impulsive behavior, more than the occasion would seem to warrant. Some part of the tendency for the violence to be so explosive and disproportionate is obvi-

27. Kakar, *The Colors of Violence*, p. 180, notes that anger is an antidote to a paralyzing anxiety deriving from a sense of persecution. For people in such a position, "violent assertion . . . is psychically mobilizing . . . ."

28. For a different view, see Robert Cribb, "Problems in the Historiography of the Killings in Indonesia," in Robert Cribb, ed., *The Indonesian Killings, 1965–1966: Studies from Java and Bali* (Clayton, Victoria, Australia: Monash Papers on Southeast Asia, no. 21, 1990), pp. 1–43, at pp. 33–34.

29. Jack Katz, *Seductions of Crime: Moral and Sensual Attractions in Doing Evil* (New York: Basic Books, 1988), pp. 10, 135–38.

30. Ibid., p. 180.

31. See Cribb, "Problems in the Historiography of the Killings in Indonesia," p. 31, referring to "a delight in gratuitous violence . . . ."

32. Katz, *Seductions of Crime*, p. 183.

33. Ibid., p. 187.

34. See, e.g., C.R. Hallpike, *Bloodshed and Vengeance in the Papuan Mountains* (Oxford: Clarendon Press, 1977), p. 210.

ously explicable by the self-selection of rioters who especially enjoy violence. But additional features of the arousal of the crowd are involved.
The surfeit of violence is due to the ability of people to store anger, to the
physically threatening character of pre-riot events and relationships, and
to collective effects on individual behavior.

In fashioning their response, as I have explained, rioters are disinclined to abide by a precisely bounded specification of the precipitant.
Rioters are able to link precipitants to antecedent events because of
mechanisms that facilitate the expression of pent-up anger all at once.
We have seen that anger can grow over time and be stored and redirected, as it is in displaced aggression. There has been a good deal of theorizing about how the memory of prior aversive events can be tapped by
a current event to enhance the level of anger. The mechanism is still not
wholly clear,[35] but almost certainly it is connected to the variable tendency among people to ruminate on their grievances.[36] Among some,
anger dissipates rapidly. But those individuals and (presumably) groups
that have keen memories of earlier events and that harbor thoughts of
vengeance are likely to produce outbursts disproportionate to the most
recent provocations. Memories of this sort are perpetuated and amplified
by their ideologization in the course of ethnic politics.

There is evidence that individuals who are provoked connect the most
recent provocation to earlier provocations in a series. They recount experiencing "continued hostility" and "lasting grievances" from the earlier
incidents.[37] Such people often stifle the expression of their anger at the
earlier stages but eventually "respond to the series of provocations by
expressing the accumulated anger," with a magnitude that, to them,
"seems entirely appropriate to the multiple offenses."[38] On the other
hand, those who see the last incident before the outburst as a discrete
event — and this, the research reveals, includes those who do the provoking[39] — view the discharge of the accumulated anger as an overreaction.

35. See Leonard Berkowitz, "On the Formation and Regulation of Anger and
Aggression," *American Psychologist* 45, no. 4 (April 1990): 494–503.

36. Katrina Collins and Robert Bell, "Personality and Aggression: The Dissipation-
Rumination Scale," *Personality and Individual Differences* 22, no. 5 (May 1997): 751–55;
Gian Vittorio Caprara, "Indicators of Aggression: The Dissipation-Rumination Scale,"
Personality and Individual Differences 7, no. 6 (November 1986): 763–69. Unfortunately,
the experimental setting leads most laboratory researchers to inquire into dissipation and
rumination over minutes and hours, rather than longer periods. But see note 37, below.

37. Baumeister, Stillwell, and Wotman, "Victim and Perpetrator Accounts of Interpersonal Conflict," p. 1001.

38. Ibid., p. 1002.

39. Ibid.

The asymmetric interpretation of the precipitant by the provoker and the provoked is a key to understanding the magnitude of the violence. In divided societies, there is plenty of accumulated anger, and the riot, with the anonymity it affords, is conducive as a gateway for release. Inhibitions are exceptionally low, the environment bristles with justification, and the immediately preceding events are evocative of the whole course of relations and the issues subsisting between the antagonists. All groups, after all, have a folk history of relations with others. The evocativeness of the precipitants must be particularly influential in triggering associated memories and drawing out stored anger. As Sudhir Kakar says, the riot can be seen as another step in an intermittent, drawn-out war.[40]

The intensity of the violence is also connected to the specifically physical character of the relationships and events that precede it. Not all target-group characteristics involve the possibility of fighting with the targets, but several — reputation for aggression, traditional antagonism (usually manifested by earlier combat), and opposition in war — certainly do. The same is true of precipitants, several of which entail palpable demonstrations of the physical danger posed by the targets. By the time the riot begins, there is a good chance that the transaction has been conceived as a trial of physical strength against powerful antagonists.

If part of the explanation for the explosiveness of the violence lies in the psychology of anger and its storage, while another part rests with the aggressive frame in which pre-riot events are set, crowd effects also intensify the violence. At various points, I have elicited evidence that, all else equal, collectivities behave more aggressively than individuals do. In laboratories, they administer more intense shocks and advance more hostile proposals; on the streets, they engage in more vicious violence.[41] When conventional behavioral norms are inoperative, the practitioners of sadism and dread, who are ordinarily avoided by their communities, come into their own, and local fighters become models for emulation. The situation that provides bullies and killers newfound respect is the same situation that allows ordinary people to cast off the uncomfortable restraints that prevent them from acting on their anger. That situation also sets up a market in escalation. A participant in the Chinese Cultural Revolution turned sociologist has described the peer pressure that prevails at the moment of aggression: "[T]he one beginning the beating wants to attract public attention. After the first hit, the beatings are

40. Kakar, *The Colors of Violence*, p. 70.
41. See Michael Argyle, *The Social Psychology of Everyday Life* (New York: Routledge, 1992), pp. 172–73. See also Chapter 3, pp. 116–17, above.

impossible to stop. Everyone needs to express their hatred to their enemies. . . . Beating someone to death usually involves more than one person, a whole group. No one dared to show any weakness in beating. . . .
Sympathy during that period was unheard of."[42] We have no comparable
testimony from ethnic riot participants, but it seems improbable in the
extreme that the same crowd dynamic that magnifies violence could be
inoperative. In the study of collective violence, crowds and crowd effects
need to be taken seriously.

One mechanism that may support the even-greater violence of genocides but that is not present in riots consists of threats against those who
are reluctant to participate. In the Rwanda genocide of 1994, for example, Hutu who refused to kill Tutsi were sometimes killed by other Hutu,
and it has been suggested that the magnitude of genocidal violence is
attributable, in part, to the willingness of organizers to kill ingroup members who are reluctant to be conscripted for interethnic killing.[43] State
sponsorship of genocides makes this a logical inference. But deadly ethnic rioters do not kill ingroup members, reluctant or not. Occasionally,
crowd members are taunted by bystanders to encourage them to violence, but there is no evidence of punishment of nonparticipants. Participation in the deadly riot is voluntary and authentic.

THE DEEP STRUCTURE OF HATRED
AND THE DESTRUCTIVE ENTHUSIASM OF THE RIOT

As the riot arises out of specific situations that seem to demand a violent
response, the riot is also a product of underlying antipathy. Events alone
do not explain the outbreak. "You know our fashion," a Papuan leader
told an anthropologist. "We look at these people; we look at them for a
long time. We say they are there: good we kill them. We think of this all
the time, and when our bellies get too hot, we go and kill them."[44] Bellies
do get hot, and they get especially hot against those who are already disliked. Equally provocative actions undertaken by potential target groups
against whom there is less antipathy are interpreted in less hostile terms

42. Xiaoxia Gong, "The Logic of Repressive Collective Action: A Case Study of
Violence in the Chinese Cultural Revolution," forthcoming in Kam-yee Law, ed., *Beyond
a Purge and a Holocaust: The Chinese Cultural Revolution Reconsidered* (London:
Macmillan, 2000), MS. p. 24.

43. David Backer and Ravi Bhavnani, "Localized Ethnic Conflict and Genocide: Accounting for Differences in Rwanda and Burundi" (paper presented at the annual meeting of
the American Political Science Association, Boston, September 3–6, 1998), pp. 17, 19.

44. Hallpike, *Bloodshed and Vengeance in the Papuan Mountains*, p. 208.

by prospective perpetrators and deemed worthy of a milder response or none at all.[45] Intergroup antipathy is thus a necessary condition for the deadly riot. (I am not referring here, of course, only to traditional antagonism or so-called ancient hatreds, which, as I have made clear, are by no means the predominant sources of interethnic antipathy.)

Where group identities are salient, group characteristics affect the way actions are interpreted. Group membership is the lens through which ingroup members explain the behavior of outgroup members. Outgroup members are seen as having more powerful intentions to cause harm than are ingroup members, and harmful behavior by outgroup members is evaluated more negatively than is identical behavior by ingroup members.[46] Anger is easier to evoke when there is prior hostility and produces a more severe response than when there is not.[47] There are differential tendencies to retaliate for identical offensive behavior, depending on whether there is positive or negative attraction to a provoker;[48] and even proxies for negative attraction produce differential responses.[49]

The events that precede the riot are interpreted against the background of group hostility. The events are attached to a whole relationship. This has two consequences. Since the events are interpreted in group terms, there is an accompanying imputation of malevolence, and the events are taken to require a far more serious response than they would otherwise receive. The brutality of the crowd thus expresses more widely shared sentiments about what the targets deserve. Behind the crowd stands the community. Recall, again, pervasive social support for the riot and subsequent lack of remorse.

Antipathy, hostility, and *animus* are terms that denote strong opposition, antagonism, or aversion, which may shade over into *hatred.* By

45. Hatred is, as Marilynn B. Brewer has argued, the product of more than ingroup favoritism alone. Brewer, "Ingroup Identification and Intergroup Conflict: When Does Ingroup Love Become Outgroup Hate?" forthcoming in R. Ashmore, L. Jussim, and D. Wilder, eds., *Social Identity, Intergroup Conflict, and Conflict Reduction* (Oxford: Oxford University Press, 2000). Ingroups may thus exhibit favoritism vis-à-vis many other groups without experiencing hatred toward them.

46. Sandra Schuijer et al., "The Group-Serving Bias in Evaluating and Explaining Harmful Behavior," *Journal of Social Psychology* 134, no. 1 (February 1994): 47–53.

47. Leonard Berkowitz, *Aggression: A Social-Psychological Analysis* (New York: McGraw-Hill, 1962), pp. 152–60.

48. Andrew Nesdale, Brendan Gail Rule, and Kenneth A. Hill, "The Effect of Attraction on Causal Attributions and Retaliation," *Personality and Social Psychology Bulletin* 4, no. 2 (April 1978): 231–34.

49. Russell Veitch and Anthony Piccione, "The Role of Attitude Similarity in the Attribution Process," *Social Psychology* 41, no. 2 (June 1978): 165–69.

some definitions, hatred is an enduring collection of aggressive impulses toward a person or category. Characterized by "habitual bitter feeling and accusatory thought,"[50] hatred, like antipathy, the milder version of the same emotion, is stubborn. Since both emotions are durable, they are available for invocation in response to acts and events as they come along. Whereas antipathy and hatred are a function of a whole course of relations, anger is produced by single events that may be interpreted singly; it can be produced even in a laboratory with subjects and instigators who have had no prior experience with each other.

A single event that might, without such prior experience, give rise to an angry response focused directly and narrowly on the instigator is, however, interpreted by the person who entertains antipathy to call up all of the dangerous proclivities imputed to the object of antipathy. The first thing that ethnic antipathy or hatred does is to take anger-producing events and convert them into the acts of the entire ethnic group. They are not merely acts of those individuals directly responsible for the events. Antipathy or hatred toward the class or category means precisely a disposition toward generalization and away from individuation of targets within the group. By focusing anger on the whole target group, antipathy makes the violence indiscriminately *ethnic*.

Antipathy (or hatred, where it exists) also contributes to the brutality and magnitude of the violence. For to interpret events through the lens of "bitter feeling and accusatory thought" is to impart to those events greater significance than would be accorded by those viewing them without that lens. Just as antipathy colors the interpretation of stimuli, attributing them to a deindividuated collectivity, so does it shape the response to stimuli, for the lives of strangers against whom there is animus are believed to be of lesser value than those of ethnic kin, perhaps even of trivial value.

The degree of antipathy is individually and temporally variable. One ingroup member may be angered by a precipitating event; another may dislike the outgroup associated with it; a third may actively hate that group. Within individuals, too, the balance among these sentiments may shift over time. Precipitating events probably shift the balance in a more hostile direction, individually and in the aggregate. (As we saw in Chapter 10, recurrent riots have the effect of increasing intergroup

---

50. Gordon W. Allport, "The Nature of Hatred," in Robert M. Baird and Stuart E. Rosenbaum, eds., *Bigotry, Prejudice and Hatred* (Buffalo, N.Y.: Prometheus Books, 1992), pp. 31–34, at p. 31.

antipathy.) "The angry man," says Aristotle, "wishes the object of his anger to suffer in return; hatred wishes its object not to exist."[51] The riot entails the infliction of both suffering and destruction. In its intimations of extinction of the target group, the riot certainly expresses mass hatred.

It is important to make clear that I am not explaining aggression in a tautological way, by citing aggressive impulses, or explaining destruction by the wish to destroy. Beneath ethnic antipathy and hatred, which are dispositions awaiting occasions, lie causes in group relations. The target-group characteristics identified in Chapter 5 have a common threatening thread. The perpetrators see themselves in danger of being outdone, controlled, or victimized by the targets. That the initiator group has ceded important areas of superiority to the target group is the foundation for hostility. This sensibility informs the hostile dispositions of the initiators.

An understanding of hatred, that most understudied of emotions, facilitates the understanding of indiscriminate violence against members of the target group. Ethnic hatred consists of at least four elements: (1) a growing focus on the hated group, to the neglect of others; (2) a belief that the hated group possesses fixed characteristics and dispositions to action; (3) a compression of intragroup differences attributed to members of the hated group; and (4) a sense of repulsion toward the group and its members. Some of these elements are merely extreme versions of ethnic attitudes in general, while others are features of negative affect; but the amalgam is powerful.

Hatred concentrates the attention of whoever holds that emotion. It is, as Gordon W. Allport has said, "an enduring organization of aggressive impulses . . . a stubborn structure in the mental-emotional life of the individual."[52] Hatred has an obsessive aspect. I have noted that a great deal of severe conflict is associated with growing bipolarity between groups that come to view each other as opposite types. Hatred is scrupulously focused on a single (collective) object. Such a tendency contributes to what I called the economy of antipathy that accompanies violence, screening out lesser antipathies and rendering them irrelevant for the time being. Hatred and selective targeting go hand in hand.

This keenly sensed opposition is characterized by widely distributed

---

51. Aristotle, *The Rhetoric*, Bk. II, § 4, p. 107. Hatred is "the affect that accompanies the wish to destroy an object." Richard Galdston, "The Longest Pleasure: A Psychoanalytic Study of Hatred," *International Journal of Psychoanalysis* 68, no. 3 (1987): 371–78, at p. 373.

52. Gordon W. Allport, *The Nature of Prejudice* (Garden City, N.Y.: Anchor Books, 1958), p. 341.

beliefs in the reputations of groups. Those who hate believe that the object of their hatred has properties that do not change. They believe that, in a certain sense, the objects of hatred cannot help themselves, that their attributes are embedded in their nature.

Subgroup differences are perceived more keenly by members of the group said to possess them than they are by outgroup members, who assume a high degree of homogeneity among others.[53] To the belief that the targets are unlike the perpetrators in important ways is added the belief that all members of the target group share a common repertoire. Believing in the homogeneity of the targets, as well as in the embeddedness of the polarity, rioters are certainly not social constructivists. These beliefs underpin indiscriminate targeting within the target group. When such beliefs change, the deadly riot declines.

Finally, there is sharply negative affect, a sense of repulsion that motivates the wish that the targets no longer share the same environment. This emotion is undoubtedly a function of unflattering comparisons feared by those who experience the emotion, and it is strongly felt by groups who complain of being outdone by ethnic strangers or who sense that aggressive newcomers are taking over the environment.

These four qualities that form part of the deep structure of hatred make possible the imputation of collective guilt and, consequently, the infliction of indiscriminate violence on the targets, but they do not require either. A moment's reflection on lynching, which is also born of hatred but is not indiscriminate, makes that clear. What is required, in addition to hatred, is a collective offense by the targets. Whereas lynching is preceded by an individual offense, and by collective action the lynching crowd warns others in the offending category against its repetition, the riot is preceded by a decidedly collective offense; there are no others left to warn. This is one reason the crowd carries the violence so far: it is tempted to finish the victims off, rather than merely teach them a lesson.

An especially forceful, brutal, and lethal response is thought to be commensurate with the danger posed, not by the proximate events alone (those merely produce anger), but by the fundamental character traits of — and thus the behavior that can be expected of — the targets. Observers who think that even trivial precipitants can produce ethnic riots are nearly always wrong, but perhaps what they really mean to say is that the response to a precipitant is, to outsiders, startlingly dispropor-

53. As this statement indicates, the perception of outgroup homogeneity is a generalized one, but it can be falsified. Those who entertain ethnic hatred find it dangerous to learn of the heterogeneity of the group that is the object of their hatred.

tionate, *when the precipitant is considered as a one-time event*. Antipathy never permits consideration of a precipitant as a one-time event. Just as the rioters do not individuate their own violent action, but tie it to the earlier actions of the targets, thus facilitating justification of the violence and inhibiting the growth of remorse, they also do not individuate the precipitant or its author but consider it to be part and parcel of the ongoing conduct of an entire ethnic group — and, as such, a further manifestation of group character and intentions. As ontologists, rioters again show themselves to be prodigious unifiers, who assiduously link together events in a single, unbounded chain and link targets in an indivisible group. They do not reason the way social scientists do, by partitioning variables, which is one reason social science has had so much trouble understanding them.

STRATEGIC AND RATIONALIST APPROACHES TO ETHNIC VIOLENCE

A spate of writing following the dissolution of the former Yugoslavia argues that ethnic warfare can be understood in terms of strategic dilemmas or rational action. Most of the arguments are applicable only to highly organized civil or separatist warfare, but some need to be assessed for their more general implications for ethnic riots.

SECURITY DILEMMAS AND RIOTS

One line of argument is founded on the classical security dilemma encountered in international relations. A security dilemma arises when, in a situation of anarchy, it becomes difficult to distinguish an opponent's defensive preparations from what may be its offensive intentions. Under these uncertain circumstances, an actor is better off launching preemptive warfare if offense is better than defense and if the actor's current military advantage would be eroded by inaction.

Some security-dilemma theorists, most notably Barry R. Posen,[54] who pioneered the application of the security dilemma to ethnic war, are careful to limit themselves to warfare between incipient states in the anarchic situation resulting from the collapse of Yugoslavia.[55] They make no spe-

---

54. Barry R. Posen, "The Security Dilemma and Ethnic Conflict," *Survival* 35, no. 1 (Spring 1993): 27–47.

55. For a looser sense of what is meant by anarchy, see David A. Lake and Donald Rothchild, "Spreading Fear: The Genesis of Transnational Ethnic Conflict," in David A.

cial claims for the rationality of all aspects of the decision to go to war. On the contrary, Posen underscores that, while the record of earlier violent transactions affects the participants' views of the likelihood of attack from the other side and thus the need to strike first, interpretations of the intentions of opponents will be skewed toward the imputation of malevolence if there is a history of ethnic violence.[56]

Some riot episodes bear a partial resemblance to warfare that emerges from the security dilemma. Precipitants sometimes back a group into what it sees as a corner, and a few precipitants may suggest a need to strike first. This is especially true of precipitating events, such as large, disorderly processions, that themselves verge on violence or evoke violent imagery. Even so, many processions precipitate violence because they embody an affront or an unacceptable political challenge, or perhaps because they cue aggressive responses, rather than because they create a realistic fear in the initiators that they will be subject to attack if they themselves do not strike first.

Many other features of riots confound any analogy to the security dilemma. The genuine uncertainty about intentions that characterizes the security dilemma is, in the riot, overlaid by elements of projection and imagined aggressive acts. During the lull that typically follows the last precipitant, both sides do not mobilize for violence. Only the initiator group does, and so the dilemma in which neither side can assess whether the other will strike first does not exist.[57] The attack takes place at a moment of safety, not a moment of special danger. That safety for the rioters is typically provided by the expectation that the police will not interfere. Whereas the true security dilemma is created by international anarchy, in which self-help is a necessary strategy of preemptive defense, for rioters there is no anarchy. Rather, there is a supportive environment. Knowing this, the targets do not attack or prepare to attack, except in very unusual circumstances. Even then, their first violent steps will be overwhelmed by the initiators' violent response, facilitated by a supportive environment.[58]

Of course, hostile behavior on the part of the target group precedes the violence. It is not the existence of a threat that is at issue, but the spe-

Lake and Donald Rothchild, eds., *The International Spread of Ethnic Conflict* (Princeton: Princeton University Press, 1998), pp. 3–32, at p. 8.

56. Posen, "The Security Dilemma and Ethnic Conflict," pp. 30–31.

57. Consistent patterns of targeting over time and space also confirm the unlikelihood that either side could strike first. The same side does, again and again.

58. See, e.g., Brass, *Theft of an Idol,* pp. 214–21, on Kanpur (1992).

cific threat of violence from the targets and the depiction of that threat as presenting a security dilemma.[59]

FEAR, ANTIPATHY, AND RIOTS

More general rationalist arguments for ethnic violence, not so easily confined to international warfare, bear heavily on a larger issue that threads its way through the riot materials: whether emotions can be subsumed in reason. Rationalists have generally argued against explanations that provide an independent place for passion, suggesting instead that conflict and violence derive from the suboptimal consequences of rational action. A number of these accounts concern an emotion central to the riot — fear — and this adds to their pertinence here.

Two attributes pervade rationalist accounts of ethnic violence: a profound antipathy to antipathy as an explanatory variable and a strong role for manipulative elites as progenitors of violent action. A third, a tendency to interpret ethnic violence as the outgrowth of frictions in interpersonal relations, is present in some accounts but not others. A fourth, alternating with the third, is a view of ethnic violence as the product of collective fear, conceived as a rational response to a very significant threat; and a fifth, which follows from the fourth, is an inference that violence occurs when the risks of failing to engage in violence are great.

On several points, there are contrasts with the account rendered here. I have argued that antipathy is a necessary condition for the deadly ethnic riot. The riot is a mass phenomenon, from which leaders attempt to benefit. Intergroup, rather than interpersonal, conflicts produce ethnic violence. Fear does indeed underlie violence, but it is fear characterized by faulty reasoning and magnification of danger, rather than clear-eyed rationality and an accurate assessment of the risks of refraining from violence.

I have dealt with a number of rationalist arguments about ethnic riots — such as the view that violence flows from random shocks or from disturbances in interpersonal relations — in other chapters. But two challenges to the role of passion are worth considering separately because of

59. Neither does the riot result from other components of strategic dilemmas invoked by David A. Lake and Donald Rothchild, "Containing Fear: The Origins and Management of Ethnic Conflict," *International Security* 21, no. 2 (Fall 1996): 41–75: information failure or the inability of groups to commit themselves credibly to fulfill agreements they make. That is not to say that these components may not aid in explaining other forms of ethnic violence.

their large implications for riot behavior, even if, in both cases, the focus of the accounts is on ethnic warfare. The first is a claim for the rationality of fear; the second, a claim for the rationality of atrocities.

Fear of the immediate or more distant future is a pivotal element in a number of approaches to ethnic warfare. In one carefully framed account, by Robert Bates, Rui de Figueiredo, and Barry Weingast, the ethnification of politics is the product of mass fear that the other side *may* strike first, the reinforcement of this fear by ambitious ethnic-group leaders, who convince followers of the plausibility that the other group *will* strike first, and the unintended cooperation of the other group by acting in ways that seem to confirm the fear.[60] Fear induces people to support even very costly violence, because the choice seems to be between becoming a victim or becoming a participant. In the former Yugoslavia, the Serbs had had experience of genocide by Croats during World War II.[61] When, in the early 1990s, the Croats opted for independence and for state symbols reminiscent of the Ustasha-led fascist republic of World War II, and when Serb police were dismissed and guerrilla warfare began inside Croatia, the Croats signaled the reasonableness of Serb fears, manipulated by Slobodan Milosevic, who needed the Croat issue to secure his power. According to this approach, a high degree of affect is expressed when the stakes are large (genocide involves large stakes), and so emotion follows a rational assessment by ordinary people of their situation. The improbability of genocide is not decisive, for the stakes are too high to chance it.

On this view, there is a place for fear in ethnic conflict that does not consign it to the realm of irrationality. Without imputing to proponents of this view positions they might not take—for they advance the argument for the rationality of fear in connection with warfare rather than

60. Robert H. Bates, Rui J.P. de Figueiredo, Jr., and Barry R. Weingast, "The Politics of Interpretation: Rationality, Culture, and Transition," *Politics and Society* 26, no. 2 (June 1998): 221–56, at pp. 242, 245–46; Barry R. Weingast, "Constructing Trust: The Political and Economic Roots of Ethnic and Regional Conflict," in Karol Soltan, Eric M. Uslaner, and Virginia Haufler, eds., *Institutions and Social Order* (Ann Arbor: University of Michigan Press, 1998), pp. 163–200; Rui de Figueiredo and Barry R. Weingast, "The Rationality of Fear: Political Opportunism and Ethnic Conflict" (unpublished paper, Department of Political Science, Stanford University, February 1997); Robert H. Bates and Barry R. Weingast, "Rationality and Interpretation: The Politics of Transition" (paper presented at the annual meeting of the American Political Science Association, Chicago, August 31–September 3, 1995).

61. Posen, "The Security Dilemma and Ethnic Conflict," first proposed that groups seeking to assess the intentions of others will attempt to recall how the others behaved on a similar occasion in the past.

riots — I believe it is worth asking whether this could be a way to view the emotions of those who engage in the deadly ethnic riot.[62]

Before the violence, members of the perpetrator group are trying to judge the intentions of the target group. In making such judgments, rioters must assess the magnitude of the potential consequences of failing to act, and their assessments are colored by recollections of target-group behavior on previous occasions.

Sometimes riots are preceded by grave and dramatic changes in group relations — when, for example, the target group has essentially stolen the state in a coup d'état — but more often the threats are incremental and smaller in magnitude. The question of assessment is then critical, and ref-

62. Although I shall be concerned solely with the implications of the argument for ethnic riots, it is possible to sketch in outline a provisional counterargument to the case made for the rationality of fear in Yugoslavia. It might go along the following lines:

The account provided shows Milosevic inciting Serb fears and Serbs struggling to make a judgment of Croat intentions on the limited information provided by Croat signals. No claim is made that the Croats' intentions actually were genocidal — and certainly not in Serbia — only that Milosevic succeeded in making them appear merely plausibly so. Since the Croat signals were not necessarily omens of genocide, what can the interpretation of Milosevic's behavior mean except that leaders find means to convince followers to behave in a way that is not necessarily required by their interests. The causal variable then becomes manipulation rather than realistic fear.

The large-stakes argument can be turned around. If the stakes are genocide, on the one hand, or bloody warfare, on the other, is it not odd that the Serbs felt impelled to make their judgments on the basis of merely suggestive, "plausible" Croat signals across the border? Even if one grants that the Serbs did the best they could on the limited information they had, most people would regard this degree of factual uncertainty underlying the decision to engage in bloody warfare as an exercise in irrational, not rational, behavior. Indeed, an entire literature has grown up around the origins of World War I as an exercise in just this sort of misperception. See, e.g., Ole R. Holsti, *Crisis, Escalation, War* (Montreal: McGill-Queen's University Press, 1972); Robert Jervis, *Perception and Misperception in International Politics* (Princeton: Princeton University Press, 1976); Jack S. Levy, "Misperceptions and the Causes of War," *World Politics* 36, no. 1 (October 1983): 76–99. To be sure, several studies argue for other causes of World War I as well. Jack Snyder, "Civil-Military Relations and the Cult of the Offensive, 1914 and 1984," *International Security* 9, no. 1 (Summer 1984): 108–46; Stephen Van Evera, "The Cult of the Offensive and the Origins of the First World War," *International Security* 9, no. 1 (Summer 1984): 58–107; Sean Lynn-Jones, "Detente and Deterrence: Anglo-German Relations, 1911–1914," *International Security* 11, no. 2 (Fall 1986): 121–50. But these studies have not displaced the role of misperception.

However great or small the danger of genocide may have been for the Serbs in the Krajina region of Croatia, for the Serbs in Serbia — the people deciding whether to support the war — the danger of genocide was remote. Other groups, such as the Ibo or the Sri Lankan Tamils, targeted directly in repeated ethnic riots, hesitated long and hard before embarking on separatist warfare. If, indeed, the fear of genocide underlay the Serb decision to support a war in far less threatening circumstances, it is a stretch to label that fear rational.

erence to earlier events is likely. Analogy is a rich source of decision-making material in such events,[63] but the use of analogy is hardly flawless. People misremember past experiences and evaluate them incorrectly; they also tend to exaggerate certain extreme emotions they experienced.[64] Recollections are affected by events occurring after the memory was formed, and recollections are especially inaccurate under conditions of stress.[65] Complex analogies are especially liable to error.[66] Particularly powerful analogies are perilous, because they foster premature cognitive closure, obscuring distinctions between the present case and the previous one and — if the earlier event involved aggression — leading to overestimates of hostile intentions on the part of the adversary.[67] Overestimates of hostile intentions are a classic problem in international relations and in social psychology, where they have invariably been treated as deviations from rationality.[68]

These general findings about analogy surely apply to pre-riot reasoning. Earlier events most likely to be lodged in the collective memory of prospective rioters are the most traumatic ones. In assessing the significance of precipitants associated with the Chinese, for example, Malays in Kuala Lumpur (1969) could not have failed to recall the attempt of Chinese guerrillas to take control of Malaya before the British returned in 1945–46 and the Communist, largely Chinese, insurrection of 1948–60. Both of these movements were far more serious than anything that was happening in 1969, when opposition parties precipitated a riot by celebrating a marginal victory at the ballot box in a single state of the federation. And both of the earlier, hostile Chinese actions were decisively defeated, thus refuting the need for very early Malay action of a preemptive sort. The Malaysian example, scarcely atypical, is consistent with the skewing that characterizes the use of analogies, and it points to a strong bias toward overestimates of the dangers posed by the target group.[69]

63. Cf. Howard Schuman and Cheryl Rieger, "Historical Analogies, Generational Effects, and Attitudes toward War," *American Sociological Review* 57, no. 3 (June 1992): 315–26.

64. Daniel Kahneman, "New Challenges to the Rationality Assumption," *Journal of Institutional and Theoretical Economics* 150, no. 1 (March 1994): 18–36, at pp. 27–32.

65. Joseph LeDoux, *The Emotional Brain* (New York: Simon & Schuster, 1996), pp. 210–11, 242.

66. John Anderson, *Cognitive Psychology and Its Implications,* 3d ed. (New York: W.H. Freeman, 1990), pp. 239–42.

67. Jervis, *Perception and Misperception in International Politics,* pp. 218–20, 274–75.

68. Ibid.; Henry A. Murray, Jr., "The Effect of Fear on Estimates of the Maliciousness of Other Personalities," *Journal of Social Psychology* 4, no. 3 (August 1933): 310–29.

69. The bias of prospective rioters toward recollection of the most extreme events is another reason in support of bright-line strategies of prevention, for to avoid one serious violent episode is likely to help in avoiding subsequent episodes as well.

If the action of target groups on previous occasions colors interpretations of their current intentions, so, too, do target-group reputations. Target groups, I have shown, are sometimes selected on the basis of reputation for aggression or of traditional antipathy to the perpetrator group. This is not surprising, given experimental findings that those with a history of doing harm are more likely than others are to trigger aggressive responses.[70] These imputed attributes, however, are not necessarily accurate reflections of present threats. The targets' reputation for aggression is typically false for the targets collectively in the current period, for it is perfectly clear that the targets do not attack on some occasions and receive attacks on others. Rather, they are consistently subject to attack. This cannot be merely because the perpetrator group is appropriately alert to impending attacks from the targets. Even the most rational actors could hardly preempt every attack by the targets, were they inclined to attack.[71] And repeated preemption ought to encourage the targets whose aggressive intentions are preempted to strike sooner and with greater surprise in the next episode, lest they be struck preemptively again. Yet they do not strike at all. The targets' reputation for aggression may be accurate for the distant past, or parts of the past viewed selectively; but, as I noted in Chapter 5, some part of that reputation may reflect current ethnic differences in proclivities to violence *among individuals*, rather than propensities to intergroup violence.

Like reputation for aggression, traditional enmity may have a historical foundation. Nevertheless, the contemporary, one-sided reading of history among groups in conflict is likely to ignore strong elements of historical intergroup cooperation and to exaggerate earlier warfare, as we have seen for Sri Lanka.[72]

These facts all constitute profound limitations on the rationality of fear in the decision to riot. But even if depictions of the targets' previous dispositions to aggression and enmity were more accurate than they are, projection of past behavior into the present, without a careful appraisal of the current context, constitutes a recurrent cognitive tendency that is conducive to error.[73]

The literature on misperception of the intentions of enemies indicates

70. Russell G. Geen, *Human Aggression* (Milton Keynes: Open University Press, 1990), p. 127.

71. Indeed, the perpetrators do not succeed in preempting attacks by guerrillas or terrorists drawn from the target group.

72. On selective recollection and selective forgetting, see James Fentress and Chris Wickham, *Social Memory* (Oxford: Blackwell, 1992), pp. 127–37.

73. See Jervis, *Perception and Misperception in International Politics*, pp. 266–79.

that, with high tension, the chance of misperception increases, as threats are magnified and discrepant information is rejected.[74] If misperception leads to decisions that would not otherwise be taken, the results it produces are irrational. (If the misperception is the result of projecting hostile intentions onto the targets, then it cannot be said that the perpetrators are genuinely engaged in a rational process of evaluating danger. I shall say more about this issue in a moment.)

I have said repeatedly that precipitants must be evocative for the riot to occur. On the whole, the most serious precipitants give rise to the most serious riots. Both of these facts suggest strongly that serious assessment is being performed by prospective perpetrators before the riot. The phenomenon of a surfeit of violence points to deficiencies in assessing not the direction of the danger but its magnitude. Although the target group typically behaves provocatively before the riot, it rarely sends anything like a signal that it is prepared to engage in mass violence. Such a signal might actually deter rioters, for they are inclined to attack strong targets at weak moments, not at moments when the targets are well prepared. In short, the perpetrator group and the target group are not locked into a situation in which to abjure violence is to lay oneself open to it and from which, therefore, there is no peaceful extrication.

Furthermore, the notion of a choice to kill or be killed, which ought to have a fortiori application to ethnic riots, does not accord with the behavior of the targets of riots. They, more than the citizens of states engaged in civil wars, would face something close to a kill-or-be-killed predicament, if one existed: the rioting, with its civilian focus, is closer and more immediate for them. Yet, with great consistency, they choose versions of a third option: to hide or to flee. Even the threat of mass killing does not necessarily give rise to a kill-or-be-killed choice.

A specific challenge to the role of antipathy in violence is presented in an argument for separatist warfare as the result of a failure of credible commitment.[75] In the course of an account of ethnic warfare as the product of insecurity, James D. Fearon displays great skepticism of an expla-

74. See, e.g., Ole R. Holsti, "Crisis Decision Making," in Philip E. Tetlock et al., eds., *Behavior, Society, and Nuclear War*, Vol. 1 (New York: Oxford University Press, 1989), pp. 8–84, at p. 40.

75. Fearon, "Ethnic War as a Commitment Problem" (paper presented at the 1994 annual meeting of the American Political Science Association, New York). A simpler version appears as "Commitment Problems and the Spread of Ethnic Conflict," in Lake and Rothchild, eds., *The International Spread of Ethnic Conflict*, pp. 107–26, but I use the earlier version, to which Fearon refers readers in ibid., p. 116 n. 26.

nation that could incorporate any affective state that might accompany insecurity. Fearon speculates that atrocities inflicted in the course of separatist warfare are not produced by passion but are intended to make later cohabitation of the groups impossible by deliberately deepening hatred or by generating such fear of the target group's revenge on the part of even moderate members of the group perpetrating the atrocities that they will be unable to live anywhere near surviving members of the target group.[76]

If the warfare is initiated by separatists, this explanation might account for atrocities inflicted by them, but it could hardly account for atrocities inflicted by those who wish to keep the country united.[77] In any case — and here the point is directly pertinent to atrocities in riots — if future hatred can be engendered by inflicting atrocities, why is it not plausible to consider that the current atrocities are the result of an earlier-engendered hatred, rather than the result of a deliberate strategy? How can hatred always be a consequence but never a cause? Do the emotions produced by a strategic use of violence dissipate, so that they do not become independent variables in later episodes of violence? If they do dissipate, of what use is the strategy of engendering hatred? If affect is intended to be a result of action, then it follows that it must also be a cause of action, unless the present actors who seek to engender hatred are behaving irrationally. The antipathy to antipathy leads to an argument that proves too much.

ATROCITIES IN WARFARE AND IN RIOTS: A NONSTRATEGIC EXPLANATION

A nonstrategic explanation of atrocities in international warfare is provided by historians. According to such accounts, brutality of soldiers in combat is seen by responsible authorities as something akin to a cost of doing business. (By *cost*, I mean, for example, that torture and murder of

76. Fearon, "Ethnic War as a Commitment Problem," p. 3. In this and the following paragraph, I am borrowing from an essay written under the auspices of the World Bank: "Structure and Strategy in Ethnic Conflict: A Few Steps toward Synthesis," in Boris Plescovic and Joseph E. Stiglitz, eds., *Annual World Bank Conference on Development Economics, 1998* (Washington, D.C.: The World Bank, 1999), pp. 345–70.

77. Of course, a strategic view of atrocities would have to deal with issues of compliance: it would be necessary to motivate those who are to commit the atrocities. That motivation would surely be cast in emotional rather than coldly strategic terms. The willingness of people to do what the strategists wanted them to do would depend on their feelings. If so, this would leave us back where we were.

prisoners may incite the enemy to fight harder and not to surrender.) Efforts of superiors to draw the line at killing combatants, rather than civilians and prisoners, and to prevent torture and mutilation founder on sympathy for the battlefield predicament of soldiers and fear of demoralizing them by punishment for excess.[78] Once aggressive impulses are stimulated in soldiers, it is generally thought, they cannot be expected to draw neat lines about killing. The atrocities themselves, some of them identical to those committed in ethnic riots,[79] are not strategic in origin. Superiors do not like atrocities, but they sense the difficulty of stopping them. By default rather than condonation, they provide social support. Some soldiers take delight in face-to-face killing (even as many others assiduously avoid it), or see it as a form of sport, an activity that generates great pleasure and joy.[80]

In warfare, anger (about what the enemy has done to one's comrades) and hatred (an emotion military authorities attempt to cultivate) are present.[81] In addition to hatred, there are three other elements that contribute to atrocities. The enemy is paradigmatically an outgroup, the battlefield is, by definition, dedicated exclusively to fighting — if soldiers give the enemy half a chance, it is feared, the enemy will exterminate them — and there are very powerful group effects from comrades on every soldier's behavior. The battlefield turns out to be an extreme case of a disinhibited setting, in which extremes of violence can occur.

The scene of a riot is another such setting. In riot, as in war, brutal killing and mutilation reduce dangerous antagonists to utter helplessness — a transformation that would seem to animate the joy of killing in warfare and in rioting. Accounts of atrocities in war are broadly similar to accounts of those in riot, the strategic setting of warfare notwithstanding. Despite these atrocities, I shall argue below that there is much less inclination in the West toward collective killing than there was formerly.

---

78. See Niall Ferguson, *The Pity of War* (New York: Basic Books, 1999), pp. 373–84; Joanna Bourke, *An Intimate History of Killing: Face-to-Face Killing in Twentieth-Century Warfare* (London: Granta Books, 1999), pp. 184–92; John Keegan, *The Face of Battle* (New York: Viking Press, 1976), pp. 49–50.

79. See, e.g., Bourke, *An Intimate History of Killing*, pp. 15, 37–39.

80. For these themes, see Ferguson, *The Pity of War*, pp. 360–62; Bourke, *An Intimate History of Killing*, pp. 15, 30–43, 233, 369–71. Keegan, *The Face of Battle*, p. 324, stresses the other side, the coercion required to keep soldiers in "the killing zone."

81. Hatred and revenge are the motives stressed most by Ferguson, *The Pity of War*, pp. 362–63, 377, 382–83. Bourke, *An Intimate History of Killing*, pp. 141–42, 151–59, 166–70, 182, acknowledging hatred, also emphasizes love for one's comrades, revenge, and the thrill of brutal killing.

REASON AND PASSION:
HYPERVIGILANCE, CIRCUMSPECTION,
AND BEING OF MORE THAN ONE MIND

Given what I have said repeatedly, I scarcely need to reiterate that the riot is not a wholly irrational affair. If there were nothing to fear, there would be no occasion for collective violence. But this does not conclude the issue of how much there is to fear from the targets, what forces in the environment or in collective sentiment magnify and distort the danger, or what level of response might be appropriate. Actions may be caused by rational assessments or by emotions or by a fusion of the two. Consider the variable role of reason and emotion in three riot decisions: (1) the decision that the precipitant warrants unrestrained violence; (2) the decision to conduct the violence at times and places that entail only minimal risk to the perpetrators; and (3) the decision(s) to kill indiscriminately within the target group but scrupulously to avoid killing outside the target group.

The ultimate danger for rioters is the one I identified earlier: alien rule, with the subordination and cruelty that have historically attended it. (As the rioters make clear in the course of their violent actions, they know what alien rule can entail; their own violence exemplifies its worst excesses.) But the precipitants are usually at a considerable remove from this danger; and, even when they are proximate to it, it is far from the case that mass violence is the only way to counter it. The presence of authoritative social support for the violence implies that there would also be support for lesser measures. How, then, do the perpetrators arrive at their judgments?

At the outset, their reasoning is not defective: just as they act prudently to reduce the risks to themselves, they get the facts of the provocation right. We know this from the recurrent pattern of precipitants and from events that are habitually insufficient to provoke violence. What the perpetrators get wrong are the facts about the facts: they exaggerate the significance of the precipitants. Then, before the violence begins, they add false facts or exaggerated facts: rumors of nonexistent aggression, nonexistent armies on the march, nonexistent atrocities performed by the target group, poisoned water supplies, skirmishes reported as massacres. Rioters imagine themselves engaged in self-defense even when the physical aggressiveness of their opponents has been manufactured.

The hypervigilance of the rioters manifests itself in cognitive errors. Those errors are, presumably, reinforced by the attitudinal conformity that accompanies ethnic antipathy and, in particular, by the widely distributed social approval that precedes riots. In these conditions, challenges to faulty reasoning in a group are uncommon. I shall return to this point in due course.

Anxiety is an emotional state impairing cognitive processes. It is conventional to distinguish anxiety from fear, depending on whether the reaction is disproportionate or not.[82] Danger sometimes leads to accurate and sometimes to inaccurate assessments of risk.[83] These assessments are affected by their social acceptability,[84] which suggests that, in dealings with disliked ethnic strangers, something other than realistic appraisal of risk can be expected. By providing early warning of danger, apprehensiveness has survival value, but hypervigilance is usually dysfunctional.[85] The hypervigilance of the rioter is anxiety-laden. Anyone who doubts this might recall the incident in Bombay (1992), when Hindu perpetrators shone searchlights out to sea in order to detect the arrival of Pakistani forces that they imagined were on the way.

The violence produced by these mental processes bursts the shackles of restraint, jeopardizing any message the rioters may have wished to send. Psychologists distinguish instrumental from impulsive violence.[86] Some psychologists emphasize instrumental goals in generating aggression,[87] others the affect that flows from frustration.[88] Most hold that the two motives can be separated. In deadly riots, the distinction is not com-

82. Charles Rycroft, *Anxiety and Neurosis* (Harmondsworth: Penguin Books, 1968); Isaac M. Marks, *Fears, Phobias, and Rituals* (New York: Oxford University Press, 1987).

83. Terry L. Baumer, "Testing a General Model of Fear of Crime: Data from a National Sample," *Journal of Research in Crime and Delinquency* 22, no. 3 (August 1985): 239–55; Kenneth F. Ferraro, *Fear of Crime: Interpreting Victimization Risk* (Albany: SUNY Press, 1995).

84. Marshall D. Spiegler and Robert M. Liebert, "Some Correlates of Self-Reported Fear," *Psychological Reports* 26, no. 3 (June 1970): 691–95.

85. Michael W. Eysenck, *Anxiety: The Cognitive Perspective* (Hove, East Sussex, England: Lawrence Erlbaum Associates, 1992), pp. 4–5.

86. Leonard Berkowitz, *Aggression: Its Causes, Consequences, and Control* (Philadelphia: Temple University Press, 1993), pp. 142, 149–50; Leonard Berkowitz, "Some Varieties of Human Aggression: Criminal Violence as Coercion, Rule-Following, Impression Management and Impulsive Behavior," in Anne Campbell and John J. Gibbs, eds., *Violent Transactions: The Limits of Personality* (Oxford: Basil Blackwell, 1986), pp. 87–103; Leonard Berkowitz, "Some Determinants of Impulsive Aggression," *Psychological Review* 81, no. 2 (March 1974): 165–76; Russell and Arms, "False Consensus Effect, Physical Aggression, Anger, and a Willingness to Escalate a Disturbance," p. 382.

87. See, e.g., Alfred Lange and Ad van de Nes, "Frustration and Instrumentality of Aggression," *European Journal of Social Psychology* 3, no. 2 (1973): 159–77.

88. See, e.g., Don Fitz, "A Renewed Look at Miller's Conflict Theory of Aggression Displacement," *Journal of Personality and Social Psychology* 33, no. 6 (June 1976): 725–32.

pletely lost, but the motives are commingled. The perpetrators can simultaneously act on the wish to destroy and exterminate the victims, the wish to turn the tables by torturing them and treating them as playthings, the wish to break free of restraint in general and make a holiday of killing. In the expression of these wishes, any embryonic message of conditional coexistence is inevitably lost in the excess that declares coexistence on any terms, except possibly (and even then most doubtfully) utter subordination, to be beyond contemplation. As the riot fails as a proportionate, angry response to frustration, it fails as a calibrated political response to a threatened change in the status quo.

Following the duality of fear and anxiety and of instrumental and impulsive aggression, theorists of aggressive behavior have posited that aggression has a dual source: cognition or judgment and excitation or arousal. Cognition can reduce arousal and curtail hostile behavior at moderate levels of excitation, but it fails to do so at high levels, at which point impulsive aggression, with its propensity to excess, prevails.[89] Which brings me precisely to the point I want to emphasize here: the fusion of emotions and reason in the decision to riot and the triumph of the former over the latter in that decision.

If emotion is joined to reason, emotion will have a powerful influence on behavior. By definition, a reasoned response is measured (reasonable), whereas an emotional response is not. Emotions affect reasoned judgment, as Jon Elster has pointed out,[90] by fostering mistakes about the beliefs and intentions of other people, by prompting action without regard to consequences, by emphasizing short-term over long-term preferences, by distorting estimates of probability and credibility, and by excluding trade-offs between a strong emotional preference and other values held by those who experience the emotion. Rioters are inclined to several of these tendencies, to which I would add their ontological proclivities for merging events and failing to discriminate among members of the target group who are and are not responsible for the actions that provoke them. Short-lived emotions, such as anger (for the moment, leave aside the storage of anger), contends Elster, induce people to jump to conclusions. The conclusions may concern what others will do or what the actor's own wishes are. Durable emotions, such as contempt or hatred, have effects that are not so limited, for they become consuming

89. Dolf Zillmann, "Cognition-Excitation Interdependencies in Aggressive Behavior," *Aggressive Behavior* 14, no. 1 (1988): 51–64.

90. Elster, *Alchemies of the Mind*, pp. 261–62, 284–87, 298, 304–06.

passions that take over the actor's preference structure, rather than merely skew it toward short-term gratification.[91]

Elster also advances something approaching a spiral model of emotional actions and reactions. With considerable plausibility, he shows how the behavior of a first actor, triggering an emotion in a second, can then lead the second to a mistaken interpretation of the emotion of the first that responded to the emotion of the second, and this mistake can then lead to a mistaken view by the second of the actual motivation of the first. At each point, the emotion experienced by the second increases the malevolence imputed to the first. The escalation in malevolence is accompanied by more aggressive action-tendencies appropriate to each more severe assessment.[92]

We have seen something like this at work in the interpretation of precipitants, which are evaluated as challenges to group relations, then as challenges accompanied by the hostility of the target group toward the perpetrator group, and finally as challenges motivated by the desire of the targets to kill the perpetrators. Projection is the mechanism that animates the final jump from one interpretation to the next. Although projection is a mechanism with roots in psychoanalytic theory, nonpsychoanalytic versions are perfectly serviceable. If I wish to kill you, I may assume you harbor the same wish toward me, either because I believe you sense the mortal danger from me, or because I believe a wish to kill me is reasonable in the light of our uncompromising opposition, or because I know that feelings of extreme hostility tend to be reciprocated. None of these surmises necessarily makes my belief true. Against a background of antipathy or hatred, the action-tendency of which is to hurt or extinguish its object, the projection of aggressive impulses onto the targets in the course of the interpretive process is easy to understand. In a passage apposite to projection, Elster makes it clear that irrational emotions often accompany irrational beliefs. "Because our self-esteem may not allow us to harbor emotions that we cannot defend to ourselves and to others, we invent some kind of story to justify even the most irra-

---

91. "In brief summary," Elster says neatly, "the short-lived passions undermine the theory of the rational actor, whereas the durable ones undermine the theory of *homo economicus*." Ibid., p. 306.

92. Ibid., pp. 261–62. Here is the clearest example: "If you buy a car that is fancier than mine, I may be envious. If I also believe that you enjoy my envy, it may turn into resentment. If I believe that you bought the car in order to make me envious, it may become murderous. In the first case, the emotion is triggered by (my belief about) your action; in the second case, by (my belief about) your emotion; in the third case, by (my belief about) the motivation behind your action." Ibid., p. 262.

tional reactions."[93] Such a story, as Elster recognizes, can have lethal results.

Although emotion triumphs over reason in interpreting the stimuli leading to the riot decision, there is, at least figuratively, a wall that prevents the flow of emotions from jeopardizing the rioters' own security. The perpetrators do not allow their fury to spill over and induce them to make cognitive mistakes that might imperil their lives. As they go about the killing, their risk aversion is unimpaired by the hypervigilant arousal that leads them to riot and to indulge in excess and sadism along the way. Their reasoning about risk is not flawless — witness their proclivity for charms and amulets — but there is a stark contrast between their capacities in reasoning well about risk to themselves and reasoning poorly about and exaggerating the risk to the group to which they belong. Each assessment seems uncontaminated by the other.

A different mix is on display in target selection. Intensely focused hatred imputes responsibility to all members of the target group, but the arousal that characterizes the riot is nonetheless compatible with a coolly scrupulous, precise choice of targets that leaves third groups unharmed. Although the rioters command the streets, they do not succumb to temptations in the heat of the moment to victimize people outside the specified class. Fury is in command, but it does not impede meticulous categorization and careful assessment in individual cases that could fall on either side of the boundary.

In debates about rationality and emotion, composite activity of this sort has not generally been scrutinized. The coexistence of passion and calculation — their compartmentalization in one respect, their causal interaction in another — demonstrates the complexity of the episode and the variety of mental processes underlying violence. The riot is a supremely furious episode, but the survival of limited, partitioned spheres of rationality means that arousal does not quite swamp everything.

It is as if the rioters are of more than one mind. They feel impelled to act, and act without restraint, against the victimized class, but they will not bear any serious risk to do so, and they will recognize no gradation between the fury reserved for the victims and the immunity accorded everyone else. Anyone acquainted with theories of the modularity of the mind might suspect that more than one mental process was at work here.[94] The hypervigilance and fury of rioters resemble "prepackaged

93. Ibid., p. 314.
94. For the existence of many emotional systems and their distinction from cognitive functioning, see LeDoux, *The Emotional Brain*, pp. 106, 127. For behavior as the outcome of a struggle among specialized mental modules, see Steven Pinker, *How the Mind Works* (New York: W.W. Norton, 1997), pp. 21, 27, 42, 396.

emotional reactions"[95] characteristic of rapid defenses against danger under conditions of stress. Such reactions are crude, and they typically do not involve the deliberative input of the neocortex.[96] The decision to kill, and kill furiously, has the stamp of an impulsive decision not counter-manded once made. On the other hand, the sophisticated risk assessment of the perpetrators reflects a far more deliberative process,[97] while the mix of fury and circumspection that characterizes rioters as they approach prospective victims, who need to be categorized before they can be attacked, has elements of both processes. Once many prospective rioters have apprehended a group danger, it seems probable that group interaction effects confirm and amplify their apprehension, effectively blocking a sober evaluation of the danger, but do not prevent them from thinking through the best plans for carrying out violence.

I make no pretense, of course, to identifying the neural systems involved in rioters' decisions. All I mean to do is mark resemblances and underscore that these features of riot behavior possess characteristics that are quite different from each other. These characteristics are con-nected to some standard modes by which people respond to stimuli. This behavioral complexity makes it impossible to see the deadly riot as either a wholly rational or a wholly irrational affair, and it ought to open the door to a more discerning assessment of the variable roles of reason and emotion in various aspects of complex episodes.

THE DECLINE OF THE DEADLY
ETHNIC RIOT IN THE WEST

Ethnic cleavages can change over time,[98] and so can the forms of vio-lence. It is all too easy to see both as fixed. Lynching died out in the United States, and individual amok has more or less disappeared in Southeast Asia. Why does the deadly ethnic riot also seem to have died

95. LeDoux, *The Emotional Brain*, p. 175.

96. See ibid., pp. 165, 247, 285, 299, 303.

97. See ibid., p. 176. Steven Pinker has called my attention to the "rich bi-directional connections" that exist between the limbic system and the frontal cortex of the brain. These, he suggests, might produce a response that is simultaneously excessive and prudent. Personal communication, June 4, 2000.

98. What seems now to be the ineluctable Sinhalese-Tamil conflict in Sri Lanka was preceded by severe conflict and violence between religious and caste groups, as well as between Sinhalese and Moors (and Sinhalese and Tamils), in the nineteenth century. In the nineteenth-century United States, cleavages were sharply drawn along religious lines and between old and new immigrants, and then between those of northern European origin and those of southern and eastern European origin, as well as between whites and blacks.

out in the West? On this singularly important but unrecognized transformation, some speculations are warranted.

Deadly riots in the United States in the nineteenth and early twentieth centuries had all the characteristics of such episodes: indiscriminate targeting of anyone in the victim group, mass killing and burning, and mutilation of victims.[99] But since the first half of the twentieth century, these episodes have been absent.[100] And what is true of the United States is equally true of divided societies elsewhere in North America and Western Europe. Canada, Belgium, Corsica, Catalonia, and the Basque country of Spain have not experienced deadly ethnic riots.[101] Of course, the Western world is by no means free of all forms of ethnic violence; witness terrorism in Spain and Northern Ireland, black protest violence of the 1960s in the United States, and Maghrébin protest violence of the 1980s in France.[102] Yet, from 1967 to 2000, ethnic conflict in Quebec claimed only one life; and, although anti-immigrant assaults are not uncommon in Western Europe, even mass assaults there are rarely lethal.[103] These striking facts demonstrate that the deadly riot need not be a permanent feature of divided societies.

Prosperity might be thought to undermine the deadly riot, but if so the connection must be most indirect. We have witnessed deadly riots in countries experiencing good times and witnessed quiescence in bad times. The United States was slow to abandon the riot, despite growing prosperity.[104] Prosperity alone cannot explain the decline in ethnic riot behavior. I have expressed similar skepticism in Chapter 12 about democracy

99. See Joel Williamson, *A Rage for Order: Black/White Relations in the American South since Emancipation* (New York: Oxford University Press, 1986), pp. 127–51.

100. With the partial exception of Miami (1980) and Los Angeles (1992), both of which were violent protest demonstrations mixed with killing.

101. A revealing example is provided by what followed the execution of a Spanish politician by the Basque separatist group ETA in July 1997. In Pamplona, an anti-ETA crowd attacked ETA supporters and tried to burn the offices of Herri Batasuna, a political organization affiliated to ETA. But there were no random ethnic attacks.

102. For France, see Sophie Body-Gendrot, *The Social Control of Cities? A Comparative Perspective* (Oxford: Blackwell, 2000), pp. 83, 216–17.

103. A rather serious episode occurred in Spain's Costa del Sol in February 2000, when Moroccans were subject to crowd attacks for three days. Hundreds were beaten, and a great deal of property was destroyed, but there were no deaths. *New York Times*, February 12, 2000, p. A3. The precipitants were three killings of Spaniards in two separate incidents — not the sort likely to produce deadly riots.

104. Maurice Pinard argues that, in the postmaterialist West, affluence is conducive to growing militancy about ethnic issues. Maurice Pinard, "The Quebec Independence Movement: A Dramatic Resurgence" (unpublished paper, Department of Sociology, McGill University, Montreal, Spring 1992), pp. 17–19.

as the other obvious explanation for the decline of deadly riots in the West.[105]

An important clue to the end of riots in the West is provided by its timing. In the United States, the deadly riot receded and the violent protest demonstration by the former targets took its place during World War II. Detroit (1943) was the last major antiblack riot, and Harlem (1943) was the second major black violent protest demonstration.[106] The violent protest demonstration is aimed at ethnic equality and, more to the point, does not require attitudes justifying killing in the way that deadly riots do.[107]

Important attitudinal changes were in progress in the West during the first half of the twentieth century. Following World War I, nationalism — that is, extreme manifestations of ethnic sentiment — began to be discredited; and, although ethnic sentiment revived in the 1960s and '70s, World War II delegitimized the most extreme manifestations.[108] Partly in response to the Detroit riot, from 1943 through 1945 more than 200 public and private organizations were established in the United States to deal with ethnic and racial issues.[109] This extraordinary number provides a sense of the forces being deployed for change. A "general rethinking" was under way during the war.[110] Immediately after World War II, there was accelerated concern about ethnic relations in the West, a concerted assault on the asserted biological foundations of ethnic hostility, and a variety of proposals to counter prejudice and reduce discrimination.[111] The focus was on the irrationality and unscientific character of judg-

105. Unless democracy is accompanied by specific measures to foster the reduction of ethnic conflict.

106. Harlem had experienced a violent protest in 1935. Interestingly enough, 1943 was also the year in which the Daughters of the American Revolution reversed themselves and permitted Marian Anderson, the celebrated African-American contralto, to appear before a racially mixed audience in the DAR's Constitution Hall in Washington, D.C.

107. In Harlem (1943), African-American opinion was divided on the justification for protest violence, let alone interpersonal killing. See Ted Robert Gurr, *Why Men Rebel* (Princeton: Princeton University Press, 1970), p. 167 n. 25.

108. See Edward Shils, "Nation, Nationality, Nationalism and Civil Society," *Nations and Nationalism* 1, no. 1 (March 1995): 93–118, at p. 99.

109. Louis Wirth, "The Unfinished Business of American Democracy," *The Annals* 244 (March 1946): 1–9, at p. 6. These developments proceeded simultaneously, of course, with manifestations of ethnic distrust, perhaps most notably Jim Crow in the armed forces and the confinement of Japanese Americans.

110. Howard Schuman, Charlotte Steeh, and Lawrence Bobo, *Racial Attitudes in America*, 2d ed. (Cambridge: Harvard University Press, 1988), p. 124. The few attitudinal measures for which survey data were available at the time show positive trends.

111. See Ivan Hannaford, *Race: The History of an Idea in the West* (Washington, D.C.: Woodrow Wilson Center Press, and Baltimore: Johns Hopkins University Press, 1996),

ments about whole groups, occasionally on prejudice as a reflection of psychological disturbance, and on the incompatibility of intolerance with the democratic creed. From this attack on the ideological underpinnings of ethnocentrism, a new orthodoxy of tolerance worked its way into public culture, especially into education, and most notably in the United States. Where, for example, in 1944, anti-Semitism increased with the social status of the respondent,[112] within 25 years anti-Semitism decreased with social status.[113] This is a mark of how elite opinion had changed and how powerful were the postwar forces favoring cosmopolitanism and tolerance.[114]

This is not the place to trace those attitudinal changes, and certainly not for the West as a whole, except to note that, on such matters, Western societies were in close touch with each other[115] and that the new tolerance was not merely rhetorical, although it may not have begun that way: the best evidence indicates it was genuine.[116] The results were not visible for some decades after the war, as new conceptions took hold, particularly in the schools, but they were manifested eventually across a spectrum of activity. The new tolerance furnished support for movements of ethnic equality, sometimes, ironically enough, accompanied by other forms of violence, in the United States, Canada, Northern Ireland, and Spain.

The declining legitimacy of ethnic antipathy eliminated support for the deadly ethnic riot. For if interpersonal ethnic violence is not justifiable, rioters may not gather. If they do gather, they undertake consider-

pp. 385–89. For the thinking of the period in the United States, and the (accurate) sense that a great change was about to occur, see Robert M. MacIver, *The More Perfect Union* (New York: Macmillan, 1948); Robin M. Williams, Jr., *The Reduction of Intergroup Tensions* (New York: Social Science Research Council, 1947).

112. See MacIver, *The More Perfect Union*, p. 33 n. 7.

113. See Gertrude J. Selznick and Stephen Steinberg, *The Tenacity of Prejudice* (New York: Harper & Row, 1969), pp. 71, 75, 83.

114. Cf. Samuel Stouffer, *Communism, Conformity and Civil Liberties* (Gloucester, Mass.: Peter Smith, 1963), pp. 107, 236. I am indebted to Paul Sniderman for this reference, for the reference in the preceding footnote, and for a helpful conversation about the sources of change in Western patterns of violence.

115. For example, an active program to utilize science to counter prejudice was launched under the auspices of UNESCO. Ethnic movements were similarly unconfined by national boundaries. The Québécois movement and the movement of Catholics in Northern Ireland were, in part, inspired by developments in the United States and borrowed some motifs from the civil rights movement of the 1960s.

116. See Paul M. Sniderman and Edward G. Carmines, *Reaching beyond Race* (Cambridge: Harvard University Press, 1997), p. 70. Cf. Schuman, Steeh, and Bobo, *Racial Attitudes in America*, pp. 163–92. Ethnic tolerance is accompanied by political tolerance. See Paul M. Sniderman et al., "Principled Tolerance and the American Mass Public," *British Journal of Political Science* 19, part 1 (January 1989): 25–45.

able risk, for the police cannot be counted on for indifference, the targets cannot be counted on for passivity, and public authorities cannot be counted on for impunity. Provocations may still exist, but an ideology that rejects homogeneous group characteristics makes it impossible to attribute to all target-group members indiscriminately the acts of some. Recall from Chapter 12 the language of survey respondents in Northern Ireland identifying members of other groups as ordinary people like themselves. Save perhaps for precipitants, all the conditions underlying the deadly riot have been altered by changing ethnic attitudes.

At the same time, another set of changes, with different origins, was taking place in the West: a growing aversion to mass violence in general. This change is harder to pin down, but various pieces of evidence point in its direction. Consider the results of separate surveys conducted in the United States and Canada in the 1960s. In the former, even strong anti-Semites did not advocate the use of violence against Jews; in the latter, not a single Québécois respondent among the 40 percent of respondents favoring separatism supported the use of violence for that purpose.[117] A sharp change in attitudes toward ethnic violence had taken place independently of changes in ethnic attitudes.

This point is made trenchantly with respect to warfare by Western armies — and then extrapolated to other forms of face-to-face killing — by John Keegan.[118] Keegan points out that army officers, who have a choice of whether or not to kill in battle, do so less and less. The arms they carry are increasingly ornamental and decreasingly effective, from purely ceremonial swords in the nineteenth century to walking sticks or, at most, holstered pistols in the twentieth. Similarly, coercion is often needed to keep soldiers in the killing zone. Conscientious objection is conceded even by Western states formerly hostile to it. Capital punishment has been abolished in nearly all Western states. All of this, argues Keegan, indicates that killing "is not an activity which seems to carry widespread approval."[119] Indeed, he concludes, "in the aftermath of two world wars," the West has "become suffused with a deep antipathy to violence and to conflict."[120]

There is, of course, counterevidence, and atrocities are still committed in warfare. Nevertheless, much evidence exists, on and off the battlefield,

---

117. Selznick and Steinberg, *The Tenacity of Prejudice*, 13–15; Gurr, *Why Men Rebel*, p. 173.

118. Keegan, *The Face of Battle*, pp. 314–15, 319, 320–21, 324.

119. Ibid., p. 314.

120. Ibid., p. 319.

to support Keegan's view. The small fraction of infantrymen in World War II who actually fired their weapons,[121] the absence of civil war anywhere in the West (outside Latin America) after World War II, the preference for risk-averse aerial combat strategies after the Vietnam War, and the extent to which ethnic terrorists, in order to retain a modicum of support among members of their own group, have had to adopt rules of targeting that show great respect for civilians of the target group: all of these bespeak a popular aversion to face-to-face mass killing that is fundamentally at odds with the exigencies of the deadly ethnic riot, not to mention the atrocities that accompany it.

The conjunction of attitudes of ethnic tolerance and of antipathy to mass violence is a powerful combination of forces inimical to the deadly ethnic riot. The same maximalist path to the decline of the deadly riot is not likely to be traversed soon outside the West. Long-term change in ethnic attitudes in the West was built on individualism, supported by a strongly scientific ethos, which could be used to undermine thinking in group terms. Individualism is very much a Western product. The aversion to mass violence may have more diffuse sources, but they may be equally idiosyncratic.

There are, undoubtedly, less arduous paths to the decline of deadly riots. The conjunction of multiple conditions to produce a riot means the riot can be thwarted by change at any of several points. To the extent that fear of subordination and uncertainty about relative group status underlie the riot, this points toward a renewed appreciation of the value of political stability, which allows people to redirect their waking watchfulness about others into activities that cannot be performed while those others are a constant danger. Since the fear of change in group relations is so frequently implicated in deadly riots, the ability of governments to manage ethnic change becomes surpassingly important. This, however, is a challenge that governments have recurrently failed to meet. In many places, the wind still blows.

121. S.L.A. Marshall, *Men against Fire: The Problem of Battle Command in Future War* (New York: William Morrow, 1947), pp. 53–54.

Index

Compositor: BookMatters, Berkeley
Text: 10/13 Sabon
Display: Sabon
Printer and Binder: Edwards Brothers